Frommer's

Belgium, Holland & Luxembourg

12th Edition

by George McDonald

Wiley Publishing, Inc.

ABOUT THE AUTHOR

George McDonald has lived and worked in both Amsterdam and Brussels, as deputy editor of the in-flight magazine for KLM and as editor-in-chief of the in-flight magazine for Sabena. Now a freelance journalist and travel writer, he has written extensively on both the Netherlands and Belgium for magazines and for travel books. In addition to *Frommer's Belgium, Holland & Luxembourg,* he is the author of *Frommer's Amsterdam* and a coauthor of *Frommer's Europe and Frommer's Europe by Rail.*

Published by:
WILEY PUBLISHING, INC.
111 River St.
Hoboken, NJ 07030-5774

ISBN 978-0-470-88766-0 (paper); ISBN 978-1-118-06149-7 (ebk); ISBN 978-1-118-06150-3 (ebk); ISBN 978-1-118-06151-0 (ebk)

Editor: Jennifer Reilly
Production Editor: Jonathan Scott
Cartographer: Roberta Stockwell
Photo Editor: Richard Fox
Production by Wiley Indianapolis Composition Services
Front Cover Photo: Bruges. ©Nagelestock.com / Alamy Images.
Back Cover Photo: Place Guillaume in Luxembourg City. ©Bert Hoferichter / Alamy Images.

For information on our other products and services or to obtain technical support, please contact our Customer Care Department within the U.S. at 877/762-2974, outside the U.S. at 317/572-3993 or fax 317/572-4002.

Wiley also publishes its books in a variety of electronic formats. Some content that appears in print may not be available in electronic formats.

Manufactured in the United States of America

5 4 3 2 1

CONTENTS

4 SUGGESTED BENELUX ITINERARIES 58

5 PLANNING YOUR TRIP TO BELGIUM 71

6 BRUSSELS 82

7 BRUGES 133

8 GHENT & ANTWERP 159

9 THE BELGIAN COAST & YPRES 100

10 LIÈGE, THE MEUSE RIVER & HAINAUT 208

11 THE ARDENNES 237

12 PLANNING YOUR TRIP TO HOLLAND 253

13 AMSTERDAM 266

14 HAARLEM & NOORD-HOLLAND 330

15 THE HAGUE, ROTTERDAM & ZUID-HOLLAND 357

16 FRIESLAND, GRONINGEN & DRENTHE 396

17 UTRECHT, GELDERLAND, OVERIJSSEL & FLEVOLAND 426

18 ZEELAND, NOORD-BRABANT & LIMBURG 452

19 PLANNING YOUR TRIP TO LUXEMBOURG 483

20 LUXEMBOURG 490

21 FAST FACTS 513

Index 523

LIST OF MAPS

HOW TO CONTACT US

In researching this book, we discovered many wonderful places—hotels, restaurants, shops, and more. We're sure you'll find others. Please tell us about them, so we can share the information with your fellow travelers in upcoming editions. If you were disappointed with a recommendation, we'd love to know that, too. Please write to:

Frommer's Belgium, Holland & Luxembourg, 12th Edition
Wiley Publishing, Inc. • 111 River St. • Hoboken, NJ 07030
frommersfeedback@wiley.com

AN ADDITIONAL NOTE

Please be advised that travel information is subject to change at any time—and this is especially true of prices. We therefore suggest that you write or call ahead for confirmation when making your travel plans. The authors, editors, and publisher cannot be held responsible for the experiences of readers while traveling. Your safety is important to us, however, so we encourage you to stay alert and be aware of your surroundings. Keep a close eye on cameras, purses, and wallets, all favorite targets of thieves and pickpockets.

FROMMER'S STAR RATINGS, ICONS & ABBREVIATIONS

Every hotel, restaurant, and attraction listing in this guide has been ranked for quality, value, service, amenities, and special features using a **star-rating system.** In country, state, and regional guides, we also rate towns and regions to help you narrow down your choices and budget your time accordingly. Hotels and restaurants are rated on a scale of zero (recommended) to three stars (exceptional). Attractions, shopping, nightlife, towns, and regions are rated according to the following scale: zero stars (recommended), one star (highly recommended), two stars (very highly recommended), and three stars (must-see).

In addition to the star-rating system, we also use **seven feature icons** that point you to the great deals, in-the-know advice, and unique experiences that separate travelers from tourists. Throughout the book, look for:

special finds—those places only insiders know about

fun facts—details that make travelers more informed and their trips more fun

kids—best bets for kids and advice for the whole family

special moments—those experiences that memories are made of

overrated—places or experiences not worth your time or money

insider tips—great ways to save time and money

great values—where to get the best deals

The following **abbreviations** are used for credit cards:

AE American Express **DISC** Discover **V** Visa

DC Diners Club **MC** MasterCard

TRAVEL RESOURCES AT FROMMERS.COM

Frommer's travel resources don't end with this guide. Frommer's website, **www.frommers.com**, has travel information on more than 4,000 destinations. We update features regularly, giving you access to the most current trip-planning information and the best airfare, lodging, and car-rental bargains. You can also listen to podcasts, connect with other Frommers.com members through our active-reader forums, share your travel photos, read blogs from guidebook editors and fellow travelers, and much more.

THE BEST OF BELGIUM, HOLLAND & LUXEMBOURG

1

Although they're small, each of these three countries contains a diversity of culture, language, and tradition that defies easy definition. Belgium is fractured along the age-old European divide between the Germanic north and the Latin south. This division is expressed in the constant regional bickering between Dutch-speaking Flanders and French-speaking Wallonia that threatens to split the country entirely.

Holland (the Netherlands) has its great divide, too, along the "three great rivers"—the Maas, the Waal, and the Rhine. The northerners are strait-laced and Calvinist and (to hear the southerners say it) know what to do with a glass of beer only because they've been shown by the exuberant, Catholic southerners. Then there's the matter of nations within the nation. Friesland, Zeeland, and Limburg have their notions of separateness and their own languages to back them up.

As for Luxembourg, you'd think a country so small that—even on a big map—its name can't fit within its borders would be simpler. Not a bit. Luxembourgers are such a mixed bag they're still trying to sort out the mess left behind when the Germanic tribes overran the Roman Empire's Rhine defenses in A.D. 406.

Diversity is the greatest asset of the Benelux countries. The visitor from afar may be equally impressed by their shared characteristics, which include a determined grasp on the good life, as by the differences that separate them.

THE best TRAVEL EXPERIENCES

- **Seeing the Grand-Place for the First Time** (Belgium): There's nothing quite like strolling onto the Grand-Place. You'll never forget your first look at this timelessly perfect cobbled square, surrounded by gabled guild houses and the Gothic tracery of the Hôtel de Ville (Town Hall) and Maison du Roi (King's House). See chapter 6.

- **Admiring Art Nouveau** (Belgium): Brussels considers itself the world capital of Art Nouveau, and local architect Victor Horta (1861–1947) was its foremost exponent. View the master's colorful, sinuous style at his former home, now the Horta Museum, and in buildings around town. See chapter 6.
- **Time-Traveling in Bruges** (Belgium): Without a doubt, Bruges is one of Europe's most handsome small cities. Its almost perfectly preserved center sometimes seems like a film set or museum, with buildings that run the gamut of architectural styles from medieval times to the 19th century. The picturesque canals are the icing on Bruges's cake. See chapter 7.
- **Riding the Kusttram** (Coast Tram; Belgium): Onboard the Kusttram, the 2-hour ride along the Belgian coast, from De Panne on the French border to Knokke-Heist near the Dutch border, still seems like an old-fashioned adventure. Along the way, stop off at inviting resorts, beaches, horseback-riding trails—whatever takes your fancy. See chapter 9.
- **Touring the Ardennes** (Belgium and Luxembourg): The Ardennes, which covers the eastern third of Belgium, beyond the Meuse River and on into Luxembourg, is unlike any other Benelux landscape. Steep river valleys and thickly forested slopes set it apart. This region of castles, stone-built villages, and farms has resort towns like Spa and Bouillon; unequaled cuisine created from fresh produce and game; winter skiing; nature and fresh air in abundance; and towns like Bastogne and Ettelbruck that recall the sacrifice American soldiers made for victory in the Battle of the Bulge. See chapters 11 and 20.
- **Skating on the Canals** (Holland): When the thermometer drops low enough for long enough, the Dutch canals freeze over, creating picturesque highways of ice through the cities and countryside. At such times, the Dutch take to their skates. Joining them could be the highlight of your trip. See p. 317.
- **Relaxing in a Brown Cafe** (Holland): Spend a leisurely evening in a brown cafe, the traditional Amsterdam watering hole. These time-honored Dutch bars are unpretentious, unpolished institutions filled with camaraderie, like a British pub or an American neighborhood bar. See chapter 13.
- **Following the Tulip Trail** (Holland): The place to see the celebrated Dutch tulips in their full glory is Keukenhof Gardens at Lisse, where vast numbers of tulips and other flowers create dazzling patches of color in the spring. Combine your visit with a trip through the bulb fields between Leiden and Haarlem. See chapter 14.
- **Checking Out the Windmills at Zaanse Schans** (Holland): In flat Holland, wind is ever present, so it's not surprising that the Dutch have used windmills to assist with their hard labor, from draining polders to sawing wood. At one time, the Zaan district, northwest of Amsterdam, had more than 1,000 windmills. Of the 13 that survive, five have been reconstructed at Zaanse Schans, together with other historical buildings reminiscent of the area's past. See chapter 14.
- **Celebrating Carnival in Maastricht** (Holland): The country never seems so divided by the great rivers as it does during Carnival season. Southerners declare that their celebrations are superior, and if you ever run into a southern Carnival parade, you'll have to admit they know how to party. In Maastricht the festivities are especially boisterous—people parade through the streets in an endless procession of outrageous outfits and boundless energy. See p. 258.
- **Driving the Wine Trail** (Luxembourg): Follow the Route du Vin along the banks of the Moselle River from Echternach to Mondorf-les-Bains. Here the low hills of

Luxembourg are covered with vineyards. Several wineries open their doors to visitors, offer guided tours, explain how their wine is produced, and treat you to a little of what they have stored in their barrels. See chapter 20.

THE best CASTLES & STATELY HOMES

- **Beersel** (near Brussels, Belgium): This 13th-century castle, 8km (5 miles) south of Brussels, is a castle just like Disney makes them, with turrets, towers, a drawbridge, a moat, and the spirits of all those who have, willingly or unwillingly, resided within its walls. It looks like the ideal place for pulling up the drawbridge and settling in for a siege—so long as the owners have the foresight to amply stock the rustic Auberge Kasteel Beersel restaurant inside. See p.131.
- **Gravensteen** (Ghent, Belgium): Even 900 years after it was constructed, the castle of the Counts of Flanders in Ghent can still summon up a feeling of dread as you peruse its gray stone walls. It's a grim reminder that castles were not all for chivalrous knights and beautiful princesses. This one was intended as much to subdue the independent-minded citizens of Ghent as to protect the city from foreign marauders. Inside are the tools of the autocrat's profession: torture instruments that show that what the Middle Ages lacked in humanity, they made up for in invention. See p. 162.
- **Bouillon** (near Dinant in the Ardennes, Belgium): This was the seat of the valiant but hardhanded Godfrey of Bouillon, who led the First Crusade in 1096. His castle still stands today, atop a steep bluff overlooking the town, the bridge over the Semois River, and the road to Paris. Tour its walls, chambers, and dungeons. See p. 238.
- **Menkemaborg** (Uithuizen, in Groningen province, Holland): A *borg* is the Groningen version of a stately home, developed from an earlier, defensive structure. Once home to Groningen landed gentry, Menkemaborg is a fine example of the style. Rebuilt in the 1700s, it was owned by the same family until the beginning of the 20th century. Nowadays it's a museum, with period furnishings re-creating a vivid picture of the life and times of a wealthy provincial squire. See p. 417.
- **Rijksmuseum Paleis Het Loo** (near Apeldoorn, Holland): William III, who became king of England, had a royal hunting lodge built here in the forests surrounding Apeldoorn. Subsequent members of the House of Orange made alterations to the palace, especially during the 19th century. Restoration has revealed much of the original decoration, and what couldn't be saved has been redesigned according to the original plans. The gardens have been restored to their original 17th-century splendor. See p. 435.
- **Kasteel Ammersoyen** (near 's-Hertogenbosch, Holland): This magnificent example of a moated fortress, with sturdy towers at each corner, dates from the second half of the 13th century. Ammersoyen's history was turbulent—it burned down in 1590 and was left in ruins for half a century before being rebuilt. See p. 467.

THE best MUSEUMS

- **Musées Royaux des Beaux-Arts de Belgique** (Brussels, Belgium): Paintings by many of the finest Belgian artists are assembled in this museum's neoclassical Museum of Historical Art. An entire section is devoted to Pieter Bruegel the Elder, and there are works by Peter Paul Rubens, Anthony van Dyck, Hieronymus Bosch, and many others. Go underground to the Modern Art Museum for works by René Magritte, Paul

Delvaux, James Ensor, Félicien Rops, and Pierre Alechinsky, as well as the Musée Magritte, boasting more than 150 works by the surrealist artist Magritte. See p. 112.

- **Koninklijk Museum voor Schone Kunsten Antwerpen** (Royal Fine Arts Museum; Antwerp, Belgium): If you want to see the Flemish Masters in all their glory, head to Antwerp, where the Fine Arts Museum has the world's best collection of their works, including the largest group of Rubens masterpieces in existence. See p. 117.
- **Musée de la Vie Wallonne** (Museum of Walloon Life; Liège, Belgium): Set in a 17th-century convent, this museum rambles through the history and culture of Belgium's French-speaking region of Wallonia. The exhibits wander through the building that houses them, covering everything from popular arts and crafts to industry and agriculture. There's an interesting section on theater marionettes. See p. 212.
- **Rijksmuseum** (State Museum; Amsterdam, Holland): The Rijksmuseum houses some of the Netherlands's most important works of art: many paintings by Rembrandt, among them the world-famous *The Night Watch,* four of Jan Vermeer's miniatures, and numerous works by Frans Hals. All in all, this is one of the most impressive collections of Old Masters in the world. Unfortunately, until 2013 you'll be viewing a lot fewer than before, since most of the museum is closed for refurbishment. But in the sole wing that remains open, the museum has assembled The Masterpieces, highlights from its collection of 17th-century Dutch Golden Age collections. See p. 301.
- **Van Gogh Museum** (Amsterdam, Holland): An extensive collection of van Gogh's work is here: 200 paintings and 500 drawings, ranging from the famous *Sunflowers* to earless self-portraits. The permanent collection includes important works by van Gogh's 19th-century contemporaries, and frequent temporary or visiting exhibits concentrate on the same period. See p. 304.
- **Mauritshuis** (The Hague, Holland): An intimate museum set in the 17th-century palace of a Dutch count, it contains a small but impressive collection of Golden Age art treasures. See p. 360.
- **Museum Boijmans Van Beuningen** (Rotterdam, Holland): This eclectic museum features a range of art forms, from visual to applied arts, covering a period of over 7 centuries. Here you see paintings by the likes of Pieter Bruegel and Jan van Eyck, and surrealists like René Magritte and Salvador Dalí. See p. 375.
- **Musée National de l'Histoire Militaire** (National Museum of Military History; Diekirch, Luxembourg): There's something special about this tribute to the heroes of the Battle of the Bulge (1944–45), something gritty and immediate that sets it apart from other war museums. Its centerpiece is a series of dioramas that give you an eerie sense of being there in the battle, in the snow, with danger all around. See p. 506.

THE best CATHEDRALS & CHURCHES

- **Onze-Lieve-Vrouwekerk** (Church of Our Lady; Bruges, Belgium): The spire of this church soars 122m (400 ft.) high and can be seen from a wide area around Bruges. The church holds a marble *Madonna and Child* by Michelangelo, a painting by Anthony van Dyck, and the 15th-century bronze tomb sculptures of Charles the Bold and Mary of Burgundy. See p. 150.
- **Onze-Lieve-Vrouwekathedraal** (Cathedral of Our Lady; Antwerp, Belgium): It's hard to miss this towering example of the Flemish Gothic style if you visit Antwerp or even

pass close to the city—its spire is 123m (404 ft.) high and dominates the area. This is the biggest church in the Benelux countries, with seven naves and 125 pillars. But oversize statistics are not Our Lady's only attraction—no fewer than four Rubens masterpieces are inside, along with paintings by other prominent artists. See p. 176.

- **Cathédrale Notre-Dame** (Cathedral of Our Lady; Tournai, Belgium): With a harmonious blending of the Romanesque and Gothic styles, this cathedral has five towers, magnificent stained-glass windows, and paintings by Peter Paul Rubens and Jacob Jordaens. Equally interesting are the opulent objects in the Treasury, especially a gold-and-silver reliquary, The Shrine of Our Lady, dating from 1205. See p. 232.
- **Westerkerk** (West Church; Amsterdam, Holland): The Westerkerk's tower, the Westertoren, is, at 85m (277 ft.) high, the tallest in Amsterdam, providing a spectacular view of the city. Anne Frank could hear every note of the carillon's dulcet tones while in hiding from the Nazis in her house nearby. See p. 310.
- **Sint-Bavokerk** (Church of St. Bavo; Haarlem, Holland): The moment you enter Haarlem's main square, this church is revealed in all its splendor. Completed after an unusually short construction period, it has a rare unity of structure and proportion. Regular concerts are given here on the famous organ built by Christian Müller in 1738. The young Mozart once played on this instrument. See p. 383.
- **Sint-Janskerk** (Church of St. John; Gouda, Holland): At 122m (400 ft.), this is the longest church in Holland, and it has magnificent stained-glass windows. See p. 390.
- **Domkerk** (Cathedral; Utrecht, Holland): This magnificent cathedral was begun in the 13th century. Its tower, which is 111m (365 ft.) high and dominates old Utrecht's skyline, affords great views of the city. See p. 428.
- **Sint-Servaasbasiliek** (Basilica of St. Servatius; Maastricht, Holland): One of Holland's oldest churches, this basilica was built over the grave of St. Servatius, the first bishop of Holland. Over the centuries, people have honored St. Servatius with gifts, and now the Treasury holds a collection of incredible richness and beauty. Most impressive are the reliquaries of St. Thomas and of St. Servatius, created by Maastricht master goldsmiths in the 12th century. See p. 474.
- **Cathédrale Notre-Dame** (Cathedral of Our Lady; Luxembourg City): The cathedral was built late for the Gothic style—in the early 17th century—but is nevertheless a great Gothic monument, albeit one clearly influenced by Renaissance ideals. The Octave of Our Lady of Luxembourg takes place here every year before the statue of the Virgin, which is said to have miraculous powers. See p. 496.

THE best OUTDOOR ACTIVITIES

- **Sand-Yachting at De Panne** (Belgium): Conditions on the beach at De Panne are ideal for this exciting, unusual sport. See p. 203.
- **Hiking Across the Hautes Fagnes** (Belgium): Wooden walkways stretch like the Yellow Brick Road across the high, bleak moorland plateau of Hautes Fagnes Nature Reserve in eastern Belgium, between Eupen and Malmédy. On these walkways, you explore the remnants of an ancient morasslike landscape that has claimed lives in bad weather through the centuries and into recent times. It is a beautiful, wild place and satisfying to cross at any time of year. A fine summer's day may be best, but venturing onto the moor, adequately clothed, in the middle of a snowbound winter night also has its attractions. See p. 250.

- **Skiing the Ardennes** (Belgium and Luxembourg): Some years it snows and some years it doesn't. But when it does snow enough, the Ardennes is a very pleasant place to ski. You'll find a dozen or so downhill centers, but most skiing in the Ardennes is cross-country. A particularly good location is Hautes Fagnes Nature Reserve between Eupen and Malmédy, but skiing is permitted only on the designated trails because this is a protected landscape. See chapters 11 and 20.
- **Biking in Holland:** To fully engage in the Dutch experience, you positively have to board a bicycle and head out into the wide green yonder. The tourism authorities have marked out many cycling tour routes and have published descriptive booklets and maps to go along with them, available from VVV tourist offices. Many rail stations around the country have bikes for rent. See p. 264.
- **Walking on the Wadden Sea** (Holland): At low tide, the Wadden Sea, between the northern coast and the Wadden Islands, virtually disappears, and if you're up for a walk in the mud, join a Wadden Walking *(Wadlopen)* trip and plow your way over land to one of the islands. If you're lucky, you might encounter seals gallivanting in pools left by the retreating tide or sunbathing on the flats. See p. 412.
- **Riding White Bikes in Hoge Veluwe National Park** (Holland): It was tried once in Amsterdam—providing free white bikes for everyone to use—but the bikes mysteriously disappeared and turned up in private hands with fresh coats of paint. The scheme has worked much better in this beautiful national park, which apparently doesn't shelter as many bike thieves. Just head to Hoge Veluwe's parking lot, pick up a bike, and explore the traffic-free scenery. See p. 436.
- **Canoeing in the Biesbosch** (Holland): This unique natural park of marshland, meadows, and willow woods was formed during the St. Elizabeth floods of 1421, when 16 villages were submerged and polderland became an inland sea. There are several possibilities for exploring the Biesbosch, including a tour boat, but paddling your own canoe is the best way to get close to nature. See p. 465.

THE best DELUXE HOTELS

- **Métropole** (Brussels, Belgium; ✆ **02/217-23-00**): This century-old hotel in the heart of Brussels maintains the Belle Epoque splendor of its first days and combines it with modern furnishings and service. Its **L'Alban Chambon** restaurant is one of Brussels's best. See p. 89.
- **Hotel des Indes** (The Hague, Holland; ✆ **070/361-2345**): Within this opulent hotel, simply lean over the balustrade on the first-floor landing to watch the cream of The Hague's society having tea in the lounge, and the lights of chandeliers reflecting in the polished marble pillars. The rooms are equally grand and comfortable. See p. 361.
- **Bilderberg Landgoed Lauswolt** (Beetsterzwaag, near Leeuwarden, Holland; ✆ **0512/381-245**): This 19th-century country house has been converted into a luxury hotel equipped with the latest amenities and leisure facilities. Some 2,700 acres of forest and heather offer ample opportunity for walking or horseback riding. Play golf or tennis, or swim in the heated indoor pool. All this activity will surely stir your appetite—luckily, the cuisine in the restaurant **De Heeren van Harinxma** is of the same high standard as the other comforts in the hotel. See p. 400.
- **Romantik Hotel-Auberge de Campveerse Toren** (Veere, Holland; ✆ **0118/501-291**): This ancient inn guards the harbor of Veere. With the Veerse Meer (Lake Veere) lapping at the walls below your room, you overlook the length of the lake to

the harbor where pleasure boats are moored. Little is as calming to the spirit as a walk through the old streets of Veere at dusk. Later, back in your room at the inn for the night, you'll be gently lulled to sleep by the murmuring lake waters. See p. 460.

- **Kasteel Wittem** (Wittem, Holland; © **043/450-1208**): This romantically idyllic 12th-century castle is also a hotel. It's the perfect place to stay after exploring the south of Holland's Limburg province. In the summer, dine or have breakfast on a magnificent terrace overlooking the garden and moat. See p. 478.
- **Grand Hotel Cravat** (Luxembourg City; © **22-19-75**): The Cravat has been a Luxembourg institution for a century. And for fine dining nearby, you won't need to look farther than its own **Le Normandy.** See p. 499.

THE best MODERATELY PRICED HOTELS

- **Welcome** (Brussels, Belgium; © **02/219-95-46**): This is the best little hotel in Brussels, a small place with a big welcome, and the standard of the rooms is high. Try to get proprietor Michel Smeesters to tell you about his hotel's history, preferably over a glass or two of Kwak beer—but be careful: It's a long story, and Kwak is strong beer. See p. 92.
- **Egmond** (Bruges, Belgium; © **050/34-14-45**): Think of the Egmond as your own country mansion, for not much more than a hundred bucks a room. There's just one problem with this image: The Egmond is not actually in the country. In compensation, it has its own grounds and gardens, and stands next to the Minnewater (Lover's Lake). See p. 137.
- **Firean** (Antwerp, Belgium; © **03/237-02-60**): Some hotels would be notable enough if they only shared the Firean's Art Deco style and Tiffany glass decor. So having an inventively fitted-out interior, a fine restaurant, and proprietors who care about service makes this one stand out from the crowd. See p. 180.
- **Seven Bridges** (Amsterdam, Holland; © **020/623-1329**): At some hotels, the owners aren't just running a business—they're doing what they love. The Seven Bridges is that kind of place. Pierre Keulers and Günter Glaner have found both their hobby and their profession in this fine hotel in Amsterdam. It's no exaggeration to say that all the furniture, fixtures, and fittings have been selected with loving care, and guests receive the same conscientious attention. See p. 281.
- **Amrâth Hotel DuCasque** (Maastricht, Holland; © **043/321-4343**): The Hotel DuCasque overlooks the Vrijthof, which basks in its reputation as the liveliest square in the liveliest city in the country. Despite its prestigious address, this hotel is about as moderately priced as you're likely to find in Maastricht. See p. 476.

THE best RESTAURANTS

- **Comme Chez Soi** (Brussels, Belgium; © **02/512-29-21**): An irony about this culinary holy of holies is its name: "Just Like Home." A hallowed silence descends on diners as they sample their first mouthful of French specialties with added Belgian zest. This being Belgium, the silence doesn't last long, but the taste and the memory linger. See p. 95.
- **In 't Spinnekopke** (Brussels, Belgium; © **02/511-86-95**): For a different kind of Brussels eating experience, try this down-home restaurant dating from 1762. Here

traditional Belgian dishes are given the care and attention expected of more refined—though not necessarily tastier—cuisine. See p. 102.

- **Le Sanglier des Ardennes** (Durbuy, Belgium; ✆ **086/21-32-62**): This restaurant, in a hotel in one of the prettiest of Ardennes villages, has the rustic looks and ideal location to go along with its fine country food. Walking in the surrounding wooded hills is the perfect preparation for lunch or dinner here. See p. 244.
- **De Echoput** (Apeldoorn, Holland; ✆ **055/519-1248**): Game features prominently on the menu at this restaurant, set amid the forests near Apeldoorn, on the edge of the Royal Wood. During the hunting season, try wild boar, venison, and any kind of fowl—always succulent and prepared with flair. In spring and summer, the menu's just as delectable, and in fair weather, dine on the terrace in the fresh forest air. See p. 436.
- **Château Neercanne** (Maastricht, Holland; ✆ **043/325-1359**): "To live like a god in France" goes the proverb expressing the pinnacle of earthly pleasure. You might imagine yourself to be both a god and in France if you dine at this château, which was designed following French models. What's more, in true French culinary style, the food here is seductively elegant and the wine cellar is unique and impressive—the wines are kept under perfect conditions in the marlstone caves behind the château. See p. 478.
- **Le Bouquet Garni/Salon Saint-Michel** (Luxembourg City; ✆ **26-20-06-20**): The Saint-Michel occupies a little side street in the Old Town, but it lights up the entire city with classic French cuisine that makes no concessions where quality is concerned. See p. 500.

THE best CAFES & BARS

- **Falstaff** (Brussels, Belgium; ✆ **02/511-87-89**): Le Falstaff deserves the highest accolades for its eclectic, accomplished mix of Art Nouveau and Art Deco, and its extensive drink list. This is self-satisfied, bourgeois Brussels at its best. See p. 129.
- **'t Dreupelkot** (Ghent, Belgium; ✆ **09/224-21-20**): Ghent has no shortage of fine cafes, and you can just about guarantee that any one you enter will provide pleasant memories. 't Dreupelkot adds a particularly warm glow of appreciation, but you should know that its stock in trade is *jenever,* one of the most potent alcoholic liquids known to humankind. Actually, some of 't Dreupelkot's 100 varieties are fairly mild, while others have been flavored with herbs and spices. The atmosphere in the cafe is great—it's filled with *jenever* buffs, not drunks. See p. 171.
- **Den Engel** (Antwerp, Belgium; ✆ **03/233-12-52**): There are cafes in Antwerp with a lot more action, but for a genuine Antwerp bar, it's hard to beat this one. A location on a corner of the Grote Markt adds to the attraction. To experience Den Engel's crowning glory, order a glass of Antwerp's own, lovingly poured De Koninck beer—a golden-brown liquid in a glass called a *bolleke* (little ball) that glows like amber in sunlight streaming through Den Engel's windows. See p. 184.
- **Cafe 't Smalle** (Amsterdam, Holland; ✆ **020/623-9617**): This cozy, crowded brown cafe on Amsterdam's Egelantiersgracht is usually thick with *jenever* vapor and lively conversation. Escape the crush on the splendid canal-side terrace, a perfect place to watch cyclists and cars rushing past while you rest your legs on the terrace railing. See p. 326.
- **In den Ouden Vogelstruys** (Maastricht, Holland; ✆ **043/321-4888**): This friendly, popular Maastricht watering hole was already well-trodden territory when

it came under artillery fire in some war or another in 1653 and took a hit from a cannonball that remains lodged in one of its walls. The place attracts a broad—in some individual cases, very broad—cross section of Maastricht society. See p. 479.

THE best SHOPPING

- **Antiques** (Brussels, Belgium): You'll need luck to score a bargain at the weekend antiques market on place du Grand Sablon—the dealers are well aware of the precise worth of each item in their stock and are calmly determined to get it. But it's still fun to wander the market, browsing and haggling, and who knows? You just might stumble on that hard-to-find affordable treasure. See chapter 6.
- **Chocolates** (Belgium): The Swiss might want to argue the point, but the truth is that Belgian handmade chocolates, filled with various fresh-cream flavors, are the best in the universe. You won't go wrong if you buy chocolates made by Marcolini, Wittamer, Nihoul, Leonidas, and Neuhaus, available in specialist stores all over Belgium (and in Holland and Luxembourg, too). See chapter 6.
- **Lace** (Belgium): There are two kinds of Belgian lace: exquisitely handmade pieces, and machine-made stuff. Machine-made lace is not necessarily bad, but this is the form used to mass-produce pieces of indifferent quality to meet the demand for souvenirs. The highest-quality lace is handmade. Brussels, Bruges, and Ghent are the main, though not the only, points of sale. See chapters 6, 7, and 8.
- **Diamonds** (Antwerp, Belgium): One thing is for sure: You'll be spoiled for choice in Antwerp's Diamond Quarter. Much of the trade here is carried on by the city's Orthodox Jewish community, whose conservative ways and traditional black clothing make a striking contrast to the glitter of their stock in trade. See chapter 8.
- **Flower Bulbs** (Holland): It's difficult to choose from the incredible variety of bulb shapes and colors offered in Holland. Some bulbs flower early in January; others wait until the warmer months of May or June. Knowing this, choose bulbs with different flowering times, so you'll enjoy their blooming over a long period in spring. In Amsterdam buy them from the Floating Flower market on the Singel canal. See chapter 13.
- **Delftware** (Holland): Originally, the pottery made in the factories at Delft was white, imitating tin-glazed products from Italy and Spain. But during the 16th century, blue Chinese porcelain was imported to Holland, and this was soon recognized to be of superior quality. So the Delftware factories started using a white tin glaze to cover the red clay and decorating the pottery in blue. This Delft Blue became famous the world over, along with Makkumware, which is pottery produced in the Dutch town of Makkum. Delftware and Makkumware are for sale in specialized stores all over the country, but it's far more interesting to go to one of the workshops in the towns themselves and see how it's made. Little has changed over the centuries, and all the decorating is still done by hand. See chapters 15 and 16.
- **Wine** (Luxembourg): Holland's and Belgium's modest output notwithstanding, Luxembourg is the only major wine producer in the Benelux countries. The vintage in question is the highly regarded Moselle wine, perhaps not as well known outside the Grand Duchy and its immediate neighbors as German and French wines, but fine stock nonetheless. See chapter 20.

2

BELGIUM, HOLLAND & LUXEMBOURG IN DEPTH

Nobody who lives in one of these countries—with the exception of politicos and bureaucrats—speaks routinely of the "Benelux." Whenever you read that word in this book, be advised that it's merely a convenient shorthand that does away with the need to write "Belgium, the Netherlands (Holland), and Luxembourg." No one from the Benelux—not even politicos and bureaucrats—thinks of themselves as a Beneluxian.

Despite being buffeted by the economic storms roiling the world at the time of writing, the three Benelux countries continue to enjoy an enviable standard of living, and a quality of life that makes good use of it. Their societies become more multicultural by the day, a development that's seen most clearly in the region's towns and cities—these lands are among the most urbanized on earth. For the most part, this has only added to their contemporary vibrancy, but the process has not been without stress. Even Amsterdam's famed tolerance is showing signs of strain.

Belgium is a small country. Not so small that if you blink you'll miss it, but small enough that a couple of hours of focused driving will get you from the capital, Brussels, to any corner of the realm. Yet the variety of culture, language, history, and cuisine crammed into this space would do credit to a land many times its size. Belgium's diversity is a product of its location at the cultural crossroads of western Europe. The boundary between the Continent's Germanic north and Latin south cuts clear across the country's middle.

Like an Atlantis in reverse, Holland has emerged from the sea. Much of the country was once a pattern of islands, precariously separated from the North Sea by dunes. As the centuries rolled past, these islands were patiently stitched together by Dutch ingenuity and hard work. The outcome is a canvas-flat, green-and-silver Mondrian of a country, with nearly half its land and two-thirds of its 16 million inhabitants below sea level.

The Grand Duchy of Luxembourg is tiny. Its borders seem unlikely to enclose so many worthy travel delights. Yet within this country are the remnants of a rich history and a landscape with scenery that varies from wild highlands to peaceful river valleys fringed by vineyards to plains dotted with picturesque villages and farmlands.

To make themselves even more livable than they already are, the big cities of Brussels, Amsterdam, Antwerp, Rotterdam, and The Hague have been building out their rapid-transit systems, redeveloping decayed or decaying inner-city and harbor zones, and expanding their cultural offerings. All the while, more ethnic eateries and shops are springing up. Other cities, such as Bruges, Ghent, Liège, Utrecht, Maastricht, and Luxembourg City (to name just a few!), are doing no less, and I recommend that you get out of the big cities and find out what's up in these other places during your visit to the Benelux.

BELGIUM TODAY

After a long history of occupation by foreign powers, Belgium has emerged as a site for European nations to come together. Brussels—which hosts the headquarters of both the European Union and NATO—is now home to the world's largest concentration of international diplomats.

Modern Belgium is a parliamentary democracy under a constitutional monarch, King Albert II. The government exists in a more-or-less permanent state of crisis due to the cultural and linguistic divide. And that's when there even is a government with ambitious regional politicians, particularly in Flanders, often pushing the country to the brink of dissolution. In 2010 Flanders was once again threatening to break away and form its own government, in light of inconclusive election results and Wallonia's weaker economic status. Still, reports of Belgium's death have been published before and have always turned out to be greatly exaggerated, and it seems likely to be no different this time around.

For a graphic picture of Belgium's two ethnic regions, Dutch-speaking Vlaanderen (Flanders) and French-speaking Wallonie (Wallonia), draw an imaginary east-west line across the country just south of Brussels. North of the line is Flanders, where you find the medieval cities of Bruges, Ghent, and Antwerp, and Belgium's North Sea coastline. South of the line is Wallonia. Then there's Brussels, the capital, roughly in the geographic middle, and going off on a trajectory of its own as the "capital of Europe."

It has been said that Belgium suffers severely from linguistic indigestion. The inhabitants of Flanders speak *Nederlands* (Low Countries Speech), which is generally rendered in English as Dutch, although you may hear the language referred to as *Vlaams* (Flemish) in Flanders. The inhabitants of Wallonia speak French, and a minority still speak the old Walloon dialect. In Brussels the two languages mingle, but French has the upper hand. So strong is the feeling for each language in its own region that, along the line where they meet, it's not unusual for French to be the daily tongue on one side of a street and Flemish on the other. Throughout the country, road signs acknowledge both languages by giving multiple versions of the same place name—Brussel/Bruxelles or Brugge/Bruges, for example. There's even a small area in eastern Belgium where German is spoken. Belgium, then, has not one, but three, official languages: Dutch, French, and German.

In short, far from being a homogeneous, harmonious people with one strong national identity, Belgians take considerable pride in their individualistic attributes.

The vast majority of Belgians are Catholic, though there's more than a smattering of Protestants, a small Jewish community, and a rising proportion of immigrant Muslims and their locally born children. Down the centuries, Belgians—nobles and peasants alike—have proclaimed their Christian faith by way of impressive cathedrals, churches, paintings, and holy processions. The tradition continues today.

Folklore still plays a large part in Belgium's national daily life, with local myths giving rise to some of the country's most colorful pageants and festivals, such as Ypres's Festival of the Cats, Bruges's Pageant of the Golden Tree, and the stately Ommegang in Brussels. In Belgium's renowned puppet theaters, marionettes based on folkloric characters identify their native cities—Woltje (Little Walloon) belongs to Brussels, Schele to Antwerp, Pierke to Ghent, and Tchantchès to Liège.

Undoubtedly, Belgians have a finely tuned appreciation for the good things in life; when standards are met, watch Belgian eyes light up. Appreciation then moves very close to reverence, whether inspired by a great artistic masterpiece, or a homemade mayonnaise of just the right lightness, or one of Belgium's more than 450 native beers. If you have shared that experience with a Belgian companion, chances are you'll find your own sense of appreciation taking on a finer edge.

LOOKING BACK AT BELGIUM

Julius Caesar first marched his Roman legions against the ancient Belgae tribes in 58 B.C. For nearly 5 centuries thereafter, Belgium was shielded from the barbarians by the great Roman defense line on the Rhine.

From the beginning of the 5th century, Roman rule gave way to the Franks. In 800, their great king Charlemagne was named emperor of the West. He instituted an era of agricultural reform, setting up local rulers known as counts, who rose up to seize more power after Charlemagne's death. In 843, Charlemagne's grandsons signed the Treaty of Verdun, which split French-allied (but Dutch-speaking) Flanders in the north from the southern (French-speaking) Walloon provinces.

Then came Viking invaders. A Flemish defender known as Baldwin Iron-Arm became the first count of Flanders in 862; his house eventually ruled over a domain that included the Low Countries and lands as far south as the Scheldt (Escaut) in France. Meanwhile, powerful prince-bishops controlled most of Wallonia from their seat in Liège.

Flanders Rising

As Flanders grew larger and stronger, its cities thrived, and its citizens wrested more and more self-governing powers. Bruges emerged as a leading center of European trade; its monopoly on English cloth attracted bankers and financiers from Germany and Lombardy. Ghent and Ypres (Ieper) prospered in the wool trade. Powerful trade and manufacturing guilds emerged and erected splendid edifices as their headquarters.

As towns took on city-state status, the mighty count of Flanders, with close ties to France, grew less and less mighty; in 1297, France's Philip the Fair attempted to annex Flanders. However, he had not reckoned on the stubborn resistance of Flemish common folk. Led by Jan Breydel, a lowly weaver, and Pieter de Coninck, a butcher, they rallied to face a heavily armored French military. The battle took place in 1302 in the fields surrounding Kortrijk. When it was over, victorious artisans and craftsmen scoured the bloody battlefield, triumphantly gathering hundreds of golden spurs from slain French knights. Their victory at the "Battle of the Golden Spurs" is celebrated by the Flemish to this day.

The Burgundian Era

Philip the Good, duke of Burgundy in the mid-1400s, gained control of virtually all the Low Countries. His progeny, through a series of marriages, consolidated their holdings into a single Burgundian "Netherlands," or Low Countries. Brussels, Antwerp, Mechelen, and Leuven attained new prominence as centers of trade, commerce, and the arts.

This era was one of immense wealth, much of which was poured into fine public buildings, impressive mansions, and soaring Gothic cathedrals that survive to this day. Wealthy patrons made possible the brilliant works of Flemish artists such as Jan van Eyck, Hieronymous Bosch, Rogier van der Weyden, and German-born Hans Memling. Flemish opulence became a byword around Europe.

By the end of the 1400s, however, Charles the Bold, last of the dukes of Burgundy, had lost to the French king on the field of battle, and once more French royalty turned a covetous eye on the Low Countries. To French consternation, Mary of Burgundy, the duke's heir, married Maximilian of Austria. The provinces became part of the Austrian Habsburg Empire.

A grandson of that union, Charles V, born in Ghent and reared in Mechelen, presided for 40 years over most of Europe, including Spain and its New World possessions. He was beset by the Protestant Reformation, which created dissension among the once solidly Catholic populace. It all proved too much for the great monarch, and he abdicated in favor of his son, Philip II of Spain.

The Spanish Invasion

Philip ascended to power in an impressive ceremony at Coudenberg Palace in Brussels in 1555. An ardent Catholic who spoke neither Dutch nor French, he brought the infamous instruments of the Inquisition to bear on an increasingly Protestant—and increasingly rebellious—Low Countries population. The response from his Protestant subjects was violent: For a month in 1566, they went on a rampage of destruction, the Beeldenstorm (Iconoclastic Fury), that saw churches pillaged, religious statues smashed, and other religious works of art burned.

An angry Philip ordered the duke of Alba to lead 10,000 Spanish troops in a wave of retaliatory strikes. The atrocities Alba and his "Council of Blood" committed as he swept through the Spanish Netherlands are legendary. He was merciless—when the Catholic counts of Egmont and Hornes tried to intercede with Philip, he put them under arrest for 6 months, and then had them publicly beheaded on the Grand-Place in Brussels.

Instead of submission, this sort of intimidation gave rise to a brutal conflict that lasted from 1568 to 1648. Led by William the Silent and other nobles who raised private armies, the Protestants fought on doggedly until, finally, independence was achieved for the seven undefeated provinces to the north, which became the fledgling country of the Netherlands. Those in the south remained under the thumb of Spain and gradually returned to the Catholic Church.

An Independent Nation

In 1795, Belgium wound up once more under the rule of France. It was not until Napoleon Bonaparte's crushing defeat at Waterloo—just miles from Brussels—that Belgians began to think of national independence as a real possibility. Its time had not yet come, however; under the Congress of Vienna, Belgium was once more united with the provinces of Holland. But the Dutch soon learned that governing the unruly Belgians was more than they had bargained for, and the 1830 rebellion in Brussels was the last straw. A provisional Belgian government was formed with an elected National Congress. On July 21, 1831, Belgium officially became a constitutional monarchy when a German prince, Leopold of Saxe-Coburg-Gotha, became king.

The new nation set about developing its coal and iron natural resources, and its textile, manufacturing, and shipbuilding industries. The country was hardly unified by this process, however, for most of the natural resources were to be found in the French-speaking Walloon region, where prosperity grew much more rapidly than in Flanders.

The Flemish, while happy to be freed from the rule of their Dutch neighbors, resented the greater influence of their French-speaking compatriots.

War & Peace

It took another invasion to bring a semblance of unity. When German forces swept over the country in 1914, the Belgians mounted a defense that made them heroes of World War I—even though parts of the Flemish population openly collaborated with the enemy, hailing them as "liberators" from Walloon domination.

With the coming of peace, Belgium found its southern coal, iron, and manufacturing industries reeling, while the northern Flemish regions were moving steadily ahead by developing light industry, especially around Antwerp. Advanced agricultural methods yielded greater productivity and higher profits for Flemish farmers. By the end of the 1930s, the Flemish population outnumbered the Walloons by a large enough majority to install their beloved language as the official voice of education, justice, and civil administration in Flanders.

With the outbreak of World War II, Belgium was once more overrun by German forces. King Leopold III decided to surrender to the invaders, remain in Belgium, and try to soften the harsh effects of occupation. The Belgian Resistance was among the most determined and successful of the underground organizations that fought against Nazi occupation in Europe. On the other side, Flemish and Walloon quislings formed separate Waffen-SS formations that fought for the Nazis in Russia. By the war's end, the king was imprisoned in Germany and a regent was appointed as head of state. His controversial decision to surrender led to bitter debate when he returned to the throne in 1950, and in 1951 he stepped down in favor of his son, Baudouin.

Unity & Disunity

During King Baudouin's 42 years on the throne, much progress was made in achieving harmony among Belgium's linguistically and culturally diverse population. In the

Invented Here

Betcha didn't know that a Belgian invented the Internet . . . kind of. In 1934, Paul Otlet wrote a paper titled *Traité de Documentation* in which he foresaw a Universal Network for Information and Documentation. Access would be through multimedia workstations. These didn't exist yet—an inconvenient fact that, since he was a lawyer, Otlet was perfectly able to disregard.

1970s, efforts were made to grant increasing autonomy to the Flemish and Walloons in the areas where each was predominant, and to apportion power to each group within the national government and the political parties. Finally, in 1993, the constitution was amended to create a federal state, made up of the autonomous regions of Flanders and Wallonia (and its semiautonomous German-speaking community), together with the bilingual city of Brussels.

Baudouin died in 1993, removing one of the pillars of unity. His successor, his brother Albert II, has won respect for his conscientious efforts but has not made the same personal connection with the people.

BELGIAN ART & ARCHITECTURE

Art

Despite its small geographic size, Belgium has exerted a significant influence on Western art. The works of Bosch, Bruegel, Rubens, van Dyck, van Eyck, and Magritte represent only a fraction of the treasures you see gracing the walls of the notable art museums in Brussels, Bruges, Ghent, and Antwerp.

The golden age of Flemish painting occurred in the 1400s, a century dominated by the so-called Flemish Primitives—so dubbed because they were "first," not because they were unsophisticated—whose work was almost always religious in theme, usually commissioned for churches and chapels, and largely lacking in perspective. As the medieval cities of Flanders flourished, more and more princes, wealthy merchants, and prosperous guilds became patrons of the arts.

Art's function was still to praise God and illustrate religious allegory, but **Jan van Eyck** (ca. 1390–1441), one of the earliest Flemish Masters, brought a sharp new perspective to bear on traditional subject matter. His *Adoration of the Mystic Lamb,* created with his brother Hubert for St. Bavo's Cathedral in Ghent, incorporates a realistic landscape into its biblical theme. The Primitives sought to mirror reality, to portray both people and nature exactly as they appeared to the human eye, down to the tiniest detail, without classical distortions or embellishments. These artists would work meticulously for months—even years—on a single commission, often painting with a single-haired paintbrush to achieve a painstakingly lifelike quality.

The greatest Flemish artist of the 16th century, **Pieter Bruegel the Elder** (ca. 1525–69), lived and worked for many years in Antwerp. From 1520 to 1580, the city was one of the world's busiest ports and banking centers, and it eclipsed Bruges as a center for the arts. Many of the artists working here looked to the Italian Renaissance

Masters for their models of perfection. Bruegel, who had studied in Italy, integrated Renaissance influences with the traditional style of his native land. He frequently painted rural and peasant life, as in his *Wedding Procession,* on view at the Musée de la Ville in Brussels.

In 1563, Bruegel moved to Brussels, where he lived at rue Haute 132. Here his two sons, also artists, were born. **Pieter Brueghel the Younger** (ca. 1564–1637) became known for copying his father's paintings; **Jan Brueghel the Elder** (1568–1625) specialized in decorative paintings of flowers and fruits.

Peter Paul Rubens (1577–1640) was the most influential baroque painter of the early 17th century. The drama in his works, such as *The Raising of the Cross,* housed in the Antwerp cathedral, comes from the dynamic, writhing figures in his canvases. His renditions of the female form gave rise to the term "Rubenesque," which describes the voluptuous women who appear in his paintings.

Portraitist **Anthony van Dyck** (1599–1641), one of the most important talents to emerge from Rubens's studio, served as court painter to Charles I of England, though some of his best religious work remains in Belgium. Look for the *Lamentation* in the Koninklijke Museum voor Schone Kunsten in Antwerp, and the *Crucifixion* in Mechelen Cathedral.

Belgium's influence on the art world is by no means limited to the Old Masters. **James Ensor** (1860–1949) was a late-19th-century pioneer of modern art. One of his most famous works is the *Entry of Christ into Brussels.* Ensor developed a broadly expressionistic technique, liberating his use of color from the demands of realism. He took as his subject disturbing, fantastic visions and images.

Surrealism flourished in Belgium, perhaps because of the earlier Flemish artists with a penchant for the bizarre and grotesque. **Paul Delvaux** (1897–1989) became famous, but the best known of the Belgian surrealists is unquestionably **René Magritte** (1898–1967). His fantastical images of pipes that are not pipes, bowler-hatted men who fall like black rain from the skies, and much more have become widely recognized images in popular culture. Many of these modern works can be seen in the Musées Royaux des Beaux-Arts (p. 112) in Brussels and the Koninklijke Museum voor Schone Kunsten (p. 175) in Antwerp. The fine-arts museums in Ghent, Tournai, and Liège, and the modern art museums in Antwerp and Ostend, are also major sources.

Carrying the flag into modern times are artists like **Marcel Broodthaers** (1924–76), the founding father of Belgian conceptual art, and **Pierre Alechinsky** (b. 1927), a member of the post-war Cobra group of artists.

Architecture

Examples of Gothic civic architecture abound in Flanders. The great ecclesiastical examples are St. Michael's Cathedral in Brussels, in which the choir is the earliest Gothic work in Belgium, and the churches of Our Lady in Mechelen, St. Peter's in Leuven, and St. Bavo's in Ghent. Antwerp Cathedral is perhaps the most imposing example of late Gothic; it was begun in 1352 at the east end and the nave was completed in 1474.

Among the finest examples of commercial Gothic architecture are the Cloth Hall at Ypres (built 1200–1304), the Cloth Hall in Mechelen, the Butchers Guildhall in

Ghent, and the Butchers Guildhall in Antwerp. Gothic style remained dominant until the early 16th century, when Renaissance decorative elements began to appear.

Around the turn of the 20th century, Belgium produced one of the greatest exponents of the new Art Nouveau style of architecture and interior design, the prime materials of which were glass and iron, worked with decorative curved lines and floral and geometric motifs. The work of **Victor Horta** (1861–1947) can be seen in Brussels at the Tassel House (1893), the Hôtel Solvay (1895), and the ambitious Maison du Peuple (1896–99), with its concave, curved facades and location within an irregularly shaped square.

BELGIUM IN POPULAR CULTURE

Books

Belgium's most prolific man of letters—indeed, one of the most prolific authors of all time—is Georges Simenon (1903–89), whose prodigious output very nearly defies belief. The Liège-born author wrote some 200 novels and 150 novellas, along with many other works, from autobiographical books to magazine and newspaper articles, and still found time to produce dozens more novels under a variety of pseudonyms. He is undoubtedly best known for the 75 novels and dozens of short stories in the Inspector Maigret detective series, most of them set in Paris.

The two best-known Belgian novels would likely be *Het Verdriet van België* (*The Sorrow of Belgium;* 1983) by Hugo Claus, which deals with the Nazi occupation; and *Bruges-la-Morte* (*Dead Bruges;* 1892) by Georges Rodenbach, which deals with themes of love and loss, but is perhaps best known for having put Bruges on the European map as a tourist destination.

Brussels-born author Marguerite Yourcenar (1903–88), the first woman to be elected to the French Academy, and who spent a considerable part of her life living in Maine, wrote *Alexis* (1929), *Memoirs of Hadrian* (1951), and *The Abyss/Zeno of Bruges* (1976).

Comics

Belgium produces 30 million comic-strip books annually, and exports 75% of them. The Tintin books alone have sold more than 200 million copies since the youthful adventurer first appeared in 1929, created by the Belgian Georges Rémi, better known as Hergé (the initials of his name reversed and written as they would be pronounced in French). Like all good comic-strip characters, Tintin and his companions—the dog Snowy, short-fused Captain Haddock, the dopey near-look-alike detectives Thomson and Thompson, and absent-minded Professor Calculus—are ageless.

Lucky Luke, the cowpoke who beats his shadow to the draw and whose horse, Jolly Jumper, plays a mean hand at poker, stars in more than 80 adventures—each of which ends with the hero riding into the sunset singing "I'm a poor lonesome cowboy," and it has been adapted for television and computer games. His creator, illustrator Morris (real name Maurice de Bevere), a native of Kortrijk, died at age 77 in 2001.

Themes of displacement and anomie run through the stories in *Thorgal*, though the attractions of a good fight are not passed up. Thorgal Aegirsson, born in space and sent to earth by his mother after his father and grandfather quarreled over whether to invade the planet, lives during the Viking era and knows how to use a broadsword and battle-ax to defend himself, his beautiful wife, Aarcia, and their two children. He has the Norse gods on his case and must contend against them along with a gallery of cruel human enemies.

There's also a darker side to comic strips: *Bande Dessinée Erotique*. Many of these books are harmlessly titillating productions; others feature graphic images of rape, bestiality, torture, and what verges on pedophilia.

Film

I think it's fair to say that Belgium is not one of the world's great movie powers. It's a rare Belgian film that's seen by more than about 10 people outside of the cast and the crew and their relatives. Then again, Belgium has given Hollywood a star in Jean-Claude "the Muscles from Brussels" Van Damme, and Agatha Christie's ageless fictional detective Hercule Poirot has often graced the silver screen.

Dominique Deruddere's *Everybody Famous* was nominated in 2000 for the Academy Award for Best Foreign Language Film, but it didn't win. Bruges starred alongside Colin Farrell, Brendan Gleeson, Ralph Fiennes, and Clémence Poésy in the 2008 hit movie (literally) *In Bruges,* about two contract killers who take refuge in Bruges when a hit goes wrong.

Belgian comic-strip characters have gotten the Hollywood treatment for a few new releases. Announced for summer 2011, *The Smurfs Movie* is a live-action/CGI/animated film based on *les Schtroumpfs,* which features small blue creatures, better known in English as the Smurfs, created by Belgian cartoonist Peyo (Pierre Culliford; 1928–92) and made famous internationally via a 1980s American TV franchise. The movie is projected to be the first of a Smurfs trilogy. Next up, later in 2011, is Steven Spielberg's *The Adventures of Tintin: Secrets of the Unicorn,* based on three of the Tintin tales written and illustrated by Belgian cartoonist Hergé (Georges Remi; 1907–83). Peter Jackson may direct a second Tintin movie, and Spielberg and Jackson may collaborate on a third.

Music

Where would jazz be today if it weren't for Belgium? If you are scratching your head trying to come up with the name of a great Belgian jazz musician, don't bother (though virtuoso harmonica player Jean "Toots" Thielemans, who played theme music for movies such as *Midnight Cowboy, The Sugarland Express,* and *The Getwaway,* would be a decent answer). But if it hadn't been for Adolphe Sax (1814–94), nobody would have invented the saxophone—and then where would jazz be today?

Singer/songwriter Jacques Brel (1929–78) brought unequalled passion to his performances of songs of love, comedy, low life, and more. His discography includes *Quand On n'a que l'Amour* (*If We Only Have Love*) and *Ne Me Quitte Pas* (*If You Go Away*). Should you want to dig into Brel's Belgian oeuvre, listen to songs like *Le Plat Pays, l'Ostendaise, Knokke-Le Zoute Tango, Bruxelles,* and *Marieke.*

And then there's the still very much alive schmaltzy singer Helmut Lotti.

EATING & DRINKING IN BELGIUM

Cuisine

Belgian chefs may be influenced by the French, but they add their own special touches. Native specialties in Wallonia include *jambon d'Ardenne* (ham from the hills and valleys of the Ardennes) and savory *boudin de Liège* (a succulent sausage mixed with herbs). Almost every menu lists *tomates aux crevettes* (tomatoes stuffed with tiny, delicately sweet North Sea shrimps and light, homemade mayonnaise), which is filling enough for a light lunch and delicious as an appetizer. A special treat awaits visitors in May and June in the form of Belgian asparagus, and from October to March there's chicory, which is known as *endive/witloof* in Belgium.

Belgian cuisine is based on the country's own regional traditions and produce, such as asparagus, chicory (endive), and the humble Brussels sprout. Of course, Belgium is also known for its selection of more decadent treats like waffles. Street vendors throughout the country sell Liège waffles, a concoction that's sweet and rich enough not to need any toppings, as well as the rectangular-shaped Belgian or Brussels waffles, which are lighter and less sweet and often topped with cream or fresh fruit.

Handmade Belgian chocolates (known generically as *pralines*) are the world champs, so lethally addictive they ought to be sold with a government health warning. This applies in particular to those made by artisanal Chocolatier Mary and arty Marcolini in Brussels, and more widely available brands like Wittamer, Nihoul, Neuhaus, and Leonidas. Purchase them loose, in bags weighing from 100 grams or boxes of 2 kilograms or more. Take a prepared box, or simply point to those you want, or ask the assistant to select a mixture. Made with real cream, they do not keep well—but you weren't planning on keeping them for long anyway, were you?

Most places serve both a *plat du jour/dagschotel* (plate of the day) and a good-value two- or three-course menu. A tradition in Brussels is to cook with local beers like gueuze and faro. Flanders has added its own ingredients to the mix of Belgian cuisine. The Flemish share the Dutch fondness for raw herring, generally eaten with equally raw onions, while *sole à l'Ostendaise* (sole in a white-wine sauce) and the small, gray North Sea shrimps are firm favorites. River fish used to be the main ingredient of the Flemish souplike stew called *waterzooï,* but today's rivers being polluted, chicken is now a more familiar ingredient.

If you're basically a potatoes person, you're in good company, for Belgians dote on their *steak-frites,* available at virtually every restaurant—even when not listed on the menu. These are twice-fried potatoes, as light as the proverbial feather. They're sold in paper cones on many street corners and (in my opinion) are best when topped with homemade mayonnaise, though you may prefer tomato or curry sauce. *Frites* will accompany almost anything you order in a restaurant.

Seafood anywhere in Belgium is fresh and delicious. *Moules* (mussels) are a specialty in Brussels, where you find a concentration of restaurants along Petite rue des Bouchers that feature them in just about every guise you can imagine. (Ironically,

Belgian mussels actually come from Zeeland in Holland and may, in fact, be the only Dutch products Belgians will admit to being any good.) *Homard* (lobster) comes in a range of dishes. Don't miss the heavenly Belgian creation called *écrevisses à la liègeoise* (crayfish in a rich butter, cream, and white-wine sauce). Eel, often "swimming" in a grass-green sauce, is popular in both Flanders (where it's called *paling in 't groen*) and Wallonia (*anguilles au vert*).

False Friend

Watch out for *steak Américain* on Francophone menus. This might sound like a nice, big, mouthwateringly juicy, American-style steak, but it is in fact raw chopped beef!

No matter where you eat, you should know that service will be professional but not necessarily speedy. Belgians don't just dine; they savor each course—if you're in a hurry, you're better off heading for a street vendor or an imported fast-food establishment.

Drinks

What to drink with all those tasty dishes? Why, beer, of course! Belgium is justly famous for its brewing tradition, and this tiny country has more than 100 breweries producing around 450 different brews. The majority are local beers, specialties of a region, city, town, or village. Some famous pilsners are Stella Artois, Jupiler, Maes, Primus, and Eupener; ales to look for are Duvel, De Koninck, and Kwak. Hoegaarden is a well-known wheat beer. Unique to the country are lambic beers (beer produced by spontaneous fermentation and brewed only in Brussels and the surrounding area), such as faro (a lambic sweetened with sugar), kriek (a fruit lambic made with cherries), and gueuze (a blend of lambics). Then there are the heavenly tasting beers brewed by Trappist monks (or contracted out to commercial breweries). There are six Trappist breweries in the land: Chimay, Orval, Rochefort, Achel, Westmalle, and Westvleteren.

Each local beer has a distinct, and often beautiful, glass (and bottle), which is why you can instantly tell what everyone is drinking in a Belgian bar. Needless to say, with so many choices, it may take quite a bit of sampling to find a favorite.

For a *digestif*, you might try a gin, in Flanders known as *jenever* (or, colloquially, as *witteke*), and in Wallonia known as *genièvre* (colloquially as *pèkèt*). This stiff grain-spirit is often served in glasses little bigger than a thimble. Belgium's 70 *jenever* distilleries produce some 270 varieties, some flavored with juniper, coriander, or other herbs and spices. Among notable brands are Filliers Oude Graanjenever, De Poldenaar Oude Antwerpsche, Heinrich Pèkèt de la Piconette, Sint-Pol, and van Damme. *Jenever* in a stone bottle makes an ideal gift.

In recent decades, Belgian vineyards have been slowly re-established, reversing a loss that began with the onset of the Little Ice Age in the 15th century. Most of the wineries, and five out of the seven officially recognized geographical wine regions, are in Flanders. Total annual output is less than 200,000 liters (53,000 U.S. gallons/44,000 imperial gallons), not even a quarter of neighboring Holland's, and a tiny fraction of neighboring Luxembourg's. Among the country's best labels are those of Wijnkasteel Genoels-Elderen (www.wijnkasteel.com), northeast of Tongeren, and Château

Bon Baron (www.chateaubonbaron.com), in the Meuse River valley between Dinant and Namur.

HOLLAND TODAY

The Netherlands is small enough that a burst of vigorous driving will get you from one corner of the realm to the other in a morning, and you can travel by train from Amsterdam to the farthest point of the rail network in an afternoon. The nation's 42,000 sq. km (16,500 sq. miles) are among the most densely populated in the world, holding 16 million people, or approximately 1,000 per square mile. The crowding is most noticeable in the Randstad (Rim City), the heavily populated area that includes the cities of Amsterdam, Rotterdam, The Hague, Leiden, Haarlem, Utrecht, and Delft. Elsewhere the land is much more sparsely populated.

For the visitor, Holland today presents much the same face it has over the centuries—a serene landscape and an industrious population who treasure their age-old tradition of tolerance and who welcome people of all political, religious, and ideological persuasions. Today almost a million (6%) of the country's inhabitants are Muslim. In recent years, though, there have been indications that, faced with threats from radical Islamists, the welcome mat is wearing thin. The politician Geert Wilders has become a lightning rod for the racial tensions in contemporary Dutch society, inheriting some of the anti-Islam mantle of the gay populist politician Pym Fortuyn, assassinated in 2002 by a pro-Muslim Dutch activist, and of filmmaker Theo van Gogh, murdered by a Dutch-Moroccan Islamist in 2004. Wilders heads Holland's third largest party, the Party for Freedom (PVV), which in elections in 2010 increased its representation from 9 to 24 out of 150 seats in the Lower House of Parliament. The PVV views Dutch society, culture, European values, and public safety as threatened by the growth of the Muslim community and of radical Islam. Wilders, who has described the Koran as a "fascist book," and who wants Muslim migration into Holland halted and Muslims currently living in the country to be "encouraged" to leave, lives under permanent police protection due to threats to his life. Various surveys of Dutch public opinion suggest a society that's split on his views. At press time, Wilders was on trial in Holland for inciting hatred and discrimination; the judges in the case were dismissed for alleged bias against him, and a new trial was being awaited.

Holland is a constitutional monarchy headed by Queen Beatrix of the House of Orange (opinion surveys regularly give her an 80% approval rating). The heir apparent is her oldest son, Willem-Alexander (b. 1967).

Let's clear up some matters of nomenclature. "Dutch" is the result of a 15th-century misunderstanding on the part of the English, who couldn't distinguish too clearly between the people of the northern Low Countries and the various German peoples. So to describe the former, they simply corrupted the German *Deutsch* to Dutch.

The term "Holland," too, is a bit of a misnomer as, strictly speaking, it refers only to the provinces of Noord-Holland and Zuid-Holland and not to the whole country. The Dutch themselves call their country *Nederland* (the Netherlands) and themselves *Nederlanders.* But they recognize that Holland and Dutch are popular internationally and are here to stay, so, being a practical people, they make use of them.

Dutch people have a passion for detail that would boggle the mind of a statistician—and a sense of order and propriety that sends them into a tailspin if you mess things up. They organize everything (people, land, flower beds), and they love to make schedules and stick to them. They may allow you to indulge an occasional whim, though they haven't a clue what it means to "play it by ear."

"The Dutch Disease" is what a conservative U.S. columnist called Holland's social liberalism. But not many of the hookers in Amsterdam's Red Light District are Dutch, and relatively few denizens of the smoking coffeeshops are Dutch. If Amsterdam is a latter-day Sodom and Gomorrah, it's one mainly for visitors.

The uniquely Dutch combination of tolerance and individualism impacts areas of personal and social morality that in other countries are still red-button issues. In 2001, the world's first same-sex marriage, with a legal status identical to that of heterosexual matrimony, took place in Amsterdam. The Dutch Parliament legalized regulated euthanasia ("mercy killing"), making the Netherlands the first country in the world to do so. And then there's prostitution and drug use.

Authorities are not duty bound to prosecute criminal acts, leaving a loophole for social experimentation in areas that technically are illegal. It has been wryly said that the Netherlands has one of the lowest crime rates in Europe because whenever something becomes a criminal problem, the Dutch make it legal. Don't laugh—at least not in Holland—or you may find you've touched the natives where they're tender. The Dutch will take aim at anyone, on any issue, outside their borders. Just so long as it's understood that everything *inside* has arrived at that hallowed state of perfection.

Popular opinion notwithstanding, narcotic drugs are illegal in the Netherlands. But the Dutch treat drug use mainly as a medical problem rather than purely as a crime. The authorities distinguish between soft drugs like cannabis, which are considered unlikely to cause addiction and pose a minor health risk, and hard drugs like heroin and cocaine, which are highly addictive and pose significant risks to users' health. Both types are illegal, but the law is tougher on hard drugs. Ironically, improvements in Dutch cannabis cultivation techniques have increased the concentration of the active ingredient THC from 9% to 18% in the past 10 years.

The Netherlands has significantly lower rates of heroin addiction, drug use, and addiction in general, and of drug-related deaths than Britain, France, Germany, and other European countries that criticize Holland so fiercely on this issue. Still, the Dutch "tradition" of allowing visitors to the country to pop into a "coffeeshop" to smoke an illegal but tolerated cannabis joint is under threat. A legal ruling has upheld the mayor of Maastricht's decision to end cross-border "drugs tourism" into that town by banning foreigners from its smoking coffeeshops. Rosendaal and Bergen op Zoom, two additional border towns plagued by drugs tourists, have simply shut down all of their coffeeshops. The most serious threat comes from the coalition government elected in 2010, which has announced its intention to force all of the country's surviving coffeeshops—their number reduced from a peak of close to 2,000 in 1997 to around 650, and still falling—to become members-only clubs. These would be open only to legal residents of the Netherlands, thereby shutting out the tens of thousands of drugs tourists who visit the country each year. With some Amsterdam coffeeshops claiming that 99% of their customers are tourists—though an overall estimate of 40% is widely accepted—it's clear that many coffeeshops will be forced out of business if the proposals become law.

Prostitution is legal in Holland, and prostitutes work in clean premises, pay taxes, receive regular medical checks, are eligible for welfare, and have their own trade union. The streetwalker "heroin whores" need to be excluded from this ostensibly idyllic picture of the world's oldest profession.

LOOKING BACK AT HOLLAND

The earliest inhabitants of what is now the Netherlands were three tribal groups who settled the marshy deltas of the Low Countries in the dawn of recorded history. They were the Belgae of the southern regions; the Batavii, who settled in the area of the Great Rivers; and the fiercely independent Frisii, who had taken up residence along the northern coast. Each tribe posed a challenge to Julius Caesar when he came calling in the 1st century B.C., but the Romans managed, after prolonged and effective objections from the locals, to get both the Belgae and the Batavii to knuckle under.

Having seen off the Romans, the Frisians in the 5th century repelled the next wave of would-be conquerors, hordes of Saxons and Franks who had overrun the Romano-Batavians. Although the Franks in the late 5th century embraced Christianity, not until the late 8th century did the Frisians abandon their pagan gods, and then only when the mighty Charlemagne, king of the Franks and emperor of the West, compelled them to.

Good for Business

By the 13th and 14th centuries, the nobility were busy building most of the castles and fortified manor houses throughout Holland that now attract tourists. Meanwhile the Catholic hierarchy grew both powerful and wealthy; the bishops of Maastricht and Utrecht played key roles in politics, and they preserved their legacy by erecting splendid cathedrals, abbeys, and monasteries.

During the 14th and 15th centuries, Holland's position at the mouths of the great west European rivers made it a focal point in power struggles. The House of Burgundy became the first major feudal power in the Low Countries, consolidating its hold on the region by acquiring fiefdoms one by one through the various means of marriage, inheritance, and military force. Its day soon passed, however, and the Austrian Habsburg emperor Maximilian acquired the Low Countries from the Burgundians by much the same means.

Amsterdam began its rise to commercial prosperity in 1323, when the Count of Holland Floris VI established the city as one of two toll points for the import of beer. The city's skillful merchants established guilds of craftsmen and put ships to sea to catch North Sea herring. They expanded into trade in salted Baltic herring, Norwegian salted and dried cod and cod-liver oil, German beer and salt, bales of linen and woolen cloth from the Low Countries and England, Russian furs and candle wax, Polish grain and flour, and Swedish timber and iron.

Wars of Religion

Dutch citizens began to embrace the Protestant church at the same time that the Low Countries came under the rule of Charles V, the Catholic Habsburg emperor and king of Spain. Holland became a pressure point and fulcrum for the shifting political scene that the Reformation occasioned everywhere in Europe. The rigorous doctrines of John Calvin and his firm belief in the separation of church and state began to take root.

When Charles relinquished the Spanish throne to his son Philip II in 1555, things took a nasty turn for the Dutch. An ardent Catholic, Philip was determined to defeat the Reformation and set out to hunt heretics throughout his empire. He dispatched the infamous duke of Alba to the Low Countries to carry out the Inquisition's "death to heretics" edict. The Dutch resented Philip's intrusion into their affairs and began a resistance movement, led by William of Orange, count of Holland, known as William the Silent, who loudly declared: "I cannot approve of princes attempting to control the conscience of their subjects and wanting to rob them of the liberty of faith."

Those towns that declined to join the fight were spared destruction when the Spanish invaded. Spanish armies marched inexorably through Holland, besting the defenses of each city to which they laid siege, with few exceptions. In an ingenious if desperate move in 1574, William saved Leiden by flooding the province, allowing his ships to sail right up to the city's walls.

This victory galvanized the Dutch in fighting for their independence. In 1579, the Dutch nobles formed the Union of Utrecht, in which they agreed to fight together in a united front. Although the union was devised solely to prosecute the battle against Spain, consolidation inevitably occurred, and by the turn of the 17th century, the seven northern provinces of what had been the Spanish Netherlands became the United Provinces.

The struggle with Spain continued until 1648, but a new, prosperous era was about to begin.

The Golden Age

Over the first 50 to 75 years of the 17th century, the legendary Dutch entrepreneurial gift would come into its own. These years have since become known as the Golden Age. It seemed every business venture the Dutch initiated during this time turned a profit and that each of their many expeditions to the unknown places of the world resulted in a new jewel in the Dutch trading empire. Colonies and trade were established to provide the luxury-hungry merchants at home with new delights, such as fresh ginger from Java, foxtails from America, fine porcelain from China, and flower bulbs from Turkey that produced big, bright, waxy flowers and grew quite readily in Holland's sandy soil—tulips. Holland was getting rich.

Beating the Dutch

The 17th-century Dutch got up English noses by competing for maritime trade and, in 1667, by sailing boldly up the Medway near London and trashing the English fleet. So the English added verbal abuse to their arsenal. That's why we have "Dutch courage" (alcohol-induced courage), "Dutch treat" (you pay for yourself), "going Dutch" (everybody pays their share), and "double Dutch" (gibberish). Americans were kinder to their Revolutionary War supporters, speaking of "beating the Dutch" (doing something remarkable).

Amsterdam grew into one of the world's great cities. In 1602, traders from each of the major cities in the Republic of the Seven Provinces set up the Vereenigde Oostindische Compagnie (V.O.C.), the United East India Company, which was granted a monopoly on trade in the East. It was wildly successful and established the Dutch presence in the Spice Islands (Indonesia), Goa, South Africa, and China.

Holland was becoming a refuge for persecuted groups. The Pilgrims stopped in Leiden for a dozen years before embarking for America, Jews fled the oppressive Spanish and welcomed the tolerance of the Dutch, and refugees straggled in from France and Portugal. William the Silent had helped create a climate of tolerance in Holland, which attracted talented newcomers who contributed to the expanding economic, social, artistic, and intellectual climate of the country.

Golden Age Holland can be compared to Renaissance Italy and Classical Greece for the great flowering that transformed society. "There is perhaps no other example of a complete and highly original civilization springing up in so short a time in so small a territory," wrote the historian Simon Schama.

The Dutch call 1672 the Rampjaar (Year of Disaster). France, under Louis XIV, invaded the United Provinces by land and the English attacked by sea. This war (1672–78) and the later War of the Spanish Succession (1701–13) drained the country's wealth and morale. The buccaneering, can-do, go-anywhere spirit of traders, artists, and writers began to ebb, replaced by conservatism and closed horizons.

Decline & Fall

Revolutionary France invaded Holland in 1794, capturing Amsterdam and establishing the Batavian Republic in 1795, headed by the pro-French Dutch Patriots. Napoleon brought the short-lived republic to an end in 1806 by setting up his brother, Louis Napoleon, as king of the Netherlands, and installed him in a palace that had been Amsterdam's Town Hall. Louis did such a good job of representing the interests of his new subjects that in 1810 Napoleon deposed him and brought the Netherlands formally into the empire.

When the Dutch recalled the House of Orange in 1814, it was to fill the role of king in a constitutional monarchy. The monarch was yet another William of Orange; however, because his reign was to be a fresh start, the Dutch started numbering their Williams all over again (which makes for a very confusing history). Then came Waterloo in 1815 and Napoleon's final defeat.

Modern Times

The Netherlands escaped the worst ravages of World War I by maintaining strict neutrality. Holland shared in the wealth as Europe's condition improved, but conditions were very bad during the 1930s, when the widespread unemployment brought on by the Great Depression caused the government to use the army in 1934 to control the unruly masses.

During World War II, Nazi troops invaded the country in 1940. An estimated 104,000 of Holland's 140,000 Jews were murdered, Rotterdam sustained heavy bombings, and the rest of the country suffered terribly at the hands of its invaders. The Dutch operated one of the most effective underground movements in Europe,

Dutch Heights

Maybe it's nature's way of compensating for their country being attitudinally challenged, but the Dutch are *tall.* The average man is 1.8m (6 ft.) and the average woman is 1.7m (5 ft., 7 in.), which in both cases is 5 centimeters (2 in.) more than the European average. Not only that, but a government study showed that the average height of the Dutch increases by 1.5 centimeters (½ in.) every decade.

which became an important factor in the liberation in 1945. Among those murdered in the Nazi terror was a teenage girl who came to symbolize many other victims of the Holocaust: Anne Frank (1929–45).

In the 1960s, Amsterdam was a hotbed of political and cultural radicalism. Hippies trailing clouds of marijuana smoke took over the Dam and camped out in Vondelpark and in front of Centraal Station. Radical political activity, which began with "happenings" staged by a group known as the Provos, continued and intensified. In 1966, the Provos were behind the protests that disrupted the wedding of Princess Beatrix to German Claus von Amsberg in the Westerkerk; they threw smoke bombs and fighting broke out between protesters and police. The Provos disbanded in 1967, but much of their program was adopted by the Kabouters, or Green Gnomes. This group won several seats on the city council, but they, too, eventually faded.

The Provos and Green Gnomes had long advocated environmental programs like prohibiting all motor vehicles from the city. They persuaded authorities to provide 20,000 white-painted bicycles free for citizens' use—this scheme was abandoned when most of the bicycles were stolen, to reappear in freshly painted colors as "private" property. Some of their ideas very nearly came to fruition. In 1992, the populace voted to create a traffic-free zone in the center city, but this has yet to be realized.

HOLLAND'S ART & ARCHITECTURE

Art

The 17th century was the undisputed Golden Age of Dutch art. During this busy time, artists were blessed with wealthy patrons whose support allowed them to give free reign to their talents. Art held a cherished place in the hearts of average Dutch citizens, too. The Dutch were particularly fond of pictures that depicted their world: landscapes, seascapes, domestic scenes, portraits, and still lifes. The art of this period remains some of the greatest ever created.

One of the finest landscape painters of all time was **Jacob van Ruysdael** (1628–82), who depicted cornfields, windmills, and forest scenes, along with his famous views of Haarlem. In some of his works, the human figure is very small, and in others it does not appear at all; instead the artist typically devoted two-thirds of the canvas to the vast skies filled with the moody clouds that float over the flat Dutch terrain.

Frans Hals (1581–1666), the undisputed leader of the Haarlem school, specialized in portraiture. The relaxed relationship between the artist and his subject in his paintings was a great departure from the formal masks of Renaissance portraits. With the lightness of his brushstrokes, Hals was able to convey an immediacy and intimacy. It's worth visiting the Frans Hals Museum (p. 332) in Haarlem to study his techniques.

One of the geniuses of western art was **Rembrandt Harmenszoon van Rijn** (1606–69). This highly prolific and influential artist had a dramatic life filled with success and personal tragedy. Rembrandt was a master at showing the soul and inner life of humankind, in both his portraits and illustrations of biblical stories. His most famous work, the group portrait known as *The Night Watch* (1642), is on view in the Rijksmuseum (p. 301) in Amsterdam.

A spirituality reigns over his self-portraits as well; Rembrandt did about 60 of these during his lifetime. The *Self-Portrait with Saskia* shows the artist with his wife during prosperous times, when he was often commissioned by wealthy merchants to do portraits. But later self-portraits show his transition from an optimist to a careworn old man. At the Rembrandt House in Amsterdam—which has been restored to much the way it was when the artist lived and worked there—you can see the above self-portrait along with some 250 etchings.

Perhaps the best known of the "Little Dutch Masters," who restricted themselves to one type of painting, such as portraiture, is **Jan Vermeer** (1632–75) of Delft. The main subjects of Vermeer's work are the activities and pleasures of simple home life. Vermeer placed the figure(s) at the center of his paintings, and typically used the background space to convey a feeling of stability and serenity. Vermeer excelled at reproducing the lighting of his interior scenes.

If **Vincent van Gogh** (1853–90) had not failed as a missionary in the Borinage mining region of Belgium, he might not have turned to painting and become the greatest Dutch artist of the 19th century. *The Potato Eaters* (1885) was van Gogh's first masterpiece. This rough, crudely painted work shows a group of peasants gathered around the table for their evening meal after a long day of manual labor. Gone are the traditional beauty and serenity of earlier Dutch genre painting.

In 1888, Vincent traveled to Arles in Provence, where he was dazzled by the Mediterranean sun. His favorite color, yellow, which signified love to him, dominated landscapes such as *Wheatfield with a Reaper* (1889). For the next 2 years, he remained in the south of France, painting at a frenetic pace in between bouts of madness. The Van Gogh Museum in Amsterdam (p. 304) has more than 200 of his paintings.

Before **Piet Mondrian** (1872–1944) became an originator of De Stijl (or neoplasticism), he painted windmills, cows, and meadows. His Impressionistic masterpiece, *The Red Tree* (1909)—which looks as though it's bursting into flames against a background of blue—marked a turning point in his career. With Theo van Doesburg, Mondrian began a magazine in 1917 entitled *De Stijl (The Style)* in which he expounded the principles of neoplasticism: a simplification of forms or, in other words, a purified abstraction; an art that would be derived "not from exterior vision but from interior life."

Architecture

In the 16th and 17th centuries, the **strap and scroll ornament** became quite popular. A fluid form, it frames a facade's top and resembles curled leather. The **step gable,** a nonclassical element resembling a small staircase (with varying numbers of

A New School

Between 1900 and 1940, various Amsterdam architects purveyed many different styles of architecture. One of these styles stands out above the others: The Amsterdam school of architects succeeded in creating forms of brickwork that had existed only in earlier architects' fantasies. Their buildings are massive yet fluid, and feature decorations like stained glass, wrought iron, and corner towers.

steps and varying step heights), was used on many of the buildings you see as you walk along the canals today. Often you find step gables of this period augmented by Renaissance features, such as vases and masks.

Hendrick de Keyser (1565–1621), an architect who worked in Amsterdam at the height of the Renaissance, is known for using decorative, playful elements in a way that was practical to the structure. For instance, he combined hard yellow or white sandstone decorative features (like volutes, keystones, and masks) with soft red brick, creating a visually stimulating multicolored facade, while utilizing the sandstone as protection from rain erosion. **Philips and Justus Vingboons** were architects and brothers who worked in the Renaissance style; while walking along Herengracht, Keizersgracht, and Prinsengracht, you'll see many of their buildings. With them the medieval stepped gable gave way to a more ornate one with scrolled sides, decorative finials, and other features.

Because classical elements tend to have straight lines and don't flow like the Renaissance elements did, facades shifted to a more boxed-in, central look. **Jacob van Campen** (1595–1657), who built the elaborate **Town Hall** at the Dam, now the Royal Palace, was probably the single most important architect of Amsterdam architecture's classical period.

Around 1665, **Adriaan Dortsman** (1625–82), best known for his classic restrained Dutch style, began building homes with balconies and attics, leaving off the pilasters and festoons that adorned earlier facades.

THE LAY OF THE LAND

For all that the Bible says otherwise, the Dutch insist the Creation took 8 days, not 7—on the eighth day they reclaimed their country from the sea with their own hands. "God made the earth," they tell you, "and the Dutch made Holland."

The all-important dikes, which hold back the sea, began to evolve as far back as the 1st century A.D., when the country's earliest inhabitants settled on unprotected coastal wetlands in the northern regions of Friesland and Groningen. These settlers first attempted to defend their land by building huge earthen mounds *(terpen)* on which they constructed their homes during recurring floods. Around the 8th and 9th centuries, they were building proper dikes; by the end of the 13th century, entire coastal regions were enclosed by dikes that held back unruly rivers and the sea.

If you think a dike is a high wall, you'll be surprised to see that, actually, many of them are great mounds of earth and stone that extend for miles. Indeed, many of the roads you travel on are built along the tops of dikes.

Around half of the country's land area has been reclaimed from the sea, lakes, and marshes. Some 2,600 sq. km (1,000 sq. miles) of the country was underwater just 100 years ago. Approximately 25% of Holland, an area that holds about two-thirds of its people, now lies *below* sea level, protected from flooding only by sand dunes, dikes, and Dutch engineering ingenuity. The solid, timeless buildings of Amsterdam and other cities stand where waves should, by all rights, be lapping.

In 1953, devastating North Sea storms broke through the dikes in many places along Holland's southwest coast, flooding significant areas. There was a substantial loss of life and property. To assure greater protection along its coastal areas, Holland embarked upon a long-range Delta Project to seal off the river estuaries in the southwest of the country.

In flat Holland, wind is ever present, so it is not surprising that the Dutch have made use of windmills to do their hard labor, from pumping water off the land to drain polders, to milling grain and sawing timber. Nowadays you're as likely to see the whirling blades of wind turbines, generating a growing proportion of the nation's electrical power.

Anyway, Holland still exists, despite worries about global warming and rising sea levels. Still, the government is considering bolstering the sea defenses to handle a 1-in-100,000-years superstorm, a tenfold increase over the current standard. Should holding back the tides turn out to be a lost cause, a possible solution is floating homes. Several hundred are being constructed at the IJburg development east of Amsterdam, on the IJsselmeer's southern shore. Made from timber and aluminum on a base of polystyrene-filled concrete, floating homes might one day keep Dutch heads above water.

HOLLAND IN POPULAR CULTURE

Books

If a single individual may be said to "personify" the Holocaust—a status that is surely an unbearable burden—that person must be Anne Frank. Her diary, compiled as a series of letters addressed "Dear Kitty" and kept for more than 2 years until her arrest on August 4, 1944, has come to symbolize the plight of millions of Jews during the Nazi terror. *The Diary of a Young Girl* (1947) includes photos of Anne and the people she hid with, plus a map of the secret annex in the house on Prinsengracht.

For a personal insight into Vincent van Gogh's life and art, read Ken Wilkie's *The van Gogh File: A Journey of Discovery* (1990). What began as a routine magazine assignment in 1972 to coincide with the opening of the Van Gogh Museum became exactly what the book's subtitle indicates: A journey that continued long after the article was published. Wilkie followed van Gogh's trail through the Netherlands, Belgium, England, and France. Along the way, Wilkie met some of the last surviving people to have known or met the artist.

The Booker Prize–winning short novel *Amsterdam* (1998) plays with themes of love and friendship, death and mortality, and on Amsterdam's status as a city where euthanasia laws are relatively liberal, but most of it actually takes place in England. In that sense, the city is more of a city of the mind than a real place.

Far more sense of place is provided by Nicolas Freeling's *Love in Amsterdam* (1962), the first in his series of Inspector Piet Van der Valk detective novels, and even though it's the Amsterdam of almost a half century ago, the city is easily recognizable, and something of a co-protagonist. Much the same could be said of Alistair MacLean's thriller *Puppet on a Chain* (1969).

Simon Schama's *The Embarrassment of Riches: An Interpretation of Dutch Culture in the Golden Age* (1987) lets you inside Amsterdam's greatest period. Schama, adeptly, is simultaneously lighthearted and scholarly—a chapter headed "The Pretzel and the Puppy Dog" refers to a portrait by Jacob Cuyp. Most of the 700 pages feature works of art that are explained in the text. Schama succeeds in his intention "to map out the moral geography of the Dutch mind, adrift between the fear of deluge and the hope of moral salvage."

Film

Amsterdam-born film director Paul Verhoeven is probably the best-known Dutch filmmaker—though that doesn't mean that Verhoeven's Hollywood films, such as *Basic Instinct, RoboCop,* and *Starship Troopers,* contain much (if anything) inspired by his hometown. Closer to home is his wartime resistance drama *Soldier of Orange* (1977), starring Jeroen Krabbé and Rutger Hauer. Another wartime drama, *The Assault,* won the Oscar for Best Foreign Language Film in 1986.

Amsterdam starred as the darkly atmospheric setting of the underworld in the thriller *Puppet on a Chain* (1972), based on the novel of the same name by Scottish writer Alistair MacLean—which contained a memorable chase sequence on the canals. And it played a supporting role in the James Bond movie *Diamonds Are Forever* (1971). In *Girl with a Pearl Earring* (2003), Scarlett Johansson and Colin Firth star in an appropriately moody interpretation of the "backstory" to the Vermeer painting, set and partly filmed in Delft.

Should you want to dine on a movie set, head for Chinese restaurant Nam Kee in Amsterdam, which played a notable role in the Dutch red-hot romance flick *De Oesters van Nam Kee* (*The Oysters of Nam Kee;* 2002).

Music

About the only well-known song in English to feature Holland in a starring role is "Tulips from Amsterdam" (1956), which was originally written in German. This dose of concentrated saccharine keeps the unlikely company of pot-smoking, sex-tourism, and gay parades as a popular image of the city. Kids might likely be more familiar with "A Windmill in Old Amsterdam" (1965), which tells a heart-warming tale of "a little mouse with clogs on, going clip-clippety-clop on the stair."

Hard to say for sure, but it could be that the most successful pop song in English by a Dutch band is "Venus," released in 1969 by the group Shocking Blue. It reached number one on the U.S. charts and sold a million copies within a year. Bananarama had further success with their disco version in 1986.

EATING & DRINKING IN HOLLAND

Dutch national dishes tend to be of the ungarnished, hearty, wholesome variety—solid, stick-to-your-ribs stuff. A perfect example is *erwtensoep,* a thick pea soup cooked with ham or sausage that provides inner warmth against cold Dutch winters and is filling enough to be a meal by itself. Similarly, *hutspot,* a potato-based "hotch-potch," or stew, is no-nonsense nourishment to which *klapstuk* (lean beef) is sometimes added.

Seafood, as you might imagine in this traditionally seafaring country, is always fresh and well prepared. Fried sole, oysters, and mussels from Zeeland, and herring (fresh in early June, pickled other months) are most common. In fact, if you happen to be in Holland for the beginning of the herring season, it's an absolute obligation—at least once—to interrupt your sidewalk strolls to buy a "green" herring from a pushcart. The Dutch are uncommonly fond of oily freshwater eel *(paling)* and Zeeland oysters and mussels (*Zeeuwse oesters* and *Zeeuwse mosselen*), from September to March.

At lunchtime you're likely to find yourself munching on *broodjes,* small buttered rolls usually filled with ham and cheese or beef, although a *broodje gezond* (healthy sandwich) with cheese and vegetables is a good choice for vegetarians. Not to be missed are the delicious, filling pancakes called *pannenkoeken,* often eaten as a savory dish with bacon and cheese. *Poffertjes* are a sweet, lighter, penny-size version that are especially good topped with apples, jam, or syrup. Dutch *gebak* (pastries) are fresh, varied, and inexpensive; and you will notice the Dutch sitting down for a *koffie* and one of these delicious *hapjes* (small snacks, or literally, "bites") throughout the day—why not join them?

The popular Indonesian *rijsttafel* (rice table), a feast of 15 to 30 small portions of different dishes eaten with plain rice, has been a national favorite ever since it arrived in the 17th century. If you've never experienced this minifeast, it should definitely be on your "must-eat" list for Holland—the basic idea behind the rijsttafel is to sample a wide variety of complementary flavors, textures, and temperatures: savory and sweet, spicy and mild.

For authentic Dutch dishes, look for the NEERLANDS DIS sign, which identifies restaurants specializing in the native cuisine. Then there are the numerous moderately priced restaurants and the brown cafes, which are cozy social centers with simple but tasty food, sometimes served outside on sidewalk tables in good weather. Sidewalk vendors, with fresh herring and the ubiquitous *broodjes* (sandwiches) or other light specialties, are popular as well.

Though there's no such thing as a free lunch, there is the next best thing—a *dagschotel* (plate of the day) and *dagmenu* (menu of the day). Another way to combat escalating dinner tabs is to take advantage of the tourist menu offered by many restaurants.

Beer, Gin & Wine

What to drink? Beer, for one thing. As you make the rounds of the brown cafes (traditional Dutch watering holes), you can get regular brands such as Heineken, Grolsch, or Amstel, or you could try something different. I happen to like the *witte* (white) beer, like Wiekse Witte, which is sweeter than *pils,* the regular beer.

Then there is the potent native gin known as *jenever* (the name comes from the Dutch word for "juniper"), a fiery, colorless spirit distilled from grain or malt, served ice cold and drunk neat—without any mixer, or even ice. It was once the drink of the masses in Holland, where it originated as a kind of medicine.

There are even Dutch wines, perfectly respectable, though produced in modest quantities by 150 wineries around the country. Total annual production is some 800,000 liters (211,000 U.S. gallons/176,000 imperial gallons). Some of the finest wines are produced by the Apostelhoeve (www.apostelhoeve.nl), Hoeve Nekum (www.hoevenekum.nl), and Château Neercanne (www.chateauhotels.nl) vineyards, near Maastricht, close by the Belgian border.

LUXEMBOURG TODAY

The Grand Duchy of Luxembourg is a constitutional monarchy headed by Grand Duke Henri of the House of Nassau. Economically, the strength of its banking and financial institutions has attracted more than 200 foreign banks, including the headquarters of the European Investment Bank. The 500,000 residents have among the highest income levels per capita of any country in the world.

Agriculture is still important. Around half of the total land area is farmed, though less than 5% of Luxembourgers now live and work on farms. Despite problems caused by overproduction of European wines in general, the vineyards of Luxembourg's Moselle Valley are still competitive. And the enchanting Luxembourg countryside, particularly its northern reaches in the Ardennes, is a popular vacation destination for Luxembourgers and visitors from neighboring countries.

Having played a key role in establishing the institutions that evolved into the European Union, Luxembourg today hosts the secretariat of the European Parliament, the European Court of Justice, and the European Investment Bank.

The Luxembourgers

In such a small country, with bigger neighbors on its doorstep, Luxembourgers have a distinctive individuality that even extends to the national language, Lëtzebuergesch, which is vaguely related to both French and German, yet quite different from both.

Some of their character traits are easy to pin down. They're definitely hardworking. One look at the country's well-tended farms or shops will reveal the industriousness of their owners. Go into a Luxembourg home and the cleanliness and order will speak more loudly than the proud homemaker ever could.

The people of Luxembourg are cosmopolitan. From their cuisine (a combination of the best from surrounding countries) to their culture and dress, they're at home in the world, eager to travel, and secure enough in their uniqueness to appreciate the special qualities of others. But in addition to this openness, they're essentially proud and patriotic. Centuries of domination by foreign rulers could not kill their independent spirit. They do have a reputation for smugness that's not entirely undeserved: If you are a citizen of one of the world's wealthiest countries per capita, it may be no more than human nature to assume that this pleasing fact is due to your own native industry or superiority, rather than to, for instance, enabling the citizens of less-blessed countries—like Germany and France, to name but two of many—to engage in fiscal fiddling and stash the illicit proceeds in your banks.

Some 95% of Luxembourgers are Roman Catholic. Although a significant percentage of those hasten to make it clear that they're nonpracticing, it's rare to meet someone who doesn't observe some of the customs, traditions, and mores of the church. Finally, to say that Luxembourgers are fond of eating is an understatement. If there's an important matter to discuss, decision to be made, or social crisis to resolve, Luxembourgers repair to the nearest cafe or pastry store. It goes without saying, then, that they're fond of cooking—don't leave without indulging in their luscious pastries.

LOOKING BACK AT LUXEMBOURG

Long before recorded history, the territory of today's Grand Duchy was home to Magdalenian and Celtic tribes. The Treveri, a fierce Celtic people who resisted invaders to the death, finally fell in the 1st century B.C. to Roman legions. Thereafter, one Roman emperor after another put down numerous uprisings of the independent-minded inhabitants, who stubbornly refused to give up their worship of Druidism for the paganism of Rome.

As a declining Rome suffered military defeats, the Roman hold on the region weakened. By the 5th century, the only reminders of the Romans left in Luxembourg were the bits and pieces of their urban civilization, a network of bridges, and place names like Ettelbruck (Attila's Bridge), named for the Hun warlord who dealt the knockout blow to the Western Roman Empire. Luxembourg was by then firmly in the camp of the Franks.

Along with monasteries that sprang up and flourished came educational and cultural influences that helped form the foundation of today's Luxembourg. The great Frankish leader Charlemagne brought in Saxons to settle the Ardennes, thus adding another ethnic imprint to the face of the region.

In the 10th century, Siegfried, the youngest of the counts of the Ardennes, built his castle on the ruins of Castellum Lucilinburhuc, an ancient Roman fort that had guarded the crossroads of the important roads from Paris to Trier and from Metz to Aix-la-Chapelle (Aachen). On that strategic spot grew a town and eventually a country by the name of Luxembourg.

Enlightened Female Rule

By the 12th century, the counts of Luxembourg were at the helm. They enlarged their territory by wars with other noblemen, astute marriages, and diplomatic shenanigans.

When Henry the Blind's daughter, Countess Ermesinda, reached adulthood in the early 1200s, things were in disarray. But Ermesinda was able to restore some of Luxembourg's lost territory through a few marriages, as she inherited lands previously held

A Luxembourg Artist

The Expressionist painter Joseph Kutter (1894–1941) was among Luxembourg's most important 20th-century artists. As is often the way, Kutter was largely unappreciated in his homeland until after his death, being more highly regarded in neighboring France, Belgium, and Germany. Among works by Kutter than can be viewed in the Musée National d'Histoire et d'Art (p. 496) in Luxembourg City are *Self-Portrait in a Red Shirt* (1919), *Reclining Nude* (1919), and *Venice* (1924).

Modern Art & Architecture

One of the most distinguished works of modern architecture in Luxembourg City, the Museum of Modern Art, opened in 2006. The Musée d'Art Moderne Grand-Duc Jean (p. 498), better known as MUDAM, was designed by Chinese-American architect Ieoh Ming Pei. It sits atop a 17th-century fortification designed by Vauban.

by her ailing spouses. When her last husband died in 1225, she boldly took charge of the affairs of state. Her legacy was a united nation with enlightened social standards.

Imperial Glory

In 1308, Henry VII of the House of Luxembourg became emperor of the Holy Roman Empire. He spent the rest of his life trying to unite all of Europe under his rule; by the time his great-grandson, Wenceslas, gained the throne, the House of Luxembourg ruled a territory some 500 times the size of today's Luxembourg.

The glory days did not last long, however. King Wenceslas's son, Sigismund, was far less capable than his ancestors. By the mid-1400s, Luxembourg itself was a province ruled by the dukes of Burgundy. During the next 400 years, that rule shifted among Spain, France, and Austria.

A Strong Place

To quell the locals' growing unrest, each successive ruler found it necessary to further strengthen a capital city that was already one of Europe's best defended. Luxembourg, then, became a problem for the rest of Europe: Its position was too strategic and its fortifications too strong to allow it to be self-governing—or even to be controlled by any one nation. The answer seemed to be to divide Luxembourg among several nations; therein, the Congress of Vienna in 1815 handed over most of the country to Holland's William of Orange-Nassau, and the remainder to Prussia. Then, with the Treaty of London in 1839, more than half of Holland's piece of Luxembourg was given to Belgium (the resulting Belgian province still bears the name Luxembourg).

Still, its many fortifications made it all but impregnable, so in 1867 the European powers convened in London and decided that freedom would be granted the Grand Duchy on condition that its fortifications be dismantled. Luxembourgers were overjoyed. In October 1868, they affirmed a constitution that boldly proclaimed "the Grand Duchy of Luxembourg forms a free state, independent and indivisible."

War & Peace

Twice—in World War I and World War II—Luxembourg suffered military occupation. In the winter of 1944 to 1945, part of the Battle of the Bulge was fought in the Ardennes region of northern Luxembourg. General George S. Patton's Third Army turned the tide of that battle, with an assault that relieved the besieged U.S. 101st Airborne Division at Bastogne in Belgium. The little country didn't just work to rebuild itself in the postwar years: In 1945, Luxembourg joined the United Nations; in 1948, it formed a customs union called Benelux with Belgium and the Netherlands that later became an economic union; and in 1949, it was a founding member of NATO.

EATING & DRINKING IN LUXEMBOURG

Among the national favorites are some of the best pastries you're ever likely to eat; delicious Luxembourg cheese; trout, crayfish, and pike from local rivers; Ardennes ham smoked in saltpeter; hare, wild boar, and other game during the hunting season; and in September, lovely small plum tarts called *quetsch.* Other tasty treats include the national dish of smoked neck of pork with broad beans *(judd mat gaardebounen);* a *friture* of fried small river fish such as bream, chub, gudgeon, roach, and rudd; calves' liver dumplings *(quenelles)* with sauerkraut and boiled potatoes; black pudding *(treipen)* and sausages with mashed potatoes and horseradish; and a green-bean soup *(bouneschlupp).* French cuisine features prominently on restaurant menus, and German and Belgian influences make their presence felt.

Winemaking along the Moselle has a history that dates back to the Romans. And, of course, the Moselle wines (mostly white) will top any list. Look for riesling, pinot gris, pinot noir, pinot blanc, auxerrois, rivaner, elbling, gewürztraminer, and crémant de Luxembourg, and for the National Mark, which certifies that they're true Luxembourg wines. In beers, look for such brand names as unfiltered Mousel (pronounced *Mooz*-ell), Bofferding, and Henri Funck.

3 PLANNING YOUR TRIP TO BELGIUM, HOLLAND & LUXEMBOURG

Before any trip, most of us like to do a bit of planning. The three Benelux countries are not hard to come to grips with even if you arrive cold (in the preparedness sense). They are foreign, of course, but not impossibly so, especially since many Belgians, Dutch, and Luxembourgers speak at least some English. The local tourist organizations pride themselves on being able to answer any conceivable travel question, excepting only those that are illegal, and aid any conceivable traveler, excepting only those of doubtful moral standing (and in the case of Holland, both of these provisos leave plenty of wiggle room).

The information in this chapter is intended to cover a trip to Benelux in general, and should be useful whether you are visiting one, two, or all three of them. Yet, close together though they are, they are still three separate nations. For additional help in planning your trip—when to go, what the weather's like—and for more on-the-ground resources in Belgium, Holland, and Luxembourg, please turn to the "Planning" chapters for the three countries (chapters 5, 12, and 19), along with chapter 21, "Fast Facts."

ENTRY REQUIREMENTS

Passports

Citizens of the United States, Canada, the United Kingdom, Ireland, Australia, and New Zealand need only a valid passport for a visit of less than 3 months to Belgium, Holland, and Luxembourg. If you're a citizen of another country, be sure to check the travel regulations before you leave.

It is advised to always have at least one or two consecutive blank pages in your passport to allow space for visas and stamps that need to appear together. It is also important to note when your passport expires.

Belgium, Holland, and Luxembourg require your passport to have at least 3 months left, in addition to the length of your intended stay, before its expiration to allow you into the Benelux.

For Residents of Australia: Contact the **Australian Passport Office,** R.G. Casey Building, John McEwen Crescent, Barton, ACT, 0221 (✆ **131-232;** www.passports.gov.au).

For Residents of Canada: Contact **Passport Canada,** Place du Centre, 200 Promenade du Portage, Commercial Level 2, Gatineau, QC K1A 0G3 (✆ **800/567-6868;** www.ppt.gc.ca).

For Residents of Ireland: Contact the **Passport Office,** Setanta Centre, Molesworth Street, Dublin 2 (✆ **01/671-1633** or 1890/426-888; www.foreignaffairs.gov.ie).

For Residents of New Zealand: Contact the **Passports Office,** Department of Internal Affairs, 47 Boulcott St., Wellington, 6011 (✆ **0800/225-050** in New Zealand or 04/474-8100; www.passports.govt.nz).

For Residents of the United Kingdom: Visit your nearest passport office, major post office, or travel agency, or contact the **Identity and Passport Service (IPS),** 89 Eccleston Square, London, SW1V 1PN (✆ **0300/222-0000;** www.ips.gov.uk).

For Residents of the United States: To find your regional passport office, check the U.S. State Department website (http://travel.state.gov/passport) or call the **National Passport Information Center** (✆ **877/487-2778**) for automated information.

Visas

Citizens of the United States, Canada, the United Kingdom, Ireland, Australia, and New Zealand need only a valid passport for a visit to a Benelux country of less than 3 months. If you're a citizen of another country, be sure to check the travel regulations before you leave. You can get these in English from the Ministry of Foreign Affairs in the three Benelux countries: **www.diplomatie.be** for Belgium; **www.minbuza.nl** for Holland; and **www.mae.lu** for Luxembourg.

Customs

WHAT YOU CAN BRING INTO BELGIUM, HOLLAND & LUXEMBOURG

Duty-free shopping has been abolished in all European Union countries, so standard allowances do not apply to goods purchased in one EU country and brought into another. In this case, there are no import limitations for most goods for personal use, but the following guideline limits may apply (above these limits, you could be asked to prove the goods are for personal use): 800 cigarettes, 400 cigarillos, 200 cigars, and 1 kilogram of tobacco; 10 liters of liquor, 20 liters of aperitifs (port and so on), 90 liters of wine (of which 60 liters may be sparkling wine), and 110 liters of beer.

Travelers 17 and older residing in a country outside the European Union can bring in, free of duty, 200 cigarettes, 100 cigarillos, 50 cigars, or 250 grams of tobacco; 1 liter of liquor or 2 liters of sparkling or fortified wine; 4 liters of wine and 16 liters of beer; 50 milliliters/grams of perfume; and 250 milliliters of eau de toilette. Import of most other goods is unlimited, so long as import duty is paid on amounts above the exempt allowance: 430€ for visitors arriving by air and sea, 300€ for visitors arriving by other transportation, and 175€ for children 14 and under.

Forbidden products include firearms, counterfeit goods, banned narcotic substances, and protected animals and plants and products made from these.

For more information, contact:

Belgian Customs (✆ **02/422-11-91,** or 32-2/422-11-91 from outside Belgium; http://fiscus.fgov.be).

Netherlands Customs (✆ **0800/0143,** or 31-45/574-3031 from outside the Netherlands; www.douane.nl).

Luxembourg Customs (✆ **290-19-11,** or 352/290-19-11 from outside Luxembourg; www.do.etat.lu).

WHAT YOU CAN TAKE HOME FROM BELGIUM, HOLLAND & LUXEMBOURG

For information on what you're allowed to bring home, contact one of the following agencies:

U.S.: U.S. Customs & Border Protection (CBP), 1300 Pennsylvania Ave. NW, Washington, DC 20229 (✆ **877/287-8667,** or 1-877/287-8667 from outside the U.S.; www.cbp.gov).

Canada: Canada Border Services Agency, 410 Laurier Ave. W., Ottawa, Ontario, K1A 0L8 (✆ **800/461-9999,** or 1-204/983-3500 from outside Canada; www.cbsa-asfc.gc.ca).

U.K.: HM Revenue & Customs, Crownhill Court, Tailyour Road, Plymouth, PL6 5BZ (✆ **0845/010-9000,** or 44-20/8929-0152 from outside the U.K.; www.hmrc.gov.uk).

Ireland: Irish Revenue's Customs Division, St. Conlon's Road, Nenagh, Co. Tipperary (✆ **1890/666-333,** or 353-67/63400 from outside Ireland; www.revenue.ie).

Australia: Australian Customs Service, Customs House, 5 Constitution Avenue, Canberra, ACT 2601 (✆ **1300/363-263,** or 61-2/6275-6666 from outside Australia; www.customs.gov.au).

New Zealand: New Zealand Customs, The Customhouse, 1 Hinemoa St., Harbour Quays, Wellington 6140 (✆ **0800/428-786,** or 64-9/300-5399 from outside New Zealand; www.customs.govt.nz).

Medical Requirements

No health and vaccination certificates are required. You don't need any shots before your trip, but if you suffer from a chronic illness, consult your doctor before your departure.

GETTING THERE & GETTING AROUND

Getting to the Benelux

BY PLANE

Brussels Airport (BRU), 11km (7 miles) northeast of the center city, is Belgium's main, and very nearly only, international airport. It has direct train connection to Brussels and from there to Bruges, Ghent, Antwerp, and other Belgian cities; to Amsterdam, Rotterdam, and The Hague; and to Luxembourg City. It is the hub for Brussels Airlines and is served by many international carriers. See "Orientation," in chapter 6. **Brussels South Charleroi Airport (CRL),** 46km (29 miles) south of Brussels, is served by budget airline Ryanair. **Antwerp International Airport (ANR),** just outside Antwerp to the east, is served primarily by the small Flemish carrier VLM, which operates a handful of European routes.

Amsterdam Airport Schiphol (AMS) is Holland's only real international airport. It is 13km (8 miles) southwest of Amsterdam's center city, and it has quick, direct train links to Amsterdam; to Rotterdam, The Hague, Utrecht, and other Dutch cities; and to Antwerp and Brussels. Schiphol is the hub of the Netherlands flag carrier KLM Royal Dutch Airlines, which has merged with Air France. See "Orientation," in chapter 13. Holland has other airports at **Rotterdam (RTM), Maastricht (MST), Eindhoven (EIN), Groningen (GRQ),** and **Enschede (ENS),** all of which handle a few regional flights and charters.

Luxembourg Airport (LUX), the sole airport of the tiny Grand Duchy, is 6km (4 miles) northeast of Luxembourg City. See "Essentials" under "Luxembourg City," in chapter 20.

To find out which airlines travel to Belgium, Holland, and Luxembourg, see "Airline Websites," p. 522.

BY BOAT

You might sail onboard a cruise-liner into the ocean terminal at Amsterdam, Rotterdam, or Antwerp, or on a European river-cruiser to any number of Benelux's inland and seacoast ports. More likely, though, you'll arrive onboard a car-ferry—likely a giant "cruise-ferry"—from Britain.

TO BELGIUM **P&O Ferries** (✆ **08716/64-20-20** in Britain, or 070/70-77-71 in Belgium; www.poferries.com) has daily car-ferry service between Hull in northeast England and Zebrugge. The overnight travel time is 14 to 15 hours. Trains shuttle between nearby Zeebrugge-Strand and Zeebrugge-Dorp stations and Bruges (Brugge) station, a 20-minute ride, from where there are hourly trains to Brussels, Ghent, and Antwerp. Buses shuttle between the Zeebrugge ferry terminal and Bruges (Brugge) station.

Transeuropa Ferries (✆ **01843/595522** in Britain, or 059/34-02-60 in Belgium; www.transeuropaferries.com) has three car-ferry sailings daily, from Ramsgate in southern England to Ostend; the travel time is 4 hours. This service transports only cars and other commercial and noncommercial vehicles along with their drivers and passengers; foot passengers aren't accepted.

TO THE NETHERLANDS **Stena Line** (✆ **08447/707070** in Britain, or 0174/315-811 in Holland; www.stenaline.co.uk) has twice-daily car-ferry service between Harwich in southeast England and Hoek van Holland (Hook of Holland), near Rotterdam. The travel time during the day is 6¼ hours, and 7 hours overnight. Frequent trains depart from Hoek van Holland Haven station to Rotterdam and Amsterdam.

P&O Ferries (✆ **08716/64-20-20** in Britain, or 020/200-8333 in Holland; www.poferries.com) has daily car-ferry service between Hull in northeast England and Rotterdam (into Europoort harbor). The overnight travel time is 11 to 12 hours. Ferry company buses shuttle between the Rotterdam Europoort terminal and Rotterdam Centraal Station, from where there are frequent trains to Amsterdam.

DFDS Seaways (✆ **0871/522-0955** in Britain, or 0330/333-0245 in Holland; www.dfdsseaways.co.uk) has daily car-ferry service between Newcastle in northeast England and IJmuiden on the North Sea coast, 24km (15 miles) west of Amsterdam. The overnight travel time is 15½ hours. From IJmuiden, you can go by special bus to Amsterdam Centraal Station.

BY TRAIN

Rail service to the Benelux countries by international trains from major European cities is frequent and, at least in the case of the various high-speed trains, fast.

Britain is connected to the Continent (or, as the Brits might say, the Continent is connected to Britain) through the Channel Tunnel. On the **Eurostar** high-speed train, with a top speed of 300kmph (186 mph), travel times between London's St. Pancras station and Brussels' Bruxelles-Midi station are around 2 hours. Departures are approximately every 2 hours. For Eurostar reservations, call © **08432/186186** in Britain, or 02/528-28-28 in Belgium. Or book online at **www.eurostar.com**. Tickets also are available from main train stations and travel agents.

On the **Thalys** high-speed train, travel time from Paris-Nord station to Brussels's Bruxelles-Midi station is 1 hour and 20 minutes; from Bruxelles-Midi to Amsterdam Centraal Station (via Antwerp, Rotterdam, The Hague, and Schiphol Airport) is 1 hour and 50 minutes; and from Cologne to Bruxelles-Midi is 1 hour and 50 minutes. Departures are approximately every hour. For Thalys information and reservations in France, call © **3635;** in Belgium, © **070/79-79-79;** in Germany, © **11861;** and in Holland, © **0900/9296.** Or book online at **www.thalys.com**. Tickets also are available from main rail stations and travel agents.

Further high-speed train connections are the **TGV,** which arrives in Brussels from France (excluding Paris), and the **ICE** trains that speed into both Amsterdam and Brussels from Frankfurt, Germany.

Direct, though relatively slow, international trains connect Luxembourg City with Brussels, Amsterdam, and Cologne. Of Europe's high-speed international trains, only the TGV Est from Paris's Gare de l'Est serves Luxembourg City, with seven or eight trains per day and a travel time of 2 hours and 5 minutes.

BY BUS

Eurolines has the most comprehensive bus network in Europe. For reservations, call © **08717/818181** in Britain, © **02/274-13-50** in Belgium, or © **020/560-8788** in the Netherlands. Or book online at **www.eurolines.com**.

Up to four Eurolines buses depart daily from London's Victoria bus station to Brussels's Gare du Nord bus station, and up to four daily from London's Victoria to Amsterdam's Amstel station; travel time is 8 hours to Brussels and 12 hours to Amsterdam. Luxembourg City can be reached from London, with two departures a day, and from Amsterdam, both via Brussels; travel time is 13 hours from London and 7 hours from Amsterdam.

BY CAR

The three countries are crisscrossed by a dense network of major highways connecting them with other European countries. These enter from France to the south and from Germany to the east. Traffic is very often heavy, but road conditions are generally excellent throughout the Benelux, distances between major population centers are short, service stations are plentiful, and highways are plainly signposted.

The fast and efficient **Eurotunnel** (© **08443/353535** in Britain; www.eurotunnel.com) auto-transporter trains transport your car through the Channel Tunnel from Folkestone, England, to Calais, France (a 35-min. trip). Departures are every 15 minutes at peak times, every 30 minutes at times of average demand, and every hour at night.

See also "By Car" under "Getting Around the Benelux," below.

Distances & Driving Times in the Benelux

ROUTE	DISTANCE *	TIME
Brussels-Bruges	100km/62 miles	1 hr. 10 min.
Brussels-Ghent	56km/35 miles	45 min.
Brussels-Antwerp	55km/34 miles	45 min.
Brussels-Liège	97km/61 miles	1 hr. 5 min.
Brussels-Amsterdam	212km/132 miles	2 hr. 15 min.
Amsterdam-Rotterdam	80km/50 miles	1 hr. 5 min.
Amsterdam-Groningen	180km/112 miles	1 hr. 50 min.
Amsterdam-Arnhem	105km/65 miles	1 hr. 15 min.
Amsterdam-Maastricht	215km/134 miles	2 hr. 15 min.
Maastricht-Luxembourg City	198km/123 miles	2 hr.

* In all cases, the distance is the shortest direct route, going by expressway/motorway as far as possible.

Getting Around the Benelux

In order of priority, taking ease of use, convenience, time, and cost into account, the best ways to get around in the Benelux are by train, by car, and by bus.

BY TRAIN

One of the best rail systems in the world operates in and between these small countries. There is virtually no spot so remote that it cannot easily be reached by trains that are fast, clean, and almost always on time. Furthermore, rail travel is a marvelous way to meet the locals, because the people of the Benelux countries spend as much time riding the rails as they do behind the wheel of an automobile. Schedules are exact—if a departure is set for 12:01pm, that means 12:01pm precisely, not 12:03pm—and station stops are sometimes as short as 3 or 4 minutes, which means you must be fleet of foot in getting on and off.

Rail Passes

An important consideration for anyone planning to travel a lot by train is an appropriate pass allowing reduced-rate travel. In addition to those referred to below, Belgium, the Netherlands, and Luxembourg have discount rail passes for travel within their own country's borders. In each country, there are many lower-cost options, including cheaper weekend and day returns, reductions for multiple journeys, and reductions for more than one passenger (not all options are available in each country). You should always ask about lower-cost options before buying. You'll find more details in the "Planning" chapters of each country (chapters 5, 12, and 19).

EURAIL PASSES The **Eurailpass** (www.eurail.com) allows residents of non-European countries unlimited first-class travel throughout the rail systems of many European countries, including the Benelux countries, at a cost that starts out at $849 for 10 days. The **Eurail Youth Pass** gives you the same deal at discount rates and in second class, and there are other variations. These passes should be purchased before you leave home (they're more expensive if you buy them in Europe) and are available from **Rail Europe** (✆ **800/622-8600;** www.raileurope.com) and from travel agents.

BENELUX PASS If all or most of your travel within Belgium, Holland, and Luxembourg will be by train—and provided you plan to travel by train *a lot*—a good investment may be the **Eurail Benelux Pass,** available through **Rail Europe** (see above) and through travel agents. It gives you unlimited travel in all three countries on any 5 days in a 1-month period. The pass costs $364 for first class and $248 for second class. Two to five adults traveling together should purchase instead the **Eurail Benelux Saver Pass,** to benefit from a discount of around 18%. For passengers ages 12 to 25, the **Eurail Benelux Youth Pass** (available in second class only) costs $166. Children ages 4 to 11 pay around half the adult fare, and children ages 3 and under ride free so long as they share a seat or berth with an adult.

But if you're not traveling far, or often, don't bother with this pass. It's hard to make it pay off because most trips in these three countries are so short and relatively cheap. Even if you cram in Amsterdam, Haarlem, Leiden, Delft, The Hague, Antwerp, Bruges, Ghent, and Brussels, you'll still spend on point-to-point tickets less than you'd pay for a Benelux Pass.

BY CAR

Traveling by car gives you the most freedom to ramble at your own speed, either on or off the beaten path. You'll find information on specific requirements, rules of the road, gasoline prices, maps, automobile clubs, car rental agencies, and other driving assistance resources in the "Planning" chapters for each country (chapters 5, 12, and 19).

The Benelux countries have a high density of population in relation to their size, so roads are busy. In addition, many drivers in the region have high-density road aggression, so driving can degenerate into a struggle for survival. The major roads are very often busiest precisely at the most popular vacation times, and accidents are not uncommon.

Traffic congestion in Brussels, Bruges, Ghent, Antwerp, Amsterdam, Rotterdam—in fact, any Benelux city of any size—can cause monumental tie-ups. You'll find it's best to stash your car at your hotel garage and use local public transportation or walk.

To drive in the Benelux lands, drivers need only produce a valid driver's license from their home country. The minimum age for renting a car is generally 23, and the driver's license should have been valid for at least 12 months. Virtually all major car rental agencies have offices in the three capital cities and some other large cities, though arranging a rental outside a metropolitan area can present problems.

See also "By Car" under "Getting to the Benelux," above, and "Responsible Tourism," later in this chapter.

BY BUS

Intercity bus service ranges from poor to nonexistent throughout the Benelux countries. This is not as bad as it sounds, because the rail network is among the best in the world, and fast, comfortable intercity trains do most of the work. If you really want to, you can travel intercity by bus, but the buses stop a lot en route, so trip times are long, and you often have to change at an intermediate town—for example, a trip from Brussels to Liège is two journeys: Brussels to Leuven and Leuven to Liège. Tourist offices and bus stations can furnish schedule and fare information.

The exception to the avoid-the-bus rule is in sparsely populated places where there is little or no rail service, such as Zeeland in Holland and the Ardennes in Belgium and Luxembourg. In such areas, there are more regional bus services, though the buses still may be few and far between. In general, unless you have a specific reason for wanting to go by bus, you'll always find it better to go by train.

All cities have excellent bus and/or tram (and in two cases, electric trolley bus) service. Some have metro (subway) service, which means you can easily leave your car at the hotel and avoid city driving woes.

BY PLANE

The Benelux capitals are so close together that air travel is really not worth the added expense unless time is a vital factor (and even then you might still get there quicker by train). Air service is provided by **KLM** (✆ **020/474-7747** in Holland; www.klm.com), and **Brussels Airlines** (✆ **02/723-23-45** in Belgium; www.brusselsairlines.com). KLM flies from Amsterdam to both Brussels and Luxembourg City; Brussels Airlines flies from Brussels to Amsterdam.

BY BICYCLE

Belgium, Holland, and Luxembourg are all ideal biking countries. In Holland, especially, and in parts of Flanders, there are often special bicycle tracks in towns and cities, and well-signed long-distance routes. You can also take your bike on a train. Rental bikes are usually available at major rail stations and often at smaller ones, and some even allow you to pick up and return bikes at stations at either end of a particular route. All three national tourist boards can help you plan an itinerary best suited to your physical condition and time restraints. Holland's excellent ***Cycling in Holland*** publication is especially useful.

Organized bicycle tours can be arranged through **International Bicycle Tours,** P.O. Box 754, Essex, CT 06426 (✆ **860/767-7005;** www.internationalbicycletours.com); and **Cycletours,** Buiksloterweg 7A, 1031 CC Amsterdam (✆ **020/521-8490;** www.cycletours.nl).

BY HITCHHIKING

Hitchhiking is permitted (not encouraged) in Belgium and Luxembourg, though prohibited on highways (you can, however, stand on the approach road). It's officially forbidden in Holland, but many a blind eye is turned by officialdom to those standing in a safe spot to hitchhike.

MONEY & COSTS

THE VALUE OF THE EURO VS. OTHER POPULAR CURRENCIES

Euro (€)	US$	Can$	UK£	Aus$	NZ$
1	$1.33	C$1.34	£0.85	A$1.35	NZ$1.75

Admittedly, the three Benelux countries are by no means inexpensive. Clearly, whether you agree with this statement will depend on how much you can bring to bear—or bear to bring—in the way of financial resources. If you're used to the prices in New York and London, those in Amsterdam, Brussels, and Luxembourg City likely won't seem too out of whack. But opportunities for scoring genuine bargains run a thin gamut from few and far between to nonexistent. In your favor is that the natives themselves display a reluctance to part unnecessarily with a euro. A sound rule of thumb is that if you lodge, dine, and entertain yourself in the same places where "ordinary" locals do, you can limit the financial damage.

Frommer's lists prices in the local currency. The currency conversions quoted above were correct at press time. However, rates fluctuate, so before departing consult a currency exchange website such as **www.oanda.com/currency/converter** to check up-to-the-minute rates.

The currency-exchange offices at the main train stations in Brussels, Amsterdam, and Luxembourg City offer fair rates for cash and traveler's checks, as do banks, offices of **Travelex** (www.travelex.com) in Belgium and Luxembourg, **GWK Travelex** (www.travelex.com) in Holland, and VVV tourist information offices in Holland. Exchange rates at currency-exchange offices at Brussels, Amsterdam, and Luxembourg City airports are lousy; use the airport ATMs to avoid these bad deals. Other currency-exchange offices throughout the Benelux countries, which are open regular hours plus evenings and weekends, may charge a low commission or none at all, but they give a low rate of exchange. Hotels should be avoided as a currency-exchange resource unless there's no alternative.

The Travelex and GWK Travelex offices can arrange money transfers through **Western Union.**

ATMs are widespread in Benelux cities and towns, and you can even find them in some villages. They accept bank cards and credit cards linked to the **Cirrus** (www.mastercard.com) and **PLUS** (www.visa.com) networks.

Be sure you know your personal identification number (PIN) and daily withdrawal limit before you depart. If you have a five- or six-digit PIN, also be sure to obtain a four-digit number from your bank to use in the Benelux. Some cards with five- or six-digit PINs might work, but it depends on what bank you use.

Credit cards are not as commonly accepted in general as they are in the United States and Britain. Many restaurants and stores, and some hotels, don't accept them at all, and others add a 5% charge for card payment. They are almost universally accepted by gas stations and for travel by plane, train, and even taxi (not all taxis). The smaller the business, the less likely it is to accept credit cards.

Visa and **MasterCard** (also known as **EuroCard** in Europe) are the most widely used cards in the Benelux lands. **American Express** is often accepted in the middle- and upper-bracket category. **Diners Club** is not as commonly accepted as American Express.

Americans using traditional "swipe" credit cards with a magnetic stripe may run into trouble when they encounter a European chip-and-PIN credit card terminal. The European cards have embedded encrypted microprocessor chips, and their use is authorized by entering a four-digit personal identification number. When it comes to ticket machines, automated gas-station pumps, and other automats in the Benelux, you'll likely be out of luck with a swipe card. Still, most human-operated chip-and-PIN payment terminals are capable of processing magnetic-stripe cards—provided the operator knows how to do this, or can be prodded into making the effort. For those occasions when a swipe card simply won't fly, you'll need to have cash on hand, or it's no transaction.

Beware of hidden credit-card fees while traveling. Check with your credit or debit card issuer to see what fees, if any, will be charged for overseas transactions. Recent reform legislation in the U.S., for example, has curbed some exploitative lending practices. But many banks have responded by increasing fees in other areas, including fees for customers who use credit and debit cards while out of the country—even if those charges were made in U.S. dollars. Fees can amount to 3% or more of the purchase price. Check with your bank before departing to avoid any surprise charges on your statement.

WHAT THINGS COST IN THE BENELUX	€
Taxi from the airport to downtown Amsterdam	40.00
Double room (moderate)	125.00
Double room (inexpensive)	60.00
Three-course dinner for one without wine (moderate)	25.00–40.00
Bottle of Heineken beer	2.00–4.00
Bottle of Coca-Cola	3.00
Cup of coffee	2.50–4.50
1 gallon/1 liter of premium gas	6.00/1.60
Admission to most museums	6.00–12.00

STAYING HEALTHY

No health and vaccination certificates are required. You don't need any shots before your trip, but if you suffer from a chronic illness, consult your doctor before your departure. Pack **prescription medications** in your carry-on luggage, and carry them in their original containers, with pharmacy labels. Carry the generic name of prescription medicines, in case a local pharmacist is unfamiliar with the brand name. Don't forget an extra pair of contact lenses or prescription eyeglasses.

Regional Health Concerns

There are no particular health concerns in the Benelux—if you don't count the "risk" in Amsterdam and other Dutch towns of occasionally breathing in a whiff of someone else's legally tolerated hashish smoke (and, of course, they'd likely argue that it's perfectly healthy). You will encounter few other health problems when traveling.

DIETARY ISSUES The tap water is safe to drink, and the milk is pasteurized. Vegetarian restaurants, or at least restaurants with some vegetarian dishes on the menu, are easy to find. The existence of growing Muslim populations in most towns and cities, and of Jewish communities primarily in Amsterdam, Antwerp, and Brussels, means that both halal and kosher food is available.

BUGS Ticks that may be vectors for diseases like Lyme disease can be a problem in summer. This is most likely to affect woods and forests and other country areas, but you get ticks in city parks, too.

Smoke-Free Zones

Smoke no longer gets in your eyes and up your nose as much as it used to in Belgium, Holland, and Luxembourg, since restrictions on smoking in restaurants, bars, cafes, clubs, and other places, including public spaces in hotels, were introduced. In Holland, a typical Dutch compromise applies to drug-selling "smoking coffeeshops," where patrons are still permitted to puff joints, but not cigarettes, cigars, or pipes. See p. 327 for more information.

If You Get Sick

The primarily state-owned healthcare systems in the Benelux lands are among the world's best, even if they have begun to show signs of the strain of universal healthcare for all. It's easy to get over-the-counter medicines for minor ailments, and both local brands and generic equivalents of most common prescription drugs are available. Many doctors speak English (though the words they use might be a little disturbing, like the doctor who told me he knew what "disease" I had when I reported a minor ailment).

If a medical issue arises, your hotel staff can usually put you in touch with a reliable doctor. Most hospitals have walk-in clinics for emergency cases that are not life threatening; you may not get immediate attention, but you won't pay the high price of an emergency-room visit. Embassies in Brussels and The Hague, and consulates in Amsterdam, can provide a list of area doctors who speak English. The "Fast Facts" sections for Brussels, Bruges, and Amsterdam (chapters 6, 7, and 13) list the main hospitals in those cities.

For both prescription and nonprescription medicines, go to a pharmacy (*pharmacie* in French; *apotheek* in Dutch). Regular pharmacy hours generally are Monday to Saturday from 9am to 5:30 or 6pm (some close earlier on Sat). Every pharmacy posts a list of late-night and weekend pharmacies on the door.

I list additional **emergency numbers** in chapter 21, "Fast Facts."

CRIME & SAFETY

In Holland, be wary of pickpockets on trams, buses, and Metro trains; in train and Metro stations; on busy shopping streets and in busy stores; and even in your hotel lobby. The rest of the Netherlands is not as bad in this respect as Amsterdam, though Rotterdam and The Hague are not so far behind.

Belgium is generally safe; even the big cities are low-crime areas. However, Belgium has experienced a creeping spread of drug-related crime, and crimes committed by some poorly integrated members of immigrant communities. In Brussels, the Métro has been plagued by muggers, and though increased police presence and video surveillance have brought this under control, it's still better not to venture alone into deserted Métro access corridors after dark; when other people are around, it's generally safe.

Both Brussels and Antwerp have well-defined red-light zones, in which more than a little caution is in order. Don't confuse these places with the Red Light District up the road in Amsterdam, which is a pretty big tourist attraction in its own right and mostly safe for casual visitors. Brussels's red-light zone in particular is a creepy, low-life place, and though Antwerp's is not quite so bad, it's still not really a place to go for sightseeing. Bruges and Ghent have only minimal facilities of this kind, so this is not a factor there.

And then there's Luxembourg. In the unlikely event that you become a victim of any kind of crime in the squeaky-clean Grand Duchy, watch out—you'll likely be stuffed and placed in a museum for the astonishment of future generations.

Dealing with Discrimination

Both Belgium and Holland are showing an increase in votes for right-wing political parties opposed, to one degree or another, to immigration, and even to the continued presence of immigrant communities. This applies in particular to those migrants "who do not share European values." Rising levels of muggings, break-ins, pickpocketing, bag snatching, auto theft, and other crimes, attributed, rightly or wrongly, to legal and illegal immigrants and to some ethnic minorities, appear to be fueling the trend. This attitude could translate into discrimination against nonwhite visitors, though the majority of Dutch and Belgians would have nothing to do with this.

In Amsterdam (of all places) and other Dutch cities, there is a rising incidence of gays and lesbians being verbally abused and even assaulted, and the perpetrators often are young fundamentalist—or maybe just hooligan—Muslim men and teens. Around 200 attacks are reported yearly in Holland's "gay capital," and estimates of unreported incidents in Amsterdam run as high as 5,000. Surveys show that more gays feel less safe than formerly. To protect themselves, some are turning to self-defense and aggression-avoidance techniques. The city mayor commissioned the University of Amsterdam to research the whole question of homophobic attacks. Their conclusion—that young Dutch Muslim men are not entirely comfortable with their own sexuality—doesn't seem likely to offer much of a solution.

Antwerp has both an ultra-Orthodox Haredi and Hasidic Jewish community and a significant minority of people of North African (Arab) origin. Tensions caused by the Israeli/Palestinian conflict have led to attacks on Jewish individuals and facilities. This problem has shown up in Amsterdam, Brussels, and other Benelux cities, too. Jewish visitors who dress in a way that clearly identifies them as Jewish should be aware of this, even though the chances of being a victim of harassment or assault are very small.

Note: Listing some of the possible dangers together like this can give a false impression of the threat from crime or discrimination in the Benelux lands. None of these dangers is statistically significant, and by no stretch of the imagination can any Benelux city be described as dangerous. The overwhelming probability is that you will not notice any of these problems, far less encounter one of them. But it can't hurt to be aware of them.

SPECIALIZED TRAVEL RESOURCES

In addition to the destination-specific resources listed below, please visit Frommers.com for other specialized travel resources.

LGBT Travelers

In Amsterdam, you can get information, or just meet people, by visiting **COC Amsterdam,** Rozenstraat 14 (✆ **020/626-3087;** www.cocamsterdam.nl), the Amsterdam branch of the Dutch lesbian and gay organization **COC Nederland** (✆ **020/623-4596;** www.coc.nl). The **Gay and Lesbian Switchboard** (✆ **020/623-6565;** www.switchboard.nl) can provide you with all kinds of information and advice. Call **AIDS Infolijn** (✆ **0900/204-2040**) for info on AIDS.

You shouldn't have too much trouble finding information about gay and lesbian bars and clubs because they're well publicized. Also see "The Gay & Lesbian Scene" under "Amsterdam After Dark," in chapter 13. The free biweekly listings magazine ***Shark*** is a great source of cultural information, in particular for the offbeat and alternative scenes. ***Gay News*** and ***Gay&Night,*** competing monthly magazines in both Dutch and English, are available free in gay establishments around the city. Amsterdam hosts one of the most successful Gay Pride events, in August.

See "Crime & Safety," above, for information on the problems of homophobic violence Amsterdam's gay community is currently experiencing.

In Belgium, contact the gay and lesbian community centers in Brussels **Tels Quels,** rue du Marché-au-Charbon 81 (✆ **02/512-45-87;** www.telsquels.be); and **La Maison Arc-en-Ciel,** rue du Marché au Charbon 42 (✆ **02/503-59-90;** www.rainbowhouse.be). For Flanders, contact **Çavaria,** Kammerstraat 22 (✆ **09/223-69-29;** www.cavaria.be), in Ghent; and **Holebifoon** (✆ **0800/99-533;** www.holebifoon.be). For the scene in Bruges, contact **Jong & Holebi in Brugge,** Koningin Elisabethlaan 92 (✆ **050/33-69-70;** www.j-h.be). Belgium's main Gay Pride events take place in Brussels in May and Antwerp in June.

In Luxembourg, the gay men's organization is **Rosa Lëtzebuerg,** rue des Romains 60 (✆ **26-19-00-18;** www.gay.lu), in Luxembourg City.

Travelers with Disabilities

Many hotels and restaurants in Benelux now provide easy access for people with disabilities, and some display the international wheelchair symbol in their brochures and advertising. It's always a good idea to call ahead to find out what the situation is before you book. Both Brussels Airport and Amsterdam's Schiphol Airport have services to help travelers with disabilities through the airport. There's also comprehensive assistance for travelers with disabilities throughout the railway systems of all three countries. Inquire also at the national tourist board offices in each country for specific details on the available resources.

Not all trams in Brussels, Antwerp, Amsterdam, The Hague, Rotterdam, and other cities are easily accessible for travelers in wheelchairs, but the new trams being introduced on some routes have low central doors that are accessible. The Metro systems in Brussels, Antwerp, Amsterdam, and Rotterdam are fully accessible. Taxis are likely to be difficult to some degree, but new minivan taxis are an improvement.

There's comprehensive assistance for travelers in Belgium on **SNCB** (✆ **02/528-28-28;** www.b-rail.be) trains and in stations; in Holland with **NS** (✆ **030/235-7822;** www.ns.nl); and in Luxembourg with **CFL** (✆ **24-89-24-89;** www.cfl.lu). If you give them a day's notice of your journey by visiting a station or calling ahead, they can arrange for assistance along the way.

A good source of information in the Netherlands is the Dutch national automobile and touring club **ANWB** (✆ **088/269-2222;** www.anwb.nl). Another is the Amersfoort-based national organization **ANGO** (✆ **033/465-4343;** www.ango.nl); their website is in Dutch, but you might likely get an English speaker if you phone. In Belgium, there's **VAPH** (✆ **02/225-84-81;** www.vaph.be) for Flanders, and **AWIPH** (✆ **0800/16-061;** www.awiph.be) for Wallonia. In Luxembourg, turn to **Info Handicap** (✆ **36-64-66;** www.info-handicap.lu).

Family Travel

Some of the more expensive hotels in this region offer kids' suites, and you might even find that a suite is cheaper than booking two rooms. Many hotels allow children up to a certain age to sleep free or for a reduced rate in their parent's room, and may provide an extra bed. Arrange ahead of time for such necessities as a crib, bottle warmer, and car seat (small children are not allowed to ride in the front seat).

As for keeping the children amused, what child wouldn't be happy exploring the castles that are scattered across the Benelux landscapes? Give your youngsters a head start with a short rundown on the people who constructed these fascinating structures and what happened within their walls, and you'll soon find their imaginations running wild. In the cities, small towns, and villages, the colorful pageantry of past centuries as depicted in numerous festivals will surely delight the younger set. In Holland, watch faces light up at the Lilliputian "Holland in a Nutshell" miniatures at Madurodam. In Belgium, Brussels's *Manneken-Pis* statue, a famous national monument of a little boy urinating, is usually a winner. And look for wildlife centers in all three countries. Virtually every sightseeing attraction admits children at half price, and many offer family-ticket discounts.

For a Benelux experience aimed especially at children, see "Belgium, Holland & Luxembourg for Families," in chapter 4. To locate accommodations, restaurants, and attractions that are particularly kid-friendly, refer to the "Kids" icon throughout this guide.

Women Travelers

In Amsterdam, it's safe for groups of women to go around in the city's famed (or notorious) Red Light District—always supposing they can stomach seeing other women serving purely as sex objects—but a young woman on her own, particularly after dark, could be subject to at least verbal harassment, and misrepresentation as a "working girl." All other red-light zones in Benelux cities—and especially those in Brussels and Antwerp—are best avoided by women.

Public transportation in most Benelux towns and cities is usually busy even late at night, so you generally won't have to worry about being alone in a bus, tram, or Metro train. If you feel nervous, sit close to the driver whenever possible.

Holland has long enjoyed a relaxed attitude to exposing nontrivial amounts of the undraped female form—a recent government DVD, part of a now-mandatory "education" for would-be migrants, portrays going topless at the beach as an integral part of Dutch culture. Far fewer women are actually going without at the beach or in the park these days, and those who do are less likely to be younger women and teens. Catholic Belgium and Luxembourg always were less relaxed about this, and remain so.

Senior Travel

Mention that you're a senior when you make your travel reservations. By far the best way to get around in the Benelux lands is by public transportation—Metro trains, trams, and buses for short journeys, and trains for longer journeys. All three countries offer discounts for seniors on public transportation. For train travel, these discounts begin at age 65 in Belgium, and at age 60 in Holland and Luxembourg. Bus companies may have different starting ages for discounted tickets and passes. Many sightseeing attractions and tour companies offer senior discounts, but these might apply only to local residents when they produce an appropriate ID. Be sure to ask when you buy your ticket.

A group of local seniors run so-called "Mee in Mokum" guided tours on foot through Amsterdam—"Mokum" is the name Amsterdam's once-thriving Jewish community used for the city, and it's still used informally by the populace. The name means something like "Going with Amsterdam." People of any age can go on the tours, which are not exclusively for seniors, but that they are led by seniors makes it more likely the pace will be suitable. The guides speak English and know their beloved city inside out, as you might expect from people who have lived there for decades. Tours depart Tuesday to Sunday from the **David & Goliath** restaurant, Kalverstraat 92 (at the Amsterdams Historisch Museum); they last 2 to 3 hours and cost 5€. You can reach the guides at ✆ **020/625-4450,** or look them up at www.gildeamsterdam.nl.

Student Travel

Check out the **International Student Travel Confederation** (**ISTC;** www.istc.org) website for comprehensive travel services information and details on how to get an **International Student Identity Card (ISIC),** which qualifies students for substantial savings on rail passes, plane tickets, entrance fees, and more. It also provides students with basic health and life insurance and a 24-hour help line. The card is valid for a maximum of 18 months. You can apply for the card online or in person at **STA Travel** (✆ **800/781-4040** in North America, 134 782 in Australia, or 0871/230-0040 in the U.K.; www.statravel.com), the biggest student travel agency in the world; check out the website to locate STA Travel offices worldwide. If you're no longer a student but are still under 26, you can get an **International Youth Travel Card (IYTC)** from the same people, which entitles you to some discounts. **Travel CUTS** (✆ **866/246-9762;** www.travelcuts.com) offers similar services for both Canadians and U.S. residents. Irish students may prefer to turn to **USIT** (✆ **01/602-1906;** www.usit.ie), an Ireland-based specialist in student, youth, and independent travel.

Single Travelers

Amsterdam is Europe's ideal singles city: Countless singles from around the world come there to have a great time. The other major Benelux cities, not so much (Antwerp and Rotterdam could be the big exceptions). Amsterdam is not that difficult of a place to get to and get to grips with for a person traveling alone. There are lots of hotels and restaurants in all price ranges, and it's easy to meet other people around the bars and clubs, on canal-boat tours and bicycle tours, and in other ways.

I don't know if anybody ever went to Brussels, Bruges, or Ghent for a no-holds-barred wild-party vacation—and for sure not to The Hague, Liège, or Luxembourg City. I don't mean to say there are no decent bars and dance clubs amid the fine dining, art galleries, history museums, and other sober-sided goings-on in these places, but that's not really where their heart and soul lie.

Companies that specialize in solo travel to the Benelux lands are thin on the ground. The **Singles Travel Company,** 56 N. Santa Cruz Ave., Los Gatos, CA 95030 (✆ **888/286-8687,** or 408/354-3871; www.singlestravelcompany.com), takes in Amsterdam as a part of its European tour.

RESPONSIBLE TOURISM

The Dutch take the environment seriously. Living in a small country that's so heavily populated they need to recover land from the sea, they must. More than 60% of household waste is sorted, collected, and recycled. As a visitor, you are expected to play your part and not to just toss stuff without first checking if it's recyclable or reusable. **Greenpeace International** (www.greenpeace.org) has its headquarters in Amsterdam.

Generating power from the wind—an age-old Dutch skill—is growing apace. In 2010 Holland had around 2,000 wind turbines (100 offshore and the remainder on land), producing 9% of its electricity from this renewable resource, a figure that's due to more than double by 2020. Dutch airline KLM offers a voluntary program of paying a little more for your flight and flying CO_2-neutral. KLM invests the additional sum in selected sustainability projects.

All those bicycles you see in Holland take plenty of cars off the street. Anyone who's not riding a bike is likely to be walking or getting around by tram; visitors are encouraged to do likewise. There are many places where you can rent bikes, and public transportation is both easy to use and efficient. This commitment to going by bicycle applies absolutely everywhere in Holland, and to all age groups.

Belgium's Dutch-speaking Flanders region comes close to sharing the Dutch commitment to getting around by bike, particularly in areas close to the Dutch border and along the coast. In much of Francophone Belgium and in Luxembourg, the hilly terrain makes the bicycle not an ideal mode of transportation, though it is used enthusiastically for sport, fitness, and touring.

Benelux cities have excellent integrated public transportation systems, and using them helps with reducing greenhouse-gas emissions. Even if you must rent a car for getting around, the main car rental firms (see "By Car" under "Getting Around the Benelux," earlier in this chapter) offer green options to one degree or another. That might involve renting a low-emissions car, or making a payment to a CO_2-offset program, so that you can drive carbon-neutral.

Green living extends to what people eat throughout the Benelux countries. Restaurants in Amsterdam such as **Bolhoed** (p. 293), **Golden Temple** (p. 295), and **De Kas** (p. 298); **Shanti** (p. 101) in Brussels; and **Lotus** (p. 143) in Bruges use "bio" and vegan products and ingredients in the meals they serve. In food-crazy Belgium, there's a small but perhaps significant sign that the environment doesn't get quite the same care and attention. The Flemish soup-like stew *waterzooï,* one of the country's signature dishes and traditionally made with freshwater fish, is generally made with chicken today, because rivers like the Scheldt and the Meuse are still too polluted.

Many Dutch and Belgian hotels have signed up for sustainable operations agreements, which provide for becoming more energy efficient in all areas of operation, conserving water, decreasing the amount of unsorted waste, and more. Check hotel reviews throughout this book for details on specific sustainable properties.

Luxembourg is also hard at work on its green credentials, with construction projects around the Grand Duchy utilizing wind and solar energy and commercial data centers expanding their use of renewable sources of power. The government has launched an **Eco-Technology Action Plan** to support such endeavors. In the hospitality industry, there's an official **Ecolabel,** awarded to hotels for instituting a broad range of green improvements, like reducing water use, reusing air-conditioning energy, emphasizing the use of public transportation over private cars and limos, and using organic produce in their restaurants. Among the hotels to pick up this award is Le Royal (p. 499) in Luxembourg City.

SPECIAL INTEREST & ESCORTED TRIPS

Academic Trips & Language Classes

If you want to get fluent and have fun doing it, take a language course in Belgium, Holland, or Luxembourg. There are countless language schools; you can explore your options at **www.language-directory.com**, **www.goabroad.com**, or find an online partner to practice your new skills with at **www.mylanguageexchange.com**.

About half of Belgians are native French speakers, even if there might be a few differences between Belgian French and that of *la belle France*—for instance, *septante* and *nonante* instead of *soixante-dix* and *quatre-vingts-dix*, for "seventy" and "ninety," respectively—so no big deal. A good if pricey school where you can learn French, Dutch, German, and other languages is **CERAN,** av. des Petits Sapins 27, 4900 Spa (✆ **087/79-11-22;** www.ceran.com). You lodge at the Château du Haut-Neubois, just outside Spa. They do courses for adults and for children ages 10 to 18.

Maybe you've always dreamed of learning Dutch. Well, it can be done in Amsterdam. All three of the city's universities offer Dutch courses: **Universiteit van Amsterdam,** Spui 21, 1012 WX Amsterdam (✆ **020/525-9111;** www.uva.nl); **Volksuniversiteit,** Rapenburgerstraat 73, 1011 VK Amsterdam (✆ **020/626-1626;** www.volksuniversiteitamsterdam.nl); and **Vrije Universiteit Amsterdam,** De Boelelaan 1105, 1081 HV Amsterdam (✆ **020/598-9898;** www.vu.nl).

Learning Luxembourg's language *Lëtzebuergesch* may seem a mite specialized—and indeed it is—but you can do this, too. More practically, French and German are options to learn. Among the schools in the Grand Duchy that offer these courses is the **Institut National des Langues,** bd. de la Foire 21, 1528 Luxembourg-Ville (✆ **26-44-301;** www.insl.lu).

Adventure & Wellness Trips

The terrain in Belgium, Holland, and Luxembourg doesn't lend itself readily to adventure—but it does lend itself wonderfully to bicycling, and for some that will be adventure enough. If you want an active, typically Dutch vacation, **VBT Bicycling Vacations,** 614 Monkton Road, Bristol, VT 05443-0711 (✆ **800/245-3868;** www.vbt.com), has a 7-day "Holland: Bike and Barge" tour. You get 3 days on a barge visiting historic towns along the shore of the IJsselmeer Lake, followed by 4 days of bicycling in the Hoge Veluwe National Park and around nearby Arnhem. Ask about VBT's "Air Package Plus," which includes round-trip airfare to Amsterdam and pre- and post-tour accommodations. The aptly named **Tulip Cycling,** Boerhaar 37, 8131 SV Wijhe (✆ **0570/545-030;** www.tulipcycling.com) does a range of great cycling vacations through this bike-crazy country.

In addition to covering Holland, **Pure Adventures** (✆ **800/960-2221** in the U.S.; www.pure-adventures.com), takes in the Flemish part of Belgium, with the cities of Bruges and Ghent.

Food & Wine Trips

Belgium boasts one of the Continent's great culinary traditions, even if it is a largely unsung one compared with France, Italy, and Spain. Going with **Gordon's Guide Culinary Tours** (www.culinary-vacations.gordonsguide.com) is a good way to get to the heart of the matter.

"Dutch cooking is not a widely known cuisine," admits a reviewer of *The Art of Dutch Cooking* (1997) by Corry Countess Van Limburg Stirum. True. Traditional Dutch cuisine has not had much of a distinctive identity beyond its sterling meat-and-potatoes heritage, though "New Dutch cuisine" is a term that's often bandied about for a contemporary style that employs the best of Dutch ingredients in refreshing new ways, and mixes and matches from the vast range of ethnic styles that are now served up in Dutch cities. **De Kookfabriek,** De Flinesstraat 4, 1099 CB Amsterdam-Duivendrecht (✆ **020/463-5635;** www.kookfabriek.nl), is one organization that offers a variety of Dutch cooking classes.

Volunteer & Working Trips

Here's a list of companies offering educational and volunteer opportunities in Benelux:

- **http://jobs.goabroad.com:** Listings for jobs throughout Europe, as well as links to study and volunteer options.
- **www.idealist.org**: Resources and tips on volunteering abroad, along with volunteer and paid postings.
- **www.volunteerabroad.com**: Extensive listings for European volunteer opportunities.
- **www.concordiafarms.org**: Concordia is a UK-based organization with extensive volunteering opportunities in European countries, among them Belgium and Holland.

Escorted General Interest Tours

With a good escorted group tour, you'll know ahead of time what your trip will cost, and you won't have to worry about transportation, luggage, hotel reservations, communicating in foreign languages, and other basics—an experienced guide will take care of all that and lead you through all the sightseeing. The downside of a guided tour is that you trade much of the freedom and personal free time independent travel grants you and often see only the canned postcard-ready side of Europe through the tinted windows of a giant bus. You get to *see* Europe, but rarely do you get the chance to really *know* it. Consult a good travel agent for the latest offerings and advice.

Virgin Vacations (✆ **888/937-8474;** www.virgin-vacations.com) organizes great escorted tours of Amsterdam alone, with bus, bike, and boat options; and of Belgium and Holland together, taking in Amsterdam, Delft, Brussels, Bruges, and Antwerp.

The Amsterdam-based company **Artifex,** Rapenburgerstraat 123, 1011 VL Amsterdam (✆ **020/620-8112;** www.artifex.nu), offers everything from architecture walks to painting classes on canal boats. Its tailor-made tours aren't exactly cheap (the price depends on what you want to do), but its multilingual guides—trained art historians—can get you into private collections, the Royal Palace even when it's closed to the public, the Amsterdam School's Scheepvaarthuis (now a hotel), and many more places. Some clients wind up spending half their day in a cozy brown cafe.

With more than 450 different beers being produced in a nation of just 10 million inhabitants, you can easily see that beer is a big deal in Belgium. Some of these are run-of-the-mill *pilsener* beers, but many are lovingly crafted specialty beers with their own distinct bottle and glass. Getting to grips with a bottle of Belgium's best is made easier on an escorted beer tour run by **BeerTrips.com,** PO Box 7892, Missoula, MT 59807 (✆ **406/531-9109;** www.beertrips.com).

Tiny Luxembourg is more likely to be included in a more general escorted tour than to be a destination in its own right. An example is the Imperial Capitals Tour offered by **Cosmos Tours** (✆ **800/942-3301;** www.escortedcosmostours.com), which covers Belgium and Luxembourg in addition to other European countries.

For more information on escorted general-interest tours, including questions to ask before booking your trip, see Frommers.com.

STAYING CONNECTED

Mobile Phones

If your phone has GSM (Global System for Mobiles) capability and you have a world-compatible phone, you should be able to make and receive calls from the Benelux countries. Only certain phones have this capability, though, and you should check with your service operator first. Call charges can be high. Alternatively, you can rent a phone through **Cellhire** (✆ **877/244-7242;** www.cellhire.com in the U.S.; or ✆ **0800/280-0415;** www.cellhire.co.uk in the U.K.;), or **Global Mobility Group** (✆ **1300/791-033;** www.globalmobilitygroup.com.au). After a simple online registration, they will ship a phone (usually with a U.K. number) to your home or office. Usage charges can be high, so read the fine print.

U.K. mobiles work in the Benelux countries; call your service provider before departing your home country to ensure that the international call bar has been switched off and to check call charges, which can be high. Also remember that you are charged for calls you *receive* on a U.K. mobile used abroad.

To rent a GSM mobile phone in Belgium, go to **Rent2Connect** (✆ **02/652-14-14;** www.locaphone.be), in the Arrivals hall at Brussels Airport. In Holland, go to **Telecom Rentcenter** (✆ **020/653-0999;** www.rentcenter.nl), in the Arrivals hall at Schiphol Airport.

If you have Web access while traveling, consider a broadband-based telephone service (in technical terms, **Voice over Internet Protocol,** or **VoIP**) such as Skype (www.skype.com) or Vonage (www.vonage.com), which allow you to make free international calls from your laptop or in a cybercafe. Neither service requires the people you're calling to also have that service (though there are fees if they do not). Check the websites for details.

Internet & E-mail

More and more hotels, hostels, bars, coffeehouses, and cafes have terminals and/or Wi-Fi hotspots with Internet access. At presstime, Amsterdam's Schiphol Airport offered free Wi-Fi for up to 1 hour throughout all its terminals. To find public Wi-Fi hotspots, go to **www.jiwire.com**; its Global Wi-Fi Finder holds the world's largest directory of public wireless hotspots. Bring a **connection kit** of the right power and phone adapters, a spare phone cord, and a spare Ethernet network cable—or find out whether your hotel supplies them to guests.

One effect of the growth in Wi-Fi has been to all but kill the market for dedicated cybercafes, which have become an endangered species in the Benelux lands. You'll still find them, just not as many as formerly.

Newspapers & Magazines

The main British and Irish daily newspapers, and the *International Herald Tribune, Wall Street Journal Europe, USA Today, Time, Newsweek, Business Week, Fortune, The Economist,* and more are available from news vendors at major train stations, and from other outlets in Benelux towns and cities.

If you are so starved of news that you need to get it somehow from a Dutch paper, the main dailies in Holland are *Het Parool* (center-left afternoon paper); *NRC Handelsblad* (centrist, intellectual evening paper); *De Volkskrant* (Catholic, left-liberal morning paper); and *De Telegraaf* (right-wing morning paper). The highbrow weekly news magazine is *Elsevier.*

In Belgium you have the luxury of choice between French- and Dutch-language dailies. On the French side of the aisle, there's *Le Soir* (liberal and authoritative); *La Libre Belgique* (Catholic and traditional); and *La Dernière Heure* (popular and breathless). Flemings get their news fix from *De Standaard* (centrist and authoritative); *De Morgen* (progressive and righteous); and *De Tijd* (popular and colorful). The authoritative weekly news magazines are the Flemish *Knack* and the French *Le Vif L'Express*. There's even a daily newspaper, the *Grenz-Echo* (independent and traditional), for the small German-speaking community in the east of the country.

In Luxembourg you have the German-language dailies *d'Wort* (which contains a section written in Lëtzebuergesch), *Tageblatt,* and *Lëtzebuerger Journal;* and in French, *La Voix du Luxembourg* and *Le Quotidien*.

Telephones

BELGIUM

The country code for Belgium is **32.** When calling Belgium from abroad, you do not use the initial **0** in the area code. For example, if you're calling a Brussels number (area code **02**) from outside Belgium, you dial the international access code (which is **011** when calling from North America, and **00** from elsewhere in Europe) and then **32-2,** followed by the subscriber number.

You only dial the initial **0** of the area code if you're calling within Belgium (and this includes if you're calling another number in the same area-code zone). When you call someone in Belgium, you always need to use the area code even if you're calling from inside the same area. There are two main formats for Belgian phone numbers. In the main cities, a two-digit area code followed by a seven-digit number; and for other places, a three-digit area code followed by a six-digit number. For instance, Brussels's tourist information number is **02/513-89-40;** Ypres's is **057/23-92-20.**

For information in English, both domestic and international, dial ✆ **1404.**

To make international calls from Belgium, first dial **00** and then the country code. To call the United States or Canada, dial **00** (the international access code) + **1** (the country code) + the area code + the number. Other country codes are: United Kingdom, **44;** Ireland, **353;** Australia, **61;** New Zealand, **64.** International calls, per minute, cost: **U.S., Canada, U.K., Ireland:** 0.35€; **Australia, New Zealand:** 1€.

You can use most pay phones with a Belgacom *telecard* (phone card), selling for 5€, 10€, and 20€ from post offices. Some pay phones take coins, of 0.10€, 0.20€, 0.50€, 1€, and 2€. Both local and long-distance calls from a pay phone are 0.30€ a minute at peak time (Mon–Fri 8am–7pm) and the same amount for 2 minutes at other times. Calls dialed direct from hotel room phones are usually more than twice the standard rate.

To charge a call to your calling card, contact: **AT&T** (✆ 0800/100-10), **Sprint** (✆ 0800/100-14), **Australia Direct** (✆ 0800/100-61), **Canada Direct** (✆ 0800/100-19), **British Telecom** (✆ 0800/100-24), and **Telecom New Zealand** (✆ 0800/100-64).

HOLLAND

The country code for the Netherlands is **31.** When calling Holland from abroad, you do not use the initial **0** in the area code. For example, if you're calling an Amsterdam number (area code **020**) from outside Holland, you dial the international access code (which is **011** when calling from North America, and **00** from elsewhere in Europe) and then **31-20,** followed by the subscriber number. You only dial the initial **0** of the area code if you're calling within Holland.

When making local calls in Holland, you won't need to use the area codes shown in this book. You do need to use an area code between towns and cities. The two main formats for Dutch phone numbers are: for cities and large towns, a three-digit area code followed by a seven-digit number; and for small towns and villages, a four-digit area code followed by a six-digit number.

For operator assistance, call ✆ **0800/0410.** For information inside Holland, dial ✆ **0900/8008;** for international information, dial ✆ **0900/8418** for multiple numbers. Numbers beginning with 0800 within Holland are toll-free. Watch out for the special Dutch numbers that begin with 0900; calls to these are charged at a higher rate than ordinary local calls. Depending who you call, they can cost up to 1€ a minute.

To make international calls from the Netherlands, first dial **00** and then the country code. To call the United States or Canada, dial **00** (the international access code) + **1** (the country code) + the area code + the number. Other country codes are: United Kingdom, **44;** Ireland, **353;** Australia, **61;** New Zealand, **64.** International calls, per minute, cost: **U.S.** and **Canada:** 0.30€; **U.K.** and **Ireland:** 0.35€; **Australia** and **New Zealand:** 0.40€.

You can use pay phones with a KPN *telekaart* (phone card). KPN cards are 5€, 10€, 20€, and 50€, from post offices, train-station ticket counters, and some tobacconists and newsstands. Some pay phones take credit cards. A few take coins of 0.10€, 0.20€, 0.50€, 1€, and 2€. Both local and long-distance calls from a pay phone are 0.30€ a minute.

There's a sustained dial tone, and a beep-beep sound for a busy signal. On card and coin phones, a digital reading tracks your decreasing deposit so you know when to add another card or more coins. To make additional calls when you still have a coin or card inserted, briefly break the connection, and you will get a new dial tone for another call.

To charge a call to your calling card, call **AT&T** (✆ 0800/022-9111), **Sprint** (✆ 0800/022-9119), **Canada Direct** (✆ 0800/022-9116), **British Telecom** (✆ 0800/022-9944), **Australia Direct** (✆ 0800/022-0061), or **Telecom New Zealand** (✆ 0800/022-4295).

LUXEMBOURG

The country code for Luxembourg is **352.** The entire country is in the same local dialing area, so no **area codes** are used. For example, if you're calling a Luxembourg City number from outside Luxembourg, you dial the international access code (which is **011** when calling from North America, and **00** from elsewhere in Europe) and then **352,** followed by the local number.

When you're calling a Luxembourg number from anywhere in Luxembourg, you need only dial the local number. These numbers can be confusing enough, since you might need to dial a five-, six-, seven-, eight-, or even nine-digit subscriber number.

Almost all pay phones accept phone cards; these cost 5€, 10€, and 25€, and are sold at post offices and newsstands. Some phones accept 0.20€, 0.50€, and 1€ coins. To charge a call to your calling card, phone: **AT&T** (✆ 800/20-111), **Sprint** (✆ 800/20-115), **Canada Direct** (✆ 800/20-119), **British Telecom** (✆ 800/20-044), or **Telecom New Zealand** (✆ 800/20-064).

TIPS ON ACCOMMODATIONS

Traditional European hotels tend to be simpler than American ones and emphasize cleanliness and friendliness over amenities. For example, even in the cheapest American chain motel, free cable is as standard as indoor plumbing. In Europe, few hotels below the moderate level have in-room TVs.

Unless otherwise noted, all hotel rooms in this book have private en suite bathrooms. However, the standard European hotel bathroom might not look like what you're used to. For example, one European concept of a shower is a nozzle stuck in the bathroom wall and a drain in the floor. Shower curtains are optional. In some cramped private bathrooms, you have to relocate the toilet paper outside the bathroom before turning on the shower and drenching the whole room. Another interesting fixture is the "half tub," in which there's only room to sit, rather than lie down. Hot water may be available only once a day and not on demand—this is especially true with shared bathrooms. Heating water is costly, and many smaller hotels do so only once daily, in the morning.

Belgium, the Netherlands, and Luxembourg established the Benelux Hotel Classification System back in 1978 and updated the standards in 1994. Each establishment that accepts guests must publicly display a sign indicating its classification (from "1" for those with minimum amenities to "5" for deluxe, full-service hotels). The national tourist boards do an excellent job of providing full accommodations listings and advance booking for visitors.

Should the idea of vacationing on a working farm, or in a château (an old-fashioned country home), or even in an old school converted to a character-filled lodging hold some charms for you, Belgium has two organizations that can smooth your path to the front door. In Wallonia, contact **Gîtes de Wallonie,** av. Prince de Liège 1/21, 5100 Jambes-Namur (**© 081/31-18-00;** www.gitesdewallonie.be); for Flanders, contact **Plattelandstoerisme in Vlaanderen,** Diestsevest 40, 3000 Leuven (**© 016/28-60-35;** www.hoevetoerisme.be).

In all three countries, you can choose among luxury hotels in city or rural locations; smaller urban hotels with moderate rates and somewhat limited facilities; and charming, family-run country inns. No matter what end of the price scale it's on, each lodging will be spotlessly clean and will feature a staff dedicated to personal attention and excellent service. The rates quoted include the service charge (usually 15%), tax, and, in most cases, breakfast.

Be sure to inquire about discounts when you book your room. Many hotels have a variety of room rates. It's sometimes possible to pay less if you settle for a shower instead of full bathroom facilities. Also, weekend or midweek rates are often available.

For tips on surfing for hotel deals online, visit Frommers.com.

SUGGESTED BENELUX ITINERARIES

4

The quintessential Benelux experience is a city one. Not many foreign visitors come for the Belgian beaches, even fewer for the Dutch mountains, and none at all for Luxembourg's vast empty spaces. On the other hand, Benelux cities—big and small—are among Europe's cultural and historical glories. This doesn't mean there are no places of scenic beauty; there are actually more than you might think.

Most important, bring as much time with you as you can afford. You might want to indulge yourself by stepping onboard an occasional slow train rather than always rushing to catch the high-speed Thalys or an InterCity Express; and drive on at least some country roads instead of zipping along on expressways. Even going by bicycle isn't out of the question.

Getting around Belgium, Holland, and Luxembourg is a snap, but deciding what to take in and what to leave out is difficult. I hope these suggested itineraries will help you organize your time as you plan your own trip to the Benelux.

THE COUNTRIES IN BRIEF

Taken together, the Benelux nations of Belgium, Holland (the Netherlands), and Luxembourg cover a small area, a mere 75,000 sq. kilometers (29,000 sq. miles)—around one-fifth the size of neighboring Germany, and not much larger than West Virginia. But arguably, no other comparably sized place in Europe compresses so many points of interest. Topping the list are artistic masterpieces, cultural events, and substantial reminders of a long and colorful history. Space remains for scenery that, while mostly lacking in drama, can still be lyrically beautiful. Then there are the more mundane (but agreeable) advantages of convenience, economy, and friendly populations, not to mention a host of other travel delights—the exquisite food and drink of Brussels, the exuberant sociability of Amsterdam, and Luxembourg's sidewalk cafes.

BELGIUM For a graphic image of Belgium's two ethnic regions, Dutch-speaking Vlaanderen (Flanders) and French-speaking Wallonie (Wallonia), draw an imaginary east-west line across the country just south of Brussels. North of the line is Flanders, where you find the medieval cities of Bruges, Ghent, and Antwerp, and Belgium's North Sea coastline. South of the line is Wallonia. The art cities of Tournai and Mons, and the scenic resort towns of the Meuse River valley and the Ardennes, are the attractions of this region. Then there's Brussels, the capital, roughly in the geographic middle, and going off on a trajectory of its own as the "capital of Europe."

HOLLAND The Netherlands is a WYSIWYG kind of country: What you see is what you get. There are no dramatic canyons or towering peaks. The nation's highest point wouldn't top the roof of a New York City skyscraper, and its average altitude is just 11m (37 ft.) above sea level. This makes for few panoramic vantage points; you can't see most of its canals and lakes until you're about to fall into them. Does this mean the views are boring? The answer is a flat "no." As the famous 17th-century Dutch landscape painters showed the world, vistas in Holland are among the most aesthetic anywhere: wide-angle views of green pastures and floating clouds, with tiny houses, church spires, and grazing cattle silhouetted against the horizon.

LUXEMBOURG At first sight, Luxembourg—a county-size nation with a population barely bigger than a small- to medium-size city—might appear to have an obvious provincial aspect. But size isn't everything, and, in this case at least, small really is beautiful. Luxembourg packs into its handful of square miles a fascinating little capital city and an enviable roster of cultural diversity and scenic splendor.

BELGIUM & HOLLAND IN 1 WEEK

Few countries can boast of cities more justly celebrated than Amsterdam, Brussels, and Bruges. Not far behind are Ghent, Antwerp, The Hague, Maastricht, Delft, Leiden, and Luxembourg City, among others. Some of these stellar places can't fit on this itinerary. (Don't blame me: It was you who decided to come for only a week!) Travel between the cities listed here is easy—I recommend getting around by car or riding Belgium and Holland's excellent trains.

Day 1: Arrive in Amsterdam ★★★

Get in early and get going—time is of the essence! First up is a 1-hour **canal cruise** (p. 314). This is the Dutch capital's tourist-trap par excellence, but it is also *the very best* way to view much of this canal-threaded city in a reasonable time. Now choose *just one*—a tough decision that will depend on your own interests—from Amsterdam's three standout museums: the **Van Gogh Museum** (p. 304), the **Rijksmuseum** (p. 301), or the **Anne Frank House** (p. 300). A walk in the old hippie paradise **Vondelpark** (p. 314) to clear your head can be followed by drinks at **Café Americain** (p. 295) on Leidseplein. Dine in the evening at a traditional Dutch restaurant like **Haesje Claes** (p. 287) or an Indonesian one like **Tempo Doeloe** (p. 294).

Day 2: The Hague ★★★

The Dutch seat of government is a 50-minute train ride from Amsterdam. Parliament is in the heart of town, in the **Binnenhof** and **Ridderzaal** (p. 360), and you can take a guided tour if you've planned ahead. Visit the **Koninklijk Kabinet van Schilderijen** (p. 362), in the **Mauritshuis** palace, for its superb paintings by the Old Dutch and Flemish Masters. Then hop on a tram and take a short ride to the seacoast at **Scheveningen** (p. 368), where you can breathe fresh sea air and have coffee at the

Suggested Benelux Itineraries

Enjoying Belgium, Holland & Luxembourg with Kids

Wadden Islands
Waddenzee
NORTH SEA
IJsselmeer
Enkhuizen
Lelystad
Zandvoort
Amsterdam
Harderwijk
NETHERLANDS
Rotterdam
Kinderdijk
GERMANY
Ostend
Bruges
Antwerp
Brussels
BELGIUM
Han-sur-Lesse
FRANCE
LUXEMBOURG
0 50 mi
0 50 km

Seeing Belgium & Holland in One Week

Wadden Islands
Waddenzee
NORTH SEA
IJsselmeer
Amsterdam
NETHERLANDS
The Hague
GERMANY
Bruges
Antwerp
Ghent
Brussels
BELGIUM
FRANCE
LUXEMBOURG
0 50 mi
0 50 km

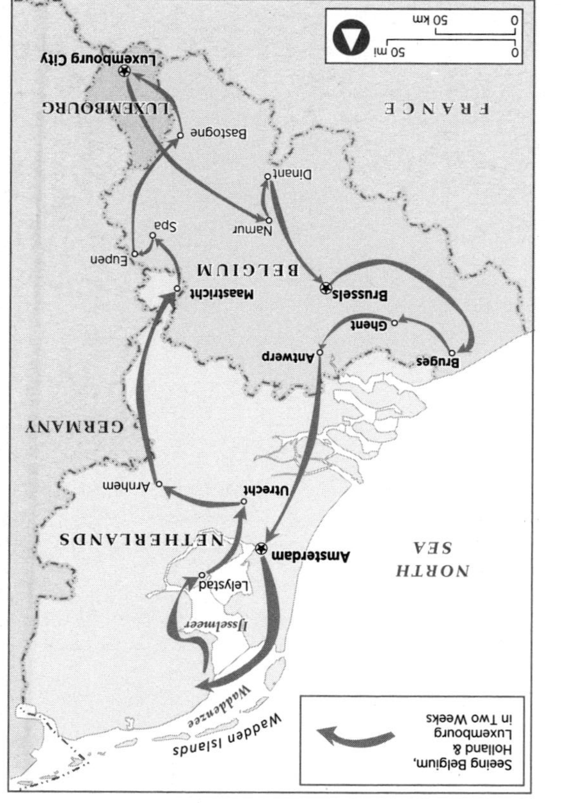
Seeing Belgium, Holland & Luxembourg in Two Weeks
Wadden Islands
Waddenzee
IJsselmeer
Lelystad
Amsterdam
Utrecht
Arnhem
NETHERLANDS
GERMANY
NORTH SEA
Antwerp
Ghent
Bruges
Brussels
Maastricht
BELGIUM
Eupen
Spa
Namur
Dinant
Bastogne
LUXEMBOURG
Luxembourg City
FRANCE
0 50 mi
0 50 km

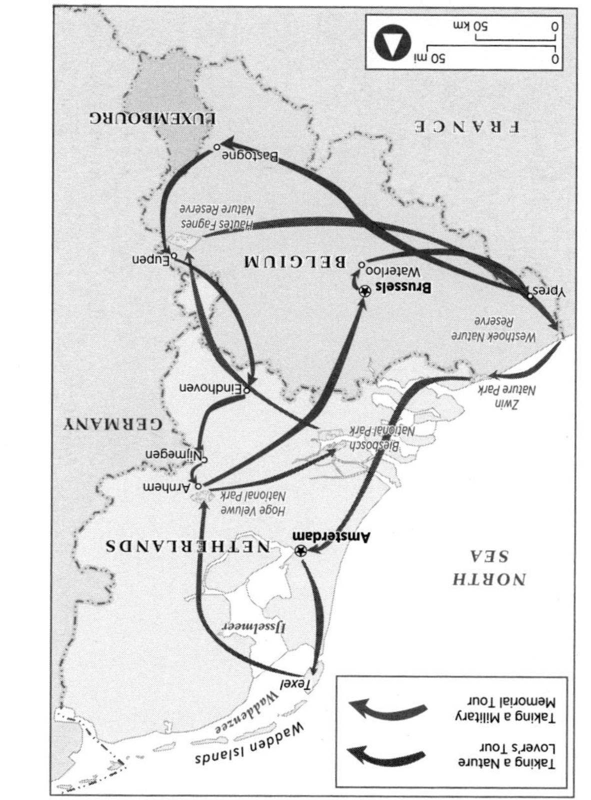
Taking a Nature Lover's Tour
Taking a Military Memorial Tour
Wadden Islands
Waddenzee
Texel
IJsselmeer
Amsterdam
NETHERLANDS
Hoge Veluwe National Park
Arnhem
Nijmegen
GERMANY
Eindhoven
Biesbosch National Park
NORTH SEA
Zwin Nature Park
Westhoek Nature Reserve
Ypres
Brussels
Waterloo
BELGIUM
Eupen
Hautes Fagnes Nature Reserve
Bastogne
LUXEMBOURG
FRANCE
0 50 mi
0 50 km

splendid **Steigenberger Kurhaus Hotel** (p. 371) before taking the tram back to The Hague to catch a late-afternoon train to Brussels.

Day 3: Brussels ★★★

If you don't want to be packing and unpacking every day, lodge in Brussels and do Belgium's other historic cities as easy day trips. In the "capital of Europe," start out at the **Grand-Place** (p. 103), taking time to absorb the magnificent old square's architectural details and animated spirit. A date with Rubens, Bruegel, Magritte, and other notable Belgian artists awaits you in the elegant **Musées Royaux des Beaux-Arts de Belgique** (p. 112). Next you might want to stroll amid trees, fountains, and lawns in the **Parc de Bruxelles** (p. 117), and view the **Palais Royal** (p. 113) and the Belgian Parliament building, the **Palais de la Nation** (p. 117), on opposite sides of the park. In the evening, dine at **'t Kelderke** (p. 99), a traditional Brussels restaurant on the Grand-Place.

Day 4: Bruges's Medieval Splendor ★★★

By train, Bruges is just an hour from Brussels. Once you arrive, hire wheels at the rail station or at a store in town and you can easily tour the city by **bicycle** (p. 135). A must-do is a **canal cruise** (p. 153); this will mark you indelibly as a tourist, but what you lose in street cred you'll make up for by seeing a lot in a short time. Later, stroll around the connected medieval central squares **Burg** (p. 145) and **Markt** (p. 144). On the Burg, visit the **Basiliek van het Heilig-Bloed** (p. 145) for a glimpse of a relic that's said to be drops of Christ's blood; on the Markt, climb the **Belfry** (p. 144) for splendid city views. Next, head to the **Kantcentrum** (p. 149) and watch how Bruges's handmade lace is crafted.

Day 5: Ghent ★★

Just a half-hour train ride from Brussels, Ghent has a different, thoroughly Flemish character. Scoot to the center of town by tram, and get your bearings by climbing the stairs or taking the elevator up above the city's rooftops to the 14th-century **Belfry's** (p. 162) viewing platform. Across elegant Sint-Baafsplein from the Belfry, **Sint-Baafskathedraal** (p. 163) holds a great medieval artwork: Jan van Eyck's altarpiece *The Adoration of the Mystic Lamb* (1432). From the cathedral, stroll to the medieval inner harbor along **Korenlei** and **Graslei** (p. 165 and 165), past the forbidding castle of the counts of Flanders, the **Gravensteen** (p. 162), and then go through the restored medieval **Patershol** district (p. 167).

Day 6: Antwerp ★★

Forty minutes by train from Brussels, Antwerp is Belgium's second-largest city. Make the most of your time here by riding a tram to the center of town. Visit the **Grote Markt** (p. 177) to view its dramatic Brabo sculpture-fountain, and then stop for a *bolleke* (round glass) of Antwerp's De Koninck beer at the grand old tavern **Den Engel** (p. 184), on the square. Antwerp means Rubens; to learn more about the artist, go to his former home, the **Rubenshuis** (p. 176), and view his paintings at the **Koninklijk Museum voor Schone Kunsten Antwerpen** (p. 175). Back at Antwerp Centraal Station, stroll briefly around the city's celebrated (though not exactly handsome) **Diamond Quarter** (p. 178) before catching your train.

Day 7: Back to Amsterdam

If you have an early flight home from Amsterdam's **Schiphol Airport,** you'll be happy to know that Thalys high-speed and InterCity Express trains to Amsterdam from Brussels and Antwerp stop at Schiphol. If, on the other hand, you have time to kill in Amsterdam but don't want to stray too far from Centraal Station, take a short ride onboard a **harbor ferry** (p. 271) from the Waterplein-West dock behind the station, for fine views of Amsterdam harbor. More time might permit you to visit historic **Haarlem** (p. 330).

BELGIUM, HOLLAND & LUXEMBOURG IN 2 WEEKS

If you have 2 weeks in the Benelux lands, you'll breathe more easily. You can stroll where you might otherwise have needed to hop on a city tram or bus, and you'll have time to visit Luxembourg. Yes, there's a lot to be said for having 2 weeks. This itinerary is designed for you to travel by car, but you can do most of it by train and an occasional bus. You'll just need to modify some elements to allow for the additional time it will take to get around.

Day 1: Arrive in Amsterdam ★★★

With 2 weeks, you can take your time—all the while looking cool and laid-back. But before you do the cool thing, I suggest you don a disguise and step onboard a touristy **canal cruise boat** (p. 314). The view of Amsterdam is best from the water, and how else are you going to get it? Afterward, stroll along the 17th-century Golden Age **Canal Belt** (p. 292)—comprising the Herengracht, Keizersgracht, and Prinsengracht canals—starting out at the **Westerkerk** (p. 310) and going by way of **Leidseplein** (p. 269) to **Rembrandtplein.** For dinner, head to the fine canal-side *eetcafé* **De Prins** (p. 295).

Day 2: More of Amsterdam's Best

This morning you have to make a choice—between the **Van Gogh Museum** (p. 304), the **Rijksmuseum** (p. 301), or the **Anne Frank House** (p. 300). (If you want to visit Anne's wartime refuge, try to go as early as possible.) In the afternoon, tour the **Red Light District** (p. 313), or, if that sounds like an indecent proposal, walk instead through the old artisans'—now trendified—**Jordaan** district (p. 312). For dinner, try **Haesje Claes** (p. 287), a traditional Dutch restaurant, or **Tempo Doeloe** (p. 294) for Indonesian cuisine.

Day 3: The IJsselmeer ★★

Today go by car north out of Amsterdam along the western shore of the **IJsselmeer** (p. 337), a freshwater lake that was once a sea known as the Zuiderzee. Go through **Marken** (p. 339), **Monnickendam** (p. 339), **Volendam** (p. 338), **Edam** (p. 340), **Hoorn** (p. 342), **Enkhuizen** (p. 343), and **Medemblik** (p. 345). Cross over the **Afsluitdijk** (p. 346), the great barrier completed in 1932 that closed off the mouth of the Zuiderzee. Turn south along the eastern IJsselmeer shore, through **Makkum** (p. 401), **Hindeloopen** (p. 402), **Stavoren** (p. 403), and **Urk** (p. 450), before driving across the flat polders of **Flevoland** province (p. 426) back to Amsterdam.

Day 4: Driving to Arnhem

Get on the road again, heading southeast to Arnhem. Places worth taking in along the way include **Breukelen** (p. 432), the village from which Brooklyn, New York, takes its name (it even has a Breukelen Bridge!) and **Utrecht** (p. 426) for a brief stroll through this historic ecclesiastical city's canal-threaded Old Town. **Arnhem** (p. 438) was the target of a gallant but doomed Allied airborne assault in World War II. Visit the nearby **Hoge Veluwe National Park** (p. 436)—where you can get around slowly on foot, or faster by borrowing a free white bicycle—and the surprising **Kröller-Müller Museum** (p. 437) at its heart, which contains no fewer than 278 works by Vincent van Gogh.

Day 5: Drive to Maastricht

This morning head south to **Nijmegen** (p. 441), once a Roman legionary fortress and later a favorite seat of the Frank king Charlemagne. When you hit the Maas River at **Grave,** follow its course south. A brief side excursion through **Thorn** (p. 480), the comely "white village," can break up the journey on your way to **Maastricht** (p. 470). This most southerly Dutch city's squares and cobblestone streets are filled with southern charm, not to mention plenty of fine restaurants and cafes.

Day 6: Spa ★★

Just over an hour's drive from Maastricht is Spa, Belgium's elegant "town of waters." When you arrive, tour the mineral springs in the forests around the town. Then follow an easy circuit from Spa through the northern **Ardennes** (p. 237). Along the way, take in **Eupen** (p. 249), the diminutive "capital" of Belgium's small German-speaking community, and the **Hautes Fagnes Nature Reserve** (p. 250), where you might want to take time out for a hike on this invariably wind-swept high moorland. Then pass through **Malmédy,** the attraction park at **Coo (Trois Ponts),** and **Stavelot.**

Day 7: Luxembourg City ★★

Driving south through the Ardennes in Belgium and Luxembourg, by way of **Bastogne** (p. 241), today you'll make your way toward Luxembourg-Ville, the capital of the Grand Duchy of Luxembourg. Stroll its streets and squares, with their affluent yet somewhat Ruritanian air. View the dramatic gorge that separates the Old Town from the New Town, and take in the **casemates** (p. 496), remnants of once powerful fortifications; the grand duke's seat in the **Palais Grand-Ducal** (p. 497); and the elegant **Cathédrale Notre-Dame** (p. 496).

Day 8: Namur ★★

On the eighth day, a 2-hour drive on the expressway from Luxembourg City brings you to Namur, on the Meuse River. For a more scenic route, go by way of **Abbaye Notre-Dame d'Orval** (p. 240), which will add an hour or two to your drive. In Namur visit the hilltop **Citadelle** (p. 218), and stroll through **Le Corbeil** (p. 219), the town's oldest quarter. A short, charming out-of-town excursion is along the Meuse to **Dinant** (p. 224), which you can combine with a visit to some magnificent gardens, the **Jardins d'Annevoie** (p. 222). In the evening, try your luck at Namur's **casino** (p. 222).

Day 9: Brussels ★★★

Today, you'll scoot along the expressway to Belgium's capital. The magnificent **Grand-Place** (p. 103) is an ideal staring point for the drive. You might also want to fit in a "pilgrimage" to the nearby ***Manneken-Pis*** statue (p. 110). Following this, stop off at the **Musées Royaux des Beaux-Arts de Belgique** (p. 112) to view works by Rubens, Bruegel, Magritte, and other notable Belgian artists. Then stroll amid Masonic symbols in the **Parc de Bruxelles** (p. 117), stopping to view the **Palais Royal** (p. 113) and the **Palais de la Nation** (**Parliament;** p. 117)—on opposite sides of the park. In the evening, dine on the Grand-Place at **'t Kelderke,** a traditional Bruxellois restaurant.

Day 10: More of Brussels's Best

After breakfast, go shopping (or even just window-shopping) at the 19th-century **Galeries Royales St-Hubert** (p. 122), and then make your way to the **Cathédrale des Sts-Michel-et-Gudule** (p. 114). Go up onto rue Royale and take a tram to **place du Grand Sablon** (p. 109) to browse its antiques stores (or, on weekends, the antiques market). When you're finished there, cross over rue de la Régence to tranquil **place du Petit Sablon** (p. 109) and enjoy a rest in its central garden. In the afternoon, take a trip to the **Atomium** (p. 118) and the **Bruparck** (p. 85) complex on Brussels's northern edge or to the **battlefield of Waterloo** (p. 130), just south of the city.

Day 11: Bruges ★★★

Not much more than an hour on the expressway (once you've broken free from Brussels's congested ring road), Bruges is the Benelux's prime medieval property. Do a **canal cruise** (p. 153) to give yourself an easy introduction to the city's layout and character. Afterward, stroll around the connected medieval **Burg** (p. 145) and **Markt** (p. 144) central squares. On the Burg, visit the **Basiliek van het Heilig-Bloed** (p. 145) for a glimpse of a relic that's said to be drops of Christ's blood; on the Markt, climb the **Belfry** (p. 144) for splendid city views. In the late afternoon, go to the **Kantcentrum** (p. 149) and see how Bruges's handmade lace is crafted.

Day 12: More of Bruges's Best

This morning, try to visit the **Groeningemuseum** (p. 148) to view its fine collection of works by the Flemish Old Masters dubbed the "Flemish Primitives." Next, stroll through the courtyard of the 15th-century, Burgundian-era Palace of the Lords of Gruuthuse, now the **Bruggemuseum-Gruuthuse** (p. 149). On the way to the **Prinselijk Begijnhof ten Wijngaarde** (p. 150), pop into **Onze-Lieve-Vrouwekerk** (p. 150) to see its *Madonna and Child* sculpture by Michelangelo. In the afternoon, if you have time, consider taking a side trip to the nearby canal-side village of **Damme** (p. 157).

Day 13: Ghent ★★ & Antwerp ★★

These two Flemish cities are close to Bruges and close together—by road, Ghent is 53km/33 miles from Bruges; Antwerp is 91km/56 miles from Bruges and 64km/40 miles from Ghent. When you arrive in Ghent, head to its central district and up to the top of the 14th-century **Belfry** (p. 162) for beautiful city views. In nearby **Sint-Baafskathedraal** (p. 163), you'll lay eyes on a medieval masterpiece: Jan van Eyck's *The Adoration of the Mystic Lamb* (1432). From the cathedral, stroll to the medieval inner harbor along **Korenlei** and **Graslei** (p. 165 and 165). Next it's on to Antwerp. Here visit the **Grote Markt** (p. 177) and view its dramatic Brabo sculpture-fountain. For an insight into the artist Rubens, visit his home, the **Rubenshuis** (p. 176).

Day 14: Back to Amsterdam

From Antwerp, Amsterdam's Schiphol Airport is just a couple hours up the expressway. If you have time before your flight, consider spending it in one of the following places (all close to the airport): In spring, breathe in the scent from millions of flowers at **Keukenhof Gardens** (p. 350), in Lisse; at other times of year, tour sites in **Leiden** (p. 390) associated with the Pilgrims. Should neither option appeal, perhaps you'd prefer a visit to the beach at **Zandvoort** (p. 335).

BELGIUM, HOLLAND & LUXEMBOURG FOR FAMILIES

The young folks'll be pleased to learn there's more to the Benelux lands than paintings by Old Masters *(sigh!)*; Gothic architecture *(groan!)*; struggling with French, Dutch, and Lëtzebuergesch *(aak!)*; and eating mussels *(no way!)*. Actually, you don't need to worry too much about the lingo throughout most of this region since many natives speak English. And there are hundreds of fun family-friendly things to see and do in these three countries—remember, Benelux burghers have kids, too!

Day 1: Brussels ★★★

Whenever the kids step out of line in Brussels, uttering these magic words should get their attention: "Maybe we should tour the European Union administrative buildings today." I'd wager that they (and you) would prefer the **Atomium** (p. 118). And while you're there, in the city's northern Bruparck district, think about touring **Mini-Europe** (p. 119). Back in the center of town, treat the kids to an exposé of bold little ***Manneken-Pis*** (p. 110); grown-ups usually wonder what all the fuss is about, but kids love him. By the way: Going around the city by **tram** (p. 86) can't hurt.

Day 2: More of Brussels

Boys, especially, might want to take a look under the hood of **Autoworld** (p. 113) today. And is it being sexist to suggest that the girls might prefer costumes and lace at the **Musée du Costume et de la Dentelle** (p. 116)? Both genders will likely agree that the comic strips and characters at the **Centre Belge de la Bande-Dessinée** (p. 118) are pretty cool.

Day 3: Bruges ★★★

In this historic Flemish city, you can swerve past Old Masters, Gothic architecture, and mussel-slurping diners in one fast move. Achieve this satisfying feat by visiting the **Boudewijn Seapark** (p. 153) or the **Kinderboerderij Domein De Zeven Torentjes** (p. 153)—or both. The open-top **canal cruise boats** (p. 153) are another good bet. And it's safe to go around by rented **pedal-bike** (p. 135) in the center of town.

Day 4: The Belgian Coast

A day at the seacoast is a no-brainer for families, especially in summer—building sand-castles on the beach, swimming in the sea, and riding beach buggies. You can go from one end of Belgium's seacoast to the other onboard the amazing **Coast Tram** (p. 190). At Ostend there's the **Noordzeeaquarium** (p. 194), and the museum ships ***Mercator*** (p. 193) and ***Amandine*** (p. 194). Up the coast at Knokke-Heist, allow some time to check out the bird sanctuary at **Provinciaal Natuurpark Zwin** (p. 197).

Day 5: Antwerp ★★

Begin the fifth day in Antwerp, with a visit to Belgium's only traditional **zoo** (p. 179). Then, in the afternoon, cross over to **Aquatopia** (p. 179). For other options, consider a **cruise** (p. 180) downriver to the harbor.

Days 6 & 7: The Ardennes

From Antwerp, the drive here takes long enough that I'd suggest allocating 2 days for your family's visit to **Han-sur-Lesse** (p. 243). On the first day, drive to the village and visit the **Grottes de Han** underground caverns; the next day, spend some time at the **Réserve d'Animaux Sauvages** (p. 243) before moving on.

Day 8: Rotterdam ★

Today make your way to the **Euromast** (p. 375) for the greatest views of Rotterdam. Afterward, you'll probably need to choose between a **boat tour** (p. 377) through the city's vast harbor and a visit to the outstanding **Blijdorp Zoo** (p. 377), but if you have time for both, by all means fit them in.

Day 9: Amsterdam ★★★

Going around Amsterdam by **tram** (p. 270) is fun for the whole family. I'm not sure, though, about going by **bicycle** (p. 272); parents might need to spend too much time watching out for the kids. I suppose it all depends on what age the children are, and how good they are on strange bikes. A **canal boat cruise** (p. 314) is a good idea. A visit to the **Anne Frank House** (p. 300) is interesting and thought-provoking for children, in particular for those as old as Anne was when she hid from the Nazis here and wrote her famous diary. After this, try the **Artis Zoo** (p. 311), or—if you've had enough of zoos by now—go onboard the *Amsterdam,* a full-size replica 18th-century ocean-going sailing ship. The Maritime Museum that is the ship's usual home is closed until the summer of 2011, but the ship is still open for business, tied up just across the water at NEMO (see below).

Day 10: More of Amsterdam

Today choose between a visit to **Madame Tussaud's** (p. 311) and the **Science Center NEMO** (p. 311)—either one is worthwhile, but both in a single day can be too much, unless it's raining. By way of variation, you could try **in-line skating** in Vondelpark (p. 314), ice skating at **Jaap Eden IJsbanen** (p. 317), or bowling at **Knijn Bowling** (p. 316).

Day 11: Dolphins & Sailing Ships

From Amsterdam (your base), drive east today to Harderwijk and visit the outstanding **Dolfinarium Harderwijk** (p. 435). Cross over into Flevoland province and head to Lelystad. Here, at **Batavia Wharf** (p. 449), a full-size replica of a 17th-century sailing ship, the *Batavia,* is moored, and a man-of-war from the same century, *De Zeven Provinciën,* is being constructed.

Day 12: Enkhuizen ★

This town lies on the western shore of the IJsselmeer, a freshwater lake that until 1932 was a sea known as the Zuiderzee. Enkhuizen hosts the superb **Zuiderzeemuseum** (p. 344), which aims to recreate traditional life around the transformed sea. Between getting to and from Enkhuizen and visiting both sections of this large museum, you'll need most of a day to do it all justice.

Day 13: Zandvoort

Always supposing the weather is good, there's nothing your standard young Amsterdammer likes more than to take a train for the short ride to Amsterdam's favorite seacoast resort, **Zandvoort** (p. 335), on the North Sea. The locals will do this in all but the most abysmal weather, but if it's really too bad for the seacoast, try instead the neat little Visitor Center at the **Amsterdamse Bos** (**Amsterdam Wood;** p. 314). You can peruse the nature displays here and get out and about in the park if the weather picks up.

Day 14: Back to Brussels

One way to break the monotony of a 3-hour drive back to Brussels is to stop off at the cluster of windmills at **Kinderdijk** (p. 383), close to Rotterdam.

A NATURE LOVER'S TOUR

The natural world exists in Benelux, and not only in the great landscape paintings by 17th-century Dutch Old Masters. This tour takes you to some of the region's prettiest nature reserves, national parks, and scenic places.

Day 1: Arrive in Amsterdam

In your rented car from Schiphol Airport, swing nimbly past the city's Red Light District haunts and dope dens, on the ring road expressway. Head north to **Den Helder** (p. 352), at the tip of the Noord-Holland peninsula. From the harbor, cross over on the ferry (with or without your car) to **Texel** (p. 353), the largest of Holland's string of Wadden Islands. Departing from the **EcoMare** visitor center (p. 354), tour groups visit nature reserves that together cover a third of the island, and observe the many different species of birds that pass this way.

Day 2: Drive to Apeldoorn

Spend the morning on Texel before crossing over on the ferry back to Den Helder. Drive to "Royal Apeldoorn," a good home base for visiting the Hoge Veluwe National Park tomorrow.

Day 3: Hoge Veluwe National Park ★★

Enjoy a full day at the **national park** (p. 436), which has a landscape consisting of heathland, sand drifts, and forest. The park's animal inhabitants include deer, wild boar, and mouflon. Get around by borrowing a free national park bicycle.

Day 4: Drive to Dordrecht

Dordrecht, a town close to Rotterdam, is the northern access point to the **Biesbosch National Park** (p. 465), a freshwater tidal zone of wetlands, marshes, and partly drowned islands in the Maas and Waal river estuary. Visit the northern sector today, from the **Biesboschcentrum Dordrecht** (p. 465).

Day 5: The Southern Biesbosch

On the fifth day, drive to the southern access point for the **Biesbosch National Park** (p. 465) at Drimmelen, and tour the southern sector from the **Biesbosch Bezoekerscentrum Staatsbosbeheer**, in Drimmelen (p. 465).

Day 6: Drive to Eupen

A small town that's the "capital" of Belgium's German-speaking East Cantons district, **Eupen** (p. 249) is a convenient base for getting out to the nearby **Hautes Fagnes Nature Reserve** (in German, the Hohes Venn; p. 250).

Day 7: The Hautes Fagnes ★★★

Walk along the boardwalks and forest trails that snake through the **Hautes Fagnes** (p. 250). Stop by the **Botrange Visitor Center** (p. 250) and other access points at **Mont-Rigi** and **Baraque Michel.** If there's time, check out another piece of the park on the Eupen-Monschau (Germany) road, **Haus Ternell.**

Day 8: Drive to De Panne ★

At the opposite end of Belgium, right next to the French border, this North Sea coast resort is home to the **Westhoekreservaat (Westhoek Reserve)** dunes landscape (p. 202). Take a few hours to tour the reserve.

Day 9: Het Zwin Nature Reserve ★

Today drive to the northern end of the Belgian coast and visit **Het Zwin** (p. 197), a small but important breeding and feeding ground for seabirds and wetlands birds.

Day 10: Back to Amsterdam

Head north into Holland's Zeeland province, and cross over the Western Schelde estuary by the road tunnel. Continue to Rotterdam and the expressway north to Schiphol Airport.

A MILITARY BUFF'S TOUR OF THE BENELUX

I call this a "military buff's tour," but it may be more appropriate to think of it as a military memorial tour. Belgium and Luxembourg have long histories as battlefields, usually in other countries' quarrels. Belgium was particularly badly handled in World War I, and Holland had a similar experience in World War II. Although this itinerary revolves around a grim subject, it also passes through scenic parts of all three countries. The tour is best done by car.

Day 1: Waterloo ★

South of Brussels, the French emperor Napoleon Bonaparte met final defeat at the **Battle of Waterloo** (p. 130) in 1815. A tour of this largely preserved battlefield and a visit to the duke of Wellington's headquarters, now the **Musée Wellington** (p. 131), afford a fascinating insight into the great and decisive battle.

Day 2: Drive to Ypres (Ieper)

A 2-hour drive from Brussels, bypassing Ghent and Kortrijk, brings you to the medieval cloth town of **Ypres** (p. 203), a crucible of fighting on the World War I Western Front that claimed the lives of 500,000 Allied and German soldiers. The now peaceful Flanders fields are sprinkled with military cemeteries and a few remaining sections of trenches.

Day 3: Drive to Bastogne

Drive east past Tournai and Mons, to the Meuse River at **Namur** (p. 219). Continuing eastward into the rolling **Ardennes** hills (p. 237), you'll pass the scenes of many a hard-fought action from the Battle of the Bulge in the winter of 1944 to 1945, at places like Marche-en-Famenne, Rochefort, and La Roche-en-Ardenne. None was harder than the epic struggle surrounded U.S. troops waged to hold the strategic crossroads town of **Bastogne** (p. 241). Afterward, visit the star-shaped **Mardasson Memorial** (p. 242) outside of town.

Day 4: Drive to Eupen

Cross into Luxembourg today. Starting at **Echternach** (p. 509), follow the Our River upstream along the German border. This was a thinly manned but staunchly defended U.S. front line on December 16, 1944, when the surprise German offensive in the Ardennes erupted. Pass through **Vianden** (p. 508) and **Clervaux** (p. 507); then take the road in Belgium the GI's dubbed the "Skyline Drive," to Sankt-Vith. From Losheim to Rocherath-Krinkelt, you'll cross the assault route taken by Hitler's elite SS divisions. Foxholes once held by American troops still exist in the forests. The U.S. Fifth Corps headquarters was in **Eupen** (p. 249).

Day 5: Drive to Nijmegen

Take the expressway via Liège and Maastricht, for rapid deployment to **Eindhoven** (p. 468), the scene of action for the U.S. 101st Airborne Division during the Allied offensive into Nazi-occupied Holland in September 1944. Follow the bitterly contested "Hell's Highway" north through Veghel and Grave to **Nijmegen** (p. 441). The U.S. 82nd Airborne Division suffered heavy losses taking and holding the Groesbeek Heights east of town, and the bridges over the Maas River at Grave and the Waal River in Nijmegen.

Day 6: Arnhem ★

From Nijmegen north to **Arnhem** (p. 438) is just 16km (10 miles)—a distance that proved fatal for Britain's 1st Airborne Division, which landed on heathland west of the city to take Arnhem's bridge over the Rhine—the famous "bridge too far." The British held out for a week at **Oosterbeek** (p. 439). Polish paratroops landed at nearby Driel.

Day 7: Return to Brussels

An expressway goes southwest from Arnhem to connect with the north-south expressway at Breda. From there go south via Antwerp to Brussels.

PLANNING YOUR TRIP TO BELGIUM

Belgium is not a difficult country to come to grips with—thanks to its widespread use of English, relatively small size, and excellent tourist infrastructure—but a little forethought when planning your trip can still save you precious time and effort. This chapter gives you some of the practical information you need to plan your trip.

For information that covers planning and tips for the Benelux countries in general, see chapter 3.

THE REGIONS IN BRIEF

Modest little Belgium has never been known to boast of its charms, yet its variety of language, culture, history, and cuisine would do credit to a country many times its size. Belgium's diversity stems from its location at the cultural crossroads of Europe. The boundary between the Continent's Germanic north and Latin south cuts clear across the nation's middle, leaving Belgium divided into two major ethnic regions: Dutch-speaking Flanders and French-speaking Wallonia.

Although international attention is focused on Brussels as the "capital of Europe," there's another Belgium waiting in the wings, of Gothic cathedrals, medieval castles, cobblestone streets, and tranquil canals. The timeless beauty of Bruges and Ghent are accessible even to the most hurried visitor, and to get away from it all, there's no better place than the unhurried Ardennes.

BRUSSELS In a sense, Brussels has a split personality. One is the brash "capital of Europe," increasingly aware of its power and carrying a padded expense account in its elegant leather pocketbook. The other is the old Belgian city—once a seat of emperors, but lately more than a little provincial, tenaciously hanging onto its heritage against the wave of Euro-construction that has swept over it.

These two cities intersect, of course, generally in a popular bar or restaurant, though they may sit together uneasily. Most foreigners who live here long enough, or who stay on an extended vacation, find they need to choose between the two. As an outsider, it's easy enough to live in the Eurocity. Getting below the surface to the real Brussels is more difficult, but worth the effort.

BRUGES From its 13th-century origins as a cloth-manufacturing town to its current incarnation as a tourism mecca, the main town of West Flanders province seems to have changed little. As in a fairy tale, swans glide down the winding canals, and the stone houses look as if they're made of gingerbread. Even though glass-fronted stores have taken over the ground floors of ancient buildings, and swans scatter before tour boats chugging along the canals, Bruges has made the transition from medieval to modern with remarkable grace. The town seems revitalized rather than crushed by the tremendous influx of tourists.

GHENT & ANTWERP The old town at the confluence of the Scheldt and Leie rivers has been spruced up, and **Ghent** has never looked so good. Although this former seat of the powerful counts of Flanders is larger and seems more like a "real" city than Bruges, it has enough cobblestone streets, meandering canals, and antique Flemish architecture to make it nearly as magical as its more famous sister.

Antwerp is a port city, with all the liveliness, sophistication, and occasional seediness that goes along with this. The city is the acknowledged "Diamond Center of the World," the leading market for cut diamonds and second only to London as an outlet for raw and industrial diamonds. It boasts a magnificent cathedral, a fine-arts museum full of Flemish masterpieces, a maze of medieval streets in the town center, and a vibrant cultural life.

THE BELGIAN COAST & YPRES At the center of the seacoast is **Ostend,** the "Queen of the Coast." It retains a little of the cachet and some of the ambience of its great days as a 19th-century beach resort. It's complemented by more modern resorts such as **Knokke-Heist** and **De Panne.**

Having suffered through centuries of intermittent warfare and almost total destruction during World War I, **Ypres (Ieper)** has picked itself up in the years since, its indomitable spirit intact—a spirit that shines in the perseverance underlying its 20th-century rebuilding of 13th-century buildings.

LIÈGE, THE MEUSE RIVER & HAINAUT The rugged Meuse River valley, the heartland of French-speaking Wallonia, is speckled with resort towns in which fine cuisine is a way of life. A visit to **Liège, Namur, Huy,** and **Dinant** after traveling to Brussels and the Flemish art cities of Bruges and Ghent adds another dimension to Belgium.

> **Visitor Information**
>
> **For contact details of the Belgian tourist offices in the United States, Britain, and other countries, see "Visitor Information," in chapter 21.**

Tucked into an area south of Brussels that stretches to the French border, Hainaut, Belgium's "Green Province," can seem isolated from the mainstream of Belgian life, yet it possesses prime assets in the historic towns of **Mons** and **Tournai.**

THE ARDENNES Belgium's wildest, most heavily forested region—part of the rugged Ardennes-Eifel Massif, which stretches across into Germany, Luxembourg, and France—is its least populated. French is the most common language, but in the northeast, in the area called the Ostkantone (East Cantons), you most often hear German spoken, a residue from the years before 1919 when this part of the Ardennes belonged to Germany.

Belgium

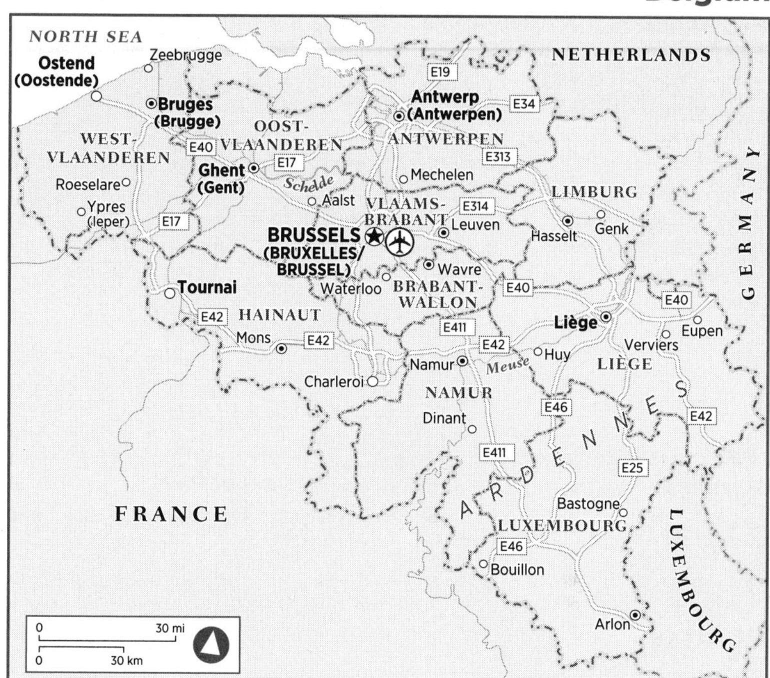

WHEN TO GO

"In season" in Belgium means from mid-April to mid-October. The peak of the tourist season is July and August, when the weather is at its finest, but you'll find Belgium every bit as attractive during other months. Not only are airlines, hotels, and restaurants cheaper and less crowded during this time (with more relaxed service, which means you get more personal attention), but some very appealing events are going on. For example, Brussels swings into its rich music season in April, and Tournai turns out for the colorful thousand-year-old Procession of the Plague the second Sunday in September.

Climate

Although there is a world of difference between the seacoast on a summer's day and the high moorland of the Hautes Fagnes in the Ardennes in the dead of winter, Belgium's climate is generally moderate, with few extremes in temperature either in summer or winter. It does rain a lot, though there are more showers than downpours. (It's a good idea to pack a raincoat.) Temperatures are lowest in December and January, when they average 42°F (6°C), and highest in July and August, when they average 73°F (23°C).

In the springtime, when the parks are coming up flowers, the first sidewalk tables put in a tentative appearance, but the weather can be variable. July and August are the best months for soaking up rays at a sidewalk cafe, dining at an outdoor restaurant in the evening, and swimming and sunbathing at the seacoast. September usually has a few weeks of fine late-summer weather, and there are even sunny spells in winter, when brilliant, crisp weather alternates with clouded skies.

In the hilly, forested Ardennes, autumn's falling leaves bring out visitors searching for the finest fall colors. It's not quite New England, but it's spectacular enough, and any shortcomings on the color spectrum are compensated for by the culinary feasts on the menus of the many great restaurants here, during the hunting season for wild game. Winter snow in the Ardennes attracts cross-country and downhill skiers to the region's handful of ski lifts and short runs.

Winters at the coast, moderated a touch by the North Sea, most often are rainy. Expect lots of gray skies in Brussels—Eurocrats from sunny Mediterranean lands confess to going stir-crazy for the sight of blue skies and sun during winter in the capital.

You're well advised to pack a fold-up umbrella at any time of year; likewise, carry a raincoat (with a wool liner for winter). Second, pack a sweater or two (even in July), and be prepared to layer your clothing at any time of year. Don't worry: In the summer, you can leave some space for T-shirts, skimpy tops, and sneakers.

For local weather forecasts, go to **www.meteo.be**.

Brussels's Average Monthly Temperature & Days of Rain

	JAN	FEB	MAR	APR	MAY	JUNE	JULY	AUG	SEPT	OCT	NOV	DEC
TEMP. (°F)	38	38	44	48	55	60	64	64	59	52	44	40
TEMP. (°C)	3	3	7	9	13	16	18	18	15	11	7	4
DAYS OF RAIN (OR SNOW)	21	17	17	18	16	15	17	18	13	17	20	19

Holidays

National holidays are January 1 (New Year's Day); Easter Sunday and Monday; May 1 (Labor Day); Ascension Thursday; Pentecost Sunday and Monday; July 21 (Independence Day); August 15 (Assumption); November 1 (All Saints); November 11 (World War I Armistice Day); and December 25 (Christmas Day). In Flanders only, July 11 is Flemish Community Day, the anniversary of the Battle of the Golden Spurs in 1302. In Wallonia only, September 27 is French Community Day, recalling liberation from Dutch rule in 1830.

Belgium Calendar Of Events

Belgium is big on festivals. You could arrive in a town or village to find the populace turned out in costume to honor with all due solemnity (followed by some fun and games) the local cheese. The country has a lively and colorful Carnival tradition that includes, in the otherwise unremarkable town of Binche, one that's among the most spectacular in Europe.

The Festival of Flanders cultural program runs throughout Flanders from September to June. Contact **Festival van Vlaanderen** (✆ **012/23-57-19;** www.festival.be). The Festival of Wallonia puts on classical music throughout Wallonia from September to June. Contact **Festival de Wallonie** (✆ **081/73-37-81;** www.festivaldewallonie.be).

More information about what's on and where, is available from **www.agenda.be**. For an exhaustive list of events beyond those listed here, check **http://events.frommers.com**, where you'll find a searchable, up-to-the-minute roster of what's happening in cities all over the world.

JANUARY

Bommelfeesten (Festival of Fools), Ronse. The main action of this traditional festival in the East Flanders town, with its masked characters called Bommels, has been moved from Zotte Maandag (Crazy Monday) to the preceding Saturday. Contact **Dienst Toerisme Ronse** (✆ **055/23-28-16;**

www.ronse.be). Weekend (Sat–Mon) closest to the Epiphany (Jan 6).

Brussels Antiques and Fine Arts Fair. The top Belgian antiques dealers and selected dealers from abroad get together to show off their wares in the Tour & Taxis convention center at the city's old port. Contact **BRAFA** (✆ **02/513-48-31;** www.brafa.be). Last 10 days of January.

FEBRUARY

Carnival, Eupen. Five days of pre-Lenten revelry in the capital town of Belgium's German-speaking district. Highlight is the Rosenmontag (Rose Monday) Procession. Contact **Tourist Info Eupen** (✆ **087/55-34-50;** www.eupen-info.be). Thursday to Shrove Tuesday (the day before Ash Wednesday).

Carnival ★, Malmedy. The pre-Lenten festival brings good-natured mayhem to the streets of this otherwise sober town. On Sunday's big parade, costumed characters called Banes Courants chase people through the streets, and others called Haguètes snare passersby with long wooden pincers. Contact **Royal Syndicat d'Initiative de Malmedy** (✆ **080/79-96-35;** www.malmedy.be). Saturday to Shrove Tuesday.

Carnival, Aalst. Three days of pre-Lenten festivities, including the Giants' Parade with the horse Bayard, onion-throwing from the roofs of the Grote Markt, and the parade of Vuil Jeannetten—men dressed as women. Contact **Dienst Toerisme Aalst** (✆ **053/73-22-70;** www.aalst.be). Sunday to Shrove Tuesday.

Carnival ★★★, Binche. One of Europe's most colorful street carnivals, led on Shrove Tuesday by the sumptuously costumed Gilles de Binche, modeled, or so it is believed, on Inca nobles. Contact **Office du Tourisme de Binche** (✆ **064/33-67-27;** www.binche.be). Sunday to Shrove Tuesday.

MARCH

Bal du Rat Mort (Dead Rat's Ball), Ostend. This outrageous fancy-dress event takes its grisly name from a chic Paris cafe. Proceeds go to charity. Contact **Toerisme Oostende** (✆ **059/70-11-99;** www.visitoostende.be or www.ratmort.be). First Saturday in March.

Carnival, Stavelot. The Blancs Moussis, characters with long red noses and hooded white costumes, are the stars of the town's Laetere procession. Contact **Office du Tourisme de Stavelot** (✆ **080/86-27-06;** http://tourisme.stavelot.be). Sunday 3 weeks before Easter.

Carnival, Fosses-la-Ville. Costumed characters called Chinels parade through the streets. Contact **Syndicat d'Initiative Fosses-la-Ville** (✆ **071/71-46-24;** www.fosses-la-ville.be). Saturday and Sunday 3 weeks before Easter.

APRIL

Sablon Spring Baroque Music Festival, Brussels. Open-air concerts on place du Grand Sablon. Contact **Brussels International Tourism** (✆ **02/513-89-40;** www.brusselsinternational.be). April/May.

Brussels International Fantastic Film Festival. Science fiction and fantasy films are screened at several movie theaters around the city. Contact **Peymey Diffusion** (✆ **02/201-17-13;** www.bifff.org). April 7 to 19, 2011; similar dates in 2012.

Meieavondviering (May Day's Eve Festival), Hasselt. Celebrants plant a May Tree on the Grote Markt and burn dummies representing winter, while participants costumed as witches dance on the square. Contact **VVV Hasselt** (✆ **011/23-95-40;** www.hasselt.eu). April 30.

MAY

Queen Elisabeth Contest ★, Brussels. For promising young musicians, featuring a different instrument each year. Generally at Bozar (Palais des Beaux-Arts) and a few other venues. Contact **Concours Reine Elisabeth** (✆ **02/213-40-50;** www.concours-reine-elisabeth.be). Throughout May.

Kunstenfestivaldesarts, Brussels. Arts festival famed across the cultural universe for its irritatingly scrunched-up name, which means Arts Festival in both Dutch and French. It spotlights stage events, putting an emphasis on opera, theater, and dance, but finds space for cinema, music concerts, and fine-arts exhibits. Various auditoriums and venues around town. Contact **Kunstenfestivaldesarts** (✆ **02/219-07-07;** www.kfda.be). Three weeks in May.

Kattenstoet (Cat Parade) ★, Ypres (Ieper). During the traditional Festival of the Cats, toy cats (it used to be live ones!) are thrown from the town hall belfry. Contact **Toerisme Ieper** (✆ **057/23-92-20;** www.ieper.be). Every third year on the second Sunday in May (May 13, 2012).

Heilig-Bloedprocessie (Procession of the Holy Blood) ★, Bruges. The bishop of Bruges carries a relic of the Holy Blood through the streets, while costumed characters act out biblical scenes. Contact **Toerisme Brugge** (✆ **050/44-46-46;** www.brugge.be). Ascension Day (fifth Thurs after Easter): generally May, but June 2, 2011; May 17, 2012.

Brussels Jazz Marathon. Enjoy a long weekend of jazz of all kinds at a slew of concerts on the Grand-Place, place du Grand Sablon, and place Ste-Catherine; at other open-air venues around town; and in jazz clubs, cafes, and hotel bars. Contact **Jazztronaut** (✆ **02/456-04-84;** www.brusselsjazzmarathon.be). May 28 to 30, 2011; similar dates in 2012.

JUNE

Quatres Cortèges (Four Parades), Tournai. The annual parades feature flower-decked floats, a military band, and the highlight: a procession of giants representing historical characters, including King Childeric of the Franks and France's King Louis XIV. Contact **Office du Tourisme de Tournai** (✆ **069/22-20-45;** www.tournai.be). Second weekend in June.

Ducasse de Mons (Festival of Mons) ★. Religious procession of guilds and the reliquary of Ste-Waltrude (St. Waudru) mounted on a golden coach. This is followed by a folkloric street performance, the *Lumeçon,* in which St. George slays the dragon. Contact **Maison du Tourisme du Pays de Mons** (✆ **065/33-55-80;** www.monsregion.be). Holy Trinity Sunday (first Sun after Pentecost): June 19, 2011; June 3, 2012.

International Cartoon Festival, Knokke-Heist. A celebration of Belgium's national fascination with the "Ninth Art," as comic-strip art is dubbed by its practitioners and aficionados. Contact **Toerisme Knokke-Heist** (✆ **050/63-03-80;** www.knokke-heist.info). Mid-June to early September.

Couleur Café Festival, Brussels. Three days of Afro, Caribbean, and Latin music and dance, ably supported by heaps of soul food, at the Tour & Taxis cultural complex, in a former warehouse zone next to the Willebroeck Canal dock. Contact **Couleur Café** (www.couleurcafe.be). June 24 to 26, 2011; similar dates (Fri–Sun) 2012.

Brussels Film Festival. A 9-day feast of European films, primarily of first or second features, and by independent directors, screened at the Flagey cultural center. Contact **Festival du Film Européen de Bruxelles** (✆ **02/649-40-89;** www.fffb.be). Late June to early July.

JULY

Entertainment, Grand-Place, Brussels. Concerts, theater, dance, exhibits, and other forms of entertainment "animate" the Grand-Place. Contact **Brussels International Tourism** (✆ **02/513-89-40;** www.brusselsinternational.be). Entire month.

Ommegang ★★★, Brussels. A dramatic annual historical pageant that dates from the 13th century and represents the city guilds, magistrates, and nobles honoring the Virgin Mary. Participants wearing period costume from the time of the "joyous entry" of Emperor Charles V into Brussels in 1549, escorted by a mounted cavalcade and waving medieval banners, go in procession from place du Grand Sablon to the Grand-Place. Contact **Ommegang-Brussels Events** (✆ **02/512-19-61;** www.ommegang.be). First Tuesday and Thursday in July.

Brosella Folk and Jazz Festival, Brussels. A small-scale specialized music fest that takes place over a weekend at the Théâtre de Verdure in Parc d'Osseghem. Contact **Les Amis de Brosella** (✆ **02/474-06-41;** www.brosella.be). July 9 and 10, 2011; similar dates in 2012.

Cactus Festival, Bruges. A prickly summer rock festival unfolds over 3 days and attracts big names to the city. Contact **Cactus Muziekcentrum** (✆ **050/33-20-14;** www.cactusfestival.be). Mid-July.

Belgian National Day, Brussels. Marked throughout Belgium but celebrated most in Brussels, with a military procession and music at the Royal Palace. Contact **Brussels International Tourism** (✆ **02/513-89-40;** www.brusselsinternational.be). July 21.

Gentse Feesten (Ghent Festivities) ★. Free street entertainment of music, dance, theater, puppet shows, and general fun and games marks the annual Ghent Festivities. Contact **Dienst Feestelijkheden** (✆ **09/ 269-46-30;** www.gentsefeesten.be). July 16 to 25, 2011; July 14 to 23, 2012.

AUGUST

Visiting the Palais Royal, Brussels. Exceptionally, the Royal Palace on place des Palais is open to free guided tours. King Albert and Queen Paola won't be there, however. Contact **Palais Royal** (✆ **02/551-20-20;** www.monarchie.be). Throughout August (dates vary year by year but generally include the last week or so of July and the first week or so of Sept).

Planting of the Meyboom (May Pole), Brussels. Despite the name, this does happen in August, on the eve of the Feast of St. Lawrence, at the corner of rue des Sables and rue du Marais, and celebrates Brussels's victory over Leuven in 1311 (nowadays it's more a celebration of summer). Contact **Brussels International Tourism** (✆ **02/ 513-89-40;** www.brusselsinternational.be). August 9.

Tapis des Fleurs (Carpet of Flowers) ★★, Grand-Place, Brussels. The historic square is carpeted with two-thirds of a million begonias arranged in a kind of tapestry. Contact **Brussels International Tourism** (✆ **02/513-89-40;** www.brusselsinternational.be). Mid-August in even-numbered years.

Marktrock, Leuven. Three days of rock and jazz on the square in front of Leuven's medieval Stadhuis (Town Hall). Contact **Dienst Toerisme Leuven** (✆ **016/20-30-20;** www.leuven.be). Mid-August.

Outremeuse Festival, Liège. Music, dance, and theater performances go along with appearances by the city's two favorite folklore characters, Tchantchès and Nanesse. Contact **Office du Tourisme de Liège** (✆ **04/221-92-21;** www.liege.be). August 15.

Reiefeesten (Canal Festival) ★★, Bruges. Around 600 costumed participants celebrate the city's storied history with a series of concerts, spectacles, short theater pieces, and other events. Contact **Toerisme Brugge** (✆ **050/44-46-46;** www.brugge.be). Every third year: August 15 to 31, 2011.

Praalstoet van de Gouden Boom (Pageant of the Golden Tree) ★★★, Bruges. Some 2,000 costumed participants, along with giant mannequins, and parade floats reenact the lavish spectacle that accompanied the wedding of Duke of Burgundy Charles the Bold and Margaret of York in 1468. Contact **Toerisme Brugge** (✆ **050/ 44-46-46;** www.brugge.be). Every fifth year: August 19, 2012.

SEPTEMBER

Liberation Parade, Brussels. The *Manneken-Pis* statue is dressed in a Welsh Guard's uniform in honor of the city's liberation in 1944. Contact **Brussels International Tourism** (✆ **02/513-89-40;** www.brusselsinternational.be). September 3.

Grande Procession, Tournai. Commemorates a religious procession that first took place in 1090 to thank Notre-Dame des Malades (Our Lady of the Sick) for warding off the plague. Contact **Office du Tourisme de Tournai** (✆ **069/22-20-45;** www.tournai.be). Second Sunday in September.

Journées du Patrimoine (Heritage Days), Brussels. Taking a different theme each year, this program allows you to visit some of the finest buildings in town that are usually closed to visitors. Contact **Brussels International Tourism** (✆ **02/513-89-40;** www.brusselsinternational.be). Third weekend: September 18 and 19, 2011; September 15 and 16, 2012.

OCTOBER

Ghent Film Festival. Belgium's top international film festival, and an event that has grown in stature to become one of Europe's main movie showcases. As many as 150 full-length movies and 100 shorts are screened over 12 days. Contact **Filmfestival Gent** (✆ **09/242-80-60;** www.filmfestival.be). Midmonth: October 11 to 22, 2011; October 9 to 20, 2012.

NOVEMBER

Snow & Ice ★, Bruges. Cool works of ice sculpture with a too-short shelf life can be viewed on Stationsplein in front of the rail station. Contact **Snow & Ice** (✆ **050/20-04-65;** www.ijssculptuur.be). For 2 weeks anytime from the third week of November to mid-January.

DECEMBER

Christmas Market, Brussels. Stands selling seasonal trinkets, craft items, and food and drink are set up on place Ste-Catherine. Contact **Brussels International Tourism** (✆ **02/513-89-40;** www.brusselsinternational.be). Throughout the month, daily from 11am to 10pm.

Christmas Market, Bruges. Stands selling seasonal trinkets, craft items, and food and drink, alongside an ice-skating rink, are set up on the Markt. A second market is on Simon Stevinplein, daily from 11am to 7pm. Contact **Toerisme Brugge** (✆ **050/44-46-46;** www.brugge.be). Throughout the month, daily from 11am to 10pm.

Christmas Market, Ghent. Stands selling seasonal trinkets, craft items, and food and drink are set up on Sint-Baafsplein. Contact **Dienst Toerisme Gent** (✆ **09/210-10-10;** www.gent.be). Throughout the month, daily from 11am to 10pm.

Nativity Scene and Christmas Tree, Grand-Place, Brussels. The crib on display at this Christmas nativity scene has real animals. Contact **Brussels International Tourism** (✆ **02/513-89-40;** www.brussels international.be). Throughout the month.

Winter Fun, Brussels. An ice-skating rink and a big wheel are set up on the Marché aux Poissons; on neighboring place Ste-Catherine, there's a baroque carousel. Contact **Brussels International Tourism** (✆ **02/513-89-40;** www.brusselsinternational.be). Throughout the month.

GETTING THERE & GETTING AROUND

Getting There

There is no shortage of travel routes into the kingdom, which occupies one of Western Europe's transportation hubs (for the full details, see "Getting There & Around," in chapter 3). Virtually all international flights to Belgium arrive at Brussels Airport; the only exceptions are a handful of short-haul services that fly into Antwerp, and those of budget carrier Ryanair to its base at Charleroi.

In addition, there are ferry services from Britain to the ports of Zeebrugge and Ostend; high-speed trains from London, Paris, Amsterdam, and Cologne to Brussels (and some to Antwerp, Bruges, and Liège), along with "ordinary" international trains from around Europe; Eurolines bus service from many European cities; and multiple expressways/motorways from France, Germany, and Holland.

The Euro

Belgium's currency is the euro (see "Money & Costs," in chapter 3).

Getting Around

Belgium's compact size makes it easy on travelers. The roads are excellent (though often busy), and the comprehensive rail net is one of Europe's best.

BY TRAIN

All major tourist destinations in Belgium can be done easily in a day trip by train from Brussels, on the network of the **Société Nationale des Chemins de Fer Belges/ SNCB,** or **NMBS** in Dutch (✆ **02/528-28-28;** www.b-rail.be). Antwerp is just 35 minutes away; Ghent, 34 minutes; Namur, 59 minutes; Bruges, 60 minutes; and Liège, 51 minutes. These times are by the fast InterCity (IC) trains; InterRegio (IR) trains are somewhat slower; Local (L) trains are the network's tortoises, stopping at every station on the way.

If all or most of your travel will be by train, a good investment is a **Rail Pass,** good for 10 single journeys anywhere on the network, except stations at international borders, within a month of it being issued. It costs 74€ in second class and 113€ in first class. The same pass for passengers ages 4 to 25 (traveling in second class only) is called a **Go Pass,** and costs 50€.

In addition to Belgian Railways's regular one-way *(billet simple/enkele reis)* and round-trip *(aller et retour/retour)* tickets, look for discounted **B-Excursion** and **Weekend Ticket** options. These various tickets are valid only in Belgium, and can be purchased only from train stations and other sales points in Belgium. Reduced-rate tickets and passes are available for seniors, young adults, and children.

BY BUS

Brussels, Bruges, Ghent, Antwerp, Liège, and other important cities and towns have excellent local bus service. Express InterCity bus service is not available, though you *can* go by bus between cities with the aid of some complicated timetable and route planning—expect this to be slow and to require transfers at intermediate points. Regional buses serve every area of Belgium, from whichever is the nearest city or large town. In general, the only part of the country where it makes sense to plan on going by bus instead of by train is the Ardennes, which has few rail lines.

Fares and schedules are available from **STIB** (✆ **070/23-20-00;** www.stib.be) for Brussels and **De Lijn** (✆ **070/22-02-00;** www.delijn.be) for Flanders. **TEC** (www.infotec.be), which operates bus service in Wallonia, has six separate area phone numbers to call for information; you'll find these listed on the website and in the appropriate chapters of this book.

BY CAR

Driving conditions are excellent in Belgium, with lighted highways at night. Belgian drivers, though, are not as excellent. They're notoriously fast and aggressive and have clocked some of the worst road-accident statistics in Europe, so drive with care.

RENTALS Rental cars are available from **Avis** (✆ **800/331-2112** in the U.S., or ✆ 070/22-30-01 in Belgium; www.avis.be); **Europcar** (✆ **02/348-92-12;** www.europcar.be); **Hertz** (✆ **800/654-3001** in the U.S., and ✆ 02/717-32-01 in Belgium; www.hertz.be); and **SIXT** (✆ **02/753-25-60;** www.sixt.co.uk). All four companies have desks at Brussels Airport, and rental offices (or agencies) in Brussels, Antwerp, Bruges, Ghent, and Liège, among other places. For a subcompact auto with gearshift, expect to pay from 60€ a day and 90€ for a weekend, including insurance and other charges, and for unlimited mileage.

DRIVING RULES To drive in Belgium, you need only a passport, a driver's license, and car registration papers. The minimum age for drivers is 18. On highways, speed limits are 70kmph (43 mph) minimum, 120kmph (74 mph) maximum; in all cities and urban areas, the maximum speed limit is 50kmph (31 mph). Lower limits

driven CRAZY

The behavior of many Belgian car drivers could easily be described as "hoglike," a moderate term employed because finding the pertinent adjective would tax even the considerable powers of the English language as an instrument of personal abuse.

Part of the blame attaches to the *priorité à droite* (priority from the right) traffic rule, whereby in some cases (not always), traffic from the right has the right of way. You won't believe how this plays at multiple-street intersections, particularly since many Belgians will give up their *priorité* under no known circumstances, cost what it might. Be ready to stop instantly at *all* such intersections. ***Note:*** Poles with yellow diamond signs, which you see mostly on main roads, mean that the right of way lies with traffic already on the road, so if you are on one of these, you don't have to stop.

At rotaries, traffic entering the rotary has the right of way over traffic already on it, unless STOP lines on the road indicate otherwise. This system has caused so much mayhem it's being changed at some accident hotspots and obvious danger zones. Not everyone knows about the changes or acts according to them, so stay alert.

Hoglike driver behavior is extended to pedestrians. Don't expect cars to stop for you just because you're crossing at a black-and-white pedestrian crossing. Only in recent years have drivers been obliged legally to stop at these, and many don't seem to have received or understood the message yet.

might be posted. Seat belts must be worn in both the front seats and in the back. In the car, you need to have a fire extinguisher, a basic medical kit, a red reflective warning triangle, and a reflective jacket. If you are driving a car from Britain or Ireland with the wheel on the right side, be sure to attach adapter kits that change the angle of your headlight beams.

An important Belgian driving rule to be aware of is the *priorité à droite* (priority from the right), which makes it perfectly legal most of the time to pull out from a side road to the right of the flow of traffic. That means, of course, that you must keep a sharp eye on the side roads to your right (see "Driven Crazy," below).

ROAD MAPS Tourist offices provide excellent city, regional, and country maps. Michelin map nos. 213 and 214 cover the country; they are detailed and reliable, and are available from bookstores, news vendors, some supermarkets, and other outlets.

BREAKDOWNS/ASSISTANCE A 24-hour nationwide emergency road service is offered by **Touring** (**✆ 070/34-47-77;** www.touring.be).

BY BICYCLE

Main rail stations, and some minor ones, have bicycles for rent. If you travel by train and would like to have a trusty steed awaiting you when you arrive, use the Belgian Railways *Train + Vélo/Trein + Fiets* (Train + Bicycle) formula to reserve a bike at the same time you buy your ticket.

ON FOOT

A network of special walking, cycling, and horseback-riding routes in Wallonia provides a healthy alternative to touring by car and links scenic, off-the-beaten-track parts of the region. RAVeL (Résau Autonome des Voies Lentes/Independent Slow Routes Network) has given new life to old ways by employing disused rail and tram routes, river and canal towpaths, and other minor paths, connected by purpose-built sections. Four main RAVeL routes and a web of secondary ones crisscross the region. Guides with maps are available from local tourist offices.

6 BRUSSELS

Brussels—the headquarters of the European Union—both symbolizes Europe's vision of unity and is a bastion of officialdom, a breeding ground for the regulations that govern and often exasperate the rest of the Continent.

The Bruxellois have mixed feelings about their city's transformation into a power center. At first the waves of Eurocrats brought a new cosmopolitan air to a somewhat provincial city (though once the seat of emperors), but as old neighborhoods were leveled to make way for office towers, people wondered whether Brussels (pop. 1,080,000) was losing its soul. After all, this city doesn't only mean politics and business. It inspired surrealism and Art Nouveau, it worships comic strips, it prides itself on handmade lace and chocolates, and it serves each one of its craft beers in a unique glass.

Fortunately, not all of Brussels's individuality has been lost in this transition, and though the urban landscape has suffered from wanton development, the city's spirit survives in traditional cafes, bars, bistros, and restaurants. Whether elegantly Art Nouveau or eccentrically festooned with posters, curios, and knickknacks, such centuries-old establishments provide a convivial ambience that is peculiarly Belgian.

ORIENTATION

Arriving

BY PLANE

For details on air travel to Belgium, see "Getting There & Around," in chapter 3. The country's main international airport, **Brussels Airport** (✆ **0900/70-000** in Belgium, or 02/753-77-53 from abroad; www.brusselsairport.be), is 11km (7 miles) northeast of the center city. The **Brussels Airport Express** train service to Brussels's three main rail stations (Bruxelles-Nord, Bruxelles-Central, and Bruxelles-Midi) has up to four departures hourly between 5:30am and 11:30pm, for a one-way fare of 5.10€ in second class and 6.70€ in first class. The ride to Bruxelles-Central takes around 20 minutes. Most airport trains have wide corridors and extra space for baggage.

The **Airport Line bus** no. 12 (Mon–Fri express) or no. 21 (Sat–Sun and holidays) depart from the airport about every half-hour to the European District in the city; the fare is 3€ for a one-way ticket purchased from a ticket machine before boarding the bus and 5€ for one purchased onboard. **De Lijn bus** no. 471 connects the airport every half-hour with

Bruxelles-Nord train station; it costs 2€ for a ticket purchased pre-boarding and 3€ for a ticket purchased onboard the bus.

Taxis that display an orange sticker depicting a white airplane offer reduced fares from the airport to the center city. Others charge about 35€, and some offer reduced rates for a reserved return journey (ask your driver for details). Go to the taxi stand and wait your turn. Be sure to use only licensed cabs.

BY TRAIN

High-speed Eurostar trains from London; Thalys from Paris, Amsterdam, and Cologne; TGV from France (not Paris); and ICE from Frankfurt zip into town from all points of the compass. The Brussels metropolitan area has three main rail stations: **Bruxelles-Central,** Carrefour de l'Europe; **Bruxelles-Midi,** rue de France (the Eurostar, Thalys, TGV, and ICE terminal); and **Bruxelles-Nord,** rue du Progrès. All three are served by Métro, tram, or bus lines, and have taxi stands outside. For train information and reservations, call © **02/528-28-28** or visit **www.sncb.be**.

Warning: Attracted by rich pickings from international travelers, bag snatchers roam the environs of Gare du Midi, and pickpockets work the interior. Do not travel to or depart from the station on foot if you can avoid doing so; take a taxi or use public transportation. Inside, keep a close eye on your possessions.

BY BUS

Eurolines (© **02/274-13-50;** www.eurolines.com) buses from London, Paris, Amsterdam, and other cities arrive at the bus station below Bruxelles-Nord train station.

BY CAR

Major expressways to Brussels are E19 from Amsterdam and Paris, and E40 from Bruges and Cologne. If possible, avoid driving the "hell on wheels" R0 Brussels ring road. And once you're settled at a hotel, do yourself a favor: Leave the car at a parking garage.

Visitor Information

The city tourist organization, **Brussels International Tourism & Congress** (© **02/513-89-40;** fax 02/513-83-20; www.brusselsinternational.be), has several offices around the city. Good information is available from these offices, including a comprehensive visitors' booklet, *Brussels Guide & Map,* and they can make last-minute reservations for city hotels. For both administration and walk-in service, head to rue Royale 2, 1000 Bruxelles (tram: 92 or 94), at place Royale (daily 10am–6pm). The most centrally located office is in the Hôtel de Ville, Grand-Place (Métro: Gare Centrale), on the ground floor of the Town Hall (Jan–Mar Mon–Sat 9am–6pm; Apr–Oct daily 9am–6pm; Nov–Dec Mon–Sat 9am–6pm, Sun 10am–2pm). There are tourist information desks in the Arrivals hall at Brussels Airport (daily 8am–9pm) and in the main hall at Gare du Midi rail station (May–Oct Sat–Thurs 8am–8pm, Fri 8am–9pm; Nov–Apr Mon–Thurs 8am–5pm, Fri 8am–8pm, Sat 9am–6pm, Sun and holidays 9am–2pm). The office at rue Wiertz 43 (Bus: 22 or 54) is for visitors to the European Parliament (Mon 1–5pm, Tues–Thurs 9am–5pm, Fri 9am–noon). All offices are closed on January 1 and December 25.

For English-speaking visitors, a most useful publication is the weekly what's-on guide ***Brussels Unlimited,*** containing information on cultural events, shopping, and more. Its sister publication, the monthly magazine ***The Bulletin,*** covers local news and current affairs.

Damage Assessment

As Brussels's architectural heritage has taken a hit—by unscrupulous property developers, venal local officials, and the steamroller of Euroconstruction—the phenomenon has been dubbed "Bruxellisation": the destruction of beautiful old buildings and their replacement by dreary office towers.

City Layout

Brussels is divided into 19 *communes* (districts)—"Brussels" being both the name of the central commune and of the city as a whole (which comprises Belgium's Brussels Capital Region). The center city, once ringed by fortified ramparts, is now encircled by broad boulevards known collectively as the **Petite Ceinture.** Most of the city's premier sightseeing sights are in this zone. Around 14% of the zone's total area of 160 sq. km (63 sq. miles) is occupied by parks, woods, and forest, making this one of Europe's greenest urban centers.

Brussels sits smack-dab on Europe's often edgy interface between its Latin south and Germanic north. You'll hear both French and Dutch (along with a Babel of other tongues) spoken in its streets. The city is bilingual: Bruxelles in French and Brussel in Dutch, and street names and places are in both languages. Grand-Place is Grote Markt in Dutch; Théâtre Royal de la Monnaie is Koninklijke Munttheater. ***Note:*** For convenience and to save space, I use only the French names in this chapter.

STREET MAPS Go to Brussels International Tourism and pick up its *Brussels Guide & Map,* which has a fairly detailed street map of the inner city marked with principal tourist attractions. If you need a comprehensive street map, purchase the *Géocart Bruxelles et Périphérie* at most news vendors and bookstores.

Neighborhoods in Brief

Brussels is flat in its center and western reaches, where the now-vanished Senne River once flowed. To the east, a range of low hills rises to the upper city, which is crowned by the Royal Palace and has some of the city's most affluent residential and prestigious business and shopping districts. The **Grand-Place** stands at the heart of Brussels and is both a starting point and reference point for most visitors.

The Lower Town The **Bas de la Ville,** the core area of the Old Center, has at its heart the **Grand-Place** and its environs. Two of the most traveled lanes nearby are restaurant-lined **rue des Bouchers** and **Petite rue des Bouchers,** part of an area known as the **Ilot Sacré (Sacred Isle).** A block from the Grand-Place is the classical colonnaded **Bourse (Stock Exchange).** A few blocks north, on **place de la Monnaie,** is the Monnaie opera house and ballet theater, named after the coin mint that once stood here. Brussels's busiest shopping street, pedestrianized **rue Neuve,** starts from place de la Monnaie and runs north for several blocks. Just north of the center lies **Gare du Nord** and nearby place Rogier. Central Brussels also includes the **Marché-aux-Poissons** (Fish Market) district.

The Upper Town The **Haut de la Ville** lies east of and uphill from the Grand-Place, along rue Royale and rue de la Régence and abutting the unpretentious, working-class **Marolles** district. Lying between the Palais de Justice and Gare du Midi, the Marolles has cozy cafes, drinking-man's bars, and inexpensive restaurants; its denizens even speak their own dialect. The Upper Town is spread along an escarpment east of the center, where you find the second great square, **place du Grand-Sablon,** as well as the Royal Museums of Fine Arts and the Royal Palace. If you head southwest and cross the broad **boulevard de Waterloo,** where you find the most exclusive designer stores, you come to **place Louise.**

Avenue Louise Beyond the city center, things start to get hazier. From place Louise, Brussels's most fashionable thoroughfare, **Avenue Louise,** runs south all the way to a large wooded park called the **Bois de la Cambre.** On either side of **Avenue Louise** are the classy districts of **Ixelles** and **Uccle**; they're both good areas for casual, inexpensive restaurants, bars, cafes, and shopping, and both border the wide green spaces of the Bois de la Cambre and the Forêt de Soignes.

European District East of the city center lies a part of Brussels whose denizens are regarded by many Bruxellois with the same suspicion they might apply to just-landed extraterrestrials. I refer, of course, to the **European Union district** around place Schuman, where the European Commission, Parliament, and Council of Ministers buildings jostle for space in a warren of offices populated by civil servants, journalists, and lobbyists (the area also is home to a wealth of restaurants and cafes that cater to Euro-appetites). A quaint old neighborhood was made to disappear to make way for these noble edifices. North of Ixelles, the modern European Union district surrounds **place Schuman.** The **Cinquantenaire,** a park criss-crossed with tree-lined avenues, extends from just east of the European District to the Porte de Tervuren and is bisected east to west by avenue John F. Kennedy. At the park's eastern end are the monumental Palais du Cinquantenaire and the Arc du Cinquantenaire**.**

Bruparck In the north of the city (and something of a leap of the imagination) is the **Bruparck.** Inside this recreation complex, you'll find the Mini-Europe theme park; the 26-screen Kinepolis multiplex movie theater; a made-to-order village with stores, cafes, and restaurants; and the Océade water recreation center. Beside it is the Atomium, Brussels Planetarium, Roi Baudoin Soccer Stadium, and the Parc des Expositions congress center.

GETTING AROUND

Brussels's center city is small enough that walking is a viable option. There's no better way to explore the historical core, especially around Grand-Place. You'll likely also enjoy strolling uptown around place du Grand Sablon. Yet city traffic can be both heavy and frantic, creating a tiring experience for strollers. The best solution, if you have several days, is to divide your time into walking tours. Otherwise, a combination of walking and using the excellent public transportation is best. In any case, beyond the center city, using public transportation is a necessity.

Be careful when crossing roads at the black-and-white pedestrian crossings with no signals. Astonishingly, pedestrians at these crossings haven't always had legal priority over cars! Watch out for cars turning (legally) right or left at traffic lights, even when the green "walking man" indicates you are allowed to cross.

By Public Transportation

Maps of the city's excellent, fully integrated transit network—Métro (subway), tram (streetcar), and bus—are available free from the city tourist office, from offices of the **STIB** public transportation company at av. de la Toison d'Or 15 (✆ **070/23-20-00;** www.stib.be; Métro: Louise), and from the Porte de Namur, Rogier, and Gare du Midi Métro stations. In addition, transit maps are posted at all Métro stations and on many bus and tram shelters. The full network operates from 6am to midnight, after which a limited night-bus network takes over. If possible, avoid the crush at morning and evening rush hours. Watch out for pickpockets, especially at busy times, and avoid walking alone in deserted access tunnels, particularly after dark—the risk of being mugged is small but not entirely absent.

FARE INFORMATION & DISCOUNT PASSES Tickets for a one-ride JUMP ticket (JUMP is the name for a Brussels transit ticket) are 2€ when purchased onboard and 1.70€ when purchased before boarding. It costs 7.30€ for a five-ride JUMP ticket, 12€ for a 10-ride JUMP ticket, 4.50€ for a 1-day JUMP ticket, and 9.50€ for a 3-day ticket. A round-trip ticket valid for 24 hours costs 3.30€. The 5-ride, 10-ride, and 1-day tickets cannot be purchased onboard trams or buses of the STIB city transit authority, rather only from sales points and ticket machines; they can, however, be purchased onboard buses of the regional transit companies De Lijn and TEC that have stops inside the city limits. The 3-day ticket can be used only with STIB and must be purchased before boarding. Finally, whatever ticket you want, if you plan to use it on Métro trains, you must purchase it before boarding. Children 6 to 11 ride free on the STIB transit network; they need to get a free pass called an Abonnement J. A maximum of four children 5 and under can ride free per paying adult.

STIB has introduced an electronic stored-value card, the **MOBIB,** available from KIOSK and BOOTIK sales points at some train and Métro stations. It is more complicated to purchase and use this card compared with the ordinary tickets detailed above, and short-stay visitors may not find it to be worth the extra hassle. Still, there's a savings of around 10% off the price of ordinary tickets for ticket classes that have a MOBIB option.

VALIDATION You validate your card by inserting it into the orange electronic machines inside buses and trams and at the access to Métro platforms. Though the card must be revalidated each time you enter a new vehicle, you're allowed multiple transfers within a 1-hour period of the initial validation, so you can hop on and off Métros, trams, and buses during that time and only one journey will be canceled by the electronic scanner. If more than one person is traveling on one card, the card must be validated each time for each traveler.

BY TRAM & BUS An extensive network of tram lines provides the ideal way to get around the city. Both trams and urban buses are painted in gray-and-brown colors. Their stops are marked with red-and-white signs and often have a shelter. You stop a tram or bus by extending your arm as it approaches so the driver can see it; if you don't signal, the bus or tram might not stop. Two bus companies provide service to points outside the city (and stop at some points within it): **TEC** (**© 010/23-53-53;** www.infotec.be), which provides yellow buses covering French-speaking Wallonia, and **De Lijn** (**© 070/22-02-00;** www.delijn.be), which has white buses covering Dutch-speaking Flanders.

Ride the Rails

Though not as fast as the Métro, trams are generally faster than buses and are a great way to get around, not least because you get to view the cityscape while you ride. Line nos. 92 and 94 pass by key sights along rue Royale and rue de la Régence as far as avenue Louise.

BY METRO The Métro is quick and efficient, and covers many important center-city locations, as well as the suburbs, the Bruparck recreation zone, and the Heysel congress center. Stations are identified by signs with a white M on a blue background. A trip underground takes you into an art center: Métro stations are decorated with specially commissioned paintings, installations, and other artworks by contemporary Belgian artists.

By Taxi

Taxi fares start at 2.40€ daily from 6am to 10pm and at 4.40€ between 10pm and 6am, increasing by 1.35€ per kilometer inside the city (tariff 1) and 2.70€ per kilometer outside (tariff 2)—make sure the meter is set to the correct tariff. Tip and taxes are included on the meter price, and you need not add an extra tip unless there has been extra service, such as help with heavy luggage (though drivers won't refuse tips). All taxis are metered. They cannot be hailed on the street, but there are taxi stands on many principal streets, particularly in the center city, and at rail stations. To request a cab by phone, call **Taxis Bleus** (✆ **02/268-00-00;** www.taxisbleus.be) or **Taxis Verts** (✆ **02/349-49-49;** www.taxisverts.be).

By Car

Driving in Brussels is akin to life during the Stone Age: nasty and brutish—though it's rarely short. Normally polite citizens of Brussels turn into red-eyed demons once they get behind the steering wheel. Driving is fast, except at rush hour, and always aggressive. At rush hour (which actually lasts about an hour to either side of 9am and 5pm), it is almost impossible to move on main roads inside the city and on the R0 outer ring road (beltway). Sunday and early morning are better, and evening is not too bad.

Park your car either at your hotel or in one of the many public parking garages—your hotel can furnish the address of the nearest one—and do not set foot in it again until you're ready to leave the city. Good public transportation and an occasional taxi ride will get you anywhere you want inexpensively and hassle-free.

If you must drive, watch out for the notorious *priorité de droite* (priority from the right) traffic system (see "Driven Crazy," in chapter 5).

RENTALS See "Getting Around," in chapter 5.

[FastFACTS] BRUSSELS

Airport See "Orientation," earlier in this chapter.

Area Code Brussels's area code is **02;** always use this when calling a number in Brussels, even when you are calling from Brussels itself. When calling from outside the Netherlands, the area code for Brussels is **2.**

Business Hours See "Fast Facts: Belgium," in chapter 21. Friday is late shopping evening in Brussels, when some stores stay open to 9pm.

Doctors & Dentists For doctors, call **Médi Garde** (✆ **02/479-18-18**) or **SOS Médecins** (✆ **02/513-02-02**) and ask for an English-speaking doctor. For emergency dental care, call ✆ **02/426-10-26.**

Embassies & Consulates See "Fast Facts: Belgium," in chapter 21.

Emergencies For police assistance, call ✆ **101.** For an ambulance or the fire department, call ✆ **100.** For routine police matters, go to **Brussels Central Police Station,** rue du Marché au Charbon 30 (✆ **02/279-79-79;** Métro: Bourse), just off the

Grand-Place. Some Brussels police officers have a poorly developed sense of public service, and a surly and unconcerned attitude to visitors' problems is not uncommon, even at this office where tourists in difficulty often end up. Many officers do, however, speak at least some English.

Hospital **Cliniques Universitaires St-Luc,** av. Hippocrate 10 (✆ **02/764-11-11;** www.saintluc.be; Métro: Alma), has an emergency department.

Mail Most post offices—the national mail company is known as **bpost** (✆ **02/21-23-45;** www.depost laposte.be)—are open Monday to Friday from 9am to 5pm. The office at Centre Monnaie, bd. Anspach 1 (Métro: De Brouckère), is open Monday to Friday from 8:30am to 6pm and Saturday from 10am to 4pm. The office at Gare du Midi, av. Fonsny 1E/F (Métro: Gare du Midi), is open Monday to Friday from 8am to 7:30pm and Saturday from 10:30am to 4:30pm. See "Fast Facts: Belgium," in chapter 21.

Newspapers & Magazines English-language newspapers and magazines are available from **Waterstone's,** bd. Adolphe Max 71 (✆ **02/219-27-08;** www.waterstones.com; Métro: Rogier). Newsstands at Brussels Airport and the Bruxelles-Central, Bruxelles-Midi, and Bruxelles-Nord train stations stock many international publications.

Toilets Should you have a toilet emergency in Brussels, a very good place to find relief is the **Métropole hotel** (p. 89). See "Fast Facts: Belgium," in chapter 21 for more info on restrooms.

Safety Brussels is generally safe, but there is a growing trend of pickpocketing, theft from and of cars, and muggings in places such as Métro station foot tunnels and quiet streets just off the center of town. There's no need to overestimate the risk, but take sensible precautions, particularly in obvious circumstances such as on crowded Métro trains and when withdrawing cash from an ATM at night. See "Crime & Safety," in chapter 3.

WHERE TO STAY

The most popular Brussels districts in which to stay are the center of town, broadly defined as the extended zone around the **Grand-Place;** in the upper town district around place Stéphanie and boulevard de Waterloo; and along **avenue Louise.** The most noticeable lodgings in these areas are large, glittering three- and four-star establishments, yet there are numbers of decent medium-priced and even budget hotels in the streets around the Grand-Place and in the Ixelles district to the south of the upmarket axis of avenue Louise. Other mixed-category concentrations of hotels can be found on and around the **Marché aux Poissons (Fish Market),** and around the **Bruxelles-Nord** and **Bruxelles-Midi** train stations (in the case of Bruxelles-Nord, keep to the south side of the station, not to the scuzzy north side). The **European District** presents something of a special case: Its hotels are convenient for visiting Eurocrats, politicians, lobbyists, and media people, but that won't necessarily make them a good choice for tourists.

Hotels in the upper price range, including deluxe hotels of just about every international chain that wants to be represented in the "capital of Europe," have a wealth of facilities and efficient, though invariably impersonal, service. At every level, hotels fill up during the week and empty out on weekends and during July and August. In off-peak periods, rates can drop as much as 50% from those quoted below; be sure to ask for lower rates and confirm that you're quoted the correct rates, which include 6% value-added tax (TVA) and a 16% service charge.

Brussels International Tourism (see "Visitor Information," earlier in this chapter) makes reservations for the same day if you go to their offices in person and pay a small fee (which is deducted by the hotel from its room rate).

Around the Grand-Place

VERY EXPENSIVE

Amigo ★★★ In Brussels slang, an *amigo* is a prison, and indeed a prison once stood here, in a highly convenient location (both then and now) across the street from the Town Hall. But any resemblance to the former accommodations is nominal. The Amigo is among the city's finest hotels. Its Spanish Renaissance architecture, stately corridors, and flagstone lobby are right at home in this ancient neighborhood. Some of the previous incarnation's antiques, sculptures, wall tapestries, and wood accents have been retained, to good effect. The rooms are quite spacious and traditionally elegant, but with touches of modern Flemish design to brighten things up. Motifs from the comic strip series *The Adventures of Tintin* add an element of whimsy. Ask for a room with a view of the Town Hall's fantastic Gothic spire.

Rue de l'Amigo 1–3 (off Grand-Place), 1000 Bruxelles. ✆ **02/547-47-47.** Fax 02/513-52-77. www.hotelamigo.com. 173 units. 300€–600€ double; from 900€ suite. AE, DC, MC, V. Valet parking 30€. Métro: Bourse. **Amenities:** Restaurant; bar; lounge; babysitting; concierge; executive rooms; health club; room service. *In room:* A/C, TV, fax, hair dryer, Internet (20€/24 hr.), minibar.

EXPENSIVE

Le Dixseptième ★ This graceful, 17th-century house that was once the official residence of the Spanish ambassador stands close to the Grand-Place in a neighborhood of restored dwellings. Guest rooms, reached via a carved-wood stairway, have wood paneling and marble chimneys, and are as big as suites in many hotels; some have balconies. All are in 18th-century style and are named after Belgian painters from Bruegel to Magritte. Two beautiful lounges are decorated with carved-wood medallions and 18th-century paintings.

Rue de la Madeleine 25 (off place de l'Albertine), 1000 Bruxelles. ✆ **02/517-17-17.** Fax 02/502-64-24. www.ledixseptieme.be. 24 units. 200€–270€ double; 350€–430€ suite. Rates include buffet breakfast. AE, DC, MC, V. Limited street parking. Métro: Gare Centrale. **Amenities:** Bar. *In room:* A/C, TV, hair dryer, Internet (15€/24 hr.), minibar.

Métropole ★★ Even if you're not staying here, the hotel is worth a visit on its own account. An ornate, marble-and-gilt interior distinguishes this late-19th-century hotel several blocks from the Grand-Place, intimating Victorian elegance without rejecting the convenience of modern amenities. Soaring ceilings, potted palms, and lavishly decorated public rooms add to the Belle Epoque allure. Spacious guest rooms have classic furnishings and some modern luxuries, including heated towel racks, hair dryers, and trouser presses. An elegant French restaurant, **L'Alban Chambon,** caters to the sophisticated diner, and the sumptuous Belle Epoque **Le 19ième Bar** and the sidewalk **Cafe Métropole** (p. 98) to the sophisticated cafe hound.

Place de Brouckère 31 (close to Centre Monnaie), 1000 Bruxelles. ✆ **02/217-23-00.** Fax 02/218-02-20. www.metropolehotel.com. 305 units. 250€–450€ double; from 650€ suite. Rates include buffet or continental breakfast. AE, DC, MC, V. Valet parking 20€. Métro: De Brouckère. **Amenities:** Restaurant; lounge; cafe; concierge; health club & spa; room service. *In room:* TV, hair dryer, minibar, Wi-Fi (free).

Radisson Blu Royal ★★ Modern, yet in harmony with its neighborhood a few blocks from the Grand-Place, this highly regarded hotel incorporates part of the medieval city wall. The large rooms are decorated in a variety of styles, including

Where to Stay & Dine in Brussels

ACCOMMODATIONS ■

Agenda Louise **35**
Albert **26**
Amigo **18**
Floris Arlequin Grand Place **12**
George V **2**
Izán Avenue Louise Boutique Hotel **36**
La Vieille Lanterne **22**
Le Dixseptième **25**
Louise **34**
Métropole **8**
Mozart **21**
Radisson Blu Royal **10**
Sabina **27**
Thon Hotel Bristol Stephanie **37**
Thon Hotel Stanhope **29**
Welcome **7**

DINING ◆

Aux Armes de Bruxelles **11**
Au Vieux Bruxelles **31**
Belga Queen **9**
Café Métropole **8**
Chez Léon **13**
Comme Chez Soi **4**
De l'Ogenblik **14**
François **6**
In 't Spinnekopke **3**
La Grande Porte **30**
La Maison du Cygne **19**
La Manufacture **1**
La Mirabelle **41**
La Quincaillerie **40**
La Roue d'Or **23**
La Table de l'Abbaye **39**
Le Marmiton **16**
Le Paon Royal **5**
Le Pain et le Vin **32**
Le Scheltema **15**
Le Stévin **28**
Paradiso **24**
Shanti **38**
Taverne du Passage **17**
't Kelderke **20**
Villa Lorraine **33**

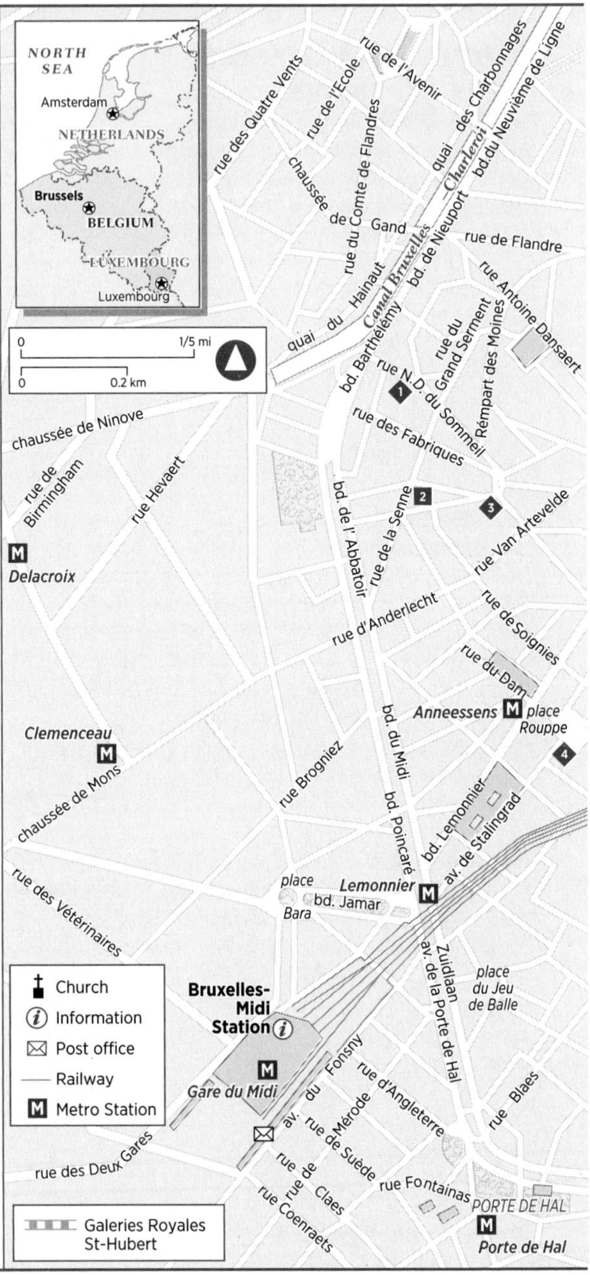

NORTH SEA
Amsterdam
NETHERLANDS
Brussels
BELGIUM
LUXEMBOURG
Luxembourg

0 1/5 mi
0 0.2 km

rue des Quatre Vents
rue de l'Ecole
rue de l'Avenir
quai des Charbonnages
bd. du Neuvième de Ligne
chaussée de Gand
rue du Comte de Flandres
Canal Bruxelles–Charleroi
bd. de Nieuport
rue de Flandre
quai du Hainaut
bd. Barthélémy
rue Antoine Dansaert
rue du Grand Serment
Rempart des Moines
rue N.D. du Sommeil
rue des Fabriques
chaussée de Ninove
rue de Birmingham
rue Hevaert
bd. de l' Abbatoir
rue de la Senne
rue Van Artevelde
Delacroix
rue d'Anderlecht
rue de Soignies
rue du Dam
Anneessens
place Rouppe
Clemenceau
chaussée de Mons
rue Brogniez
bd. du Midi
bd. Poincaré
bd. Lemonnier
av. de Stalingrad
rue des Vétérinaires
place Bara
Lemonnier
bd. Jamar
av. de la Porte de Hal
Zuidlaan
place du Jeu de Balle
Bruxelles-Midi Station
Gare du Midi
av. du Fonsny
rue d'Angleterre
rue Blaes
rue de Mérode
rue de Suède
rue des Deux Gares
rue de Claes
rue Coenraets
rue Fontainas
PORTE DE HAL
Porte de Hal

Church
Information
Post office
Railway
Metro Station

Galeries Royales St-Hubert

place de l'Yser
Yser
bd. d'Ypres
bd. Baudouin
Jacqmain
rue du Marché
rue du Progrès
Bruxelles-Nord Station
bd. St-Lazare
rue de la Poste
rue Royale
chaussée de Haecht
rue Van Dyck
place Rogier
Rogier
quai au Foin
rue du Canal
rue de Laeken
rue du Pélican
bd. Emile
JARDIN BOTANIQUE
bd. du Jardin Botanique
rue du Moulin
rue Tiberghien
rue du Méridien
rue la Limite
Botanique
bd. Adolphe Max
rue Neuve
rue du Marais
bd. Pacheco
rue Potagère
quai-au-Bois-à-Brûler
quai aux Briques
rue de Flandre
place de Brouckère
De Brouckère
place des Martyrs
bd. Bisschoffsheim
place Ste-Catherine
Sainte-Catherine
place de la Monnaie
Théâtre Royal de la Monnaie
rue des Comédiens
rue Royale
place de la Liberté
Madou
chaussée de Louvain
bd. Anspach
rue de l'Ecuyer
bd. de Berlaimont
rue des Bouchers
place de la Bourse
Bourse
rue du Midi
Grand-Place
bd. de l'Impératrice
rue de la Croix de Fer
rue de Louvain
av. des Arts
rue Marie-Thérèse
Parc
Palais de la Nation
rue de la Loi
Gare Centrale
Bruxelles-Central Station
rue Joseph II
Arts-Loi
rue du Lombard
rue du Chêne
place St-Jean
place de l'Albertine
rue Royale
PARC DE BRUXELLES
rue Ducale
bd. du Régent
av. des Arts
rue du Commerce
rue de la Science
rue des Alexiens
bd. de l'Empereur
place Royale
place des Palais
rue Belliard
rue d'Arlon
place du Grand-Sablon
place de la Chapelle
Trône
rue Montoyer
rue du Miroir
rue de la Régence
place du Petit-Sablon
rue de Namur
rue du Luxembourg
rue de l'Industrie
place du Luxembourg
rue des Capucins
rue Allard
rue de Minimes
rue Haute
place Poelaert
Porte de Namur
bd. de Waterloo
Palais de Justice
Louise
chaussée de Wavre
rue du Trône
MAROLLES
rue aux Laines
av. de la Toison d'Or
rue des Chevaliers
rue de Stassart
chaussée d'Ixelles
rue Goffart
bd. de Waterloo
av. Louise
rue de la Concorde
rue du Prince Royal
rue Sans-Souci
Hôtel des Monnaies
rue Jourdan
rue Bosquet
rue Keyenveld
place Fern. Cocq
rue Berckmans
1
5
6
7
8
9
10
11
12
13
14
15
16
17
18
19
20
21
22
23
24
25
26
27
28
29
30
31
32
33
34
35
36
37
38
39
40
41

Scandinavian, Asian, and Italian, and the Royal Club rooms are plushly upholstered. There's a huge atrium with cafe terraces and fountains; some rooms look out on this atrium rather than the outside world. The **Sea Grill** restaurant wins deserved plaudits for its seafood, and the **Bar Dessiné** (which has a roster of 200 Scotch malt whiskeys) has a Belgian comic strip theme. The Radisson has a local Eco-Dynamic label, for its implementation of sustainable operations.

Rue du Fossé aux Loups 47 (close to Galeries Royales St-Hubert), 1000 Bruxelles. ✆ **800/333-3333** in the U.S. and Canada, or 02/219-28-28. Fax 02/219-62-62. www.radissonblu.com. 281 units. 250€–450€ double; from 500€ suite. AE, DC, MC, V. Valet parking 30€. Métro: Gare Centrale. **Amenities:** 2 restaurants; bar; lounge; babysitting; concierge; health club & spa; room service. *In room:* A/C, TV, hair dryer, minibar, Wi-Fi (free).

MODERATE

Floris Arlequin Grand Place You can't get closer to the heart of the city than this property, with the restaurant-lined rue des Bouchers right outside the hotel's back entrance. Then there's the fine view, from some rooms, of the Town Hall spire on the neighboring Grand-Place (which is spectacular when lit at night), and of the Old City's rooftops and narrow medieval streets from the top-floor breakfast room. The guest rooms themselves are not quite so spectacular, but all have modern, comfortable furnishings, and most have plenty of natural light. The more expensive rooms have air-conditioning.

Rue de la Fourche 17–19 (off rue des Bouchers), 1000 Bruxelles. ✆ **02/514-16-15.** Fax 02/514-22-02. www.florishotels.com. 92 units. 105€–210€ double. Rates include buffet breakfast. AE, DC, MC, V. No parking. Métro: Bourse. **Amenities:** Bar, exercise room, room service. *In room:* TV, hair dryer, Wi-Fi (15€/24 hr.).

INEXPENSIVE

La Vieille Lanterne A tiny place with two rooms on each floor and no elevator, this family-owned hotel is diagonally across a narrow street from the *Manneken-Pis*. It can be hard to spot, as you enter through the side door of a trinket store selling hundreds of *Manneken-Pis* replicas. You should feel quite at ease in rooms that are plainly furnished but bright and clean, with old-style leaded windows and small bathrooms with marble counters and tiled walls. Breakfast is served in your room. It's advisable to reserve well ahead.

Rue des Grands Carmes 29 (facing *Manneken-Pis*), 1000 Bruxelles. ✆ **02/512-74-94.** Fax 02/512-13-97. www.lavieillelanterne.be. 6 units. 75€–95€ double. Rates include continental breakfast. AE, DC, MC, V. Limited street parking. Métro: Bourse. *In room:* TV, Wi-Fi (free).

Mozart ★ Go up a flight from the busy, cheap-eats street level, and guess which famous composer's music wafts through the lobby? Salmon-colored walls, plants, and old paintings create a warm, intimate ambience that's carried into the rooms. Furnishings are in Louis XV style, and exposed beams lend each unit a rustic originality. Several are duplexes with a sitting room underneath the loft bedroom. Top-floor rooms have a great view.

Rue du Marché aux Fromages 23 (close to Grand-Place), 1000 Bruxelles. ✆ **02/502-66-61.** Fax 02/502-77-58. www.hotel-mozart.be. 47 units. 100€–150€ double. AE, DC, MC, V. No parking. Métro: Gare Centrale. **Amenities:** Lounge. *In room:* TV, hair dryer.

Around the Fish Market

MODERATE

Welcome ★★ The name of this gem of a hotel, overlooking the Fish Market, couldn't be more accurate, thanks to the untiring efforts of the husband-and-wife

Passport to Brussels

One of the best discounts is the Brussels Card (www.brusselscard.be), available from the Brussels International tourist office on the Grand-Place, hotels, museums, and offices of the STIB city transit authority. Valid for 1, 2, or 3 days, for 24€, 34€, and 40€, respectively, it allows free use of public transportation; free and discounted admission to about 30 of the city's museums and attractions; and discounts at some restaurants and other venues, and on some guided tours.

proprietors, Michel and Sophie Smeesters. Think of it as a country *auberge* (inn) right in the heart of town. Rooms are furnished and styled on individual, unrelated international and travel themes, such as Provence, Tibet, Egypt, Africa, Jules Verne, and Laura Ashley, all to a high standard. Reserve as far ahead of time as possible, for the Welcome's regular guests are fiercely loyal. You'll find several very good seafood-dining options on the Marché aux Poissons.

Quai au Bois-à-Brûler 23 (at the Marché aux Poissons), 1000 Bruxelles. ✆ **02/219-95-46.** Fax 02/217-18-87. www.hotelwelcome.com. 17 units. 100€–155€ double; 170€–200€ suite. Rates include buffet breakfast. AE, DC, MC, V. Parking 13€. Métro: Ste-Catherine. **Amenities:** Lounge; room service. *In room:* A/C (some rooms), TV, hair dryer, Wi-Fi (free).

INEXPENSIVE

George V This agreeable little hotel is tucked away in a corner of the center city that looks more down at the heels than it really is; it has been reborn as a trendy shopping and eating area. The George, in a renovated town house from 1859 within easy walking distance of the Grand-Place, has rooms that are plain but clean and have new furnishings.

Rue 't Kint 23 (off place du Jardin aux Fleurs), 1000 Bruxelles. ✆ **02/513-50-93.** Fax 02/513-44-93. www.hotelgeorge5.be. 16 units. 60€–90€ double. Rates include continental breakfast. AE, MC, V. Limited street parking. Métro: Bourse. **Amenities:** Bar. *In room:* TV, hair dryer, minibar, Wi-Fi (9€/stay).

Around Avenue Louise

EXPENSIVE

Thon Hotel Bristol Stephanie ★★ Every feature of this sleek hotel on one of the city's toniest shopping streets, from its lobby fittings to furnishings in the kitchenette suites, is streamlined, functional, and representative of the best in Nordic design. Some rooms have four-poster beds and anti-allergy hardwood floors; all are furnished to a high level of modern style and comfort. The rooms are quite large, but if you need more space, it's worth paying a bit more to upgrade to a far larger executive room. Try to get a room in the main building; the security in the back building is good, but nothing beats a 24-hour doorman. Restaurant **Le Chalet d'Odin** has a refined Continental menu, and the breakfast room serves a pretty reasonable American-style buffet breakfast.

Av. Louise 91–93, 1050 Bruxelles. ✆ **02/543-33-11.** Fax 02/538-03-07. www.thonhotels.be. 142 units. 240€–320€ double; from 500€ suite. AE, DC, MC, V. Parking 25€. Métro: Louise. **Amenities:** Restaurant; lounge; bar; babysitting; concierge; executive rooms; exercise room & sauna; room service. *In room:* A/C, TV, hair dryer, minibar, Wi-Fi (18€/24 hr.).

Thon Hotel Stanhope ★ An old convent and some neighboring properties in the upmarket shopping district around avenue Louise and Porte de Namur have been transformed into this graceful hotel. The ambience of the Stanhope combines that of a country retreat with a prime metropolitan location. All guest rooms are individually decorated in variations of Old English style. Despite the hotel's English image, the in-house restaurant **Brighton,** under the guidance of master-chef Gérard Souillet, majors in French cuisine.

Rue du Commerce 9 (off rue du Trône), 1000 Bruxelles. ✆ **02/506-91-11.** Fax 02/512-17-08. www.thonhotels.be. 108 units. 160€–360€ double; from 500€ suite. AE, DC, MC, V. Parking 25€. Métro: Trône. **Amenities:** Restaurant; bar; babysitting; concierge; executive rooms; health club & spa; room service. *In room:* A/C, TV, minibar, Wi-Fi (10€/24 hr.).

MODERATE

Agenda Louise ★ This fine, small, middle-of-the-road hotel affords a good balance of advantages both for leisure visitors who are looking for modern comforts without spending too much to get them, and for business visitors who don't have sheaves of locked-and-loaded plastic to get by on. The guest rooms have been spiffily upgraded with new beds and integrated color schemes and deco, to good effect. They have enough room to swing a cat, so long as it's not an overly big one, and some complete kitchens are available. The bathrooms have tiled walls and floors, and they just about break out of the shoehorned-in syndrome that afflicts many moderately priced city hotels. Ask for a room that overlooks the inner courtyard for the best view.

Rue de Florence 6 (off av. Louise), 1000 Bruxelles. ✆ **02/539-00-31.** Fax 02/539-00-63. www.hotel-agenda.com. 37 units. 160€–180€ double. Rates include buffet breakfast. AE, DC, MC, V. Parking 17€. Métro: Louise. **Amenities:** Lounge. *In room:* TV, hair dryer, minibar, Wi-Fi (free).

Izán Avenue Louise Boutique Hotel ★ Being on a quiet-ish side street right off chic avenue Louise, this fine refurbished hotel has location in spades, and there's a ton of great restaurants in the neighborhood. You'll find typically English country-house decor here, down to the fireplace in the lobby. The spacious, attractively furnished guest rooms all have private bathrooms and writing desks; some have kitchenettes. An English-style buffet breakfast is served in a pleasant and intimate breakfast room—so if you like your ham 'n' eggs done with a touch of class, this gem of a hotel could be the place for you.

Rue Blanche 4 (off av. Louise), 1000 Bruxelles. ✆ **02/535-95-00.** Fax 02/535-96-00. www.hotelizanavenuelouise.com. 80 units. 130€–260€ double; 360€ suite. Rates include buffet breakfast. AE, DC, MC, V. Parking 15€. Métro: Louise. **Amenities:** Bar; babysitting. *In room:* TV, Wi-Fi (20€/24 hr.).

Louise ★ New owners have taken this property by the scruff of its neck and given it new status, taste, and levels of comfort. They started out with some advantages—a graceful, well-maintained 19th-century town house in a hot part of town. The hotel has some unusually spacious rooms and some so small you'll need to shoehorn yourself and your luggage into them. If you need one of the larger rooms, you'll want to check it out first, if possible, or confirm how large it is when you reserve.

Rue Veydt 40 (off chaussée de Charleroi), 1050 Bruxelles. ✆ **02/537-40-33.** Fax 02/534-40-37. www.louisehotel.com. 49 units. 140€–180€ double. AE, DC, MC, V. Limited street parking. Métro: Louise. **Amenities:** Bar. *In room:* A/C (in some), TV, hair dryer, minibar (in some), Wi-Fi (free).

Around Bruxelles-Nord Station

INEXPENSIVE

Albert ★ A modern hotel next to the bronze-domed 19th-century Eglise Royale Ste-Marie and close to an enclave of the most authentic Turkish restaurants in town (which should more than compensate for its lack of an in-house restaurant), Albert has clean, bright, rooms with a touch of design flair and tiled bathrooms. Next door, guests of the Résidence Albert have access to large studio apartments with refrigerators. Although the hotel is on the outer edge of the city center, trams from a nearby stop take you straight to the Royal Palace, the Royal Museums of Fine Arts, and the Sablon antiques district.

Rue Royale-Ste-Marie 27–29 (off place de la Reine), 1030 Bruxelles. ✆ **02/217-93-91.** Fax 02/219-20-17. www.hotelalbert.be. 19 units. 70€–75€ double; 75€–90€ studio apartment. Rates include continental breakfast. MC, V. Free parking. Tram: 25 to Lefrancq; 92 to Robiano; or 94 to Sainte-Marie. **Amenities:** Bar. *In room:* TV, hair dryer, Wi-Fi (free).

Sabina This small hostelry is like a private residence, presided over by hospitable owners who keep the place up to modern standards with regular small but thoughtful touches. A grandfather clock in the reception area and polished wood along the restaurant walls give it a warm, homey atmosphere. Rooms vary in size, but all are comfortable and simply yet tastefully done in a modern style with twin beds. None of them measure up to the elegant public spaces, but they are adequately furnished, with comfortable beds and soft carpeting. It's in a slightly awkward place to reach, between public transportation stops, however.

Rue du Nord 78 (at place des Barricades), 1000 Bruxelles. ✆ **02/218-26-37.** Fax 02/219-32-39. www.hotelsabina.eu. 24 units. 57€–92€ double. Rates include buffet breakfast. AE, DC, MC, V. Limited street parking. Métro: Madou. *In room:* TV, hair dryer.

WHERE TO DINE

Food is a passion in Brussels, which boasts more Michelin-star restaurants per head than Paris. People here regard dining as a fine art and their favorite chef as a grand master. It's just about impossible to eat badly, no matter what your price range. The city has no fewer than 1,500 restaurants. Even if you're on a tight budget, you should try to set aside the money for at least one big splurge in a fine restaurant—nourishment for both the soul and the stomach.

The Brussels restaurant scene covers the entire city, but there are one or two culinary pockets you should know about. It has been said that you haven't truly visited this city unless you've dined at least once along **rue des Bouchers** or its offshoot, **Petite rue des Bouchers,** both of which are near the Grand-Place. Both streets are lined with an extraordinary array of ethnic eateries, most with a proudly proclaimed specialty, and all with modest prices. Reservations are not usually necessary in these colorful, and often crowded, restaurants; if you cannot be seated at one, you simply stroll on to the next one.

Then there's the cluster of fine restaurants at the **Marché aux Poissons (Fish Market),** a short walk from the Grand-Place around place Ste-Catherine. This is where fishermen once unloaded their daily catches from a now-covered canal. Seafood, as you'd expect, is the specialty. A well-spent afternoon's occupation is to stroll through the area to examine the bills of fare exhibited in windows and make your reservation for the evening meal. Don't fret if the service is slow: People take their time dining out here.

Around the Grand-Place

VERY EXPENSIVE

Comme Chez Soi ★★★ CLASSIC FRENCH A visit to the revered, Art Nouveau "Just Like Home," which sports two Michelin stars, will surely be the culinary

QUICK bites

In business since 1873, the snack bar **Au Suisse,** bd. Anspach 73–75 (✆ **02/512-95-89;** www.ausuisse.be; Métro: Bourse), serves great sandwiches with fresh ingredients and homemade sauces. This is the place to try a raw-herring sandwich (the seafood in general is ace), and you can sip an iced *frappé* on the sidewalk terrace at lunchtime. **Cap Sablon,** rue Lebeau 75 (✆ **02/512-01-70;** Bus: 34, 48, 95, or 96), just off place du Grand Sablon, is great for salads.

For a chic yet still tasty breakfast, lunch, or snack, head for the convivial **Roi des Belges ★**, rue Jules Van Praet 35–37 (✆ **02/503-43-00;** Métro: Bourse), on the corner of trendy place St-Géry. The soup of the day or a decent salad won't set you back more than a few euros, or you can just nurse a coffee while reading the newspaper or chatting with your neighboring diners.

Another seductive invitation is the aroma of **fresh Brussels waffles,** sold from street stands around the city. Generally thicker than American waffles, they cost about 3€ and are smothered in sugar icing. The stands are all pretty decent and there's not much reason to try one over another. Should you want to sample an impressive range of toppings and accompaniments, head to the specialist **Aux Gaufres de Bruxelles,** rue du Marché aux Herbes 113 (✆ **02/514-01-71;** www.belgiumwaffle.com; Métro: Gare Centrale).

Then there are all the **little Greek, Turkish, Arab,** and **Israeli** places around the Grand-Place, where you can fill up on moussaka, kebabs, salad, and falafel for as little as 5€.

And don't forget those *frites* (fries). Belgians usually eat this salty snack with mayonnaise rather than ketchup. Prices run from around 2.50€ to 4€ for a *cornet* (cone); toppings, such as peanut, tartare, samurai (hot!), or curry, cost extra. Brussels is dotted with dozens of fast-food stands serving *frites* in paper cones. One of the best, **Maison Antoine ★**, place Jourdan 1 (✆ **02/230-54-56;** www.maisonantoine.be; Métro: Schuman), in the European District, has existed since the 1940s and counts both homegrown and foreign celebrities among its devotees. You'll have to join the line at peak times, but the wait for its fries, made from fresh-peeled potatoes, should be worthwhile.

highlight of your trip—though the food is a long way from being what most people actually eat at home. Under the influence of chef Lionel Rigolet, the dishes have been looking lighter in recent times—even the Burgundian Bruxellois are having to conform to a faster, slimmer world. Ask for a table in the kitchen, where you can watch the masters at work. Book for dinner as far ahead as possible; getting a table at short notice is more likely at lunchtime.

Place Rouppe 23 (at av. de Stalingrad). ✆ **02/512-29-21.** www.commechezsoi.be. Reservations required. Main courses 43€–173€; fixed-price menus 84€–191€. AE, DC, MC, V. Tues–Sat noon–1:30pm and 7–9:30pm. Métro: Anneessens.

La Maison du Cygne ★ BELGIAN/FRENCH This grande dame of Brussels's internationally recognized restaurants overlooks the Grand-Place from the former guild house of the Butchers Guild—where Karl Marx and Friedrich Engels cooked up *The Communist Manifesto* during a 3-year sojourn in Brussels. The service, though a tad stuffy, is as elegant as the polished walnut walls, bronze wall sconces, and green velvet. The menu has haute cuisine Belgian and French classics, such as *waterzooï de* *homard* (a souplike lobster stew), veal sautéed with fresh wild mushrooms, and *tournedos* (filet steak) with green peppercorns. There are fine chicken and fish dishes, and specialties such as *huîtres au champagne* (oysters in champagne) and *goujonette de sole mousseline* (sole mousse). Because of its location, the restaurant is usually crowded at lunchtime, but dinner reservations are likely to be available.

Grand-Place 9 (entrance at rue Charles Buls 2). ✆ **02/511-82-44.** www.lamaisonducygne.be. Reservations recommended. Main courses 36€–40€; fixed-price lunch 40€, dinner 65€. AE, DC, MC, V. Mon–Fri noon–2:15pm and 7pm–midnight; Sat 7pm–midnight. Métro: Gare Centrale.

EXPENSIVE

Aux Armes de Bruxelles TRADITIONAL BELGIAN A Brussels institution since it opened in 1921, this family-owned establishment offers gracious, rather formal service, combined with a casual, relaxed ambience. It's an excellent place for your introduction to Belgian cooking, since it combines traditional cuisine with great quality and offers just about every regional specialty you can think of, including mussels in every conceivable style. To save valuable eating time at busy lunchtimes, do as many regulars do and just order *un complet*—within minutes a pan of steamed mussels accompanied by french fries and a beer will land on your table. Sample anything from an excellent beef stewed in beer to a delicious *waterzooï* (fish or chicken stew) to a steak with pepper-and-cream sauce, all at fair prices.

Rue des Bouchers 13 (off Grand-Place). ✆ **02/511-55-98.** www.auxarmesdebruxelles.be. Main courses 15€–44€; lunch menu 23€; fixed-price menus 35€–50€. AE, DC, MC, V. Daily noon–11:15pm. Métro: Gare Centrale.

Belga Queen ★ CONTEMPORARY BELGIAN Light and space are the signature design themes of a restaurant for which the description "brasserie" seems a mite too cramped, not to say convivial. Set in a Belle Epoque building that belonged to the plush 19th-century Hôtel de la Poste and later housed a branch of the French Crédit du Nord bank, Belga Queen fills its vast space with cool diners. You'll tuck into food that runs from Namurois snail soup, through gray Ostend shrimp and tender Charolais beef sirloin, to roasted Mechelen cuckoo, and you'll be served by a waitstaff fully apprised of the august nature of their calling. In addition to a restaurant, the Belga Queen contains an oyster bar, a beer bar, and a club and cigar lounge.

Rue du Fossée aux Loups 32 (at rue Neuve). ✆ **02/217-21-87.** www.belgaqueen.be. Reservations recommended on weekends. Main courses 20€–45€; fixed-price lunch 16€, dinner 30€–45€. AE, DC, MC, V. Daily noon–2:30pm and 7–11pm. Métro: De Brouckère.

Le Scheltema BELGIAN This is one of those solid restaurants in the Ilot Sacré district that keeps going day in, day out, year after year, serving up much the same fare but never forgetting that quality counts. Good service and fine atmosphere complement the seafood specialties at this brasserie-style restaurant, which is similar to others in the district but always goes the extra mile in class and taste. Pâté, *bisque d'homard* (lobster soup), *croquettes aux crevettes* (prawn croquettes), mussels (in season), and a wide range of fish and meat options all grace the excellent menu.

Rue des Dominicains 7 (off rue des Bouchers). ✆ **02/512-20-84.** www.scheltema.be. Main courses 21€–41€; seafood platter 35€–58€; fixed-price menus 27€–39€. AE, DC, MC, V. Mon–Sat noon–3pm and 6:30pm–midnight. Métro: Gare Centrale.

MODERATE

De l'Ogenblik ★ FRENCH/BELGIAN In the elegant surroundings of the Galeries Royales St-Hubert, you'll find this Parisian bistro-style restaurant. It often gets busy, but the ambience in the split-level, wood-and-brass-outfitted dining room, with a sand-strewn floor, is convivial, though a little too tightly packed when it's full. Look for garlicky meat and seafood menu dishes, and expect to pay a smidgeon more for atmosphere than might be strictly justified by the results on your plate. If you like duck, try the *magret du canard mulard aux deux poivres, gratin dauphinois* (filet of duck with peppers and potatoes gratin). A good seafood choice is the *ragoût de coquilles St-Jacques et gambas, sauce diable* (scallop and prawn stew in a "devil"—spicy—sauce).

Galerie des Princes 1 (in the Galeries Royales St-Hubert). ✆ **02/511-61-51.** www.ogenblik.be. Main courses 23€–28€; *plat du jour* (lunch only) 11€. AE, DC, MC, V. Mon–Sat noon–2:30pm and 7pm–midnight. Métro: Gare Centrale.

La Roue d'Or ★ TRADITIONAL BELGIAN With dark wood, mirrors, a high frescoed ceiling, Magritte images on the walls, and marble-topped tables, this welcoming Art Nouveau brasserie has a loyal local following. An extensive menu, ranging from grilled meats to a good selection of cooked salmon and other seafood, and old Belgian favorites like *stoemp* (mashed potatoes and carrots with sausage, a steak, or other meat), caters to just about any appetite. The beer, wine, and spirits list is equally long.

Rue des Chapeliers 26 (off Grand-Place). ✆ **02/514-25-54.** Main courses 14€–25€. AE, DC, MC, V. Daily noon–12:30am. Métro: Gare Centrale.

Le Marmiton BELGIAN/FRENCH A welcoming environment, hearty servings, and commitment to satisfying customers are hallmarks of this cozy, two-floor restaurant. On a menu that emphasizes fish, the seafood cocktail starter is a heap of shellfish and crustaceans substantial enough to be a main course, and the sole is excellent. Meat dishes are available, too. The menu is complemented by an excellent wine list selected by Portuguese/Belgian owner and chef Antonio Beja da Silva, whose love of his own cooking shows in his waistline and in the attention he devotes to his customers.

Rue des Bouchers 43A (off Grand-Place). ✆ **02/511-79-10.** www.lemarmiton.be. Main courses 16€–28€; fixed-price menus 16€–22€. AE, DC, MC, V. Mon–Fri noon–3pm and 6–11:30pm; Sat–Sun noon–midnight. Métro: Gare Centrale.

INEXPENSIVE

Café Métropole ★ LIGHT FARE Many Brussels visitors never get beyond the pleasant heated-sidewalk section of this massive Victorian-style cafe. Inside, in the associated Le 19ième Bar, you find a casually elegant decor, highlighted by a marble fireplace, colorful wood puppets hanging from the high ceilings, and comfortable leather seating arranged in cozy groupings. The menu includes sandwiches, soups, quiches, and other light meals. The bar menu fills no fewer than six pages, including some rather exceptional specialties from the head barman.

On Your Guard in the Ilot Sacré

A few restaurants (not reviewed here) in this colorful restaurant district just off the Grand-Place take advantage of tourists. If you decide to dine at a restaurant not reviewed here—and you don't want to get fleeced—be sure to ask the price of everything *before* you order it. Most visitors leave the Ilot Sacré with no more serious complaint than an expanded waistline, but a little caution is in order.

Place de Brouckère 31 (in the Hôtel Métropole). ✆ **02/217-23-00.** www.metropolehotel.com. Reservations not accepted. *Plat du jour* 12€; light meal 10€–15€. AE, MC, V. Mon–Sat 11am–2am; Sun 3–11pm. Métro: De Brouckère.

Chez Léon SEAFOOD/BELGIAN Think of it as the mussels from Brussels. This big, basic restaurant is the city's most single-minded purveyor of that marine delicacy. Léon has been flexing its mussels since 1893 and now has clones all over Belgium, among them one at the Bruparck amusements complex. The mollusks in question are top quality, at low prices, in a variety of styles, such as *moules marinières* (mussels boiled in vegetable stock) and *moules au vin blanc* (mussels in white-wine sauce). If you don't like mussels, the menu features plenty of other fishy delights—including eels in green sauce, cod, and bouillabaisse.

Rue des Bouchers 18 (off of Grand-Place). ✆ **02/511-14-15.** www.chezleon.be. Main courses 11€–27€; *menu Formule Léon* 13€; mussel plates 11€–22€. AE, DC, MC, V. Sun–Thurs 11:30am–11pm; Fri–Sat 11:30am–11:30pm. Métro: Gare Centrale.

Paradiso ITALIAN This great little Italian restaurant is close enough to the Grand-Place to be convenient, but just far enough away to not be immediately obvious to the crowds. As such, it is one of Brussels's best-kept secrets. Owner/chef Santino Trovato has created a little gem, with pasta and pizza just like mamma used to make and a list of fine Italian wines as long as your arm.

Rue Duquesnoy 34 (off place St-Jean). ✆ **02/512-52-32.** www.resto-paradiso.be. Main courses 13€–19€. No credit cards. Tues–Sat noon–3pm and 6:30pm–midnight. Métro: Gare Centrale.

Taverne du Passage ★ TRADITIONAL BELGIAN Surrealist painter René Magritte (1898–1967) was a regular at this classic Art Deco brasserie in a glass-roofed arcade. It's easy to imagine him strolling through the door in his bowler hat, sitting at his favorite banquette, and ordering from one of the white-jacketed waiters. The menu hasn't changed much since Magritte's day: Belgian staples like shrimp croquettes, *waterzooï,* endive with ham, and roast beef carved tableside. The prices are a little steep, but it's worth it for the atmosphere alone. Plus, the food's great—a real Brussels treat.

Galerie de la Reine 30 (in the Galeries Royales St-Hubert). ✆ **02/512-37-31.** www.tavernedupassage.com. Main courses 16€–27€; *plat du jour* 15€. AE, DC, MC, V. Daily noon–midnight. Métro: Gare Centrale.

't Kelderke ★ TRADITIONAL BELGIAN Despite being on the square that is the focus of tourism in Brussels, this is far from being a tourist trap. As many Bruxellois as tourists throng the long wood tables in a 17th-century, brick-arched cellar, and all are welcomed with time-honored respect, even if that should be perceived as being a little rough and ready. Memorable traditional Belgian fare, with little in the way of frills, is served up from an open kitchen. This is a great place to try local specialties such as *bloedpens* (blood sausage) *à la Bruxelloise, stoemp* (mashed potato and vegetable) with *boudin* (sausage), *carbonnades à la Flamande* (Flemish beef stew), *lapin à la gueuze* (rabbit in Brussels beer), and big steaming pans piled high with Zeeland mussels.

Grand-Place 15. ✆ **02/511-09-56.** www.restaurant-het-kelderke.be. Main courses 11€–19€; *plat du jour* 11€. AE, DC, MC, V. Daily noon–2am. Métro: Gare Centrale.

Around Avenue Louise

EXPENSIVE

La Quincaillerie ★★ MODERN FRENCH/SEAFOOD In the Ixelles district, where fine restaurants are as common as streetlights, this spot stands out, even though it may be a little too aware of its own modish good looks and a shade pricey. The setting is a traditional former hardware store from 1903 with a giant rail-station clock, wood paneling, and masses of drawers, designed by students of Art Nouveau master Victor Horta. It's busy enough to get the waitstaff harassed and absent-minded, yet they're always friendly. Seafood dishes dominate the menu. Specialties include *escalope du saumon rôti au gros sel* (salmon in roasted rock salt) and *canette laquée au miel et citron vert* (baby duck with a crust of honey and lime). You don't need to look much further than a crisp Sancerre as the ideal wine accompaniment to most dishes.

Rue du Page 45 (at rue Américaine). ✆ **02/533-98-33.** www.quincaillerie.be. Main courses 17€–46€; lunch menu 13€; fixed-price menus 25€–30€. AE, DC, MC, V. Mon–Sat noon–2:30pm and 7pm–midnight; Sun 7pm–midnight. Tram: 81 to Trinité.

Le Pain et le Vin ★ MEDITERRANEAN The owners of this restaurant were once steeped in the Michelin-star milieu but have jettisoned the rigorous requirements of that system to concentrate on having some good, clean, tasty fun instead. "Bread and Wine" fits the bill perfectly—and the bill won't be excessive either. The restaurant, in a converted house, looks out onto a garden. There's a terrace for alfresco dining in good weather. Whether the dish is chicken, fish, meat, or vegetables, the preparation concentrates on bringing out the natural taste, rather than smothering it with over-rich sauces. For interesting variations on common dishes, try the chicken ravioli with basil and Parmesan, or the lobster and shrimp lasagna with ginger sauce. Vegetarian dishes are available on request, and vegetable side dishes form a big part of the menu offerings.

Chaussée d'Alsemberg 812A. ✆ **02/332-37-74.** www.painvin.be. Main courses 31€–39€; lunch menu 24€; fixed-price menus 52€–69€. AE, MC, V. Mon–Fri noon–2pm and 6–10pm; Sat 6–10pm. Tram: 51 to Rittweger.

MODERATE

Au Vieux Bruxelles BELGIAN/SEAFOOD This convivial, brasserie-style restaurant from 1882 specializes in mussels, which it serves in a wide variety of ways. In Belgium, the personality of the humble but tasty mussel is a staple of conversation as much as of diet, and people assess the quality of each year's crop with the same critical eye that other countries reserve for fine wines. Au Vieux Bruxelles, a kind of temple to the Belgian obsession with mussels, serves the shellfish in 15 different ways, including raw (accompanied only by a light white-wine sauce), baked, fried, grilled, and broiled, and in traditional dishes like *moules marinières* (boiled in water with vegetables) and *moules au vin* (boiled in wine). Should you not wish to work on the mussels, there are great steaks like *steak au poivre flambé* (flamed pepper steak), *escargots* (snails), and crepes.

Rue St-Boniface 35 (close to Porte Namur). ✆ **02/503-31-11.** www.auvieuxbruxelles.com. Reservations not accepted. Main courses 11€–21€; mussel plates 18€–20€. AE, MC, V. Tues–Thurs 6:30–11:30pm; Fri–Sat 6:30pm–midnight; Sun noon–3pm and 6:30–11:30pm. Métro: Porte de Namur.

La Mirabelle ★ TRADITIONAL BELGIAN Due to its "democratic" prices, convivial atmosphere, and consistently good food, this brasserie-restaurant in Ixelles is popular both with students from the nearby Université Libre de Bruxelles and with Bruxellois in general. Plainly decorated, with wooden tables crowded together, it looks more like a bar than a restaurant and often has a boisterous pub-style atmosphere to match. The *steak-frites* (steak with french fries), a Belgian staple, is particularly good here. The garden terrace is a great setting for alfresco dining in summer.

Chaussée de Boondael 455 (at av. Arnaud Fraiteur). ✆ **02/649-51-73.** www.mirabelle.be. Main courses 13€–25€; *plat du jour* 9.20€. MC, V. Daily noon–3pm and 6pm–1:30am. Bus: 71, 72, or 95 to Cimetière d'Ixelles.

La Table de l'Abbaye ★ FRENCH If you're a French-cuisine enthusiast who likes things done just so and you're not too enamored of nouvelle cuisine, La Table de l'Abbaye is for you. The setting is a well-appointed town house near the tranquil grounds of the Abbaye (Abbey) de la Cambre. The food here is hard to beat, and its prices are not excessive, considering the quality of the fare and its presentation. Look for many French favorites, all best accompanied with a fine wine—from France, of course. Lobster flexes its claws in several interesting ways on the menu here: in pancakes with caviar butter, in a mixed salad, and with a pepper-cream sauce. Lamb marinated in Bourgogne wine is another specialty. In a romantically atmospheric touch, candlelight provides the main illumination for the classic decor, enlivened by sculptures and paintings.

Rue de Belle-Vue 62 (off av. Louise). ✆ **02/646-33-95.** www.la-table-abbaye.be. Main courses 15€–25€. AE, DC, MC, V. Mon–Fri 12:30–2:30pm and 6–10:30pm; Sat 6–10:30pm. Tram: 94 to Abbaye.

INEXPENSIVE

La Grande Porte TRADITIONAL BELGIAN It's hard to think of a Brussels eatery that is more traditionally Belgian than this archetypal place in the down-at-the-heels Marolles district. A decor comprised of dark-wood furnishings, paper lanterns, marionettes hanging from the ceiling, old posters, and fashionably shabby walls, and background noise that calls to mind a canned French cabaret, combine to create a cozy, convivial dining space. The mostly regional main courses are served in bountiful portions. Sure to impart a warm glow of appreciation are hearty standards like the *carbonnades à la flamande* (beef braised in beer), *waterzooï à la Gantoise* (chicken stew), and *stoemp* (mashed potatoes and carrots) with sausage. But a touch of bistro-level sophistication in starters such as the chicory with smoked salmon and the warm goat's cheese salad lifts the menu out of the plain class. The late-night hours are an added plus.

Rue Notre-Seigneur 9 (off rue Blaes). ✆ **02/512-89-98.** Main courses 11€–14€. MC, V. Mon–Fri noon–3pm and 6pm–2am; Sat 6pm–2am. Bus: 27 or 48 to Chapelle.

Shanti ★ VEGETARIAN An exotic look here is consistent with the restaurant's multicultural menus: Lots of greenery and flowers create a gardenlike feel, and crystal lamps, mirrors, and old paintings adorn the walls. Try Neptune's Pleasure, crab with avocado and seaweed, as a starter. For a main course, shrimp masala with mixed vegetables and coriander is excellent, as is eggplant with ricotta in a tomato-and-basil sauce.

Av. Adolphe Buyl 68 (at bd. Général Jacques). ✆ **02/649-40-96.** www.shanti-restaurant.com. Main courses 9€–14€; fixed-price menus 20€–25€. AE, DC, MC, V. Tues–Sat noon–2pm and 6:30–10pm. Tram: 94 to Buyl.

West of the Bourse

EXPENSIVE

François ★★ SEAFOOD A bright and cheerful ambience complements fine cuisine at this restaurant on the ground floor of a 19th-century *maison de maître* (town house) that has housed a fishmongers and *traiteur* (restaurant or catering business that sells takeout food) since 1922, and the tradition is taken seriously. Tiled walls and dark wood tables grace a small dining room. "Superb" is the best word to describe seafood specialties, like the *sole Ostendaise* (North Sea sole cooked in butter) and the bouillabaisse, and their signature lobster dishes, mussels, and Zeeland oysters. The menu includes a few meat choices. The presentation is professional yet relaxed. In fine weather, dine on a great sidewalk terrace across the street on the old Fish Market square. If you're dining indoors, try to get one of the window tables that have a view of the square.

Quai aux Briques 2 (corner of place Ste-Catherine and Marché aux Poissons). ✆ **02/511-60-89.** www.restaurantfrancois.be. Main courses 28€–58€; fixed-price menus 35€–39€; mussel plates 14€–28€. AE, DC, MC, V. Tues–Sat noon–2:30pm and 7–11:30pm. Métro: Ste-Catherine.

MODERATE

In 't Spinnekopke ★★ TRADITIONAL BELGIAN "In the Spider's Web" occupies a stagecoach inn from 1762, just far enough off the beaten track downtown to be frequented mainly by those in the know. You dine in a tilting, tiled-floor building, at plain tables, and more likely than not squeezed into a tight space. This is one of Brussels's most traditional cafe/restaurants—so much so, in fact, that the menu lists its hardy standbys of regional Belgian cuisine in the old Bruxellois dialect. *Stoemp mi sossisse* is hotchpotch with sausage, and *toung ave mei* is sole. The bar stocks a vast selection of traditional beers. ***Tip:*** Just one click on its website's home page takes you to a recording of Jacques Brel's beautiful song "Le Plat Pays."

Place du Jardin aux Fleurs 1 (off rue Van Artevelde). ✆ **02/511-86-95.** www.spinnekopke.be. Main courses 16€–30€; *plat du jour* 13€; mussel plates 23€–28€. AE, DC, MC, V. Mon–Fri noon–3pm and 6–11pm; Sat 6pm–midnight. Bar Mon–Fri 11am–midnight; Sat 6pm–midnight. Métro: Bourse.

La Manufacture ★ FRENCH/INTERNATIONAL Even in its former incarnation, this place was concerned with style—it used to be the factory of chic Belgian leather-goods maker Delvaux. Fully refurbished, with hardwood floors, leather banquettes, polished wood, and stone tables, all set amid iron pillars and exposed air ducts, it produces trendy world cuisine on a French foundation, for a mostly youthful public. You may find it a little disconcerting at first to mix Asian menu dishes like dim sum and sushi with Moroccan couscous, Lyon sausage, sliced ostrich filets with mango and green pepper, and Belgian specialties like *waterzooï,* but you soon get the hang of it (the menu changes seasonally, so these particular dishes might not be available). Some evenings there's live piano music. On sunny days in summer, you can dine outdoors on a terrace shaded by giant bamboo plants.

Rue Notre-Dame du Sommeil 12–20 (off place du Jardin aux Fleurs). ✆ **02/502-25-25.** www.manufacture.be. Main courses 14€–27€; lunch menu 15€; fixed-price menus 35€–55€. AE, DC, MC, V. Mon–Fri noon–2pm and 7–11pm; Sat 7pm–midnight. Métro: Bourse.

INEXPENSIVE

Le Paon Royal BELGIAN One of my favorite small, family-owned restaurants, this typically Bruxellois treat is in a house dating from 1631 that has a rustic wood-and-exposed-brick interior and timber-beamed ceiling. Have just a snack with one of the 65 brands of beer, six of them draft beers, behind the tiny bar (some of which are used in the cooking), or try the hearty *plat du jour,* invariably a traditional Belgian dish offered at lunchtime only. Specialties of the house are roast suckling pig in a mustard sauce, and cod filet in a Hoegaarden (Belgian white beer) sauce. In fine weather, chairs are generally set beneath a cluster of plane trees in a little park just across the street.

Rue du Vieux Marché aux Grains 6 (at rue Ste-Catherine). ✆ **02/513-08-68.** www.paonroyal.com. Main courses 15€–26€. AE, DC, MC, V. Tues–Sat 11:30am–9:30pm. Métro: Ste-Catherine.

The European District

MODERATE

Le Stévin BELGIAN/FRENCH If you're experiencing an uncontrollable desire to rub shoulders with the European Union's politicos and bureaucrats—including an occasional commissioner or government minister from an EU member state—this tranquil town house is the place to go. True, that's not much of a recommendation, but fine food can make all the difference. Belgian specialties are prepared in a light, modern way that makes a pleasant change from the weightbound portions in traditional Belgian eateries. Have a premeal drink at an Art Deco bar, and in fine weather, dine alfresco in a garden at the back. The traditional wood-paneled setting features antique furnishings and old pictures of Brussels. Popular dishes here are sole, red mullet, and grilled or roast lamb. Wild mushrooms make a nice accompaniment for any of these meat and fish dishes.

Rue St-Quentin 29 (off Sq. Ambiorix). ✆ **02/230-98-47.** www.le-stevin.com. Main courses 15€–30€; fixed-price menus 20€–24€. AE, DC, MC, V. Mon–Fri noon–2:30pm and 7–11:30pm. Métro: Schuman.

South Brussels

VERY EXPENSIVE

Villa Lorraine ★★ TRADITIONAL FRENCH You'll find one of the city's top kitchens in this renovated château on the fringes of the Bois de la Cambre park. The dining rooms are spacious, with wicker furnishings, flower arrangements, and a skylight. In good weather, enjoy drinks outside under the trees. Among the classic French offerings are saddle of lamb in a delicate red wine–and-herb sauce, cold salmon in an herb sauce, partridge cooked with apples, and baked lobster with butter rose.

Av. Du Vivier d'Orie 75. ✆ **02/374-31-63.** www.villalorraine.be. Main courses 38€–95€; fixed-price lunch 45€, dinner 85€–100€. AE, DC, MC, V. Mon–Sat noon–3:30pm and 7–9:30pm. Closed 3 weeks in July. Bus: 41 to Gendarmes.

SEEING THE SIGHTS

Brussels has such a variety of things to see and do that it can sometimes be overwhelming. There are more than 75 museums dedicated to just about every special interest under the sun, in addition to impressive public buildings, leafy parks, and interesting squares. History is just around every corner. Fortunately, numerous sidewalk cafes offer respite for weary feet, and there's good public transportation to those attractions beyond walking distance of the compact, heart-shaped center city, which contains many of Brussels's most popular attractions.

The City's Principal Squares

GRAND-PLACE ★★★

Ornamental gables, medieval banners, gilded facades, sunlight flashing off gold-filigreed rooftop sculptures, a general impression of harmony and timelessness—there's

Free Culture

Be sure to take advantage of the free admission some museums offer on the first Wednesday afternoon of every month.

Arc du Cinquantenaire **28**
Atomium **2**
Autoworld **31**
Bois de la Cambre **34**
Bourse **7**
Bruxella 1238 **6**
Cathédrale des Sts-Michel-et-Gudule **26**
Centre Belge de la Bande Dessinée **4**
Eglise Notre-Dame du Sablon **17**
Eglise St-Jacques-sur-Coudenberg **21**
Eglise St-Nicolas **8**
European District **32**
Forêt de Soignes **35**
Grand-Place **10**
Hôtel de Ville (Town Hall) **11**
Hôtel Ravenstein **23**
Jardin Botanique **3**
Manneken-Pis **14**
Mini-Europe **1**
Musée de la Brasserie **12**
Musée de la Ville de Bruxelles **9**
Musée du Cinquantenaire **29**
Musée du Costume et de la Dentelle **13**
Musée Horta **36**
Musée Magritte **20**
Musée René Magritte **39**
Musée Royal de l'Afrique Centrale **33**
Musée Royal de l'Armée et d'Histoire Militaire **30**
Musées Royaux des Beaux-Arts de Belgique **18**
Palais de Justice **37**
Palais de la Nation **25**
Palais Royal **22**
Parc de Bruxelles **24**
Parc du Cinquantenaire **27**
place des Martyrs **5**
place du Grand Sablon **15**
place du Petit Sablon **16**
place Royale **19**
Porte de Hal **38**

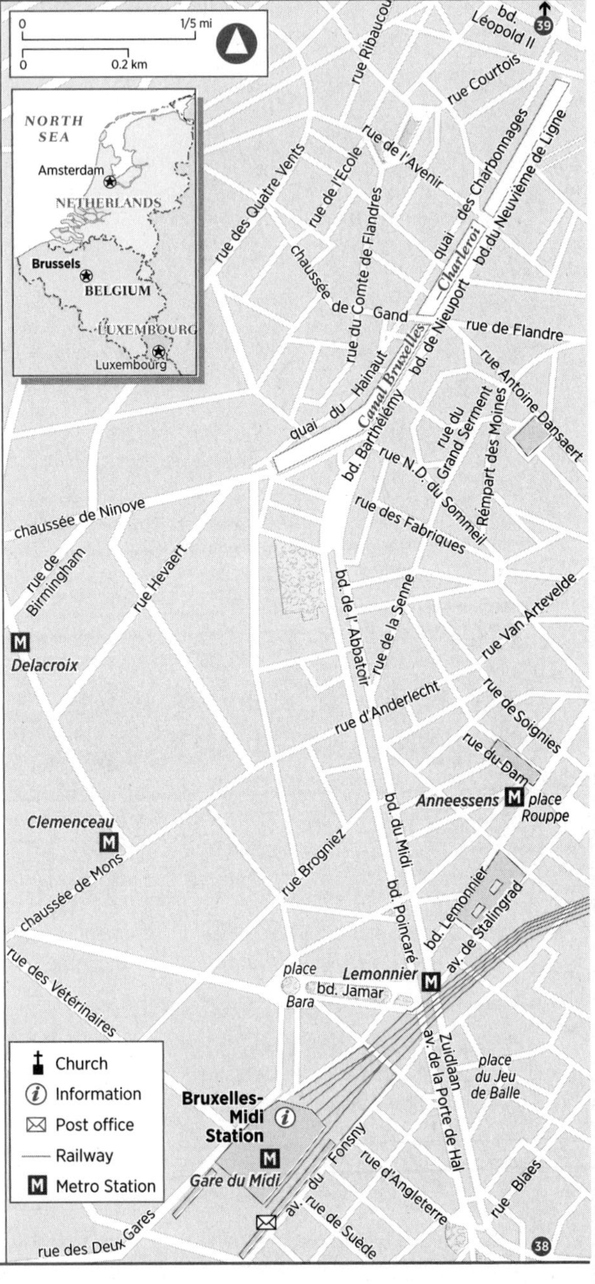

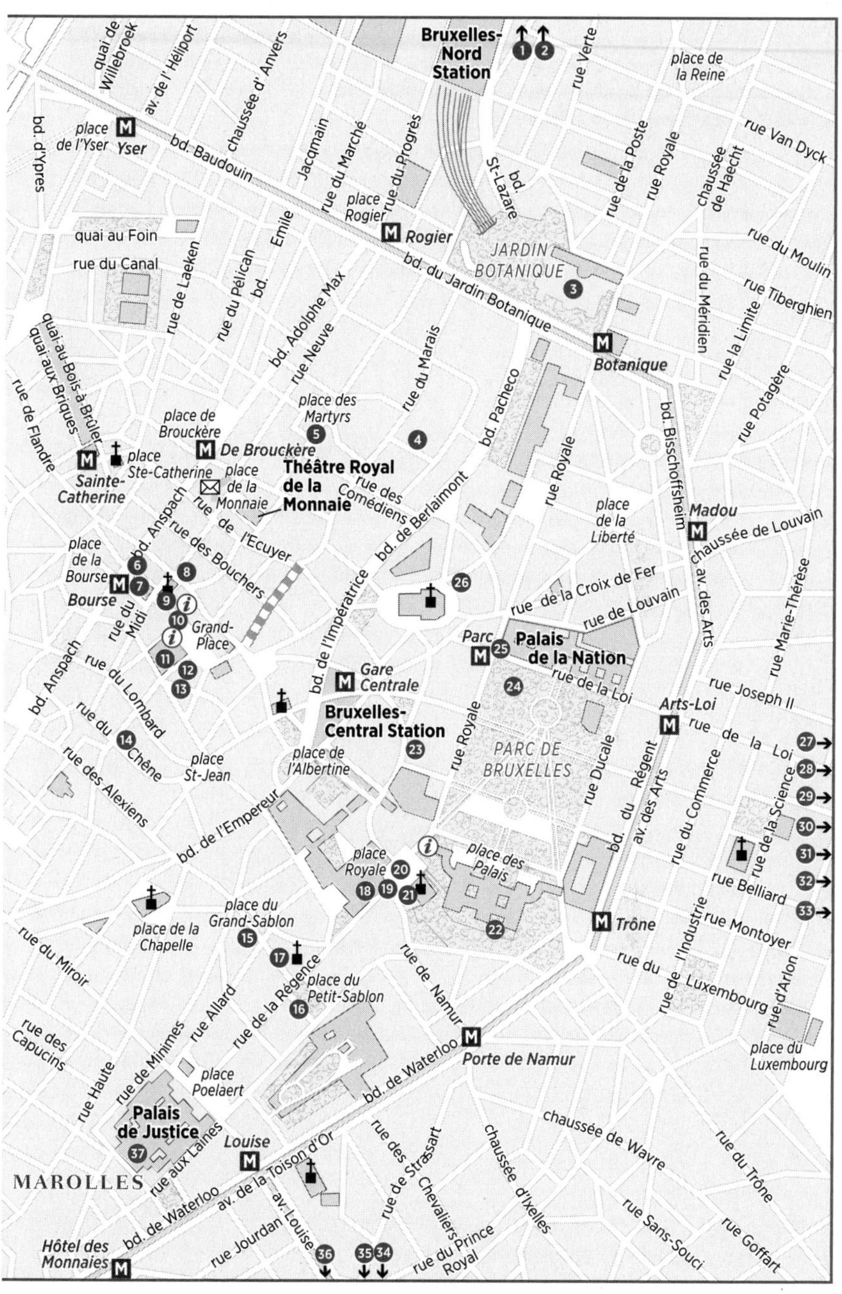
Bruxelles-Nord Station
Bruxelles-Central Station
Théâtre Royal de la Monnaie
Palais de la Nation
Palais de Justice
JARDIN BOTANIQUE
PARC DE BRUXELLES
MAROLLES
Grand-Place
place Rogier
place de Brouckère
place des Martyrs
place Ste-Catherine
place de la Monnaie
place de la Bourse
place de la Liberté
place de la Reine
place de l'Yser
place St-Jean
place de l'Albertine
place Royale
place des Palais
place du Grand-Sablon
place du Petit-Sablon
place de la Chapelle
place Poelaert
place du Luxembourg
Yser
Rogier
Botanique
De Brouckère
Sainte-Catherine
Bourse
Madou
Parc
Gare Centrale
Arts-Loi
Trône
Porte de Namur
Louise
Hôtel des Monnaies
bd. Baudouin
bd. du Jardin Botanique
bd. d'Ypres
bd. Adolphe Max
bd. Emile Jacqmain
bd. Anspach
bd. Pacheco
bd. de Berlaimont
bd. de l'Impératrice
bd. de l'Empereur
bd. Bischoffsheim
bd. du Régent
bd. de Waterloo
bd. St-Lazare
quai de Willebroek
quai au Foin
quai au Bois-à-Brûler
quai aux Briques
av. de l' Héliport
av. des Arts
av. de la Toison d'Or
av. Louise
chaussée d' Anvers
chaussée de Haecht
chaussée de Louvain
chaussée de Wavre
chaussée d'Ixelles
rue du Marché
rue du Progrès
rue Verte
rue de la Poste
rue Royale
rue Van Dyck
rue du Moulin
rue Tiberghien
rue du Méridien
rue la Limite
rue Potagère
rue du Canal
rue de Laeken
rue du Pélican
rue Neuve
rue du Marais
rue de Flandre
rue des Comédiens
rue de l'Ecuyer
rue des Bouchers
rue du Midi
rue du Lombard
rue du Chêne
rue des Alexiens
rue de la Croix de Fer
rue de Louvain
rue de la Loi
rue Joseph II
rue Marie-Thérèse
rue Ducale
rue du Commerce
rue de la Science
rue Belliard
rue Montoyer
rue de l'Industrie
rue du Luxembourg
rue d'Arlon
rue de Namur
rue de la Régence
rue Allard
rue de Minimes
rue Haute
rue du Miroir
rue des Capucins
rue aux Laines
rue Jourdan
rue de Stassart
rue des Chevaliers
rue du Prince Royal
rue du Trône
rue Sans-Souci
rue Goffart
1 2 3 4 5 6 7 8 9 10 11 12 13 14 15 16 17 18 19 20 21 22 23 24 25 26 27 28 29 30 31 32 33 34 35 36 37

Up Close & Personal

In styles ranging from Gothic through Flemish Renaissance and baroque to neo-Gothic, the Grand-Place has a wealth of architectural and decorative elements. Bring a small pair of binoculars so you won't miss even the tiniest details.

a lot to take in all at once when you first enter the **Grand-Place** (Métro: Gare Centrale or Bourse). Once the pride of the Habsburg Empire, the Grand-Place has always been the heart of Brussels. Jean Cocteau called it "a splendid stage."

Its present composition dates mostly from the late 1690s, thanks to France's Louis XIV: In 1695 his army lined up its artillery on the heights of Anderlecht and blasted away at the medieval Grand-Place, using the Town Hall spire as a target marker. The French gunners destroyed the square, but ironically the Town Hall spire escaped undamaged. The timber-fronted buildings of the city's trading and mercantile guilds were not so fortunate. But the Bruxellois weren't about to let a mere French king do away with their centuries-old corporate headquarters. The guildsmen had the place up and running again within 4 years, on the same grand scale as before but in the baroque style known as the Flemish Renaissance. The Town Hall, though badly damaged by Louis's guns, is the real thing, however, dating from the early 1400s.

Don't miss the cafes lodged within the opulent wood-beamed interiors of old guild houses; their upper-floor windows overlooking the Grand-Place give some of the best views in Europe. And be sure to take in the ***son-et-lumière*** on summer evenings. This sound-and-light show, in which a series of colored lamps on the Hôtel de Ville (Town Hall) are switched on and off in sequence to appropriately grand music, is admittedly kind of kitsch. But who cares? It's magical.

Top honors go to the Gothic **Hôtel de Ville (Town Hall)** and the neo-Gothic **Maison du Roi (King's House),** which houses the **Musée de la Ville de Bruxelles** (**Museum of the City of Brussels).** See below for info on these.

A Detailed Tour of the Grand-Place

The Grand-Place deserves both a generalized visual sweep to absorb the ensemble, and a close-up perusal of the myriad details. Going clockwise around from rue de la Colline, you begin with nos. 13–19, a harmonious array of seven mansions behind a single facade, known as the **Maison des Ducs de Brabant (House of the Dukes of Brabant)** ★. The house dates from 1698 and is adorned with busts of 19 dukes on the pilasters, and it has a curved pediment below which is a sculptured allegory of Abundance. The seven mansions are: no. 19, La Bourse (the Stock Exchange)—not to be confused with the city's main Bourse (see "Important Buildings & Monuments," below); no. 18, La Colline (the Hill), formerly the Stonemasons' Guild House; no. 17, Le Pot d'Etain (the Pewter Tankard), formerly the Carpenters' Guild House; no. 16, Le Moulin à Vent (the Windmill), formerly the Millers' Guild House; no. 15, La Fortune (Fortune), formerly the Tanners' Guild House—the traditional Belgian restaurant **'t Kelderke** is in the cellar (p. 99); no. 14, L'Ermitage (the Hermitage), also known as L'Ecrevisse (the Crayfish); and no. 13, La Renommé (Fame). Next door, no. 12A is a private residence called **L'Alsemberg.**

Cross over rue des Chapeliers. On this side of the Grand-Place are two relatively unadorned private homes: **Le Mont Thabor,** from 1699, at no. 12, named after Mt.

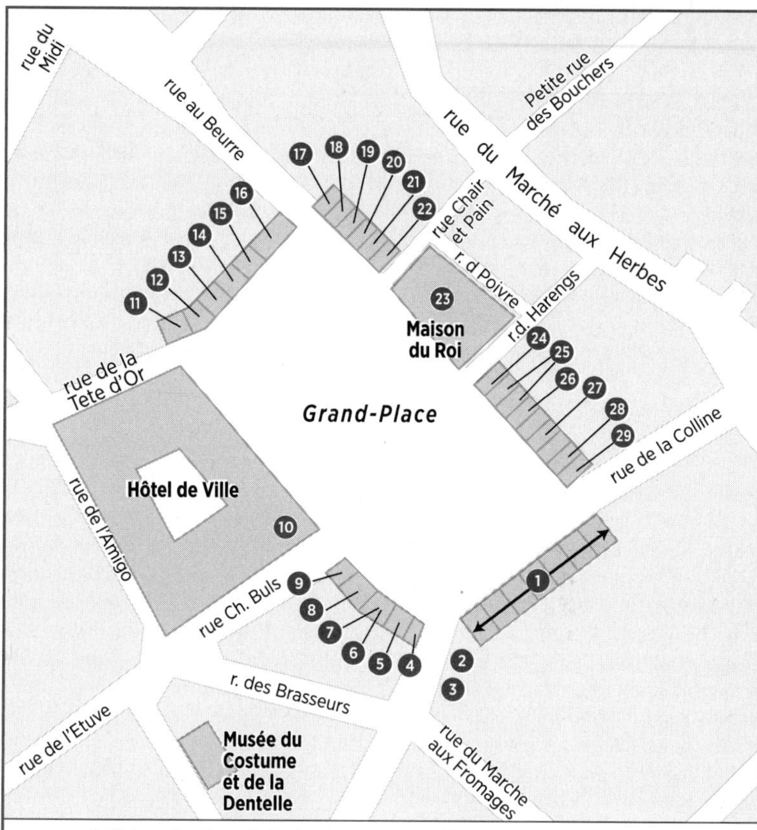

1 Maison des Ducs de Brabant
2 't Kelderke
3 L'Alsemberg
4 Le Mont Thabor
5 La Rose
6 L'Arbre d'Or
7 Musée de la Brasserie
8 Le Cygne
9 L'Etoile
10 Hôtel de Ville
11 Le Renard
12 Le Cornet
13 La Louve
14 Le Sac
15 La Brouette
16 Le Roy d'Espagne
17 L'Ane
18 Ste-Barbe
19 Le Chêne
20 Le Peitit Renard
21 Le Paon
22 Le Heaume
23 Maison du Roi
24 La Chambrette de l'Amman
25 Le Pigeon
26 La Chaloupe d'Or
27 L'Ange
28 Joseph et Anne
29 Le Cerf

Tabor in Israel, where Christians believe the Transfiguration of Jesus took place; and **La Rose (the Rose),** from 1702, at no. 11, named for the Van der Rosen family who lived in an earlier incarnation of the house during the 15th century, and which now houses the rustic Belgian bistro La Rose Blanche.

Continuing around, no. 10, dubbed **L'Arbre d'Or (the Golden Tree),** from 1698, is headquarters of the Brewers' Guild and is the location of the neat little **Musée de la Brasserie** (p. 115). On the roof is a gilded equestrian sculpture from 1901 of Duke Charles of Lorraine. The next house, no. 9, also from 1698, is known as **Le Cygne (the Swan),** for the sculptured swan above the doorway. Formerly the Butchers' Guild House, it now houses the refined restaurant **La Maison du Cygne** (p. 96), and the entrance is around the corner on rue Charles Buls. Standing as if on stilts, no. 8, **L'Etoile (the Star),** is a small house that was built in 1897 over the archway on rue Charles Buls. Do what every visitor does here and ensure good luck by rubbing the bronze deathbed sculpture of Everard 't Serclaes, a 14th-century local hero who freed the city from the counts of Flanders and died resisting another would-be conqueror.

The monumental Gothic building across rue Charles Buls is the **Hôtel de Ville (Town Hall),** a glorious statement of Brussels's medieval pride and prestige (p. 111).

Cross over rue de la Tête d'Or. No. 7, **Le Renard (the Fox),** formerly the Haberdashers' Guild House, dates from 1699. Look for reliefs of typical haberdashery tasks on the busy facade, along with sculptures representing Africa, Europe, Asia, and the Americas, and on the roof a statue of St. Nicholas, the guild's patron saint. Among the most interesting houses on the square is no. 6, the Italian-Flemish **Le Cornet (the Horn),** from 1697, which takes its name from a relief of a horn above the doorway. This was the Boatmens' Guild House, as you might well guess from the nautical images on the facade and the pediment in the shape of a sailing ship's stern. Images of ancient Rome adorn the facade of no. 5, **La Louve (the She-Wolf)**—also in the Italian-Flemish style, from 1696—among them the classic image of Romulus and Remus being suckled by a she-wolf. Look out also for the medallions of emperors Trajan, Tiberius, Augustus, and Julius Caesar, on a building that was the Archers' Guild House.

No. 4, **Le Sac (the Sack),** formerly the Carpenters' and Coopers' Guild House, is notable in that the lower floors survived the 1695 bombardment, and this part of the house dates from 1644. The post-bombardment rebuilding of the upper floors followed the original style. Likewise, no. 3, **La Brouette (the Wheelbarrow),** survived the French guns more or less intact, though the 1645 facade was embellished in later years, and there's a sculpture of St. Gilles, the guild's patron saint, on the gable of what's now a tavern.

The Bakers' Guild clearly wasn't short of cash in those days, and they invested plenty in their guild house at no. 1–2, **Le Roy d'Espagne (the King of Spain) ★,** from 1697. A neoclassical Italianate look extends to a cupola surmounted by a gilded weather vane. Medallions sport images of Roman emperors Marcus Aurelius, Nerva, Decius, and Trajan. This ornate building houses one of Brussels's finest cafes, so be sure to invest some time in a drink at one of the upstairs tables, looking out on the grand cobbled square.

Cross over rue au Beurre. The houses from nos. 39 to 34 form the plainest segment on the Grand-Place, allowing you a break from detailed facade-perusing. From left to right, the six are called **L'Ane (the Donkey), Ste-Barbe (St. Barbara), Le Chêne (the Oak Tree), Le Peitit Renard (the Little Fox), Le Paon (the Peacock),** and **Le Heaume (the Helmet).** Across rue Chair et Pain is the neo-Gothic **Maison du Roi (King's House),** which houses the city museum (p. 111).

Moving on across rue des Harengs, you arrive at the final segment. No. 28 has a strange name (even by Grand-Place standards): It's called **La Chambrette de l'Amman (the Little Chamber of the Amman),** and it dates from 1709. The Amman was the name for a kind of early mayor, a minion of the dukes of Brabant. An alternate name is Le Marchand d'Or (the Gold Merchant), because it was once a gold merchant's premises. No. 26–27, **Le Pigeon (the Pigeon),** from 1697, was the Painters' Guild House. In the 1850s, Victor Hugo spent part of his time in exile from France here, firing off literary broadsides at Napoleon III until the City Fathers told him to leave town. Now the house is home to a fine lace store, the **Maison Antoine** (p. 125), and a branch of Neuhaus pralines.

St. Boniface, a native of Brussels, blesses passersby from the roof of no. 24–25, known as **La Chaloupe d'Or (the Golden Sloop),** or the Maison des Tailleurs (House of the Tailors), whose guild house it once was. Nowadays, under its first-mentioned name, it's another of the Grand-Place's standout cafes. A bust of St. Barbara, the patroness of tailors, is above the doorway of what is now the deluxe lace store Rubbrecht Dentelles. No. 23, **L'Ange (the Angel),** from 1697, is a private house in the Italian-Flemish style, graced by Doric and Ionic pilasters. Nos. 21–22 and 20, respectively known as **Joseph et Anne (Joseph and Anne),** from 1700, and **Le Cerf (the Stag),** from 1710, are relatively plain private dwellings. Godiva Chocolates now sets out its store in the Joseph et Anne, and Le Cerf is a traditional Belgian restaurant.

PLACE DU GRAND SABLON ★

Though the traffic passing through it diminishes the experience, **place du Grand Sablon** (tram: 92 or 94) is filled with sidewalk cafes and lined with gabled mansions. Locals consider it a classier place to see and be seen than the Grand-Place. The Grand Sablon is antiques territory; many of its mansions house antiques stores or private art galleries with pricey merchandise on display. The dealerships have spread onto neighboring side streets as well. The statue of Minerva on the square dates from 1751. Saturday and Sunday mornings, an excellent antiques market sets up its stalls in front of **Notre-Dame du Sablon** (**© 02/511-57-41**). This flamboyantly Gothic church, with no fewer than five naves, was paid for by the city's Guild of Crossbowmen in the 15th century. The church is open Monday to Friday from 9am to 5pm, and weekends from 10am to 6:30pm. Admission is free.

PLACE DU PETIT SABLON

Just across rue de la Régence is the Grand Sablon's little cousin, **place du Petit Sablon** (tram: 92 or 94). An ornamental garden with a fountain and pool, it's a magical little retreat from the city bustle. The 48 bronze statuettes adorning the surrounding wrought-iron fence symbolize Brussels's medieval guilds. Two statues in the center commemorate the Catholic counts of Egmont and Hornes, who were beheaded in 1568 for protesting the cruelties of Spain's Holy Inquisition in the Low Countries.

PLACE ROYALE

Brussels's royal square, **place Royale** (tram: 92 or 94), is at the meeting point of rue de la Régence and rue Royale, two streets that hold many of the city's premier sights. The 18th-century square, which was laid out in neoclassical style, is graced by a heroic **equestrian statue** of the leader of the First Crusade, Duke Godefroid de Bouillon. The inscription describes him as the "First King of Jerusalem," a title Godefroid himself refused, accepting instead that of "Protector of the Holy Places" (which amounted to the same thing). On the north face of the square is the **Eglise St-Jacques-sur-Coudenberg.** Archaeologists have excavated the foundations of the Royal Palace of Emperor Charles V on the square, and the site has been covered over again.

PLACE DES MARTYRS

Some years back, the once-elegant 18th-century **place des Martyrs** (Métro: Brouckère), in the lower city near the Théâtre Royal de la Monnaie, was in a sorry state, literally crumbling to the ground. It entombs the "500 Martyrs" of Belgium's 1830 War of Independence. The square has been extensively restored, and though it lost some of its former ragged charm in the process, the square is once again an important and attractive public place.

Important Buildings & Monuments

The celebrated ***Manneken-Pis*** statue ★, on the corner of rue du Chêne and rue de l'Etuve (Métro: Gare Centrale), 2 blocks from the Grand-Place, is Brussels's favorite little boy, gleefully doing what a little boy's gotta do. More often than not, he's watched by a throng of admirers snapping pictures. Children especially seem to enjoy his bravura performance; adults, on the other hand, are more inclined to wonder what all the fuss is about. This is not the original statue, which was prone to theft and anatomical maltreatment and was removed for safekeeping.

It's known that the boy's effigy has graced the city since at least the time of Philip the Good, who became count of Flanders in 1419. Among the speculations about the boy's origins are that he was the son of a Brussels nobleman who got lost and was found while answering nature's call; another is that he was a patriotic Belgian kid who sprinkled a hated Spanish sentry passing beneath his window. Perhaps the best theory is that he saved the Town Hall from a sputtering bomb by extinguishing it—like Gulliver—with the first thing handy.

Louis XV of France began the tradition of presenting colorful costumes to "Little Julian" to make amends for the French abduction of the statue in 1747. Since then the statue has acquired around 800 outfits, which are housed in the Musée de la Ville on the Grand-Place.

The ornately decorated **Bourse (Stock Exchange),** rue Henri Maus 2 (✆ **02/509-12-11;** Métro: Bourse), at boulevard Anspach, a landmark of the French Second Empire architectural style, dates from 1873. It's a temple to the venerable religion of making money and is not open to casual visitors. Along its north facade, on rue de la Bourse, visit the interesting little **Bruxella 1238** museum (see below).

You may not want to spend too much time around the **Palais de Justice (Palace of Justice),** place Poelaert (✆ **02/508-65-78;** Métro: Louise), adjacent to place Louise. This is, after all, where people who have run afoul of the law go directly to jail. Nonetheless, it's worth viewing architect Joseph Poelaert's extravagant (some would say megalomaniacal) 19th-century neoclassical temple dedicated to the might

The Lost River

Believe it or not, Brussels is constructed on a river called the Senne. In the 19th century, the City Fathers had it covered up, but traces of the missing river can still be seen at courtyards off place St-Géry in the Lower Town.

Impressions

The principal [fountain] whereof is the Mannicke Piss, being the figure of a brass boy erected upon a pedestal, the water issuing from his privy member (at a good distance) into a stone cistern.

—William Lord Fitzwilliam, *Touring the Low Countries: Accounts of British Travellers, 1660–1720,* Amsterdam University Press

and majesty of the law. The palace's domed magnificence stands on the old Galgenberg hill, once an open-air place of execution where criminals were hanged in public. It looms over the rebellious, working-class Marolles district, a none-too-subtle warning. A modern elevator out on the palace's esplanade brings you down the steep hillside to the Marolles. Visit the reception hall of the palace, which is open Monday to Friday from 9 to 11:30am and 1:30 to 3pm. Admission is free.

Not much has survived of the architecture of Burgundian-era Brussels; even most of the royal palace of the Burgundians and their Habsburg successors bit the dust due to fire. Part of the 15th- to 16th-century palace survives aboveground, 2 blocks east of Gare Centrale, in the redbrick **Hôtel Ravenstein,** rue Ravenstein 1–3 (Métro: Gare Centrale). Like the Hôtel de Ville, this is not a hotel at all. It houses a professional institute and the fancy French restaurant Le Relais des Caprices. But it does give you some idea of what Burgundian Brussels looked like—at least in those parts of the city occupied by the blue bloods.

The only surviving gateway from Brussels's once imposing 14th-century defensive walls is the squat and imposing **Porte de Hal,** at the junction of avenue de la Porte de Hal and chaussée de Waterloo (Métro: Porte de Hal).

The Top Museums & Attractions

Hôtel de Ville (Town Hall) ★★ The facade of the dazzling Town Hall, from 1402, shows off Gothic intricacy at its best, complete with dozens of arched windows and sculptures—some of these, like the drunken monks, a sleeping Moor and his harem, and St. Michael slaying a female devil, displaying a sense of humor. A tower 66m (215 ft.) high sprouts near the middle, yet it's not placed directly in the center. A colorful but untrue legend has it that when the architect realized his "error," he jumped from the summit of the tower.

Visit the interior on 40-minute tours, which start in a room full of paintings of the past foreign rulers of Brussels, who have included the Spanish, Austrians, French, and Dutch. The spectacular mirrored Gothic Hall, open for visits when the city's aldermen are not in session, has baroque decoration. In other chambers are 16th- to 18th-century tapestries. One of these depicts the Spanish duke of Alba, whose cruel features reflect the brutal oppression he and his Council of Blood imposed on the Low Countries; others show scenes from the life of Clovis, first king of the Franks.

Grand-Place. ✆ **02/548-04-42.** Admission (for guided tours only) 3€ adults, 2.50€ seniors and students, 1.50€ children 6–15, free for children 5 and under. Guided tours in English Apr–Sept Tues–Wed 3:15pm, Sun 10:45am and 12:15pm; Oct–Mar Tues–Wed 3:15pm; tours at other times in French or Dutch. Closed Jan 1, May 1, Nov 1 and 11, and Dec 25. Métro: Gare Centrale.

Musée de la Ville de Bruxelles (Museum of the City of Brussels) ★ This museum is in the neo-Gothic Maison du Roi (King's House), which, despite its name, never housed a king. Exhibits inside document the history of Brussels. Among the

COMIC murals

No fewer than 44 (and counting) large comic-strip murals and sculptures have been scattered around Brussels since the city began in 1993 to celebrate Belgium's passionate love affair with *bande-dessinée* (comic-strip art). Among the cartoon characters honored on the sides of houses and other ordinary buildings are Tintin (rue de l'Etuve 37; Métro: Bourse), running down a fire escape together with Captain Haddock and Snowy, as if searching for the nearby *Manneken-Pis;* Lucky Luke (rue de la Buanderie 21; Métro: Anneessens), as always drawing his Colt faster than his shadow; and just along the street, Asterix and Obelix (rue de la Buanderie 33; Métro: Anneessens), leading a charge of the gallant Gauls against the rotten Romans.

There's a catch for visitors who want to take in as many of these heroic figures as possible: A lot of them are in off-the-beaten-track districts. Getting there will give you an idea of what Brussels looks like away from its tourist heartlands—not greatly inspiring, it must be said—at the cost of a great deal of Métro-, tram-, and bus-hopping, and considerable shoe leather. Both the Brussels International tourist office (see "Visitor Information" under "Orientation," earlier in this chapter) and the Centre Belge de la Bande-Dessinée (see below) have information on the mural locations, which have been put together as a *Parcours BD* (Comic-Strip Tour). In addition, the English version of the Brussels city website (www.brussels.be) has pictures of the murals; look under Photo Albums/Admiring Brussels/Comic Book Walls in Brussels.

most fascinating displays are old paintings and modern scale reconstructions of the historic center city, particularly those depicting riverside activity along the now-vanished Senne. There are exhibits on traditional arts and crafts, such as tapestry and lace. The museum is most proud of its 800 costumes—among them an Elvis suit—donated to outfit Brussels's famous *Manneken-Pis* statue; each one is equipped with a strategically positioned orifice so that the little sculpture's normal function is not impaired.

Grand-Place 1. ✆ **02/279-43-50.** www.brusselsmuseums.be. Admission 3€ adults, 2.50€ seniors and students, 1.50€ visitors with limited mobility and children 6–15, free for children 5 and under. Tues–Sun 10am–5pm. Closed Jan 1, May 1, Nov 1 and 11, and Dec 25. Métro: Gare Centrale.

Musées Royaux des Beaux-Arts de Belgique (Belgian Royal Fine Arts Museums) ★★★ In a vast museum of several buildings, this complex combines the **Musée d'Art Ancien** and the **Musée d'Art Moderne** under one roof, as well as the Musée Magritte (connected by a passage; p. 116). The collection shows off works, most of them Belgian, from the 14th to the 20th centuries. In the historical section are Hans Memling portraits from the late 15th century, which are marked by sharp lifelike details; works by Hieronymus Bosch; and Lucas Cranach's *Adam and Eve*. You should particularly seek out the subsequent rooms featuring Pieter Bruegel the Elder, including his *Adoration of the Magi* and *Fall of Icarus*. Don't miss his unusual *Fall of the Rebel Angels,* with grotesque faces and beasts. But don't fear—many of Bruegel's paintings, like those depicting Flemish village life, are of a less fiery nature. Later artists represented here include Rubens, van Dyck, Frans Hals, and Rembrandt.

Next door, in a circular building connected to the main entrance, the modern art section has an emphasis on underground works—if only because the museum's eight floors are all below ground level. The overwhelming collection includes works by van Gogh, Matisse, Dalí, Tanguy, Ernst, Chagall, and Miró, as well as local boys Magritte, Delvaux, De Braekeleer, and Permeke.

If you want to do this fantastic museum any kind of justice at all, you'll need 3 to 4 hours; a serious art lover won't bat an eyelid at spending a full day, taking time out only for lunch. In fast-track mode, you could do the Bruegel, Rubens, and Magritte collections in an hour.

Place Royale 1-3. ✆ **02/508-32-11.** www.fine-arts-museum.be. Admission 8€ adults; 5€ students, seniors, and visitors with disabilities; free for children 11 and under; free for everyone 1st Wed afternoon of the month (except during special exhibits). Tues–Sun 10am–5pm. Closed Jan 1, May 1, Nov 1 and 11, and Dec 25. Métro: Parc.

Palais Royal (Royal Palace) ★ The King's Palace, which overlooks the Parc de Bruxelles, was begun in 1820 and had a grandiose Louis XVI–style face-lift in 1904. The older side wings date from the 18th century and are flanked by two pavilions, one of which sheltered numerous notables during the 1800s. Today the palace is used for state receptions. It contains the offices of King Albert II, though he and Queen Paola do not live there—their *pied à terre* is the Royal Palace at Laeken. The national flag flies when the sovereign is in Belgium.

Place des Palais. ✆ **02/551-20-20.** www.monarchie.be. Free admission. From 3rd week of July to late Sept (exact dates announced yearly). Tues–Sun 10:30am–4:30pm. Métro: Parc.

Parc du Cinquantenaire ★

Designed to celebrate the half-centenary of Belgium's 1830 independence, the Cinquantenaire (Golden Jubilee) Park was a work in progress from the 1870s until well into the 20th century. Extensive gardens have at their heart a triumphal arch, the **Arc du Cinquantenaire,** topped by a bronze quadriga (four-horse chariot) sculpture, representing *Brabant Raising the National Flag,* and flanked by pavilions that house several fine museums.

Autoworld ☺ Even if you're not a car enthusiast, you'll likely find this display of 500 historic cars set in the hangarlike Palais Mondial fascinating. The collection starts with early motorized tricycles from 1899 and moves on to a 1911 Model T Ford, a 1924 Renault, a 1938 Cadillac that was the official White House car for FDR and Truman, a 1956 Cadillac used by Eisenhower and then by Kennedy during his June 1963 visit to Berlin, and more.

Parc du Cinquantenaire 11. ✆ **02/736-41-65.** www.autoworld.be. Admission 6€ adults, 4.70€ students and seniors, 3€ children 6–13, free for children 5 and under. Apr–Sept daily 10am–6pm; Oct–Mar daily 10am–5pm. Closed Jan 1 and Dec 25. Métro: Mérode.

Musée du Cinquantenaire ★ This vast museum shows off an eclectic collection of antiques, decorative arts (sculptures, tapestries, lace, porcelain, silver, furniture, toys, stained glass, jewels, folklore, and old vehicles including 18th-century coupes, sedan chairs, sleighs, and royal coaches), and archaeology. Some highlights are an Assyrian relief from the 9th century B.C., a Greek vase from the 6th century B.C., a tabletop model of imperial Rome in the 4th century A.D., the A.D. 1145 reliquary of Pope Alexander, some exceptional tapestries, and colossal statues from Easter Island.

Parc du Cinquantenaire 10. ✆ **02/741-72-11.** www.kmkg-mrah.be. Admission 5€ adults; 4€ students, seniors, and children 13–17; 1.50€ visitors with disabilities; free for children 12 and under; free admission every 1st Wed afternoon of the month (except during special exhibits). Tues–Fri 9:30am–5pm; Sat–Sun and holidays 10am–5pm. Closed Jan 1, May 1, Nov 1 and 11, and Dec 25. Métro: Mérode.

Drive-In Movie Palace

In summer the Arc du Cinquantenaire becomes the backdrop for the screen of a drive-in movie theater set around the fountain between the Porte de Tervuren and the Palais du Cinquantenaire.

Musée Royal de l'Armée et d'Histoire Militaire (Royal Museum of the Armed Forces and Military History) ☺ Because Belgium is not and never has been a great military power, this is one of Brussels's often forgotten museums. But its huge collection is one of the finest in Europe. It includes an extensive display of armor, uniforms, and weapons from various Belgian campaigns (like the Congo), a massive amount of World War I artillery, an aircraft hangar of 130 impressive planes (among them a Spitfire and a Hurricane that recall Belgian pilots' gallant service with the Royal Air Force during the Battle of Britain in 1940), and a World War II collection of Nazi flags that brings to mind the Nürnberg rallies. Anyone interested in military history shouldn't miss this superb though cluttered collection.

Parc du Cinquantenaire 3 (opposite Autoworld). ✆ **02/737-78-11.** www.klm-mra.be. Free admission. Tues–Sun 9am–noon and 1–4:45pm. Closed Jan 1, May 1, Nov 1, and Dec 25. Métro: Merode.

Sights of Religious Significance

Cathédrale des Sts-Michel-et-Gudule ★ Victor Hugo considered this magnificent church, dedicated to the city's patron, St. Michael, and to St. Gudula, to be the "purest flowering of the Gothic style." Its choir is Belgium's earliest Gothic work. Begun in 1226, it was officially consecrated as a cathedral only in 1961. The 16th-century Habsburg Emperor Charles V donated the superb stained-glass windows. Apart from these, the spare interior decoration focuses attention on soaring columns and arches. The bright exterior stonework makes a fine sight. On Sunday at 10am, the Eucharist is celebrated with a Gregorian choir. In July, August, and September, polyphonic Masses are sung by local and international choirs at 10am. From August to October, chamber-music and organ concerts are occasionally performed on weekdays at 8pm. In spring and autumn at 12:30pm, Mass is sung accompanied by instrumental soloists and readings by actors (in French).

In the crypt and an associated archaeological zone are foundations and other construction elements from an earlier church dating from the 11th century. The Trésor (Treasury) is also worth visiting, for its religious vessels in gold, silver, precious stones, and ecclesiastical vestments.

Parvis Ste-Gudule (off bd. de l'Impératrice 2 blocks west of Gare Centrale). ✆ **02/217-83-45.** www.cathedralestmichel.be. Admission: cathedral free; crypt, archaeological zone 2.50€; treasury 1€. Mon–Fri 8am–6pm; Sat–Sun 8:30am–6pm. Métro: Gare Centrale.

Eglise Notre-Dame du Sablon (Church of Our Lady of the Sablon) ★ This flamboyant late-Gothic church, dating from around 1400 to about 1594, was paid for by the city's Guild of Crossbowmen, who optimistically called it Notre-Dame des Victoires (Our Lady of Victories), and it was their guild church. It is noted for its four-fold gallery with brightly colored stained-glass windows, illuminated from the inside at night, in striking contrast with the gray-white arches and walls. Worth seeing are the two baroque chapels decorated with funeral symbols in white marble. Inside is a celebrated statue of St. Hubert with an interesting history: It was actually stolen from Brussels and taken to Antwerp but was seized and returned to the church in 1348, where it has remained ever since.

Rue Bodenbroek 6 (at place du Grand Sablon). ✆ **02/511-57-41.** Free admission. Mon–Fri 9am–5pm; Sat–Sun 10am–6:30pm. Tram: 92 or 94 to Petit Sablon.

Eglise St-Nicolas (Church of St. Nicholas) This delightful little church behind the Bourse is almost hidden by the fine old houses surrounding it, just as its 11th-century Romanesque lines are hidden by a 14th-century Gothic facade and the repairs made after the French bombardment of 1695. The church holds a small painting by Rubens, the *Virgin and Sleeping Child;* a bronze shrine dedicated to the Catholic Martyrs of Gorcum (Gorinchem), tortured and killed by Protestant Dutch rebels in 1572; and the *Vladimir Icon,* painted by an artist from Constantinople in 1131.

Rue au Beurre (facing the Bourse). ✆ **02/513-80-22.** Free admission. Mon–Fri 8am–6:30pm; Sat 9am–6pm; Sun and holidays 9am–7:30pm; closed to casual visitors during services. Métro: Bourse.

More Museums & Attractions

The Brussels Bourse (Stock Exchange) stands on the grounds of a Franciscan convent, Les Récollets, which succumbed over the centuries to wars, fire, and religious conflict. Excavations begun in 1988 uncovered the convent's foundations and a bunch of medieval tombs. There's now a small underground museum, **Bruxella 1238,** rue de la Bourse (✆ **02/279-43-50**), on the site. The most important tomb is that of Duke of Brabant Jean I, who died in 1294. You visit here only on guided tours that depart from the Musée de la Ville (see "Grand-Place" under "The City's Principal Squares," earlier in this chapter), Wednesday 10:15am (English), and 11:15am and 3pm (French). The tour costs 3€.

Jardin Botanique This graceful 19th-century glass-and-wrought-iron palace is no longer the Botanical Gardens of Brussels, but it merits a visit as a monument of 19th-century architecture. There's still a fine ornamental garden outside. Nowadays the Botanique functions as a cultural center in which theater, music and dance performances, and visiting art exhibits are held.

Rue Royale 236 (at bd. du Jardin Botanique). ✆ **02/226-12-11.** Free admission to gardens and main building; admission varies for cultural events. Métro: Botanique.

Musée de la Brasserie (Brewing Museum) Operated by the Confederation of Belgian Breweries, this museum is housed in the Maison des Brasseurs, the home of the Brewers' Guild, the Knights of the Mash Staff. A permanent exhibit on modern

Underground Art

Most of Brussels's Métro stations have been decorated with works of art—a painting, sculpture, mosaic, or installation—by leading Belgian modern artists. Taken together, they form an underground museum that you can tour for the price of a Métro ticket. Among interesting Métro stations are: Bourse, in the center city, which has a mural of old Brussels trams by the surrealist painter Paul Delvaux; Stockel, the eastern terminus of line 1B, where the walls are decorated with strips from the comic series *Tintin,* which was created by local hero Hergé; and Horta, south of Gare du Midi, which pays homage to Brussels's Art Nouveau architect Victor Horta, by way of elements from some of the buildings and interiors he designed.

high-tech brewing methods has joined an old one on traditional techniques. You'll find numerous paintings, stained-glass windows, and collections of pitchers, pint pots, and old china beer pumps. And you get a chance to sample some of your host's finished product.

Grand-Place 10. ✆ **02/511-49-87.** www.beerparadise.be. Admission 5€ adults. Apr–Dec daily 10am–5pm; Jan–Mar Sat–Sun noon–5pm. Closed Jan 1 and Dec 25. Métro: Gare Centrale.

Musée du Costume et de la Dentelle (Costume and Lace Museum) The collections here include fine examples of historical Belgian lace styles from the once-renowned factories of Mechelen, Bruges, Antwerp, Binche, Turnhout, Poperinge, and Sint-Truiden. In addition, the museum houses displays of costumes, including an array of dresses from the 16th to the 19th centuries.

Rue de la Violette 12 (near Grand-Place). ✆ **02/213-44-50.** Admission 3€ adults, 1.50€ children 6–16, free for children 5 and under. Mon–Tues and Thurs–Fri 10am–12:30pm and 1:30–5pm (until 4pm Oct–Mar); Sat–Sun 2–4:30pm. Closed Jan 1, May 1, Nov 1 and 11, and Dec 25. Métro: Gare Centrale.

Musée Horta (Horta Museum) ★ Art Nouveau might take its name from the gallery opened by art dealer Siegfried Bing in Paris in 1895, but Brussels considers itself the capital of this medley of related art styles that burst across the Western world at the end of the 19th century and drew on exotic sources, including Celtic, Viking, Asian, and Islamic art. The city owes much of its rich Art Nouveau heritage to the inspired creative vision of Victor Horta, a resident architect who led the style's development. His home and an adjoining studio have been restored to their original condition and are now a museum. They showcase his use of flowing, sinuous shapes and colors in interior decoration and architecture.

Rue Américaine 25 (off chaussée de Charleroi). ✆ **02/543-04-90.** www.hortamuseum.be. Admission 7€ adults, 3.50€ seniors and students, 2.50€ children 5–18, free for children 4 and under. Tues–Sun 2–5:30pm. Closed holidays. Tram: 81 to Trinité.

Musée Magritte ★★ ***Note:*** This museum should not be confused with the museum in Belgian artist René Magritte's Brussels home (see next item). The Magritte Museum opened in 2009 in the Hôtel Altenloh, a neoclassical mansion dating from 1779 and an aristocratic setting for his fantastical visions that Magritte himself surely would have considered suitably surrealist. Its collection, bequeathed by the Musée d'Art Moderne of the Musées Royaux des Beaux-Arts de Belgique (p. 112), comprises more than 150 works, making it the world's largest Magritte catalog, covering all periods of the artist's oeuvre and the multiple genres to which he applied his imagination and skill. The gallery has divided Magritte's career into three broad phases, providing compelling visual evidence of his artistic evolution and culminating in signature works such as versions of his series *The Dominion of Light* and *The Domain of Arnheim*.

Rue de la Régence 3 (at Coudenberg). ✆ **02/508-32-11.** www.musee-magritte-museum.be. Admission 8€ adults (13€ combination ticket with Musées Royaux des Beaux-Arts de Belgique), 5€ seniors, 2€ students, free for children 17 and under. Tues–Sun 10am–5pm (until 8pm Wed). Closed Jan 1, May 1, Nov 1 and 11, and Dec 25. Métro: Parc.

Musée René Magritte From 1930 to 1954, the great Belgian surrealist artist René Magritte lived and worked in an undistinguished town house in suburban Jette in northwest Brussels. Now restored, that 19-room house is a museum of the artist's life. You're allowed to visit most of the rooms, but you can only view through glass the dining room–cum-studio where he painted many of his fantastical masterpieces while wearing a three-piece suit. You even get to look through the famous window, with a

A Stroll Through the Marolles

The scuzzy Marolles district, lying beneath the long shadow of the Palace of Justice, is a special place where the old Brussels dialect called *Brusseleir* can still be heard. The generally poor community is under constant threat of encroachment and gentrification from neighboring, far wealthier areas—a process the Marolliens seem to want nothing to do with. Locals remain resolutely unimpressed by the burgeoning "capital of Europe."

view of nothing in particular, onto which Magritte projected images that would revolutionize art and the way we look at the world. Be warned, though, that there's little to see—*This is not a studio,* you might think—even though the museum's founders have been diligent in uncovering bits and pieces of the artist's banal private life. On the first and second floors are a few original sketches; his easel and trademark bowler hat; a pipe; his passport; his checkbook and will; household objects; and letters and photographs illustrating his commercial work, negotiations with museums about exhibits, and contacts with art dealers.

Rue Esseghem 135 (off bd. de Smet de Naeyer). ✆ **02/428-26-26.** www.magrittemuseum.be. Admission 7€ adults, 6€ ages 9–23, free for children 8 and under. Wed–Sun 10am–6pm. Closed Jan 1 and Dec 25. Tram: 51 or 94 to Cimetière de Jette.

Musée Royal de l'Afrique Centrale/Koninklijk Museum voor Midden Afrika (Royal Museum of Central Africa) ★★ Originally founded to celebrate Belgium's colonial empire in the Belgian Congo (now the Democratic Republic of Congo), this museum has moved beyond imperialism to feature exhibits on ethnography and environment, mostly in Africa, but also in Asia and South America. The beautiful grounds of this impressive museum are as much a draw as the exhibits inside. The collection includes some excellent animal dioramas, African sculpture, and other artwork, and even some of the colonial-era guns and artillery pieces that no doubt helped make Belgium's claim to its African colonies more persuasive. A modern perspective is added by environmental displays that explain desertification, the loss of rainforests, and the destruction of habitats.

Leuvensesteenweg 13, Tervuren (a suburban Flemish *gemeente*/district just east of Brussels). ✆ **02/769-52-11.** www.africamuseum.be. Admission 4€ adults, 3€ seniors, 1.50€ children 13–17, free for children 12 and under. Tues–Fri 10am–5pm; Sat–Sun 10am–6pm. Closed Jan 1, May 1, and Dec 25. Tram: 44 from Métro Montgomery station to Tervuren terminus.

Palais de la Nation (National Palace) The Parliament building opposite the Parc de Bruxelles is quite an elegant place, if you ignore the politicians squabbling in the Chamber of Representatives and the Senate—bickering, after all, is part of democracy's charm. The building dates from 1783 and was constructed originally to house the Sovereign Council of Brabant. You're permitted to enter only during sessions of either house.

Rue de la Loi 16. ✆ **02/519-81-36.** Free admission. Métro: Parc.

Green Brussels

Brussels is a green city with a great extent of parks and gardens. Once a hunting preserve of the dukes of Brabant, the **Parc de Bruxelles (Brussels Park),** rue Royale (Métro: Parc), between Parliament and the Royal Palace, was laid out in the

Ferry Tale

Taking a ferryboat trip in the Bois de la Cambre is a literal moment. The ferry in question is a tiny, electrically operated pontoon that makes a 1-minute crossing to Robinson's Island in the lake at the heart of the park.

18th century as a landscaped garden. In 1830, Belgian patriots fought Dutch regular troops here during the War of Independence. Later it was a fashionable place to stroll and to meet friends. Although not very big, the park manages to contain everything from carefully trimmed borders to rough patches of trees and bushes, and it has fine views along its main paths, which together with the fountain form the outline of Masonic symbols. Diseased chestnut trees have been cut down and lime trees replaced with sturdier specimens; statues have been restored and cleaned; and the 1840s bandstand by Jean-Pierre Cluysenaer has been refurbished so it now hosts regular summer concerts. The cleanup diminished the various unwholesome nighttime activities in the park.

The big public park called the **Bois de la Cambre** begins at the top of avenue Louise (tram: 94) in the southern section of Brussels. Its centerpiece is a small lake with an island in its center that can be reached by a neat little electrically operated pontoon. The park gets crowded on sunny weekends. A few busy roads with fast-moving traffic run through it, so be careful with children. The **Forêt de Soignes,** south of the Bois, is no longer a park with playing areas and regularly mown grass, but a forest that stretches almost to Waterloo. This is a great place to escape the maddening crowds and fuming traffic, particularly in the fall, when the colors are dazzling.

Especially for Kids

Atomium ★ ☺ There's nothing quite like this cluster of giant spheres representing the atomic structure of an iron crystal enlarged 165 billion times, rising 102m (335 ft.) like a giant plaything of the gods that's fallen to earth. The model was constructed for the 1958 World's Fair. Whatever you think of its founding impulse, it's a fair bet that when you stand underneath this vast schematic, you'll be suitably impressed. There may be something last-century about this paean of praise to the wonders of science and technology, but the Atomium has somehow moved beyond this, taking on a monumental life of its own. The view from the deck on the top sphere is marvelous, and you can even wander around inside the spheres.

Sq. de l'Atomium, Heysel (at Bruparck). ✆ **02/475-47-75.** www.atomium.be. Admission 11€ adults; 8€ seniors, students, and children 12–18; 4€ children 6–11; free for children 5 and under. Daily 10am–6pm. Métro: Heysel.

Centre Belge de la Bande-Dessinée (Belgian Center for Comic-Strip Art) ★★ ☺ Grown-ups will love this place as much as kids do. Called the CéBéBéDé for short, the center, on a side street not far from the Gothic spires and baroque guild houses of the Grand-Place, is dedicated to comic strips and takes a lofty view of what it calls "the Ninth Art." As icing on the cake, it's in a restored Art Nouveau department store from 1903, the Magasins Waucquez (designed by Victor Horta), which was slated for demolition before the center took it over. A model of the red-and-white checkered rocket in which Hergé's Tintin and Snowy flew to the Moon, long before Armstrong and Aldrin did it in mere fact, takes pride of place at the top of the elegant staircase. Beyond is a comic-strip wonderland. All the big names appear in a library of 30,000 books and in permanent and special exhibits, including Tintin, Asterix, Thorgal, Lucky Luke, the Smurfs, Charlie Brown, Andy Capp, Suske and Wiske—yes, even Superman, Batman, and the Green Lantern—along with many lesser heroes.

Rue des Sables 20 (off bd. de Berlaimont). ✆ **02/219-19-80.** www.cbbd.be. Admission 7.50€ adults; 6€ students, seniors, and children 12–18; 3€ children 6–11; free for children 5 and under. Tues–Sun 10am–6pm. Closed Jan 1 and Dec 25. Métro: Gare Centrale.

Mini-Europe ★ ☺ Kids and adults alike will get a kick out of strolling around such highlights from member states of the European Union as London's Big Ben, Berlin's Brandenburg Gate, the Leaning Tower of Pisa, the Bull Ring in Seville (complete with simulated sounds of fans yelling *¡Olé!*), and Montmartre in Paris, as well as more modern emblems of Continental achievement such as the Channel Tunnel and the Ariane rocket. Meanwhile, Mount Vesuvius erupts, gondolas float around the canals of Venice, and a Finnish girl dives into the icy waters of a northern lake. As the scale is 1:25, the kids will feel like giants.

Bruparck, Heysel (facing the Atomium). ✆ **02/478-05-50.** www.minieurope.com. Admission 13€ adults, 10€ children 12 and under, free for children under 1.2m (4 ft.) accompanied by parents. Mid-Mar to June and Sept daily 9:30am–6pm; July–Aug daily 9:30am–8pm (mid-July to mid-Aug Fri–Sun 9:30am–midnight); Oct–Dec and 1st week Jan daily 10am–6pm. Métro: Heysel.

The European District

Home to the European Commission, European Parliament, Council of Ministers, and related institutions, Brussels has no less than 1.2 million sq. m (12.7 million sq. ft.) of office space packed with 20,000-plus Eurocrats to back up its "capital of Europe" tag. Entire neighborhoods full of character were swept away to make room for them.

To tour the heartland of European Union governance, take the Métro to Schuman station. If you wish to view that exotic species, the European civil servant, in its native habitat, you'll want to do this tour Monday to Friday; the district is dead during the weekend. Grab a bite to eat in one of the fancy restaurants favored by the Euro-crowd or a drink in one of the Irish bars that speckle the district. When you're done, head for the Schuman or Maelbeek Métro stations for the fast track back to civilization.

Your first sight is the X-shaped **Palais de Berlaymont (Berlaymont Palace),** the commission's former headquarters, at Rond-Point Schuman. Across rue de la Loi, the Council of Ministers headquarters, the **Consilium,** is instantly recognizable for its facade's lavish complement of rose-colored granite blocks. On its far side, a soothing stroll through little Parc Léopold brings you to the postmodern **European Parliament** and **International Conference Center,** an architectural odyssey in white marble and tinted glass. Take the passageway through the building's middle to place Léopold, an old square that looks lost and forlorn in comparison to its powerful new neighbors.

An island of green and tranquillity—and perhaps even sanity—at the heart of the Euro District, the graceful, small 19th-century **Parc Léopold,** laid out around a pond, was originally conceived as a zoo and science park. The zoo didn't fly for long, but a cluster of scientific institutes dating from the late 19th and early 20th centuries still occupies part of the terrain. Among these is the **Institut de Sociologie** from 1902, which contains the magnificently ornate Solvay Library. At the south end of Parc Léopold is the **Institut Royal des Sciences Naturelles,** which houses the Natural Sciences Museum and the Musée Wiertz.

A New Art

A new design style appeared toward the end of the 19th century and flourished for a few decades. It was called Art Nouveau in the United States and Britain. Art Nouveau's prime materials were glass and iron, which were worked with decorative curved lines and floral and geometric motifs. Belgium produced one of its greatest exponents in **Victor Horta** (1861–1947); his work can be seen in Brussels, where the **Tassel House** (1893) and the **Hôtel Solvay** (1895) are forerunners of the ambitious **Maison du Peuple** (1896–99), with its concave, curved facades and location within an irregularly shaped square. His most famous building was the Innovation department store (1901), which was destroyed by fire.

Fans of the city's superb legacy of Art Nouveau architecture should check out the works of **Gustave Strauven** (1878–1919), the Brussels-born student of Horta. Strauven's signature is his use of blue and yellow bricks. He designed the **Maison St-Cyr** on square Ambiorix (see below), and about 100 private homes in Brussels and Tournai. A private enthusiast has restored **Strauven's own Brussels home** (1902), at rue Luther 28 (Bus: 29), a few blocks north of square Ambiorix.

THE ART NOUVEAU SQUARES ★

It's fortunate that the European District has at least one neighborhood that has yet to be engulfed by marble and glass: a 19th-century bourgeois residential neighborhood just off its northern flank. You can reach this Art Nouveau area by a short walk along bd. Charlemagne or rue Archimède from the Palais du Berlaymont (Métro: Schuman or Maelbeek).

The first thing you notice are the central gardens laid out along a gentle east-west slope. At the heart of **square Ambiorix** is an ornamental garden that continues across the street on **square Marguerite.** This is a good place for a sandwich-box lunch in fine weather, and many Euro civil servants take advantage of it. **Square Marie-Louise,** downhill via **avenue Palmerston,** is dominated by a large artificial pond in which a fountain plays, and it has artificial grottoes along its eastern bank.

Outside of the gardens—ignoring as best you can both the expensive but undistinguished interloping modern apartments and the giant parking lot that the surrounding streets have become—stroll around for a close-up look at the town houses and mansions, in Art Nouveau and other styles, that border the squares. Perhaps the finest is the slender **Maison Saint-Cyr** (1903) at sq. Ambiorix 11, a flamboyant, almost sensuous masterpiece of curling wrought-iron, curved windows, and swirling brick, designed for the artist Georges Léonard de Saint-Cyr by Gustave Strauven, a then 22-year-old student of Art Nouveau master Victor Horta. Close by, the **Hôtel Van Eetvelde** (1898), at av. Palmerston 4, was designed by Horta for an industrious exploiter of Belgium's Congo colony. Tolerably sober on the outside, it has a wealth of precious and exotic materials inside. The **Hôtel Deprez-Van de Velde** (1896), at no. 3, and its neighbor at no. 2 are also by Horta. The nearby **Villa Germaine** (1897), at av. Palmerston 24, is interesting for its eclectic style and multicolored brickwork, tiles, and mosaics.

Organized Tours

BY BUS Bus tours, which last 3 hours and operate throughout the year, are available from **Brussels City Tours,** rue du Marché aux Herbes 82 (✆ **02/513-77-44;**

www.brussels-city-tours.com; Métro: Gare Centrale). The tours start at 24€ for adults and 12€ for children. Reservations can be made through most hotels, and hotel pickup is often available.

From June 15 to September 15, **Le Bus Bavard,** rue des Thuyas 12 (✆ **02/673-18-35;** www.busbavard.be), operates a daily 3-hour "chatterbus" tour at 10am from the Galeries Royales St-Hubert (Métro: Gare Centrale), a mall next to rue du Marché aux Herbes 90, a few steps off the Grand-Place. A walking tour covers the historic center city, followed by a bus ride through areas the average visitor never sees. You hear about life in Brussels and get a real feel for the city. Most tours costs around 8€. You don't need a reservation for this fascinating experience—just be there by 10am.

ARAU, bd. Adolphe Max 55 (✆ **02/219-33-45;** www.arau.org; Métro: De Brouckère), organizes tours that help you discover not only Brussels's countless treasures but also problems the city faces. It runs 3-hour themed coach tours: "Grand-Place and Its Surroundings," "Brussels 1900—Art Nouveau," "Brussels 1930—Art Deco," "Surprising Parks and Squares," and "Alternative Brussels." Reserve ahead. Tours by bus are 15€ for everyone over 25 and 12€ for those 25 and under; tours by foot are 10€. They take place on Saturday mornings from March to November; private group tours can be arranged year-round.

SPORTS & RECREATION

BOWLING The top bowling alley (with a laser-games facility, Q-Zar) is **Bowling Crosly,** bd. de l'Empereur 36 (✆ **02/512-08-74;** www.crosly.be; bus: 27 or 48).

HORSEBACK RIDING In the south of Brussels, both the Bois de la Cambre and the Forêt de Soignes are great places for horseback riding. Contact **Centre Equestre de la Cambre,** chaussée de Waterloo 872 (✆ **02/375-34-08;** bus: W, 136, 137, or 365); and **Royal Etrier Belge,** champ du Vert Chasseur 19 (✆ **02/374-28-60;** www.royaletrierbelge.be; bus: W, 136, 137, or 365).

ICE SKATING There's ice skating from September to May at **Poseidon,** av. des Vaillants 4 (✆ **02/762-16-33;** www.ijsbaanposeidon.be; Métro: Tomberg).

SOCCER The top local soccer club is **RSC Anderlecht,** av. Théo Verbeeck 2 (✆ **02/522-15-39;** www.rsca.be; Métro: Sint-Guido), which is always in contention for Belgian prizes and usually in the running for European honors. During Continental tournaments, crack European soccer squads can often be seen in action at the stadium in Anderlecht.

SHOPPING

Brussels is not the place to come expecting bargains. It's expensive, though no more so than Paris, Amsterdam, and Cologne. Still, there are reasonable prices to be found, even some bargains. A lot depends on where and when you shop. As a general rule, the upper city around avenue Louise and Porte de Namur is more expensive than the lower city around rue Neuve and the center-city shopping galleries around La Monnaie and place de Brouckère. But this is not a fixed rule. For example, rue Haute, in the upper city, is inexpensive, while the Galeries Royales St-Hubert, in the lower city, is expensive.

Shopping hours are generally from 9 or 10am to 6pm Monday to Saturday. On Friday evening, many center-city stores, particularly department stores, stay open

SOME BRUSSELS specialties

Bruxellois know a thing or two about chocolate. So addictive are theirs that they really should be sold with a government health warning. Just ask anyone who has ever bitten into one of those devilish little creations—handmade pralines, made and sold by **Wittamer** (p. 125); **Nihoul,** chaussée de Vleurgat 111 (✆ **02/648-37-96;** www.nihoul.be; tram: 94); **Neuhaus** (p. 125); **Leonidas,** place du Grand Sablon 41 (✆ **02/513-14-66;** www.leonidas.com; tram: 92 or 94); and . . . well, it's a long list. Many branches of the city's best chocolatiers are congregated at **place du Grand Sablon.** You'll find some of the finest confections at **Mary** (p. 125) and **La Maison des Maîtres Chocolatiers Belges** (p. 125).

Lace is another old favorite that's widely available in the city, particularly in and around the Grand-Place. Purchase from **Maison Antoine** (p. 125) or **Manufacture Belge de Dentelle** (p. 125).

For local beers like gueuze, kriek, and faro—among the 450 or so different Belgian beers—head for **A la Mort Subite** (see "Brussels After Dark," below).

Other traditional products include *jenever* (gin), of which there are some 270 brands produced by 70 distilleries; crystal, particularly superb Val-Saint-Lambert crystal from Liège; ceramics; jewelry; hand-beaten copper or bronze; and even diamonds, though Brussels is nowhere near as sparkling in this respect as Antwerp.

Finally, sweet-toothed shoppers should try **Dandoy** (p. 125).

until 8 or 9pm. A useful source of shopping information is the weekly English-language what's-on guide *Brussels Unlimited,* which keeps tabs on the latest shopping ideas and trends, and reviews individual stores.

Shopping Promenades

Many of Brussels's most interesting stores are clustered along certain promenades or arcades. **Rue Neuve,** which starts at place de la Monnaie and extends north to place Rogier, is practically a pedestrian shopping mall; this busy and popular area is home to many boutiques and department stores, including City 2, a modern shopping complex. **Boulevard Anspach,** which runs from the Stock Exchange up to place de Brouckère, is home to a number of fashion boutiques, chocolate stores, and electronic-appliance stores. The **Anspach Center** (near place de la Monnaie) is a shopping mall.

One of Europe's oldest "malls," the glass-roofed **Galeries Royales St-Hubert ★★** (www.galeries-saint-hubert.com; Métro: Gare Centrale) is a light and airy arcade hosting boutiques and other upmarket stores (Davenport, Ganterie Italienne, Delvaux, Oriande, Belgique Gourmande, and more), sidewalk cafes, a theater and a movie theater, and street musicians playing classical music. Constructed in Italian neo-Renaissance style and opened in 1847, architect Pierre Cluysenaer's gallery offers shopping with a touch of class and is well worth strolling through even if you have no intention of window-shopping. The elegant gallery has three connected wings—Galerie du Roi, Galerie de la Reine, and Galerie des Princes—and was the forerunner of other city arcades like the Burlington in London. It is just north of the

Grand-Place, between rue du Marché aux Herbes and rue d'Arenberg, and is split by rue de Bouchers. There are entrances on all three of these streets.

Avenue Louise and the nearby **boulevard de Waterloo** attract those in search of world-renowned, high-quality goods from such stores as Cartier, Burberry's, Louis Vuitton, and Valentino. A different kind of style rules amid the boutiques on trendy **rue Antoine Dansaert** (Métro: Bourse), a long street that runs from close to the Bourse northwest to canalside boulevard de Nieuport. Along its length are names like **Princesse tam.tam,** at no. 9 (✆ **02/514-57-01;** www.princessetamtam.com), for sexy lingerie; **Plus One,** at no. 60 (✆ **02/503-02-90;** www.plus1.be), for fashionable pregnancy apparel; and **Christa Reniers,** at no. 196 (✆ **02/510-06-60;** www.christareniers.com), for designer jewelry.

The **Galerie Agora** (off Grand-Place) offers a wide variety of modestly priced merchandise, including leather goods, clothing, souvenirs, records, and jewelry.

Outdoor Markets

At the **Vieux Marché** ★ flea market on place du Jeu de Balle, a large square in the Marolles district, you'll find some exceptional decorative items, many recycled from the homes of the "recently deceased," and unusual postcards, clothing, and household goods. So you should be able to snap up a bargain on everything from the weird to the wonderful. The market is held daily from 7am to 2pm.

Every weekend the place du Grand Sablon hosts a fine **Antiques Market.** The salesmanship is low-key, the interest is pure, the prices are not unreasonable (don't expect bargains, though), and the quality of the merchandise—which includes silverware, pottery, paintings, and jewelry—is high. The market is open Saturday from 9am to 6pm and Sunday from 9am to 2pm.

May to October, Tuesday to Sunday, the Grand-Place hosts a **Flower Market** that's open from 8am to 6pm. Nearby, at the top end of rue du Marché aux Herbes, in a square called the place de l'Agora, there's a weekend **Crafts Market,** with lots of fine specialized jewelry and other items, mostly inexpensive.

From mid-May to September, painters, sculptors, potters, photographers, and other artists sell their work—and some of them produce it, too—at the **Marché d'Art,** Parvis Saint-Pierre, Uccle. The market is open Sunday from 10am to 1pm.

Two weekends before Christmas is the occasion for the **European Union Christmas Market** on and around place Ste-Catherine. From Friday evening until Sunday evening, the square is a hub of activity, as each country of the EU sets out its stall with traditional foods and products. There's music, singing, and dancing, and the festive spirit is fueled by mulled wine and typical national drinks. The main problem is that, at times, the square gets so busy that it is almost impossible to move. Still, this is a colorful and memorable event.

In a part of Ixelles district that has its share of restaurants, bars, and shops, place du Châtelain and its environs (tram: 81, 93, or 94) host a trendy crowd on Wednesday from 2 to 7pm for the bustling weekly **green food market,** a medley of scents, color, and organic produce. Browse the market stalls for an impromptu picnic.

Shopping A to Z

Here's a short list of my personal recommendations, only a small sampling of Brussels's best shopping and the wealth of chocolatiers in the city; many of the chocolate shops listed below have multiple locations.

An Affordable Wine Source

If you're planning to purchase wine by the bottle, don't be fooled into the idea that you have to go to an expensive wine store to get something worthwhile. The midprice **Delhaize** supermarket chain has built up an enviable reputation and a loyal local following for the quality of its wine department. Delhaize's buyers look for good value in all price categories and have an adventurous streak that makes them look beyond the classic names. There are Delhaize supermarkets all over Brussels (and Belgium). Ask at your hotel desk for the nearest branch.

ART

Ma Maison de Papier ★ Owner Marie-Laurence Bernard is an enthusiast for vintage posters—she has written three books on the subject—that do more than hide a crack on your bathroom wall. Many kinds of posters are here, from a 1930s cigarette ad to a reproduction Toulouse-Lautrec, as well as original Art Nouveau and Art Deco works by Belgian, French, and other masters of the genre. Galerie de la Rue de Ruysbroeck 6 (off place du Grand Sablon). ✆ 02/512-22-49. www.mamaisondepapier.be. Tram: 92 or 94 to Petit Sablon.

BOOKS

Waterstone's It's not so easy to find a wide selection of English-language books in Brussels, but the major British bookstore chain does have a full-size branch here that sells magazines, newspapers, and books. The books, however, usually cost 30% to 60% more than in Britain. Bd. Adolphe Max 71 (at rue du Pont Neuf). ✆ 02/219-27-08. www.waterstones.com. Métro: Rogier.

CHILDREN

Boutique de Tintin ★ Forget computer games and other electronic toys. If you need to buy a gift for the kids, take home some Tintin mementos from this excellent, if somewhat pricey and stuffy (surprising, considering the stock in trade), store. Rue de la Colline 13 (off Grand-Place). ✆ 02/514-51-52. Métro: Gare Centrale.

EURO-STUFF

Eurotempo One of the most surprising marketing phenomena of recent years has been the popularity of the European Union's symbol: a blue flag with a circle of 12 stars. At Eurotempo you find this logo on an astonishing range of products: umbrellas, T-shirts, pens, golf balls, watches, hats, knives, towels—you name it. Where better to buy Euro stuff than in the capital of Europe? Rue du Marché aux Herbes 84 (off rue du Marché aux Peaux). ✆ 02/503-39-53. www.eurotempo.com. Métro: Gare Centrale or Bourse.

FASHION & APPAREL

Delvaux ★★ At its Galeries Royales St-Hubert store, this local company, founded in 1829, makes and sells some of the best—and priciest—handbags and leather goods in Belgium. Galerie de la Reine 31 (off Grand-Place). ✆ 02/512-71-98. www.delvaux.com. Métro: Gare Centrale or Bourse.

Ganterie Italienne This is a glove store with Italian style, founded in 1890, selling attractive handwear that keeps out the winter cold. It's open Monday to Saturday from 10am to 12:30pm and 1:30 to 6pm. Galerie de la Reine 3 (off Grand-Place). ✆ 02/512-75-38. Métro: Gare Centrale or Bourse.

Olivier Strelli ★ This top-rated Belgian fashion designer is just one of several big names with boutiques in this area. His store is strong on elegant, ready-to-wear items. Av. Louise 72 (at place Stéphanie). ✆ 02/512-56-07. www.strelli.be. Métro: Louise.

FLOWERS

Daniël Ost This flower store, in a superb Art Nouveau location, is just the place for that important bouquet. Rue Royale 13 (at rue de la Croix de Fer). ✆ 02/217-29-17. Métro: Botanique.

FOOD & WINES

Dandoy ★★ Founded in 1829, Dandoy is still *the* place for sweet-toothed cookies-'n'-cakes fans. Try the traditional Belgian house specialties: spicy *speculoos* cookies (made with brown sugar, cinnamon, ginger, and almonds, and baked in wood molds), and *pain à la grecque* (thin, spicy caramelized, sugary flaky pastries). Rue au Beurre 31 (off Grand-Place). ✆ 02/511-03-26. www.biscuiteriedandoy.be. Métro: Bourse.

De Boe ★ Don't miss this small store near the Fish Market. It has a superb selection of roasted and blended coffees and wines in all price categories, and an array of specialty crackers, nuts, spices, teas, and gourmet snacks, many of which are canned, making them suitable for transport home. Rue de Flandre 36. ✆ 02/511-13-73. Métro: Ste-Catherine.

La Maison des Maîtres Chocolatiers Belges ★ Housed in one of the few Grand-Place guild houses that at least in part survived the 1695 French artillery bombardment, this chocolatier is a showcase for handmade chocolates created by a team of artisans from around the country. Grand-Place 4. ✆ 02/888-66-20. www.mmcb.be. Métro: Gare Centrale or Bourse.

Mary ★★ Supplier of pralines to the Belgian royal court—which tells you right away that these are no plain chocolates—Mary is a small store, but its wares look every bit as good as they taste. Rue Royal 73 (at rue du Congrès). ✆ 02/217-45-00. www.mary-choc.com. Métro: Parc.

Neuhaus This chocolatier sells some of the best of the dangerously delicious Belgian handmade chocolates. Purchase gift pralines here. Galerie de la Reine 25-27 (off Grand-Place). ✆ 02/512-63-59. www.neuhaus.be. Métro: Gare Centrale or Bourse.

Wittamer Wittamer makes some of the best handmade pralines in the world. Its rolls, breads, pastries, and cakes have been winning fans here since 1910. Place du Grand Sablon 12 (at rue Ste-Anne). ✆ 02/512-37-42. www.wittamer.com. Tram: 92 or 94 to Petit Sablon.

LACE

Maison Antoine This lace boutique is one of the best in Brussels and surely has the best location, a former guild house where Victor Hugo lived in 1852. The quality is superb, the service friendly, and the prices decent. Grand-Place 26. ✆ 02/512-48-59. Métro: Gare Centrale or Bourse.

Manufacture Belge de Dentelle Unlike the many Belgian lace stores that sell machine-made and imported lace, this store, which has been based in the Galeries Royal St-Hubert since 1847, sells top-quality handmade Belgian lace. Galerie de la Reine 6–8 (off Grand-Place). ✆ 02/511-44-77. www.mbd.be. Métro: Gare Centrale or Bourse.

MULTIMEDIA

FNAC This good-value books, electronics, and photo chain has a branch in the giant City2 multistory mall on the city's main shopping drag. It also sells concert tickets. Rue Neuve (at bd. du Jardin Botanique). ✆ 02/275-11-11. Métro: Rogier.

BRUSSELS AFTER DARK

Brussels may not be internationally known for its nightlife, but that's partly because it's overshadowed by the worldwide reputations of neighboring capitals like Paris and London. Nightlife is actually alive and doing rather well in Brussels, and if the range is inevitably thinner than in bigger cities, the quality is not.

There's little doubt that the most splendid nightlife outlook in town is from the bars and cafes around the central **Grand-Place** (Métro: Gare Centrale or Bourse) and, to a lesser degree, **place du Grand Sablon** (tram: 92 or 94). Still, these places are admittedly more than a little touristy, and there are spots not too far away that have a far cooler cachet. The **place Ste-Catherine** (Métro: Sainte-Catherine) and **place St-Géry** (Métro: Bourse) neighborhoods, west of boulevard Anspach, are good for trendy bars and cafes that attract the young and hip, and on the near side of this boulevard to the Grand-Place, **rue du Marché au Charbon** (Métro: Bourse) is good for both lively bars and gay nightlife.

For African vibes, music, late-night shopping, and more, head to the **Matonge** quarter (Métro: Porte de Namur), named after a district in Kinshasa and centered on rue Longue-Vie between chaussée de Wavre and chaussée d'Ixelles. Also in Ixelles, **place du Châtelain** (tram: 81, 93, or 94) and its environs is another hotspot for trendy bars and cafes. Spanish and Portuguese spots can be found toward the southern end of rue Haute and neighboring streets in the **Marolles** district (Métro: Porte de Hal).

For current information on after-dark entertainment during your visit, purchase the weekly English-language what's-on guide *Brussels Unlimited.*

The Performing Arts

OPERA & BALLET An opera house in the grand style, the **Théâtre Royal de la Monnaie ★★**, place de la Monnaie (✆ **070/23-39-39;** www.lamonnaie.be; Métro: De Brouckère), is home to the Opéra Royal de la Monnaie—which has been called the best in the French-speaking world—and the Orchestre Symphonique de la Monnaie. The resident modern dance company, Anne Teresa de Keersmaeker's group **Rosas ★** (✆ **02/344-55-98;** www.rosas.be), is noted for its original moves. The box office is open Tuesday to Saturday from 11am to 6pm. Tickets run 10€ to 170€; those 25 and under may be able to get tickets for 10€ just before a show.

CLASSICAL MUSIC **BOZAR ★**, rue Ravenstein 23 (✆ **02/507-82-00;** www.bozar.be; Métro: Gare Centrale)—the Palais des Beaux-Arts—is home to Belgium's National Orchestra. The box office is open Monday to Saturday from 11am to 6pm, with tickets running 10€ to 75€.

Heritage Celebration

On the third weekend in September, the annual Journées du Patrimoine (Heritage Days) program allows you to visit some of the finest buildings in town that are usually closed to visitors. Sixty or so sites are open. For more details, visit the information center in the Halles St-Géry, place St-Géry 23 (✆ 02/502-44-24; www.hallessaintgery.be; Métro: Bourse), open daily from 10am to 6pm (admission is free).

puppet SHOWS: A BELGIAN PASSION

A special word is in order about a special sort of theater—that of the wooden marionettes that have entertained Belgians for centuries. In times past, puppet theaters numbered in the hundreds nationwide (Brussels alone had 15), and the plays were much like our modern-day soap operas. The story lines went on and on, sometimes for generations, and working-class audiences returned night after night to keep up with the *Dallas* of the times. Performances were based on folklore, legends, or political satire. Specific marionette characters came to personify their home cities: A cheeky ragamuffin named Woltje (Little Walloon) was from Brussels; Antwerp had the cross-eyed, earthy, ne'er-do-well Schele; Pierke, from Ghent, was modeled on the traditional Italian clown; and Liège's Tchantchès stood only 16 inches high and always appeared with patched trousers, a tasseled floppy hat, and his constant companion, the sharp-tongued Nanesse (Agnes). Today a few Belgian puppet theaters still survive, and their popularity has increased in recent years.

Concerts are performed at the **Cirque Royal,** rue de l'Enseignement 81 (✆ **02/218-20-15;** www.cirque-royal.org; Métro: Parc), which was formerly a real circus but is now a venue for music, opera, ballet, and more. The box office is open Tuesday to Saturday from 11am to 6pm, with tickets for 10€ to 75€.

Le Botanique, rue Royale 236 (✆ **02/218-37-32;** www.botanique.be; Métro: Botanique), generally focuses on small-scale modern and avant-garde performances, not only of classical music but also of jazz and other forms.

THEATERS Brussels theater is important among French-speaking countries, with more than 30 theaters presenting performances in French, Dutch, and (occasionally) English. Among the most important is the **Théâtre Royal du Parc ★★**, rue de la Loi 3 (✆ **02/505-30-40;** www.theatreduparc.be; Métro: Parc), a magnificent edifice occupying a corner of the Parc de Bruxelles, where classic and contemporary drama and comedies are performed. The **Théâtre National de la Communauté Française,** bd. Emile Jacqmain 111–115 (✆ **02/203-53-03;** www.theatrenational.be; Métro: De Brouckère), is mainstream; and the **Théâtre Royal des Galeries,** Galerie du Roi 32 (✆ **02/512-04-07;** www.trg.be; Métro: Gare Centrale), is known for its range of offerings, including drama, comedy, and musicals.

Also important is **Le Botanique,** rue Royale 236 (✆ **02/218-37-32;** www.botanique.be; Métro: Botanique), inclined toward the experimental in mostly French theater. Bringing theater to the city in Dutch is the **Koninklijke Vlaamse Schouwburg,** quai aux Pierres de Taille/Arduinkaai 9 (✆ **02/210-11-12;** www.kvs.be; Métro: Yser), in a restored neo-Renaissance-style building dating from 1887.

Puppet Theater

Toone ★ Look for the small wooden sign in the tiny alleyway—impasse Schuddeveld—to reach this theater, in an upstairs room in a bistro of the same name. It's the latest in the Toone line of puppet theaters, which dates back to the early 1800s—the title being passed from one puppet master to the next—and it may be the most popular theater in Brussels. At Toone, puppet master José Géal presents his adaptation of such classic tales as *The Three Musketeers, Faust,* and *Hamlet* in the Brussels dialect, Brussels Vloms, and in English, French, Dutch, and German. In any case, language should present no difficulties since it's easy to follow the action on stage. Impasse Ste-Pétronille, rue du Marché aux Herbes 66. ✆ 02/511-71-37. www.toone.be. Ticket prices and performance times vary; check in advance. Métro: Gare Centrale.

Jazz & Blues Clubs

L'Archiduc, rue Antoine Dansaert 6 (✆ **02/512-06-52;** www.archiduc.net; Métro: Bourse), had the brilliant idea of putting on after-shopping jazz concerts on Saturday beginning at 5pm, and then went one better by repeating the idea (minus the shopping) on Sunday. For those who like their licks a little more restrained, there's a jazz brunch at the **Sheraton Brussels Airport Hotel,** facing the terminal building (✆ **02/710-80-00;** www.sheratonbrusselsairport.com; train: Brussels Airport), once a month on Sunday from noon to 3pm. **Le Sounds,** rue de la Tulipe 28 (✆ **02/512-92-50;** www.soundsjazzclub.be; bus: 54 or 71), in the Ixelles district, has daily jazz concerts, and a workshop on Mondays at 7:30pm.

During the 3-day, late-May **Brussels Jazz Marathon** (✆ **02/456-04-84;** www.brusselsjazzmarathon.be), there are more than 125 concerts, covering all known jazz forms, at outdoor venues like the Grand-Place and Place du Grand Sablon, and at clubs, bars, and indoor cultural venues around town. Outdoor concerts are free; a pass for all indoor concerts is 15€, and 12€ if you reserve ahead of time.

Dance Clubs

Nothing in life changes quite so fast as the "in" places. But there are a few that stand the test of time—and that, of course, makes them anathema to genuine dance hounds. Since the turnover rate is so high, be sure to check locally to see if the following are still in operation before setting out for the night. Sophisticated and central, **Duke's Nightclub,** in the Royal Windsor Hotel Grand Place, rue Duquesnoy 5 (✆ **02/505-55-55;** royalwindsorbrussels.com; Métro: Gare Centrale), is in full swing every night from Thursday to Sunday. **Mirano Brussels,** chaussée de Louvain 38 (✆ **02/227-39-70;** www.mirano.be; Métro: Madou), north of the city center and reopened after major refurbishing, is a classy place for those whose wildest years are a few years behind them but who still like to enjoy themselves. A few blocks north of the Grand-Place, **Nostalgia Club,** rue de la Fourche 49–51 (✆ **02/513-32-91;** www.nostalgia-club.be; Métro: De Brouckère), is similar, with hits from the '60s, '70s, and '80s.

You ★★, rue Duquesnoy 18 (✆ **02/639-14-00;** www.leyou.be; Métro: Gare Centrale), is just off the Grand-Place and features a consistently up-to-date approach to music. West of the Grand-Place, **Cartagena ★**, rue du Marché au Charbon 70 (✆ **02/502-59-08;** www.cartagenasalsabar.be; Métro: Bourse), is as hot as a salsa night in, well, Cartagena, and dispenses drinks and music from all over Latin America. If only techno will do (along with a dab of house), **Fuse ★★**, rue Blaes 208 (✆ **02/511-97-89;** www.fuse.be; Métro: Porte de Hal), in the Marolles district, is the place for you.

Bars

Now you're talking. Bars are where Brussels lives. It's hard to be disappointed, whether you pop into a neighborhood watering hole where a *chope* or *pintje* (a glass of beer) will set you back a mere 2.50€, or whether you prefer to fork out several times as much in one of the trendier places. The following are only a few of the many Brussels pubs and bistros worthy of recommendation.

Brews from Brussels

Brussels is known for its lambic beers, which use naturally occurring yeast for fermentation, are often flavored with fruit, and come in bottles with champagne-type corks. They're almost akin to sweet sparkling wine. Gueuze, a blend of young and aged lambic beers, is one of the least sweet. If you prefer something sweeter, try raspberry-flavored framboise or cherry-flavored kriek. Faro is a low-alcohol beer, sometimes sweetened or lightly spiced.

A Brussels favorite, **A la Mort Subite ★**, rue Montagne aux Herbes Potagères 7 (✆ **02/513-13-18;** Métro: Gare Centrale), is a bistro of rather special character whose name translates to "Sudden Death," which is the name of one of the beers sold here. Don't worry, the name is just a name—it comes from a dice game regulars used to play. The decor consists of stained-glass motifs, old photographs, paintings, and prints on the walls; and plain wood chairs and tables on the floor. Specialties are traditional Brussels beers: gueuze, lambic, faro, and kriek, and abbey brews like Chimay, Maredsous, and Grimbergen. In a quite different vein is **La Fleur en Papier Doré ★**, rue des Alexiens 55 (✆ **02/511-16-59;** Métro: Anneessens), in a 16th-century house. From its beginnings in 1846, this bistro and pub has been a mecca for poets and writers. Even now, about once a month, young Brussels poets gather here informally for poetry readings—the dates vary, but you might inquire by phone or, better yet, drop by and ask in person. This is a wonderfully atmospheric old pub, much like a social club, where patrons gather for good conversation and welcome all newcomers. The place serves what is possibly the best onion soup in Brussels, a great late-night snack.

The following are only a few of the many Brussels pubs and bistros worthy of recommendation. **Au Bon Vieux Temps,** impasse St-Michel, rue du Marché aux Herbes 12 (✆ **02/217-26-26;** Métro: Bourse), at the end of a narrow alleyway, is a gloomily atmospheric old tavern that seems to hearken back to a bygone era. You should try the appropriately named Duvel (Devil) beer here—just go easy, that's all. Nearby, **A l'Imaige Nostre-Dame,** impasse des Cadeaux, rue du Marché aux Herbes 8 (✆ **02/219-42-49;** Métro: Bourse), is a good, quiet place to drink and reflect if you're alone, or to converse with a friend without having to compete with a blaring jukebox.

Le Cirio, rue de la Bourse 18 (✆ **02/512-13-95;** Métro: Bourse), is across the road from the Stock Exchange, and indeed many of the bar's customers look like they've just made a killing on the stock market and have retired to a state of genteel splendor. And what better place to do it in? Le Cirio is a quiet, refined sort of place to sip your beer, in attractive surroundings that make the whole exercise seem worthwhile. On the other side of the Bourse (Stock Exchange), **Falstaff ★★**, rue Henri Maus 19 (✆ **02/511-87-89;** Métro: Bourse), a legendary 1904 Art Nouveau tavern, has stunning decor, stained-glass scenes in the style of Pieter Bruegel the Elder depicting Shakespeare's Falstaff tales, and reasonably priced brasserie food. Two blocks to the west, **L'Archiduc ★**, rue Antoine Dansaert 6 (✆ **02/512-06-52;** Métro: Bourse), remains a font of local chic (and a purveyor of jazz; see above).

Gay & Lesbian Bars

Rue des Riches-Claires and **rue du Marché au Charbon** host some gay and lesbian bars. **Macho Sauna,** rue du Marché au Charbon 106 (✆ **02/513-56-67;**

Métro: Bourse), a block from rue des Riches-Claires, houses a gay men's sauna, pool, steam room, and cafe. It's open Monday to Thursday from noon to 2am, Friday and Saturday from noon to 4am, and Sunday from noon to midnight. Both the **Fuse** and **You** dance clubs (see above) have gay nights.

For more information, stop by the gay and lesbian community center, **Tels Quels,** rue du Marché au Charbon 81 (✆ **02/512-45-87;** www.telsquels.be; Métro: Bourse), open Saturday to Thursday from 5pm to 2am and Friday from 5pm to 4am. Or, on the same street, stop by the meeting rooms and cafe at **La Maison Arc en Ciel,** rue du Marché au Charbon 42 (✆ **02/503-59-90;** www.rainbowhouse.be; Métro: Bourse).

Movies

Since most movies in Brussels are shown in the original language, you'll always be able to find many English-language films in the theaters. Major cinemas in the center city, several of them multiplexes, are: **Actor's Studio,** Petite rue des Bouchers 16 (✆ **02/512-16-96;** http://actorsstudio.cinenews.be; Métro: Bourse); **Arenberg,** Galerie de la Reine 26 (✆ **02/512-80-63;** www.arenberg.be; Métro: Gare Centrale); **Aventure,** Galerie du Centre 57, rue des Fripiers 17 (✆ **02/219-92-02;** www.cinema-aventure.be; Métro: Bourse); **UGC Toison d'Or,** av. de la Toison d'Or 8 (✆ **0900/10-440;** www.ugc.be; Métro: Porte de Namur); and **UGC De Brouckère,** place de Brouckère 38 (✆ **0900/10-440;** www.ugc.be; Métro: De Brouckère).

Kinepolis, bd. du Centenaire 20 (✆ **0900/00-555** or 02/474-26-03; www.kinepolis.com; Métro: Heysel), is the best equipped and the biggest, with 26 screens and an IMAX theater. Part of the Bruparck recreation complex beside the Atomium, Kinepolis is likely to have something for everyone. Most movies shown are big releases, usually from Hollywood, which is no doubt the main reason why the place is so popular. **Nova,** rue d'Arenberg 3 (✆ **02/511-24-77;** www.nova-cinema.org; Métro: Gare Centrale), is an art-house cinema. The **Musée du Cinema,** rue Baron Horta 9 (✆ **02/507-83-70;** Métro: Gare Centrale), at the Palais des Beaux-Arts (BOZAR), often features little-seen films from the past.

SIDE TRIPS FROM BRUSSELS

The lovely Brabant countryside around Brussels offers scenic beauty and several sightseeing attractions well worth the short trip.

Waterloo ★★

10km (6 miles) S of Brussels

The battle that ended Napoleon's empire was fought on rolling farmland near **Waterloo,** just south of Brussels. On June 18, 1815, 72,000 British, Dutch, Belgian, and German troops, aided before the day's end by around 40,000 Prussians, defeated the mighty Napoleon Bonaparte and his 76,000 French, leaving 40,000 dead and wounded on the field. Napoleon survived, but his attempt to rebuild his empire was crushed; he was exiled to the island of St. Helena, where he died 6 years later.

The battlefield remains much as it was on that fateful day. To visit, though, you don't go to the town of Waterloo, which is a pleasant suburb of Brussels—and the capital town of Brabant-Wallon (Walloon Brabant) province. The Battle of Waterloo wasn't fought there. A stretch of rolling farmland several miles to the south around Mont-St-Jean, speckled with stoutly constructed manor-farmhouses, got that "honor."

Before touring the field, you should study a 360-degree **Panoramic Mural** featuring the massed French cavalry charge led by Marshal Ney and see a short audiovisual presentation of the battle, including scenes from Sergei Bondarchuk's epic movie *Waterloo,* at the **Centre du Visiteur (Visitor Center) ★★**, route du Lion 315, Waterloo (✆ **02/385-19-12;** www.waterloo1815.be). To survey the battlefield, climb the 226 steps to the top of the nearby **Butte du Lion (Lion Mound),** a conical hill surmounted by a bronze lion, behind the center—it takes an active imagination to fill the peaceful farmland with slashing cavalry charges, thundering artillery, and nearly 200,000 colorfully uniformed, struggling soldiers. Across the road from the Visitor Center is the **Musée des Cires (Waxworks Museum),** where Napoleon, Wellington, Blücher, and other key participants appear as wax figures.

Draw rations from one of the cafes or restaurants, which have names like Le Hussard and Les Alliés. Souvenir stores sell everything from Napoleonic corkscrews to hand-painted model soldiers. Beside the crossroads at the Brussels-Charleroi road are monuments to the Belgians and Hanoverians; to Colonel Gordon, Wellington's aide; and to General Picton, shot down at the head of his division. A little way down the Brussels-Charleroi road is La Haie–Sainte, a farmhouse that played a crucial role in Napoleon's defeat by shielding Wellington's center from direct assault.

These four sites are open daily April to October from 9:30am to 6:30pm, and November to March from 10am to 5pm (closed Jan 1 and Dec 25). Admission to the Visitor Center is free; admission to its audiovisual presentation and the four on-site attractions is 8.70€ for adults, 6.50€ for seniors and students, 5.50€ for children 7 to 17, and free for children 6 and under. From Brussels, TEC bus W (Brussels–Waterloo–Braine-l'Alleud) departs twice hourly from Bruxelles-Midi train station (Métro: Gare du Midi). The 18km (11-mile) ride takes 55 minutes and costs 4.20€. The bus stops at both the Wellington Museum in Waterloo (see below) and at the battlefield Visitor Center, south of the town. By car from Brussels, take the ring road/beltway (R0) to exit 27 for Waterloo, and then N5 south to the battlefield.

In Waterloo itself is the well-ordered **Musée Wellington (Wellington Museum),** chaussée de Bruxelles 147 (✆ **02/357-28-60;** www.museewellington.com), in an old Brabant coaching inn that was the duke's headquarters. It was from here that Wellington sent his historic victory dispatch. The museum is open April to September daily from 9:30am to 6:30pm, and October to March daily from 10am to 5pm (closed Jan 1 and Dec 25). Admission, which includes an audio guide (except for children 5 and under), is 5€ for adults, 4€ for seniors and students, 2€ for children 6 to 17, and free for children 5 and under.

Beersel

9km (5½ miles) SW of Brussels

The only local example of a still-intact fortified medieval castle is **Kasteel van Beersel ★**, on Lotsestraat (✆ **02/359-16-46;** www.historische-woonsteden.be). The three-towered, 13th-century castle is set in a wooded area and surrounded by a moat, which you cross via drawbridge. Pick up the excellent English-language guidebook at the entrance for a detailed history of the castle and its inhabitants, and then wander through its rooms for a trip back through time. End your visit with a stop at the magnificent mausoleum that holds the alabaster effigies of Henry II of Witthem and his wife, Jacqueline de Glimes, who lived here during the early 1400s. The castle is open

An Adventure with Tintin

Head to Louvain-la-Neuve, 27km (17 miles) southeast of Brussels, to visit the ★ Musée Hergé, rue du Labrador 26 (✆ 010/488-421; www.museeherge.com), which opened in 2009 to celebrate the *œuvre* of Tintin creator Georges Remi (1907–83), better known as Hergé. The museum is open Tuesday to Friday from 10:30am to 5:30pm, and weekends from 10am to 6pm (closed Jan 1, Dec 25). Admission is 9.50€ for adults, 7€ for students and "large" family groups (per person), 5€ for children ages 7 to 14, and free for children 6 and under.

March to mid-November Tuesday to Sunday from 10am to noon and 2 to 6pm, and mid-November to February Saturday and Sunday from 10am to noon and 2 to 6pm. Admission is 2.50€ for adults, 1.25€ for seniors and children 5 to 12, free for children 4 and under, and 7.50€ for a family. Beersel station is a 40-minute train ride from Brussels; the castle is a walk of 400m (440 yd.) west of the train station.

Leafy pathways through the castle grounds make this a favorite retreat for Brussels residents, especially during the summer months. At the entrance to the park, you find **Auberge Kasteel Beersel,** Lotsestraat 65 (✆ **02/377-10-47;** www.auberge-beersel.be), a charming rustic restaurant with a decor of dark wood, exposed brick, and accents of copper and brass. In good weather, there's service on the shaded outdoor terrace. Light meals (omelets, salads, soups, and sandwiches) are available, and complete hot meals are offered for both lunch and dinner. Prices are moderate. If you don't want a meal, you're welcome to stop in for a draft of Belgian beer.

Gaasbeek

13km (8 miles) SW of Brussels

The ancestral **château of the counts of Egmont** is at Gaasbeek, beyond the village of Vlezenbeek. The furnishings of **Kasteel van Gaasbeek ★★**, Kasteelstraat 40 (✆ **02/531-01-30;** www.kasteelvangaasbeek.be), are magnificent, as is the castle itself. All the rooms are splendid, and far from presenting a dead "museum" appearance, they create the eerie impression that the counts and their families may come walking through the door any moment. Before each guided tour, a slide show augments your appreciation of the castle's countless works of art, silver items, religious objects, and priceless tapestries. The castle is open April to early November Tuesday to Sunday from 10am to 6pm; the park is open daily from 8am to 8pm (to 6pm Oct–Mar). Admission to the castle is 7€ for adults, 5€ for seniors and people with disabilities, 1€ for those ages 7 to 26, and free for children 6 and under. Admission to the park is free. To get there by car from Brussels, take the R0/E19 Brussels ring road west to exit 15A, for Vlezenbeek, and continue through this village to the castle; by public transportation, take De Lijn bus no. 142 (Gaasbeek-Leerbeek) from Bruxelles-Midi station, or from the end-of-the-line Métro station Erasmus, and get out at the Kasteel van Gaasbeek stop.

BRUGES

Graceful Bruges has drifted down the stream of time with all the self-possession of the swans that cruise its canals. To step into the old town is to be transported back to the Middle Ages, when Bruges (Brugge in Dutch) was among the wealthiest cities of Europe. Unlike so many European cities that have had their hearts torn out by war, Bruges has remained unravaged, its glorious monumental buildings intact. UNESCO has awarded the entire historical city center World Cultural Heritage status.

The city (pop. 117,000, of whom 20,000 live in the Old Town) is the capital town of West-Vlaanderen (West Flanders) province, and the pride and joy of all Flanders.

Medieval Gothic architecture is the big deal here. Oh, there's a layer of Romanesque; a touch of Renaissance, baroque, and rococo; a dab of neoclassical and neo-Gothic; and a smidgeon of Art Nouveau and Art Deco. But Gothic is what Bruges does, in quantities that come near to numbing the senses—and likely would do so if it wasn't for the distraction of the city's contemporary animation. In the 15th century, Bruges was a center for the Hanseatic League and has a rich heritage of civic buildings from that period: guildhalls, exchanges, warehouses, and the residences of wealthy merchants.

ORIENTATION

Arriving

BY TRAIN

Two trains arrive in Bruges every hour from Brussels, four or five from Ghent, two from Antwerp, and up to three every hour from the ferry ports of Zeebrugge and Ostend (Oostende). The travel time is around 1 hour from Brussels, 25 minutes from Ghent, 1 hour and 20 minutes from Antwerp, and 15 minutes from both Ostend and Zeebrugge. Train information is available from Belgian Railways (✆ **02/528-28-28;** www.b-rail.be).

From London, passengers can ride the Eurostar high-speed trains through the Channel Tunnel and transfer for Bruges either at Lille in northern France or in Brussels. From Paris, Thalys high-speed trains go via Brussels direct to Bruges; on the slower and cheaper international trains, you transfer in Brussels. From Amsterdam, go via Antwerp or Brussels, either on Thalys or on international and InterCity (IC) trains. From Cologne, Thalys trains stop in Brussels, and international trains via Brussels to Ostend stop in Bruges.

folklore EVENTS IN BRUGES

One of the most popular and colorful folklore events in Belgium is Bruges's **Heilig-Bloedprocessie (Procession of the Holy Blood) ★**, which dates back to at least 1291 and takes place every year on Ascension Day (fifth Thurs after Easter). During the procession, the bishop of Bruges proceeds through the city streets carrying the golden shrine containing the Relic of the Holy Blood (see "The Burg," later in this chapter). Residents wearing Burgundian-era and biblical costumes follow the relic, acting out biblical and historical scenes along the way. The procession takes place on June 2, 2011, and May 17, 2012.

Every 3 years, the canals of Bruges are the subject and location of the **Reiefeest (Canal Festival) ★★**. This multi-day evening event takes place on 6 nonconsecutive days in August and is a combination of historical tableaux, dancing, open-air concerts, and lots of eating and drinking. The next Reiefeest is between August 15 and 31 in 2011.

The **Praalstoet van de Gouden Boom (Golden Tree Pageant) ★★★** recalls the great procession and tournament held on the Markt to celebrate the 1468 marriage of duke of Burgundy Charles the Bold to Margaret of York. It takes place every 5 years in the second half of August; the next one will be on August 19, 2012.

Although the city is called Bruges in both English and French, look out for its Flemish name, BRUGGE, written on the station name boards. The station is on Stationsplein, 1.6km (1 mile) south of the center of town, a 20-minute walk or a short taxi or bus ride—choose any bus labeled CENTRUM and get out at the Markt.

BY BUS

Buses are less useful than trains for getting to Bruges, though there is frequent service from Zeebrugge, Ostend, and other Belgian seacoast resorts. The Bruges bus station adjoins the rail station. Schedule and fare information is available from **De Lijn** (✆ **070/22-02-00;** www.delijn.be).

Eurolines (see "By Bus" under "Getting to the Benelux," in chapter 3) operates daily bus service from London, Amsterdam, Paris, Cologne, and other cities around Europe, to Brussels or Bruges, or to both.

BY CAR

Bruges is 92km (57 miles) northwest of Brussels and 51km (32 miles) northwest of Ghent on A10/E40; 102km (63 miles) west of Antwerp on A14/E17 and A10/E40; 16km (10 miles) south of the ferry port of Zeebrugge on N31 and N371; and 30km (19 miles) southeast of Ostend on A10/E40. From Calais, France, and the Channel Tunnel, take E40 east.

Visitor Information

Bruges's tourist office's mailing address and contact information is **Toerisme Brugge,** P.O. Box 744, 8000 Brugge (✆ **050/44-46-46;** fax 050/44-46-45; www.brugge.be). The organization's walk-in office is **In&Uit Brugge,** Concertgebouw, 't Zand 34, inside the city's Concert Hall, about midway between the rail station and the heart of town. The office is open daily from 10am to 6pm (closed Jan 1 and Dec 25). The efficient staffers here can make last-minute hotel reservations and provide brochures that outline walking, coach, canal, and horse-drawn carriage tours. Ask for the free annual ***events@brugge*** brochure and monthly ***Exit*** newsletter; both are directories of current goings-on.

City Layout

You could liken Bruges's Old Town to a circular archery target outlined by the ring canal, with two bull's-eyes representing the side-by-side monumental squares called the Markt and the Burg. Beyond these central points are other more or less concentric circles of places of interest, and these attractions are generally thicker on the ground the closer in to the center of town you are, and more spread out as you move through a network of narrow streets that fan out from the two squares. The ring canal opens at its southern end to become the Minnewater (Lake of Love), filled with swans and other water birds and bordered by the Begijnhof and a fine park. Beyond the southern rim of the Minnewater is the rail station.

Outside the ring canal are residential neighborhoods—they were formerly separate *gemeenten* (districts) with their own local government and not part of Bruges at all. These districts have relatively few points of interest when compared to the attractions-packed center, so the likelihood is you won't see much of them on your visit.

GETTING AROUND

The center of Bruges is compact and filled with pedestrians-only streets, which makes walking the best way to get around. Just be sure to wear comfortable shoes; those charming cobblestones can be hard on your feet.

By Bus

Most city and regional buses, operated by **De Lijn** (**© 070/22-02-00;** www.delijn.be), depart from the bus station beside the train station, or from a secondary station at a large square known as 't Zand, and many buses stop at the Markt in the Old Town. Purchase your ticket from a De Lijn sales point or automat (ticket machine) before boarding and you'll pay less (the "twin" prices listed here reflect this distinction). An *enkele rit* (one-way) ticket costs 1.20€/2€ for two zones and 2€/3€ for three or more zones. A *dagkaart* (day card), valid for the entire city network, costs 5€/6€ for 1 day; 10€/12€ for 3 days; and 15€/18€ for 5 days. A 1-day pass for children 6 to 11 is 1.50€/2€, and children 5 and under ride free.

By Bicycle

Cycling is a terrific way to get around Bruges, or to get out of town to the nearby village of Damme (see "A Side Trip to Damme," later in this chapter) by way of scenic canal-side roads. Unlike most Belgian cities, Bruges has made cyclists privileged road users. They can travel in both directions on many of the narrow, one-way streets in the center city—but some streets are one-way only, and you'll be fined if you're caught riding against the traffic flow. Ride with caution, because the streets are filled with visitors, many of whom have no experience of bikes en masse and are liable to step in front of you without looking.

Rent a pedal-bike from the rail station, for 9.50€ per day plus a returnable guarantee of 13€. In addition, many hotels rent bikes to guests, and there are at least a dozen rental stores around town. A good rental store is **De Ketting,** Gentpoortstraat 23 (**© 050/34-41-96;** www.deketting.be), which has bikes for 6€ a day.

By Car

Don't drive. Leave your car at your hotel parking garage (if it has one); one of six big, prominently labeled underground parking garages in the center (these get expensive for long stays); one of four cheap park-and-ride lots next to the train station; or a free parking zone outside the city center. It's a short walk into the heart of the Old Town from any of the parking lots. Driving the narrow streets, many of them one-way, can be confusing. Parking rules are firmly enforced, and unlawfully parked cars will be ticketed, wheel-clamped, or towed.

By Taxi

There are taxi stands at the Markt (✆ **050/33-44-44**) and outside the rail station on Stationsplein (✆ **050/38-46-60**).

[Fast FACTS] BRUGES

Currency Exchange The tourist office (see "Visitor Information," above) is a good place to change money and traveler's checks, as are banks. ATMs can be found around the Markt and at numerous other points in the city center.

Doctors For a doctor on night and weekend duty, call ✆ **078/15-15-90.**

Emergencies For the police, dial ✆ **101;** for firefighters and ambulance, call ✆ **100.**

Hospital Bruges's main hospital is the **AZ Sint-Jan,** Ruddershove 10 (✆ **050/45-21-11;** www.azbrugge.be).

Mail The main post office, Markt 5 (✆ **050/33-14-11**), is open Monday to Friday from 9am to 6pm and Saturday from 9am to 3pm.

Pharmacies A pharmacy is an *apotheek* in Dutch. Regular pharmacy hours are Monday to Saturday 9am to 6pm (some close earlier on Sat). Try **Steve Baert,** Wollestraat 7 (✆ **050/33-64-74**), just south of the Markt. All pharmacies have details of the nearby all-night and Sunday pharmacies posted on the door.

Police (Politie) In an emergency, call ✆ **101.** In non-urgent situations, go to the **Central Police Station,** Hauwerstraat 3 (✆ **050/44-88-44**). Bruges police officers are likely to be both professional and helpful to visitors with problems, and you're almost sure to be attended to by an officer who speaks English.

Restrooms The finest place to find relief in the center of Bruges has to be the **Crown Plaza Brugge Hotel,** on the Burg. There are tolerable public restrooms on the west side of the Minnewater lake, close to the Begijnhof.

Safety Bruges is safe, and there are no areas you need be leery of going into. That said, since it's a big tourist center, it can't hurt to take routine precautions against pickpocketing and other types of theft.

WHERE TO STAY

If a high-rise luxury hotel is your cup of tea, I suggest you stay in Brussels and commute to Bruges. But if you like the idea of small, atmospheric accommodations, perhaps on the banks of a picturesque canal, with modern (and in some places, luxurious) facilities, opt for one of the places reviewed below. Try to arrive with a reservation. Considering the four million visitors it welcomes each year, Bruges is Belgium's premier tourist destination. Even though many visitors are day-trippers, it's essential to make your hotel reservations at least 2 weeks in advance if you plan to stay overnight. Having said that, if you do come into town without a place to stay, head immediately to the tourist office, which has a last-minute reservation service. Accommodations are more likely to be full on weekends.

Note that where hotels have no private parking, there's another option beyond the "limited street parking" that might be listed in the service information. Bruges's small city center holds six large public parking garages, all clearly marked on access roads. There will always be at least one within a short walk of your hotel.

Expensive

Die Swaene ★★ This small hotel on the beautiful Groenerei canal in the center city has rightly been called one of the most romantic in Europe. The rooms are elegantly and individually furnished, and the lounge, from 1779, was formerly the Guildhall of the Tailors. You might be expected to lodge in an annex, across the canal, where the rooms are luxurious enough but not so convenient—you have to recross the canal to take advantage of the main building's amenities, for instance. The seafood and regional cuisine at the in-house restaurant **Wine&Dine Pergola Kaffee** has deservedly earned favorable reviews from guests and food critics alike.

Steenhouwersdijk 1 (across the canal from the Burg), 8000 Brugge. ✆ **050/34-27-98.** Fax 050/33-66-74. www.dieswaene-hotel.com. 32 units. 195€–295€ double; 360€–480€ suite. AE, DC, MC, V. Parking 15€. Bus: 6 or 16 to Vismarkt. **Amenities:** Restaurant; bar; lounge; babysitting; concierge; exercise room; heated indoor pool; sauna; Wi-Fi in lobby (free). *In room:* A/C (some rooms), TV, hair dryer, minibar.

The Pand Hotel ★★★ On a side street just off Bruges's handsome central canal, this hotel in a restored 18th-century mansion is an oasis of tranquillity, surrounded by plane trees and built around a courtyard garden with a fountain. Although it provides modern conveniences, its exquisite, old-fashioned furnishings lend special grace to rooms that (except for the suites) may be a little small for some tastes, though that's not unusual for old buildings in Bruges. Guests praise Mrs. Chris Vanhaecke-Dewaele for her hospitality and attention to detail. The suites each have a whirlpool bath.

Pandreitje 16 (across the canal from the Burg), 8000 Brugge. ✆ **050/34-06-66.** Fax 050/34-05-56. www.pandhotel.com. 26 units. 185€–363€ double; 279€–443€ suite. AE, DC, MC, V. Parking 24€. Bus: 1 or 6 to Vismarkt. **Amenities:** Bar; babysitting; concierge; access to nearby health club; room service; sauna. *In room:* A/C, TV, hair dryer, minibar, Wi-Fi (free).

Moderate

Egmond ★ The Egmond has just eight rooms, in a rambling mansion next to the Minnewater Park, but the lucky few who stay here will find ample space, plenty of family ambience, abundant local color, and lots of peace. All rooms have been redecorated recently and are furnished in individual styles with views of the garden and the Minnewater Park. Every afternoon, free coffee and tea are served on the garden terrace or in the lounge, which has an 18th-century fireplace. There's an "honesty bar," where you help yourself to a drink and leave payment. Some rooms have air-conditioning.

Minnewater 15 (at Minnewater Park), 8000 Brugge. ✆ **050/34-14-45.** Fax 050/34-29-40. www.egmond.be. 8 units. 98€–140€ double. Rates include buffet breakfast. MC, V. Parking 10€. Bus: 1 to Begijnhof. *In room:* TV, hair dryer, Wi-Fi (free).

Heritage ★★ A short walk from the Markt in a mansion dating from 1869, the Heritage has a well-established reputation. Its rooms are not overly big, but they are warmly furnished and decorated. Everything has been upgraded here in recent years

Where to Stay & Dine in Bruges

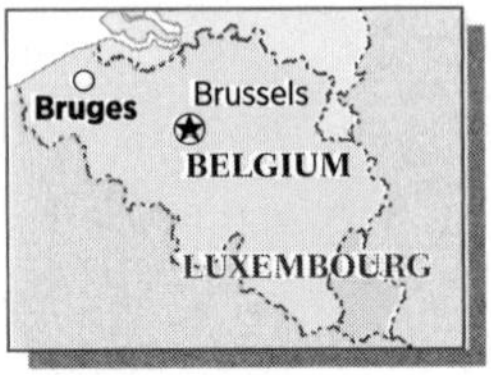

ACCOMMODATIONS ■

- Die Swaene **9**
- Egmond **20**
- Fevery **2**
- Heritage **6**
- Lucca **5**
- Martin's Relais Oud Huis Amsterdam **3**
- The Pand Hotel **15**
- Rosenburg **17**
- Ter Duinen **1**
- 't Keizershof **19**

DINING ◆

- Bhavani **13**
- Brasserie Erasmus **10**
- Breydel-De Coninck **12**
- Central **7**
- De Florentijnen **4**
- De Karmeliet **18**
- De Visscherie **11**
- Lotus **8**
- 't Huidevettershuis **14**
- 't Pandreitje **16**

Church
Canal boat tours
Information
Parking
Post office
Railway

0 — 1/4 mi
0 — 0.25 km

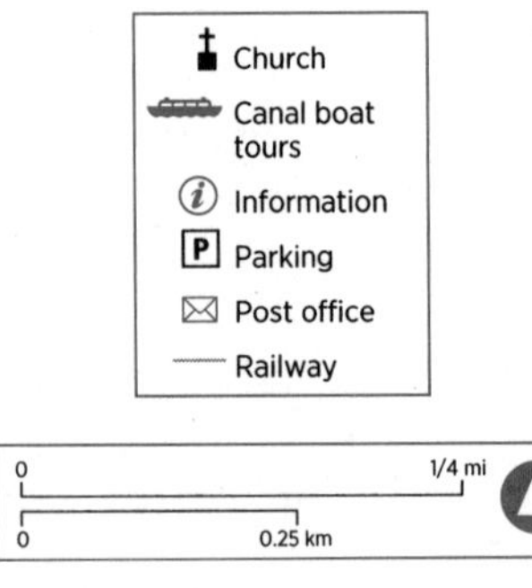

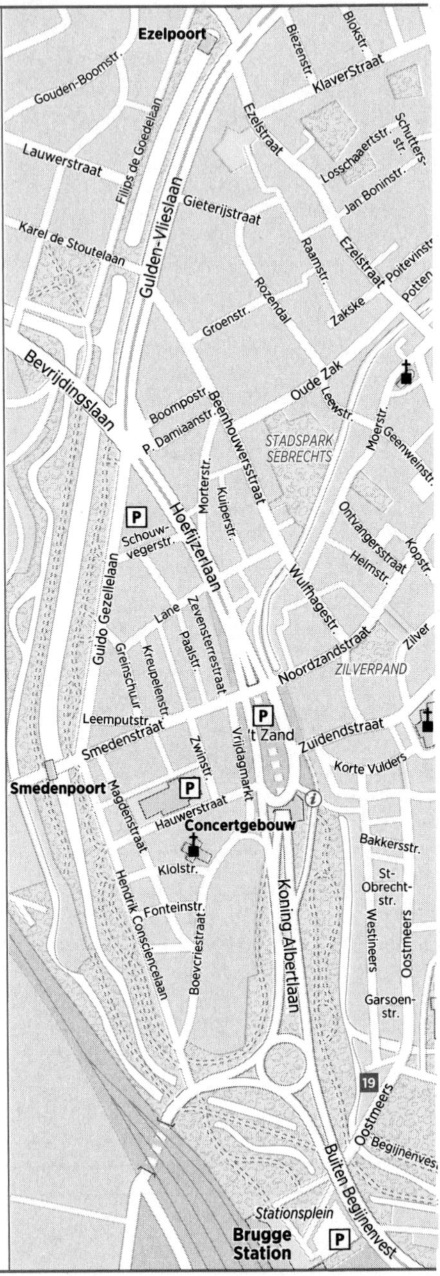

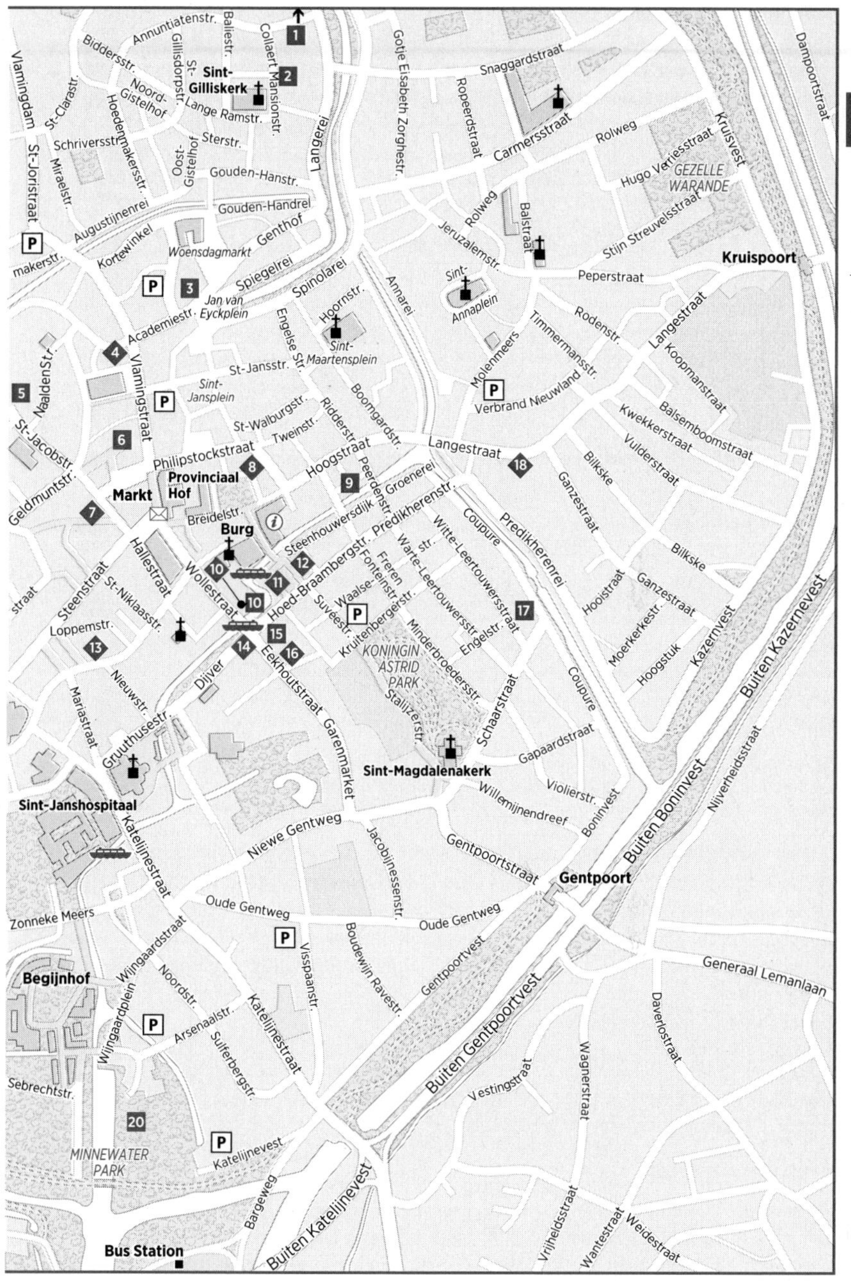
Annuntiatenstr.
Baliestr.
Collaert Mansionstr.
1
2
Biddersstr.
Gillisdorpstr.
St-
Sint-
Gilliskerk
Vlamingdam
St-Clarastr.
Noord-
Gistelhof
Hoedenmakersstr.
Lange Ramstr.
Langerei
Gotje Elisabeth Zorghestr.
Ropeerdstraat
Snaggardstraat
Dampoortstraat
Carmersstraat
Rolweg
Kruisvest
Hugo Verriesstraat
GEZELLE
WARANDE
Schriversstr.
St-Jorisstraat
Miraelstr.
Sterstr.
Oost-
Gistelhof
Gouden-Hanstr.
Gouden-Handrei
Augustijnenrei
Genthof
Woensdagmarkt
Kortewinkel
makersstr.
P
3
Spiegelrei
Spinolarei
Jan van
Eyckplein
Academiestr.
Rolweg
Balstraat
Jeruzalemstr.
Stijn Streuvelsstraat
Kruispoort
Sint-
Annaplein
Peperstraat
Annarei
Hoornstr.
Sint-
Maartensplein
Engelse Str.
4
Naaldenstr.
5
St-Jansstr.
Sint-
Jansplein
Vlamingstraat
Rodenstr.
Timmermansstr.
Langestraat
Koopmanstraat
Molenmeers
Verbrand Nieuwland
Balsemboomstraat
Kwekkerstraat
St-Jacobstr.
6
St-Walburgstr.
Tweinstr.
Ridderstr.
Boomgaardstr.
Philipstockstraat
8
Provinciaal
Hof
Markt
Hoogstraat
9
Langestraat
18
Vulderstraat
Bilkske
Ganzestraat
Geldmuntstr.
7
Breidelstr.
Burg
Steenhouwersdijk
Groenerei
Peerdenstr.
Predikherenstr.
Coupure
Predikherenrei
Witte-Leertouwersstraat
Hallestraat
Wollestraat
10
11
12
Hoed-Braambergstr.
Fonteinstr.
Freren
Warte-Leertouwersstr.
str.
Bilkske
Hooistraat
Ganzestraat
Steenstraat
straat
St-Niklaasstr.
Waalse-
Suveestr.
Kruitenbergerstr.
Minderbroedersstr.
Engelstr.
17
Moerkerkestr.
Hoogstuk
Kazernvest
Buiten Kazernevest
Loppemstr.
13
15
14
16
Eekhoutstraat
KONINGIN
ASTRID
PARK
Stalijzerstr.
Schaarstraat
Coupure
Mariastraat
Nieuwstr.
Dijver
Gruuthusestr.
Garenmarkt
Sint-Magdalenakerk
Gapaardstraat
Violierstr.
Willemijnendreef
Boninvest
Buiten Boninvest
Nijverheidsstraat
Sint-Janshospitaal
Katelijnestraat
Niewe Gentweg
Jacobijnessenstr.
Gentpoortstraat
Gentpoort
Zonneke Meers
Oude Gentweg
Oude Gentweg
Wijngaardstraat
Visspaanstr.
Boudewijn Ravestr.
Gentpoortvest
Generaal Lemanlaan
Begijnhof
Noordstr.
Arsenaalstr.
Katelijnestraat
Buiten Gentpoortvest
Daverlostraat
Wijngaardplein
Sulferbergstr.
Wagnerstraat
Vestingstraat
Sebrechtstr.
20
MINNEWATER
PARK
Katelijnevest
Bargeweg
Buiten Katelijnevest
Vrijheidsstraat
Wantestraat
Weidestraat
Bus Station

in a classic French and Italian style, with individual coordinated color schemes in blue, lime, brown, and boudoir red. At the risk of seeming sexist, they have lots of feminine touches—plush elegance without a sign of stuffiness, manorial without the shooting-trophy baggage that often goes with that. The staff are friendly and the ambience welcoming. In the breakfast room is an ornamental ceiling that's a reminder of the building's respectable origins.

Niklaas Desparsstraat 11 (off Vlamingstraat), 8000 Brugge. ✆ **050/44-44-44.** Fax 050/44-44-40. www.hotel-heritage.com. 20 units. 167€–265€ double; 375€–451€ suite. AE, DC, MC, V. Parking 21€. Bus: 3 or 13 to Kipstraat. **Amenities:** Lounge; exercise room; sauna. *In room:* A/C, TV/DVD, hair dryer, minibar, Wi-Fi (free).

Martin's Relais Oud-Huis Amsterdam ★★ A fine hotel has been carved out of four canal-side buildings, parts of which date back to the 1300s. Rooms are large and sumptuously furnished. The colors and decorative accents hearken back to the building's origins, based on meticulous research and restoration. Some of the bathrooms have whirlpool tubs. The elegant guest rooms in the front overlook the canal; those in back overlook the garden and picturesque rooftops. In the rear, there's a charming little courtyard with umbrella tables and a garden off to one side—the setting for Sunday concerts in June.

Genthof 4A (at Spiegelrei), 8000 Brugge. ✆ **050/34-18-10.** Fax 050/33-88-91. www.martins-hotels.be. 44 units. 149€–181€ double; 328€ suite. AE, DC, MC, V. Parking 15€. Bus: 4, 14, or 43 to Jan van Eyckplein. **Amenities:** Restaurant; bar; babysitting; room service. *In room:* A/C (some rooms), TV, hair dryer, high-speed Internet.

Rosenburg This ultramodern brick hotel set alongside a lovely canal artfully combines old Bruges style with modern amenities and fittings. Its spacious guest rooms are restfully decorated in cool colors that accent blue and yellow in the bed covers, sofa covers, cushions, and other fabrics, alongside relatively plain brown furnishings. The hotel is a short walk west from the city center, and most rooms have a view of the canal at Coupure.

Coupure 30 (at Schaarstraat), 8000 Brugge. ✆ **050/34-01-94.** Fax 050/34-35-39. www.rosenburg.be. 27 units. 110€–170€ double; 200€–350€ suite. AE, DC, MC, V. Limited street parking. Bus: 6 or 16 to Schaarstraat. **Amenities:** Bar; lounge; room service. *In room:* TV, hair dryer, minibar, Wi-Fi (15€/stay).

Ter Duinen ★ Here's an ideal marriage of classical style and modern conveniences. Proprietors Marc and Lieve Bossu-Van Den Heuvel take justified pride in their charming hotel and extend a friendly welcome to guests. Brightly decorated guest rooms are ample in size and have modern furnishings. Some rooms have wooden ceiling beams, and some have a great view overlooking the tranquil Langerei canal, just north of the town center and within easy walking distance. The most expensive rooms have canal views.

Langerei 52 (at Kleine Nieuwstraat), 8000 Brugge. ✆ **050/33-04-37.** Fax 050/34-24-55. www.terduinenhotel.eu. 20 units. 130€–159€ double; 175€ suite. Rates include buffet breakfast. AE, DC, MC, V. Limited street parking. Bus: 4, 14, or 43 to J&M Sabbestraat. **Amenities:** Lounge. *In room:* A/C (some rooms), TV, hair dryer, Wi-Fi (free).

Inexpensive

Fevery ★ Don't be put off by the name: It's pronounced *fay*-ver-ee, not fever-y as in "feverish." This family-owned hotel is on a side street in a quiet part of town, facing the Sint-Gilliskerk (St. Giles's Church), a short walk north of the center city. The modern and comfortably furnished guest rooms are cheery and immaculate, with new bathrooms and monogrammed pressed sheets. One room is a quad. There's a downstairs lounge and breakfast room. The proprietor, Mr. Asselman, has a wealth of local information and clearly takes great pride in his establishment. In 2009, his hotel was the first in Bruges to be awarded a "Green Key" for its sustainable practices.

Collaert Mansionstraat 3 (off Langerei), 8000 Brugge. ✆ **050/33-12-69.** Fax 050/33-17-91. www.hotelfevery.be. 12 units. 50€–90€ double. Rates include buffet breakfast. MC, V. Parking 8€–10€. Bus: 4, 14, or 43 to Snaggaardbrug. **Amenities:** Lounge; bikes. *In room:* TV, hair dryer, Wi-Fi (free).

Lucca Built in the 14th century by a wealthy merchant from Lucca, Italy, this mansion right in the heart of romantic Bruges has high ceilings and wide halls that convey a sense of luxury. The welcome is warm, and the guest rooms are in fair condition and sport pine furnishings. Rooms with bathrooms have TVs. Breakfast is served in a cozy medieval cellar decorated with antiques.

Naaldenstraat 30 (off Kuipersstraat), 8000 Brugge. ✆ **050/34-20-67.** Fax 050/33-34-64. www.hotellucca.be. 19 units, 14 with bathroom. 53€ double without bathroom; 68€–88€ double with bathroom. Rates include buffet breakfast. AE, DC, MC, V. Limited street parking. Bus: 3 or 13 to Normaalschool. *In room:* TV (some rooms).

't Keizershof Despite being one of the least expensive hotels in Bruges, 't Keizershof gets high marks for having clean, comfortable accommodations in a quiet, peaceful location. The couple who own and operate this hotel speak several languages and are very helpful to guests planning their stay in Bruges. I like the subtle encouragements they give to potential guests, including one slogan that goes: "When you are sleeping, we look just like one of those big fancy hotels."

Oostmeers 126 (across from the rail station), 8000 Brugge. ✆ **050/33-87-28.** www.hotelkeizershof.be. 7 units, none with bathroom. 44€ double. Rates include continental breakfast. No credit cards. Free parking. All buses to Bruges station. *In room:* No phone.

WHERE TO DINE

Half of Bruges seems like one big museum, another half seems like one big drinkery, and yet another half (yes, I know, that's a half too many) seems like one big eatery. You'll be practically tripping over restaurants within the central zone. Pretty much all of them are tourist-orientated to one degree or other; it would be hard to be otherwise, considering the throngs of visitors.

The Markt and the streets leading off this central square (though not the adjacent Burg) are the happiest hunting grounds. Close to the Vismarkt (Fish Market), Pandreitje and Huidenvettersplein have decent choices; so, too, do Simon Stevinplein and Katelijnestraat, near Sint-Salvatorskathedraal and Onze-Lieve-Vrouwekerk, respectively. North of the Markt, Academiestraat and Jan van Eyckplein are good bets.

The least touristy restaurants and local bars with eats generally are to be found out toward the ring canal and beyond this moat. They're thin on the ground.

Very Expensive

De Karmeliet ★★★ BELGIAN/FRENCH In 1996, chef Geert van Hecke became the first Flemish chef to be awarded three Michelin stars. He has described his award-winning menu as "international cuisine made with local products" that aims to combine French quality with Flemish quantity. A good example of this is van Hecke's deceptively plain-sounding common Zeebrugge sole served with North Sea shrimps. The result is outstanding fine cuisine dished out in an elegant setting. You'll find the local Oud Brugge cheese both as an ingredient and on the cheese board, and some sauces are made using Belgian *jenever* (gin) and Belgian beers.

Langestraat 19 (off Hoogstraat). ✆ **050/33-82-59.** www.dekarmeliet.be. Reservations required. Main courses 55€–75€; fixed-price menus 80€–180€. AE, DC, MC, V. Tues–Sat noon–2pm and 7–9:30pm; Sun 7–9:30pm. Bus: 6 or 16.

Expensive

De Florentijnen ★ CONTINENTAL It's a fair bet that the Renaissance-era Florentine merchants who once stayed here wouldn't recognize their gabled old house. It now houses this sophisticated restaurant, a dazzlingly white confection in which shades are a useful accessory. The menu is more than a little showy, with items like a 50g (1.7 oz.) dollop of caviar starter that costs more than twice the most expensive main course, and Barents Sea king crabs. Still, most dishes live up to both their billing and their tab. The price of some added-cost fixed-price menus, with enough wine and liquor to breach the legal driving limit, includes complementary limo pickup and an arranged but noncomplementary taxi for the return ride.

Academiestraat 1 (at Vlamingstraat). ✆ **050/67-75-33.** www.deflorentijnen.be. Main courses 34€–63€; fixed-price lunch 24€, dinner 39€–65€. AE, DC, MC, V. Tues–Sat noon–2pm and 7–9:30pm; Sun 7–9:30pm. Bus: 3 or 13.

De Visscherie ★★ SEAFOOD Deservedly much-admired, "The Fishery" couldn't be closer to a supply of its prime ingredient: It's just steps from Bruges's Vismarkt (Fish Market), in the center of town. Specialties here include a delicious lobster stew, "fruits of the sea" (shellfish in many guises; try the spotted scallops with roe), and Channel sole. Inside, white-gloved waiters pad around the soft chairs on a stone floor, amid a restful pastel-orange and brown color scheme. When a chilly Flanders winter howls beyond the windows, you can warm your spirits at the open fire. Outside on the square, a sidewalk terrace with wicker chairs soaks up both the sun and Fish Market ambience in good weather.

Vismarkt 8 (at Steenhouwersdijk). ✆ **050/33-02-12.** www.visscherie.be. Main courses 32€–53€; fixed-price lunch 35€, dinner 78€. AE, DC, MC, V. Wed–Mon noon–2pm and 7–10pm. Bus: All buses to Markt.

't Pandreitje ★ FRENCH/BELGIAN This restaurant sits in the shade of the medieval Market Hall's bell tower, just off the Rozenhoedkaai, one of the most beautiful canalsides in Bruges. The interior of this Renaissance-era private home has been turned into an elegant Louis XVI setting for a menu of classic dishes. The four-course a la carte meal is superb, and the menu of preselected choices is excellent. Try the sea bass served with fennel, parsley sauce, and sautéed potatoes, or the salad of Dublin Bay prawns with artichoke and a truffle vinaigrette.

Pandreitje 6 (off Rozenhoedkaai). ✆ **050/33-11-90.** www.pandreitje.be. Reservations required. Main courses 35€–48€; fixed-price menus 75€–95€. AE, DC, MC, V. Mon–Tues and Thurs–Sat noon–2pm and 7–9:30pm. Bus: 1, 6, 11, or 16.

Moderate

Bhavani ☺ INDIAN For a change from traditional Belgian food, try the better of Bruges's pair of traditional Indian restaurants. It's a consistently fine performer across a wide range of subcontinental cuisine—*thali* (a sampling platter), tandoori, curry, vegetarian, and seafood—without being exactly outstanding in any category. You shouldn't have to count your rupees too closely, and the set meals are a good value. The chicken *tikka Maharaja* is a good bet, as is the vegetarian *thali*. A mix of coziness, colonial atmosphere, Indian music, and exotic charm marks a setting that gives traditional Indian motifs a modern slant. There's a menu for kids who can't handle spicy Indian food.

Simon Stevinplein 5 (off of Oude Burg). ✆ **050/33-90-25.** www.bhavani.be. Main courses 16€-25€; fixed-price menus 19€-27€. AE, DC, MC, V. Daily 4:30pm-12:30am. Bus: 6, 12, or 14.

Breydel-De Coninc SEAFOOD An aquarium of tropical fish at the entrance sets a marine mood in this seafood restaurant just off the Markt. The wood-beam ceilings and plaid upholstery are cheerful, but the real attraction is the seafood. The specialties here are mussels, eels, and lobsters prepared with white wine, cream, or garlic sauces that enhance the flavor of the seafood without overwhelming it. Try a pail full of plain mussels, or go for something with a little more zest, like the *moules Provençal* (mussels in a light red sauce with mushrooms, peppers, and onions). The homemade ice cream with caramel sauce is a good way to wind up any meal.

Breidelstraat 24 (between the Markt and the Burg). ✆ **050/33-97-46.** Main courses 10€-21€; fixed-price menus 16€-36€. AE, MC, V. Thurs-Tues noon-3pm and 6-9:30pm. Bus: All buses to Markt.

Central FLEMISH The medieval Markt square is such a romantic setting for a meal that few visitors can resist it. Central has both outdoor dining and a glassed-in room that overlooks the square. You can't go too far wrong with the basic Flemish *steak-frites* (steak with fries), but this restaurant does the regional cuisine more justice with a fine range of mussels dishes, and other seafood offerings like a tasty North Sea bouillabaisse, the *sole à l'Ostendaise* (Ostend sole), and lobster.

Markt 31 (in the Central Hotel). ✆ **050/33-18-05.** www.restaurantcentral.be. Main courses 12€-32€; fixed-price menu 14€-32€. AE, DC, MC, V. Daily 10am-10pm. Bus: All buses to Markt.

't Huidevettershuis ★ FLEMISH/SEAFOOD This charmer, right on a canal in the town center, is in a stone building dating from 1630 with flowers blooming in diamond-paned windows. It used to be the Ambachtshuis der Huidevetters (Tanners' Guild House) and now houses a cozy, intimate room downstairs and a pleasant, larger one upstairs. Look for Flemish specialties such as the souplike *waterzooï* (with chicken), in addition to ham, rabbit, and herring dishes.

Huidenvettersplein 10-11 (at Rozenhoedkaai). ✆ **050/33-95-06.** www.huidevettershuis.be. Main courses 22€-48€; fixed-price lunch 20€, dinner 29€. AE, DC, MC, V. Wed-Mon noon-2pm and 6-10pm. Bus: All buses to Markt.

Inexpensive

Brasserie Erasmus ★ FLEMISH Small but popular, this is a great stop after viewing the cathedral and nearby museums. It serves a large variety of Flemish dishes, all prepared with beer. Try the typically Flemish souplike stew dish *waterzooï,* which is served with fish here, as it's supposed to be—although they also make it with chicken instead, a style that has become the norm elsewhere. If that doesn't grab you, how about *lapin à la bière* (rabbit in a beer sauce)? More than 200 different brands of Belgian beer are available (for drinking, that is), 16 of them on tap.

Wollestraat 35 (in the Hotel Erasmus, off the Markt). ✆ **050/33-57-81.** www.hotelerasmus.com. Main courses 15€-25€; fixed-price menus 35€-43€. MC, V. Tues-Sun noon-4pm (also Mon in summer) and 6-11pm. Bus: All buses to Markt.

Lotus VEGETARIAN Even nonvegetarians likely will enjoy the delicious lunch here. There are just two menu options—but at least you get to choose from a small, medium, or large serving—each with a hearty assortment of imaginatively prepared vegetables, served in a tranquil but cheery Scandinavian-style dining room. Locally sourced organic produce is used as much as possible. There's a small but decent selection of Belgian beers to accompany your meal—look out for the relatively rare unfiltered Poperings Hommelbier from the West Flanders region around Ypres (Ieper).

Wapenmakersstraat 5 (off the Burg). ✆ **050/33-10-78.** www.lotus-brugge.be. Fixed-price lunch 9€–12€. No credit cards. Mon–Sat 11:45am–2pm. Bus: All buses to Markt.

SEEING THE SIGHTS

A leading contender for the title of Europe's most romantic small city, Bruges is really one big attraction—a fairy-tale mixture of gabled houses, meandering canals, magnificent squares, and narrow cobblestone streets. Perhaps the most astonishing thing is the consistently warm welcome its residents provide to the swarms of visitors. The basis for this is more than mere economics—those who live in Bruges love their city and appreciate that others want to experience it.

The Markt

Heraldic banners float from venerable facades on the Markt. This square, along with the Burg (see below), is the heart of Bruges and the focal point of your sightseeing. Most major points of interest in the city are little more than 5 or 10 minutes' walk away.

Bruggemuseum-Belfort (Belfry) ★★ The Belfry was, and is, the symbol of Bruges's civic pride. What poet Henry Wadsworth Longfellow in 1856 called "the beautiful, wild chimes" of its magnificent 47-bell carillon peal out over the city every quarter-hour, and several times a day in longer concerts during the summer. The tower stands 83m (272 ft.) high. Its lower section dates from around 1240, with the corner turrets added in the 14th century and the upper, octagonal section in the 15th century. Climb the 366 steep steps to the Belfry's summit for panoramic views of Bruges and the surrounding countryside all the way to the sea. Pause for breath at the second-floor Treasury, where the town seal and charters were kept behind multiple wrought-iron grilles. From the 13th to the 16th century, much of the city's commerce was conducted in the **Hallen (Market Halls),** below the Belfry. A consortium of local art dealers now uses the Hallen as a space for exhibits. ***Note:*** The Belfry is under renovation until summer 2011, and views are obscured until then.

Markt. ✆ **050/44-87-11.** Admission 8€ adults, 6€ seniors, 4€ ages 6–25, free for children 5 and under. Daily 9:30am–5pm. Closed Jan 1, Ascension Day afternoon, and Dec 25.

OTHER SIGHTS AROUND THE MARKT

The **sculpture group** in the center of the Markt depicts a pair of Flemish heroes, butcher Jan Breydel and weaver Pieter de Coninck. The two led an uprising in 1302 against the wealthy merchants and nobles who dominated the guilds, and went on to win an against-the-odds victory over French knights later that same year in the Battle of the Golden Spurs. The small, castlelike building called the **Craenenburg** (it's now a restaurant), at the corner of Sint-Amandsstraat, was used by a rebellious citizenry to imprison the Habsburg Crown Prince and future Emperor Maximilian of Austria in 1488 over a small matter of increased taxes. In revenge for that humiliation, Maximilian later wounded Bruges's pride by transferring his capital to Ghent and hit the city's pocketbook by transferring its trading rights to Antwerp. The large neo-Gothic

Swans Forever

In addition to locking up the heir to the Habsburg throne, Bruges's vexed 15th-century taxpayers removed the head of his counselor Pieter Lanchals, who had argued for the tax increase in the first place. Lanchals's family emblem was a swan, and for this crime, Maximilian exacted a "penalty" from the citizens that has added a note of pure beauty to the city ever since: He obliged them to keep swans on the canals forever.

Provinciaal Hof (Provincial Palace) dates from the 1800s and houses the government of the province of West Flanders.

The Burg

The Burg, a public square just steps away from the Markt, holds an array of beautiful buildings, which together add up to a kind of trip through the history of European architecture. On this site, Baldwin Iron Arm, count of Flanders, once built a fortified castle (or "burg"), around which a village developed into Bruges.

Basiliek van het Heilig-Bloed (Basilica of the Holy Blood) ★ A 12th-century Romanesque basilica with a Gothic upper floor, this church houses a venerated relic of Christ and is well worth a visit for the richness of its design and its other treasures. It is the repository of a fragment of cloth stained with what is said to be the blood of Christ, wiped from his body after the crucifixion by Joseph of Arimathea. Legend says the relic was brought to Bruges at the time of the Second Crusade by Count of Flanders Diederik van de Elzas, who received it from the patriarch of Jerusalem and donated it to the church in 1150. More likely, it arrived later from the Byzantine capital Constantinople, which in 1204 was sacked by the Crusader army of Count of Flanders Baldwin IX.

The relic is embedded in a rock-crystal vial, which itself is held inside a small glass cylinder adorned at each end with a golden crown. Normally the relic is kept in a magnificent tabernacle on a side altar in the upstairs chapel, but it is brought out regularly so the faithful can kiss it. In the Basilica Museum, a reliquary created in 1617 by Bruges goldsmith Jan Crabbe has a gem-encrusted hexagonal case to hold the relic, and at the top a golden statue of the Virgin. A second reliquary, dating from 1612, with a lid from 1716, is silver with a golden flower garland added in 1890. Every year, in the colorful Procession of the Holy Blood, on Ascension Day, the bishop of Bruges leads the relic through the streets, accompanied by costumed residents acting out biblical scenes.

Burg 10. ✆ **050/33-67-92.** www.holyblood.com. Admission: basilica free; museum 1.50€ adults, 1€ children 5–18, free for children 4 and under. Apr–Sept daily 9:30am–noon and Thurs–Tues 2–6pm; Oct–Mar daily 10am–noon and Thurs–Tues 2–4pm. Museum closed Jan 1, Nov 1, and Dec 25.

Bruggemuseum-Brugse Vrije (Liberty of Bruges) Dating in part from a rebuilding that took place between 1722 and 1727 and in part from earlier periods, the Landhuis (Palace) of the Liberty of Bruges was the seat of a district of the county of Flanders around Bruges from the Middle Ages onward. The palace later became a courthouse and now houses the city archives. Inside, at no. 11A, is the **Renaissancezaal (Renaissance Hall) ★★**, the council chamber, which has been restored to its original 16th-century condition. The hall has a superb black marble fireplace

What to See & Do in Bruges

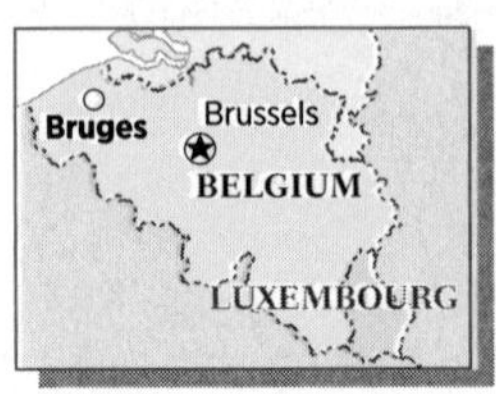

Basiliek van het Heilig-Bloed **19**
Begijnhof **35**
Begijnhuisje **34**
Bruggemuseum-Belfort (and Hallen) **18**
Bruggemuseum-Brugse Vrije **22**
Bruggemuseum-Gruuthuse **26**
Bruggemuseum-Stadhuis **24**
Bruggemuseum-Volkskunde **10**
Bonne-Chièremolen **5**
Boudewijn Seapark **37**
Brouwerij De Halve Maan **31**
Burg **21**
Choco Story–The Chocolate Museum **12**
Craenenburg **17**
Diamantmuseum Brugge **32**
Ezelpoort **1**
Gentpoort **28**
Godshuis De Vos **33**
Groeningemuseum **27**
Hof Bladelin **13**
Jeruzalemkerk **9**
Kantcentrum **8**
Kinderboerderij Domein De Zeven Torentjes **6**
Koeleweimolen **3**
Kruispoort **7**
Markt **15**
Memling in Sint-Jan/Hospitaalmuseum **30**
Nieuwe Papegaaimolen **2**
Onze-Lieve-Vrouwekerk **29**
Onze-Lieve-Vrouw ter Potterie **2**
Oude Civiele Griffie **23**
Poertoren **36**
Proosdij **20**
Provinciaal Hof **16**
Sint-Jakobskerk **14**
Sint-Janshuismolen **4**
Sint-Salvatorskathedraal **25**
Sint-Walburgakerk **11**
Smedenpoort **38**

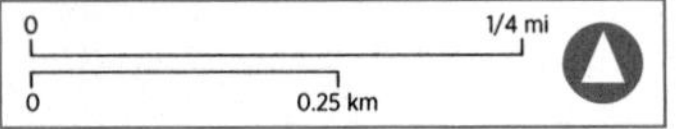

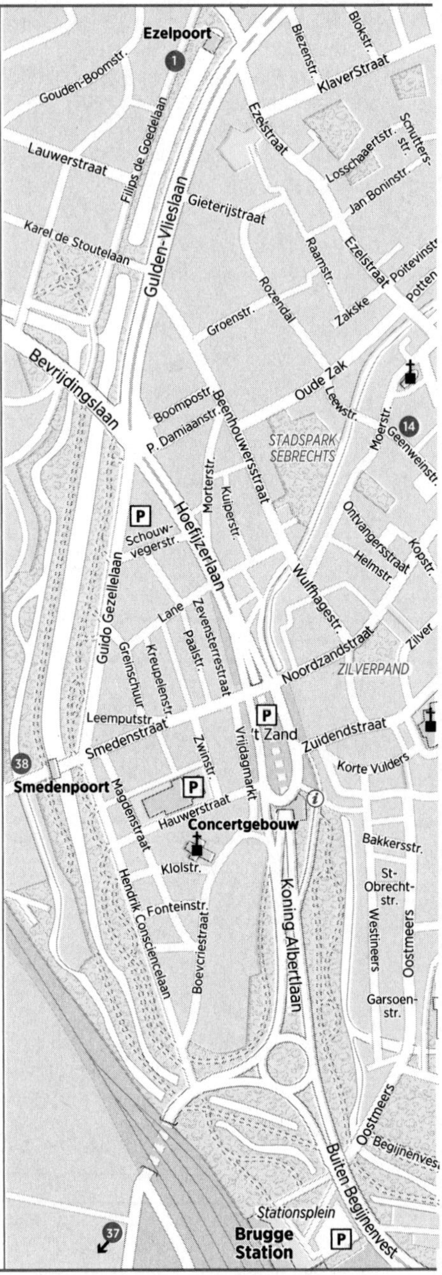

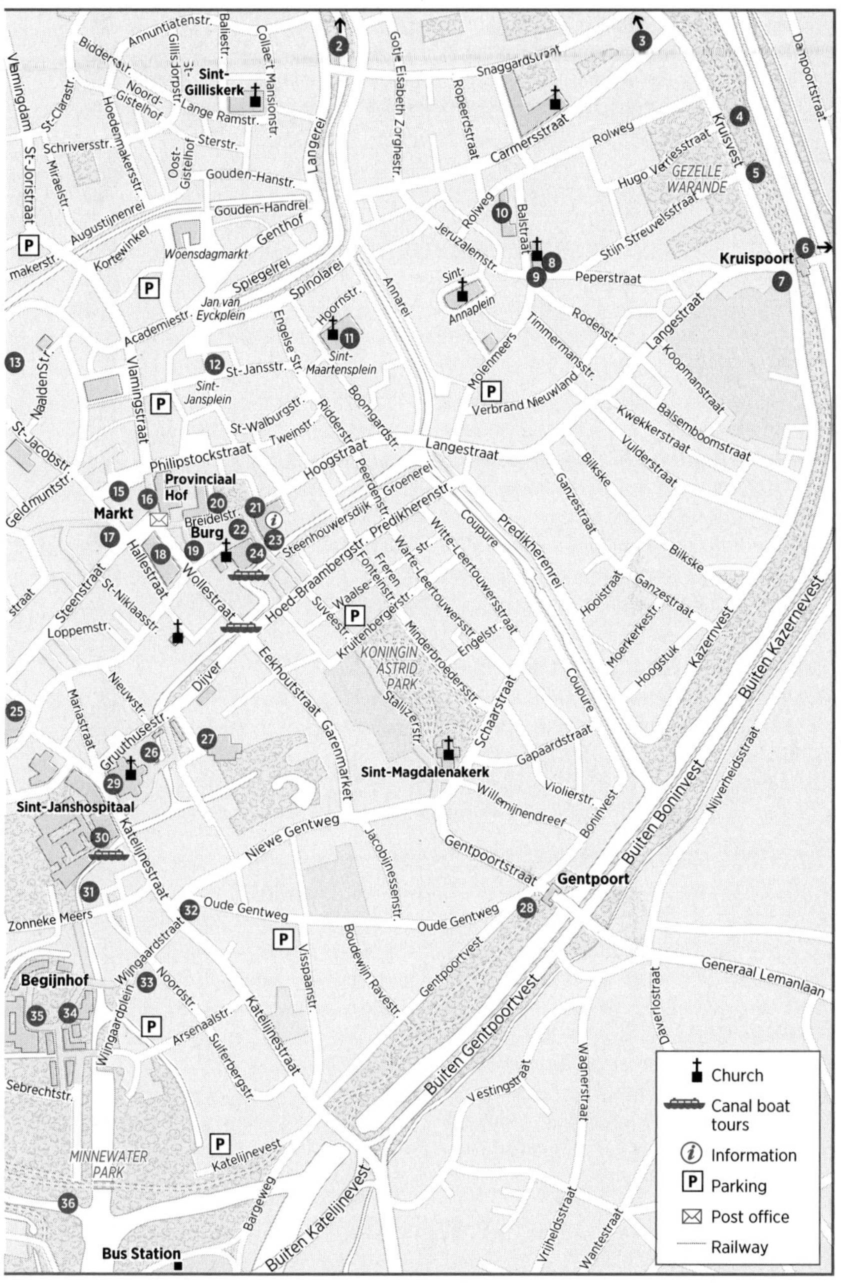
Church
Canal boat tours
Information
Parking
Post office
Railway
Sint-Gilliskerk
Kruispoort
Provinciaal Hof
Markt
Burg
Sint-Magdalenakerk
Sint-Janshospitaal
Gentpoort
Begijnhof
Bus Station
GEZELLE WARANDE
KONINGIN ASTRID PARK
MINNEWATER PARK
Sint-Annaplein
Sint-Maartensplein
Sint-Jansplein
Jan van Eyckplein
Woensdagmarkt
Annuntiatenstr.
Baliestr.
Collaert Mansionstr.
Biddersstr.
Gillis Dorpstr.
Noord-Gistelhof
Lange Ramstr.
Vlamingdam
St-Clarastr.
Hoedenmakersstr.
Schriversstr.
Sterstr.
Oost-Gistelhof
Gouden-Handstr.
Gouden-Handrei
St-Joristraat
Miraelstr.
Augustijnenrei
Genthof
Langerei
Gotje Eisabeth Zorghestr.
Ropeerdstraat
Snaggaardstraat
Carmersstraat
Rolweg
Kruisvest
Hugo Verriesstraat
Stijn Streuvelsstraat
Balstraat
Jeruzalemstr.
Peperstraat
Dampoortstraat
Kortewinkel
Spiegelrei
Spinolarei
Annarei
Hoornstr.
Academiestr.
Engelse St.
St-Jansstr.
Vlamingstraat
Naaldenstr.
St-Jacobstr.
Molenmeers
Timmermansstr.
Rodenstr.
Langestraat
Koopmanstraat
Verbrand Nieuwland
Kwekkerstraat
Balsemboomstraat
Vulderstraat
Bilkske
Ganzestraat
Boomgaardstr.
Ridderstr.
St-Walburgstr.
Tweinstr.
Philipstockstraat
Hoogstraat
Geldmuntstr.
Breidelstr.
Peerdenstr.
Groenerei
Steenhouwersdijk
Predikherenstr.
Coupure
Predikherenrei
Witte-Leertouwersstraat
Warte-Leertouwersstr.
Hoed-Braambergstr.
Fonteinstr.
Freren
Waalse-str.
Suvéestr.
Kruitenbergstr.
Minderbroedersstr.
Engelstr.
Hooistraat
Moerkerkestr.
Hoogstuk
Kazernvest
Buiten Kazernevest
Hallestr.
Steenstraat
St-Niklaasstr.
Wollestraat
Loppemstr.
Dijver
Eekhoutstraat
Nieuwstr.
Mariastraat
Gruuthusestr.
Garenmarkt
Stalijzerstr.
Schaarstraat
Gapaardstraat
Violierstr.
Willemijnendreef
Boninvest
Buiten Boninvest
Nijverheidsstraat
Katelijnestraat
Niewe Gentweg
Jacobijnessenstr.
Gentpoortstraat
Oude Gentweg
Zonneke Meers
Wijngaardstraat
Visspaanstr.
Boudewijn Ravestr.
Gentpoortvest
Buiten Gentpoortvest
Generaal Lemanlaan
Daverlostraat
Noordstr.
Wijngaardplein
Arsenaalstr.
Sulferbergstr.
Sebrechtstr.
Vestingstraat
Wagnerstraat
Katelijnevest
Bargeweg
Buiten Katelijnevest
Vrijheidsstraat
Wantestraat

Size Isn't Everything

Here's your chance to compare codpieces . . . ahem, I mean, to admire the finely carved suits of armor of the statues of Emperor Charles V, Emperor Maximilian of Austria, and King Ferdinand II of Aragon on the chimney piece in the Hall of the Liberty of Bruges. (I say Charles's is the biggest.)

decorated with an alabaster frieze and topped by an oak chimneypiece carved with statues of Emperor Charles V, who visited Bruges in 1515, and his grandparents: Emperor Maximilian of Austria, Duchess Mary of Burgundy, King Ferdinand II of Aragon, and Queen Isabella I of Castile.

Burg 11. ✆ **050/44-87-11.** Admission: courtyard free; Renaissance Hall 2€ adults, 1€ seniors and ages 6–25, free for children 5 and under. Daily 9:30am–12:30pm and 1:30–5pm. Closed Jan 1, Ascension Day afternoon, and Dec 25.

Bruggemuseum-Stadhuis (Town Hall) This Gothic structure was built in the late 1300s, making it the oldest Town Hall in Belgium. Don't miss the upstairs **Gotische Zaal (Gothic Room) ★★** with its ornate decor and wall murals depicting highlights from Bruges's history. Most spectacular of all is the vaulted oak ceiling, dating from 1402, which features scenes from the New Testament. The statues in the niches on the Town Hall facade are 1980s replacements of the originals, which had been painted by Jan van Eyck and were destroyed by pro-French rebels in the 1790s.

Burg 12. ✆ **050/44-87-11.** Admission 2€ adults, 1€ seniors and ages 6–25, free for children 5 and under. Daily 9:30am–5pm. Closed Jan 1, Ascension Day afternoon, and Dec 25.

OTHER SIGHTS AROUND THE BURG

The **Oude Civiele Griffie (Old Civic Registry),** built beside the Town Hall as the offices of the town clerk, has the oldest Renaissance facade in the city, dating from 1537, and now houses the city archives. Facing the Town Hall is the baroque **Proosdij (Provost's House),** dating from 1666, which used to be the residence of the bishop of Bruges and is now occupied by government offices of West Flanders province.

Top Museums & Attractions

Groeningemuseum ★★★ The Groeninge ranks among Belgium's leading traditional museums of fine arts, with a collection that covers painting in the Low Countries from the 15th to the 20th centuries. The Gallery of Flemish Primitives holds some 30 works—many of which are far from primitive—by painters such as Jan van Eyck, Rogier van der Weyden, Hieronymus Bosch *(The Last Judgment),* and Hans Memling. Works by Magritte and Delvaux also are on display. Among works by van Eyck in the museum are his beautiful altarpiece *The Madonna and Child with Canon Joris van der Paele* (1436), in which the Flemish cardinal is being presented to the Virgin Mary and the infant Jesus, and a portrait of van Eyck's wife created in 1439. In addition, Sint-Salvatorskathedraal (see below) has given the museum for permanent safekeeping its magnificent *Martyrdom of St. Hippolytus* altarpiece by Dirk Bouts, with a side panel by Hugo van der Goes. ***Note:*** Due to limited space, the exhibits on display rotate and may not reflect exactly what is listed in this review.

Dijver 12. ✆ **050/44-87-11.** Admission (combined ticket with neighboring Arentshuis) 8€ adults, 6€ seniors, 1€ ages 6–25, free for children 5 and under. Tues–Sun 9:30am–5pm (also Easter Mon and Pentecost Mon). Closed Jan 1, Ascension Day afternoon, and Dec 25.

Bruggemuseum-Gruuthuse The Flemish nobleman and herb merchant Lodewijk van Gruuthuse, who was a counselor to the dukes of Burgundy in the 1400s, lived in this ornate Gothic mansion. Among the 2,500 numbered antiquities in the house are paintings, sculptures, tapestries, lace, weapons, glassware, and richly carved furniture.

Dijver 17 (in a courtyard next to the Groeningemuseum). ✆ **050/44-87-11.** Admission 6€ adults, 5€ seniors, 1€ ages 6–25, free for children 5 and under. Tues–Sun 9:30am–5pm (also Easter Mon and Pentecost Mon). Closed Jan 1, Ascension Day afternoon, and Dec 25.

Bruggemuseum-Volkskunde (Folklore Museum) Housed in the low white-washed houses of the former Shoemakers Guild Almshouse, the Folklore Museum aims to recreate life in Bruges in times gone by. Exhibits depict a primary school class, a cooper's and a milliner's workshop, a spice store and a candy store, and everyday household scenes. A new emphasis is on the history of the important regional textile industry. Most refreshing of all is an old inn, De Zwarte Kat (the Black Cat), which has real beer on tap. In summer, children and adults can play traditional games in the garden.

Balstraat 43 (at Rolweg). ✆ **050/44-87-11.** Admission 2€ adults, 1€ seniors and ages 6–25, free for children 5 and under. Tues–Sun 9:30am–5pm (also Easter Mon and Pentecost Mon). Closed Jan 1, Ascension Day afternoon, and Dec 25. Bus: 6 to Kruispoort.

Kantcentrum (Lace Center) This combination workshop, museum, and salesroom is where the ancient art of lace making is passed on to the next generation. You'll get a firsthand look at the artisans making many of the items for future sale in all those lace stores. Your ticket is valid also in the neighboring Jeruzalemkerk (Jerusalem Church; see "More Churches," below).

Peperstraat 3A (at Jeruzalemstraat). ✆ **050/33-00-72.** www.kantcentrum.eu. Admission 2.50€ adults; 1.50€ seniors, students, and children 7–12; free for children 6 and under. Mon–Fri 10am–noon and 2–6pm; Sat 10am–noon and 2–5pm. Closed national holidays. Bus: 6 or 16 to Langestraat.

Memling in Sint-Jan/Hospitaalmuseum This museum is housed in the former Sint-Janshospitaal (Hospital of St. John), where the earliest wards date from the 13th century. To get a sense of the vastness of the wards when this was a functioning hospital, take a look at the old painting near the entrance that shows small, efficient bed units set into cubicles along the walls. The 17th-century apothecary in the cloisters near the entrance is furnished exactly as it was when this building's main function was to care for the sick. Nowadays visitors come to see the typical medieval hospital buildings filled with furniture and other objects that illustrate their history, and the magnificent collection of paintings by the German-born artist Hans Memling (ca. 1440–94), who moved to Bruges from Brussels in 1465 and became one of the city's most prominent residents. At this museum, you find such Memling masterpieces as the three-paneled altarpiece of St. John the Baptist and St. John the Evangelist, which

Impressions

The difference between Bruges and other cities is that in the latter, you look about for the picturesque, and don't find it easily, while in Bruges, assailed on every side by the picturesque, you look curiously for the unpicturesque, and don't find it easily.

—British novelist Arnold Bennett, *The Journals*, 1896–1931

TRANQUIL escapes

Through the centuries, since it was founded in 1245 by the Countess Margaret of Constantinople, the **Prinselijk Begijnhof ten Wijngaarde (Princely Beguinage of the Vineyard)** ★, Wijngaardstraat (✆ **050/33-00-11**), at the Lake of Love, has been one of the most tranquil spots in Bruges, and so it remains today. *Begijns* were religious women, similar to nuns, who accepted vows of chastity and obedience but drew the line at poverty, preferring to earn a living by looking after the sick and making lace. They provided an option for women to live without a husband and children without becoming a nun—there was little in the way of alternatives at the time.

The *begijns* are no more, but the Begijnhof is occupied by Benedictine nuns who try to keep the *begijns'* traditions alive. This beautiful little cluster of 17th-century whitewashed houses surrounding a lawn with poplar trees and flowers makes a marvelous escape from the hustle and bustle of the outside world. One of the houses, the **Begijnhuisje (Beguine's House),** has been made over into a museum and can be visited, as can the convent church during a service. The Begijnhof courtyard is always open and admission is free. The Beguine's House is open from March to November Monday to Saturday from 10am to noon and 1:45 to 5:30pm, Sunday from 10:45am to noon and 1:45 to 5:30pm; from December to February, hours are Monday, Tuesday, and Friday from 11am to noon and 1:45 to 4:15pm, Wednesday and Thursday from 1:45 to 4:15pm, Saturday from 10am to noon and 1:45 to 5:30pm, and Sunday from 10:45am to noon and 1:45 to 5:30pm. Admission is 2€ for adults, 1.50€ for seniors, 1€ for students and children 6 to 18, and free for children 5 and under.

A fine example of the *godshuizen* (houses of God, or almshouses), built by the rich in Bruges from the 13th century onward as refuges for widows and the poor is the **Godshuis de Vos (De Vos Almshouse),** from 1713, at the corner of Noordstraat and Wijngaardstraat, near the Begijnhof. The moneybags weren't being entirely altruistic, since the residents had to pray for their benefactors' souls twice a day in the chapel that was an integral part of an almshouse's facilities. The pretty courtyard garden here is surrounded by a chapel and eight original houses, now converted to six, which are owned by the city and occupied by seniors.

consists of the paintings *The Mystic Marriage of St. Catherine, Shrine of St Ursula,* and *Virgin with Child and Apple.*

Mariastraat 38 (across from Onze-Lieve-Vrouwekerk). ✆ **050/44-87-11.** Admission 8€ adults, 6€ seniors, 1€ ages 6–25, free for children 5 and under. Tues–Sun 9:30am–5pm (also Easter Mon and Pentecost Mon). Closed Jan 1, Ascension Day afternoon, and Dec 25.

Historical Churches

Onze-Lieve-Vrouwekerk (Church of Our Lady) ★★ It took 2 centuries (13th–15th) to build this church, whose soaring 122m (400-ft.) spire can be seen for miles around Bruges. Among the many art treasures here is a beautiful Carrara marble sculpture of the ***Madonna and Child*** ★★★ by Michelangelo. This statue, made in 1504, was the only one of Michelangelo's works to leave Italy in his lifetime and today is one of the few that can be seen outside Italy. It was bought by a Bruges merchant, Jan van Mouskroen, and donated to the church in 1506. The church holds a painting of the *Crucifixion* by Anthony van Dyck, and the impressive side-by-side **bronze tomb sculptures ★** of duke of Burgundy Charles the Bold, who died in 1477, and his daughter, Mary of Burgundy, who died in 1482 at age 25, after falling from her horse. A windowpane under the tombs allows you to view the 13th- and 14th-century graves of priests.

Onze-Lieve-Vrouwekerkhof Zuid. ✆ **050/44-87-11.** Admission: church and *Madonna and Child* altar free; chapel of Charles and Mary and museum 2€ adults, 1€ seniors and ages 6–25, free for children 5 and under. Mon–Fri 9am–12:30pm and 1:30–5pm; Sat 9am–12:30pm and 1:30–4pm; Sun 1:30–5pm.

Sint-Salvatorskathedraal (Holy Savior's Cathedral) This mainly Gothic church with a 100m (328-ft.) belfry has been Bruges's cathedral since 1834 (its predecessor, Saint Donatian's on the Burg, was demolished by the French around 1800). Flanking the altar, the 15th-century wooden choir stalls bear a complete set of escutcheons of the Knights of the Golden Fleece, who held a chapter meeting here in 1478. The Cathedral Museum (Mon–Fri 2–5pm; Sun 3–5pm) houses gold and silver religious vessels, reliquaries, and Episcopal vestments.

Sint-Salvatorskerkhof (off Steenstraat). ✆ **050/33-68-41.** www.sintsalvator.be. Admission: cathedral free; museum 2.50€ adults, 1.50€ students, free for children 18 and under. Cathedral Mon 2–5:45pm; Tues–Fri 8:30–11:45am and 2–5:45pm; Sat 8:30–11:45am and 2–3:30pm; Sun 9–10:15am and 2–5:45pm. Closed to casual visitors during services. Museum Sun–Fri 2–5pm.

MORE CHURCHES

There's no shortage of notable churches in Bruges, but you probably don't want to spend *all* your time visiting them. Anyone with a particular interest in churches, however, should try to visit at least a few of these.

The magnificent **Sint-Walburgakerk (St. Walburga's Church),** in Sint-Maartensplein (1619–43), is one of the few baroque monuments in this Gothic-fixated city. It has a satisfying amount of marble and a notable altar, pulpit, and communion bench. Sint-Walburgakerk was the Jesuit church of Bruges until 1774.

The wealthy Adornes merchant family constructed the **Jeruzalemkerk (Jerusalem Church),** Peperstraat 3, beside the Lace Center, between 1471 and 1483, along the lines of the Church of the Holy Sepulcher in Jerusalem. A replica of Christ's Tomb is in the crypt underneath the choir. Admission to the Lace Center (p. 149) allows you to visit this church as well.

Also owing much of its ornamentation to wealthy benefactors is **Sint-Jakobskerk (St. James's Church)** in Sint-Jakobsplein. This heavy-looking 15th-century Gothic construction has an intricately carved wooden pulpit, with figures at the base representing the continents.

Founded in 1276 as a hospice, **Onze-Lieve-Vrouw ter Potterie (Our Lady of the Pottery),** Potterierei 78–79, is now a seniors' home. Part of it houses the **Potterie Museum** (✆ **050/44-87-11**), which has a collection of tapestries, 15th- to 17th-century furniture, silverware, religious objects, books, and early Flemish paintings. The adjoining 14th-century church, with a fine baroque interior, was the Potters Guild chapel. The museum is open Tuesday to Sunday from 9:30am to 12:30pm and 1:30 to 5pm (closed Jan 1, Ascension Day afternoon, and Dec 25). Admission is 2€ for adults, 1€ for seniors and ages 6 to 25, and free for children 5 and under.

Other Sights of Interest

Brouwerij De Halve Maan The brewery here was mentioned in dispatches as early as 1546 and has been in use in "modern" times since 1856. Today, it produces the famous (in Belgium) Brugse Zot and Straffe Hendrik beers, strapping brews that can be sampled in the brewery's own brasserie.

Walplein 26. ✆ **050/44-42-22.** www.halvemaan.be. Admission 5.50€. Guided visits on the hour: Apr-Oct Sun-Fri 11am-4pm, Sat 11am-5pm; Nov-Mar Mon-Fri 11am-3pm, Sat-Sun 11am-4pm. Closed Dec 25-26 and Jan 1 (and other dates in Jan; see website for details).

Choco Story-The Chocolate Museum ☺ Although Bruges is far from being a powerhouse of Belgian handmade pralines, it has decided to squeeze itself into this important tourism sector via this museum. That said, the museum is an interesting trip down chocolate's memory lane. The exhibits cover chocolate's beginnings with the Aztecs, move on to the way it took Europe's royal courts by storm, and end up with Belgium's winning ways with the confection. Quizzes about chocolate are aimed at child visitors.

Wijnzakstraat 2 (at Sint-Jansplein). ✆ **050/61-22-37.** www.choco-story.be. Admission 6€ adults, 5€ seniors, 4€ children 6-12, free for children 5 and under. Daily 10am-5pm. Closed Jan 1 and Dec 24-25 and 31.

Diamantmuseum Brugge (Bruges Diamond Museum) Diamond polishing has been an important local industry for centuries, ever since Antwerp dealers, looking for cheaper skilled labor, brought the craft to Bruges. The technique of polishing diamonds using diamond powder on a rotating disk may have been invented by the Bruges goldsmith Lodewijk van Berquem around 1450. This museum focuses on the history of diamond polishing in Bruges, with demonstrations and displays of the equipment employed by the craftspeople.

Katelijnestraat 43B (at Oude Gentweg). ✆ **050/34-20-56.** www.diamondmuseum.be. Admission: museum 7€ adults, 6€ seniors, 5€ students/children 7-18, free for children 6 and under; diamond-polishing demonstration and museum 10€ adults, 9 € seniors, 7.50€ students, 8€ children 7-18, free for children 6 and under. Daily 10:30am-5:30pm; diamond-polishing demonstration daily 12:15pm. Closed Jan 1, 2nd and 3rd week in Jan, and Dec 24-25.

Hof Bladelin (Bladelin House) This 15th-century mansion, which is now a seniors' home, was built by Pieter Bladelin, treasurer to Duke Philip the Good. The Medici Bank of Florence took over in 1466 and gave the place an Italian look, particularly in the courtyard, which is thought to be the earliest example of the Renaissance style in the Low Countries. On the facade are medallions depicting Lorenzo de Medici and his wife, Clarice Orsini.

Naaldenstraat 19 (off Kuipersstraat). ✆ **050/33-64-34.** Admission 1€. Apr-Sept Mon-Sat 10am-noon and 2-5pm, Sun and holidays 10:30am-noon; Oct-Mar Mon-Sat 10am-noon and 2-4pm, Sun and holidays 10:30am-noon.

City Gates

The now-vanished city wall once boasted nine powerfully fortified gates dating from the 14th century. The four that survive are (clockwise from the rail station) the imposing **Smedenpoort; Ezelpoort,** which is famed for the many swans that grace the moat beside it; **Kruispoort,** which looks more like a castle with a drawbridge; and **Gentpoort,** now reduced in status to a traffic obstacle. Only one defensive tower remains, the **Poertoren,** which was used as a gunpowder store and overlooks the Lake of Love.

Windmills

The park that marks the line of the city walls between Kruispoort and Dampoort in the northeast is occupied by a row of photogenic windmills. They are (from south to

Strolling the Back Streets

You don't need to visit the top 10 highlights to enjoy Bruges. Shut your guidebook, put away the street map, and just wander, taking time out to make your own discoveries. Bruges's inhabitants live their everyday lives in absurdly beautiful surroundings and aren't always engaged in putting on a show for the tourists.

north): the **Bonne-Chièremolen** (1888), moved here from Olsene in East Flanders in 1911; the **Sint-Janshuismolen** (1770; open May–Aug daily 9:30am–12:30pm and 1:30–5pm; admission 2€ adults, 1€ seniors and ages 6–25, free for children 5 and under); the **Nieuwe Papegaaimolen** (1790), an oil mill rebuilt here in 1970; and the **Koeleweimolen** (1765), rebuilt here in 1996 (open July–Aug daily 9:30am–12:30pm and 1:30–5pm; admission 2€ adults, 1€ seniors and ages 6–25, free for children 5 and under).

Especially for Kids

Boudewijn Seapark ★, Alfons de Baeckestraat 12 (✆ **050/38-38-38;** www.dolfinarium.be; bus no. 7 or 17), in the southern suburb of Sint-Michiels, is a big favorite with children, who for some reason seem to prefer its rides, paddleboats, dolphins, and sea lions to Bruges's many historical treasures. Strange but true! Admission is 24€ for adults; 20€ for seniors, visitors with reduced mobility, and children over 1m (39 in.) and up to age 12; and free for children under 1m (39 in.). The park is open June to August daily from 10:30am to 5pm, and during Easter week and weekends in September from 11am to 5pm. The Dolfinarium is open intermittently at other times in April and May.

In the eastern suburbs, **Kinderboerderij Domein De Zeven Torentjes (Seven Towers Estate Children's Farm),** Canadaring 41, Assebroek (✆ **050/35-40-43;** bus no. 2), is a 14th-century manor farm that has been transformed into a children's farm, with pigs, hens, horses, and other animals. All the buildings—the farmhouse, barns, coach house, bakery, and more—have been restored and a large playpark added. An on-site cafeteria has a kids-friendly menu. A 16th-century dovecote has niches for 650 doves. The farm is open Monday to Friday from 8:30am to 5:15pm, Saturday from 10am to 6pm, and Sunday from 1 to 6pm. Admission is free.

Both the theme park and the farm can be reached by bus from either the rail station or the Markt.

Organized Tours & Excursions

A must for every visitor is a **boat cruise ★★** on the city canals. There are several departure points, all marked with an anchor icon on maps available at the tourist office. Those open-top canalboats can be scorching in hot weather and bracing in cold, but they're fun and they give you a uniquely satisfying view of the city. They operate March to November daily from 10am to 6pm, and December to February on weekends, school vacations, and public holidays from 10am to 6pm (except if the canals are frozen!). A half-hour cruise is 6.90€ for adults, 3.20€ for children 4 to 11 accompanied by an adult, and free for children 3 and under. Wear something warm if the weather is cold or windy.

Another delightful way to tour Bruges is by **horse-drawn carriage** (✆ **050/34-54-01;** www.hippo.be). From March to November, carriages are stationed on the Markt (on Wed on the Burg). A 35-minute ride is 36€ per carriage for up to five people.

Minivan tours by **Sightseeing Line** (✆ **050/35-50-24;** www.citytour.be) last 50 minutes and depart hourly daily from the Markt. The first tour departs at 10am; the last tour departs at 8pm July to September, at 7pm April to June, at 6pm October, at 5pm March, and at 4pm November to February. Fares are 15€ for adults, 8.50€ children 6 to 11, and free for children 5 and under.

From March to October, get some exercise and at the same time visit little-known parts of Bruges—or head out of town to explore the nearby flat Flemish countryside and the village of Damme—on a bike tour, with commentary in English, led by **QuasiMundo Biketours** (✆ **050/33-07-75;** www.quasimundo.eu). Tours are 24€ for adults, 20€ for students and ages 8 to 26, and free for children 7 and under. Call ahead to make a reservation. The meeting and departure point is the Burg.

If you'd like a trained, knowledgeable guide to accompany you in Bruges, the tourist office can provide one for 50€ for the first 2 hours and 25€ for each additional hour. Or in July and August, join a daily guided tour at 3pm that leaves from the tourist office; it costs 9€ for adults and is free for children 11 and under.

SHOPPING

No one comes here for stylish shopping—for that you need Brussels or Antwerp. What Bruges is famous for is **lace.** Most of it is machine-made, but there's still plenty of genuine, high-quality (if expensive) handmade lace to be found. Souvenirs of a more perishable nature include Oud-Brugge **cheese,** and local **beers** such as Straffe Hendrik, Brugs Tarwebier, and Brugge Tripel. The contents of a stone bottle of ***jenever*** (gin) and a box of handmade chocolate **pralines** should go down well.

Upmarket stores and boutiques can be found on the streets around the Markt and 't Zand squares, among them Geldmuntstraat, Noordzandstraat, Steenstraat, Zuidzandstraat, and Vlamingstraat. There are souvenir, lace, and small specialty stores everywhere. Most stores are open Monday to Saturday from 9am to 6pm, with late-night shopping to 9pm on Friday. Many open on Sunday, especially in summer.

Shopping A to Z

Shopping in Bruges caters primarily, but not exclusively, to tourist tastes and needs. Here's a short list of interesting and useful stores.

BOOKS

Brugse Boekhandel K. Demeester Stocks a moderate range of English-language books, with a focus on travel guides, as well as maps, newspapers, and magazines. Dijver 2. ✆ 050/33-29-52. www.brugseboekhandel.be.

Tips on Buying Lace

When you purchase lace, ideally you should specify that you want handmade lace, which is more expensive and of higher quality than the machine-made stuff. The most famous laces to look for are *bloemenwerk, rozenkant,* and *toversesteek.*

DEPARTMENT STORES

Galeria Inno This is Bruges's main department store, which sells a wide range of goods. Steenstraat 11-13. ✆ 050/33-06-03. www.inno.be.

DIAMONDS

Brugs Diamanthuis ★ Housed in a handsome building dating from 1518, this store has a sparkling array of diamonds. The company has a second store at the Diamond Museum (see "Other Sights of Interest," above). Cordoeaniersstraat 5 (off Vlamingstraat). ✆ 050/34-41-60. www.diamondhouse.net. Second location: Katelijnestraat 43 (at Oude Gentweg). ✆ 050/33-64-33.

FOOD, DRINK & CHOCOLATES

Malesherbes A French delicatessen, with all that implies in terms of taste and the range of artisanal products. It has a salon de dégustation for tasting its fine pâté, cheese, and wine. Stoofstraat 3–5. ✆ 050/33-69-24.

Van Tilborgh The owner's lip-smacking pralines are made from her own recipe. Noordzandstraat 1. ✆ 050/33-59-04.

Woolstreet Company ★ One of several stores along this street selling a wide range of Belgian beers, mainly locally produced. Wollestraat 31A. ✆ 050/34-83-83.

GIFTS

Callebert Should you tire of the traditional in Bruges, you can shop here for stylish, modern gifts and toys. Wollestraat 25. ✆ 050/33-50-61. www.callebert.be.

LACE

Kantuweeltje ★★ You can see fine lace pieces being made by hand at this lace and tapestry specialist, in business since 1895. Philipstockstraat 11. ✆ 050/33-42-25.

Markets

The **Antiques and Flea Market** on Dijver is a fine show in a scenic location beside the canal. It runs from March to October Saturday and Sunday from noon to 5pm. There are **general markets** on the Markt every Wednesday from 8am to 1pm, and on 't Zand and nearby Beursplein every Saturday from 8am to 1pm. The **fish market** on the colonnaded Vismarkt, dating from 1821, may be less important—although ready-to-eat prawns and raw herring are available here—but it's still interesting to see; it takes place Monday to Saturday from 8am to 1pm.

BRUGES AFTER DARK

For information on what to do after dark, pick up the free monthly brochure ***Exit*** and the free monthly newsletter ***events@brugge*** from the tourist office, hotels, and performance venues. The monthly newspaper ***Brugge Cultuurmagazine,*** free and available at these locations, is in Dutch, but its performance dates and venue details are fairly easy to follow.

The Performing Arts

The new, ultramodern **Concertgebouw** ★★, 't Zand (✆ **070/22-33-02;** www.concertgebouw.be), the home base of the **Symfonieorkest van Vlaanderen** (**Flanders Symphony Orchestra;** ✆ **050/84-05-87;** www.symfonieorkest.be), is the city's main venue for opera, classical music, theater, and dance. This has left the former principal venue for these events in Bruges, the **Koninklijke Stadsschouwburg (Royal Municipal Theater),** Vlamingstraat 29 (✆ **050/44-30-60;** www.cultuurcentrumbrugge.be), from 1869, to back up the new mother ship by mounting smaller-scale performances. Theater at both venues is likely to be in Dutch or French, and rarely, if ever, in English.

Another important performance venue is the **Joseph Ryelandtzaal,** Achiel van Ackerplein 3 (✆ **050/44-80-12**). Smaller-scale events, such as recitals, are often held at **Sint-Salvatorskathedraal, Sint-Jakobskerk,** and other churches (see "Historical Churches," earlier in this chapter).

A different kind of theater is on the menu at **Brugge Anno 1468 (Bruges Year 1468)** ★, Celebrations Entertainment, Vlamingstraat 86 (✆ **050/34-75-72;** www.celebrations-entertainment.be). In the atmospheric setting of the neo-Gothic former Heilige-Hartkerk (Sacred Heart Church), from 1885, which belonged to the Jesuit Order, actors recreate the wedding of duke of Burgundy Charles the Bold to Margaret of York, while visitors tuck into a medieval banquet. Performances are April to October Thursday to Saturday from 7:30 to 10:30pm; November to March Saturday from 7:30 to 10:30pm. Tickets are 45€ to 76€ for adults, 50% of the adult price for children 11 to 14, 13€ for children 6 to 10, and free for children 5 and under.

LIVE MUSIC & DANCE

The **Cactus Muziekcentrum** ★ presents an eclectic and very often prickly concert schedule Friday and Saturday nights in the **Magdalenazaal (MaZ),** Magdalenastraat 27 (✆ **050/33-20-14;** www.cactusmusic.be), just southwest of the Old Town. Jazz from bebop to modern along with the blues (and a smidgeon of French and Dutch chanson) are all belted out at **De Versteende Nacht** ★, Langestraat 11 (✆ **050/68-81-77;** www.deversteendenacht.com), across the canal from central Hoogstraat.

For a raucous dancing-on-the-tables kind of night, head to **Café de Vuurmolen,** Kraanplein 5 (✆ **050/33-00-79;** www.vuurmolen.com), a few blocks north of the Markt; it's open nightly 10pm until the wee hours. **Ma Rica Rokk,** 't Zand 6 (✆ **050/33-83-58;** www.maricarokk.be), attracts a young and (for a medieval town like Bruges) trendy crowd to its DJ evenings.

Cool as a cucumber, **kaffee L'aMaRaL,** Kuipersstraat 10 (✆ **0497/39-19-29;** www.lamaral.be), does cocktails and hip DJs. More DJ licks, along with cocktails and more-than-decent food, are served up at chic **B-IN,** in the rambling Oud Sint-Jan building, off Mariastraat, south of the city center (✆ **050/31-13-00;** www.b-in.be).

BARS

Bruges's ability to peel back the centuries is on stellar display in the city's oldest tavern, **Café Vlissinghe** ★★, Blekersstraat 2 (✆ **050/34-37-37;** www.cafevlissinghe.be), which dates from 1515 and is tucked into a side street off Sint-Annarei. **'t Brugs Beertje** ★, Kemelstraat 5 (✆ **050/33-96-16;** www.brugsbeertje.be), off Steenstraat, is a traditional cafe that serves more than 300 different kinds of beer. Even that stalwart number is outdone by **Bierbrasserie Cambrinus,** Philipstockstraat 19 (✆ **050/33-23-28;** www.cambrinus.eu), in a building that dates from 1699, just off the Burg, and which has no fewer than 400 Belgian brews on its drinks list. **Grand Café de Passage,** Dweersstraat 26 (✆ **050/34-02-32;** www.passagebruges.com), is a quiet and elegant cafe that serves inexpensive meals.

A SIDE TRIP TO DAMME ★

This small town (pop. 11,000), just 7km (4½ miles) from Bruges, was once the city's outer harbor, where seagoing ships loaded and unloaded their cargoes, until the Zwin inlet silted up in 1520. The marriage of duke of Burgundy Charles the Bold and Margaret of York, daughter of England's duke of York, was celebrated here in 1468—which indicates the importance of Damme at the time. Today, visitors come to view the picturesque Markt (which holds a statue of 13th-century native Jacob van Maerlant, the "Father of Flemish Poetry"), and the canal-side scenery en route from Bruges. It's easy to make a day trip to Damme.

The Essentials

GETTING THERE A delightful way to get to Damme is to sail there onboard the small sternwheeler *Lamme Goedzaak* ★. Departures are from Noorweegse Kaai in the north of Bruges, five times daily from April to mid-October. The half-hour cruise on the poplar-lined canal takes you past a landscape straight out of an old Flemish painting. Round-trip tickets are 7.50€ for adults, 6.50€ for seniors, 5.50€ for children 3 to 11, and free for children 2 and under. Schedules and other details are available from **Rederij Doornzele** (✆ **09/233-84-69;** www.bootdamme-brugge.be).

De Lijn **bus no. 43** departs up to seven times daily from the train station and the Markt in Bruges to Damme. Other options are to drive, bike, or even walk from Bruges to Damme, along the scenic canal-side road Daamse Vaart Zuid from Dampoort in Bruges.

VISITOR INFORMATION **Toerisme Damme,** Jacob van Maerlantstraat 3, 8340 Damme (✆ **050/28-86-10;** fax 050/37-00-21; www.toerismedamme.be), faces the Stadhuis (Town Hall) on the Markt. The office is open mid-April to mid-October Monday to Friday from 9am to noon and 1 to 6pm, and weekends and holidays from 10am to noon and 2 to 6pm; and mid-October to mid-April Monday to Friday from 9am to noon and 1 to 5pm, and weekends and holidays from 2 to 5pm.

Seeing the Sights

The Gothic **(Stadhuis) Town Hall** on the Markt dates from 1464 to 1468. On its facade are statues of duke of Burgundy Charles the Bold and his wife, Margaret of York, among other historical notables. Out front stands a statue of the poet Jacob van Maerlant (1230–96), who wrote his most important works in Damme. Across from the Town Hall, at Jacob van Maerlantstraat 13, is a 15th-century mansion, the **Saint-Jean d'Angély Huis** ★, where in 1468 Charles the Bold married Margaret of York.

Along the street, at Jacob van Maerlantstraat 3, is another 15th-century mansion, **Huyse de Groote Sterre.** This was the Spanish governor's residence in the 17th century and is now occupied by Damme's tourist office and the **Uilenspiegelmuseum.** Tijl Uilenspiegel is a 14th-century German folk-tale character (Till Ulenspiegel) who came to Damme by a roundabout route and has been adopted by the village. The museum has the same contact details and open hours as the tourist office (see above). Admission is 2.50€ for adults, 1.50€ for students and children 6 to 18, free for children 5 and under, and 5€ for a family.

On Kerkstraat, which runs south from the Markt, is the Gothic **Sint-Janshospitaal (St. John's Hospital)** at no. 33, a hospital for the poor, endowed in 1249 by Countess Margaret of Constantinople. This now houses a small period museum that's open Monday and Friday from 2 to 4:30pm, Tuesday to Thursday from 11am to noon and 2 to

4:30pm, and weekends from 11am to noon and 2 to 6pm. Admission is 1.50€ for adults, 1€ for people with reduced mobility, .75€ for children 6 to 17, free for children 5 and under, and 3€ for a family. Nearby stands the **Onze-Lieve-Vrouwekerk (Church of Our Lady),** dating from around 1340.

Across the bridge over the Bruges-Sluis Canal, at Dammesteenweg 1, is the 18th-century whitewashed **De Sint-Christoffelhoeve (St. Christopher's Farm).** Note the ornamental gate and the monumental barn with its mansard roof. A little way to the west along Daamse Vaart is the **Schellemolen,** a windmill built in 1867.

Beside the jetty where the *Lamme Goedzaak* ties up is a modern **sculpture group** featuring the legend of Tijl Uilenspiegel.

Where to Dine

The sophisticated French/Flemish restaurant **De Lieve ★★**, Jacob van Maerlantstraat 10 (✆ **050/35-66-30;** www.delieve.com), in the center of Damme, has main courses for 27€ to 29€, and a fixed-price *Menu Uilenspiegel* for 34€. Along the canal to Bruges, the rustic **Smoefelhuis 't Meiliedje,** Daamse Vaart Zuid 5 (✆ **050/35-24-78;** www.meiliedje.be), has pancakes and other snacks; in addition, it serves fish and meat main courses for 9€ to 18€ and also has a fixed-price menu for 23€.

GHENT & ANTWERP

Although Ghent and Antwerp can't match Bruges for sheer medieval good looks, many Belgians consider them the true heartland of Flemish culture. Both cities have a gritty, lived-in feel when compared with Bruges's museum-piece air, and neither yields a millimeter in any argument over relative historical importance and artistic heritage. When it comes to contemporary vibrancy, they are the hands-down winners.

8

Standing at the confluence of the Schelde (Scheldt) and Leie rivers, **Ghent** has always been a pivotal point for Flanders. The city was a seat of the counts of Flanders, who built a great castle here in the 12th century, but local fortifications predate their reign, back to the 900s. The medieval treasures in the Old Town are preserved not as dry, showcase relics, but as living parts of the city.

Antwerp owes its life to the Schelde (Scheldt) River. Rubens is the greatest of several artistic masters who left their mark on the face of this city and a great love of beauty in the hearts of its inhabitants. You see that love expressed in their buildings, their public works of art, and the contents of some 20 museums.

GHENT ★★

48km (30 miles) NW of Brussels; 46km (29 miles) SE of Bruges

Ghent (pop. 235,000) is often considered a poor relation of Bruges, with historical monuments and townscapes that aren't as distinguished as those in its sister city. Many people might suggest you visit Ghent only if you have time after visiting Bruges. There is some validity in this recommendation—but not much. Life moves faster in the capital town of Oost-Vlaanderen (East Flanders) province (Gent in Dutch; Gand in French), an important inland port and industrial center, and Ghent compensates for its less precious appearance with a vigorous social and cultural scene.

Essentials

GETTING THERE Ghent is a 35-minute train ride from Brussels, and there are at least three trains every hour from the capital. The regular one-way fare is 8.10€ in second class and 13€ in first class; the round-trip/return fare is 16€ in second class and 25€ in first class. Ghent's main train station, **Gent-Sint-Pieters,** on Koningin Maria-Hendrikaplein, 2km (1½ miles) south of the center city, dates from 1912. To get quickly and easily to the center of town, take tram no. 1 from the nearest platform under the bridge to your left as you exit the station, and get out at Korenmarkt. Unless you need to count every euro, don't walk there; it's a dull route. Save your energy for sightseeing once you've arrived.

By **car,** take A10/E40 from both Brussels and Bruges, and A14/E17 from Antwerp.

VISITOR INFORMATION The city tourist office is the **Dienst Toerisme Gent Infokantoor,** in the cellar of the **Belfry,** Botermarkt 17A, 9000 Gent (✆ **09/266-56-60;** fax 09/266-56-73; www.visitgent.be; tram: 1 or 4). This office is open mid-March to mid-October daily from 9:30am to 6:30pm, and mid-October to mid-March daily from 9:30am to 4:30pm (closed Jan 1 and Dec 25). In addition to providing information, they can make last-minute hotel reservations.

GETTING AROUND Ghent has an excellent **tram** and **bus** network, and a single **electric trolley-bus** line (see the box "Silent Running," below), operated by **De Lijn** (✆ **070/22-02-00;** www.delijn.be). Many lines converge at Korenmarkt and Gent-Sint-Pieters rail station. All four of the city's tram lines (1, 4, 21, 22) stop at the station and at multiple points in the heart of town. Walking is the best way to experience the Old Town at a human pace. Farther out, you're better off using public transportation, particularly the trams. The city's **bus station** adjoins Gent-Sint-Pieters train station.

Purchase your ticket from a De Lijn sales point or automat (ticket machine) before boarding and you'll pay less (the "twin" prices listed here reflect this distinction). An *enkele rit* (one-way) ticket costs 1.20€/1.60€ for two zones and 2€/3€ for three or more zones. A *dagkaart* (day card), valid for the entire city network, costs 5€/6€ for 1 day, 10€/12€ for 3 days, and 15€/18€ for 5 days. A 1-day pass for children 6 to 11 is 1.50€/2€. Children 5 and under ride free.

Silent Running

Ghent has Belgium's only remaining electric trolley-bus service (line 3). It hums quietly through the center of town on an east-west route and is useful for getting to some places of interest—but you might want to step aboard as much for the novelty value of the ride as for any other reason.

For taxis, call **Vtax** (✆ **09/222-22-22;** www.v-tax.be).

SPECIAL EVENTS During 10 days around July 21, plunge into the swirl of Belgium's greatest extended street party, the **Gentse Feesten** (**Ghent Festivities;** ✆ **09/210-10-10;** www.gentsefeesten.be), a time of free music, from classical through Tin Pan Alley to alternative rock and the latest dance beats, along with street theater, dance, performance art, puppet shows, a street fair, special museum exhibits, and generally riotous fun and games in the heart of town.

City Layout

The city's central district is known as Het Kuip van Gent (the Barrel of Ghent), and this is where in times past the local big wheels had their residences. **Korenmarkt** lies at the center of the city. Most of Ghent's important sights—including the Town Hall, St. Bavo's Cathedral, and the Belfry—lie within 1km (⅓ mile) of Korenmarkt. **Patershol,** a medieval enclave not far from the Castle of the Counts, is now something of a gastronomic center sprinkled with restaurants in renovated old buildings. The **Leie River** winds through the center of town to connect with the Scheldt River

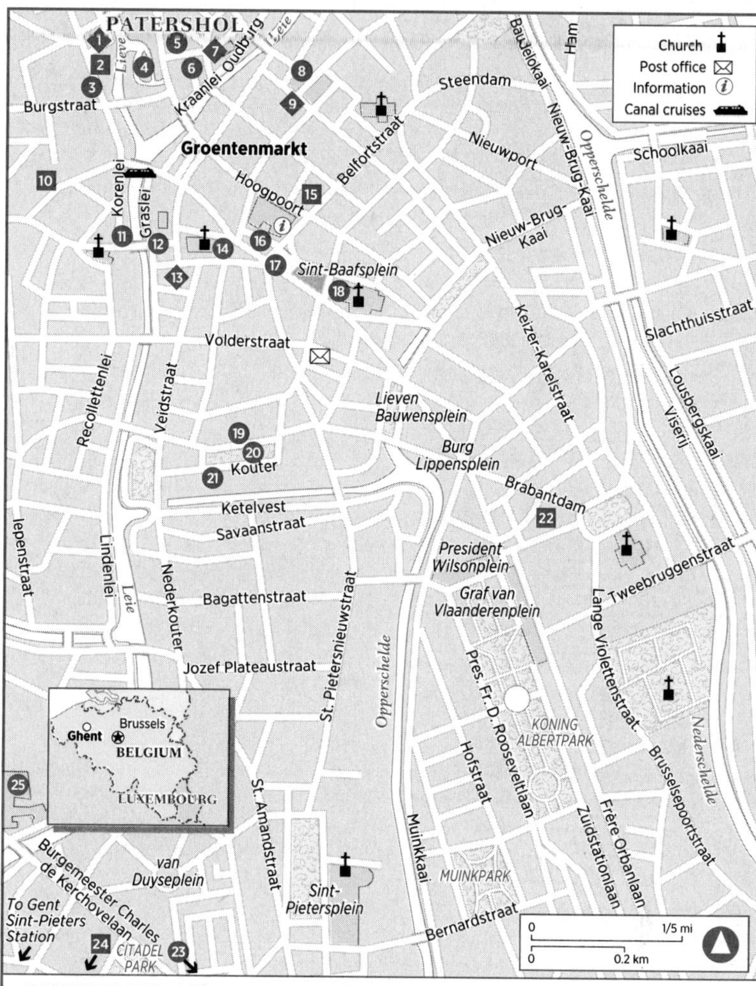

ACCOMMODATIONS ■
Adoma **24**
Eden **22**
Erasmus **10**
Gravensteen **2**
NH Gent Belfort **15**

DINING ◆
Amadeus **7**
Brasserie Pakhuis **13**
Jan Breydel **1**
Keizershof **9**

ATTRACTIONS ●
Belfort en Lakenhalle **17**
Design museum Gent **3**
Graslei **12**
Gravensteen **4**
Het Huis van Alijn **6**
Hoofdwacht/ Handelsbeurs **21**
Hotel Falligan **19**
Korenlei **11**
Kouter **20**
Museum voor Schone Kunsten Gent **23**
Patershol **5**
Sint-Baafskathedraal **18**
Sint-Niklaaskerk **14**
Stadhuis **16**
STAM/Stadsmuseum van Gent **25**
Vrijdagmarkt **8**

and a network of canals that lead to the busy port area. **Citadel Park,** location of the Fine Arts Museum, is in the south, near Gent-Sint-Pieters station.

Seeing the Sights

This is a city best seen by walking its streets, gazing at its gabled guild houses and private mansions, and stopping on one of its bridges to look down at the canal or river. Ghent's historical monuments have not all been prettified; some of them look downright gray and forbidding, which, oddly enough, gives them a more authentic feel. The castle of the counts of Flanders, for instance, was *meant* to look gray and forbidding, since the citizens of Ghent were so often in revolt against its overlord.

THE TOP ATTRACTIONS

The "Three Towers of Ghent" that have become a signature image of the city are **St. Bavo's Cathedral, the Belfry,** and **St. Nicholas's Church.** They form a virtually straight line pointing toward St. Michael's Bridge.

Belfort en Lakenhalle (Belfry and Cloth Hall) ★ Across the square from the cathedral, the Belfry tower and Cloth Hall form a glorious medieval ensemble. The 14th-century Belfry holds the great bells that have rung out Ghent's civic pride through the centuries, the most beloved being a giant bell known as Roeland (1315), destroyed by emperor Charles V in 1540 as punishment for Ghent's insubordination. No fewer than 28 of the 54 bells that now make up the tower's huge carillon were cast from Roeland's broken pieces. The massive Triomfanten bell, cast in 1660, now rests in a small park at the foot of the Belfry, still bearing the crack it sustained in 1914. Take the elevator to the Belfry's upper gallery, 66m (217 ft.) high, to see the bells and take in fantastic panoramic views of the city. A great iron chest was kept in the Belfry's *Secreet* (strongroom) to hold the all-important charters that spelled out privileges the guilds and the burghers of medieval Ghent wrested from the counts of Flanders.

Your Passport to Ghent

One of the best discounts in town is the Gent museumpas, available from the Infokantoor (see "Visitor Information," above) for 20€. The pass, valid for 3 days, affords free use of the city's public transportation and admission to 15 key museums and monuments.

The Cloth Hall dates from 1425 and was the gathering place of wool and cloth merchants. A baroque extension from 1741 on Goudenleeuwplein was used until 1902 as a prison, dubbed De Mammelokker (the Suckler). The name comes from a relief above the doorway that depicts the Roman legend of Cimon, starving to death in prison, being suckled by his daughter Pero. Appropriately, this newer section is now the office for the city's *ombudsvrouw* (ombudswoman).

Sint-Baafsplein (at Botermarkt). ✆ **09/233-39-54.** www.belfortgent.be. Admission 5€ adults, 3.75€ seniors and ages 19–26, free for children 18 and under. Daily 10am–6pm; free guided tours of Belfry daily Tues–Sun 2:30 and 3:30pm. Tram: 1 or 4 to St-Baafsplein.

Gravensteen (Castle of the Counts) ★ "Grim" is the word that comes to mind when you first see this gray fortress crouching like a great stone lion. The counts of Flanders clearly designed the Gravensteen to keep the populace in line by sending a "don't-even-think-about-it" message to a rebellion-inclined citizenry. It was built by count of Flanders Philip of Alsace, soon after he returned from the Crusades in

Naked Truth

A prudish 18th-century Austrian Emperor Joseph II ordered *The Adoration of the Mystic Lamb*'s naked figures of Adam and Eve replaced by others with fig leafs covering their genitals.

Today, the original Adam and Eve are back in their birthday-suit glory, and you can view the faintly ridiculous replacement panels attached to columns near the cathedral's entrance.

1180 with images of crusader castles in the Holy Land. If its walls (2m/6 ft. thick), battlements, and turrets failed to intimidate attackers, the count could always turn to a well-equipped torture chamber inside. Relics of the chamber—a small guillotine, spiked iron collars, branding irons, thumb screws, and a special kind of pitchfork designed to ensure that people being burned at the stake stayed in the flames—are displayed in a small museum. Climb up to the ramparts of the high central building, the donjon, which has great views of Ghent's rooftops and towers.

Sint-Veerleplein 11 (at Kraanlei). ✆ **09/225-93-06.** www.gent.be/gravensteen. Admission 8€ adults, 6€ seniors and ages 19–26, free for children 18 and under. Apr–Sept daily 9am–6pm; Oct–Mar daily 9am–5pm. Closed Jan 1 and Dec 24–25 and 31. Tram: 1 or 4 to Sint-Veerleplein.

Sint-Baafskathedraal (St. Bavo's Cathedral) ★★★ Even if you see nothing else in Ghent, you shouldn't miss this massive cathedral. Don't be put off by its rather unimpressive exterior, a mixture of Romanesque, Gothic, and baroque architecture. The interior is filled with paintings, sculptures, memorials, and carved tombs. St. Bavo's showpiece is the 24-panel altarpiece *The Adoration of the Mystic Lamb* ★★, commissioned by a wealthy city alderman and completed by Jan van Eyck in 1432. Van Eyck's luminous use of oils and naturalistic portrayal of nature and people represented a giant step away from the rigid style of Gothic religious art. But besides its importance in the history of art, the *Mystic Lamb* is simply spellbinding. Other art treasures in the cathedral include Rubens's *The Conversion of St. Bavo* (1623), in the Rubens Chapel on the semicircular ambulatory behind the high altar. In the vaulted nave is a remarkable pulpit in white marble entwined with oak.

Sint-Baafsplein. ✆ **09/269-20-45.** www.sintbaafskathedraal-gent.be. Admission: cathedral free; *Mystic Lamb* chapel and crypt 4€ adults (includes audio guide in English), 1.50€ children 8–12, free for children 7 and under. Cathedral Apr–Oct Mon–Sat 8:30am–6pm, Sun 1–6pm; Nov–Mar Mon–Sat 8:30am–5pm, Sun 1–5pm. *Mystic Lamb* chapel and crypt Apr–Oct Mon–Sat 9:30am–5pm, Sun 1–5pm; Nov–Mar Mon–Sat 10:30am–4pm, Sun 1–4pm. Tram: 1 or 4 to Sint-Baafsplein.

MORE MUSEUMS & ATTRACTIONS

Design museum Gent ★ Something of a split personality, this worthwhile museum is housed in the Hotel de Coninck (1755), a baroque mansion with a modern extension at the rear. In the old wing, the exhibits range through period rooms furnished and decorated in 18th- and 19th-century style. Tapestries and a collection of Chinese porcelain are among the prized antique items. Some of these belonged to France's King Louis XVIII, who passed a period of exile in Ghent in 1815 during Napoleon's brief return to power. The new wing is strong on Art Nouveau—from Belgian Masters of the genre such as Victor Horta, Henry van de Velde, and Paul Hankar, among others—Art Deco, and contemporary design. You can take in most everything of importance here in around an hour.

Jan Breydelstraat 5 (off Korenlei). ✆ **09/267-99-99.** http://design.museum.gent.be. Admission 5€ adults, 3.75€ seniors, 1€ ages 19–26, free for children 18 and under. Tues–Sun 10am–6pm. Closed Jan 1 and Dec 25–26 and 31. Tram: 1 or 4 to Korenmarkt.

Het Huis van Alijn (Alijn House) ☺ Ghent's fascinating folklore museum is in a *godshuis* (almshouse) founded in the 1300s and rebuilt in the 1500s, which functioned as a children's home and hospital. Set around a grassy courtyard, it creates an oasis of tranquillity. Inside the cluster of folksily restored cottages are replicas of typical rooms in Ghent homes at the turn of the 20th century and workshops where weaving, metalwork, carpentry, and other crafts were practiced. Visit the almshouse's late Gothic **Sint-Catharinakapel (St. Catherine's Chapel),** dating from 1540. A marionette theater troupe, **Poppenkast Pierke,** presents performances for children (in Dutch, but young kids might be enchanted by the action even if they can't understand the words) on specified days of the week. While the kids are being thusly entertained, the grown-ups can kick back over drinks at the museum's traditional tavern, **'t Cafeetse.**

Kraanlei 65 (across the Leie River from Vrijdagmarkt). ✆ **09/269-23-50.** www.huisvanalijn.be. Admission: museum 5€ adults, 3.75€ seniors, 1€ ages 19–26, free for children 18 and under; marionette theater 3€. Museum Tues–Sat 11am–5pm; Sun 10am–5pm. Marionette theater Sept–June Wed and Sat 2:30pm (also Thurs 2:30pm during school vacations). Closed Jan 1 and Dec 25. Tram: 1 or 4 to Sint-Veerleplein.

Museum voor Schone Kunsten Gent (Ghent Fine Arts Museum) ★★ Ancient and modern art masterpieces, many of them by Belgian artists ranging from early Flemish Primitives to 19th-century Symbolists, are displayed here on the edge of Citadelpark, south of the center of town. Highlights include works by Peter Paul Rubens, Anthony van Dyck, Hieronymus Bosch, and Théodore Géricault, along with such moderns as James Ensor, Theo van Rysselberghe, George Minne, and Constant Permeke. Among the most notable works is Bosch's painting *The Bearing of the Cross* (ca. 1500), a respectful rendition of Christ on his way to being crucified while surrounded by a gaggle of rather grotesque-looking Flemish characters.

Fernand Scribedreef 1, Citadelpark (near Gent-Sint-Pieters train station). ✆ **09/240-07-00.** www.mskgent.be. Admission 5€ adults, 3.75€ seniors, 1€ ages 19–26, free for children 18 and under. Tues–Sun 10am–6pm. Closed Jan 1 and Dec 24–25 and 31. Tram: 1 to Kortrijksesteenweg.

Sint-Niklaaskerk (St Nicholas's Church) A mixture of surviving Romanesque elements and the Flemish Schelde Gothic architectural style, the impressive 13th- to 15th-century church, a veritable mountain of blue Tournai limestone, was paid for by Ghent's wealthy medieval merchants and guilds. In recent decades, it has undergone extensive renovation work that's still ongoing. The tower is one of the "three towers of Ghent"—in fact, it was the first of the three to grace the city skyline. A baroque high altar and other rich decorations embellish the interior; all of these date from after the Protestant *Beeldenstorm* (Iconoclastic Fury) of 1566, during which Catholic churches across the Low Countries were ransacked.

Korenmarkt (entrance on Cataloniëstraat). ✆ **09/234-28-69.** Free admission. Mon 2–5pm; Tues–Sun and holidays 10am–5pm. Tram: 1 or 4 to Korenmarkt.

STAM/Stadsmuseum van Gent Weapons, uniforms, musical instruments, coins, clothing, glass objects, tapestries, and household items from daily life long ago are on view in a 14th-century former Cistercian convent (14th–17th c.), the Bijlokeabdij (Bijloke Abbey). Art from Ghent and Flanders is exhibited inside the House of the Abbess.

Godshuizenlaan 2 (south of the Coupure canal). ✆ **09/267-14-00.** www.stamgent.be. Admission 5€ adults, 3.75€ seniors, 1€ ages 19–26, free for children 18 and under. Tues–Sun 10am–6pm. Closed Jan 1 and Dec 24–25 and 31. Tram: 1 to Charles de Kerchovelaan.

The Medieval Harbor ★★★

Graslei and Korenlei, two beautiful canal-side quays just west of Korenmarkt, are each home to a solid row of towering, gabled former guild houses, warehouses, and other harbor installations. These were built in a variety of architectural styles between the 1200s and 1600s, when the Leie waterway between them formed the city's busy commercial harbor, the **Tussen Bruggen (Between the Bridges).** A considerable amount of restorative nip and tuck has been done to them over the centuries, right up to the present day, and many now house cafes and restaurants.

GRASLEI

The building at Graslei no. 8, the Brabant Gothic **Gildehuis van de Metselaars (Stonemasons' Guild House),** has graceful pinnacles and is decorated with a medallion of an angel (hence its other name: Den Enghel/the Angel) and reliefs of the *Quatuor Coronati,* four Roman martyrs who were the guild's patrons. It claims to date from 1527 but is actually a 1912 reconstruction of a 16th-century guild house located in another part of Ghent (on Cataloniëstraat).

No. 9, dating from 1435, was the first **Korenmetershuis (House of the Grain Measurers),** where officials weighed and assessed the quality of imported grain before it was transported to market on Korenmarkt. Next door, at no. 10, is the solidly constructed **Het Spijker (Stockpile House),** dating from around 1200, where taxed corn was stored. The front of its outward-leaning Romanesque facade reaches up to Belgium's oldest step gable. Inside is the chic restaurant and live-music club Belga Queen.

The tiny building at no. 11 is the **Tolhuisje (Little Customs House),** which was constructed in 1682 in the Flemish Renaissance style as the office of the city's corn revenue agent. It now houses a great little cafe, Het Tolhuisje. Nos. 12–13, the second, or annex, **Korenmetershuis (House of the Grain Measurers),** dates from 1540 and has ornamental elements from 1698 on its facade of red brick and white stone.

No. 14, with a facade dating from 1531 covering the 14th-century building underneath, was the ornate Brabant Gothic **Gildehuis van de Vrije Schippers (Guild House of the Free Boatmen) ★**. This is one of the finest sights on Graslei, decorated with symbols of sailing ships and sailors on its sandstone facade.

KORENLEI

Across the water from Graslei by the Sint-Michielsbrug (St. Michael's Bridge), on Korenlei, stands the once (and perhaps future) restaurant Graaf van Egmond, housed in a **16th-century mansion.** Below the shuttered restaurant, at Korenlei 24, is another, the equally venerable and atmospheric Crypte. An adjoining step-gabled 16th-century house of red bricks at no. 23, dubbed **De Lintworm (the Tapeworm),** was formerly the Brewers' Guild House.

The stunning Marriott Ghent Hotel has installed itself in a bunch of restored guild houses, with the main entrance at no. 10. Next door, the redbrick, step-gabled building called **De Swaene (the Swans),** at no. 9, a former brewery from 1609, has a pair of gilded swan medallions on the facade. It later (though not any more) housed that vital installation in any self-respecting harbor district—a bordello.

At no. 7 is the pink-and-white-shaded **Gildehuis van de Onvrije Schippers (Guild House of the Tied Boatmen) ★**. Dating from 1739 and dubbed Den Ancker (the Anchor), it is a masterpiece of Flemish baroque architecture and has on the roof a gilded sailing ship weathervane. This was the proud symbol of the rivals to the Free Boatmen, whose home base lay just across the Leie on Graslei (see above). Note the carved dolphins and lions on the facade, and the graceful bell gable. Inside is the chic restaurant Allegro Moderato and, at ground level, a bar called De Onvrije Schipper, which spreads a terrace out onto the quay next to a tour-boat dock.

MORE ATTRACTIONS & PLACES OF INTEREST

Ghent's large **Stadhuis (Town Hall),** Botermarkt/Hoogpoort (✆ **09/223-99-22;** tram: 1 or 4), turns a rather plain Renaissance profile to Botermarkt and an almost garishly ornamented Gothic face to Hoogpoort. Its appearance came about because construction, begun in 1518, was interrupted, began again at the end of the century, halted once more in the early 1600s, and wasn't completed until the 18th century. The changing public tastes of those years are reflected in the building's styles. In its Pacificatiezaal (Pacification Room), the Pacification of Ghent was signed in 1567. This document declared the repudiation by the Low Countries provinces of Spanish Habsburg rule and their intention to permit freedom of religion within their boundaries, a progressive ideal that didn't stand the test of time. May to October, the Town Hall can be visited on guided tours that depart from the tourist office in the Belfry cellar Monday to Thursday at 2:30pm; the tour costs 4€ per person.

Vrijdagmarkt

Ghent's main square—huge, tree shaded, ever bustling—is surrounded by old guild houses and mansions, most of which these days host restaurants and cafes that sprout sidewalk terraces when the sun shines. In addition, Vrijdagmarkt (Friday Market Sq.) is the scene of lively street markets on Friday (7:30am–1pm) and Saturday (11am–6:30pm), as well as the Sunday bird market (7am–1pm).

Throughout the city's long history, when trouble erupted in Ghent, as it so often did, Vrijdagmarkt was nearly always the rallying point, and until 1863 it was a venue for public executions. But there were also jousting tournaments, parades, and other happy events. When the future Habsburg Emperor Charles V was born in Ghent during the bitterly cold winter of 1500, the square was flooded so that the populace could skate on the ice.

The bronze statue of **Jacob van Artevelde** (1863) is a tribute to a 14th-century rebel leader. Its base is adorned with the shields of 52 medieval guilds and four female figures representing the maids of Flanders, Ghent, Bruges, and Ypres (Ieper). Van Artevelde was assassinated amid scenes of factional violence on "Evil Monday" in 1345 that saw the Vrijdagmarkt heaped with corpses.

A curiously shaped, step-gabled building is on the square's east side (nos. 33–36), incorporating a round tower. This is the 15th-century **Gildenhuis van de Huidevetters (Tanners' Guild House),** and the guild's talisman—a mermaid—forms the weathervane on top. A poetry society now occupies the building. The round tower, dubbed the **Toreken (Little Tower),** was once used by the city's cloth commission. Any bolt of cloth that didn't pass muster was hung from a metal ring on the outside of the tower for all to see. What was then the commission's own premises, the **Lakenmetershuis** (**Cloth Measurers' House;** 1770), stands on the square's north side at no. 25.

On the west side is the remarkable **Ons Huis (Our House).** This approximately Art Nouveau confection, dating from 1902, was headquarters of the Ghent Socialist Workers society Vooruit (Forward). Still spelled out (in Dutch) in large gold letters on the facade is Karl Marx's famous call to proletarian solidarity: WERKLIEDEN ALLER LANDEN VEREENIGT U (WORKERS OF THE WORLD UNITE). Ons Huis is now the offices of a local welfare organization.

Among the most notable of Vrijdagmarkt's multifarious eateries and drinkeries are the restaurant **Keizershof** at no. 47 (p. 170) and, a few doors along, the cafe **Dulle Griet** at no. 50 (see "Ghent After Dark," below).

Off the west end of Vrijdagmarkt, a smaller square, **Groot Kanonplein,** is named after the large red cannon, Dulle Griet (Mad Meg), emplaced there. Measuring more than 5m (16 ft.) and weighing in at 16,400 kilograms (18 tons), it served in the 1400s during military operations of the Burgundian dukes but cracked a century later while defending Protestant Ghent against a besieging Spanish Catholic army.

Patershol ★

Few traditional sights clutter the small yet beguiling **Patershol** neighborhood that lies just west of the center of town, along the west bank of the Leie River and north of the Lieve Canal. Yet the area is charming and provides an authentic taste of Old Ghent; about 100 of its buildings are protected monuments.

The district's name comes from the monks of the Caermersklooster (Carmelite Monastery), founded in the 13th century and expanded over the centuries, which still stands (more or less) on Vrouwebroersstraat. The 16th- to 17th-century monastery church now houses the **Provinciaal Centrum voor Kunst en Cultuur (Provincial Art and Cultural Center).** Don't let that provincial tag put you off—it means the facility belongs to East Flanders province and is not a comment on the quality of the exhibits. The center is open Tuesday to Saturday from 10am to 5pm; admission is free.

Patershol's nest of narrow, pedestrianized streets and tightly packed small brick houses replaced the medieval tanners' quarter and was built in the 17th century for the city's weavers, craftsmen, and tradesmen. This modest nature remains even though renewal and gentrification were carried out in the 1980s.

A new generation of entrepreneurs has revitalized the old neighborhood (which had degenerated into a slum and red-light district), turning some of the little houses into trendy restaurants, bustling cafes, and offbeat stores. The number of these is regulated, so as not to destroy Patershol's residential character. Still, its "indigenous" residents are alive and well and show no sign of succumbing to the gentrification going on around them.

Kouter

This large, sober square (tram: 1, 21, or 22) south of the city center dates from the 18th century and has a quite different look compared to Ghent's Old Flemish squares. On the south face, the rococo **Hoofdwacht** (**Guard House;** 1739), designed by local architect David 't Kindt, was originally a barracks of the Austrian Imperial Guard. It later became the city's Handelsbeurs (Commercial Exchange) and is now a concert hall, **HA',** Kouter 29 (✆ **09/265-9165;** www.handelsbeurs.be), which features classical, jazz, rock, folk, and world music. A highlight in the elegant interior is an ultracool cafe-restaurant, likewise called HA'.

Across the square at no. 172, the rococo **Hotel Falligan** (1755) is fronted by Corinthian columns. A pair of sculptures dating from 1884 on the mansion's ocher

THE good news FROM GHENT

On Christmas Eve 1814, John Quincy Adams, the future sixth president of the United States, signed the Treaty of Ghent that brought to an end the War of 1812 with Great Britain. Peace came too late to save the White House, though: Along with most other public buildings in Washington, DC, it was burned by the British when they captured the city in August 1814 and chased President James Madison out of his capital. It took weeks for word of the treaty to cross the Atlantic, affording Andrew Jackson time to exact a measure of revenge by repelling the British assault on New Orleans in January 1815.

Adams and the other U.S. peace commissioners resided at the Hotel Schamp, an 18th-century baroque mansion at Veldstraat 45–47, south of Korenmarkt. The building now houses a tobacconist and a fashion store, and sports a 1964 plaque from the United States Daughters of 1812, thanking the people of Ghent for their hospitality to the U.S. delegation.

facade paradoxically have Apollo, the god of the arts, wielding a bow, and Diana, the goddess of hunting, with a harp. The building houses a private society, the Club des Nobles, that doesn't permit tours of the opulent interior.

Sunday is **Grote Bloemenmarkt (Big Flower Market)** day on Kouter, from 7am to 1pm. On the same day in summer, the bandstand (1878) occasionally hosts concerts. As you stroll the central part of the square, you'll notice that the central sculptured bronze leaf by contemporary U.S. artist Jessica Diamond is accompanied by other bronze leaves embedded in the stones—each leaf is pictured in Jan van Eyck's *Adoration of the Mystic Lamb* altarpiece in St. Bavo's Cathedral.

SIGHTSEEING TOURS

The tourist office can arrange qualified guides for private **walking tours** at a charge of 55€ per person for the first 2 hours (Mon–Fri) and 25€ for each additional hour. Ask them about organized group-walking tours sometimes conducted during summer months at a fee of 7€ for adults and free for children 11 and under (admission to view *The Adoration of the Mystic Lamb* in St. Bavo's Cathedral is included).

A **cruise** ★ on the canals with **De Bootjes van Gent-Rederij Dewaele** (✆ **09/223-88-53;** www.debootjesvangent.be; tram: 1 or 4) is a good way to view the city's highlights. Tour boats sail from Graslei and Korenlei, April to October daily from 10am to 6pm and November to March on weekends from 11am to 4pm, for a basic 40-minute city tour. Cruises begin at 6€ for adults; 5.50€ for seniors, students, and ages 13 to 25; 3.50€ for children 3 to 12; and free for children 2 and under. Longer tours are available.

From Easter to October, tours by **horse-drawn carriage** offered by **De Koetsen van Gent** (✆ **0475/82-16-20;** www.koetsenvangent.be; tram: 1 or 4) depart from Sint-Baafsplein and Korenlei from 10am to 6pm for half-hour rides that cost 25€ per coach (for four to five passengers).

Where to Stay

EXPENSIVE

Gravensteen ★★ The entrance to this lovely mansion—built in 1865 as the home of a Ghent textile baron—is through an old carriageway (made up of ornamented pillars and a wall niche occupied by a marble statue), which sets the tone for what's inside. The elegant, high-ceilinged parlor is a sophisticated blend of pastels, gracious modern furnishings, and antiques, with a small bar tucked into one corner. The rooms are attractive and comfortably furnished. Those in front look out on the moated Gravensteen castle (p. 162), while those to the back have city views. A top-floor lookout has windows that afford fine city views.

Jan Breydelstraat 35 (close to the Castle of the Counts), 9000 Gent. ✆ **09/225-11-50.** Fax 09/225-18-50. www.gravensteen.be. 49 units. 126€–210€ double. AE, DC, MC, V. Parking 10€. Tram: 1 or 4 to Gravensteen. **Amenities:** Bar; lounge; exercise room; sauna. *In room:* A/C in some units, TV, hair dryer, minibar, Wi-Fi (12€/24 hr.).

NH Gent Belfort If you like to experience historical towns while sleeping in modern and comfortable accommodations, this might be the place for you. The chain's often bland style is mitigated here—it was designed to at least partly fit into its venerable surroundings, and it sits atop medieval cellars and foundations. Plus, it's set in an ideal location just across the road from Town Hall, within easy distance of the city's premier tourist attractions. The rooms have most of the level of style and comforts expected by international business travelers. Belgian specialties and international dishes are served in the Van Artevelde Brasserie, and outside on the patio in good weather; drinks are served in the cellar bar.

Hoogpoort 63 (at Botermarkt), 9000 Gent. ✆ **09/233-33-31.** Fax 09/233-11-02. www.nh-hotels.com. 172 units. 104€–245€ double; 315€ suite. AE, DC, MC, V. Parking 15€. Tram: 1 or 4 to Sint-Niklaasstraat. **Amenities:** Restaurant; bar; babysitting; concierge; executive rooms; health club; room service. *In room:* A/C, TV, hair dryer, minibar, Wi-Fi (11€/24 hr.).

MODERATE

Erasmus ★ Each room is different in this converted pair of 17th-century Flemish mansions, and all are plush, furnished with antiques and knickknacks. Rooms have high oak-beam ceilings, and bathrooms are modern. Some rooms have leaded-glass windows, some overlook a carefully manicured inner garden, and some have elaborate marble fireplaces. You can, if you so choose, hide yourself away in the attic den. Breakfast is served in an impressive room that would have pleased the counts of Flanders, as well as in the garden—weather permitting.

Poel 25 (off Sint-Michielsstraat), 9000 Gent. ✆ **09/224-21-95.** Fax 09/233-42-41. www.erasmushotel.be. 11 units. 99€–150€ double. Rates include buffet breakfast. AE, MC, V. Limited street parking. Tram: 1 or 4 to Korenmarkt. **Amenities:** Bar. *In room:* TV, hair dryer.

INEXPENSIVE

Adoma The facilities and atmosphere at this hotel have taken a big leap forward in recent years, and an ongoing upgrading and renovation program continue the story, yet the rates remain reasonable. Rooms are spacious and brightly decorated, with contemporary furnishings that don't have any great pretention to being stylish. You'll find it to be a comfortable, if not luxurious, experience.

Sint-Denijslaan 19 (behind Gent-Sint-Pieters rail station), 9000 Gent. ✆ **09/222-65-50.** Fax 09/245-09-37. www.hotel-adoma.be. 15 units. 67€–92€ double. MC, V. Free parking. Tram: 21 or 22 to Sint-Denijslaan. *In room:* TV.

Eden ★ You climb a flight of stairs in this personable small hotel to reach the reception, where an elevator awaits you. Each of the decent-size guest rooms has a wall tapestry, adding an old-fashioned Flemish touch to rooms that otherwise have mostly functional furnishings, such as faux-leather armchairs, and are painted in pastel tones. A toilet, basin, and shower are crammed into the smallest bathrooms;

larger ones have a bathtub. The hotel stands on a busy street with easy access to the center of town and is close to shops, bars, and restaurants—and to Ghent's small red-light district, though you likely won't even be aware of this if you stick to the main drag. Rooms at the back are quieter than those at the front.

Zuidstationstraat 24 (at Sint-Annaplein), 9000 Gent. ✆ **09/223-51-51.** Fax 09/233-34-57. www.edenonline.be. 29 units. 70€–115€ double. Rates include buffet breakfast. MC, V. Parking 7.50€. Tram: 21 or 22 to Gent-Zuid. *In room:* TV, hair dryer, Wi-Fi (free).

Where to Dine

EXPENSIVE

Jan Breydel ★★ SEAFOOD/FRENCH High honors go to this exquisite restaurant on a quaint street near the Castle of the Counts. Its interior is a garden delight of greenery, white napery, and light woods. Proprietors Louis and Pat Hellebaut see to it that dishes issued from their kitchen are as light as the setting, with delicate sauces and seasonings enhancing fresh ingredients. Seafood and regional specialties like the traditional Ghent souplike fish stew *waterzooï* are all superb. Dine in summer on an outdoor terrace beside the confluence of the Leie River and the Lieve canal, next to a pretty little garden called Appelbrug Parkje.

Jan Breydelstraat 10 (facing Design museum Gent). ✆ **09/225-62-87.** www.janbreydel.com. Main courses 19€–33€; fixed-price menus 32€–48€. AE, DC, MC, V. Mon 7–10pm; Tues–Sat noon–2pm and 7–10pm. Tram: 1 or 4 to Korenmarkt.

MODERATE

Brasserie Pakhuis ★ FLEMISH/CONTINENTAL In a beautifully restored 19th-century warehouse down a narrow lane, this see-and-be-seen hangout is replete with painted cast-iron pillars, green pipes and tubing, ceiling fans, track lighting, soaring wrought-iron balconies, oak and marble tables with specially designed table settings, and a granite mosaic floor. Although a bit too conscious of its own sense of style, Pakhuis is stocked in matters of taste. The oyster and seafood platters are notable, and you won't go wrong with meat-based offerings like baked ham in a mustard sauce, or Flemish favorites like chicken *waterzooï* and *garnaalkroketten* (shrimp croquettes). Outside of lunch and dinner times, join the local smart set for afternoon tea or a late-night drink at the curving oak-and-riveted-copper bar.

Schuurkenstraat 4 (off Veldstraat). ✆ **09/223-55-55.** www.pakhuis.be. Main courses 11€–21€; fixed-price lunch 13€, dinner 26€–42€. AE, DC, MC, V. Mon–Thurs 11:30am–1am; Fri–Sat 11:30am–2am (full meals at lunch and dinner only). Tram: 1 or 4 to Korenmarkt.

Keizershof ★ BELGIAN/CONTINENTAL Despite being modern in tone and, to an extent, in cuisine by offering plenty of salads and other light fare, Keizershof is too smart to let you miss out on traditional Belgian standbys like *Gentse stoverij* (Ghent stew) and *mosselen* (mussels). Convivial and trendy, this place on the garish market square has an attractively informal ambience and a positive price-to-quality ratio. Behind its narrow, 17th-century baroque facade, even a capacity crowd of 150 diners can seem sparsely dispersed at the plain wood tables on multiple floors around a central stairwell. The decor beneath the timber ceiling beams is spare, tastefully tattered, and speckled with paintings by local artists. Service for office workers doing lunch is fast but not furious; in the evenings, you're encouraged to linger. In summertime dine alfresco in a courtyard at the back.

Vrijdagmarkt 47. ✆ **09/223-44-46.** www.keizershof.net. Main courses 14€–21€. AE, MC, V. Tues–Sat noon–2:30pm and 6–11pm. Tram: 1 or 4 to Geldmunt.

INEXPENSIVE

Amadeus RIBS/CONTINENTAL Sure, there are vegetarian and fish plates, but all of Ghent comes to this venerable institution in the Patershol district for the all-you-can-eat spareribs dinner: a slab of cooked ribs with a choice of sauces and a baked potato. If you're up to it, order another and another and another. A bottle of wine is on the table, and you pay only for what you drink from it. The decor is a sumptuous mix of Old Flemish and Art Nouveau with burnished wood, mirrors, and colored glass, and the ambience is relaxed.

Plotersgracht 8–10 (at Hertogstraat). ✆ **09/225-13-85.** www.amadeusspareribrestaurant.be. Main courses 13€–17€; spareribs dinner 14€. MC, V. Mon–Thurs 6:30–11pm; Sat–Sun 6–11;30pm. Tram: 1 or 4 to Geldmunt.

Ghent After Dark

THE PERFORMING ARTS

From October to mid-June, international opera is performed in the 19th-century **De Vlaamse Opera,** Schouwburgstraat 3 (✆ **09/268-10-11;** www.vlaamseopera.be; tram: 1, 21, or 22). Ghent venues for those marvelous Belgian puppet shows are the folklore museum (see earlier in this chapter), **Het Huis van Alijn,** Kraanlei 65 (✆ **09/269-23-50;** www.huisvanalijn.be; tram: 1 or 4), and **Teater Taptoe,** Abrahamstraat 15 (✆ **09/223-67-58;** www.theatertaptoe.be).

BARS & TAVERNS

In typical Flemish fashion, Ghent's favorite after-dark entertainment is frequenting atmospheric cafes and taverns. You should have a memorable evening in any one you choose. At the Old Flemish tavern **Herberg de Dulle Griet,** Vrijdagmarkt 50 (✆ **09/224-24-55;** www.dullegriet.be; tram: 1 or 4), you'll be asked to deposit one of your shoes before being given a potent Kwak beer in the too-collectible glass, which comes with a wood frame that allows the glass to stand up—you, too, might need artificial support if you drink too many of this or any of the other 250 different beers in stock. The smallest building on Graslei, the former Toll House, is now a nice little tavern called **Het Tolhuisje,** Graslei 11 (✆ **09/224-30-90;** tram: 1 or 4).

Groentenmarkt, near the Gravensteen, makes for a good pub crawl in an easily navigable area. In an old canal house, **Het Waterhuis aan de Bierkant,** Groentenmarkt 9 (✆ **09/225-06-80;** www.waterhuisaandebierkant.be; tram: 1 or 4), has more than 100 different Belgian beers, including locally made Stopken. Of all the gin joints in town, **'t Dreupelkot,** Groentenmarkt 12 (✆ **09/224-21-20;** www.dreupelkot.be; tram: 1 or 4), has to be the best. Ask owner Paul to recommend one of his 100 or so varieties of *jenever* (a stiff spirit similar to gin), served in tiny (but deadly) glassfuls. Or walk straight in and boldly go for a 64-proof Jonge Hertekamp or a 72-proof Pekèt de Houyeu. If they don't knock you down, you may be up for an 8-year-old 100-proof Filliers Oude Graanjenever or a 104-proof Hoogspanning. Across the tramlines, **'t Galgenhuisje,** Groentenmarkt 5 (✆ **09/233-42-51;** tram: 1 or 4), the oldest drinking spot in town, is an intimate place popular with students.

ANTWERP ★★

48km (30 miles) N of Brussels; 51km (32 miles) NE of Ghent

Until a few years ago, Antwerp (pop. 475,000) was one of Western Europe's most hidden gems. Its reputation as a port and diamond trade center is well deserved, but that's far from being all there is to say about this lively, sophisticated, and—in parts—seedy

Antwerp

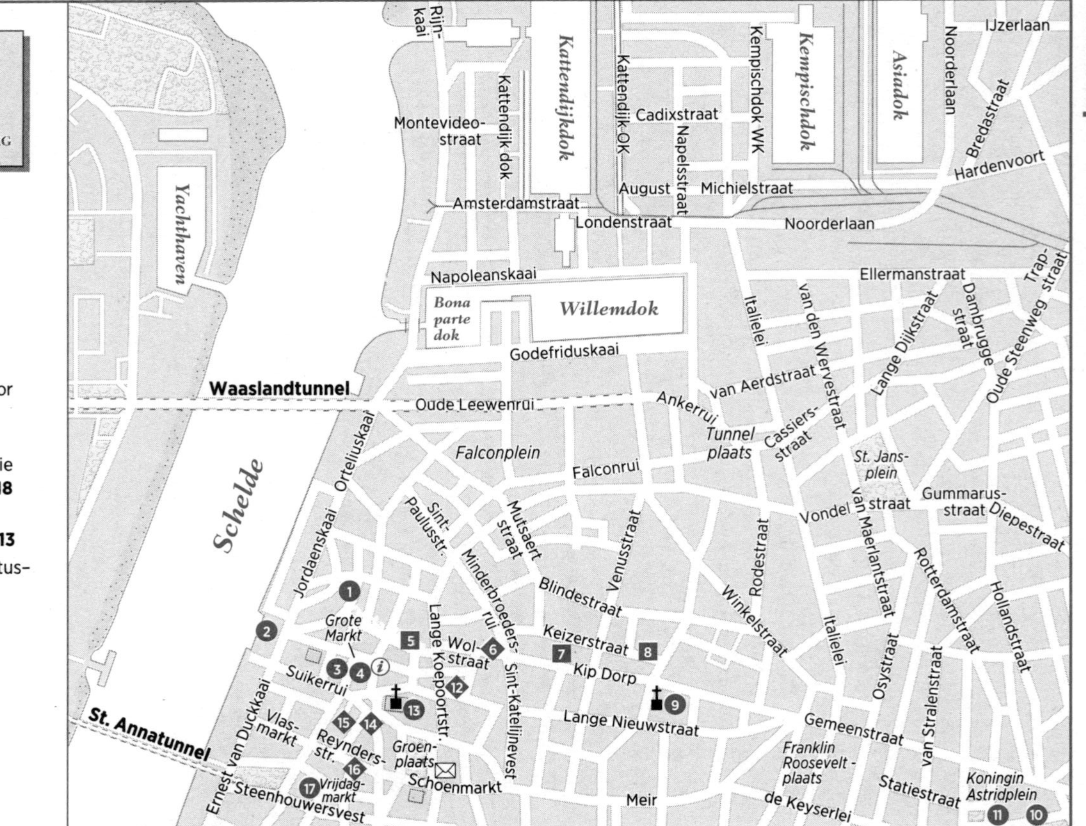

ATTRACTIONS ●

Aquatopia **11**
De Steen **2**
Diamantkwartier **22**
Diamantmuseum **10**
Grote Markt **4**
Koninklijk Museum voor Schone Kunsten Antwerpen **23**
ModeMuseum Provincie Antwerpen-MoMu **18**
Onze-Lieve-Vrouwekathedraal **13**
Museum Plantin-Moretus-Prentenkabinet **17**
Museum Vleeshuis **1**
Rubenshuis **20**
Sint-Jacobskerk **9**
Stadhuis **3**
Zoo Antwerpen **21**

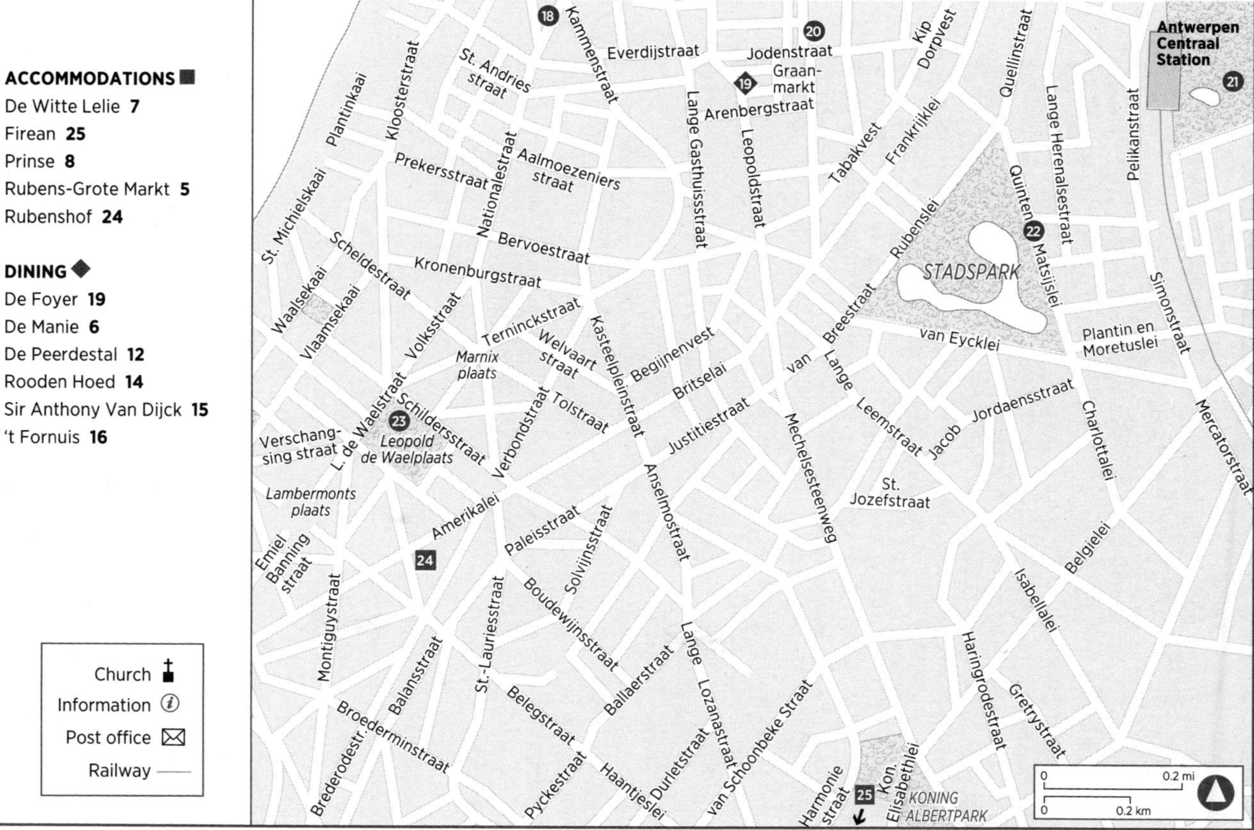
ACCOMMODATIONS
De Witte Lelie 7
Firean 25
Prinse 8
Rubens-Grote Markt 5
Rubenshof 24
DINING
De Foyer 19
De Manie 6
De Peerdestal 12
Rooden Hoed 14
Sir Anthony Van Dijck 15
'T Fornuis 16
Church
Information
Post office
Railway
Antwerpen Centraal Station
Kammenstraat
Everdijstraat
Jodenstraat
Graan-markt
Arenbergstraat
Kip Dorpvest
Quellinstraat
Lange Herenalsestraat
Pelikanstraat
St. Andries straat
Plantinkaai
Kloosterstraat
Lange Gasthuisstraat
Leopoldstraat
Tabakvest
Frankrijklei
Prekersstraat
Nationalestraat
Aalmoezeniers straat
St. Michielskaai
Rubenslei
Quinten Matsijslei
Bervoestraat
Kronenburgstraat
Scheldestraat
STADSPARK
Simonstraat
Waalsekaai
Vlaamsekaai
Volksstraat
Ternickstraat
Welvaart straat
Kasteelpleinstraat
Begijnenvest
Breestraat
van Eycklei
Plantin en Moretuslei
Marnix plaats
Britselai
van Lange Leemstraat
Jordaensstraat
Charlottalei
Mercatorstraat
Verschang-sing straat
L. de Waelstraat
Schildersstraat
Leopold de Waelplaats
Tolstraat
Verbondstraat
Justitiestraat
Mechelsesteenweg
Jacob
St. Jozefstraat
Lambermonts plaats
Amerikalei
Anselmostraat
Paleisstraat
Solvijnsstraat
Belgielei
Emiel Banning straat
Montiguystraat
St.-Lauriesstraat
Boudewijnsstraat
Isabellalei
Lange Lozanastraat
Haringrodestraat
Balansstraat
Belegstraat
Ballaerstraat
van Schoonbeke Straat
Gretrystraat
Broederminstraat
Brederodestr.
Pyckestraat
Haantjeslei
Durletstraat
Harmonie straat
Kon. Elisabethlei
KONING ALBERTPARK
0 0.2 mi
0 0.2 km

city. The capital town (Antwerpen in Dutch; Anvers in French) of Antwerpen province boasts monuments from its wealthy medieval, Renaissance, and baroque periods; a magnificent cathedral; a fine-arts museum full of Old Flemish masterpieces; a maze of medieval streets in the center of town; and a vibrant nightlife and cultural scene. Given all this, it's no surprise that international visitors to Belgium have been remedying their former neglect of the city. The new trend is to pour in from all over, to soak up everything Antwerp has to offer.

Essentials

GETTING THERE

BY PLANE **Brussels Airport** is the main international airport for Antwerp (see "Orientation," in chapter 6). Only a very few scheduled international flights arrive at **Antwerp Airport** (✆ **03/285-65-00;** www.antwerp-airport.be), at Deurne, 7km (4½ miles) east of the city. De Lijn bus no. 14 shuttles between the airport and Rooseveltplein, close to Antwerp Centraal Station, in around 20 minutes. Taxi fare to downtown is around 15€.

BY TRAIN Antwerp's two stations are **Antwerpen Centraal Station,** 1.5km (1 mile) east of the Grote Markt, on the edge of the center city, and **Antwerpen-Berchem,** 4km (2½ miles) south of the city center. Antwerp is on the **Thalys** high-speed train network that connects Paris, Cologne, Brussels, and Amsterdam; most Thalys trains stop at Berchem, but a few go to Centraal Station. For schedule and fare information, and for all train reservations, contact Belgian Railways (✆ **02/528-28-28;** www.b-rail.be).

Antwerpen Centraal Station is a domed, cathedral-like edifice dating from 1905, and it was recently refurbished. A 2009 article in *Newsweek* magazine named the station the world's fourth most beautiful (behind London's St. Pancras, New York's Grand Central, and Mumbai's Chhatrapati Shivaji).

BY BUS **Eurolines** international buses arrive and depart from a **bus stop** at van Stralenstraat 8, a short distance northwest of Centraal Station.

BY CAR Major roads connecting to Antwerp's R1 Ring Expressway (beltway) are A1/E19 from Brussels via Mechelen and from Amsterdam; A12 from Brussels via Laeken; A14/E17 from Ghent; and N49 from Knokke, Bruges, and Zeebrugge.

VISITOR INFORMATION

Toerisme Antwerpen, Grote Markt 13, 2000 Antwerpen (✆ **03/232-01-03;** fax 03/231-19-37; www.antwerpen.be; tram: 2, 3, 4, 8, or 15) is open Monday to Saturday from 9am to 5:45pm, Sunday and holidays from 9am to 4:45pm (closed Jan 1 and Dec 25). An **Info Desk** at Centraal Station is open the same hours as the main tourist office.

Impressions

The art is amazing, and it's everywhere you look; the fashion scene is vibrant, and the design is gorgeous; there's a cool café culture, and the streets are practically paved with diamonds. When you think about it, there's not much about Antwerp that is less than totally adorable. . . . Antwerp is the secret city with sex appeal.

Vanity Fair, **April 2009**

THE SEVERED hand OF ANTWERP

A legend of ancient days tells of a giant named Druon Antigon, who levied exorbitant tolls on every Scheldt boatman who passed his castle. If anyone would not pay up, the big man cut off the miscreant's hand and threw it into the river. Druon's comeuppance came from a Roman centurion, Silvius Brabo, who slew the giant and cut off *his* hand and threw it into the river. The Flemish *handwerpen* (throwing a hand) eventually became Antwerpen.

This explanation had a certain appeal to citizens who were traders to their fingertips, and who resented tolls of any size. Historians tell a different story, that after Viking raiders erased an original settlement in 836, the surviving populace moved to a more defensible mound, or *aanwerp,* where the Steen castle was later built. But to the people who live here, the severed, bleeding "Red Hand of Antwerp" is the symbol of their city. Two statues commemorate the Roman's act of revenge, and replicas of the giant's hand appear in everything from chocolate to brass.

GETTING AROUND

Antwerp is a good place to walk around. Its major sightseeing attractions are easily reached from one major street that changes its name as it goes along: Italiëlei, Frankrijklei, Britselei, and Amerikalei. Most sights are within easy walking distance of the center of town, but if the cobblestone streets start to bother your feet, hop onto a tram.

Besides walking, the tram is the best way to get around the city. The most useful trams for tourists are lines 2, 3, 5, and 15, which run between Centraal Station and Groenplaats, near the cathedral; and lines 10 and 11, which run past the Grote Markt. Public transportation information is available from a kiosk inside Centraal Station and from **De Lijn** (**✆ 070/22-02-00;** www.delijn.be).

Purchase your ticket from a De Lijn sales point or automat before boarding and you'll pay less (the "twin" prices listed here reflect this distinction). An *enkele rit* (one-way) ticket costs 1.20€/1.60€ for two zones and 2€/3€ for three or more zones. A *dagkaart* (day card), valid for the entire city network, costs 5€/6€ for 1 day, 10€/12€ for 3 days, and 15€/18€ for 5 days. A 1-day pass for children 6 to 11 is 1.50€/2€. Children 5 and under ride free.

The people to call for a taxi are **Antwerp Tax** (**✆ 03/238-38-38;** www.antwerp-tax.be).

Seeing the Sights

The most colorful part of Antwerp is the medieval Old Town that fans out from the Grote Markt in a warren of winding streets. South of there, on the streets around Vlaamsekaai and Waalsekaai, is a fascinating district of shipping warehouses renovated into trendy bars, restaurants, and art galleries.

THE TOP ATTRACTIONS

Koninklijk Museum voor Schone Kunsten Antwerpen (Antwerp Royal Museum of Fine Arts) ★★★ Housed in this impressive neoclassical building is the KMSKA's world-class collection of paintings by Flemish Masters. More masterpieces by Peter Paul Rubens are here than anywhere else, including frescoes by the artist in the marble entrance hall. To view Rubens's paintings, pass through the ground-floor exhibits of modern artists' canvases (including works by Belgian artists René Magritte, James Ensor, Constant Permeke, and Paul Delvaux) and ascend to the second floor, where you'll find Rubens, along with the Flemish Old Masters Jan van Eyck, Rogier van der Weyden, Dirck Bouts, German-born Hans Memling, Peter Bruegel the Elder and his several younger Brueghel (with an "h") relatives, and the Dutch Old Masters Rembrandt and Frans Hals. All told, these walls hold paintings spanning 5 centuries.

Leopold de Waelplaats 2 (at Museumstraat). ✆ **03/238-78-09.** www.kmska.be. Admission 6€ adults, 4€ students, 1€ ages 19–25, free for seniors and children 18 and under. Tues–Sat 10am–5pm; Sun 10am–6pm. Closed Jan 1–2 and Dec 25. Tram: 8 to Museum.

Onze-Lieve-Vrouwekathedraal (Cathedral of Our Lady) ★★ A masterpiece of the Brabant-Gothic architectural style, this towering edifice is the largest church in the Low Countries. There are seven aisles and 125 pillars in the cathedral, but of the original design's five towers, only one was completed. This one is the tallest church spire in the Low Countries, 123m (404 ft.) high, and the idea that the designers could have planned to construct five such behemoths is a graphic indication of the wealth and power of Antwerp at that time. Begun in 1352 and completed by around 1520, it stands on the site of a 10th-century chapel dedicated to the Virgin that later grew to be a church in the Romanesque style. The cathedral's history included a destructive fire in 1533, devastation by Protestant rebels during the religious wars of the 16th century, deconsecration by anticlerical French revolutionaries in 1794 (resulting in the removal of its Rubens paintings), and a slow rebirth that began after Napoleon's final defeat in 1815.

Its interior embellishment is a mix of baroque and neoclassical. Today the cathedral houses four Rubens masterpieces, all of them altarpieces: *The Raising of the Cross* (1610), *The Descent from the Cross* (1614), *The Resurrection* (1612), and *Assumption of the Virgin* (1626). Also outstanding is Nicolas Rombouts's *Last Supper* (1503), an impressive stained-glass window. Among many other notable works of art is a superb *Madonna and Child* (ca. 1350) in Carrrara marble by the anonymous Master of the Maasland Marble Madonnas. During July and August, the cathedral bells peal out in a carillon concert on Sunday from 3 to 4pm and on Monday from 8 to 9pm.

Mean Streets

The area around Centraal Station, east of De Keyserlei and Koningin Astridplein, is more than a little seedy and has problems with drug dealing and prostitution.

Groenplaats 21 (at Handschoenmarkt). ✆ **03/213-99-51.** www.dekathedraal.be. Admission 5€ adults, 3€ seniors and students, free for children 11 and under. Mon–Fri 10am–5pm; Sat 10am–3pm; Sun and religious holidays 1–4pm. Closed to tourist visits during services. Tram: 2, 3, 5, or 15 to Groenplaats.

Rubenshuis (Rubens House) ★ Touch Antwerp's cultural heart at the house where Antwerp's most illustrious son, the artist Peter Paul Rubens (1577–1640), lived and worked. Far from being the stereotypical starving artist, Rubens amassed a tidy fortune from his paintings that allowed him to build this impressive mansion in 1610, along what was then a canal, when he was 33. Today you stroll past the baroque portico into its reconstructed period rooms and through a Renaissance garden, and you come away with a good idea of the lifestyle of a patrician Flemish gentleman of that era. Examples of Rubens's works, and others by Master painters who were his contemporaries, are sprinkled throughout. In the dining room, look for a self-portrait painted when he was 47 years old, and in another room a portrait of Anthony van Dyck as a boy. Rubens collected Roman sculpture, and some of the pieces in his sculpture gallery appear—reproduced in amazing detail—in his paintings. Don't just stay inside the house: The superb, restored ornamental garden is well worth a stroll around and a nice place to take a breather in fine weather.

Wapper 9-11 (off Meir). ✆ **03/201-15-55.** www.rubenshuis.be. Admission 6€ adults; 4€ ages 19-26; free for seniors, visitors with disabilities and companion, and children 18 and under; free for all visitors last Wed of month. Tues-Sun (also Easter Mon and Pentecost Mon) 10am-5pm. Closed Jan 1-2, May 1, Ascension Day, Nov 1-2, and Dec 25-26. Tram: 2, 3, 5, or 15 to Meir.

AROUND THE GROTE MARKT

A lively 16th-century square lined with sidewalk cafes and restaurants, the Grote Markt, though not quite as dramatic as Brussels's Grand-Place, is no less the focus of the city's everyday life. The fountain in the middle recalls the city's founding legend of Druon and Brabo.

Stadhuis (City Hall) The Renaissance City Hall (1561–65), designed by Cornelius Floris de Vriendt, is an outstanding example of the Flemish mannerism that replaced the formerly supreme Gothic style. It was burned during the city's sack by Spanish troops in 1576, an episode the city still recalls with a shiver as the "Spanish Fury," and then rebuilt as you see it now. Look for the frescoes by Hendrik Leys, a 19th-century Antwerp painter; murals; and, in the burgomaster's chamber, an impressive 16th-century fireplace.

Grote Markt. ✆ **03/221-13-33.** Free guided tours Mon-Wed and Fri-Sat 2pm and 3pm (council business permitting). Tram: 10 or 11 to Sint-Katelijne.

Museum Vleeshuis (Butcher's Hall Museum) Around the square and on nearby streets are fine examples of 16th-century guild houses. One worth a visit is this magnificent Gothic structure. It functions now as a museum of archaeology, ceramics, arms, religious art, sculpture, musical instruments, coins, and medieval furnishings. The collections give a good general idea of daily life in Antwerp during the 16th century, as do the historical paintings (look for the striking *The Spanish Fury,* picturing Antwerp's darkest hour).

Vleeshouwersstraat 38-40. ✆ **03/292-61-00.** www.museumvleeshuis.be. Admission 5€ adults; 3€ ages 19-26; free for seniors, visitors with disabilities and companion, and children 18 and under; free for all visitors last Wed of month. Tues-Sun (also Easter Mon and Pentecost Mon) 10am-5pm. Closed Jan 1-2, May 1, Ascension Day, Nov 1-2, and Dec 25-26. Tram: 10 or 11 to Sint-Katelijne.

MORE ATTRACTIONS WORTH A VISIT

ModeMuseum Provincie Antwerpen-MoMu ★ The collections of the Antwerp Province Fashion Museum consist of clothing, lace, embroidery, fabrics, and tools for textile processing dating back to the 16th century, complemented with pieces by contemporary Belgian designers, some of them highly touted. "MoMu" combines a varied exhibits policy with publications, a library and spacious public reading room, lectures, conferences, workshops, and movies. Together with the Flanders Fashion Institute (FFI) and the renowned fashion department of the Antwerp Royal Academy of Fine Arts, the museum is housed in the beautifully restored 19th-century ModeNatie building in the cultural and historical heart of town.

Nationalestraat 28 (at Drukkerijstraat). ✆ **03/470-27-70.** www.momu.be. Admission 7€ adults, 5€ students and seniors, 1€ visitors with disabilities and companion, and ages 12-25, free for children 11 and under. Tues-Sun 10am-6pm. Closed Jan 1-2 and Dec 25-26, early closing Dec 24 and Dec 31. Tram: 4 or 8 to Kammenstraat.

Museum Plantin-Moretus-Prentenkabinet Printer Christoffle Plantin established a workshop in this stately patrician mansion in 1555. Its output included an astonishing multilanguage (Hebrew, Greek, Syriac, Latin, and Aramaic) edition of the Bible, and translations of other great works of literature. Plantin's grandson, Balthasar Moretus, was a contemporary and close friend of Rubens, who illustrated many of the books published by the Plantin-Moretus workshop and painted the family portraits you see displayed here. The museum's exhibits include an antique *Librorium Prohibitorum,* a catalog of books proscribed by the church as being unsuitable for pious eyes. Vrijdagmarkt 22-23. ✆ **03/221-14-50.** www.museumplantinmoretus.be. Admission 6€ adults; 1€ ages 19–26; free for seniors, visitors with disabilities and their companion, and children 18 and under; free for all visitors last Wed of month. Tues–Sun (also Easter Mon and Pentecost Mon) 10am–5pm. Closed Jan 1–2, May 1, Ascension Day, Nov 1–2, and Dec 25–26. Tram: 2, 3, 5, or 15 to Groenplaats.

Sint-Jacobskerk (St. James's Church) ★ A short walk north from the Rubens House, this flamboyant Gothic church with a baroque interior is the final resting place of the artist Peter Paul Rubens (1577–1640). His vault is in the Rubens Chapel, one of seven chapels bordering the opulent semicircular ambulatory behind the high altar. Several of Rubens's works are here, as are some by Antoon van Dyck and other prominent artists. Rubens is joined in his eternal slumber by a glittering array of Antwerp's one-time high and mighty, and a glittering collection of gold and silver religious objects. Lange Nieuwstraat 73–75 (at Sint-Jacobsstraat). ✆ **03/232-10-32.** www.topa.be. Admission 2€ adults, free for children 11 and under. Apr–Oct daily 2–5pm. Closed to tourist visits during services. Tram: 10 or 11 to Sint-Jacob.

ANTWERP'S PORT

When you come down to it, if there were no Schelde (Scheldt) River, there would be no Antwerp. The city's prime location just above the point where the river meets the tidal Westerchelde (Western Scheldt) Estuary made it an important port as far back

THE diamond TRADE

The raw facts and figures are sparkling enough: 80% of the world's rough diamonds, 50% of its cut diamonds, and 40% of its industrial diamonds are traded here annually—together they're valued at around $10 billion. Antwerp is the world's leading market for cut diamonds and second only to London as an outlet for raw and industrial diamonds. The trade, with its diamond cutters and polishers, workshops, brokers, and merchants, is centered on the city's **Diamantkwartier (Diamond Quarter),** a surprisingly down-at-the-heels-looking area, only steps away from Centraal Station. It is supervised by the Antwerp World Diamond Center and is mostly, though not exclusively, run by members of the city's Hasidic Jewish community.

In addition to perusing the stores and visiting a workshop (see "Shopping," later in this chapter), a good place to get close to the city's diamond trade is the **Diamantmuseum (Diamond Museum),** Koningin Astridplein 19–23 (✆ **03/202-48-90;** www.provant.be; Métro: Diamant or Astrid). Exhibits trace the history, geology, mining, and cutting of diamonds. Diamond-cutting and polishing demonstrations are on Saturday from 1:30 to 4:30pm. The museum is open Thursday to Tuesday (and Wed when national holiday) from 10am to 5:30pm (closed Jan 1–2 and Dec 25–26). Admission is 6€ for adults, 4€ for seniors and ages 12 to 25, and free for children 11 and under.

as the 2nd century B.C. Antwerp was a trading station of the powerful medieval Hanseatic League but, unlike Bruges, did not have the status of a full-fledged *Kontor,* with its own separate district and mercantile installations. In the early days, ships moored along the city's own wharves, where the Steen (see below) stands; nowadays the port has moved 13km (8 miles) downstream to huge excavated docks that jam up against the Dutch border. Antwerp is Europe's second biggest port (after Rotterdam) for goods handled, and the third biggest (after Rotterdam and Hamburg) for containers. The port is well worth a visit, if only to appreciate its vast size.

On the waterfront in the center of town, Antwerp's oldest building, **De Steen (The Castle)** ★, Steenplein 1 (at the Scheldt River), is a glowering 13th-century fortress on the banks of the Scheldt, just along the street from the Grote Markt.

ESPECIALLY FOR KIDS

Futuristic **Aquatopia,** Koningin Astridplein 7 (✆ **03/205-07-40;** www.aquatopia.be; Métro: Centraal Station), in the Park Plaza Astrid Antwerp building, has 40 aquaria filled with around a million liters (264,172 gal.) of saltwater and houses 3,500 marine creatures, from sea horses to sharks. Tropical rainforests, mangroves, wetlands, coral reefs, the ocean floor—all, and more, are featured. No doubt your biggest thrill will be walking through a clear-walled "shark tunnel" while watching smallish examples of these toothy fish swimming around you. Multimedia applications and interactive computer displays complement the live action; even Nemo puts in an appearance. You may want to spend at least 2 hours here. Aquatopia is open daily from 10am to 6pm (closed Dec 25). Admission is 14€ for adults, 9.50€ for seniors and children 3 to 12, free for children 2 and under, and 20€ or 32€ for a family (the price varies according to the size of the family).

The Belgian Muppets

Take the kids to the delightful Koninklijke Poppenschouwburg (Royal Puppet Theater) van Campen, Lange Nieuwstraat 3 (✆ 03/237-37-16; www.van-campen.be; tram: 10 or 11), a handsome little theater with 120 seats, where the plot lines are always easy to follow (even when the language isn't).

Zoo Antwerpen ★★ ☺ This 10-hectare (25-acre) zoo is a great place to take the kids. Its large collection of animals from around the world roam through spaces bounded for the most part by artificial reproductions of natural barriers. There's an aquarium, winter garden, Egyptian temple (which houses elephants), anthropoid house, museum of natural history, deer parks, Kongo peacock habitat, and planetarium. The zoo is something of an Art Nouveau masterpiece, though whether or not the animals appreciate this is hard to say.

Koningin Astridplein 26 (just east of Centraal Station). ✆ **03/202-45-40.** www.zooantwerpen.be. Admission 20€ adults, 16€ seniors, 14€ visitors with disabilities and companion and children 3–11, free for children 2 and under. Jan–Feb and Nov–Dec daily 10am–4:45pm; Mar–Apr and Oct daily 10am–5:30pm; May–June and Sept daily 10am–6pm; July–Aug daily 10am–7pm. Métro: Centraal Station.

ORGANIZED TOURS

WALKING TOURS From July to September, a daily guided tour of the center city in English (and French) departs at 2pm from the tourist office; the cost is 8€ per person if purchased at departure and 6€ if purchased ahead of time. Beyond this basic introduction, there is a variety of specialized tour options. There are also clearly marked self-guided walks, for which brochures are available from the tourist office.

BY BOAT Try to take a cruise around Antwerp's awesome harbor. Departures are from the Scheldt waterfront next to the Steen. **Rederij Flandria** (✆ **03/231-31-00;** www.flandria.nu) runs a 2½-hour harbor cruise for 13€ for adults; 11€ for seniors, people with disabilities, and children 3 to 12; and free for children 2 and under. A 50-minute excursion on the river is less interesting but still worthwhile, with half-hourly departures during summer months, for 5€ for adults and free for children 2 and under.

BY BUS The **Antwerp Diamond Bus** (✆ **02/513-77-44;** www.brussels-city-tours.com) is a double-decker bus that tours the city's main sights on a regular circuit. Hop on and hop off at various stops along the way. Tickets, valid for 24 hours, are 11€ for adults, 10€ for seniors and students, 6€ for children 5 to 12, and free for children 4 and under.

Where to Stay

VERY EXPENSIVE

De Witte Lelie ★★ A centrally located boutique hotel, the "White Lily" is set in three renovated and converted 17th-century gabled town houses with a garden courtyard. The property artfully combines old-fashioned ambience, exposed beams, marble fireplaces, antiques, and impeccable service, with a fine sense of modern style, distinctive design elements, and works of contemporary art. Each of the bright, tastefully furnished rooms has an individual character, and a "less is more" sensibility means that, though on the small side, they are not cluttered. While the white of the hotel's name is the presiding tone—the luxurious bathrooms are dazzlingly white—color shows up in drapes, rugs, flowers, and other touches. The breakfast room looks out on the courtyard.

Keizerstraat 16–18 (close to the Rockoxhuis), 2000 Antwerpen. ✆ **03/226-19-66.** Fax 03/234-00-19. www.dewittelelie.be. 11 units. 215€ double; 365€–565€ suite. AE, DC, MC, V. Parking 25€. Tram: 4 or 7 to Keizerstraat. **Amenities:** Lounge; room service. *In room:* TV, minibar, Wi-Fi (free).

EXPENSIVE

Rubens-Grote Markt ★★ Only steps away from the Grote Markt, this comfortable hotel with an attentive staff combines the classical elegance of a 16th-century mansion with plush, modern furnishings. The spacious rooms are individually decorated in a style that's a modern take on old-fashioned coziness, and from some of them you can see the cathedral steeple. Shady rooms are perked up with bright, tropical colors; sunny rooms have more muted, pastel tones. Bathrooms are not large but have marble fittings. Some of the rooms open onto an enclosed garden patio at the rear with an original colonnade, where breakfast is served in the summer; at other times, you breakfast in an elegant dining room with a marble fireplace.

Oude Beurs 29 (1 block north of the Grote Markt), 2000 Antwerpen. ✆ **03/222-48-48.** Fax 03/225-19-40. www.hotelrubensantwerp.be. 36 units. 150€–230€ double; 250€–445€ suite. Rates include buffet breakfast. AE, DC, MC, V. Parking 16€. Tram: 10 or 11 to Melkmarkt. **Amenities:** Bar; room service. *In room:* A/C, TV, hair dryer, minibar, Wi-Fi (12€/24 hr.).

MODERATE

Firean ★ 🎁 In a superb, restored Art Deco mansion from 1929, replete with delicate enamel work and Tiffany glass, this family-owned hotel is a bit off the beaten track south of the center city. The Deco elements are offset, and given added warmth, by a wealth of Persian rugs, antiques, and chandeliers. Each of the individually styled rooms is a cozy delight of pastel tones, tasteful furnishings, armchairs or sofas, and

Room for Misunderstanding

A word of warning to budget travelers: The phrase "tourist room," which in other cities means an accommodations bargain in a private home, means something rather different in Antwerp—It's a discreet way of advertising very personal services that have nothing to do with a room for the night.

comfortable beds. Breakfast is served in the garden in fine weather, and having the hotel's elegant French/Belgian restaurant Minerva just a few steps away should make a trip to one of the center-city eateries for dinner all but superfluous.

Karel Oomsstraat 6 (at Koning Albertpark), 2018 Antwerpen. ✆ **03/237-02-60.** Fax 03/238-11-68. www.hotelfirean.com. 15 units. 169€–178€ double; 235€ suite. Rates include buffet breakfast. AE, DC, MC, V. Parking 14€. Tram: 2 or 6 to Provinciehuis. **Amenities:** Restaurant; bar. *In room:* A/C, TV, hair dryer, minibar, Wi-Fi (free).

Prinse If you like modernity and efficiency in your everyday life, but you're not averse to mixing this with a dollop of history, this hotel, on a quiet street between Centraal Station and the center of town, might be the place for you. It offers cool modern rooms in a restored 16th-century residence—over-restored, some guests might conclude. The style takes its cue from the modish lobby area and moves on with signature black leather and wood, which some might find a bit impersonal, to other interiors. Yet the effect is softened overall by a friendly, personal ambience, and in the rooms by a hushed atmosphere and comfortable beds and other furnishings. The hotel has both a pleasant terrace and a tranquil courtyard garden.

Keizerstraat 63 (at Prinsesstraat), 2000 Antwerpen. ✆ **03/226-40-50.** Fax 03/225-11-48. www.hotelprinse.be. 33 units. 135€ double; 150€ suite. Rates in suite include buffet breakfast. AE, DC, MC, V. Parking 20€. Tram: 10 or 11 to Sint-Jacob. **Amenities:** Bar/lounge. *In room:* TV, Wi-Fi (free).

INEXPENSIVE

Rubenshof ★ This small, family-owned hotel used to be a residence (1860) of the Belgian cardinal. Perhaps this explains the heavenly atmosphere. The place has a remarkably beautiful interior, with painted ceilings, chandeliers, and a great deal of ornamentation that includes beautiful wood carvings and stained-glass windows. Some of this is Art Nouveau, in a "new" wing that was added to the building in 1910 and includes the breakfast room. The guest rooms are somewhat plainer than the public spaces—with the exception of the Chinese Room—but they're still comfortably and adequately furnished and tastefully decorated.

Amerikalei 115–117 (across from the Royal Museum of Fine Arts), 2000 Antwerpen. ✆ **03/237-07-89.** Fax 03/248-25-94. www.rubenshof.be. 22 units, 14 with bathroom. 52€ double without bathroom; 76€ double with bathroom. Rates include continental breakfast. AE, MC, V. Limited street parking. Tram: 4 or 24 to Bestorming; 12 to Bres. *In room:* No phone.

Where to Dine

VERY EXPENSIVE

't Fornuis ★★ FRENCH/BELGIAN Behind the heavy doors of a 16th-century stone house, this Michelin two-star restaurant offers the finest dining in town in an intimate room furnished in oak. Chef Johan Segers comes to your table to explain each succulent dish. Although you can't go wrong with anything on the menu, the

Bretagne lobster is particularly outstanding. Guests are invited to visit the superb wine cellar, which contains 4,000 bottles of wine.

Reyndersstraat 24 (at Oude Koornmarkt). ✆ **03/233-62-70.** Reservations required. Main courses 22€–52€; fixed-price menu 55€. AE, DC, MC, V. Mon–Fri noon–3pm and 7–10pm.

EXPENSIVE

De Manie ★ FRENCH This bright, modern restaurant serves innovative dishes that change every 6 months. Recent specialties included an appetizer of quail salad with goat cheese and artichoke; filet of hare with cranberries, chicory, and juniper sauce; and grilled wood pigeon with gratinéed Brussels sprouts. The food is excellent, and the setting is laid-back.

Hendrik Conscienceplein 3 (near Sint-Katelijnevest). ✆ **03/232-64-38.** Main courses 24€–32€; fixed-price menus 35€–45€. AE, MC, V. Mon–Tues and Thurs–Sat noon–2:30pm and 6:30–9:30pm; Sun 6:30–9:30pm. Tram: 10 or 11 to Melkmarkt.

Sir Anthony van Dijck ★★ BELGIAN/CLASSIC FRENCH A location amid the delightful 16th-century Vlaeykensgang courtyard's jumble of cafes, restaurants, and antique apartments all but guarantees a pleasant atmosphere here. This used to be a Michelin star–rated restaurant, until owner and chef Marc Paesbrugghe tired of being on the Michelin treadmill and chose to do something less stressful, more fun, and reasonably priced. He reopened this place as a relaxed brasserie/restaurant in an elegantly minimalist setting flooded with natural light from the old-world courtyard. It doubles as a contemporary art gallery but retains a commitment to good food.

Oude Koornmarkt 16 (inside Vlaeykensgang). ✆ **03/231-61-70.** www.siranthonyvandijck.be. Main courses 34€–35€; gastronomic menu 47€. AE, DC, MC, V. Mon–Sat noon–1:30pm and 6:30–9:30pm. Tram: 2, 3, 5, or 15 to Groenplaats.

MODERATE

De Peerdestal CONTINENTAL In this large, rustic, two-floor restaurant, you can enjoy a light meal of a salad or indulge in heartier fare such as mussels, fish, steak, or even horse meat, which is a specialty here. Despite its size, there's something almost cozy about the place. One standout offering is the nice crispy salad with marinated goat's cheese, bacon, and a honey dressing; if you regularly take your *steak Américain* (American steak) raw, chopped, mixed with raw onions, and served with a béarnaise sauce, then you should love it here.

Wijngaardstraat 8–10 (2 blocks east of the Grote Markt). ✆ **03/231-95-03.** www.depeerdestal.be. Reservations recommended on weekends. Main courses 23€–35€; fixed-price menus 28€–43€. AE, DC, MC, V. Daily 11:30am–3pm and 5:30–10pm. Tram: 10 or 11 to Melkmarkt.

Rooden Hoed ★ BELGIAN/FRENCH This pleasant, old-fashioned restaurant is the oldest in Antwerp, having been in business for more than 250 years. It serves hearty food—a mix of regional cuisine and trendy new forms—at moderate prices. Mussels, a delicious *choucroute d'Alsace* (sausages with sauerkraut and mashed potatoes), chicken *waterzooï,* and fish specialties are all featured on the menu. Try an aperitif or a snack in the medieval cellar under the restaurant.

Oude Koornmarkt 25 (facing the cathedral). ✆ **03/233-28-44.** www.roodenhoed.be. Main courses 22€–27€; fixed-price lunch 22€; Marktmenu (daily special menu) 37€. AE, MC, V. Mon–Thurs noon–2:30pm and 6–10:30pm; Fri–Sat noon–2:30pm and 6–11pm; Sun noon–2:30pm and 6–10pm. Tram: 2, 3, 5, or 15 to Groenplaats.

INEXPENSIVE

De Foyer ★ INTERNATIONAL One of Antwerp's most popular dining addresses, this magnificent brasserie is in the foyer of the 19th-century Bourla Theater. With its ornately painted dome, potted palms, red-velvet drapes, and marble columns, you would expect prices to be a lot higher than they are. The daily lunch buffet is a bargain; it includes an array of fish and vegetable salads, soup, several hot dishes, cheese, and pastries. At least try to stop in for tea or drinks, if only to bask in the opulence.

Komedieplaats 18 (at Schuttershofstraat). ✆ **03/233-55-17.** www.defoyer.be. Reservations recommended on weekends. Light meals 9€–13€; lunch buffet 15€. MC, V. Mon–Fri noon–midnight; Sat 11am–midnight; Sun 11am–6pm. Tram: 7 or 8 to Oudaan.

Shopping

Antwerp yields not an inch to Brussels in the style wars—in fact, Antwerp is the more fashion-conscious of the two. During the '80s and '90s, youthful local fashion designers, graduates of the city's Fine Arts Academy, made a major and enduring impact within Belgium and established a substantial international reputation.

Expensive upmarket stores, boutiques, and department stores abound in De Keyserlei and the Meir. For haute couture, go to Leopoldstraat; for lace, the streets surrounding the cathedral; for books, Hoogstraat; for electronics and antiques, Minderbroedersrui; and for diamonds, Appelmansstraat and nearby streets, all near Centraal Station.

WHERE TO SHOP

A top Belgian fashion designer keeps shop at **Ann Demeulemeester ★★**, Verlaatstraat 38 (✆ **03/216-01-33;** www.anndemeulemeester.be; tram: 8), at Leopold de Waelplaats, in front of the Royal Fine Arts Museum. It offers complete lines of clothes, shoes, and accessories for both men and women by Demeulemeester, one of the city's influential fashion designers going back to the 1980s, when they were dubbed the "Antwerp Six." It's open Monday to Saturday from 10am to 7pm.

Treat your feet to shoes by Anne Demeulemeester, and other top Flemish designers Dries van Noten and Dirk Bikkembergs, at **Coccodrillo,** Schuttershofstraat 9 (✆ **03/233-20-93;** www.coccodrillo.be; tram: 7 or 8). Chic, affordable women's fashion is served up at Belgian designer **Olivier Strelli ★**, Hopland 35 (✆ **03/233-51-36;** tram: 12 or 24).

For diamonds, visit the glittering jewelry and gold stores of the **Diamantkwartier (Diamond Quarter),** around Centraal Station. At **Diamondland,** Appelmansstraat 33A (✆ **03/229-29-90;** www.diamondland.be; Métro: Centraal Station), it's fascinating to watch expert cutters and polishers transform undistinguished stones into gems of glittering beauty—the "Antwerp cut" is said to give them more sparkle. This luxurious showplace, the city's biggest, provides a firsthand look at the process on a guided tour of its workrooms.

Markets

Antwerp's famed street markets are fun and good bargain-hunting territory. If you're in town on a Saturday from Easter to October, shop for a steal at the **Antiques Market,** Lijnwaadmarkt (tram: 10 or 11), from 10am to 6pm. The outstanding **Bird Market** is a general market that features live animals, plants, textiles, and foodstuffs; it takes place Sunday mornings on Oude Vaartplaats (tram: 12 or 14), off Frankrijklei. At the **street market** on Wednesday and Friday morning on Vrijdagmarkt (Tram: 2, 3, 5, or 15), facing the Plantin-Moretus Museum, household goods and secondhand furniture are put on public auction.

Antwerp After Dark

Antwerp is as lively after dark as it is busy during the day. The main entertainment zones are Grote Markt and Groenplaats, which both contain concentrations of bars, cafes, and theaters; High Town (Hoogstraat, Pelgrimstraat, Pieter Potstraat, and vicinity) for jazz clubs and bistros; Stadswaag for jazz and punk; and the Centraal Station area for discos, nightclubs, and gay bars. The red-light district here, concentrated in Riverside Quarter, is much seedier and less tourist-oriented than the one in Amsterdam (see chapter 13).

THE PERFORMING ARTS

Antwerp takes pride in being a citadel of Flemish culture. Two of the region's stellar performance companies are based here: the **Vlaamse Opera** (**Flanders Opera; © 070/22-02-02;** www.vlaamseopera.be), and the **Koninklijk Ballet van Vlaanderen** (**Royal Flanders Ballet; © 03/224-82-67;** www.koninklijkballetvan vlaanderen.be).

Top of the line for theater and classical music is the **Stadsschouwburg,** Theaterplein 1 (**© 0900/69-900;** www.stadsschouwburgantwerpen.be; tram: 12 or 24). Contemporary music and ballet is performed at **deSingel,** Desguinlei 25 (**© 03/248-28-28;** www.desingel.be; tram: 2).

BARS

No city watering hole has a better outlook than **Den Engel ★**, Grote Markt 3 (**© 03/233-12-52;** www.cafedenengel.be; tram: 10 or 11), an old-style cafe dating from 1579 on the main square, where a round glass called a *bolleke* (little ball) of Antwerp's very own yeasty, copper-toned De Koninck beer becomes a work of liquid art. Below the cathedral's soaring spire, amid wood paneling on two separate levels, **Paeters Vaetje,** Blauwmoezelstraat 1 (**© 03/231-84-76;** www.patersvaetje.be; tram: 10 or 11), is a great place for listening to the Monday-evening carillon concert and serves up 100 different brews along with snacks.

Get into the abbey habit at **De Groote Witte Arend,** Reyndersstraat 18 (**© 03/233-50-33;** www.degrootewittearend.be; tram: 2, 3, 5, or 15), a cafe in a 17th-century former monastery, where customers are serenaded by classical music. Go underground to **De Pelgrom,** Pelgrimsstraat 15 (**© 03/234-08-09;** tram: 2, 3, 5, or 15), in a candlelit, brick-arched cellar, and get convivial at long wood benches. A huge selection of beers, including virtually every Belgian brand, is displayed behind glass and served at candlelit tables in **Kulminator,** Vleminckveld 32 (**© 03/232-45-38;** tram: 7 or 8).

An altogether different kind of drinking experience is to be had at **De Vagant ★**, Reyndersstraat 25 (**© 03/233-15-38;** www.devagant.be; tram: 2, 3, 5, or 15). It deals exclusively in *jenever* and has 220 varieties of this stiff grain spirit. An upstairs restaurant specializes in dishes with *jenever*-based sauces, and its walls are a gallery of *jenever* memorabilia.

Side Trips from Antwerp

LIER

16km (10 miles) SE of Antwerp

A pretty, small town on the banks of the Nete River, Lier (pop. 35,000) has canal-side scenes reminiscent of Bruges, just not so extensive or well advertised.

Essentials

GETTING THERE There are up to six **trains** every hour to Lier (Lierre in French) from Antwerp's Centraal Station; the fastest trains get there in 15 minutes. To go by **car,** take N10.

VISITOR INFORMATION **Toerisme Lier,** Grote Markt 57 (**✆ 03/800-05-55;** fax 03/488-12-76; www.toerismelier.be), is at Stadhuis (Town Hall), in the center of town. The office is open April to October daily from 9:30am to 12:30pm and 1:30 to 5pm; and November to March Monday to Friday from 9:30am to 12:30pm and 1:30 to 5pm.

What to See & Do

Don't miss the town's 14th-century **Zimmertoren (Zimmer Tower) ★**, Zimmerplein 18 (**✆ 03/800-03-95;** www.zimmertoren.be). It's equipped with the remarkable Centenary Clock and Wonder Clock, which were installed by astronomy enthusiast Lodewijk Zimmer to explain the workings of space and time to his fellow citizens. The clocks show the sun, moon, signs of the zodiac, seasons, and tides on the Nete River. The tower is open Tuesday to Sunday from 9am to noon and 1:30 to 5:30pm. Admission is 2.50€ for adults, 1.50€ for children 6 to 16, and free for children 5 and under.

If you have time, visit the **Stedelijk Museum (Municipal Museum),** Florent van Cauwenberghstraat 14 (**✆ 03/800-03-96**), just off the Grote Markt in the center of town. The art collections here include paintings by Rubens, Jan Brueghel and Pieter Bruegel the Elder, David Teniers the Younger, and local artist Isidore Opsomer. The museum is open Tuesday to Sunday from 10am to noon and 1 to 5pm. Admission is 2€ for adults and free for children 6 and under.

HASSELT

73km (45 miles) SE of Antwerp

The heart of Belgium's potent *jenever* industry, Hasselt (pop. 72,000) is a center for touring the Kempen moorland.

Essentials

GETTING THERE Two **trains** to Hasselt depart every hour from Antwerp's Centraal Station; the fastest trains get there in just over an hour. By **car,** go east on N10 and N2, via Aarschot.

VISITOR INFORMATION **Toerisme Hasselt,** Lombaardstraat 3 (**✆ 011/23-95-40;** fax 011/22-50-23; www.hasselt.eu), is at the Stadhuis (Town Hall), in the center of town. The office is open Monday to Friday from 9am to 5pm, Saturday from 10am to 5pm, and Sunday and holidays from 10am to 2pm (Nov–Mar closed Sun and holidays).

What to See & Do

Centuries of the loving care devoted to the fiery drink *jenever* are recalled in the exhibits of the **Nationaal Jenevermuseum (National Jenever Museum),** Witte Nonnenstraat 19 (**✆ 011/23-98-60;** www.jenevermuseum.be). These include its distillation, bottling, labeling and, of course, drinking. The *jenever* has the last word in a free sample that rounds off the visit with an appropriate glow. The museum is open April to October Tuesday to Sunday (also Mon July–Aug) from 10am to 5pm; November to March Tuesday to Friday from 10am to 5pm, and weekends and holidays from 1 to 5pm (closed Jan except school vacation days, Dec 24–25 and 31). Admission is 3.50€ for adults, 2.50€ for seniors, 1€ for ages 12 to 26, and free for children 11 and under; the admission includes one *jenever* (not for children!).

A nearby attraction that is especially interesting for children is the **Domein Bokrijk (Bokrijk Estate)** ★ (✆ **011/26-53-00;** www.funinbokrijk.be), 8km (5 miles) northeast of town. On the grounds of the large wooded estate is the **Openluchtmuseum (Open-Air Museum),** consisting of old houses that provide detailed reconstructions of everyday Flemish life in premodern times; in some, craftspeople work at traditional trades. Although all of the buildings and village sites are clearly marked, I suggest you purchase the English-language guide, which is an education in itself. In addition, the estate incorporates a big nature reserve. The open-air museum is open April to September daily 10am to 6pm; the rest of the estate is open the same hours year-round. Admission to the open-air museum is 10€ for adults, 8.50€ for seniors and visitors with disabilities, 1€ for ages 6 to 26, and free for children 5 and under. There's regular bus service from Hasselt and train service from Brussels via Hasselt (Bokrijk has its own rail station). By car, take N75 from Hasselt; parking at the estate costs 3€.

TONGEREN ★

88km (55 miles) SE of Antwerp; 20km (12 miles) SE of Hasselt

Belgium's oldest town (Tongres in French), with a history dating back to Roman times, Tongeren (pop. 30,000) is at the eastern end of the Kempen moorland region, close to the Dutch border. Ambiorix, chief of the ancient Eburones tribe, wiped out one of Julius Caesar's legions somewhere in this area in 54 B.C., earning himself a martial bronze statue (1866) on the town's Grote Markt.

Essentials

GETTING THERE There's one **train** every hour from Antwerp's Centraal Station to Tongeren, going via Hasselt; the ride from Antwerp takes 1 hour and 40 minutes. By **car,** take N20 southeast from Hasselt.

VISITOR INFORMATION **Toerisme Tongeren** is at Via Julianus 5, 3700 Tongeren (✆ **012/80-00-70;** fax 012/80-00-78; www.tongeren.be), off Maastrichterstraat, 4 blocks east of the center of town. The office is open April to June and September Monday to Friday from 8:30am to noon and 1 to 5pm, and weekends and holidays from 9:30am to 5pm; July and August Monday to Friday from 8:30am to 5pm, and weekends and holidays from 9:30am to 5pm; and October to March Monday to Friday from 8:30am to noon and 1 to 5pm, and weekends and holidays from 10am to 4pm.

What to See & Do

Tongeren is home to the imposing **Onze-Lieve-Vrouwebasiliek (Basilica of Our Lady),** a Gothic church with a Brabantine tower and a Romanesque cloister. Its rich *schatkamer* (treasury) contains rare religious objects from the Merovingian era (6th–8th c. A.D.) up to the 18th century. The basilica is open daily from 9am to 4pm (the treasury Apr–Sept). Admission to the basilica is free. Admission to the treasury is 2.50€ for adults, 2€ for seniors and students, 0.50€ for children 6 to 12 and visitors with disabilities, and free for children 5 and under.

Also worth a visit is the newly expanded **Gallo-Romeins Museum (Gallo-Roman Museum)** ★, Kielenstraat 15 (✆ **012/67-03-30;** www.galloromeinsmuseum.be), which contains 18,000 objects from prehistoric times through the Roman and Merovingian periods. The Roman period, when the town was known as Atuatuca Tungrorum, is well represented and includes huge and important collections of relics—pottery, glass objects, bronze articles, terra cotta, and sculptures—from its cemetery and the surrounding countryside. These are organized by theme to illustrate everyday life both in the town and in the country, and include exhibits on religious practices and traditions. The museum is open Tuesday to Friday from 9am to 5pm, and Saturday, Sunday, holidays, and school vacations from 10am to 6pm. It's closed on January 1 and December 25. Admission is 7€ for adults, 5€ for seniors and visitors with disabilities, 1€ for ages 4 to 26, and free for children 3 and under.

THE BELGIAN COAST & YPRES

9

Belgium's 70km (44 miles) of North Sea coastline is one continuous vista of beaches backed by sand dunes and speckled with resort towns. Except for De Haan, each resort is encumbered with a dense waterfront lineup of hotels, restaurants, and apartment buildings. Together these have been dubbed the "Atlantic Wall," after Hitler's World War II fortifications, and they all but neutralize the coast's natural beauty.

Most visitors don't seem too concerned. Even those who are will find compensation in superb seafood dining, good shopping, and general vacation hustle and bustle. Kids love the seacoast. For adults the region offers several vacation styles—sea, sand, and sun; casino and nightclub action; gustatory gluttony; or a series of sightseeing expeditions. It's possible to cover all of these options in an incredibly short amount of time.

The beaches reach back up to 500m (1,640 ft.) at low tide, and their gentle slope into the sea makes for generally safe swimming—warnings are in force against swimming along isolated stretches. Just remember that this is the North Sea, not the Caribbean—the water is gray and pretty darn cold. Visitors skim along the sand on wind-blown sail carts (there's no shortage of wind), pedal beach buggies, or join the ever-hopeful sun worshipers in search of a tan.

OSTEND ★★

110km (68 miles) NW of Brussels; 20km (12 miles) W of Bruges

The glitter of the "Queen of the Coast" has faded since its 19th-century heyday as a royal vacation spot and prestigious European watering hole, but plenty of reasons remain to justify a visit to Ostend (Oostende in Dutch; Ostende in French): great beaches, a casino, a racetrack, art museums, a spa, good shopping, an Olympic-size indoor pool, outdoor pools filled with heated seawater, sailing and windsurfing, and, last but by no means least, a legitimate reputation of being a seafood cornucopia. This lively recreational haven is very much a people's queen now, welcoming all income levels. There's culture here, too, in notable art museums and links with modern artists.

The Belgian Coast

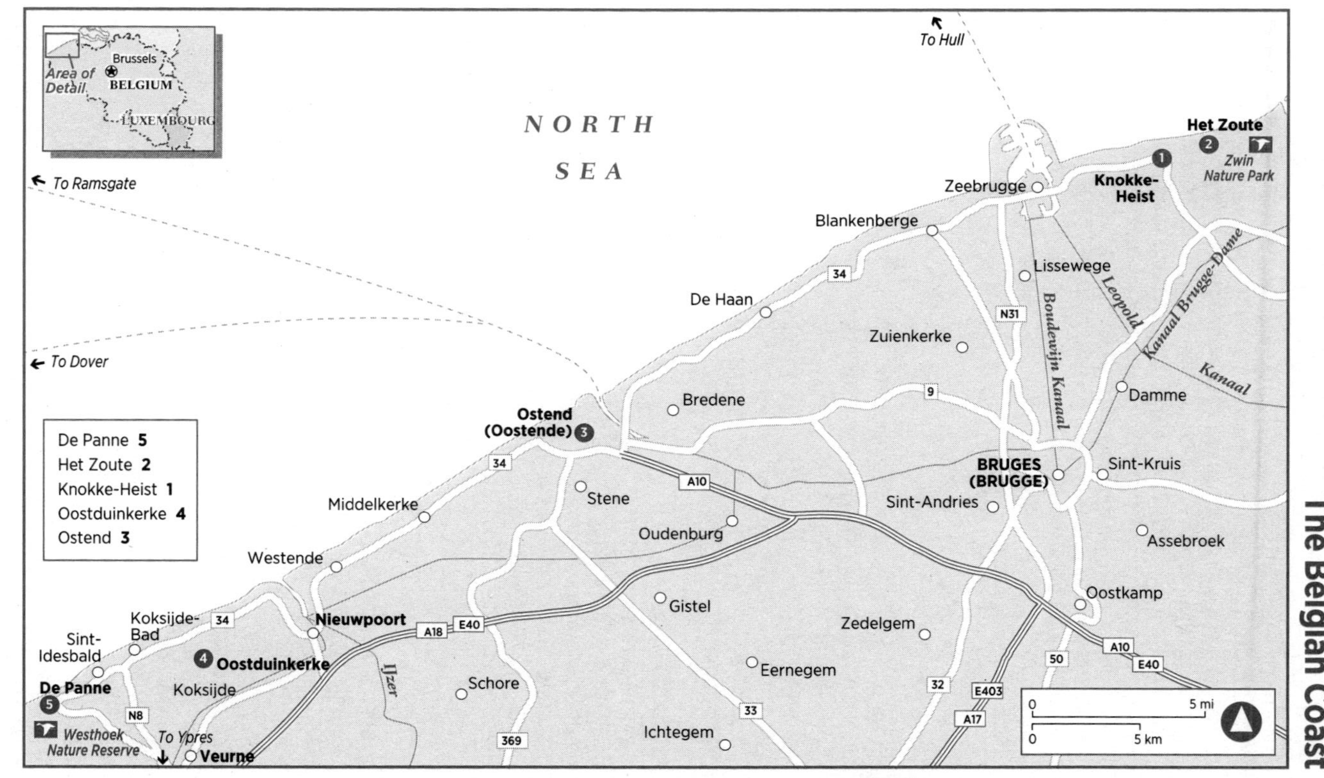

Tracks Along the Coast

The De Lijn company's **Kusttram (Coast Tram; ✆ 070/22-02-00; www.dekusttram.be)** runs the length of the seacoast between Knokke-Heist and De Panne in 2 hours and stops at 70 points along the way. Departures are every 10 to 20 minutes in summer and every 30 minutes in winter, in both directions. Purchase your ticket from a De Lijn sales point or automat (ticket machine) before boarding and you'll pay less for it (the "twin" prices listed here reflect this distinction). An *enkele rit* (one-way) ticket costs 1.20€/2€ for up to two zones and 2€/3€ for three or more zones. A *dagpas* (day pass) for adults, valid for the entire tram line, costs 5€/6€ (1 day), 10€/12€ (3 days), and 15€/18€ (5 days). For children 6 to 11, only a 1-day pass is available, costing 1.50€; children 5 and under ride free.

Ostend (pop. 70,000) has been attracting seawater enthusiasts since 1784, when the town council allowed Englishman William Hesketh to set up a drinks kiosk on the beach. He later introduced mobile beach huts that were hauled into the water by horses. Before World War II, the elevated Albert I Promenade and Zeedijk that together parallel the entire length of the 6km (4 miles) of beach were lined with elegant villas, among them vacation homes of European royalty. Wartime destruction and postwar "improvements" brought down many of these fine old houses. From the debris sprung character-free modern hotels and apartment buildings.

Essentials

GETTING THERE Two trains depart every hour from Brussels for the 80-minute ride, and up to three trains every hour from Bruges for the 15-minute ride, to **Oostende station** (**✆ 02/528-28-28;** www.sncb.be), a neo-baroque edifice (1913) at the harbor. The **Kusttram (Coast Tram)** has fast, frequent service connecting all the seacoast resorts from outside the station (see "Tracks Along the Coast," above). By car from Brussels and Bruges, take A10/E40 west; from the other coast resorts, take N34.

See "By Boat" under "Getting There & Around," in chapter 3, for ferries to Ostend from England.

VISITOR INFORMATION **Toerisme Oostende** is at Monacoplein 2, 8400 Oostende (**✆ 059/70-11-99;** fax 059/70-34-77; www.toerisme-oostende.be). The office is open May to October Monday to Saturday from 9am to 7pm and Sunday from 10am to 7pm, and November to April Monday to Saturday from 10am to 6pm and Sunday from 10am to 5pm.

GETTING AROUND Ostend is served by multiple bus lines departing from the bus station in front of the train station; if you want to get quickly to points along the coast, in either direction, take the **Coast Tram.** Bus and tram information is available from **De Lijn** (**✆ 070/22-02-00;** www.delijn.be). Pick up a **taxi** at the rail station or the Casino-Kursaal, or call **Taxibond** (**✆ 059/70-27-27**).

SPECIAL EVENTS You don't have to be crazy to take part in the annual **New Year Dive** into the North Sea, but it sure can't hurt. Around 6,000 "polar bears" nerve themselves to take the plunge into the icy North Sea waters on the first Saturday of the year.

Ostend

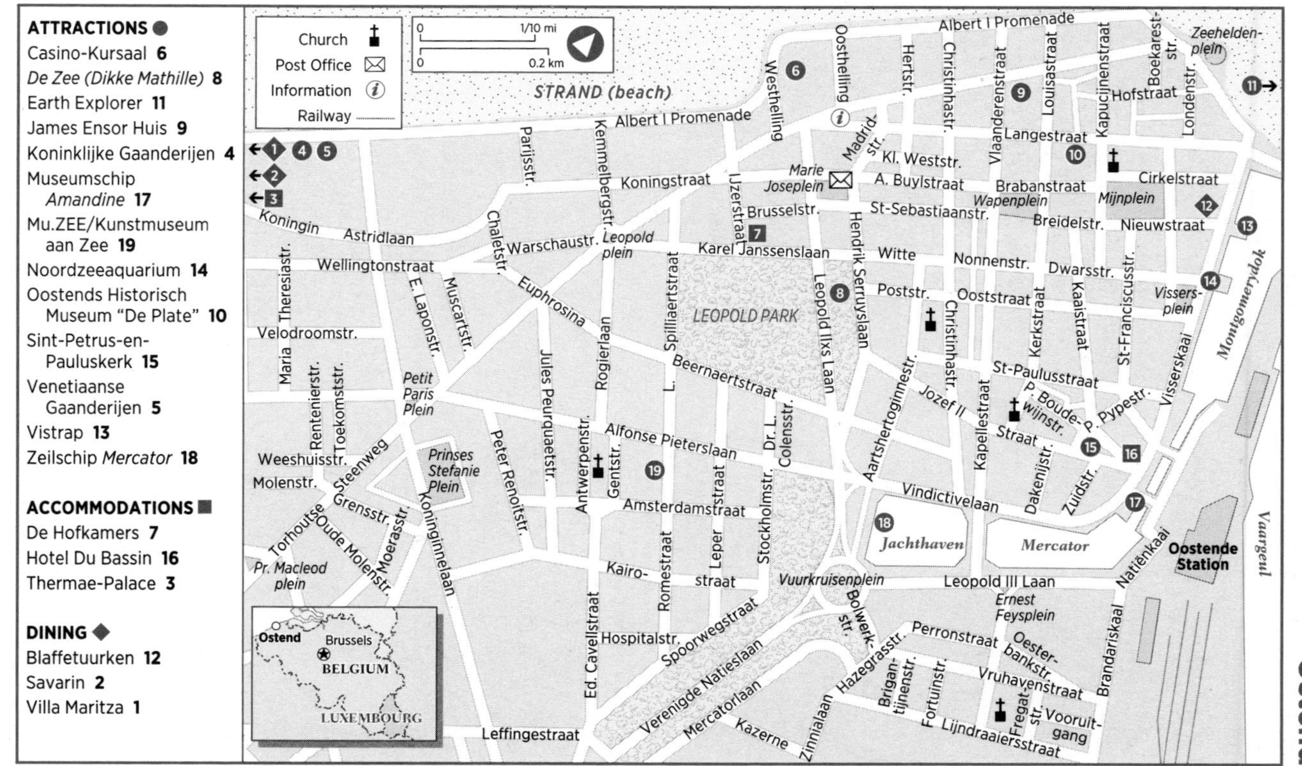

ATTRACTIONS ●
Casino-Kursaal 6
De Zee (Dikke Mathille) 8
Earth Explorer 11
James Ensor Huis 9
Koninklijke Gaanderijen 4
Museumschip Amandine 17
Mu.ZEE/Kunstmuseum aan Zee 19
Noordzeeaquarium 14
Oostends Historisch Museum "De Plate" 10
Sint-Petrus-en-Pauluskerk 15
Venetiaanse Gaanderijen 5
Vistrap 13
Zeilschip Mercator 18
ACCOMMODATIONS ■
De Hofkamers 7
Hotel Du Bassin 16
Thermae-Palace 3
DINING ◆
Blaffetuurken 12
Savarin 2
Villa Maritza 1
Church
Post Office
Information
Railway
0 1/10 mi
0 0.2 km
STRAND (beach)
Albert I Promenade
LEOPOLD PARK
Jachthaven
Mercator
Oostende Station
Vaargeul
Montgomerydok
Leopold III Laan
Leopold IIxs Laan
Hendrik Serruyslaan
Koninginnelaan
Koningin Astridlaan
Vuurkruisenplein
Marie Joseplein
Wapenplein
Mijnplein
Petit Paris Plein
Prinses Stefanie Plein
Pr. Macleod plein
Ernest Feysplein
Zeehelden-plein
Leopold plein
Vissers-plein
Ostend
Brussels
BELGIUM
LUXEMBOURG

What to See & Do

The waterfront Albert I Promenade and the Zeedijk are lined by beaches and a casino. The long beach west of the harbor has stretches that are under lifeguard surveillance in summer from 10:30am to 6:30pm, and some stretches where swimming is not permitted at any time. Look for the signs that indicate both of these, and for the green, yellow, or red flags that tell you whether the sea conditions permit swimming.

THE TOP ATTRACTIONS

James Ensorhuis (James Ensor House) The house where Ostend-born Anglo-Belgian artist James Ensor (1860–1949) lived from 1916 has been restored to its condition when his aunt kept a ground-floor shells-and-souvenir store here, and transformed into a museum of his life. Ensor's studio and lounge are upstairs. Only reproductions are displayed, but if you're familiar with his paintings, you'll recognize some of the furnishings and views from the windows. Though little understood or appreciated during his lifetime for his fantastical, hallucinatory, and sexually ambiguous visions, the pre-Expressionist painter is considered a founder of modern art. *The Entry of Christ into Brussels* (1889), first exhibited in 1929 and now in California's Getty Museum, is his most famous work. Ostend appreciates him just as much for his carnival masks inspired by the town's annual *Bal du Rat Mort* (Dead Rat Ball). Ensor is buried in the churchyard of **Onze-Lieve-Vrouw ter Duinenkerk (Our Lady of the Dunes Church)** on Dorpstraat.

Vlaanderenstraat 27 (off Wapenplein). ✆ **059/50-81-18.** Admission 2€ adults, 1€ seniors, free for children 17 and under. Wed–Mon 10am–noon and 2–5pm. Closed Jan 1 and Dec 25 (and in the event of a heavy storm).

Lady of the Sea

A bronze sculpture by Flemish artist George Grard (1901–84) depicting a generously endowed, reclining nude woman graces a fountain pond just outside Ostend's Leopoldpark. The 1955 work is formally entitled *De Zee (The Sea)*, but is known locally as *Dikke Mathille* (Fat Matilda).

Mu.ZEE/Kunstmuseum aan Zee (Art Museum by the Sea) ★ Set in a former department store, this museum's paintings, sculptures, graphics, video, and films provide a wide-ranging picture of Belgian modern art from its beginnings to the present day. It combines the collections of the town's old Museum of Modern Art and Fine Arts Museum. Paintings by native sons James Ensor, Jan de Clerck, Constant Permeke, and Léon Spilliaert, as well as by Belgian Impressionists, are featured. Among the Ensors is his racy *Bathing at Ostend* (1899), a work that scandalized polite Belgian society, though the libertine King Léopold II appreciated its saucy humor—and it is interesting to compare the beach scene then with today's. There are frequent international exhibits, a children's museum, a workshop for youngsters, slide shows, and educational projects.

Romestraat 11 (at Amsterdamstraat). ✆ **059/50-81-18.** www.kunstmuseumaanzee.be. Admission 5€ adults, 4€ seniors, 2.50€ children 12–17, free for children 11 and under. Tues–Sun 10am–6pm. Closed Jan 1 and Dec 25.

Oostends Historisch Museum "De Plate" (Ostend Historical Museum "The Plaice") Housed in King Léopold I's restored, 19th-century summer residence, the Ostend Historical museum holds displays of Neolithic and Roman objects excavated in the vicinity and exhibits depicting Ostend traditional dress, folklore, and history. There's a recreated fisherman's pub, a fisherman's home, and an old tobacco store. The Marine section deals with shipbuilding, fishing boats, and the Ostend scheduled ferry service from England, which started in 1846.

Langestraat 69 (close to Wapenplein). ✆ **059/51-67-21.** www.deplate.be. Admission 2€ adults, 1€ seniors and children 14–18, free for children 13 and under. Mid-June to mid-Sept and during school vacations Wed–Mon 10am–noon and 2–5pm; mid-Sept to mid-June (when not during school vacations) Sat 10am–noon and 2–5pm. Closed Jan 1 and Dec 25.

ROYAL OSTEND

Made fashionable by King Léopold I's decision to establish a vacation residence here in 1834, Ostend became a magnet for blue-blooded vacationers from Britain and the Continent. Remnants of this vanished glory are scattered around town. Among them are two long and elegant galleries that shielded Belgian royals and their guests from sun, wind, and rain during promenades. The **Venetiaanse Gaanderijen (Venetian Galleries;** 1903), now an exhibits hall, is on the seafront Albert I Promenade. The **Koninklijke Gaanderijen (Royal Galleries;** 1906) connected the Royal Villa with the racetrack. In 1930 the Thermae Palace Hotel (see "Where to Stay," below) was constructed at the center of the galleries.

At the entrance to the Venetian Galleries stands a sympathetic bronze sculpture (2000) of **King Baudouin** (1951–93). The "people's king" is depicted strolling in Ostend, wearing a raincoat, a long way from the hauteur of earlier royal portrayals: **Léopold I** (1831–65) adopts a heroic nationalistic pose in an equestrian sculpture on Léopold I Plein, and **Léopold II** (1865–1909), a pompous imperialistic pose in an equestrian sculpture on the seafront Zeedijk at the Venetian Galleries.

The **summer residence** of Léopold I, a surprisingly ordinary-looking town house at Langestraat 69, was eventually abandoned by the royals; it now houses the **Ostend Historical Museum** (see above). Its 1954 waterfront replacement as the Royal Villa later became the plush Oostendse Compagnie Hotel, which closed in 2005, and the building now is privately owned. Léopold II, who earned a reputation for allowing the royal libido free rein, supposedly stashed one of his mistresses, a Hungarian baroness, at the grand **Villa Maritza,** Albert I Promenade 76, one of a group of three surviving 19th-century waterfront villas and now an upscale restaurant (p. 196).

> **Impressions**
>
> ***"You had some fun there, I suppose?" I put in, thinking of—well, of Ostend in August.***
> ***"Fun! A filthy hole I call it . . . there was nothing to do on shore."***
>
> **—Erskine Childers, *The Riddle of the Sands,* 1903**

The vast, neo-Gothic **Sint-Petrus-en Pauluskerk (St. Peter and Paul Church),** from 1907, on Sint-Petrus-en-Paulusplein, close to the ferry dock, has a suite of stained-glass windows and a memorial chapel dedicated to Belgium's first queen, Marie-Louise of Orléans, who died in Ostend in 1850.

MARINE THEMES

There's plenty of sea-related stuff to see and do in Ostend. Kids will likely appreciate a ramble through the **Zeilschip *Mercator* (Sailing Ship *Mercator*),** Mercatordok (✆ **059/51-70-10;** www.zeilschip-mercator.be), moored in a dock facing the rail station. Formerly a Belgian merchant marine training ship, the *Mercator,* a

Room at the Inns

Accommodations at the seacoast can be hard to come by in July and August, despite the presence of thousands of vacation homes, apartments, and private homes offering bed-and-breakfast. Reserve well ahead for this period, either through the local tourist office or directly with your chosen lodging. Don't worry too much about this—you'll always be able to get something, but it might not be what you want, where you want, and for the price you want.

white-painted, three-masted schooner, is now a floating museum ship. The ship can be visited May to June and September daily 10am to 12:30pm and 2 to 5:30pm; July to August daily 10am to 5:30pm; and October to April daily 10am to 12:30pm and 2 to 5pm (closed Jan 1 and Dec 25). Admission is 4€ for adults, 3€ for seniors, 2€ for children 6 to 14, and free for children 5 and under.

Another worthwhile old sea dog is the **Museumschip (Museum Ship) *Amandine*,** Vindictivelaan 35Z (✆ **059/23-43-01;** www.museum-amandine.be). Launched in 1961, the trawler was the last Ostend *IJslandvaarder* (Iceland fishing boat) to work the rich northern fishing grounds. She now sits in a dry basin as a museum of the history and traditions of Ostend's Icelandic fishery. The ship can be visited Monday from 2 to 6pm, and Tuesday to Sunday from 10am to 6pm (closed Jan 1; late Nov to mid-Dec; and Dec 24, 25, and 31). Admission is 4€ for adults, 2€ for children 6 to 14, and free for children 5 and under.

Though popular with children, the small **Noordzeeaquarium (North Sea Aquarium),** Visserskaai (✆ **059/50-08-76**), by the old fishing harbor, is not exactly riveting. It features North Sea flora and fauna, including fish, mollusks, crustaceans, polyps, anemones, and shell and seaweed collections. The aquarium is open April to May daily 10am to noon and 2 to 5pm, June to September daily 10am to 12:30pm and 2 to 6pm, and October to March weekends and holidays from 10am to 12:30pm and 2 to 6pm (closed Jan 1). Admission is 2€ for adults, 1€ for children 4 to 13, and free for children 3 and under.

You need to be up early to watch the stands at the **Vistrap (Fish Market)** on Visserskaai being loaded up with North Sea fish fresh off the boats from the previous night's catch. Sole, plaice, whiting, cod, bream, brill, eels, and shrimps are the main species on view and for sale.

With water covering 71% of the surface of the "Earth," it's not much of a stretch to extend the marine theme to the entire planet. In 1992 European Space Agency astronaut Dirk Frimout flew aboard the U.S. space shuttle Atlantis as a part of NASA's "Mission to Planet Earth." Continuing in that spirit, the Belgian former spacefarer is behind **Earth Explorer,** Fortstraat 128B (✆ **059/70-59-59;** www.earthexplorer.be), a hands-on attraction that covers earth, air, fire, and water, and is especially aimed at children. The attraction is open from the Easter school vacation to August daily 10am to 6pm. Admission is 15€ for adults; 13€ for seniors, students, and visitors with disabilities; 11€ for children 4 to 12; and free for children 3 and under.

WHERE TO STAY

De Hofkamers ★★ It's been interesting to watch the Pots family continually upgrade their hotel by adding innovative amenities as well as personal touches and coordinated furnishings in the rooms, bringing some of them close to minor-boutique status. They've installed amenities such as a solarium, hammam bath, and sauna—small, perhaps, but definitely welcome. All rooms are individually decorated but in general feature bright colors and light-wood furnishings. Some have four-poster beds. In all, this is an attractive modern hotel in a convenient location, close to the beach and the casino.

IJzerstraat 5 (at Koningsstraat), 8400 Oostende. ✆ **059/70-63-49.** Fax 059/24-23-90. www.dehofkamers.be. 25 units. 90€–150€ double. Rates include buffet breakfast. MC, V. Limited street parking. **Amenities:** Bar; bikes; exercise room; sauna. *In room:* TV, hair dryer, Wi-Fi (free).

Hotel Du Bassin This pleasant hotel-restaurant, conveniently sited across the street from the train station and the ferry dock, has a bit more going for it than an undistinguished modern exterior seems to indicate. The rooms are nicely if simply furnished in contemporary style, with moody color tones that ought to be restful after a day at the beach; most also have a harbor view. On the ground floor, there's the bustling Grand Café Du Bassin, with a sidewalk terrace, where seafood is a specialty.

Visserskaai 1 (at Sint-Franciscusstraat), 8400 Oostende. ✆ **059/70-33-83.** Fax 059/80-36-78. www.hoteldubassin.be. 21 units. 79€–97€ double; 125€ suite. Rates include continental breakfast. AE, DC, MC, V. Limited street parking. **Amenities:** Restaurant; bar. *In room:* TV, hair dryer, Wi-Fi.

Thermae Palace ★ This Art Deco hotel, at the heart of the seafront architectural landmark that is the Koninklijke Gaanderijen, or Royal Galleries (see above), is beginning to show its age a touch. Constructed in the 1930s, the building is still a prominent reminder of Ostend's previous glory as a royal resort. The hotel has attractive standard guest rooms and plusher superior rooms, many of which have been upgraded with new beds, furnishings, and decor, and around half of them have a sea view. They don't quite match the grandeur of the setting, so that's part of the opportunity-cost calculation. The French restaurant **Périgord** serves high-quality cuisine in a rather formal setting; the Belgian **Bistro Paddock** is more casual.

Gaye Old Time

Marvin Gaye's 1982 classic soul torch song *Sexual Healing,* a million-selling Grammy winner, was written during an 18-month retreat the troubled singer took in 1981 and 1982 in the unlikely haven of Ostend.

Koningin Astridlaan 7 (at Kapelstraat), 8400 Oostende. ✆ **059/80-66-44.** Fax 059/80-52-74. www.thermaepalace.be. 159 units. 170€–280€ double; 350€ suite. AE, DC, MC, V. Parking 10€. **Amenities:** 3 restaurants; bar; lounge; babysitting; concierge; nearby golf course; health club. *In room:* TV, hair dryer, minibar, Wi-Fi (free).

WHERE TO DINE

Diners pile into Ostend with fish on their minds. Visserskaai (Fishermen's Wharf), along the harbor, is lined with fish restaurants and is the most obvious setting for everything from sit-down dining in plush restaurants to great handheld snacks from waterside fish stands. Fine restaurants are sprinkled along the seafront Albert I Promenade and at spots hidden away in the old town. With 250 eateries in the town, many of which have seafood on the menu, you'll have plenty of choices.

Blaffetuurken ★ SEAFOOD/BELGIAN/FRENCH With places for just 30 diners in the interior, this small restaurant has an intimate character. Some chairs painted marine blue and a few paintings of local nautical scenes are about the only visual nods to this being a seafood outlet. Instead, the owners have created a restful ambience for whatever you choose to order, whether that be the Barents Sea crab, the eel with green herbs, or the Flemish-style rabbit. A narrow sliver of outdoor terrace is protected from the elements but for some may be a tad close to the busy street when the windows are open—yet that bustle is part of the attraction on "Fishermen's Wharf."

Visserskaai 39 (facing the Vistrap/Fish Market). ✆ **059/70-42-26.** www.blaffetuurkenoostende.be. Main courses 20€–27€; fixed-price lunch 22€; fixed-price Markt menu 40€ per person (offered only per table). AE, MC, V. Fri–Tues noon–3pm and 6–10pm.

Savarin ★★ SEAFOOD/BELGIAN A titanium enclosure and a general high-tech look announces a different tack to the usual Ostend emphasis on old-fashioned elegance—new-fashioned elegance, with big chandeliers and wall mirrors. It's maybe a bit too smart and cool for its own good, but it compensates with a fine sea view. Ostend sole and seafood on the skewer are featured, and there's an outdoor terrace for fine-weather dining. If you're up for eels, try the *paling in 't groen,* eel in a grass-green vegetable sauce. More ordinary items on the menu include barbecue-grilled cod and salmon, and shrimp croquettes, a good starter choice.

Albert I Promenade 74 (at Kemmelbergstraat). ✆ **059/51-31-71.** www.savarin.be. Main courses 24€–48€; fixed-price lunch 34€, dinner 44€–84€. AE, DC, MC, V. Daily 9:30am–10:30pm.

Villa Maritza ★ SEAFOOD/FRENCH In a waterfront villa (1885) that was the vacation home of an eponymous Hungarian baroness (reputedly one of footloose King Léopold II's mistresses), this is a sophisticated restaurant that serves elegant cuisine. Seafood specialties vary with the season; all of them are culinary delights, but especially good options are the lobster with mixed vegetables and saffron, the lobster with red-wine sauce, and the pan-fried sole with green asparagus. Of the many ornate mansions that once lined the shore, this is one of the few that survived World War II bombings and destructive postwar "developers."

Albert I Promenade 76 (at Kemmelbergstraat). ✆ **059/50-88-08.** www.villa-maritza.be. Main courses 18€–36€; fixed-price menus 35€–55€. AE, DC, MC, V. Tues–Sat noon–2:30pm and 7–9:30pm; Sun noon–2:30pm.

OSTEND AFTER DARK

With gaming rooms for roulette, blackjack, craps, and stud poker, along with slot machines, **Casino Oostende,** Oosthelling 12 (✆ **059/70-51-11;** www.partouchecasinos.be), dates from 1953 and has been thoroughly modernized and refurbished. (There's been a casino at this spot since 1852, but the unlucky original occupied a prime site for a concrete bunker in Adolf Hitler's Atlantic Wall.) The gaming rooms are open daily (minimum age 21) from 3pm to 7am. Admission is free, and a passport or identity card is required. The attached **Kursaal Oostende ★**, Monacoplein (✆ **070/32-00-12;** www.kursaaloostende.be), is a venue for visiting symphonic concerts, operettas, ballet, and musicals. In its opulent interior are also a panoramic rooftop restaurant, the **Ostend Queen;** a coffeehouse; a snack bar; and a nightclub.

If you want a quiet drink in the evening, visit the Old Flemish–style **Café Rubens,** Visserskaai 44 (✆ **059/80-85-08**), or one of the cafes with sidewalk terraces around Wapenplein. For late-night dance clubs, cabarets, and bars, head for Langestraat, which runs east from Monacoplein, in front of the **Casino-Kursaal** (www.casinocity.com/be/oostende/belkursa). On this literally "Long Street," you'll find (among other hot spots) **Tao,** a fashionable loungebar, dance club, and world cuisine restaurant, at no. 24–26 (✆ **059/43-83-73;** www.tao-oostende.be); the music bar—featuring soul, jazz, and French *chanson*—**Lafayette,** at no. 12 (✆ **0475/65-89-31**); and multi-genre music bar **Twilight,** at no. 21 (✆ **059/32-50-74**).

KNOKKE-HEIST ★

24km (15 miles) NE of Bruges; 35km (22 miles) NE of Ostend

Knokke is fashionable—not as exclusive as it once was, but still fashionable. You can tell this by the very look of the place; its main shopping street features upscale jewelers, art galleries, and sporting stores adorned with internationally famous designer names. **Heist,** snuggled up close to the Dutch border, attracts classy average-income families.

The winding residential streets of the nearby **Het Zoute** suburb fairly shriek "money," and big money by Belgian standards. The villas proclaim their owners to be people of both wealth and exquisite taste (or, at any rate, what they consider exquisite taste). Whether or not you fit easily into this moneyed environment, a drive, cycle, or walk through Het Zoute provides a glimpse of Belgium's wealthy lifestyle—and if that doesn't grab you as a worthwhile way to spend 15 minutes, pass right through to the **Zwin Provincial Nature Park.**

Essentials

GETTING THERE There's frequent train and bus service from Brussels, Ghent, and Bruges. To get here from Ostend and other seafront resorts, take the **Coast Tram** (see "Tracks Along the Coast," earlier in this chapter). The combination train/bus/tram stations are at the south end of Lippenslaan, the main street. By car from Bruges, take N31 north; N34 runs the entire length of the coast, connecting all the resort towns.

VISITOR INFORMATION **Toerisme Knokke-Heist** is at Zeedijk-Knokke 660, 8300 Knokke-Heist (✆ **050/63-03-80;** fax 050/63-03-90; www.knokke-heist.info), on the seafront, at Lichttorenplein (Lighthouse Square). The office is open daily 8:30am to 6pm.

A KEY wetlands RESERVE

Along this stretch of coast in the Middle Ages, the Zwin inlet met the sea and made Bruges a leading European port. The silting up of the inlet (leaving Bruges to settle into a landlocked prominence of quite another sort) created a salty, sandy marshland. This now forms the **Het Zwin Nature Reserve (Provinciaal Natuurpark Zwin) ★**, Graaf Léon Lippensdreef 8 (✆ **050/60-70-86;** www.zwin.be), east of Het Zoute.

The park covers just 150 hectares (371 acres), yet it's one of the most important remaining wetland breeding zones for birds on Europe's northwest coast, and one of Belgium's last scraps of coastal wilderness. Among the 100 migratory and indigenous species that enjoy its facilities are avocets, storks, snipes, plovers, geese, and ducks. The spongy soil nurtures an amazing variety of vegetation, making the park a colorful place to explore, especially in summer, when it's tinged with lavender.

There's an aviary near the entrance; the **Vlindertuin (Butterfly Garden);** a restaurant, the **Châlet du Zwin;** and a bookstore. The park is open Easter to September Tuesday to Sunday (and school-vacation Mondays) from 9am to 5:30pm, and October to Easter from Tuesday to Sunday (and school-vacation Mondays) 9am to 4:30pm. Admission is 5.20€ for adults, 4.40€ for seniors, 3.20€ for children 6 to 11, and free for children 5 and under.

What to See & Do

This area's list of attractions is topped by its fine beaches, where all manner of seaside sports are available. Beach activities range from half-hour sea trips in amphibious vessels launched right from the beach to sandcastle-building competitions and kite flying.

For a different kind of fun, head to **Casino Knokke,** Zeedijk-Albertstrand 509 (✆ **050/63-05-05;** www.partouchecasinos.be), across from the Albertstrand beach. This place, which dates from the 1920s, is the epitome of elegance, with plush gaming rooms, slot machines, nostalgic bits of Art Deco, and glittering chandeliers illuminating a festive, dressed-to-the-nines clientele. Two nightclubs and a ballroom feature leading European entertainers. The magnificent Salle Magritte dining room is a tribute to surrealist painter René Magritte, whose paintings have been transformed into gigantic murals that adorn the walls. You'll need to be decked out in dressy attire, and bring your passport. The minimum age is 21, and admission is free.

Great Green Way

From Knokke-Heist, drive or cycle the 48km (30-mile) Riante Polderroute, a signposted route that takes you through wooded parks, past the Zwin, into polder farm country and along canals, to Damme (p. 157).

Golfers should find they've come to the right place. The **Royal Zoute Golf Club,** Caddiespad 14, Knokke (✆ **050/60-12-27;** www.zoute.be), has two 18-hole courses beside the dunes and accepts visiting players. Greens fees (visitors must be a member of a golf club) are 95€ for the championship course and 55€ for the executive course.

Where to Stay

Atlanta ★ Just 1 block behind the seafront, this hotel has an efficient, contemporary approach that emphasizes shiny marble over old-villa nostalgia. It fits a tolerable degree of comfort into guest rooms that are on the small side, yet they don't waste any of the available space—be careful about angled-neck syndrome when watching the wall-mounted television. The beds and other generic furnishings are new and bright, with ochre-colored prints and drapes offsetting white-painted walls; bathrooms have cold gray marble tiles but are otherwise fine. You can dine in the businesslike restaurant or, in good weather, outside on an attractive, plant-shaded terrace.

Jozef Nellenslaan 162 (at Meerminlaan), 8300 Knokke-Heist. ✆ **050/60-55-00.** Fax 050/62-28-66. www.atlantaknokke.be. 33 units. 90€–135€ double. Rates include continental breakfast. AE, MC, V. Parking 10€. **Amenities:** Restaurant. *In room:* TV, hair dryer.

Britannia ★★ Set back from the beach, the elegant Britannia is housed in a superbly restored and extended building that dates from 1929, designed in the style of a Normandy villa. It rubs elbows with other upper-income villas in classy Het Zoute and is within a cleanly struck drive of the Royal Het Zoute Golf Club. Its guest rooms have integrated furnishings and colors that aim for a cozy, contemporary style. Some rooms are small, and some of the larger ones have kitchenettes.

Elizabetlaan 85 (at Zoutelaan), 8300 Knokke-Heist. ✆ **050/62-10-62.** Fax 050/62-00-63. www.hotelbritannia.be. 30 units. 130€–175€ double. Rates include buffet breakfast. AE, DC, MC, V. Parking 15€. **Amenities:** 2 lounges; nearby golf course. *In room:* TV, hair dryer, minibar, Wi-Fi (20€/24 hr.).

Parkhotel This family-run hotel, 2 blocks back from the beach, offers well-appointed guest rooms that are furnished in a bright, modern style. Rooms at the front are exposed to some traffic noise, while those in back have a tranquil garden and, beyond that, a park for guests to look out on. Seafood is a big deal in the hotel restaurant, which overlooks the garden.

Elizabetlaan 204 (at Rozenlaan), 8300 Knokke-Heist. ✆ **050/60-09-01.** Fax 050/62-36-08. www.parkhotelknokke.be. 14 units. 95€-145€ double. Rates include continental breakfast. AE, MC, V. Parking 8€. **Amenities:** Restaurant; bar. *In room:* TV, hair dryer, minibar (most rooms), Wi-Fi (free).

Where to Dine

Aquilon ★ FRENCH/SEAFOOD A long-time local standard-bearer of fine cuisine, set in a leafy villa district close to the seafront, this elegant restaurant is widely and justifiably considered to be the most outstanding in the area. Since the portions are on a minimalist scale that accentuates delicacy over solidity, you might not want to step inside to work off a healthy appetite acquired by strolling amid stiff North sea breezes. Instead, allow time to settle back amid restful pastel tones, and take in the garden view, while savoring such specialties as filet of plaice served with steamed vegetables and (in season) filet of wild boar.

Elizabetlaan 6 (at Kustlaan). ✆ **050/60-12-74.** www.aquilon.be. Reservations required. Main courses 15€-25€; fixed-price lunch 19€, dinner 27€-56€. AE, DC, MC, V. Thurs-Mon noon-2pm and 6:30-9pm (also Wed Jul-Aug).

Brasserie Charl's ★ FRENCH/BELGIAN This farmhouse-style restaurant has a solid reputation on the coast. The wide-ranging menu emphasizes seafood. Even a straightforward dish like the *gebakken zeetong* (grilled sole) with french fries and salad comes out tasting pretty fine. Turbot, grilled lobster, and Iranian caviar are excellent seafood choices, while lamb cutlet is the best choice among the meats. A fireplace and filled bookcases add to the atmosphere.

Kalvekeetdijk 137 (at Kragendijk). ✆ **050/60-80-23.** www.charls.be. Main courses 17€-24€; fixed-price lunch 16€ (29€ Sat-Sun), dinner 35€. AE, DC, MC, V. Wed-Sun (also Mon during school vacations) noon-2pm and 6:30-10pm.

Panier d'Or SEAFOOD/BELGIAN Seafood stars at this waterfront restaurant, a medium-size place with elegant decor that's reminiscent of an ocean liner's restaurant. Menu dishes range from straightforward steaks to expensive fish dishes; the fish soup is a local legend. Standard menu items include lobster, cod, sole, and North Sea shrimps, but if you're feeling aristocratic, try the caviar on toast.

Zeedijk-Knokke 659. ✆ **050/60-31-89.** Main courses 20€-35€; fixed-price menus 28€-38€. AE, DC, MC, V. June-Sept daily noon-2:30pm and 6:30-9pm; Oct-May Wed-Mon noon-2:30pm and 6:30-9pm.

The Sea on a Plate

Many seacoast restaurants specialize in seafood, fresh off the boats from catches landed daily and prepared by chefs who have a long tradition of treating the fruits of the sea with respect. Local specialties include *sole à l'Ostendaise* (Ostend sole), *waterzooï op Oostendse wijze* (a creamy, souplike fish stew), gray North Sea *garnaalen* (shrimps), and *garnaalkroketten* (croquettes made with those shrimps).

OOSTDUINKERKE

20km (12 miles) SW of Ostend

Oostduinkerke and the neighboring resorts of **Koksijde-Bad** and **Sint-Idesbald,** with 8km (5 miles) of beach between them, are family-oriented yet hold much to interest art and nature lovers.

Essentials

GETTING THERE Ostend has the nearest **rail** station on the line from Brussels, via Ghent and Bruges, to the seacoast. Frequent **Coast Tram** service goes from Ostend. By **car,** take N34, which runs along the coast.

VISITOR INFORMATION **Toerisme Koksijde-Oostduinkerke** is at Zeelaan 303, 8670 Koksijde (✆ **058/51-29-10;** fax 058/53-21-22; www.koksijde.be), just off seafront Zeedijk in the heart of the resort. The office is open April to September daily 9am to noon and 2 to 5:45pm; and October to March Saturday, Sunday, and during school vacations from 9am to noon and 2 to 4:45pm.

What to See & Do

Oostduinkerke's chief attraction is its wide **beach ★**, the site of a special activity you find nowhere else along the coast: On days when the weather is reasonable, a group of stalwart, yellow-slickered gentlemen mount sturdy horses and wade into the surf at low tide to drag nets behind them, ensnaring *garnalen*—tiny but tasty gray North Sea shrimps. These ***Paardenvissers*** **(Horse Fishermen)** follow a tradition that dates back centuries in Oostduinkerke. Much of their catch goes into the kitchens or cafes owned by these same horsemen.

Oostduinkerke's beach is backed by impressive sand dunes, one of which, De Hoge Blekker, is the highest dune in the country, at over 30m (98 ft.).

Abdijmuseum Ten Duinen 1138 (Abbey of the Dunes Museum 1138) During much of the 12th century, this Cistercian abbey was a regional center of culture. The abbey lay in ruins for centuries. Excavations begun in 1949 have revealed objects that shed light on coastal history and the development of the abbey. A small museum presents exhibits displaying these finds. Nearby, the large abbey farmstead Ten Bogaerde includes a 12th-century barn that is now an agricultural school. It's typical of the large farm holdings of the ancient abbeys.

Koninklijke Prinslaan 6–8, Koksijde. ✆ **058/53-39-50.** www.tenduinen.be. Admission 5€ adults, 3€ seniors and students, 1€ children 6–18, free for children 5 and under. Apr–Oct Tues–Fri 10am–6pm, weekends and holidays 2–6pm; Nov–Mar weekends and holidays 2–6pm. Closed Jan 1 and Dec 25.

Nationaal Visserijmuseum (National Fishery Museum) This museum has maps of sea routes followed by local fishing fleets, and it also displays fishing implements used through the centuries, sea paintings, a fishing-harbor model, a North Sea aquarium, and a collection of fishing-boat models from A.D. 800 to the present. The interiors of typical fisherman's homes from around 1900 are other highlights.

Pastoor Schmitzstraat 5 (in a small park at the rear of the Town Hall), Oostduinkerke. ✆ **058/51-24-68.** www.visserijmuseum.be. Admission 5€ adults, 3€ seniors and students, 1€ children 6–18, free for children 5 and under. Tues–Fri 10am–6pm, weekends and holidays 2–6pm. Closed Jan 1 and Dec 25.

Paul Delvaux Museum ★ The nephew of the surrealist artist Paul Delvaux has turned a Flemish farmhouse into a modernized museum displaying his uncle's works. Delvaux's adulation of the undraped female form is conveyed in many of the paintings, as is his love of trains and railway stations (though it's hard to see the connection).

Paul Delvauxlaan 42, Sint-Idesbald. ✆ **058/52-12-29.** www.delvauxmuseum.com. Admission 8€ adults, 6€ seniors and students, free for children 6 and under. Apr–Sept Tues–Sun (and Mon holidays) 10:30am–5:30pm; Oct to 1st week of Jan Thurs–Sun 10:30am–5:30pm. Closed Jan 1, 2nd week of Jan to Mar, and Dec 25.

Where to Stay & Dine

Argos ★ This is a homey kind of place, with its own garden, in the leafy Oasis district in the center of the resort, surrounded by similar small villas. You're effectively staying at a rustic private home, with comfy beds and sofas, in rooms that are more personal than in most hotels. The restaurant **Bécassine** is deservedly highly regarded at the seacoast and serves great seafood at reasonable prices—though only as four-course menus that run 40€–50€. Tasty North Sea shrimp is the star of the show, served in shrimp soup or stuffed in potatoes and pastries. The bouillabaisse is great, too. There are just seven tables, so dining here makes most sense if you are lodging at the hotel; otherwise, reservations are required.

Rozenlaan 20 (at Zandmannetjesweg), 8670 Oostduinkerke. ✆ **058/52-11-00.** Fax 058/52-12-00. www.hotel-argos.be. 6 units. 85€ double. Rates include continental breakfast. AE, DC, MC, V. Free parking. **Amenities:** Restaurant; free station transfers; bikes. *In room:* TV.

DE PANNE

26km (16 miles) SW of Ostend; 7km (4 miles) SW of Oostduinkerke

De Panne, near Dunkirk, is Belgium's closest coastal point to France and England. During World War I, it was here that King Albert I clung to Belgian resistance against German occupying forces. Today its wide beach and spectacular sand dunes bring hordes of visitors to De Panne every year. The dunes are made all the more scenic by wooded areas that turn them into a wonderland of greenery banding the white sands of the beach and the gray sea beyond.

Essentials

GETTING THERE Ostend has the nearest **rail** station on the direct line from Brussels, via Ghent and Bruges, to the coast. A station just south of the town, at Adinkerke–De Panne, is served by trains from Bruges and Ypres. De Panne is the southern terminus of the **coast tram** line that extends north to Knokke-Heist. By **car,** take the N34 coast road from any of the coastal resorts; from Bruges, Ghent, and Brussels, take E40 to Veurne and then go north a short distance on N8.

VISITOR INFORMATION **Toerisme De Panne** is at Zeelaan 21, 8660 De Panne (✆ **058/42-16-16;** fax 058/42-16-17; www.depanne.be), on the corner of Lindelaan and Poststraat, in the center of the resort. The office is open July to August Monday to Friday from 8am to 6pm and Saturday and Sunday from 9am to 6pm; and September to June Monday to Friday from 8am to noon and 1 to 5pm, Saturday from 9am to noon and 1 to 5pm, and Sunday from 10am to noon and 2 to 5pm.

What to See & Do

A stroll through De Panne's tree-lined residential streets, with rows of delightful Art Nouveau villas from another era, and traditional fishermen's cottages still in use (on Veurnestraat), is a delight. But outdoor recreation is what people come to De Panne for. With all those dunes to explore and the beach for sunning, swimming, horseback riding, and sand-yachting—a form of overland sailing in a colorful sailboat with wheels (see box "Rolling Before the Wind," below)—no one's ever short of things to do.

NATURE RESERVES

Four nature areas around De Panne are all free and open daily. The most important, **Westhoekreservaat (Westhoek Reserve) ★**, 340 hectares (840 acres) on the western edge of De Panne, is the largest dunes landscape on the Belgian coast. Although vacation developments squeeze right up against its boundary, once you're immersed in this broad vista of sand, dubbed "the Sahara," you'll find it hard to believe you're in the same country as the overdeveloped seacoast. Vegetation varies from full-grown trees to scrubby shrubs. In the springtime, wildflowers blossom among the sands; in winter shallow rainwater pools accumulate. The dunes change both their shape and position as contrary winds imperceptibly move the grains beneath your feet.

You're obliged to tour on four signposted footpaths, because tramping on the dunes causes erosion, scares off nesting birds, and damages the fragile life-support system of rare indigenous plants, including orchids (sadly, some visitors ignore this stipulation). At a closed animal reserve are Shetland ponies, Highland cattle, and wild horses, in an attempt to mimic the scene from a century ago. The dunes continue across the border into France.

The 93-hectare (230-acre) **Cabourduinen (Cabour Dunes),** straddling the French border, is another area that affords nature walks. **Calmeynbos (Calmeyn Wood),** which covers only 45 hectares (111 acres), is the legacy of one man, Maurice Calmeyn, who in 1903 began to plant trees here to preserve the dunes. Some 25 varieties of his trees are thriving today. East of De Panne is the 60-hectare (148-acre) **Oosthoekduinen (Oosthoek Dunes),** which has more dunes and woods.

For detailed information about all these reserves and for guided tours, go to the **Bezoekerscentrum De Nachtegaal (Nightingale Visitor Center),** Olmendreef 2 (✆ **058/42-21-51;** www.vbncdenachtegaal.be).

ESPECIALLY FOR KIDS

Plopsaland ☺ It's instant enchantment for children at this adventure park, where a multitude of delightful attractions will appeal to the whole family. There's Elfira (a fairy-tale wonderland), an animal park, a jungle fantasy parrot show, a water symphony, Carioca (all sorts of playground activities), and Phantom Guild, with three different fun fairs filled with rides.

De Pannelaan 68. ✆ **058/42-02-02.** www.plopsa.be. Admission 28€ adults, 7.50€ children under 1m (3 ft., 3 in.). July–Aug daily 10am–6pm; other months generally Wed–Sun 10am–6pm, but with many variations; call ahead or check website for calendar.

Where to Stay

Hotel Donny Set among the dunes, about 150m (492 ft.) from the beach, this hotel attracts guests because of its scenery. Some of the rooms have balconies facing the sea, and all are comfortably furnished in a style that complements the contemporary look of the building.

Donnylaan 17, 8660 De Panne. ✆ **058/42-10-00.** Fax 058/42-09-78. www.hoteldonny.com. 45 units. 90€–130€ double; 160€–185€ suite. Rates include buffet breakfast. AE, DC, MC, V. Free parking. **Amenities:** Restaurant; bar; lounge; health club; heated indoor pool. *In room:* TV, hair dryer, minibar, Wi-Fi (free).

Rolling Before the Wind

The long, wide beaches, firm sand, and frequent strong winds at De Panne make for ideal conditions for sand-yachting. You're outfitted with a jumpsuit and crash helmet, given a few tips on how to handle the vehicles, and pushed out into the wind. The sand yachts are unwieldy to handle at first and heavier than they look, so maintaining stability can be difficult until you get the hang of it. But once you do, it's exhilarating.

Sand-yachting lessons are given by qualified members of the sport's local federation, the **Landelijke Zeilwagen Federatie** (✆ **058/41-57-47**; www.lazef.be). They cost 9€ per hour per sand-yacht (a course requires at least six students for a minimum time of 3 hours), plus 30€ per hour for an instructor, who can lead up to 10 students. High tides, too-high winds, and other adverse weather conditions may lead to cancellation. Due to the limited number of sand-yachts and instructors, you should reserve ahead of time.

Where to Dine

Le Fox ★★ FRENCH/SEAFOOD Although pricey, this is the best restaurant in town. The Buyens family has upheld the stellar reputation of its Michelin-star establishment into a second generation, with son Stéphane now at the helm in the kitchen. Most menu items change seasonally, but a strong contingent of seafood offerings is fairly stable. Turbot with a variety of minced mushrooms and a fennel-and-tomato ragout is a good choice; so are salmon-and-asparagus fondue and one of the French regional meat courses. Unlike most restaurants along the coast, Le Fox leaves mussels off the menu but amply makes up for this omission with oysters, scampi, langoustines (spiny lobster), and shrimp. Thoughtfully selected French wines from admirable wineries fill the wine cellar.

Walckiersstraat 2 (in the Hostellerie Le Fox, off the seafront). ✆ **058/41-28-55.** www.hotelfox.be. Main courses 25€–49€; fixed-price lunch 45€, fixed price dinner menus 48€–95€. AE, DC, MC, V. Wed–Sun noon–2:30pm; Tues–Sun 7–9:45pm.

YPRES ★★

110km (68 miles) W of Brussels; 45km (28 miles) SW of Bruges

Set among the low, gentle slopes of the West Flanders Heuvelland (Hill Country), Ypres (Ieper in Dutch) owed its early prosperity to a textile industry that peaked in the 13th century. Over the centuries, the handsome town (pronounced *ee*-pruh; pop. 35,000) was victimized by one war after another. By far the most devastating was World War I (1914–18); hardly a brick was left standing after 4 years of violent bombardments. Ypres was one of the slaughterhouses on the Western Front. In the few square miles of the Ypres salient, 250,000 soldiers from the British Empire, France, and Belgium were killed, along with an equal number of Germans. The tally of wounded on all sides reached 1.2 million.

Many visitors come to Ypres to remember those who fell on the surrounding battlefields and who now rest on the green breast of the Heuvelland. In the rolling countryside around the town, you can visit no fewer than 185 serene World War I military cemeteries.

Brick by brick, most important medieval buildings in the town have been reconstructed exactly as they were, carefully following original plans. This accounts for the pristine look of venerable monuments, instead of the moldering stones you might expect.

Essentials

GETTING THERE Because it lies in a corner of Belgium that's awkward to reach, some visitors combine a visit to Ypres with a trip to Bruges or the nearby seacoast resorts. **Trains** depart hourly from Bruges. Look out for the Dutch name, Ieper, on the station name board. The trip takes around 1 hour, and you may need to change trains at Kortrijk. Going by **bus** from Bruges is a bad option unless you have time to take in every haystack and hamlet along the way. By **car** from Bruges, take A17/E403 south to the Kortrijk interchange, and then A19 west; from the coast at De Panne, take N8 south.

VISITOR INFORMATION **Toerisme Ieper** is in the Lakenhalle, Grote Markt 34, 8900 Ieper (✆ **057/23-92-20;** fax 057/23-92-75; www.toerisme-ieper.be), in the center of town. The office is open April to September Monday to Friday from 9am to 6pm and weekends from 10am to 6pm; October to March, hours are Monday to Friday from 9am to 5pm and weekends from 10am to 5pm.

GETTING AROUND Sights in town are easily reached on foot, though if you're arriving by train, you'll save time by taking almost any **De Lijn** bus (check with the driver) from the bus station outside the train station for the 5-minute ride to the Grote Markt. Taxis generally are available at the train station, or call **Taxi Leo** (✆ **057/20-04-13**).

SPECIAL EVENTS Every 3 years on the second Sunday in May, Ypres celebrates a colorful pageant, the **Kattenstoet (Festival of the Cats),** during which the town jester throws cats from the Belfry to the people below. The custom originated centuries ago, at a time when cats were considered a "familiar" of witches, and evolved into the tradition of today's lively carnival and procession. Outraged cat lovers can simmer down; these days the flying felines are fluffy toys. The next Kattenstoet is on May 13, 2012.

Seeing the Sights

Most of the gabled guild houses and mansions around the Grote Markt are occupied now by restaurants, cafes, and hotels. At the western end of this central square, Ypres's medieval wealth is reflected in its extravagant Gothic **Lakenhalle (Cloth Hall) ★★**. The original, constructed between 1250 and 1304 along the Ieperlee River (long since banished underground), was blown to pieces between 1914 and 1918, and reconstructed with painstaking care, though the work wasn't finished until 1967. Gilded statues adorn the roof, and a statue of Our Lady of Thuyne, the patron of Ypres, stands over the main entrance, the Donkerpoort. Inside, the first-floor halls where wool and cloth were sold are now used for exhibits; the upper floor houses the **In Flanders Fields Museum** (see below).

A Flemish Renaissance extension, the arcaded Nieuwerck (1624) houses Ypres's **Stadhuis (Town Hall).** You can visit the council chamber and view its fine stained-glass window Monday to Friday from 8:30 to 11:45am when the council is not in session. Admission is free.

From the center of the Lakenhalle, the **Belfort (Belfry),** which has four corner turrets and a spire and encloses a 49-bell carillon, soars 70m (230 ft.). You get fine views over the town from here, provided you're willing and able to climb 264 steps to the upper gallery. Carillon concerts chime out on Saturday from 11am to noon and Sunday from 4 to 5pm.

The spire of the 13th-century Gothic **Sint-Martenskathedraal (St. Martin's Cathedral),** on Sint-Maartensplein, is another town landmark. Inside is the tomb of Cornelius Jansen (1585–1638), a bishop of Ypres whose doctrine of predestination, Jansenism, rocked the Catholic Church and was condemned as heretical by the pope in 1642. Britain's armed forces donated the stained-glass rose window in honor of Belgium's World War I "soldier king," Albert I. The cathedral is open to visitors daily from 8am to 8pm except during services. Admission is free.

Behind St. Martin's, the Celtic cross **Munster Memorial** honors Irish soldiers killed in World War I. Across the way, British and Commonwealth veterans made the Anglican **St. George's Memorial Church** (1929) in Elverdingsestraat (✆ **057/21-56-85**), a shrine to their fallen comrades. Wall-mounted banners and pew kneelers decorated with colorful corps and regimental badges add an almost festive air to what might otherwise be a somber scene. The church is open daily from 9:30am to dusk (4pm in winter). Admission is free.

At Meensepoort (Menen Gate), on the marble arch of the **Missing Memorial ★**, are inscribed the names of 54,896 British troops killed around Ypres between 1914 and August 15, 1917, who have no known grave. Every evening at 8 o'clock, traffic through the gate is stopped while Ypres firefighters in dress uniform sound the plaintive notes of "The Last Post" on silver bugles, in a brief but moving ceremony that dates from 1928. Adjacent to this, the **Australian Memorial** honors the more than 43,000 Aussies who lost their lives in the Ypres salient.

The impressive 17th-century **ramparts** designed by the French military engineer Vauban, fronted by a moat that once surrounded the town, are among the few structures not demolished during World War I. You reach them via stairs at the Menen Gate and walk around a pleasant park to **Rijselsepoort (Lille Gate).** On nearby Rijselsestraat, no. 204 is a timber **house** from 1575. Streets hereabouts are lined with reconstructed 17th-century facades.

A STANDOUT WAR (OR PEACE) MUSEUM

In Flanders Fields Museum ★★ "War is hell" is the clear message of this superb interactive museum. You "experience" the Great War through the eyes of the ordinary soldiers and civilians who did so without the quote marks to get an idea of the events of those 4 dreadful years. No series of dry and dusty historical exhibits, it is as much a peace museum as a war museum—it could scarcely be otherwise, considering the awesome slaughter that took place on the battlefields around the town, which makes any talk about winners and losers, or of glory, seem obscene. The museum won the 2000 Museum Award of the Council of Europe for its innovative presentation.

Lakenhalle, Grote Markt 34. ✆ **057/23-92-20.** www.inflandersfields.be. Admission 8€ adults, 1€ ages 7–25, free for children 6 and under (tickets also afford free admission to the Stedelijk Museum and Godshuis Belle Museum; see below). Apr to mid-Nov daily 10am–6pm; mid-Nov to Mar Tues–Sun 10am–5pm. Closed first 3 weeks of Jan and Dec 25.

Into the Salient

Flanders Battlefield Tours, Slachthuisstraat 58 (✆ **057/36-04-60;** www.ypres-fbt.be), and **Salient Tours,** Meensestraat 5 (✆ **057/21-46-57;** www.salienttours.com), run minibus tours of the battlefields and memorials around Ypres, ranging from 2 hours to a full day. Prices begin at 35€. The Ypres tourist office can furnish a package for the In Flanders Fields Route, a self-guided tour of 80km (50 miles) on signposted roads that cover all the main sights.

For a less ambitious, 1- to 2-hour self-guided tour by car, head out of town through the Menen Gate and take N8 to Canadalaan, close to Bellewaerde Park (see below). At the end, in **Sanctuary Wood,** is a preserved stretch of trenches peppered with shell holes and shattered trees. Amazingly, almost no other sign remains of the vast network of muddy, waterlogged trenches—nature has reclaimed the once-tortured landscape. Nearby stands the **Canadian Monument** on **Hill 62.**

Return to N8. Then take N332 and N303 through Zonnebeke in the direction of Passendale (Passchendaele in French), to the **Tyne Cot Commonwealth Military Cemetery,** with its 12,000 graves surmounted by a Cross of Remembrance in white Portland stone. In 1917, Passendale was dubbed "Passiondale" by British and Commonwealth troops, who took the village at a cost of 140,000 dead. Finally, head west from Zonnebeke to the far side of Langemark and the 44,000 graves at the **Deutscher Soldatenfriedhof (German Military Cemetery).** N313 takes you back to Ypres.

OTHER SIGHTS AROUND TOWN

In the Sint-Jansgodshuis, a reconstructed almshouse from 1270, the **Stedelijk Museum (Municipal Museum),** Ieperleestraat 31 (✆ **057/23-92-20**), recounts the town's history through paintings, antique maps, and sculpture. A fine-arts section has sculpture, silverware, porcelain, and more. The museum is open April to October Tuesday to Sunday from 10am to 12:30pm and 2 to 6pm, and November to March Tuesday to Sunday from 10am to 12:30pm and 2 to 5pm. Admission is 2.50€ for adults, 0.50€ for children 7 to 15, and free for children 6 and under.

The **Godshuis Belle Museum,** Rijselsestraat 38 (✆ **057/23-92-20**), in an almshouse from 1276, counts among its treasures the *Virgin and Child* by the anonymous Master of 1420. Other exhibits include religious paintings from the 16th to the 19th centuries, by artists such as Nicolaas van de Velde and Gilles Lamoot. In addition, there's pewter, lace, and antique furniture. The museum is open April to October Tuesday to Sunday from 10am to noon and 2 to 6pm. Admission is 2.50€ for adults, 0.50€ for children 7 to 15, and free for children 6 and under.

ESPECIALLY FOR KIDS

Check out **Bellewaerde Park,** Meenseweg 497, Ieper (✆ **057/46-86-86;** www.bellewaerdepark.be). This theme park combines white-knuckle rides with a wildlife reserve, various recreated natural environments, and a zone called KidsPark for the tiniest tots, with audiovisual specials like the 4D film *Turtle Vision*. Bellewaerde is set in what was once the wasteland of the World War I front lines. The park is open April to June daily 10am to 6pm (7pm weekends), July daily 10am to 7pm, August daily

10am to 9pm, and September to mid-October weekends from 10am to 6pm. Admission is 27€ for adults, 23€ for children between 1m and 1.4m (3 ft., 3 in.–4 ft., 7 in.), and free for children under 1m (3 ft., 3 in).

Where to Stay

Old Tom This family-owned hotel has a prime location in the center of town and reasonable rates. With only nine rooms, it fills up fast in summer. The building has plenty of antique style, and the guest rooms are comfortable and nicely, if plainly, furnished. A cafe-restaurant on the first floor has an outdoor terrace and serves regional specialties, like eels, in addition to common Flemish menu dishes.

Grote Markt 8, 8900 Ieper. ✆ **057/20-15-41.** Fax 057/21-91-20. www.oldtom.be. 9 units. 70€ double. MC, V. Parking 9€. **Amenities:** Restaurant; bar. *In room:* TV, Wi-Fi (free).

Regina ★ On the outside, the building that houses this small, neo-Gothic-style hotel looks as if it dates from Ypres's medieval heyday, but like most of the town, it was raised anew out of the rubble left behind by World War I. When you enter, you leave the somber past at the door and step into an ambience as cool as a modern-art museum. Guest rooms at the front have views of the Lakenhalle and the Grote Markt fountain. The invariably busy Regina restaurant serves West Flanders regional cuisine.

Grote Markt 45, 8900 Ieper. ✆ **057/21-88-88.** Fax 057/21-90-20. www.hotelregina.be. 17 units. 75€-100€ double. Rates include continental breakfast. AE, DC, MC, V. Limited street parking. **Amenities:** Restaurant; bar. *In room:* TV, minibar.

Where to Dine

De Waterpoort ★ FLEMISH You'll find this stylish restaurant in the north of town beyond a moat. Decorated in a spare, modern style, it's quite different from the traditional type of eatery in Ypres. It has a light, open dining room and a garden with an alfresco terrace and a play area for children. The menu offers seafood and updated versions of Flemish dishes. Some of them, like the entrecôte (steak with truffles), are cooked on an open grill. There's generally a vegetarian option on the menu.

Brugseweg 43 (6 blocks north of Grote Markt on Diksmuidestraat and Arthur Stoffelstraat). ✆ **057/20-54-52.** www.waterpoort.be. Main courses 17€-30€; fixed-price menu 35€. AE, MC, V. Thurs-Sat and Mon-Tues noon-2:30pm; Thurs-Tues 6-10:30pm.

Ter Posterie FLEMISH This traditional cafe-restaurant, down a narrow alleyway off Arthur Merghelynckstraat, serves basic Flemish fare. Look out for mussels in season, sole, and steak with french fries. These are accompanied by no less than 170 different Belgian beers, including the local—and expensive—Poperings Hommelbier, and all six of Belgium's Trappist beers, among them Westmalle Dubbel, the only Trappist beer that's on tap. Weather permitting, dine and drink outdoors in the courtyard; the plainly furnished interior is convivial when it's busy but can seem somewhat gloomy out of season.

Rijselsestraat 57 (off Grote Markt). ✆ **057/20-05-80.** www.terposterie.be. Snacks and salads 4.50€-15€; main courses 16€-21€. No credit cards. Thurs-Tues 11am-2am.

LIÈGE, THE MEUSE RIVER & HAINAUT

The steep-sided Meuse River Valley has long been an important tourist area. After rolling across northern France, the Meuse takes an L-shaped course through Belgium, and then crosses into Holland (where its name changes to the Maas). Along its Belgian banks are historic towns, strikingly situated châteaux and abbeys, impressive scenery—and aging industrial plants and smokestacks that spoil views, particularly around Liège.

10

It's best to do the Meuse Valley as a driving tour, beginning at Liège and heading upstream to Namur, Huy, and Dinant. Once you get beyond Liège's industrial environs, the riverside scenery evolves into a picturesque landscape. Due to frequent and fast connections, it's just as possible to base yourself in either Liège or Namur and tour by train and bus.

From Dinant, either head east into the Ardennes (see chapter 11) or go west into Hainaut, the lush and verdant, lake-speckled "Green Province" that stretches along most of Belgium's border with France. Tournai and Mons are the repositories of great art and historical treasures.

LIÈGE ★

89km (55 miles) SE of Brussels; 27km (17 miles) NE of Huy; 54km (34 miles) NE of Namur

Fervent, lively Liège (pop. 190,000), straddling the Meuse and with a backdrop of Ardennes foothills, has been dubbed "La Cité Ardente" ("the Passionate City"). Nowadays it exudes in part the aura of aging industrial gloom, but that seems to fade next to its gracefully down-at-the-heels 19th-century monuments, and remnants from the time of its powerful ruling prince-bishops. Liège has always had an independent spirit; its 12th-century charter decreed that the *pauvre homme en sa maison est roi* (the poor man is king in his home)—an attitude still vividly alive in Liège today.

Essentials

GETTING THERE There are two to four **trains** an hour to Liège from Brussels (59 min.) and Antwerp (2 hr. 9 min.), and one an hour from Maastricht in Holland (30 min.) and from Luxembourg (2 hr. 27 min.); all

Liège

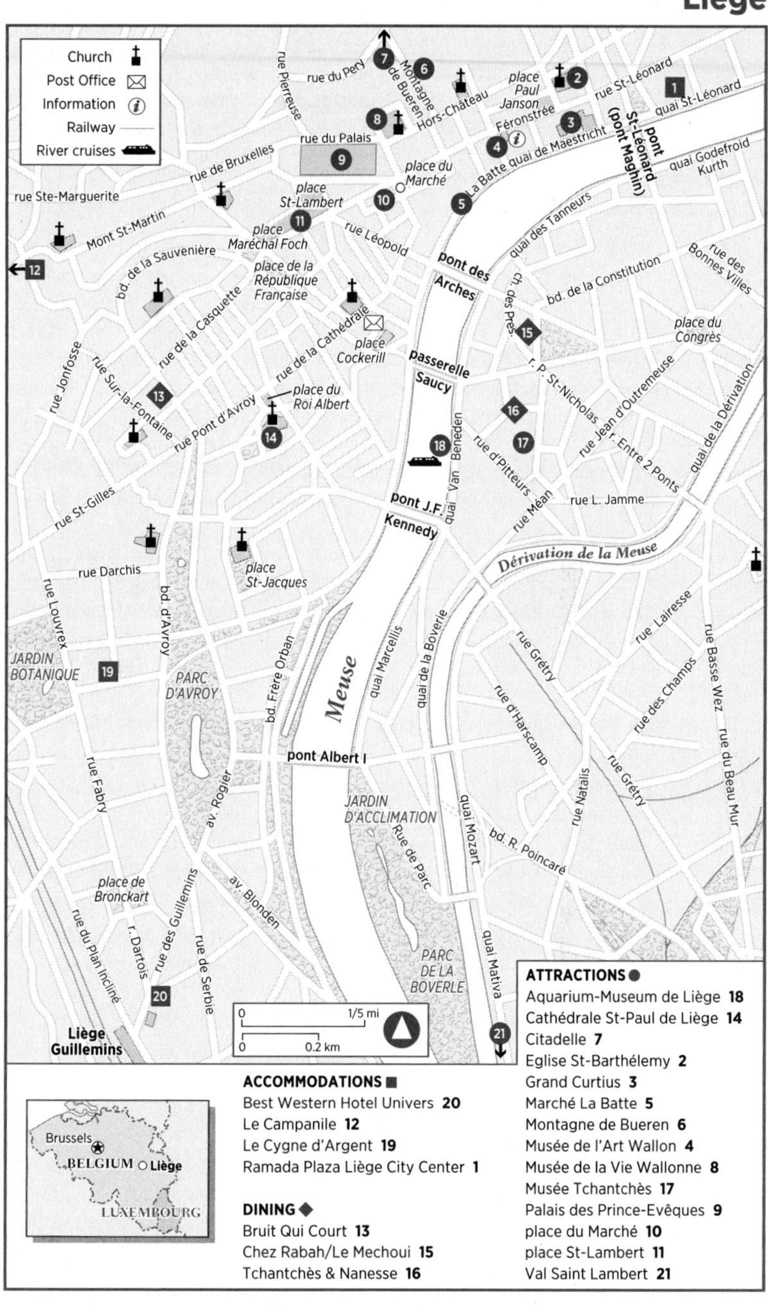
Church
Post Office
Information
Railway
River cruises
rue Pierreuse
rue du Pery
Montagne de Bueren
Hors-Château
place Paul Janson
rue St-Léonard
quai St-Léonard
Féronstrée
pont St-Léonard (pont Maghin)
quai de Maestricht
La Batte
quai Godefroid Kurth
rue du Palais
rue de Bruxelles
place du Marché
place St-Lambert
rue Ste-Marguerite
Mont St-Martin
place Maréchal Foch
rue Léopold
quai des Tanneurs
pont des Arches
bd. de la Sauvenière
place de la République Française
rue de la Casquette
ch. des Prés
bd. de la Constitution
rue des Bonnes Villes
place Cockerill
rue de la Cathédrale
place du Congrès
passerelle Saucy
r. P. St-Nicholas
rue Jean d'Outremeuse
quai de la Dérivation
rue Jonfosse
rue Sur-la-Fontaine
rue Pont d'Avroy
place du Roi Albert
quai Van Beneden
rue d'Pitteurs
r. Entre 2 Ponts
rue St-Gilles
pont J.F. Kennedy
rue Méan
rue L. Jamme
Dérivation de la Meuse
rue Darchis
place St-Jacques
rue Louvrex
bd. d'Avroy
quai Marcellis
quai de la Boverie
rue Lairesse
rue Grétry
rue Basse Wez
JARDIN BOTANIQUE
PARC D'AVROY
bd. Frère Orban
Meuse
rue d'Harscamp
rue des Champs
rue du Beau Mur
pont Albert I
rue Fabry
av. Rogier
JARDIN D'ACCLIMATION
quai Mozart
rue Natalis
Rue de Parc
bd. R. Poincaré
place de Bronckart
rue des Guillemins
av. Blonden
rue du Plan Incliné
r. Dartois
rue de Serbie
PARC DE LA BOVERIE
quai Mativa
Liège Guillemins
0 1/5 mi
0 0.2 km
Brussels
BELGIUM
Liège
LUXEMBOURG
ACCOMMODATIONS ■
Best Western Hotel Univers 20
Le Campanile 12
Le Cygne d'Argent 19
Ramada Plaza Liège City Center 1
DINING ◆
Bruit Qui Court 13
Chez Rabah/Le Mechoui 15
Tchantchès & Nanesse 16
ATTRACTIONS ●
Aquarium-Museum de Liège 18
Cathédrale St-Paul de Liège 14
Citadelle 7
Eglise St-Barthélemy 2
Grand Curtius 3
Marché La Batte 5
Montagne de Bueren 6
Musée de l'Art Wallon 4
Musée de la Vie Wallonne 8
Musée Tchantchès 17
Palais des Prince-Evêques 9
place du Marché 10
place St-Lambert 11
Val Saint Lambert 21

The Town Mascot

Liège's most beloved symbol is Tchantchès, a puppet that has been the spokesman of the streets since the 1850s. He's usually dressed in a blue smock, patched trousers, tasseled floppy hat, and red scarf, and he's constantly either grumbling or espousing every noble cause in sight—the personification of your average, everyday Liégeois. A statue of Tchantchès stands on place de l'Yser in the Outremeuse district.

times are for the fastest direct trains. In addition, the Thalys high-speed train arrives via Brussels from Paris and Amsterdam, and direct from Cologne, as well as German ICE high-speed trains from Cologne. Train information is available from **SNCB/ Belgian Railways** (✆ **02/528-28-28;** www.b-rail.be). The city's main station is **Gare Liège-Guillemins,** rue des Guillemins, just south of the center of town. In 2009, the old Guillemins station, a crumbling concrete relic from 1958, which had superceded a Belle Epoque gem from 1905, was itself replaced by a spectacular new, domed structure designed by Spanish architect Santiago Calatrava Valls. A smaller, more centrally located station, **Gare Liège-Palais,** on rue de Bruxelles, is used by some local and connecting trains.

One of the city's two main bus stations is in front of the Guillemins station; the other is right in the heart of town on place St-Lambert. Regional **buses** arrive from other places along the Meuse, such as Namur, Huy, and Dinant (and from Maastricht in Holland), and from Verviers in the Ardennes, which has connections with points like Spa and Eupen. Bus information is available from **TEC** (✆ **04/361-94-44;** www.infotec.be).

By **car** from Brussels, take A3/E40 east; from Namur, take either A15/E42 or the scenic riverside N90.

VISITOR INFORMATION The city's **Office du Tourisme** is at Féronstrée 92, 4000 Liège (✆ **04/221-92-21;** fax 04/221-92-22; www.liege.be), 6 blocks east of place St-Lambert and 1 block back from the river. It's open Monday to Friday from 9am to 5pm, Saturday 10am to 4:30pm, and Sunday from 10am to 2:30pm (closed Jan 1, May 1, Nov 1, and Dec 25).

CITY LAYOUT The **Old Town,** which contains most of Liège's sightseeing attractions, and nighttime entertainment in the student-filled **Carré** district, is on the west bank of the Meuse, bounded by rue de l'Université, boulevard de la Sauvenière, and rue Pont-d'Avroy. On the east bank, the **Outremeuse** (Across the Meuse) district has a big choice of lively bars.

GETTING AROUND Sightseeing highlights in the Old Town are close together, so central Liège is easily walkable, though traffic can be frenetic. The city's excellent bus system is not hard to figure out, since many stops have network maps. **Buses,** useful for getting to sights outside the Old Town, cost 1.40€ for a one-way ride. Discounted eight-ride **"Agglo Liège"** tickets for 6.50€ are available from booths at major route stops and at the train stations. Place St-Lambert, an important central interchange point, is reached from Gare des Guillemins by lines 1, 2, 3, and 4. City bus information is available from **TEC** (✆ **04/361-94-44;** www.infotec.be).

For a taxi, call **Liège-Tax** (✆ **0800/32-200** or 04/367-50-40; www.liege-tax.be).

What to See & Do

Monumental **place St-Lambert** and neighboring **place du Marché,** surrounded by buildings in the Mosan Renaissance style, are the hub of Liège's daily life. This is where you find the 1698-vintage **Perron Fountain,** the city's symbol of freedom, and the 18th-century **Hôtel de Ville (Town Hall).** French-inspired local revolutionaries in 1795 destroyed the sumptuous Gothic Cathédrale St-Lambert (St. Lambert's Cathedral) on place St-Lambert, a symbol of the prince-bishopric's hated *ancien régime.* Only its outline is preserved in modern paving. Excavations on the square have revealed the foundations of a Roman villa, and traces of the early medieval city dating from the 7th century.

The prince-bishops (see the box "The Belgian Rome," below), who ruled the city and the surrounding territory from 980 to 1794, constructed the world's largest secular Gothic building: the **Palais des Prince-Evêques (Prince-Bishops Palace),** on place St-Lambert. Of primary interest are the two inner courtyards, one lined with 60 carved columns depicting the follies of human nature, and the other occupied by an ornamental garden. Today, this historic building is Liège's **Palais de Justice (Palace of Justice),** housing courtrooms and lawyers' offices. The chambers, hung with antique Brussels tapestries, are not normally open to visitors, but it's sometimes possible to arrange a guided tour with the tourist office. Visit the courtyards Monday to Friday from 10am to 5pm; admission is free.

MUSEUMS

Grand Curtius ★★ Centered on a riverside Mosan Renaissance mansion, the Palais Curtius, constructed in the early 1600s by arms manufacturer Jean Curtius, is a grand museum complex uniting six important Liège collections: Archaeology, Decorative Arts, Religious Art, Mosan (Meuse Valley) Art, Weaponry, and Glass. It opened in 2009 after a long period of restoration. You can trace the history of the Meuse region from the Gallo-Roman and Frankish eras through the medieval period and on into the 18th century, gaining a remarkable glimpse of the breathtaking riches of this city's past. One room holds the relics of Prince-Bishop Notger of the 900s, whose *Evangeliary* (prayer book) is covered with exquisitely carved ivory. There are portraits and richly embroidered vestments of the prince-bishops, and furniture and works of art from homes of wealthy Liégeois. In addition, there are fine examples of Venetian, Phoenician, Roman, Chinese, and Belgian glassware. Manufacturing weapons has been a major Liège industry for centuries, and the museum displays more than 3,000 historical weapons, including a prehistoric stone ax and 15th-century muzzle-loaded firearms.

Féronstrée 136 (at rue du Mont-de-Piété). ✆ **04/221-68-17.** www.grandcurtiusliege.be. Admission 9€ adults; 5€ seniors, students, and children 12–18; free for children 11 and under; free for all visitors 1st Sun of the month; 20€ family. Wed–Mon 10am–6pm. Closed Jan 1, May 1, Nov 1–2 and 11, and Dec 25.

Musée de l'Art Wallon (Museum of Walloon Art) ★ Small but impressive, the collection of works by Walloon (French-speaking Belgian) artists and sculptors extends from the 16th century to the present. Paul Delvaux's *L'Homme de la Rue* (1940) is one of the premier works. Many other well-known, and not-so-well-known, artists from the 16th to the 21st centuries are represented, including Constant Meunier, Antoine Wiertz, Félicien Rops, René Magritte, Roger Somville, and Pierre Alechinsky.

Féronstrée 86 (at rue Velbruck). ✆ **04/221-92-31.** www.museeartwallon.be. Admission 5€ adults; 3€ seniors, students, and children 12–18; free for children 11 and under; free for all visitors 1st Sun of the month. Tues–Sat 1–6pm; Sun 11am–4:30pm. Closed Jan 1, May 1, Nov 1–2 and 11, and Dec 24–26 and 31.

Musée de la Vie Wallonne (Museum of Walloon Life) ★★ ☺ An incredible array of exhibits, housed in a 17th-century former Franciscan convent, bring to life the days of 19th-century Walloons and their rich traditions and customs. The collection affords the unusual opportunity to view in one place examples of popular art, crafts, and recreation, and even the workings of a coal mine, which is reproduced in the building's basement. Here, too, is a marvelous puppet collection, which includes the beloved Tchantchès (whose main "home" is the Museum Tchantchès; see below) and a representation of another local hero, if not perhaps one quite so beloved, the Emperor Charlemagne. The puppets occasionally "star" in shows at the museum's Marionettes Theater.

Cour des Mineurs 1 (off rue Hors-Château). ✆ **04/237-90-50.** www.viewallonne.be. Admission: museum 5€ adults, 4€ seniors and students, 3€ children 6–18, free for children 5 and under; Marionettes Theater 2€. Tues–Sun 9:30am–6pm. Closed Jan 1, May 1, Nov 1, and Dec 25.

Musée Tchantchès (Tchantchès Museum) ☺ If your children have fallen under the spell of the city's favorite puppet (see "The Town Mascot," above), come here to find a marvelous collection of his cohorts and their costumes, and to discover the remarkable history of this character, the intimate of emperors and bishops. Liège marionette theater developed during the 19th century, the puppets having a limited range of gesture and movement that makes them particularly easy for children to appreciate. And the more important the character, the bigger the puppet. From October to April, there are marionette performances; call ahead for schedules.

Rue Surlet 56 (at place Delcour, in Outremeuse). ✆ **04/342-75-75.** www.tchantches.be. Admission: museum 1€; marionette theater performance 3€. Tues and Thurs 2–4pm; also Oct–Apr during marionette theater performances Sun 10:30am and Wed 2:30pm.

SIGHTS OF RELIGIOUS SIGNIFICANCE

Cathédrale St-Paul de Liège (Cathedral of St. Paul of Liège) The formerly plain old (13th–15th c.) Church of St. Paul was raised to cathedral status to replace the city's grand Gothic Cathedral of Our Lady and St. Lambert, destroyed by French and local revolutionaries in 1795. Ask the sacristan to show you the cathedral's priceless treasures. These include a white marble–and-oak pulpit and the 13th-century polychrome *Madonna and Child* by the high altar. The **Trésor (Treasury) ★** in the church cloister holds a small but exquisite collection that includes a gold reliquary that was Burgundian Duke Charles the Bold's gift of "penance" after he wiped out the city and every able-bodied man in it in 1468. This masterpiece, the work of Charles's court jeweler, shows a repentant duke kneeling as St. George looks on (there's no word about whether the surviving populace were satisfied with this gesture). Nearby, a bas-relief depicting the Crucifixion is said to contain a piece of the True Cross. Equally impressive is the reliquary of St. Lambert, which dates from the early 1500s and holds the saint's skull.

Place de la Cathédrale (at rue Pont d'Avroy). ✆ **04/232-61-32.** www.tresordeliege.be. Admission: cathedral free; treasury 5€ adults; 3€ seniors, students, and children 6–16; free for children 5 and under. Cathedral Mon–Sat 10am–6pm; Sun 1–6pm. Treasury Tues–Sun 2–5pm. Treasury closed Jan 1 and Dec 24–25 and 31.

Eglise St-Barthélemy (Church of St. Bartholomew) ★ This twin-towered Romanesque church dates from 1108. Its **Fonts Baptismaux (Baptismal Font)** is counted among Belgium's most important historical treasures, a masterpiece of the

THE BELGIAN rome

The prince-bishops of Liège combined the roles of head of state and head of the church, but they were churchmen first and foremost—and unencumbered by the dynastic fixation of monarchs with blood lines to perpetuate.

Notger (or Notker) of Liège, at the end of the 10th century, was the first prince-bishop. Of Germanic origin, he had been an adviser to the Holy Roman Emperor Otto II and liked to keep up appearances in his new career. He constructed churches and other religious edifices, surrounded the city with a defensive wall, and in general acted to enhance the city-state's prestige. Thanks to Notger, Liège became a center of art, culture, and religion that fully deserved to be dubbed "Rome Beyond the Alps." A medieval chronicler commented that the city "owed Notger to Christ and the rest to Notger."

The prince-bishopric was overthrown with the help of the French revolutionary army in 1794.

Mosan Art style that flourished in the Meuse Valley during the Middle Ages. The big copper-and-brass font, cast in the early 1100s by master metalsmith Renier de Huy, rests on the backs of 10 sculptured oxen and is surrounded by five biblical scenes.

Place St-Barthélemy (off rue Féronstrée). ✆ **04/250-23-72.** www.st-barthelemy.be. Admission 2€ adults, 1.25€ seniors, 0.75€ students, 0.50€ children 6–12, free for children 5 and under. Mon–Sat 10am–noon and 2–5pm; Sun 2–5pm.

OTHER SIGHTS

Aquarium-Museum de Liège ★ ☺ Though owned by the University of Liège and housed in the university's neoclassical Zoological Institute, the **Aquarium** isn't a dry academic institution. Attractively presented underwater displays bring together 2,500 examples from 250 marine species. The exhibits cover a lot of ground—or water—in their 46 display tanks. Pride of place, for most younger visitors at any rate, goes to the 4,420-gallon shark tank. The Salle des Coraux (Coral Room) contains beautiful specimens collected from Australia's Great Barrier Reef by a university expedition from 1966 to 1967.

The ragged-looking **Zoological Museum** on the same premises has some 20,000 exhibits, including the skeleton of a 19m (62-ft.) whale. In its foyer is the mural *La Genèse* (*Genesis;* 1960) by Belgian artist Paul Delvaux, which depicts a kind of Garden of Eden scene, with smoke from volcanoes staining the skies of Creation.

Quai van Beneden 22 (along the Meuse at Pont Kennedy). ✆ **04/366-50-21.** www.aquarium-museum.ulg.ac.be. Admission 6€ adults; 5€ seniors, students, and children 13–18; 4.30€ children 6–12; free for children 5 and under. Sept–June (except Easter school vacation) Mon–Fri 9am–5pm, Sat–Sun and holidays 10:30am–6pm; Easter school vacation and July–Aug Mon–Fri 10am–6pm, Sat–Sun and holidays 10:30am–6pm. Closed Jan 1 and Dec 24–25 and 31.

Val Saint Lambert This place would be interesting enough if only to watch the company's craftsmen at work making the renowned hand-blown crystal that bears the Val Saint Lambert label. But you'll also find the remains of a 13th-century Cistercian abbey, the 16th-century Mosan Renaissance–style Château du Val St-Lambert, and examples of industrial archaeology from the 18th and 19th centuries. You can buy finished crystal—including slightly flawed pieces at a considerable discount—from the factory store. Housed in the château, **Cristal Discovery** (✆ **04/330-36-20;**

www.cristalpark.com) features some of Val Saint Lambert's craftsmen at work, displays particularly fine antique pieces, and takes in a tour of the workshop. Even so, I think the admission is steep enough that you'd want to be pretty sure of your interest in crystalware before stumping up.

Rue de Val 245, Seraing (southwest of Liège, beside the Meuse, on N90). ✆ **04/330-38-00.** www.val-saint-lambert.com. Admission 12€ adults, 10€ seniors, 6€ children 6–18, free for children 5 and under. Daily 9am–5pm.

THE CITADEL

For superb views of the city and the broad, curving Meuse, climb the 353 steps of the **Montagne de Bueren,** a street that ascends from rue Hors-Château. At the top of the hill, commanding even finer panoramic views, is the site of the **Citadelle (Citadel),** which has been a setting for more than its share of the bloodier side of Liège's history. It was here in 1468 that 600 citizens made a heroic but ill-considered assault on Duke Charles the Bold of Burgundy, who had sparked a revolt by installing one of his cousins as prince-bishop and was encamped with his Burgundian troops. They penetrated almost to Charles's tent before being beaten off and massacred to the man. In retaliation, Charles ordered the city's complete destruction, a task that continued for several weeks and left only the churches standing.

A decisive battle in Belgium's fight for independence from the Dutch took place here in 1830. In 1914, Belgian troops held German forces at bay long enough for the French to regroup and go on to a vitally important victory at the Battle of the Marne, thereby saving Paris. German troops again met with typically stubborn resistance from the city's defenders in 1940. The Citadel Hospital now occupies the site.

RIVER CRUISES

From April to October, hour-long **cruises** on the Meuse are operated by **Compagnie des Bateaux** (**✆ 082/22-23-15;** www.bateaux-meuse.be). They aren't wildly exciting, but they are an easy way to view the city along the river. They depart daily at 11am and 1, 3, and 5pm, from Quai van Beneden, outside the Aquarium (see above). Tickets are 6.50€ for adults, 6€ for seniors and children 13 to 18, 5.50€ for children 6 to 12, and 4.50€ for children 5 and under.

Where to Stay

Best Western Hotel Univers You won't get any closer to the city's main rail station than this, and although you trade this convenience for being close to the center-city action, you're just a few steps away from multiple buses that get you there in no time (or you can walk there in about 20 min.). There's good value in this medium-size hotel, housed in a building that dates from 1900 but has been renovated and updated—not with any great emphasis on style. The guest rooms are modest in decor but clean and bright. Though there's no restaurant on the premises, many are within walking distance.

Rue des Guillemins 116 (across from Gare Liège-Guillemins), 4000 Liège. ✆ **04/254-55-55.** Fax 04/254-55-00. www.univershotel.be. 51 units. 69€–105€ double. AE, DC, MC, V. Limited street parking. **Amenities:** Bar. *In room:* A/C, TV, hair dryer, minibar, Wi-Fi (3€/day).

Le Campanile ★ If you're touring by car, this motel-style hotel is a good choice, since it's just 200m (656 ft.) from an expressway ramp (and just 5 min. by bus to the center city). Guest rooms are spacious. A recent refurbishment, comprising new beds and color-coordinated duvets and walls in restful brown and light-brown tones, has added greatly to both their character and their comfort level, thereby extending what was an already good quality-to-price ratio. The Continental restaurant is by no means one of the city's culinary trendsetters, but it's acceptable.

Rue Jean-Baptiste Juppin 17-18, 4000 Liège. ✆ **04/224-02-72.** Fax 04/224-03-80. www.campanile-liege.be. 50 units. 65€-135€ double. AE, DC, MC, V. Free parking. **Amenities:** Restaurant; bar. *In room:* TV, Wi-Fi (free).

Le Cygne d'Argent ★ A homey atmosphere pervades this small, family-owned hotel, on a quiet side street in a leafy neighborhood just south of the center city, between the Jardin Botanique and the Parc d'Avroy. The guest rooms vary in size and have been refurbished and refitted, to a smooth design that integrates new beds, closets, desks, drapes, and carpets into a restful ensemble of pastel tones and soft lighting. All together, it affords a tolerable approach to indulgence for a hotel in this price category.

Rue Beeckman 49 (off bd. d'Avroy), 4000 Liège. ✆ **04/223-70-01.** Fax 04/222-49-66. www.cygnedargent.be. 22 units. 75€-83€ double. AE, DC, MC, V. Parking 9€. *In room:* TV, minibar, Wi-Fi (free).

Ramada Plaza Liège City Center ★★ Located beside the Meuse and a short walk from the bustling old streets rue Hors Château and Féronstrée, which lead to the heart of the city, this high-rise hotel is equipped to the latest business standards, following a top-to-bottom makeover. Front-room windows overlook the river, and though there's a busy road out front, from high up you won't notice that. All rooms have comfortable armchairs along with firm beds. The in-house restaurant, located in an arched 17th-century convent building, has some traditional Liège dishes on the menu, though they are both prepared and presented with more than the usual level of refinement for such fare.

Quai St-Léonard 36 (at rue de Marengo), 4000 Liège. ✆ **1-800/272-6232** or 04/228-81-11. Fax 04/227-45-75. www.ramadaplaza-liege.com. 149 units. 155€-275€ double; 375€ suite. Rates include buffet breakfast. AE, DC, MC, V. Free parking. **Amenities:** Restaurant; bar; babysitting; concierge; exercise room; room service. *In room:* A/C, TV, Internet (free), minibar (executive rooms only).

Where to Dine

Liège has a great diversity of restaurants, thanks in part to the various ethnic communities here. Italian, Spanish, Turkish, North African, Greek, and other immigrants have settled in the city and brought their favorite dishes with them. The popularity of Walloon cuisine adds regional specialties to the mix.

Bruit Qui Court FRENCH/BELGIAN An imposing 19th-century building, formerly a bank, confers a certain class on this establishment, which is matched by the refined cuisine. Light dishes, such as salads and quiches, predominate and often

Local Heroes

The Liégeois are especially fond of their *boudin blanc de Liège* (white sausage); *grives* (thrushes) and goose; *boulet frites avec sirop de Liège* (meatballs in a sauce made from pear-and-apple syrup, served with french fries); *tarte au riz* (rice flan); *bouquette* (a kind of pancake); *botées aux carottes ou au chou* (a kind of stew made with potatoes, cabbage, or carrots, and meat such as pork or sausage); and *salade liégeoise* (potatoes, onions, bacon pieces, vinegar, and beans).

combine flavors in unexpected ways. You are even able to dine in the ground-floor strong room, behind the original heavily armored door.

Bd. de la Sauvenière 142. ✆ **04/232-18-18.** www.bruitquicourt.be. Main courses 11€–21€. AE, DC, MC, V. Mon–Thurs 8am–midnight; Fri–Sat 8am–2am; Sun 6pm–midnight.

Chez Rabah/Le Mechoui ★ NORTH AFRICAN In a rambling, informal setting, with open wood grills in two rooms, you'll dine among Arabic ornamentation that includes a gigantic brass teapot. The menu has just a handful of main options, such as couscous (the couscous royal is ace), mushrooms, and salad, with variations provided by grilled meats, including spicy sausage, and scampi. Honey-suffused desserts lie in wait to tempt your sweet tooth. Friendly waitstaff ensure a constant supply of scented fruit tea, and little-known but surprisingly good Moroccan wines, in addition to French ones, are available. If the restaurant is full, as it often is on weekends, similar North African eateries are close by.

Chaussée des Prés 15 (1 block south of the Pont des Arches, Outremeuse). ✆ **04/343-38-56.** Main courses 9.50€–18€; fixed-price menus 24€. MC, V. Daily 6pm–3am.

Tchantchès & Nanesse WALLOON Named after two local folklore characters, this Liège institution is one of the best addresses in town for Walloon specialties, such as grilled *boudin* sausage with potatoes, the warm *salad liégeoise,* the world-famous (in Liège) meatballs with french fries in syrup, pigs' kidneys flamed in *peket* (Belgian gin), chicken in beer, and hot black pudding with sour cherries. The beer glasses hanging above the bar counter are "mail boxes"—every regular has his or her own glass in which other *habitués,* and you if you so desire, can leave messages.

Rue Grande-Bêche 35 (at rue Surlet, Outremeuse). ✆ **0475/58-36-91.** www.taverne-tchantches.be. Main courses 8€–16€; fixed-price menus 19€–35€. V. Mon–Sat 6pm–midnight.

Shopping

On Sunday mornings, the **Marché de la Batte** ★, said to be the oldest street market in Europe—and surely one of the most colorful—is strung out for a mile along quai de la Batte on the north bank of the Meuse. You'll find brass, clothes, flowers, foodstuffs, jewelry, birds, animals, books, radios, and . . . the list is endless. Shoppers from as far away as Holland and Germany join sightseers from overseas and what seems to be at least half the population of Liège. If you're anywhere near the city on a Sunday, plan to check out this marvelous shopping hodgepodge, if only to browse and people-watch.

Tip: You'll find good shopping in the several small pedestrian-only streets off place St-Lambert in the Old Town.

Liège After Dark

A short way from place Cathédrale, the pedestrian-only Carré district is the most animated part of town, a place for shopping during the day and stepping out after dark until the wee small hours.

THE PERFORMING ARTS

The highly acclaimed **Opéra Royal de Wallonie** performs at the Théâtre Royal de Liège, rue des Dominicains 1 (✆ **04/221-47-22;** www.operaliege.be). The **Théâtre Royal de LAC,** near the Church of St. Jacques, presents concerts by the city's **Orchestre Philharmonique de Liège** (✆ **04/220-00-00;** www.opl.be), along with opera and ballet. For schedules and prices of current performances, contact

Infor-Spectacles, Féronstrée 92 (✆ **04/222-11-11;** www.liege.be), Monday to Friday from 9am to 5pm.

Theaters staging puppet shows performed by the **Théâtre des Marionettes ★** (in dialect, but easy to follow) are at the Musée de l'Art Wallon (p. 211), the Musée Tchantchès (p. 212), and **Théatre Al Botroûle,** rue Hocheporte 3 (✆ **04/223-05-76**). Liégeois wit is especially apparent in the puppets' appearance; each puppet is sized according to its historical importance—for example, a huge Charles the Bold is attended by Lilliputian archers (though just how important Charles would have been without those archers is debatable!).

CAFES, TAVERNS & OTHER NIGHTSPOTS

When the sun goes down (and even when it's still up), the Liégeois head for their pick of the city's hundreds of **cafes** and **taverns** to quaff Belgium's famous beers and engage in their favorite entertainment—good conversation. If a quiet evening of the same appeals to you, you'll have no problem finding a locale. One of the best is **Tchantchès & Nanesse** (see above) in the Outremeuse district. **Café Lequet,** quai sur Meuse 17 (✆ **04/222-21-34**), a popular cafe/brasserie, is the place to encounter local characters speaking the Walloon dialect, in particular during the Sunday La Batte street market (see "Shopping," above). If you're at all musical, they'll let you pick up an instrument and do your own thing; Thursday is jazz evening.

Le Pot au Lait, rue Sœurs de Hasque 9 (✆ **04/222-07-94;** www.potaulait.be), a cafe close to the university and popular with students, is always pretty animated. If beer is your pleasure, you can't go wrong at **Le Vaudrée,** rue St-Gilles 149 (✆ **04/223-18-80;** www.vaudree-concept.be), which has a choice of some 900 different ales from around the world. If you're hungry, don't miss its delicious *pavé sur pierre* (a tender beef filet roasted on a hot stone) and the variety of dishes served in beer sauces.

In spite of having a beer cornucopia right on their doorstep, the city's imbibers are just as likely to favor the stiff Belgian perfumed grain liquor, or gin, commonly called *jenever,* and in Wallonia, *genièvre* or *pèkèt*. The table-topper in this league is **La Maison du Peket,** rue de l'Epée 4 (✆ **04/250-67-83;** www.maisondupeket.be), a traditional old cafe (it's known also by its Walloon name: Li Mohone di Pèkèt) off place St-Lambert, which has 250 varieties of *genièvre* on its drinks list. The local favorite is Peket des Houyeux. In the same building, behind the cafe, is the restaurant **Amon Nanesse,** which serves up Liège specialties.

The Prolific Touch of Georges Simenon

Liège will always be associated with one of the 20th century's most prolific and popular authors. Georges Simenon (1903–89), creator of the famed Inspector Maigret, was born at rue Léopold 24. He grew up here and did his first writing for the local newspaper, the *Gazette de Liège.* Though he later left to live in Paris and Switzerland, he never forgot his roots, and the atmosphere of Maigret's Paris owes a clear debt to the mean streets of Liège's Outremeuse district.

The Liège tourist office has marked out a Simenon itinerary, which takes you on a tour of places associated with the author.

HUY

27km (17 miles) SW of Liège; 27km (17 miles) NE of Namur

The charming Meuse River town of Huy (pop. 21,000) was noted as a center for metalworking, in particular with tin, copper, and pewter, as far back as the 7th century, and was granted its town charter back in 1066. Its most famous native son, the 12th-century goldsmith Renier de Huy, designed the baptismal font in Liège's Eglise St-Barthélemy (p. 212). Today, Huy's stores are filled with pewter bowls, goblets, pitchers, and other items. The town has several notable examples of the 16th- and 17th-century architectural style known as Mosan Renaissance.

Essentials

GETTING THERE Up to three **trains** depart every hour from Liège's train station to Huy's **Gare du Nord,** place Zenobe Gramme; the fastest trains take 27 minutes for the ride. Across the square is the town's **bus station.** By **car** from Liège, take N90 southwest.

VISITOR INFORMATION The **Maison du Tourisme** is at quai de Namur 1, 4500 Huy (✆ **085/21-29-15;** fax 085/23-29-44; www.pays-de-huy.be). It's open April to September Monday to Friday from 8:30am to 6pm and weekends and holidays from 10am to 6pm; and October to March Monday to Friday from 9am to 4pm and weekends and holidays from 10am to 4pm.

What to See & Do

On Huy's central Grand-Place, an 18th-century copper fountain known as **Li Bassinia** stands in front of the elegant neoclassical **Hôtel de Ville (Town Hall)** from the same period—with any luck, you'll be on hand when the Town Hall carillon rings out "Brave Liégeois," as it does every hour.

The 14th-century Gothic **Collégiale (Collegiate Church) Notre-Dame ★**, parvis Théoduin de Bavière (✆ **085/21-29-15**), on the Meuse's east bank, is famed for its magnificent stained-glass windows, including *Li Rondia,* a beautiful rose window, and other windows in the choir. The church is open Tuesday to Sunday from 9am to noon and 2 to 5pm; admission is free. Its **Trésor (Treasury)** contains the Romanesque reliquaries of St. Domitien and St. Mengold, and many items in chiseled copper. The Treasury is open April to the start of June the first Saturday and Sunday in the month from 2 to 4:45pm, and July to the first weekend of October Saturday and Sunday from 2 to 4:45pm. Visiting the Treasury is 3€ for adults, 2€ for students and seniors, and free for children 11 and under.

The **Musée Communal (Town Museum),** rue Vankeerberghen 20 (✆ **085/23-24-35**), a few blocks northeast of the Grand-Place in a 17th-century former monastery of the Friars Minor, displays local metalwork and glass objects. Its finest single piece is the wood crucifix from 1240 known as the *Beau Dieu de Huy* (Good Lord of Huy). The museum is open mid-May to September Monday to Friday from 2 to 4pm and weekends from 2 to 6pm, and October to mid-May Monday to Friday from 2 to 4pm. Admission is 3€ for adults, 2€ for seniors and students, 1€ for children 6 to 12, and free for children 5 and under.

A HILLTOP CITADEL

Huy is dominated by the **Fort de Huy ★**, chaussée Napoléon (✆ **085/21-53-34**), which affords marvelous views of the town, the river below, and the Roi Baudouin suspension bridge across the Meuse. The fort was constructed in 1818 on the site of

High Times

A welcome break for children awaits at the Mont Mosan Leisure Park, plaine de la Sarte (✆ 085/23-29-96; www.montmosan.be), reachable either by road or by the cable car to the Fort de Huy (see above). The park has sea lions, rides, games, and a resident clown. It's open April to September daily 10am to 8pm, and October on weekends from 10am to 8pm. Admission is 6€ per person.

earlier castles and forts that date back to the Gallo-Roman period at the very least. In World War II, the Nazis used it as a concentration camp; a museum on the site explains that history and also about the Belgian Resistance. You can reach the fort on foot or by *téléphérique* (cable car; ✆ **085/21-18-82**) from the riverside at the corner of rue d'Amérique and rue d'Arsin. Cable-car fare is 3.50€ for a one-way ticket and 4.50€ round-trip for adults, 2€ one-way and 2.50€ round-trip for children 6 to 12, and free for children 5 and under. The fort is open July and August daily 11am to 7pm; in late March to June and September, hours are Monday to Friday from 9am to 12:30pm and 1 to 4:30pm, and weekends from 11am to 6pm. Admission is 4€ for adults, 3.50€ for children 6 to 13, and free for children 5 and under.

Huy's quaint narrow streets are great for walking. Take note of the stone bas-reliefs on tiny arcaded rue des Cloîtres, which runs alongside Notre-Dame church. For a stroll through the town's history, start on Grand-Place and walk down rue des Rôtisseurs, rue des Augustins, and rue Vierset-Godin.

A RIVER CRUISE

Take a **minicruise** on the Meuse River from Huy onboard the *Val Mosan* (✆ **085/21-29-15**), which sails from quai de Namur in front of the tourist office. Departures May to August are Tuesday to Sunday (and Mon holidays) at 2, 3, and 4:30pm; and September Saturday and Sunday at 2, 3, and 4:30pm. Tickets are 5€ for adults, 3.50€ for children 6 to 12, and free for children 5 and under.

NAMUR ★★

56km (35 miles) SE of Brussels; 27km (17 miles) SW of Huy; 54km (34 miles) SW of Liège

A handsome old riverside town (pop. 108,000) at the confluence of the Meuse and Sambre rivers, the bustling capital of Belgium's French-speaking Wallonia region has fine museums and churches, a casino, and an abundance of cafes and restaurants. You'll find many good places to eat and drink along the narrow, atmospheric alleyways of **Le Corbeil,** the old quarter of rows of 17th-century brick homes, along the Sambre waterfront. The town is dominated by its brooding hilltop **Citadelle,** evidence of the strategic importance attached to Namur in centuries past.

Essentials

GETTING THERE There are two or three **trains** every hour to Namur from both Huy (23 min.) and Liège (46 min.), and two every hour from Brussels (1 hr.), to the **Gare de Namur,** square Léopold, an easy walk from the center of town. The **bus station** is out front (✆ **081/25-35-55;** www.infotec.be). By **car** from Liège, take N90 southwest via Huy; from Brussels, A4/E411 southeast.

VISITOR INFORMATION The **Maison du Tourisme** is at square Léopold, 5000 Namur (✆ **081/24-64-49;** fax 081/26-23-60; www.mtpn.be), close to the rail station. The office is open daily 9:30am to 6pm.

What to See & Do

Cathédrale St-Aubain (St. Aubain's Cathedral) The domed cathedral (1751) was designed by its Italian architect in the light, ethereal, Renaissance style of his native land, with columns, pilasters, cornices, and balustrades. It was constructed on the site of a 1047-vintage church of the same name that became the Namur cathedral in 1559; the old church's belfry still survives in the existing structure. The **Musée Diocésain et Trésor (Diocesan Museum and Treasury),** place du Chapitre 1 (✆ **081/44-42-85**), just outside the cathedral, holds a small but impressive collection of ecclesiastical relics, gold plates, and sculptures.

Place St-Aubain (off rue Lelièvre). ✆ **081/22-03-20.** www.cana.be. Admission: church free; Diocesan Museum 2.50€ adults, 1€ children 6–12, free for children 5 and under. Museum Easter–Oct Tues–Sat 10am–noon and 2:30–6pm, Sun 2:30–6pm; Nov to Easter Tues–Sun 2:30–4:30pm.

Citadelle (Citadel) ★★ ☺ To reach the hilltop Citadel, drive or walk one of two scenic ways, route Merveilleuse and route des Panoramas, that wind up the steep cliffside. A fortification has stood atop this bluff since pre-Roman times, but the Dutch are responsible for the Citadel's present shape. Today the structure is part of a wooded estate that includes a forest museum, children's playgrounds, restaurants, cafes, and craft stores. Visitors are shown a film on the Citadel's history and given a tour of the fortifications. Explore the intriguing underground caverns by torchlight on a 45-minute tour with a guide. A small excursion "train" runs through the extensive grounds on a 30-minute round-trip.

Rte. Merveilleuse. ✆ **081/65-45-00.** www.citadelle.namur.be. Admission: Citadel free; museums, guided visits, and excursion "train" 9€ adults; 6€ seniors, students, and children 4–17; free for children 3 and under. Tues–Sun 11am–6pm.

Musée Archéologique (Archaeological Museum) The 15th-century Renaissance-style building on the banks of the Sambre that houses this museum was Namur's former meat market. It displays important remains of the life and times of the Meuse Valley, from prehistoric ages through the Celtic, Roman, and Frank periods into the Middle Ages. The collections include Roman glassware, pottery, jewelry, and coins, and a relief map of the city dating from 1750.

Rue du Pont 21 (at rue des Brasseurs). ✆ **081/23-16-31.** Admission 3€ adults, 1€ children 6–12, free for children 5 and under. Tues–Fri 10am–5pm; Sat–Sun 10:40am–5pm. Closed Dec 25–Jan 2.

Musée Félicien Rops (Félicien Rops Museum) ★ Namur sometimes seems unsure of what to make of one of its best-known sons, 19th-century painter and engraver of the bizarre and the erotic, Félicien Rops. His museum is tucked away on a narrow side street, near the artist's birthplace in the old quarter of town—but inside, exposure is the name of the game. The perfection of Rops's soft-ground etchings and drypoint work is internationally recognized, and he was indisputably one of the most outstanding engravers of the late 19th century. Some important examples of his work on display are *Pornokratès* (1879), *Mors Syphilitica* (1866), and *The Beach at Heist* (1886).

Rue Fumal 12 (off rue des Brasseurs). ✆ **081/77-67-55.** www.museerops.be. Admission 3€ adults; 1.50€ seniors, students, and children 12–18; free for children 11 and under. July–Aug daily 10am–6pm; Sept–June Tues–Sun 10am–6pm. Closed Jan 1 and Dec 24–25 and 31.

Trésor du Prieuré d'Oignies (Treasury of the Oignies Priory) The Treasury of the Couvent des Sœurs de Notre-Dame (Convent of the Sisters of Our Lady), in the center of town, holds work by 13th-century master goldsmith Hugo d'Oignies. His sumptuous, jewel-studded crosses, chalices, reliquaries, and other creations are decorated with forest motifs and hunting scenes.

Rue Julie Billiart 17 (1 block east of place d'Armes). ✆ **081/25-43-00.** Admission 2€ adults, 1€ children 6-12, free for children 5 and under. Tues-Sat 10am-noon and 2-5pm; Sun 2-5pm. Closed Jan 1 and Dec 24-25 and 31.

SIGHTSEEING TOURS

In May to September, the tourist office organizes a range of **guided tours** of the old town, the Citadel, and the riverside. These start out from the Maison du Tourisme (see "Visitor Information," above).

A variety of scenic **cruises** on the Meuse and Sambre rivers is available from Namur, including trips to Dinant and Wépion, and a "Namur by Night" cruise. All of them depart from the junction of the Meuse and Sambre rivers, at boulevard Baron Louis Huart. The cruise line, **Compagnie des Bateaux** (✆ **082/22-23-15;** www.bateaux-meuse.be), is based in nearby Dinant (see below). Cruises begin at 6€ for adults, 5€ for children 6 to 12, and free for children 5 and under.

MEUSE VALLEY châteaux

The banks of the Meuse River are liberally sprinkled with grand historic châteaux, often with moats and towers. Among the finest that you can visit are:

- **Château d'Annevoie ★★★** (see "Jardins d'Annevoie," below).
- **Château de Freÿr ★**, Freÿr 12, Hastière/Waulsort (✆ **082/22-22-00;** www.freyr.be), on the left bank of the Meuse, along N96 between Hastière-Lavaux and Dinant. The 17th-century country seat of the dukes of Beaufort-Spontin has a scenic riverside location and magnificent ornamental gardens.
- **Château de Jehay ★★**, rue du Parc 1, Jehay-Bodegnée/Amay (✆ **085/82-44-00;** www.chateaujehay.be), 18km (11 miles) southwest of Liège, off N614. Its lawns and gardens are beautified with sculptures and fountains. Inside, rooms are filled with paintings, tapestries, lace, silver and gold pieces, jewels, porcelain and glass, antique furniture, and family heirlooms.
- **Château de Modave,** rue du Parc 4, Modave (✆ **085/41-13-69;** www.modave-castle.be), 12km (7½ miles) south of Huy, off N641. Once the property of Liège prince-bishops and then cardinals of the Catholic church, this fine example of the Louis Quatorze French style now belongs to the Vivaqua water-supply corporation.
- **Château de Vêves,** rue du Furfooz 2, Celles-Houyet (✆ **082-66-63-95;** www.chateau-de-veves.be), 8km (5 miles) east of the Meuse, off N94. An 18th-century re-imagining of a medieval castle, Vêves looks almost more romantic than the real thing.
- **Château du Val St-Lambert** (see "What to See & Do" under "Liège," earlier in this chapter).

Strawberry Fields

A few kilometers beyond Namur lies Wépion, a sleepy riverside village at the heart of Belgium's strawberry-growing district, and the country's self-appointed "Strawberry Capital." Wépion's Musée de la Fraise (Strawberry Museum), chaussée de Dinant 1037 (✆ 081/46-20-07; www.museedelafraise.be), is dedicated to the fruit. The museum is open mid-April to mid-September Tuesday to Saturday from 2 to 6pm, and Sunday from 10am to 6pm. Admission is 3€ for adults; 2€ for seniors, students 13–18, and visitors with disabilities; 1€ for children 6 to 12; and free for children 5 and under. In summer, you can buy strawberries from kiosks in and around Wépion.

Namur After Dark

Gamble the night away over the roulette and blackjack tables, or at the slot machines, at the **Casino de Namur,** av. Baron de Moreau 1 (✆ **081/22-30-21;** www.casinodenamur.be), below the Citadelle, on the west bank of the Meuse. Jackets and ties are required for men. The casino is open daily 2pm to dawn.

Nearby Places of Interest

Abbaie de Maredsous (Maredsous Abbey) ★ The twin towers of the neo-Gothic Benedictine abbey stand out clearly above the rugged, forested countryside outside the village of Denée, 21km (13 miles) southwest of Namur. It is famed for its own Maredsous beer, cheese, and bread, all of which can be consumed by visitors in a giant cafe on the abbey's grounds—and all of which are consumed in vast quantities at busy times. The abbey's third abbot, Dom Columba Marmion of Dublin, appointed in 1909, was beatified by Pope John Paul II in 2000.

Rue de Mardesous 11, near Denée. ✆ **082/69-82-11.** www.maredsous.be. Free admission. Daily 9am–6pm. From Annevoie, take N932 for 4.8km (3 miles), then turn left on N971.

Jardins d'Annevoie (Annevoie Gardens) ★★★ The ornamental gardens and fountains here, and the 18th-century Château d'Annevoie they surround, together make a splendid display that should top every regional sightseeing list. Annevoie, 28km (17 miles) south of Namur, is sometimes dubbed the "Belgian Versailles," and though these gardens indeed share similarities with their French cousins—and are also reminiscent of Italian and English gardens—they possess unique qualities. The fountains, waterfalls, lagoons, and canals are all engineered without the use of any artificial power. No throbbing pump or other machinery intrudes on their tranquillity and beauty. The grounds were laid out in the mid-1700s by a member of the de Montpellier family and have been tended and added to by successive generations. The present owner, Jean de Montpellier, lives here with his family. Inside the château are fine architectural details in the woodwork, stuccos, fireplaces, and family chapel. In addition to a gift store, there's a full-service restaurant and a rustic cafe.

Rue des Jardins 37A, Annevoie. ✆ **082/67-97-97.** www.annevoie.be. Admission 7.80€ adults, 5.20€ students and children 3–12, 4€ visitors with disabilities, free for children 2 and under. Gardens Apr–June and Sept to early Nov daily 9:30am–5:30pm; July–Aug daily 9:30am–6:30pm.

Where to Stay

Le Beau Vallon ★★ This elegant *chambre d'hôtes* (guest house) in a restored stone *château-ferme* (manor-farm), part of which dates from the 17th century and part from 1870, lies in a narrow, wooded valley outside Wépion, the "village of strawberries." This is one of the traditional properties that comes under the umbrella of the **Gîtes de Wallonie** organization (p. 57). Its hospitable proprietors, Marie-Jeanne and Denis de Ribaucourt, ensure that guests feel at home, perhaps by serving guests wine or local beer at a garden table beside the pool. Rooms are furnished in a comfortable, rustic style, and an 18-hole golf course is across the road.

Chemin du Beau Vallon 38 (off N92 between Wépion and Profondeville), 5100 Wépion. ✆/fax **081/41-15-91.** www.gitesdewallonie.be. 5 units. 50€–60€ double. **Amenities:** Nearby golf course. *In room:* No phone.

Leonardo Hotel Namur ★★ ☺ Despite a look that seems more suited to business travel (a character that extends to the in-house restaurant), this is a decent, up-to-date vacation lodging in a green and scenic spot along Meuse, next to a riverside walking path. There's plenty for children to do: Besides the outdoor play area, there are games, computer games, and sports like tennis and table tennis. The airy guest rooms are furnished in a functional style suited to a midlevel chain hotel, with writing desks and fine bathrooms. Ask for a room at the back, facing the river.

Chaussée de Dinant 1149 (8km/5 miles from central Namur), 5100 Wépion-Namur. ✆ **081/46-08-11.** Fax 081/46-19-90. www.leonardo-hotels.com. 110 units. 90€–175€ double. AE, DC, MC, V. Free parking. Take E411 Brussels–Luxembourg to exit 14. **Amenities:** Restaurant; bar; bikes; nearby golf course; play area; heated indoor and outdoor pools; room service. *In room:* TV, hair dryer, minibar, Wi-Fi (7.50€/60 min.).

Les Tanneurs ★ This luxuriously appointed hotel occupies a character-rich cluster of 11 restored 17th-century buildings, close to the confluence of the rivers Meuse and Sambre. Buildings in this area were falling down from neglect a few years ago, but an imaginative restoration program has recreated an old-world atmosphere. Guest rooms are individually decorated with an effective mix of antiques and modern fittings, and some have sloping walls and exposed timber beams. The most expensive rooms have a sauna or whirlpool bathtub. The French restaurant, **L'Espièglerie,** has a good local reputation.

Rue des Tanneries 13B, 5000 Namur. ✆ **081/24-00-24.** Fax 081/24-00-25. www.tanneurs.com. 32 units. 80€–215€ double. AE, DC, MC, V. Free parking. **Amenities:** 2 restaurants. *In room:* TV, minibar, Wi-Fi (6€/day).

Where to Dine

Chinda Wok ★ THAI For a change of pace from the traditional Belgian and chic French restaurants that towns along the Meuse River are pretty much filled with, try this fine Thai restaurant in the heart of town. Behind the town house facade is an elegant interior with chandeliers hanging from stucco ceilings. To this have been added images of the Buddha and minimalist Thai decor, all suffused with delicate scents. In summer tables are set up in the restful garden alongside a fish pond. Be sure to take seriously the red chili-pepper icons that accompany some dishes on the menu.

Rue Godefroid 15 (on a street leading south from the train station). ✆ **081/22-92-90.** www.chinda-wok.be. Main courses 10€–19€; fixed-price menus 20€–39€. AE, DC, MC, V. Mon–Tues and Thurs–Fri noon–2:30pm and 6–10:30pm; Sat–Sun 6–10:30pm.

La Petite Fugue ★★ FRENCH/CONTINENTAL Although it's housed in a converted 18th-century presbytery, this restaurant at the heart of the Old Town has a cool, minimalist character exemplified by vaguely New Age abstract paintings on the walls. This coolness doesn't extend to the cuisine, to which proprietor/chef Pascal Pirlot brings a passion that's mirrored in the decor's red tones. Prices are reasonable considering the exceptional food and service; the basic three-course menu is an especially good deal. The seafood items include a *sole Meunière* of heavenly simplicity. There's a decent wine selection and good advice to go with it. The interior's 20 or so places, and a sidewalk terrace in summer, tend to fill up fast.

Place Chanoine Descamps 5 (off rue du Président). ✆ **081/23-13-20.** www.lapetitefugue.be. Main courses 20€–28€; fixed-price menus 29€–55€. MC, V. Daily noon–2pm and 6:30–10pm.

L'Ermitage ★★★ FRENCH There's no more refined place to locally dine than at this magnificent château restaurant. Its location, up in the Citadel Park overlooking the town, is already an attraction even before you step into the manorial dining room, among light-filled, exposed-brick arches, and experience purringly smooth service and attention to detail. In summer you can dine in the château garden. The menu is rather short, but what's on it invariably shines. There's likely to be *foie gras* as one of the starters and something sophisticated like pintade (guineafowl) as one of the main courses, but there will also be a plainer deal, maybe *sole à l'Ostendaise*.

Av. de l'Ermitage 1 (in the Château de Namur Hotel, at the Citadelle). ✆ **081/72-99-00.** www.chateaudenamur.com. Main courses 26€–30€; fixed-price lunch 22€–30€; *menu Gourmet* 40€–50€. AE, DC, MC, V. Mon–Sat noon–2pm and 7–9pm; Sun (buffet brunch only) noon–3pm.

DINANT ★

23km (14 miles) S of Namur

A bustling riverside resort town, Dinant (pop. 13,000) has suffered from history's turmoil. In 1466, in reprisal for a rebellion, Duke of Burgundy Charles the Bold razed the town and drowned 800 citizens, tied up in pairs and thrown from the Citadel into the Meuse. In a chilling echo, the World War I German army executed 700 citizens when its troops were fired on in the town. A reminder of Dinant's military past is never far from view, for the Citadel (dating from 1530) that crowns a bluff 100m (328 ft.) high dominates the skyline.

Despite all the bloodshed, the town developed such skill in working *dinanderie* (hammered copper and brass) that its engravings were widely sought after as early as the 13th century. Charles the Bold's ruthlessness put a stop to such artistry, but in recent years the skill has come back to life, and you'll find fine examples of engravings in town stores.

Essentials

GETTING THERE There are one or two trains every hour to Dinant from Namur; the train ride takes just under a half-hour. Namur's **rail** and **bus** stations are both on rue de la Station on the west bank of the Meuse. By **car** from Namur, take N92 south.

VISITOR INFORMATION The **Maison du Tourisme** is at av. Cadoux 8, 5500 Dinant (✆ **082/22-08-70;** fax 082/22-77-88; www.dinant-tourisme.com), alongside the Meuse on the river's west bank. The office is open July to August daily 8:30am to 7pm; September to October and April to June daily 8:30am to 6pm; and November to March Monday to Friday from 8:30am to 6pm, Saturday from 9:30am to 4pm, and Sunday from 10:30am to 2pm.

What to See & Do

Abbaye Notre-Dame de Leffe An abbey that once combined its spiritual calling with brewing beer, Leffe Abbey, founded in 1152, stands at the northern edge of town on the Meuse's right (east) bank. Sadly, the abbey's Norbertin monks no longer personally brew their own traditional beer—that's been handed off to the InBev corporation and takes place at a brewery in Leuven. Still, you can taste it in many bars in Dinant and around the country, and the huge redbrick abbey is worth visiting, both for its long spiritual history and its tranquillity.

Place de l'Abbaye 1. ✆ **082/22-23-77.** www.abbaye-de-leffe.be. Free admission. Guided tours June–Aug 3pm.

Citadelle (Citadel) ★ The 16th-century Citadel, a fortress perched spectacularly on a cliff high above the town and river, can be reached by car or *téléphérique* (cable car). Alternatively, if you're feeling energetic or can't turn down the challenge, climb the 408 steep steps leading to the bluff top and spectacular views of the town and river. The **Musée d'Armes (Weapons Museum)** inside has a cannon and other firearms, and there's an audiovisual historical presentation in three languages (including English). But it's the view that takes your breath away. You might want to spend an hour or two wandering around up here.

Place Reine Astrid 3–5 (a block inland from Pont Charles de Gaulle). ✆ **082/22-36-70.** www.citadellededinant.be. Admission (includes the cable-car fare) 7€ adults, 5.40€ children 6–12, free for children 5 and under. Apr–Oct daily 10am–6pm; Nov–Dec and Feb–Mar Sat–Thurs 10am–5pm; Jan Sat–Sun 10am–5pm.

Collégiale Notre-Dame (Collegiate Church of Our Lady) Although this riverside church looks old, it was reconstructed twice during the past century, after being destroyed in both World War I and II. The original church gained collegiate status in 934. Its Romanesque successor bit the dust in 1228 when part of the neighboring cliff collapsed on top of it, and it was reconstructed in the Mosan Gothic style.

sax APPEAL

Most people would name New Orleans as the spiritual home of jazz. But Dinant can claim a part of that heritage. Adolphe Sax, inventor of the saxophone, was born here in 1814. Sax was a prolific instrument maker and designer. In 1838, he developed the bass clarinet, based on some of the same principles he later used for the sax. The first saxophone was made in 1841 or 1842, and Sax patented his new instrument in 1846.

The sax was controversial from the start, never gaining wide acceptance in the orchestra despite the support of composers Berlioz, Saint-Saens, and Massenet. Sax's saxophone class at the Paris Conservatory closed in the 1870s. Sax himself went bankrupt, and in 1894 he died a saddened man. Yet the inventor, looking down from the great sax jam in the sky, was vindicated from the 1920s and 1930s onward, as his brainchild became ever more popular in jazz, big band, and military music.

The big bulbous spire from 1697 is a majestic sight beneath the looming presence of the Citadel. Points of interest inside are the baptismal font from 1472, the 1731 lectern made from local *dinanderie,* and the fine stained-glass window that depicts scenes from the Bible. A brief visit here should suffice.

Place Reine Astrid. ✆ **082/22-22-07.** Free admission. Daily 10am–5pm.

SIGHTSEEING TOURS

Dinant is the best place on the Meuse for cruising along the scenic reaches upstream and downstream. River cruises are offered by **Compagnie des Bateaux** (✆ **082/22-23-15;** www.bateaux-meuse.be). The cruises run from Easter to October and last 45 minutes to 3½ hours. Boats depart from an east-bank dock, on avenue Winston Churchill, just south of the road bridge in the center of town. Cruises begin at 6€ for adults, 5€ for children 6 to 12, and free for children 5 and under.

Where to Stay

Auberge de Bouvignes ★ This country-style inn occupies a building dating from 1830 with thick stone walls. It started out as a riverside hostel and stables for the relays of men and horses that towed barges along the river. For all their rustic oak beams and parquet floors, the six sparely but tastefully furnished guest rooms have big new beds, and they're decorated in blue or pink and brightened with flowers and photogravures of riverside scenes. Those at the front have fine views of the Meuse. The fine French-Belgian main restaurant is open only from Friday to Sunday; at other times, there's a separate restaurant for light meals.

Rue Fétis 112, 5500 Dinant. ✆ **082/61-16-00.** Fax 082/61-45-37. www.aubergedebouvignes.be. 6 units. 69€ double. AE, DC, MC, V. Free parking. **Amenities:** 2 restaurants; bar. *In room:* TV, Wi-Fi (free). The hotel is on the Namur road (N96), 3km (2 miles) north of central Dinant, on the west bank of the Meuse.

Where to Dine

Le Trois ★ BELGIAN/FRENCH A local husband-and-wife team shook up this eatery close to the train station by taking it through a style change from old-fashioned to chic, decking it out in passionate red colors and complementary brown furnishings. Menu highlights include *truite au bleu* (oven-baked trout) and a terrific country-style *pâté de canard* (duck pâté). If you're up for it, try the grilled kidneys with mustard sauce, a local specialty.

Rue de la Station 3 (between Dinant train station and Pont Charles de Gaulle). ✆ **082/22-31-35.** www.letrois.be. Main courses 17€–24€; fixed-price menu 30€. MC, V. Tues noon–2pm; Thurs–Mon noon–2pm and 6:30–9pm.

MONS ★

51km (32 miles) SW of Brussels; 66km (41 miles) W of Namur; 43km (27 miles) SE of Tournai

Hainaut's provincial capital (pop. 91,000) started out as a fortified camp constructed by Julius Caesar's Roman legions. Today, it's home to SHAPE (Supreme Headquarters Allied Powers Europe). Between those military bookends, it saw a rich and eventful history. The Roman camp, set in a landscape of rolling hills (*mons* means "mount" in Latin), became a town when St. Waltrude, daughter of a local nobleman, founded a convent here in the 600s. Mons was fortified in the 12th century by Count Baldwin IV of Flanders, and again by the Dutch in the early 1800s.

Mons

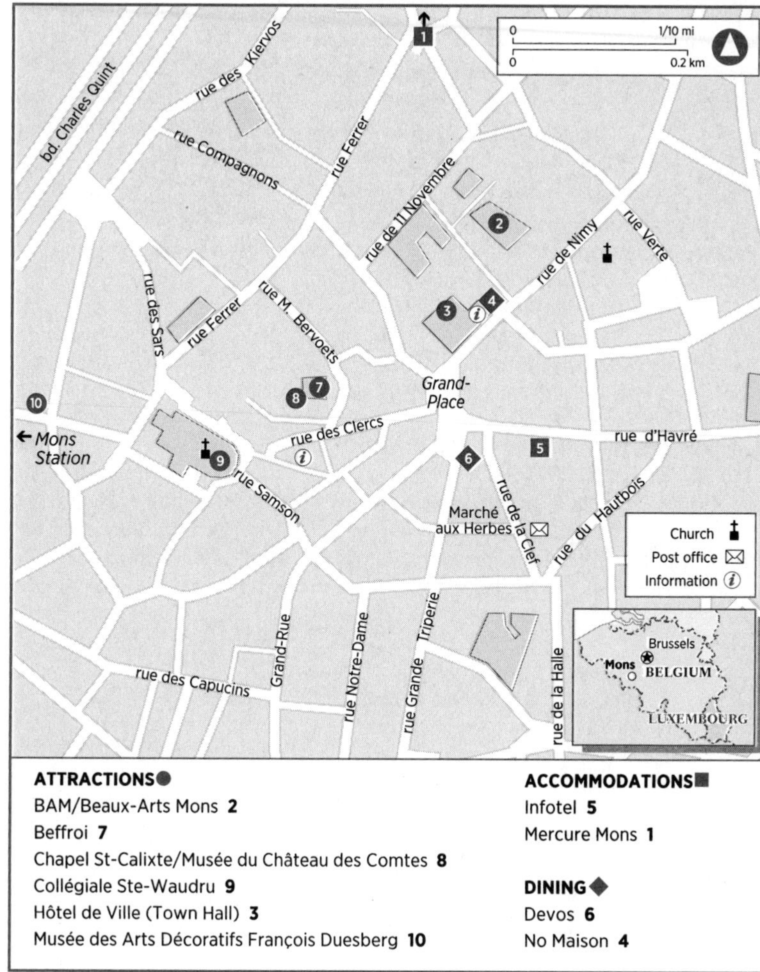

Its present character reflects its more recent history as a center of industrialization and coal mining. The Old Town, on and around the central Grand-Place, contains civic and religious buildings dating from the 11th century onward. They form a remarkably harmonious whole that gives Mons one of the most handsome townscapes in Belgium.

Essentials

GETTING THERE Mons is an easy day trip from Brussels, with **trains** departing to Mons twice hourly; the ride takes about 50 minutes. Mons station is on place Léopold, a short walk west from the center of town. To get to Mons by **car** from Brussels, take E19.

VISITOR INFORMATION The **Maison du Tourisme du Pays du Mons** is at Grand-Place 22, 7000 Mons (✆ **065/33-55-80;** fax 065/35-63-36; www.monsregion.be). The office is open Monday to Saturday from 9am to 6pm (5:30pm in winter) and Sunday from 1 to 6pm (5:30pm in winter).

GETTING AROUND Walking is the best way to get around in the Old Town, but you don't even have to walk. Free **Mons Intra Muros** "midibuses" run on three routes—circuit A, circuit B, and circuit C—between the station and the Grand-Place every 6 minutes daily from 7am to 9pm.

SPECIAL EVENTS Every year on Trinity Sunday—the first Sunday after Pentecost—Mons erupts in a burst of color, mock drama, and revelry to celebrate the **Ducasse de Mons** (or ***Doudou***) ★. This festival begins with a religious procession in which the *Car d'Or* (Golden Coach) from 1780 is drawn through the streets by a team of white horses, followed by richly dressed girls, and clerics bearing a gilded brass reliquary that holds the skull of St. Waltrude. There follows a mock battle, the *Lumeçon,* between St. George and the dragon. An evening performance by 2,000 musicians, singers, and actors brings the day to a close.

What to See & Do

THE BELFRY DISTRICT

The first thing you'll likely notice about Mons is the **Beffroi (Belfry),** a UNESCO World Heritage Site, at the highest point in town. As Victor Hugo remarked, this looks somewhat like "an enormous coffee pot, flanked below belly-level by four medium-size teapots." In Mons, the tower is referred to as *le château*—it sits near the site of an old castle of the counts of Hainaut, and even though the castle was demolished in 1866, local people have never broken the habit of using the old designation.

A short distance across square du Château from the Belfry is the **Chapelle St-Calixte,** the oldest structure in town, dating from 1051. The chapel holds the **Musée du Château des Comtes** (**Museum of the Castle of the Counts; ✆ 065/33-55-80**), which contains relics and archaeological finds. It's open May to mid-September Tuesday to Sunday from 10am to 8pm, and mid-September to April Tuesday to Sunday from 10am to 6pm. Admission is 2.50€ for adults; 1.25€ for seniors, visitors with disabilities, and children 12 to 18; and free for children 11 and under.

Collégiale Ste-Waudru (Collegiate Church of St. Waltrude) ★★ Dating from 1450, this remarkable church in the Brabant Gothic style honors the daughter of the count of Hainaut whose 7th-century convent marked the beginning of Mons as a town. The church stands below and a little to the west of the Belfry. Inside its vast vaulted space are 16th-century sculptures and wall carvings by Mons artist Jacques Du Brœucq (1505–84). Around the choir, 16th-century stained-glass windows depict biblical scenes. At the entrance of the church, the **Car d'Or (Golden Coach)** waits for its annual spring outing (see "Special Events" under "Essentials," above). The church **Trésor (Treasury)** contains richly ornamented religious objects in gold—chalices, ciboriums, monstrances, and reliquaries—many of them dedicated in honor of St. Waltrude, along with sculptures, paintings, vestments, missals, and more.

Place du Chapitre. ✆ **065/33-55-80** (church) or 065/87-57-75 (treasury). www.waudru.be. Free admission. Church Mon–Sat 9am–6:30pm; Sun 7am–6:30pm. Treasury Mar–Nov Tues–Fri 1:30–6pm; Sat–Sun 1:30–5pm.

THE GRAND-PLACE

Almost everything you'll want to see here is on, or no more than a short walk from, the Grand-Place, which is lined by fine historic buildings and surrounded by steep, cobbled streets. If you're here when the weather is good, be sure to fit in some time at a sidewalk cafe on the Grand-Place. The square's centerpiece is the 15th-century **Hôtel de Ville (Town Hall).** Access is by a free guided tour from the tourist office, July to August daily at 2:30pm (at other times by arrangement). As you go through its main entrance, look to the left and stop to rub the head of "the monkey of the Grand-Garde," an iron monkey that's been granting good luck since the 15th century. Needless to say, by this time he has a very shiny pate. Inside the Town Hall are antique tapestries and paintings. The Town Hall courtyard, occupied by the fountains, trees, flowers, and plants of the **Jardin du Mayeur (Mayor's Garden),** is a good place to relax.

Other Sights

BAM The Beaux-Arts Mons—Museum of Fine Arts—occupies a contemporary building on a side street off the Grand-Place. Its collections emphasize 19th- and 20th-century paintings and sculpture from Mons and Hainaut, and it mounts visiting exhibits that are in general more varied and interesting.

Rue Neuve 8 (beside the Jardin du Mayeur). ✆ **065/40-53-30.** www.bam.mons.be. Admission varies depending on the visiting exhibit. Tues–Sat noon–6pm; Sun 11am–6pm.

Musée des Arts Décoratifs (Museum of Decorative Arts) François Duesberg Housed in the 19th-century former National Bank of Belgium building, this museum has a fine collection of objects dating from 1775 to 1825, including exotic clocks, gilded bronzes, porcelain, crockery, gold, and silverwork. In addition, it displays 3,000 pieces of fine porcelain dating from the 17th to the 19th centuries.

Sq. Franklin Roosevelt 12 (entrance rue de la Houssière 2). ✆ **065/84-16-56.** Admission 4€ adults, free for children 17 and under. Tues–Sun 1:30–6pm.

Where to Stay

Infotel Centrally located in town and set in a handsome building dating from the 18th century, this hotel has pretty guest rooms that have thoughtful touches—wood furnishings offset by sky-blue curtains and salmon-pink walls, for example. If you want a decent amount of space, you'll need to take one of the rooms of "standing," which are slightly more expensive than the ordinary ones. The rooms look onto a quiet courtyard, giving you the impression of being in your own mansion. The staff will arrange a picnic basket for you if you ask. There's no restaurant, but that's not a problem since there are plenty within a short walk.

Rue d'Havré 32 (off the Grand-Place), 7000 Mons. ✆ **065/40-18-30.** Fax 065/35-62-24. www.hotelinfotel.be. 25 units. 60€–124€ double. AE, DC, MC, V. Free parking. *In room:* TV, hair dryer, Wi-Fi (free).

Fighting Talk

Mons has an important place in British military history, as the site of a stiff World War I battle on August 23 and 24, 1914. The outnumbered British Expeditionary Force absorbed hard blows from the Kaiser's invading army, holding up the Germans on their advance to Paris.

Mercure Mons ★ Lodging here can make sense if you're traveling by car. The hotel is outside of Mons, in quiet, rural surroundings, and not well served by public transportation. Guest rooms, while affording tranquil views of woodlands and fields, don't have much in the way of local character, and their brown color palette might seem a shade downbeat. They are, however, spacious and have large beds and bathrooms. The French restaurant Lumeçon takes more advantage of the surroundings, with serene forest views through its large picture windows.

Rue des Fusillés 12 (off N56), 7020 Mons. ✆ **065/72-36-85.** Fax 065/72-41-44. www.mercure.com. 53 units. 110€-190€ double. AE, DC, MC, V. Free parking. **Amenities:** Restaurant; bar; 2 lounges; babysitting; nearby golf courses; unheated outdoor pool. *In room:* A/C, TV, hair dryer, minibar, Wi-Fi (free).

Where to Dine

Devos ★★ MODERN FRENCH Settle back and savor the spectacle of a historic courtyard setting that traces its lineage back to 1451 as an inn, and 1879 as a restaurant. The restored decor of the main restaurant and multiple private dining rooms on several floors is that of a distinguished town house, replete with rare woods, plush-carpeting, and paintings. Yet neither the service nor the food are stuffy. The menu is relatively light on options but strong on quality, reflecting a preference to do a few things simply and well rather than to offer long lists and feature-bloat. Still, there will be three or four each of seafood and meat dishes—vegetarians, though, are out of luck.

Rue de la Coupe 7 (off Grand-Place). ✆ **065/35-13-35.** www.restaurantdevos.be. Main courses 20€-26€; fixed-price lunch 28€, dinner 45€-65€. AE, DC, MC, V. Daily noon-2pm; Mon-Tues and Thurs-Sat 7-9:30pm.

No Maison BELGIAN Thinking up a less promising name for a restaurant would be a tough proposition, but "no" is likely to become "yes" once you've tried it. A simple enough place, on three floors of an old patrician house, with a fine view over the Grand-Place from window tables, it focuses on Belgian and Mons specialties, such as *escavêche Montoise* (eel). The restaurant's dark-wood paneling is offset by colorful paintings of local festivals.

Grand-Place 21. ✆ **065/31-11-11.** Main courses 9€-17€; *plat du jour* 9€; *menu Montoise* (daily special menu) 23€. MC, V. Daily 10am-2am.

Nearby Places of Interest

Château de Beloeil (Beloeil Castle) ★★ The magnificent ancestral home of the Prince de Ligne has been called, with some justification, the "Versailles of Belgium." The palace sits amid French-style gardens in its own park, on the shores of an ornamental lake. For more than a thousand years, the de Ligne family has lived in the grand style that pervades these vast rooms, filled with priceless antiques, paintings by the Masters, historical mementos (among them a lock of Queen Marie Antoinette's hair), and more than 20,000 books, many of them rare editions.

Rue du Château 11, Beloeil (22km/14 miles northwest of Mons). ✆ **069/68-94-26.** www.chateaudebeloeil.com. Admission: château and park 8€ adults, 6€ seniors, 5.50€ children 6-18, 2.50€ visitors with disabilities, free for children 5 and under; park only 4€ adults, 3€ seniors and children 6-18, 2.50€ visitors with disabilities, free for children 5 and under. Apr-June and Sept Sat-Sun and holidays 1-6pm; July-Aug daily 1-6pm.

Grand-Hornu ★ This monument of industrial archaeology is a memorial to an idealistic—or paternalistic—employer. Mine-owner Henri de Gorge (1774–1832) constructed the complex between 1810 and 1830 in neoclassical style and attached to it some 450 well-designed and well-equipped houses for his workers. Fallen into disuse and dereliction, Grand-Hornu was restored in the 1970s. It's a fascinating, unlikely mixture of antiquarian sensibility and gritty industrial reality that showcases the Victorian entrepreneurial tradition at its best. A part of the site has been given over to the Musée des Arts Contemporains of Belgium's Francophone community and its exhibits of contemporary art.

Rue Ste-Louise 82, Hornu (13km/8 miles southwest of Mons). ✆ **065/65-21-21.** www.grand-hornu.be. Admission 6€ adults, 4€ seniors, 2€ children 6–18, free for children 5 and under, free for all visitors 1st Wed in month. Tues–Sun 10am–6pm. Closed Jan 1 and Dec 25.

Maison Van Gogh (Van Gogh House) During his days as a none-too-successful church missionary, the Dutch artist Vincent van Gogh lived in 1879 and 1880 in this miner's house, the Maison du Marais, in the Borinage coal-mining district. He preached the gospel to the mining families, while painting and drawing them and the bleak countryside. The house has been restored as a monument, with documents, an audiovisual presentation, and an original van Gogh sketch, *The Diggers* (1880).

Rue du Pavillon 3, Cuesmes (3km/2 miles south of Mons). ✆ **065/35-56-11.** Admission 5€ adults, 2.50€ children 12–17, free for children 12 and under. Tues–Sat 10:30am–12:30pm and 1:30–6pm; Sun 10:30am–noon and 2–6pm. Closed Jan 1 and Dec 25.

THE HAINAUT LAKES

Among several lakes in Hainaut are the manmade lakes of the **Barrages de l'Eau d'Heure ★**, at Boussu-lez-Walcourt in the Botte de Hainaut (Hainaut's Boot) district, south of Charleroi (off N798). The **Plate Taille** is Belgium's largest lake, covering 350 hectares (865 acres), and the entire area has been developed as a watersports center, with designated zones for windsurfing, jet-skiing, scuba diving, sailing, and water-skiing. For information on the area's ecology, go to the visitor center, the **Centre d'Accueil** (✆ **071/50-92-92;** www.lacsdeleaudheure.be), next to the Plate Taille Dam. It's open daily from 10am to 6pm (until 7pm July–Aug). Admission is free.

Farther south, near Chimay, are the **Etangs de Virelles (Virelles Lakes),** a protected nature reserve covering 100 hectares (247 acres) of natural lakes, wetlands, and forest. There are guided walking tours, and observation points for watching bird life. **Aquascope,** rue du Lac 42, Virelles-lez-Chimay (✆ **060/21-13-63;** www.aquascope.be), the lakes' nature park, has an exhibit and audiovisual presentation at its visitor center. It's open mid-March to June and September to mid-November Tuesday to Sunday (and Mon during school vacations) from 10am to 5pm; July to August, daily hours are from 10am to 7pm; and mid-November to mid-March, it's open weekends, holidays, and school vacations from 10am to 4pm (closed Jan 1 and Dec 24–25 and 31). Admission is 6€ for adults, 4€ for visitors with disabilities, 3.50€ for children 6 to 12, and free for children 5 and under; various activities in the reserve have additional charges.

TOURNAI ★★

72km (45 miles) SW of Brussels; 43km (27 miles) NW of Mons

Historic, handsome Tournai (pop. 68,000), on the Escaut (Scheldt) River, is Belgium's second-oldest town (after Tongeren). During medieval and Renaissance times, it had a position of prominence as a European ecclesiastical center. Its importance in earlier centuries was forgotten until 1653, when a workman discovered the tomb of

Childeric, king of the Franks, whose son, Clovis, founded the Merovingian dynasty that ruled for nearly 3 centuries. This led to the discovery that Tournai's predecessor, a Roman settlement known as Tornacum, was the first capital of the Frankish empire. The tomb yielded breathtaking royal treasures in gold. These were removed first to Vienna and then to Paris, where in 1831 most of the gold objects were stolen and melted down. Tournai still has magnificent works of art and architecture, the legacy of its painters, sculptors, goldsmiths, tapestry weavers, and porcelain craftsmen.

Essentials

GETTING THERE Two **trains** depart Brussels every hour for Tournai—a 1-hour ride by the fastest trains. **Tournai's station** is on the northern edge of town, on boulevard des Déportés. By **car** from Brussels, Tournai is less than an hour's drive on A8/E429.

VISITOR INFORMATION The **Office du Tourisme** is at Vieux Marché aux Poteries 14, 7500 Tournai (✆ **069/22-20-45;** fax 069/21-62-21; www.tournai.be), facing the Belfry, in the center of town. The office is open Easter to mid-October Monday to Friday from 8:30am to 6pm, Saturday from 9:30am to noon and 2 to 5pm, and Sunday and holidays from 10am to noon and 2:30 to 6pm; hours from mid-October to Easter are Monday to Friday from 8:30am to 5:30pm, Saturday from 10am to noon and 2 to 5pm, and Sunday and holidays from 2:30 to 6pm (closed Jan 1–2; Nov 1–2, 11, and 15; and Dec 24–26 and 31).

SPECIAL EVENTS On the days of the **Quatre Cortèges (Four Parades),** during the second weekend in June, episodes from Tournai's history are reenacted in a series of folklore processions and events. With the annual **Grande Procession** through the city on the second Sunday in September, the town celebrates amid splendid pageantry the intervention of Our Lady during a time of plague.

What to See & Do

To get an idea of how Tournai looked in medieval times, take a stroll along rue Barre St-Brice on the north side of the Scheldt. Although you can't go inside, you can at least peruse the exteriors of some of the oldest private houses still in existence in Europe; nos. 10 and 12 date from 1175. Closer to the center of town, 13th-century **Gothic houses** line rue des Jésuites.

Pont des Trous (Bridge of Holes) on quai Sakharov is an appropriate name for this 13th-century bridge. It has taken its lumps from any number of battles and sieges since then—most recently in 1944, when it was blown up. The bridge and its two anchoring towers once formed part of the city's defensive walls. Another military work, the 24m-high (79-ft.) **Tour Henry VIII,** on rue du Rempart, named for the English king of six-wives fame, dates from a period of English occupation from 1512 to 1518.

Beffroi (Belfry) A UNESCO World Heritage Site, the Belfry dates from the late 1100s, making it Belgium's oldest. If you're up for it, climb the 265 steps to the top of this 72m (236-ft.) tower; you'll be rewarded with glorious views of the town and surrounding countryside. The 44-bell carillon plays Saturday-morning concerts.

Vieux Marché aux Poteries. ✆ **069/22-20-45.** Admission 2€ adults, 1€ children 7–12, free for children 6 and under. Apr–Oct Tues–Sun 10am–5:30pm; Nov–Mar Tues–Sat 10am–noon and 2–5pm, Sun 2–5pm.

Cathédrale Notre-Dame (Cathedral of Our Lady) ★★★ This magnificent five-towered cathedral, a UNESCO World Heritage Site, is one of Europe's most striking examples of Romanesque architecture. Completed in the late 1100s, it's not

Tournai

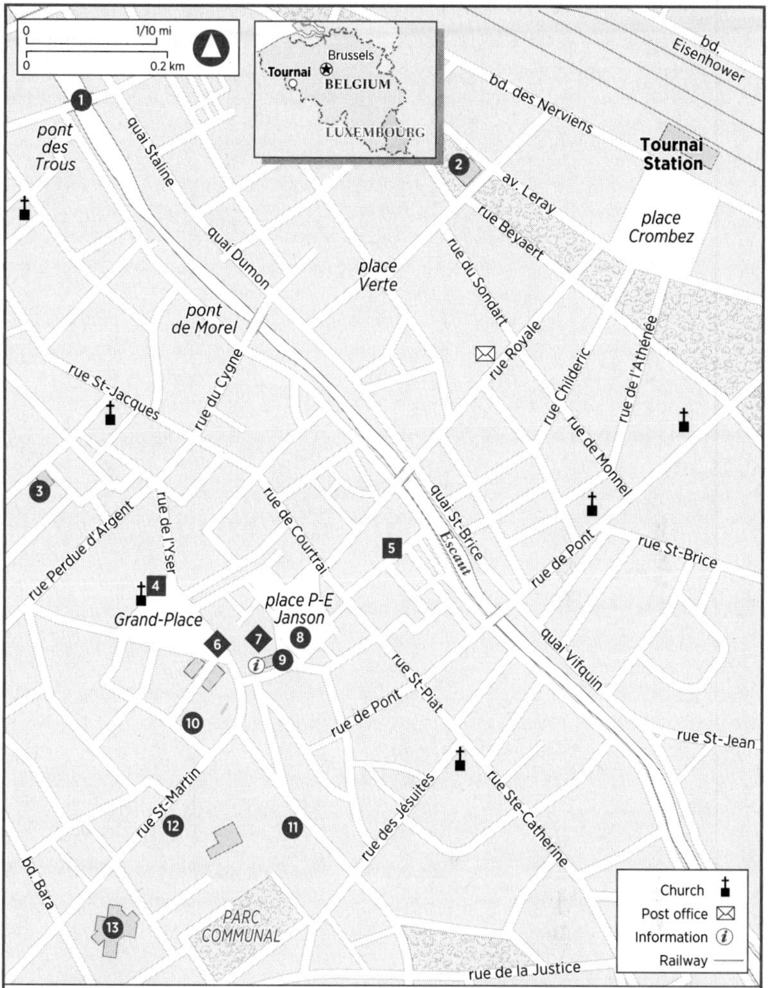

0 1/10 mi
0 0.2 km
Brussels
Tournai
BELGIUM
LUXEMBOURG
bd. Eisenhower
bd. des Nerviens
Tournai Station
av. Leray
rue Beyaert
place Crombez
pont des Trous
quai Staline
quai Dumon
place Verte
rue du Sondart
pont de Morel
rue Royale
rue Childeric
rue de l'Athénée
rue St-Jacques
rue du Cygne
rue de Monnel
rue de l'Yser
rue de Courtrai
quai St-Brice
Escaut
rue Perdue d'Argent
rue de Pont
rue St-Brice
Grand-Place
place P-E Janson
quai Vifquin
rue St-Piat
rue de Pont
rue St-Jean
rue St-Martin
rue des Jésuites
rue Ste-Catherine
bd. Bara
PARC COMMUNAL
rue de la Justice

Church
Post office
Information
Railway

ATTRACTIONS ●

Beffroi **9**
Cathédrale Notre-Dame **8**
Musée d'Archéologie **3**
Musée de Folklore **10**
Musée de la Tapisserie et des Arts du Tissu **11**
Musée d'Histoire et des Arts Décoratifs **12**
Musée des Beaux-Arts **13**
Pont des Trous **1**
Tour Henry VIII **2**

ACCOMMODATIONS ■

Hôtel Cathédrale **5**
L'Europe **4**

DINING ◆

Charles-Quint **6**
Plaisir d'Essences **7**

the first place of worship to stand on this spot. There was a church here as early as A.D. 761, and it's thought there was a pagan temple before that. The 8th-century church was replaced by another in 850, which Viking raiders burned to the ground in 881. After fire again destroyed the replacement church in 1060, it was reconstructed by 1089 and became a place of refuge for a plague-stricken population. On September 14, 1090, after the dreaded disease had abated, the bishop led a great procession through the cathedral to honor Our Lady, who was credited with miraculous cures of sick pilgrims who had poured into the cathedral to pray before her statue.

The Romanesque style was, in the eyes of a 13th-century bishop, old-fashioned compared to the Gothic buildings that were then appearing all over Europe. Before his money ran out, he had added stained-glass windows and created a soaring, graceful Gothic choir adjoining the low Romanesque nave. There's no sense of disharmony, but rather a compatible marriage of the two styles. Paintings by Rubens and Jordaens adorn the interior, along with 700-year-old murals, a Renaissance pulpit, and a stained-glass "rose window." Even these wonders pale before the display in the **Trésor (Treasury),** which houses a vast collection of priceless religious relics and antiquities. The centerpiece is a reliquary that takes the place of honor in the Procession of Tournai, the **Chasse de Notre-Dame (Shrine of Our Lady),** a masterpiece of the Mosan art style, with a gold covering created by Nicolas de Verdun in 1205.

Place de l'Evêché (just off the Grand-Place). ✆ **069/45-26-50.** www.cathedrale-tournai.be. Admission: cathedral free; treasury 2€, 3€ family. Cathedral Apr–Oct daily 9:15am–noon and 2–6pm; Nov–Mar daily 9:15am–noon and 2–5pm. Treasury Apr–Oct daily 9:30am–noon and 2–6pm; Nov–Mar daily 9:30am–noon and 2–5pm.

Musée d'Archéologie (Archaeological Museum) A 17th-century pawnshop in the center of town houses collections of Tournai relics covering virtually every period in its history. The Merovingian section features items recovered in and around the tomb of Childeric, including the skeletons of horses sacrificed during the 5th-century Frank king's funeral. There's a fine collection of glassware from the Gallo-Roman period of the 1st to the 4th century.

Rue des Carmes 8 (off place de Lille). ✆ **069/22-16-72.** Admission 3.50€ adults; 1.50€ seniors, students, and children 6–18; free for children 5 and under; free for all visitors 1st Sun of the month. Apr–Oct Wed–Mon 10am–5:30pm; Nov–Mar Mon and Wed–Sat 10am–noon and 2–5pm, Sun 2–5pm.

Musée d'Histoire et des Arts Décoratifs (Museum of History and Decorative Arts) This museum features examples of the exquisite porcelain and china made in Tournai in the 18th century, including the dinner service for the duc d'Orléans, and displays of fine silverware and historical coins.

Rue St-Martin 50 (at Cour d'Honneur). ✆ **069/33-23-53.** Admission 3.50€ adults; 1.50€ seniors, students, and children 6–18; free for children 5 and under; free for all visitors 1st Sun of the month. Apr–Oct Wed–Mon 10am–5:30pm; Nov–Mar Mon and Wed–Sat 10am–noon and 2–5pm, Sun 2–5pm.

Musée des Beaux-Arts (Museum of Fine Arts) ★★ It's hard to say which is more impressive: the museum's 700 works of art, or the building dating from 1928 that houses them. The star-shaped white stone structure, its interior illuminated by natural light, was designed by noted Art Nouveau architect Victor Horta. The art collections contain such outstanding works as *Virgin and Child* by 15th-century native son Roger de la Pasture (Rogier van der Weyden), and Edouard Manet's *Argenteuil* and *At Father Lathuille's*. Other Belgian artists represented include Pieter Brueghel the Younger, James Ensor, Henri de Braekeleer, and Sir Anthony van Dyck.

Enclos St-Martin (off rue St-Martin). ✆ **069/33-24-31.** Admission 3.50€ adults; 2€ seniors, students, and children 6–18; free for children 5 and under; free for all visitors 1st Sun of the month. Apr–Oct Wed–Mon 10am–5:30pm; Nov–Mar Mon and Wed–Sat 10am–noon and 2–5pm, Sun 2–5pm.

Musée de la Tapisserie et des Arts du Tissu (Museum of Tapestry and Cloth Art) In the late Middle Ages, Tournai was one of the great European centers of tapestry making, and this museum reflects that heritage. Several historical tapestries are displayed, but the museum focuses more on contemporary works, including pieces by modern Belgian artists like Roger Somville.

Place Reine Astrid 9 (off rue de la Wallonie). ✆ **069/84-20-73.** Admission 3.50€ adults; 2€ seniors, students, and children 6–18; free for children 5 and under; free for all visitors 1st Sun of the month. Apr–Oct Wed–Mon 10am–5:30pm; Nov–Mar Mon and Wed–Sat 10am–noon and 2–5pm, Sun 2–5pm.

Musée de Folklore (Folklore Museum) ★ A marvelous 17th-century building in the center of town, the Maison Tournaisienne, with gables and mullioned windows, provides just the right setting for a series of authentic recreations of an ancient farmhouse, a tavern, a weaver's workroom, a blacksmith's forge, and many other old scenes, aimed at preserving the atmosphere of Tournai in times gone by. A fast-food stall shows how french fries were dispensed at the turn of the 20th century.

Réduit des Sions 32–36 (off the Grand-Place). ✆ **069/22-40-69.** Admission 3.50€ adults; 2€ seniors, students, and children 6–18; free for children 5 and under; free for all visitors 1st Sun of the month. Apr–Oct Wed–Mon 10am–5:30pm; Nov–Mar Mon and Wed–Sat 10am–noon and 2–5pm, Sun 2–5pm.

A Fictional Famous Son

Elezelles, 20km (12½ miles) northeast of Tournai, has decided it must have been the birthplace of fictional Belgian detective Hercule Poirot. To prove it, a funky statue (a remarkable likeness) of Agatha Christie's famously fussy hero graces the wall of the Maison Communale (Town Hall).

SIGHTSEEING TOURS

From April until the end of August, a ***petit train touristique*** **(little tourist train)** is available to roll you through Tournai's cobblestone streets, departing from the Grand-Place at 4pm. It runs only on Sunday in April; on Saturday, Sunday, and holidays May to June; and Tuesday to Sunday (and Mon holidays) July to August. A 50-minute ride is 3.50€, and 2.50€ for children 5 and under.

Where to Stay

Hôtel Cathédrale ★ In the center of town, on a quiet square between the cathedral and the Escaut, this personable hotel is clean and bright, as is indicated by a white-painted exterior that contrasts sharply with the neighboring brick facades. Most guest rooms are quite small and pleasantly furnished in a contemporary style, but with no great pretensions to charm. A dozen somewhat larger, higher-priced executive rooms are better in all respects. An American-style buffet breakfast (extra) is served in the pleasant French/Belgian restaurant **Le Promenade,** in addition to lunch and dinner.

Place St-Pierre 2 (2 blocks east of Cathédrale Notre-Dame), 7500 Tournai. ✆ **069/25-00-00.** Fax 069/25-00-01. www.hotelcathedrale.be. 71 units. 94€–105€ double. AE, DC, MC, V. Limited street parking. **Amenities:** Restaurant. *In room:* TV, hair dryer, Wi-Fi.

L'Europe This hotel right in the central square follows the rustic style common in Tournai—except that, in this case, the style of the building is rustic Spanish—with antique paintings and lots of flowers in the public spaces. The guest rooms, plain but comfortable, have new furnishings, and some of them overlook the Grand-Place. The ground-floor cocktail bar **Tam Tam** provides more views on the square from a modestly Pacific outlook.

Grand-Place 36, 7500 Tournai. ✆ **069/22-40-67.** Fax 069/23-52-38. 8 units. 65€ double. Rates include continental breakfast. AE, DC, MC, V. Limited street parking. **Amenities:** Restaurant; cocktail bar. *In room:* TV.

Where to Dine

Charles-Quint CONTINENTAL It would be hard for a restaurant in this central location, with the Belfry just a few steps away, to not be popular, always supposing it can deliver on the plate. The "Charles the Fifth's" mirrored, Art Deco–style dining room is invariably and deservedly busy for both lunch and dinner. The kitchen's signature is combining Italian influences and ingredients—a sprinkle of Parmesan here, a touch of mozzarella there, and an occasional full dish like *osso buco*—with a Franco-Belgian base. An entrecôte (steak in butter sauce) might hit the spot just as well.

Grand-Place 3. ✆ **069/22-14-41.** www.charles-quint.be. Main courses 19€–26€; fixed-price lunch 35€; fixed-price menu 49€. AE, DC, MC, V. Wed–Sat noon–2:30pm and 7–10:30pm, Sun noon–2:30pm.

Plaisir d'Essences ★★ CONTINENTAL The antique ambience of Tournai Cathedral's 17th-century former wine press is left outside the door here, in favor of cool reds and grays, with a mere smidgeon of visible bare brick and stone. At the helm are youthful but accomplished chef François Dufour and his wife, Marie, who serve light contemporary French fare with Mediterranean and Asian touches. The menu changes constantly, varying with the seasons and what's fresh or hot at the local market. Seafood takes up around half of the menu, with lobster being one of the few regular items. You can dine on the sidewalk terrace in summer.

Vieux Marché aux Poteries 2 (facing the Cathedral). ✆ **069/76-76-55.** www.plaisirdessences.be. Main courses 22€–30€; fixed-price lunch 20€; fixed-price menus 35€–51€. MC, V. Tues, Thurs and Fri noon–2:30pm and 6–10pm; Wed and Sun noon–2:30pm; Sat 6–10pm.

THE ARDENNES

A scenic and gastronomic delight, les Ardennes (the Ardennes) makes for a welcome respite from museum hopping. With the change in landscape comes a shift in emphasis, away from treasures hoarded indoors and toward the outdoor riches of bracing air, winding roads, sparkling streams, and tranquil lakes, in a setting sculpted by the ebb and flow of ice ages. Add to that some pretty resort towns nestled in steep river valleys, and fine old country inns, and you have an idea of the Ardennes.

The region offers a cornucopia of outdoor pursuits (though the topography is one of hills, rather than genuine mountains): hiking, biking, canoeing, fishing, golf, hunting, horseback riding, skiing, swimming, tennis, and more.

Recommending an itinerary for the Ardennes is difficult. I don't think you can do better than to follow your nose. Sooner or later, you'll bump into some biggish place like Spa, Bouillon, Bastogne, or Durbuy, where you can join other wanderers. If you stick to the back roads, you'll have fun getting lost among all the stone villages and farmhouses for which the region is justly famed. Many of these were reconstructed after being destroyed during the Battle of the Bulge in the winter of 1944 to 1945.

BOUILLON ★

60km (37 miles) S of Dinant

At a strategic bend in the Semois River, this little town (pop. 5,000) guarded for centuries the major route from the Eifel to Champagne. In addition to a spectacular location in the plunging river valley, Bouillon boasts the country's finest medieval castle. The awesome 10th-century feudal castle of Godefroy de Bouillon, leader of the First Crusade to the Holy Land, still stands over the town, crouching like a great stone dragon on a steep bluff.

Bouillon is also a scenic and gastronomic stronghold. Where better to try bouillon than in the town that gave it its name?

Essentials

GETTING THERE Frequent service by **TEC bus no. 8** goes to Bouillon from the **train** station at Libramont, on the rail line connecting Namur and Luxembourg. The bus ride takes 40 minutes by the fastest bus; for bus information, contact **TEC** (✆ **081/25-35-55;** www.infotec.be). By **car** from Dinant, take N95 southeast and then N89 south to Bouillon.

The Ardennes on a Plate

Food lovers, rejoice! This region is home to the delicately smoked Ardennes ham *(jambon d'Ardenne)*, proudly served all over Belgium, and of other regional specialties, including game and fresh trout and pike. The Ardennes is famed for its wealth of gourmet restaurants, many in country inns where the innkeeper doubles as chef.

VISITOR INFORMATION The **Maison du Tourisme du Pays de Bouillon,** Quai des Saulx 12, 6830 Bouillon (✆ **061/46-52-11;** fax 061/46-52-18; www.bouillon-tourisme.be), is open daily 10am to 6pm.

Seeing the Sights

Château de Bouillon (Bouillon Castle) ★★ Once home to Duke Godefroy de Bouillon, this massive, sprawling castle is the town's dramatic centerpiece, floodlit every night during summer months. The worthy de Bouillon actually put the castle in hock to raise funds for his great venture, the First Crusade (see "Duke of Hazards," below). The mortgaged castle passed by default into the hands of the prince-bishops of Liège, who continued to hold it for 6 centuries. After the 15th century, it was conquered and reconquered several times, as local rulers and invading forces fought over this strategic spot. Within the castle's thick walls, life during its turbulent history will come alive as you walk through the ruins and visit the old prisons and gallows and the so-called Hall of Justice.

Esplanade Godefroid 1. ✆ **061/46-62-57.** Admission 5.90€ adults, 5.10€ seniors, 4.30€ students, 4€ children 6–12, free for children 5 and under; combined tickets for Bouillon Castle and Ducal Museum 8.60€ adults, 5.60€ children 6–12, free for children 5 and under. Jan–Feb and Dec Mon–Fri 1–5pm, Sat–Sun 10am–5pm; Mar and Oct–Nov daily 10am–5pm; Apr–June and Sept Mon–Fri 10am–6pm, Sat–Sun 10am–6:30pm; July–Aug daily 10am–6:30pm. Closed Dec 25.

Musée Ducal (Ducal Museum) ★ Housed in a group of four neighboring 18th-century buildings close to the Semois River, this rambling museum contains exhibits on the region's archaeology, iron industry, and folklore. It includes the Godfrey of Bouillon Museum, which holds souvenirs of the Crusades and of gallant Godfrey, including a model of Godfrey's tomb in Jerusalem as well as armor, weapons, and religious objects of the period.

Rue du Petit 1–3 (at Place Ducale). ✆ **061/46-41-89.** Admission 4€ adults, 3.50€ seniors, 3€ students, 2.20€ children 6–12, free for children 5 and under; combined tickets for Bouillon Castle and Ducal Museum 8.60€ adults, 5.60€ children 6–12, free for children 5 and under. Jan 1–Oct 31 daily 10am–6pm, Nov 1–Dec 31 Sat–Sun 10am–5pm. Closed Dec 25.

Where to Stay & Dine

Auberge Le Moulin Hideux ★★ Set beside an old water mill, with wooded hills almost at its doorstep, you'll find one of Belgium's prettiest country inns. A warm, subdued sophistication exudes from the decor. A focal point for guests is the crackling log fire, which is surrounded by luxurious leather furniture and touches of brass to complete the lounge scene. The glassed-in bar is decorated with plants. The 12 guest rooms are appointed with the same sense of style. Extras include beautiful forest walks and horse-riding trails nearby. The hotel's notable restaurant serves meals that

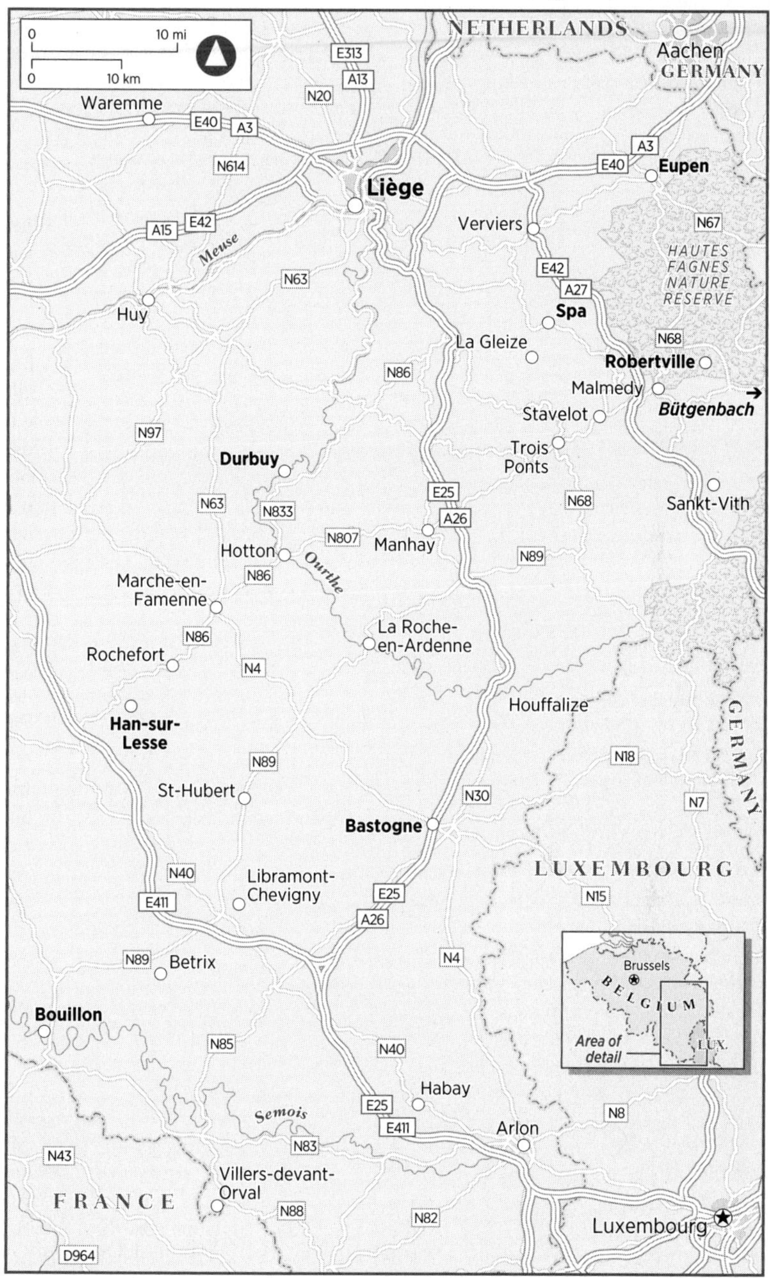
0 10 mi
0 10 km
NETHERLANDS
Aachen
GERMANY
Waremme
Liège
Eupen
Verviers
Meuse
HAUTES FAGNES NATURE RESERVE
Huy
Spa
La Gleize
Robertville
Malmedy
Bütgenbach
Stavelot
Trois Ponts
Durbuy
Sankt-Vith
Hotton
Manhay
Ourthe
Marche-en-Famenne
La Roche-en-Ardenne
Rochefort
Houffalize
Han-sur-Lesse
GERMANY
St-Hubert
Bastogne
LUXEMBOURG
Libramont-Chevigny
Betrix
Brussels
BELGIUM
Area of detail
LUX.
Bouillon
Habay
Semois
Arlon
Villers-devant-Orval
FRANCE
Luxembourg

DUKE OF hazards

Godfrey of Bouillon, duke of Lower Lorraine, was just 15 when he inherited his lands, castle, and title in 1076. He was soon fighting for them and for his life against powerful local lords who wanted all four, and who thought they would easily get them. Godfrey proved them wrong in a war that culminated in a siege of Bouillon Castle in 1086, from which he emerged victorious.

In 1095, Pope Urban II called for an "armed pilgrimage" to liberate Jerusalem from the Seljuk Turks and ensure safe passage for Christian pilgrims to the Holy Land. Godfrey was one of the first to answer the call, mortgaging his castle to the prince-bishop of Liège to finance an expedition. By June 1099, he stood before the walls of Jerusalem at the head of the combined Christian army.

On July 15, the Crusaders stormed the Holy City and massacred its Muslim inhabitants. Setting aside his armor, Godfrey put on a linen robe and prayed barefoot at the Church of the Holy Sepulcher. Offered the title King of Jerusalem, he refused it, saying he "would not wear a crown of gold in the city where Our Lord had worn a crown of thorns." He accepted instead the title Defender of the Holy Sepulcher. Godfrey did not long survive his victory: He died in 1100 and was buried in the Church of the Holy Sepulcher. The Latin inscription on his tomb reads: "Here lies the renowned Godfrey of Bouillon, who brought this whole region under Christian sway. May his soul rest in the peace of Christ."

Back in Bouillon, the prince-bishop of Liège called in the mortgage and pocketed Bouillon Castle.

feature lamb, saddle of pork, game, and fish delicacies such as baby lobsters (which are kept in a tank out in the garden). Everything is cooked to order, so be prepared to wait a bit for your dinner—your patience will be rewarded.

Rte. de Dohan (4km/2½ miles northeast of Bouillon), 6831 Noirefontaine. ✆ **061/46-70-15.** Fax 061/46-72-81. www.moulinhideux.be. 12 units. 195€ double; from 245€ suite. Rates include full breakfast. AE, DC, MC, V. Free parking. Bus: 40 from Bouillon. By car, take N865 east from Noirefontaine. **Amenities:** Restaurant; bar; lounge; heated indoor pool; tennis courts. *In room:* TV, minibar.

Hostellerie du Prieuré de Conques ★ This is a great spot to enjoy perfect tranquillity on the edge of an Ardennes forest, in an atmospheric inn on the banks of the Semois River. This hotel is set in what was once a 7th-century convent (although the oldest remains go back only as far as the 12th c.). It overlooks green lawns, rose gardens, and the river. The charming guest rooms are individual in shape and character—some have alcoves, some peek from beneath the eaves—and their comfort rates just as high as their charm. The vaulted main dining room is warmed by an open fire, and any overflow of diners spills into a bevy of smaller vaulted rooms.

Rue de Conques 2, 6820 Florenville. ✆ **061/41-14-17.** Fax 061/41-27-03. www.conques.be. 18 units. 125€–138€ double; 154€ suite. Rates include buffet breakfast. AE, DC, MC, V. Free parking. Take N83 about 23km (14 miles) south and east from Bouillon. **Amenities:** Restaurant; bar; lounge. *In room:* TV, hair dryer, minibar.

A Side Trip to Orval ★

A visit to the impressive **Abbaye Notre-Dame d'Orval (Abbey of Our Lady of Orval) ★**, Villers-devant-Orval (✆ **061/31-10-60;** www.orval.be), set in a forest, is an exercise in serenity, since there is now little to suggest the enormous power its monks wielded in past centuries. The abbey, now administered by a handful of monks, dates back to the coming of the first Cistercians in 1110, though much was left in ruins after a destructive visit from the French in 1793. Today the complex includes the old ruins, a church, and gardens. It produces two Trappist beers that are considered among the best of Belgian brews (you can taste them in bars throughout the land), and the artisanal cheese *fromage d'Orval*.

The abbey is open daily March to May and October from 9:30am to 6pm, June to September from 9:30am to 6:30pm, and November to February from 10:30am to 5:30pm. Admission to the main abbey is free; to the ruins and museum, it is 5€ for adults, 4.50€ for seniors and students, 3€ for children 7 to 14, and free for children 6 and under. To get here by car from Bouillon, take the country road 27km (17 miles) southeast through Florenville; TEC bus no. 24 from Florenville rail station passes by the monastery.

BASTOGNE ★

70km (44 miles) S of Liège

This southern Ardennes town (pop. 15,000) owes its usefulness as a touring base today to the same assets that made it a strategic target in the past—the roads that converge on it from all points of the compass. During the Battle of the Bulge in the winter of 1944 to 1945, the U.S. 101st Airborne Division, outnumbered and surrounded, held the town until a relief force could break through to them. It was a hard fight for the 101st troopers—the "Battered Bastards of Bastogne," they dubbed themselves. Their commander, Brig. Gen. Anthony MacAuliffe, answered German demands for surrender with a single word that became legend: "Nuts!" During the annual December memorial days, you'll see the division's Screaming Eagle emblem around town.

ESSENTIALS

GETTING THERE Bastogne makes a good day trip from almost any point in the Ardennes, but it's a little out of the way to use as a base for exploring. There are regular **buses** from Liège and other towns—take bus no. 6416 from Libramont rail station. By **car** from Liège, take junction 53 or 54 off the A26/E25 Liège–Luxembourg City expressway.

VISITOR INFORMATION The **Maison du Tourisme du Pays de Bastogne,** place MacAuliffe 60, 6600 Bastogne (✆ **061/21-27-11;** fax 061/21-27-25; www.paysdebastogne.be), is open daily 9:30am to 12:30pm and 1 to 5:30pm.

EXPLORING BASTOGNE

The tourism office can put you in touch with a number of local battlefield tour guides. Be aware that the scenes of action in and around Bastogne cover a considerable amount of ground, and you'll ideally need a 1-day tour to get the most out of it. A good one is run by the store **Militaria Bastogne,** place MacAuliffe 38R (✆ **061/50-10-17;** www.militariabastogne.eu). The tour, which lets you ride in a WC62 Dodge World War II truck, costs 125€ per person, including lunch.

With your own car, a self-guided tour could work. Take the road east from Bastogne through Mageret, Longvilly, and Fetsch, villages where small task forces from the U.S. 9th and 10th Armored divisions were struck by the oncoming German 2nd Panzer, Panzer Lehr, and 26th Volksgrenadier divisions, and either destroyed or driven back to Bastogne. Closer to Bastogne, the villages of Foy, Bizory, Marvie, Senonchamps, and

THE BATTLE OF THE bulge

Hitler aimed his last great offensive squarely at the Americans, because he believed that if he hit them hard enough, their multiethnic citizen army would fall apart and run. By mid-December 1944, he had assembled his last reserves of men, tanks, and guns in the hilly, misty Eifel region of Germany, opposite the thinly held American lines in the Ardennes. In one of the great failures of military intelligence, the American high command didn't know they were there.

On the morning of December 16, the German forces charged out of the forests. Their aim was far-reaching: to smash straight through the American defenses, cross the Meuse River before Allied reinforcements had time to intervene, capture Brussels and the port of Antwerp, split the American army from the British and Canadians, and break the Allied coalition.

The Führer's ambition outstripped his means, but in the Ardennes he had overwhelming strength for the attack: 300,000 against 80,000 on the first day. A few of the hard-hit American defenders "bugged out," but most held their ground until forced back or overrun. Savage struggles all across the Ardennes propelled the names of obscure towns, villages, and places into the history books: Rocherath and Krinkelt, the Elsenborn Ridge, Malmedy, Stavelot, Trois Ponts, La Gleize, Sankt-Vith, the Skyline Drive, Clervaux, Wiltz, Bastogne. The action was dubbed the Battle of the Bulge, for the shape the front took as German forces pushed through the middle of the Ardennes.

The lightly armed U.S. 82nd and 101st Airborne divisions were rushed in to stem the German armored tide until heavier reinforcements could be brought to bear. While the 82nd fought no-quarter battles with SS troops who had massacred American prisoners and murdered Belgian civilians, the 101st found itself cut off in Bastogne, holding the vital road junction there.

On December 26, the enemy spearhead was destroyed just a few miles short of the Meuse. General George S. Patton's Third Army, attacking from Luxembourg, relieved Bastogne. More weeks of heavy fighting pushed the German army back to its start line. Hitler's great gamble had failed, with German casualties above 100,000 out of 500,000 engaged.

The victors were the ordinary GI's who, in the depths of winter, outnumbered and faced with a surprise offensive by a still-powerful foe, refuted Hitler's contemptuous opinion of them. The price of victory was 81,000 American casualties out of 600,000 engaged: 19,000 killed, 47,000 wounded, and 15,000 taken prisoner. Memorials all over the Ardennes bear witness to their sacrifice. Those of America's fallen not repatriated, or still lying in the Ardennes forests, rest at the military cemeteries of **Neuville-en-Condroz** and **Henri-Chapelle.**

Champs played prominent roles in the 101st Airborne's staunch defense of the town. South of Bastogne, Lt. Col. Creighton Abrams's "B Team" from the 4th Armored Division broke through the German lines at Assenois to link up with the besieged paratroops.

American Memorial & Bastogne Historical Center ★★ ***Note:*** The Historical Center will be closed while undergoing a transformation from around mid-2011 until the end of 2012. A visit here will lay the groundwork for a better appreciation

of the great battle fought here in December 1944. General MacAuliffe of the 101st Airborne Division and his opponent, General Hasso von Manteuffel of the 5th Panzer Army, both gave advice in putting together the film, dioramas, and commentary that tell the story of the siege of Bastogne. Afterward, visitors can climb to the gigantic star-shaped memorial to America's fallen on Mardasson Hill. Key points of the battlefield are clearly posted for those interested in retracing the course of the fighting.

Colline du Mardasson (1.6km/1 mile outside Bastogne). ✆ **061/21-14-13.** www.bastognehistoricalcenter.be. Admission 8.50€ adults, 7€ seniors, 6€ children 8–12, free for World War II veterans and children 7 and under. May–Sept daily 9:30am–6pm; Mar–Apr and Oct–Dec daily 10am–5:30pm; Jan–Feb by arrangement. Closed Jan 1 and Dec 24–25 and 31.

HAN-SUR-LESSE

40km (25 miles) NW of Bastogne; 25km (16 miles) SE of Dinant

This village, sited on a scenic stretch of the Lesse River, is a particularly good stop for those traveling with children, though the two places described below should be interesting for adults as well.

Essentials

GETTING THERE **Trains** from Namur and Liège stop at nearby Jemelle, from where a frequent service by **TEC bus no. 29** goes to Han-sur-Lesse in 20 minutes. By **car** from Dinant, take N94 southeast to its junction with N86, then go northeast on this road for the last few miles.

VISITOR INFORMATION The **Office du Tourisme** is at place Théo Lannoy, 5580 Han-sur-Lesse (✆ **084/37-75-96;** fax 084/37-75-76; www.rochefort.be). The office is open March daily 9:30am to 4pm; April to June daily 9:30am to 4:30pm (to 5:30pm Sat–Sun May–June); July to August daily 9:30am to 5:30pm (to 6pm Sat–Sun); September to October daily 10am to 4:30pm (to 5pm Sat–Sun Sept); November to February Monday to Friday from 10am to 4pm.

What to See & Do

Grotte de Han (Han Cave) ★ ☺ Of the several cave complexes in the Ardennes, this one is probably the most spectacular and worth visiting. Only about one-fifth of the cave is open to the general public, though other parts are accessible to experienced speleologists. Guides take visitors on an hour-long tour to see the stalagmites and stalactites, marvel at the sometimes bizarre and sometimes graceful shapes taken on by the limestone rock of the caves, and listen to the echo in the great subterranean chambers carved out by the Lesse River. The highlight is a brief boat trip on an underground river.

Rue Joseph Lamotte 2. ✆ **084/37-72-13.** www.grotte-de-han.be. Admission (guided tours only) 13€ adults, 8.50€ children 3–12, free for children 2 and under. Jan–Mar Sat–Sun 11:30am–1pm and 2:30–4:30pm; Apr–June daily 10am–noon and 1:30–4:30pm (to 5:30pm Sat–Sun and holidays); July–Aug daily 9:30am–noon and 1:30–5pm (to 5:30pm mid-June to mid-July); Sept–Oct daily 10am–noon and 1:30–4:30pm; Christmas week daily 11:30am and 1, 2:30, and 4pm.

Réserve d'Animaux Sauvages (Wildlife Reserve) ☺ The Wildlife Reserve, which is part of the same tourist complex as the Grotte de Han, gives you a breath of fresh air after the damp and chilly caves. You can take a guided tour by train through the scenic Massif du Boine estate, where you may see wild boars, wild horses, stags, fallow deer, wolves, bison, ibex, chamois, tarpans, lynx, brown bears, and other animals—many of them are native to the area, but some are imported.

Departures from rue Joseph Lamotte 2, Han-sur-Lesse. ✆ **084/37-72-13.** www.grotte-de-han.be. Admission (guided tours only) 11€ adults, 7€ children 3-12, free for children 2 and under. Jan–Mar Sat–Sun 11:30am–1pm and 2:30–4:30pm; Apr–June daily 10am–noon and 1:30–4:30pm (to 5:30pm Sat–Sun and holidays); July–Aug daily 9:30am–noon and 1:30–5pm (to 5:30pm mid-June to mid-July); Sept–Oct daily 10am–noon and 1:30–4:30pm; Christmas week daily 11:30am and 1, 2:30, and 4pm.

DURBUY ★

31km (19 miles) S of Liège

This quaint medieval town (pop. 11,000) on a bend on the Ourthe River dubs itself "the smallest city in the world," a status it seems inordinately proud of even if it is impossible to prove—it seems to originate with it gaining town status in 1331. In any case, Durbuy makes an ideal touring base for this part of the Ardennes. Its narrow, twisting streets are lined with pretty, flower-trimmed stone houses, and there's an 11th-century castle to complete the scene.

Essentials

GETTING THERE There is a **bus** about every hour to Durbuy from the Barvaux **rail** station; the ride takes 20 minutes. By **car** from Liège, take junction 48 west from A26/E25.

VISITOR INFORMATION The **Syndicat d'Initiative** is at place aux Foires 25, 6940 Durbuy (✆ **086/21-24-28;** fax 086/21-38-81; www.durbuyinfo.be).

Exploring Durbuy

The village is pretty (though the main square is a big parking lot) without having any particularly outstanding sights. Wander around to peruse its medieval stone buildings, many of which house artists and craftspeople; or take a walk by the plunging valley of the Ourthe River or into the nearby forests. You get fine views of the town from scenic overlooks in the surrounding hills, and good exercise getting to them in the first place. Besides all that, there's minigolf for the kids. Stores abound, selling antiques, pottery, handmade jewelry, and locally produced artisanal food and drink, including chocolates, liqueur, and beer.

Where to Stay & Dine

Le Clos des Récollets In the heart of the old village, in a pedestrian zone fronted by 17th-century buildings, you'll come to Le Clos des Récollets. Housed in a structure that dates from the 17th century, it has 18th-century modifications. The interior conserves the style of the period, with oak doors, oil paintings, and wooden furnishings. Illumination is provided by candle as much as possible. The guest rooms are rather plainly furnished but quite comfortable. On the premises is a good, moderately priced Belgian restaurant, with umbrella tables on a terrace for outdoor dining. Menu items include game in season, such as pheasant, and lobster stew with vegetables.

Rue de la Prévôté 9, 6940 Durbuy. ✆ **086/21-29-69.** Fax 086/21-36-85. www.closdesrecollets.be. 8 units. 105€ double. Rates include full breakfast. AE, DC, MC, V. Free parking. **Amenities:** Restaurant; bar; lounge. *In room:* TV, minibar.

Le Sanglier des Ardennes ★★★ This stellar, centrally located hotel overlooking a shallow gorge offers comfortable rooms replete with old-fashioned charm. Those

skiing THE ARDENNES

It may not be the Alps, and it sure ain't the Rockies, but the Ardennes can be cool for skiers—so long as the snow shows up. Therein lies the problem: In the low Ardennes hills—highest point 694m (2,277 ft.) above sea level—the appearance of snow is unpredictable. Some years it stays away. Still, when the thermometer starts dropping, ski aficionados in Belgium take serious notice.

Although there are some downhill slopes, cross-country is more usual. Traversing the gentle wooded hills or the high Hautes Fagnes plateau can be a memorable experience. The main ski zones lie in the northern Ardennes, around Botrange, Robertville, Bütgenbach, Spa, Stavelot, Vielsalm, La Roche-en-Ardenne, and Bastogne. Parts of Luxembourg and Germany's neighboring Eifel region likewise have skiing facilities.

Detailed information is available from local tourist offices (some of which are listed in this chapter).

in the back overlook the Ourthe River; those in the front have a postcard-pretty view of the old town, with hills in the background. The restaurant on the ground floor is internationally famous. Fish straight from the river outside come to the table full flavored, with subtle sauces or seasonings that add to their delicacy. Regional specialties such as game and the famed smoked *jambon* (ham) take on new dimensions after passing through this extraordinary kitchen. There's a covered terrace for outdoor dining.

Rue Comte Théodule d'Ursel 14, 6940 Durbuy. ✆ **086/21-32-62.** Fax 086/21-24-65. www.sanglier-des-ardennes.be. 45 units. 120€–240€ double. AE, DC, MC, V. Free parking. **Amenities:** Restaurant; bar; lounge. *In room:* TV, hair dryer, minibar, Wi-Fi (free).

SPA ★★

28km (17 miles) SE of Liège

To uncover the origin of mineral springs, you need to go straight to the source. Where better to begin than Spa? The town (pop. 11,000) virtually floats on some of the healthiest H_2O ever to gurgle up to the surface and has been a bustling resort ever since a medieval blacksmith bought up the land holding these wondrous springs. Even earlier, the Roman geographer Pliny the Elder, in the 1st century A.D., might have been referring to these waters when he wrote about a curative spring in the country of the Tungri. The town that grew up around them has watered the likes of Charles II of England, Montaigne, the queen of Sweden, and Czar Peter the Great of Russia. So universally was its name equated with the miracles of thermal springs and mineral waters that the word "spa" is now applied to health and fitness centers of every description.

Essentials

GETTING THERE **Trains** run about hourly to Spa from Liège, but you have to transfer at Pepinster; the ride by the fastest trains takes 54 minutes. **Bus no. 388** to Spa departs regularly from in front of Verviers-Centrale rail station on the main Brussels-Liège-Eupen line; the ride takes 40 minutes. By **car** from Liège, take

A26/E25 southeast to junction 46, then follow the signs for Remouchamps, and from there take N697 east.

VISITOR INFORMATION The **Office du Tourisme** is at place Royale 41, 4900 Spa (© **087/79-53-53;** fax 087/79-53-54; www.spa-info.be), inside the 19th-century Pavillon des Petits-Jeux, in the center of town. The office is open April to September Monday to Friday from 9am to 6pm, and Saturday, Sunday, and holidays from 10am to 6pm; October to March, hours are Monday to Friday from 9am to 5pm, and Saturday, Sunday, and holidays from 10am to 5pm.

SPECIAL EVENTS In July, hundreds of thousands of visitors show up for the **Francofolies de Spa** (© **087/77-63-81;** www.francofolies.be), a 5-day musical celebration of Francophone music of all genres. August sees aficionados of an entirely different kind of noise pour in for the **Belgian Formula One Grand Prix** motor race at the nearby **Circuit de Spa-Francorchamps** (© **087/29-37-00;** www.spa-francorchamps.be), arguably the most scenic racetrack in the world.

What to See & Do

In the 18th and 19th centuries, *curistes* came from all over Europe to take the waters, gamble their money in the casino founded in 1763, and, like Victor Hugo, stroll the forested Promenade des Artistes. Visitors continue to gather in Spa both for the healing treatments and for its lively gaming action at the **Casino de Spa,** rue Royale 4 (© **087/77-20-52;** www.casinodespa.be), in the center of town. The casino is open Monday to Friday from 11am to 4am, and weekends from 11am to 5am.

There was a time when if you were here for the "cures," you would head to the neoclassical ornate mineral baths, the **Bains de Spa** (1863), on place Royale. The building is still there, but now the watery action has moved to the hilltop **Thermes de Spa ★**, Colline d'Annette et Lubin 1 (© **087/77-25-60;** www.thermesdespa.com), which opened in 2006 and can be reached by funicular from a station in the Parc de Sept Heures, close to the tourist office. Spa's ultramodern spa offers just about every kind of water cure, therapy, and relaxation known to man or woman. The spa is open Monday to Thursday and Saturday from 10am to 9pm, Friday from 10am to 10pm, and Sunday from 10am to 8pm. Admission for 3 hours is 17€ for adults (14€ after 5:30pm), 15€ for students and visitors with disabilities, 12€ for children 6 to 14 (younger children are generally not allowed in, though there are mother-and-baby sessions), 27€ for a full day for all visitors, and 39€–55€ for a family.

Another attraction in town is the **Pouhon Pierre le Grand (Peter the Great Spring),** place Pierre le Grand (© **087/79-53-53**), in what was formerly a winter garden and is now a small art gallery. The pavilion (1880) was constructed in the elegant Belle Epoque style, with lots of wrought iron and windows combining to give it a light, airy feel. The pavilion usually hosts small-scale exhibits and is open April to October daily 10am to noon and 1:30 to 5pm; November to March, hours are Monday to Friday from 1:30 to 5pm, weekends from 10am to noon and 1:30 to 5pm.

The diminutive **Lac de Warfaaz,** 2.5km (1½ miles) outside of town at Nivezé, was once a setting for Venetian-style regattas—they must have been very small regattas, considering the size of the lake, which these days is populated by pedal-powered boats that are available to rent.

On Sunday, there's a flea market (8am–2pm) in the wrought-iron Galerie Léopold II arcade, behind the tourist office.

THE ROUTE DES FONTAINES

The Route des Fontaines connects the numerous *fontaines* or *sources* (mineral springs) around Spa, and at some of them you can draw as much water as you like for free (bring your own containers). The water is full of iron and said to be very healthy, but most of it smells remarkably bad. To visit the main springs, pick up a map and brochure from the tourist office or follow this self-guided walking tour, which covers 10km (6 miles).

Go south from place Royale, uphill and into the forest on rue de Barisart, to the **Source de Barisart,** a spring of commercially bottled sparkling Spa water. This hasn't got much in the way of charm, so by all means pass by at a fast clip if time is tight. From here signs point the way on a pathway among the trees to the **Fontaine de la Géronstère,** located in a grotto. Go northeast now, on the long, straight chemin des Fontaines, past the multiple imported tree species of the **Arboretum de Tahanfagne,** to two side-by-side springs, the **Fontaine de la Sauvenière** and the **Fontaine de Groesbeeck.** Then go downhill on avenue Peltzer de Clermont to the **Fontaine du Tonnelet,** on a road that leads back into Spa.

You'll find rustic restaurants or cafes conveniently located about 10 steps from each spring—you'd almost think it had been planned that way (see "Where to Dine," below).

Where to Stay

Best Western L'Auberge This hotel in the center of town opens onto a small square; beyond that is Spa's bustling main street, rue Royale. The guest rooms are furnished in a pastel-toned contemporary style that's relatively uninspired compared with the grand look of the building itself, with its timber frames and casement windows. Tastefully furnished suites include a bedroom, a large living room, a fully equipped kitchen, and a bathroom; each of these can accommodate up to four people. The hotel's ground floor houses a genuine jewel, in its be-mirrored, Belle Epoque–style French-Belgian brasserie.

Place du Monument 3–4, 4900 Spa. ✆ **087/77-48-33.** Fax 087/77-48-40. www.auberge-spa.be. 32 units. 77€–149€ double; 120€–172€ suite. Rates include continental breakfast. AE, DC, MC, V. Parking 8€. **Amenities:** Restaurant. *In room:* TV.

La Heid des Pairs ★ Surrounded by lawns dotted with ancient trees, this villa on the southern edge of Spa was constructed for Baron Nagelmackers, whose family founded the Orient Express. It still feels like a private home. A mixture of period and functional furnishings give the inn a welcoming, homey feel. Fruit and sweets greet you in your room on arrival. Three of the rooms have private balconies; you can elect to have your breakfast served there or on the terrace downstairs.

Av. Professor Henrijean 143, 4900 Spa. ✆ **087/77-43-46.** Fax 087/77-06-44. www.hotellaheid.be. 7 units. 115€–175€ double. Rates include full breakfast. AE, MC, V. Free parking. **Amenities:** Restaurant; lounge; outdoor pool. *In room:* TV, hair dryer.

Where to Dine

Brasserie du Grand Maur ★ FRENCH/BELGIAN A 200-year-old building with creaky wooden floorboards and a cozy, U-shaped dining room is the graceful setting for a variety of seafood and regional dishes. You read the menu from a board that the owners prop beside your table, and you choose from a wide-ranging, well-considered wine list—at prices, though, that can easily double your bill. The *pâté de* *foie gras* (duck-liver pâté) is excellent, as is the *côte d'agneau d'Ecosse* (Scottish side of lamb). There's a small bar where you can enjoy your aperitif and postprandial *pousse-café*. In the summer, you can dine on a garden terrace.

Rue Xhrouet 41 (behind Pouhon Pierre le Grand). ✆ **087/77-36-16.** www.legrandmaur.com. Main courses 18€–20€; fixed-price menus 35€–45€. AE, DC, MC, V. Wed–Sun noon–2pm and 6:30–11pm.

Back in Spa, **La Tonnellerie,** Parc des Sept Heures 1 (✆ **087/77-22-84;** www.latonnellerie.be), in the park just behind the tourist office, is a good place to dine in the open air when the weather is fine.

DINING ALONG THE ROUTE DES FONTAINES

The first spring on the route, the Fontaine de Barisart (see above), has the least interesting eatery, a blocky, cafeteria-style place with all the charm of a missile silo. After that, things pick up. **La Géronstère,** rte. de la Géronstère 119 (✆ **087/77-03-72;** www.lageronstere.com), is a stone farmhouse-style building that stocks good snacks, beside the Fontaine de la Géronstère; farmhouse-style **Le Relais de la Sauvenière,** rue de la Sauvenière 116 (✆ **087/77-42-04;** www.lerelaisdelasauveniere.be), is at the Fontaine de la Sauvenière and the adjacent Fontaine de Groesbeeck; and Italian **La Fontaine du Tonnelet ★**, rte. du Tonnelet 82 (✆ **087/77-26-03**), in a red-and-white pavilion with an interior decorated in the style of a Tuscan villa, is beside the Fontaine du Tonnelet.

LA GLEIZE

14km (9 miles) S of Spa

The main claim to fame of this village—aside from a scenic location in the rugged Ambève River valley—is that it got blown to bits in December 1944 during the Battle of the Bulge. The fighting here was as important to the eventual U.S. victory in the Ardennes as the better-known struggle at Bastogne. La Gleize is on N633, between Trois Ponts and Stoumont.

> **Impressions**
>
> ***No one could say they enjoyed being here during the Battle of the Ardennes. None of us wanted to be here. But we had a job to do. We hope that what happened here will not be forgotten, because we don't want a new generation to go through the same experience.***
>
> **—Battle of the Bulge veteran Don Lassen, 82nd Airborne Division**

Spearheading the entire German offensive, Kampfgruppe Peiper, a powerful battle group from the 1st SS Panzer Division (Leibstandarte Adolf Hitler), under Oberstürmbannführer Joachim Peiper, broke through the thin American front in the Losheim Gap. Peiper's tanks and armored infantry drove west through Stavelot to Trois Ponts, where American engineers blew up the vital bridges over the Amblève in their faces. The battle group was brought to bay at La Gleize, cut off, and pounded relentlessly by artillery. Just 800 of Peiper's 6,000-strong force, minus all their tanks and other heavy weaponry, made it back to German lines.

Musée Décembre 1944 (December 1944 Museum) ★ This museum, in an old presbytery off the main street, focuses on the struggle waged in and around La Gleize by U.S. troops against Kampfgruppe Peiper. Dioramas containing 85 uniformed mannequins representing soldiers from both sides, along with military equipment, photographs, maps, and a short documentary film, illuminate the fierce fighting. A rare German Royal Tiger tank, a shot- and shell-scarred behemoth armed with a high-velocity 88-millimeter cannon, stands guard outside, having been liberated from its original allegiance. Few American weapons could dent a Royal Tiger, far less knock one out, and a close-up view of one gives you an idea why.

Rue de l'Eglise 7. ✆ **080/78-51-91.** www.december44.com. Admission 5€ adults, 3€ children 5–10, free for children 4 and under. Mar to late Nov daily 10am–6pm; late Nov to Feb Sat–Sun, holidays and school vacations 10am–6pm.

THE OSTKANTONE ★★

This rugged frontier—where Belgium meets Holland, Germany, and Luxembourg—is arguably one of the prettiest places in western Europe. The dense pine forests of the Eifel-Ardennes region alternate with rolling hills and deeply gouged river valleys, creating an outdoor playground for ramblers, cyclists, and canoeists. Known as the East Cantons (*Ostkantone* in German; *Cantons de l'Est* in French), this district in the east of Belgium is home to the country's German-speaking minority. Of its population of 100,000, two-thirds speak German and the remainder French. The whole area is sparsely populated and wonderfully scenic, with no end in sight of hills, forests, and streams. Outdoor pursuits are a way of life here.

The entire East Cantons district is a popular vacation zone and has an extensive array of hotels, guesthouses, and campgrounds. Going around by car is the only way that makes sense here. Just a few buses depart daily from key entry points, like the rail stations at Verviers and Eupen, to connect small towns and villages around the district that include Malmedy, Bütgenbach, Sankt-Vith, and Burg Reuland. Except where otherwise stated, all directions are for car travel.

For visitor information about the East Cantons in general, contact **Verkehrsamt der Ostkantone,** Mühlenbachstrasse 2, 4780 Sankt-Vith (✆ **080/22-76-64;** fax 080/22-65-39; www.eastbelgium.com).

Eupen

20km (12 miles) NE of Spa; 34km (21 miles) E of Liège

This handsome little town (pop. 17,000) is the capital of the East Cantons. It houses the German-speaking minority's local parliament, a prime minister, and a German-language television and radio station, and hosts a plethora of restaurants, bars, shops, and even nightlife venues.

ESSENTIALS

GETTING THERE There are hourly **trains** to Eupen from Brussels and Liège, some direct and some involving a transfer at Verviers; the direct train ride from Liège takes 40 minutes. By **car** from Liège, take junction 38 off A3/E40.

VISITOR INFORMATION **Tourist Info Eupen** is at Marktplatz 7, 4700 Eupen (✆ **087/55-34-50;** fax 087/55-66-39; www.eupen-info.be). The office is open Monday to Friday from 9am to 5pm, Saturday from 9am to 3pm, and Sunday (mid-July–Aug) from 9am to 3pm.

WHAT TO SEE & DO

The **Exekutive (Parliament)** of the East Cantons, Klötzerbahn 32 (✆ **087/55-34-50**), is in a handsome patrician mansion dating from 1761; guided tours are free, but you can only make one by prior arrangement. The baroque **Sankt-Nikolaus**

hautes fagnes NATIONAL PARK ★★

Eupen is a gateway to the wide green yonder. Outside the town lies the Hertogenwald Forest, with many marked walking and riding trails. Beyond the forest, in the direction of Malmedy, is Belgium's largest national park, the **Hautes Fagnes Nature Reserve,** a high, boggy fen, or moorland plateau, with unique subalpine flora, fauna, and microclimate. You can access the reserve through Baraque Michel and Mont-Rigi. Parts of the reserve are closed for some weeks in spring due to the breeding season for the endangered *coq de bruyère* (black grouse), and may be closed on occasion in summer due to the increased fire risk. At all times, you must stick to the boardwalks and signposted paths (unless accompanied by an official guide). A hike amid the stark beauty of the Hautes Fagnes (*Hohes Venn* in German) in the dead of winter is a memorable experience—but be aware that the subalpine climate can suddenly change to subarctic, so do this only if you are properly clad and equipped.

For the lowdown on the Hautes Fagnes, visit the **Centre Nature de Botrange** (✆ **080/44-03-00;** www.botrange.be), signposted off the road to Sourbrodt, which documents the reserve's history and ecology. The center is open daily 10am to 6pm. Admission to the center is free; to the museum, it is 3€ for adults, 2.50€ for seniors, 1.20€ for children 6 to 18, and free for children 5 and under.

Close by is the **Signal de Botrange,** a tower that marks the less-than-dizzying highest point in Belgium, 694m (2,277 ft.) above sea level.

Pfarrkirche (Church of St. Nicholas), Marktplatz (✆ **087/74-20-62**), incorporating part of a 14th-century church, dates mainly from 1720 to 1726. Its two bulbous spires from the late 1890s have become symbols of the town, and the Aachen style of the exterior, contrasting with an interior design typical of Liège, reflects Eupen's position on the frontier between the German and the Belgian cities. The church is open daily; admission is free.

WHERE TO STAY

Best Western Ambassador Hotel Bosten ★ On the eastern edge of town, beside the road that leads uphill to the Hertogenwald Forest and the Hautes Fagnes, this family-run hotel boasts a good location. The Weser River very nearly runs through it, and just across the street is a small park with a fountain. The guest rooms are spacious and have twin beds that can be rolled together to make a double; a comfortable sofa or armchair; and a large bathroom with a combined bathtub and shower. Every room has a balcony; ask for one over the river, or if the sound of running water sets off your own waterworks, one looking out on the hills. The warm decor features peach-colored walls and lush floral patterns on the curtains and bedcovers. The hotel's classic French restaurant, **Le Gourmet,** is well regarded.

Haasstrasse 81 (in the Unterstadt/Lower Town), 4700 Eupen. ✆ **087/74-08-00.** Fax 087/74-48-41. www.ambassador-bosten.be. 28 units. 119€–159€ double; 185€ suite. Rates include buffet breakfast. AE, DC, MC, V. Parking 12€. **Amenities:** Restaurant; lounge. *In room:* TV, hair dryer, minibar, Wi-Fi (free).

WHERE TO DINE

Le Mont-Rigi BELGIAN A few miles out of Eupen on the Malmedy road, this stone brasserie-restaurant has one of the finest outdoor terraces imaginable. It looks out over the forest-fringed Fagne de la Poleûr moorland and acts as a sun trap in good weather. The place can get busy with hikers, bikers, and day-trippers, especially on weekends in summer and during the winter ski season, but at other times it can be very quiet, which accounts for an uncertain but early closing time. Meals range from simple snacks of cheese and cold cuts, through the ubiquitous Belgian *steak-frites,* to lavish game dishes in season. In addition to outside, you can eat in either the convivial main area at no-frills wood tables or the formal restaurant section.

Rte. de Botrange 135, Mont-Rigi (at Hautes Fagnes Nature Reserve). ✆ **080/44-48-44.** www.mont-rigi.be. Main courses 11€–19€; *menu du jour* 9.95€–21€. MC, V. Tues–Sun 10am–8 or 9pm.

Robertville

20km (12 miles) S of Eupen; 18km (11 miles) E of Spa

Beyond the Hautes Fagnes, in the direction of the German border, is **Lac de Robertville,** a 62-hectare (153-acre) lake outside Robertville village that's a popular area for swimming and watersports in summer.

Burg Reinhardstein (Castle Reinhardstein) ★ This is the very image of a fairy-tale castle, a little more homey than formidable in appearance. Nevertheless, its battlemented towers stand on a rugged rocky outcrop overlooking a forest and a plunging stream. After having tumbled into near ruin, it was saved from total destruction by a Belgian castle enthusiast, the late professor Jean Overloop, and fully restored. Now you can tour its towers and chambers in the company of guides who have inherited Overloop's love for the place.

Chemin du Cheneux 50, Ovifat (signposted from the village). ✆ **080/44-68-68.** www.reinhardstein.net. Admission (guided tours only) 6€ adults, 4.80€ seniors and children 6–16, free for children 5 and under. July–Aug Mon–Fri 2:30 and 4pm; Sat–Sun 11:15am and 2:30 and 4pm.

WHERE TO STAY & DINE

Hôtel des Bains ★★ On the shores of Lac de Robertville, near the Hautes Fagnes Nature Reserve, the rooms here are notable for a chic country style that sets a relaxing tone to complement the rural location and the hotel's wellness philosophy. The hotel restaurant's classic French cuisine is served with a delicate touch. Pike from the lake comes poached and served on lettuce with a white butter sauce—*the* choice when it's available. Strolls along the lake shore are complemented by the hotel's own wellness spa, which features hydromassage, Nordic sauna and Moroccan hammam, balneotherapy, massage, and more.

Haelen 2, 4950 Robertville. ✆ **080/67-95-71.** Fax 080/67-81-43. www.hoteldesbains.be. 13 units. 145€–210€ double; 230€–260€ suite. Rates include buffet breakfast. AE, DC, MC, V. Free parking. A short way from Spa on E5 to junction A27, signposted MALMEDY-WAIMES. **Amenities:** Restaurant; lounge; heated indoor pool; spa; Wi-Fi (free). *In room:* TV, hair dryer, minibar.

Bütgenbach

10km (6 miles) SE of Robertville; 28km (17 miles) SE of Eupen

You could easily drive right through this pleasant but otherwise unremarkable village without noticing it much, even though it's at the heart of a popular vacation zone. Tourist information is available from **Tourismus Bütgenbach,** Klosterstrasse 1, 4750 Bütgenbach (✆ **080/86-47-23;** fax 080/86-47-24; www.butgenbach.be), on the village's northern edge.

Worth looking out for are signs pointing to **Sport- und Freizeitzentrum Worriken** (✆ **080/44-69-61;** www.worriken.be), a bustling sport and leisure center on the shore of **Stausee Bütgenbach,** a manmade lake set amid hills and forests on the village's eastern edge. Worriken's multitude of active offerings includes sailboating (on tiny sailboats), windsurfing, kayaking, swimming, and mountain-biking, along with a gamut of indoor sports for when the weather is poor, and a special program for kids. Among the amenities around the lakeshore are camping and trailer sites, and timber vacation chalets to rent (from the center's office). A self-service restaurant serves tolerable eats and has outdoor dining on a balcony overlooking the lake.

From Bütgenbach, N632 runs southeast for 13km (8 miles) through Büllingen to the German border at Losheimergraben.

WHERE TO STAY & DINE

There are 10 hotels and pensions in Bütgenbach and 10 more just up the road in Büllingen, along with multiple bed-and-breakfast options in the surrounding area. Many of the hotels have more-than-decent restaurants, and there are eateries ranging from plain to gourmet throughout the area.

PLANNING YOUR TRIP TO HOLLAND

12

I can just about guarantee that your trip to Holland will go well (legal eagles please note that "just about"). Of the three Benelux lands, the Netherlands is likely to be the most familiar-seeming to a visitor from the English-speaking world. But it's still a foreign country, which is why you want to go there, isn't it? A few hints on how to plan and navigate your visit can't hurt, so peruse this chapter for some practicalities.

For information that covers planning and tips for the Benelux countries in general, see chapter 3.

THE REGIONS IN BRIEF

The Netherlands might be a small country, but it boasts one of Europe's most memorable cities: Amsterdam. Around Amsterdam, the old and historic province of Holland, now divided into separate northern and southern provinces, is the economic powerhouse of the nation, and its most heavily populated region. Beyond these are three more or less natural divisions—the northern, central, and southern Netherlands.

AMSTERDAM The national capital—easygoing, prosperous, full of canals, bridges, and museums—is the natural focus of a visit to Holland. Few skyscrapers mar the clarity of the sky, and locals mostly walk or ride bicycles from place to place. The historic center of town recalls Amsterdam's 17th-century Golden Age, when it was the command post of a vast trading network and colonial empire, and wealthy merchants constructed gabled residences along neatly laid-out canals. A delicious irony is that some of the placid old structures now host brothels, smoke shops, and extravagant nightlife.

NOORD-HOLLAND You can think of North Holland province as Amsterdam's environs, because anywhere in the province is within easy reach of the capital. **Haarlem** is a graceful town of winding canals and medieval neighborhoods that hold several fine museums. A visit to the windmill-speckled, tradition-rich village of **Zaanse Schans,** on the banks of the Zaan River, makes a great short excursion. Among many other options, you can make day trips to brash **Zandvoort** or a bunch of other

Holland

0
30 mi
0
30 km
NORTH SEA
WADDEN ISLANDS
Norderney
Juist
Borkum
GERMANY
Schiermonnikoog
Ameland
Terschelling
Vlieland
Texel
Waddenzee
Delfzijl
GRONINGEN
Groningen
Leeuwarden
Harlingen
FRIESLAND
Drachten
E22
E232
A28
Den Burg
Afsluitdijk
E22
Sneek
A7
A7
Makkum
Appelscha
Assen
Den Helder
Hindeloopen
Stavoren
DRENTHE
NOORD-HOLLAND
IJsselmeer
Bergen
Medemblik
Emmen
Emmeloord
Meppel
Hoogeveen
Enkhuizen
Urk
Alkmaar
Hoorn
Markerwaarddijk
A28
Zaandijk
Purmerend
Hardenberg
Zaanse Schans
Edam
IJmuiden
Zaandam
Volendam
Lelystad
Kampen
Broek in Waterland
Marken
Monnickendam
E232
Zwolle
Zandvoort
Haarlem
Amsterdam
FLEVOLAND
A28
OVERIJSSEL
Muiden

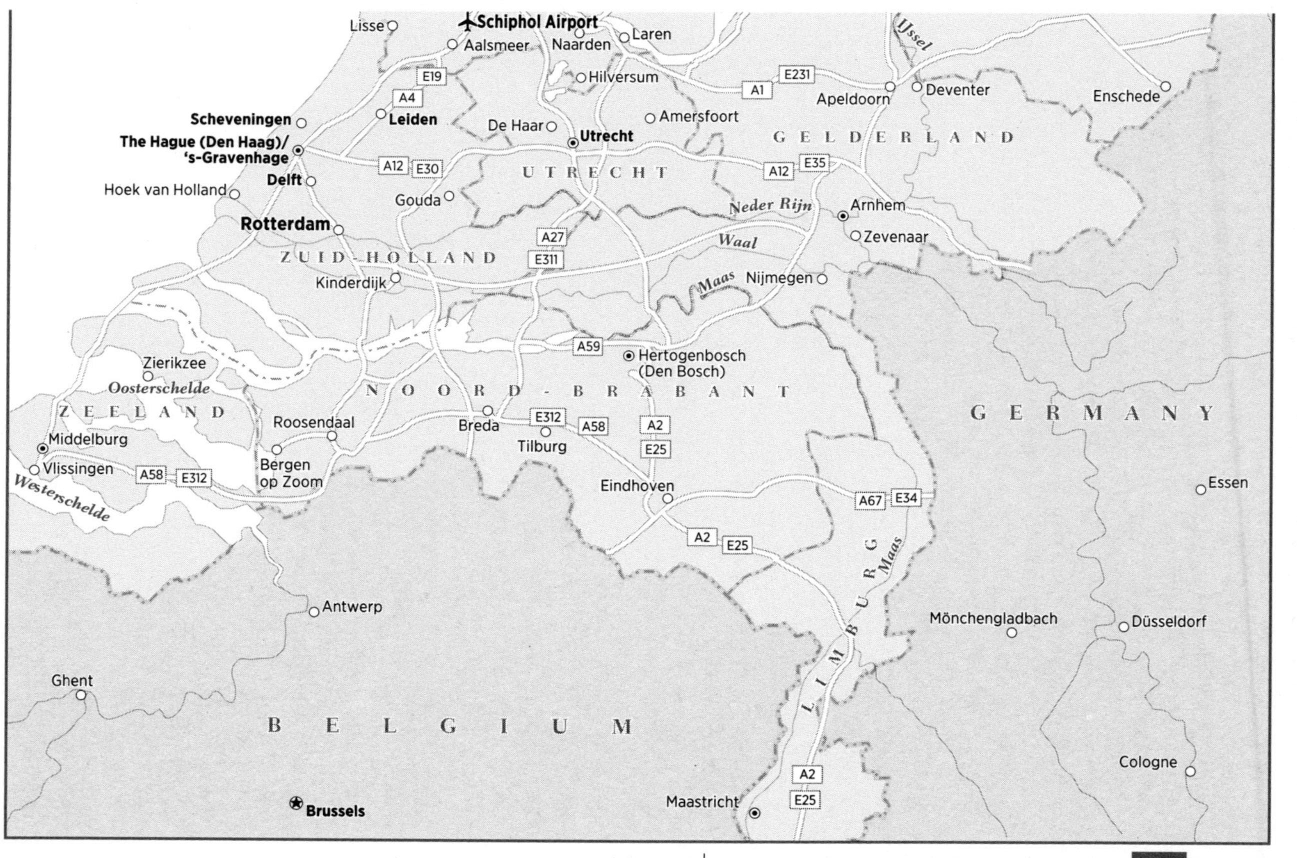
Schiphol Airport
Lisse
Aalsmeer
Naarden
Laren
Hilversum
Amersfoort
De Haar
Utrecht
Leiden
Scheveningen
The Hague (Den Haag)/
's-Gravenhage
Delft
Hoek van Holland
Gouda
Rotterdam
Kinderdijk
Apeldoorn
Deventer
Enschede
IJssel
GELDERLAND
UTRECHT
ZUID-HOLLAND
Neder Rijn
Waal
Maas
Arnhem
Zevenaar
Nijmegen
Hertogenbosch
(Den Bosch)
NOORD-BRABANT
Zierikzee
Oosterschelde
ZEELAND
Middelburg
Vlissingen
Westerschelde
Roosendaal
Bergen
op Zoom
Breda
Tilburg
Eindhoven
LIMBURG
Maastricht
GERMANY
Essen
Mönchengladbach
Düsseldorf
Cologne
BELGIUM
Antwerp
Ghent
Brussels
E19
A4
A12
E30
A1
E231
E35
A27
E311
A59
E312
A58
A2
E25
A67
E34

resorts on the North Sea coast, and to traditional IJsselmeer lakeside towns and villages such as **Volendam, Marken, Edam,** and **Hoorn.** Farther out, hop a ferry from Den Helder across to **Texel,** the closest of the Wadden Islands.

ZUID-HOLLAND South Holland province contains an awesome amount of interest for visitors. Starting with the seat of government, **The Hague,** a graceful city separated from the North Sea only by its seacoast resort of **Scheveningen,** is far more than politics. Similarly, leading-edge **Rotterdam,** which sits on the delta where the Rhine, Maas, and Waal rivers meet the North Sea, is far more than a great port. **Delft** is the town of the famous blue-and-white porcelain, the cradle of the Dutch Republic, the traditional burial place of the royal family, and the birthplace and inspiration of the 17th-century master of light and subtle emotion, painter Jan Vermeer. Famous for its associations with the Pilgrims who founded the Plymouth colony in present-day Massachusetts, **Leiden** was the birthplace of the Dutch tulip trade and of Rembrandt, and it's home to the oldest university in the country. **Gouda** is renowned for its cheese.

FRIESLAND, GRONINGEN & DRENTHE Every one of the three sparsely populated northern provinces has a different character. With its own language, traditions, and national history, lake-filled Friesland is a vacation area par excellence, particularly on its string of sea islands. Groningen has its bustling university city of the same name, and Drenthe, Holland's "Green Province," is dotted with prehistoric monuments.

UTRECHT, GELDERLAND, OVERIJSSEL & FLEVOLAND Stretching through the heartland, the four central provinces encompass a variety of scenery. Three great rivers—the **Rhine, Maas,** and **Waal**—flow through here. If it wasn't for the forests in Gelderland and Utrecht, most of Holland would consist of the flat green fields dotted with farmhouses so often depicted on the canvases of Dutch Masters. Overijssel is barely touched by tourism, and Flevoland, built on land reclaimed from the **IJsselmeer Lake** (the former Zuiderzee), has existed as a province only since 1986.

ZEELAND, NOORD-BRABANT & LIMBURG These three provinces consider themselves the Burgundian part of the Netherlands, packed to their borders with southern charm. Coastal Zeeland, the part of Holland most threatened by the sea, is protected by the **Delta Works.** These massive dams and barriers also shelter many coastal resorts (and seafood restaurants). Noord-Brabant has most of the marshy **Biesbosch National Park** on its territory, as well as the city of **Eindhoven,** home base of the giant Philips electronics corporation. **Maastricht,** a city many Dutch consider the country's second liveliest (after Amsterdam), and the country's highest "mountain"—a peak that ascends a whole 321m (1,053 ft.)—are both in the southeast province of Limburg.

Visitor Information

For contact details of the Netherlands tourist offices in the United States, Britain, and other countries, see "Visitor Information" under "Fast Facts: Holland," in chapter 21.

WHEN TO GO

"In season" in Holland means from mid-April to mid-October. The peak of the tourist season is July and August, when the weather is at its finest. But the weather here is never really extreme, and you'll find Holland every bit as attractive during shoulder- and off-season months. Not only are airlines, hotels, and restaurants cheaper and less crowded during this time (with more relaxed and personalized service), but some appealing events are going on. Case in point: Holland's bulb fields burst with color from mid-April to mid-May.

Climate

Holland has a maritime climate. Summer temperatures average about 67°F (19°C); the winter average is 35°F (2°C). Winters, moderated a touch by the North Sea, are often rainy (it's driest Feb–May). Throughout the year, you can expect some rain.

July and August are the best months to soak up rays on a sidewalk cafe terrace, dine at an outdoor restaurant in the evening, and head for the beach. September usually has a few weeks of fine late-summer weather; and there are even sunny spells in winter, when brilliant, crisp weather alternates with clouded skies.

Although the temperature doesn't always linger long below freezing in winter, remember that much of Holland is below sea level, making fog, mist, and dampness your too-frequent companions. This damp chill often seems to cut through to your very bones, so you'll want to layer yourself in Gore-Tex or something similar in the colder months. In northern provinces like Friesland, if the temperature falls far enough, canals, rivers, and lakes might freeze to become sparkling highways and playgrounds for ice skaters; the farther south you go, the less chance there is of this happening.

The Euro

Holland's currency is the euro (see "Money & Costs," in chapter 3).

To prepare for Holland's unpredictable weather, invest in a fold-up umbrella; likewise, carry a raincoat (with a wool liner for winter), pack a sweater or two (even in July), and be prepared to layer your clothing any time of year. Don't worry: You're allowed to leave space for T-shirts, skimpy tops, and sneakers.

For weather information once inside Holland, call ✆ **0900/8003.** Or visit the Royal Netherlands Meteorological Institute website **www.knmi.nl** and click the English link.

Amsterdam's Average Monthly Temperature & Days of Rain

	JAN	FEB	MAR	APR	MAY	JUNE	JULY	AUG	SEPT	OCT	NOV	DEC
TEMP. (°F)	38	37	43	47	54	59	62	62	58	51	44	40
TEMP. (°C)	3	3	6	8	12	15	17	17	14	11	7	4
DAYS OF RAIN	21	17	19	20	19	17	20	20	19	20	22	23

Holidays

Public holidays in Holland are January 1 (New Year); Good Friday; Easter Sunday and Monday; April 30 (Koninginnedag/Queen's Day); Ascension; Pentecost Sunday and Monday; and December 25 (Christmas) and December 26. The dates for Easter, Ascension, and Pentecost change each year.

In addition, there are two Remembrance Days related to World War II, neither of which is an official holiday, though you may find some stores closed: May 4, Herdenkingsdag (Memorial Day), honors all those who died in the war; and May 5 celebrates Bevrijdingsdag (Liberation Day).

Holland Calendar Of Events

Impressions

We can walk on water and see the lands we made with our own hands.
—Historian Herman Pleij (on skating frozen waterways in winter), *National Geographic,* Jan 1998

For an exhaustive list of events beyond those listed here, check http://events.frommers.com, where you'll find a searchable, up-to-the-minute roster of what's happening in cities all over the world. The website of the **Netherlands Board of Tourism & Conventions** (www.holland.com) has more information.

One of Holland's most eagerly anticipated events is the Elfstedentocht, the 11-cities race, in which skaters compete over a 200km (124-mile) course through Friesland. The first race was run in 1909, and it has been run only 15 times, most recently in 1997. If the conditions allow the race to go ahead when you are visiting, it's well worth going out of your way to watch—or even to take part. Keep a weather eye on the Fryslân Marketing website (www.beleeffriesland.nl).

JANUARY

New Year. This celebration is wild and not always wonderful. Youthful spirits celebrate the New Year with firecrackers, which they throw at the feet of passersby. This keeps hospital emergency rooms busy. January 1.

International Film Festival Rotterdam. More than 300 indie films are screened at theaters around town. Contact ✆ **010/890-9090** or www.filmfestivalrotterdam.com. January 26 to February 6, 2011; similar dates in 2012.

FEBRUARY

Carnival, Maastricht ★ and Den Bosch ('s-Hertogenbosch). Contact **VVV Maastricht** (✆ **043/325-2121;** www.vvvmaastricht.eu) and **VVV Meierei & Noordoost-Brabant** (✆ **0900/112-2334;** www.vvvdenbosch.nl). Seven weeks before Easter.

ABN AMRO World Tennis Tournament, Rotterdam. The world's top male tennis players converge on the port city for this ATP Tour event. Contact **Ahoy** (✆ **0900/235-2469;** www.ahoy.nl), or go to www.abnamrowtt.nl. February 7 to 13, 2011; similar dates in 2012.

MARCH

Windmill Days, Zaanse Schans. All five working windmills (out of eight windmills in total) are open to the public at this recreated old village and open-air museum in the Zanstreek, just north of Amsterdam. Contact **Zaans Museum** (✆ **075/681-0000;** www.zaansmuseum.nl). March to October.

The European Fine Art Fair, Maastricht. Top-rated international art and antiques fair at the Maastricht Exhibition and Congress Center (MECC). Dealers from around the world present their finest objects. Contact ✆ **0411/645-090** or www.tefaf.com. March 18 to 27, 2011; similar dates in 2012.

Opening of Keukenhof Gardens ★★, Lisse. The greatest flower show on earth blooms with a spectacular display of tulips and narcissi, daffodils and hyacinths, bluebells, crocuses, lilies, amaryllis, and many other flowers at this 32-hectare (79-acre) garden in the heart of the bulb country. There's said to be nearly eight million flowers. Contact **Keukenhof** (✆ **0252/465-555;** www.keukenhof.nl). March 24 to May 20, 2011; similar dates in 2012.

APRIL

Museumweekend. A weekend during which most museums in the Netherlands offer free or reduced admission and have special exhibits. Contact **Museumweekend** (✆ **020/551-2932;** www.museumweekend.nl). April 2 and 3, 2011; April 14 and 15, 2012.

Bloemencorso van de Bollenstreek (Bulb District Flower Parade). Floats keyed to a different floral theme each year parade from Noordwijk, through Sassenheim, Lisse, and Bennebroek, to Haarlem. Contact **Bloemencorso Bollenstreek** (✆ **0252/428-237;** www.bloemencorso-bollenstreek.nl). April 16, 2011; April 21, 2012.

Koninginnedag (Queen's Day) ★★★. Countrywide celebration honoring the queen's official birthday, with parades, street fairs, and street entertainment. Throughout Holland, but best in Amsterdam. April 30.

MAY

Herdenkingsdag (Memorial Day). Countrywide observance for victims of World War II, principally marked by 2 minutes of silence at 8pm. May 4.

Bevrijdingsdag (Liberation Day). Commemorates the end of World War II and Holland's liberation from Nazi occupation. Throughout the country, but best in Amsterdam. May 5.

National Windmill Days. Around two-thirds of the country's almost 1,000 working windmills spin their sails and are open to the public. Contact **De Hollandsche Molen** (✆ **020/623-8703;** www.molens.nl). Second weekend in May: May 14–15, 2011; May 12–13, 2012.

JUNE

Holland Festival, Amsterdam, The Hague, Rotterdam, and Utrecht. Every year, these four cities join forces to present a cultural buffet of music, opera, theater, film, and dance. The schedule includes all the major Dutch companies and visiting companies and soloists. Contact **Holland Festival** (✆ **020/788-2100;** www.hollandfestival.nl). Throughout June.

Vlaggetjesdag (Flag Day), Scheveningen. The fishing fleet opens the herring season with a race to bring the first *Hollandse Nieuwe* herring back to port (the first barrel is auctioned for charity). Contact **Stichting Vlaggetjesdag Scheveningen** (✆ **070/345-3267;** www.vlaggetjesdag.com). June 11, 2011 (unconfirmed, due to a possible conflict of events; check website); June 9, 2012.

Fietselfstedentocht (11 Cities Bicycle Tour), Friesland. The bicycling version of the Elfstedentocht ice-skating race through Friesland province (see introduction to the "Holland Calendar of Events," above), is based on the idea that roads and bikes are more reliable than frozen canals and skates. Contact **Friese Elfsteden Rijwieltocht** (✆ **0515/573-263;** www.11steden.nl). June 13, 2011; similar date in 2012.

Oerol. Open-air performances by international theater companies on the island of Terschelling. Contact **Oerol** (✆ **0562/448-448;** www.oerol.nl). June 17 to 26, 2011; June 15 to 24, 2012.

Amsterdam Roots Festival, various venues. This festival features music and dance from around the world, along with workshops, films, and exhibits. One part is the open-air **Oosterpark Festival,** a multicultural feast of song and dance held at Oosterpark in Amsterdam-Oost (East). Contact **Amsterdam Roots Festival** (✆ **020/531-8181;** www.amsterdamroots.nl). June 16 to June 19, 2011; similar dates in 2012.

Open Gardens Days. If you wonder what the fancy gardens behind the gables of some of Amsterdam's houses-turned-museums look like, this is your chance to find out. Some of the best are open to the public for 3 days. Contact **Grachten Musea** (✆ **020/320-3660;** www.grachtenmusea.nl). Third week in June.

JULY

Over Het IJ Festival. Performers stage avant-garde theater, music, and dance in Amsterdam-Noord, beside the IJ channel, at the old NDSM Wharf, TT Neveritaweg 15. Contact **Over Het IJ Festival** (✆ **010/415-9666;** www.overhetij.nl). July 7 to July 17, 2011; July 5 to July 15, 2012

North Sea Jazz Festival ★★, Ahoy, Rotterdam. One of the world's leading gatherings of top international jazz and blues musicians unfolds over 3 concert-packed days at the city's giant Ahoy venue. Last-minute tickets are scarce, so book as far ahead as possible. Contact **North Sea Jazz Festival** (✆ **015/214-8393**; www.northsea jazz.com). July 8 to 10, 2011; similar dates in 2012.

Skûtsjesilen, the Frisian Lakes and the IJsselmeer. Sailing races feature *skûtsjes,* traditional Frisian sailing ships. Go to the websites of **Fryslân Marketing** (www.beleeffriesland.nl) and **Sintrale Kommisje Skûtsjesilen** (www.skutsjesilen.nl). July 30 to August 8, 2011; similar dates in 2012.

AUGUST

Amsterdam Gay Pride ★. This is a big event in Europe's most gay-friendly city. A crowd of as many as 150,000 people turns out to watch the Boat Parade's display of 100 or so outrageously decorated boats cruising the canals. In addition, there are street discos, open-air theater, a sports program, and a film festival. Contact **Amsterdam Gay Pride** (www.amsterdamgaypride.nl). August 4 to 7, 2011 (Canal Parade Aug 7); similar dates in 2012.

Grachten Festival (Canal Festival) ★★. A 5-day festival of classical music, on a different theme each year, plays at intimate and elegant venues along the city's canals and at the Muiziekgebouw aan 't IJ. There's always a performance or two for children. The festival culminates in the exuberant **Prinsengracht Concert,** which plays on a pontoon in front of the Hotel Pulitzer. Contact **Stichting Grachtenfestival** (✆ **020/421-4542;** www.grachtenfestival.nl). August 13 to 21, 2011; similar dates in 2012.

Festival Oude Muziek (Festival of Early Music), Utrecht. Concerts of music from the Middle Ages to the Romantic era. Contact **Organisatie Oude Muziek** (✆ **030/232-9000;** www.oudemuziek.nl). August 26 to September 4, 2011; similar dates in 2012.

Uitmarkt. Amsterdam previews its cultural season with this open market of information and free performances at outdoor venues, theaters, and concert halls. The shows run the gamut of music, opera, dance, theater, and cabaret. Go to the website of **Uitmarkt** (www.uitmarkt.nl). Usually the last weekend in August, but dates are not confirmed until the preceding March.

SEPTEMBER

Open Monumentendag (Open Monument Day). A chance to see historic buildings and monuments around the country that usually are not open to the public, and to get in free. Contact **Vereniging Open Monumentendag** (✆ **020/422-2118;** www.openmonumentendag.nl). Second Saturday and Sunday: September 12 and 13, 2011; September 11 and 12, 2012.

State Opening of Parliament ★, The Hague. On Prinsjesdag (Princes' Day), Queen Beatrix rides in a splendid gold coach to the Knights' Hall in the Hague to open the legislative session by delivering the Speech from the Throne. Contact **VVV Den Haag** (✆ **070/361-8860;** www.denhaag.nl). Third Tuesday in September: September 20, 2011; September 18, 2012.

OCTOBER

Leidens Ontzet (Relief of Leiden). Procession commemorating the anniversary of the raising of the 1574 Spanish siege of Leiden. *Haring en witte brood* (herring and white bread) are distributed, just as the piratelike band of "Sea Beggars" did after helping drive the Spaniards away. Contact **VVV Leiden** (✆ **071/516-6000;** www.vvvleiden.nl). October 3 (Oct 4 when the 3rd is a Sun).

Leather Pride is a growing happening of parties and other events for gays who are into a leather lifestyle. Contact **Leather Pride Nederland** (✆ **020/422-3737;** www.get-ruff.com). Last weekend (Thurs–Sun) of October.

NOVEMBER

Horti Fair, Amsterdam. The largest exhibit of flowers, plants, and accessories in the Netherlands takes place at the RAI convention center. Contact **Horti Fair** (✆ **0297/344-033;** www.hortifair.nl). November 1 to 4, 2011; similar dates in 2012.

Crossing Border, The Hague. Literature, poetry, and music are combined in this 5-day festival. Contact **Crossing Border** (✆ **070/346-2355;** www.crossingborder.nl). Mid-November.

Sinterklaas Arrives. Holland's Santa Claus (St. Nicholas) launches the Christmas season when he arrives in Holland from Spain, accompanied by black-painted assistants, called Zwarte Piet (Black Peter), who hand out candy to kids. During the next 2 weeks, he makes his way to towns across the land. Contact local tourist offices. Third Saturday in November: November 19, 2011; November 17, 2012. He arrives the next day in Amsterdam.

Shopping Around for a Tax Break

If you live outside the European Union (E.U.), you're entitled to a refund of part of the value-added tax *(BTW/omzetbelasting)* on goods purchased in the Netherlands for personal use and totaling 50€ or more per shop in a day. Savings of up to 18% of the purchase price can be garnered. Your purchases need to be made at a store that subscribes to the refund system, identified by a TAX FREE sticker, and exported in your hand baggage or checked baggage.

To obtain the refund, ask the store for a refund cheque (or check). When you leave the E.U., present this check along with your purchases and receipts to Customs. They'll stamp the check, and you can get the refund in cash or paid to your credit card at a Refund Office. Schiphol Airport has two such locations: Global Refund in Departures Lounge 3, and ABN-AMRO in Departures Lounge 2.

A Europe-wide list of refund offices, and more information on tax-free shopping, are available from Global Refund (✆ 421-232/111-111; www.globalrefund.com). Local toll-free phone numbers and an e-mail address for inquiries can be found on the website. For a cut of your savings, VATfree.nl (✆ 084/836-7640) will handle the bureaucratic details.

DECEMBER

Winterland Maastricht. For the city's annual Christmas Market, stands selling seasonal trinkets, traditional craft items, and food and drink, alongside a nativity crib with live animals and an ice-skating rink, are all set up on the beautiful Vrijthof square. Every day there are performances by choirs and traditional bands, and Father Christmas hands out presents for the children. Contact **VVV Maastricht** (✆ **043/325-2121;** www.vvv-maastricht.eu). Throughout the month, daily from 10am to 10pm.

Sinterklaas. St. Nicholas's Eve is the traditional day in Holland for exchanging Christmas gifts. Join some Dutch friends or a Dutch family if possible. December 5.

Gouda bij Kaarslicht (Gouda by Candlelight) ★. In the evening, all the electric lights are turned off around the Markt, and Gouda's main square, the 15th-century town hall, and a giant Christmas tree are all lit up by 1,500 candles. Contact **VVV Gouda** (✆ **0900/468-3288;** www.vvvgouda.nl). Second Tuesday in December.

GETTING THERE & GETTING AROUND

Getting There

All intercontinental and virtually all intra-European flights to Holland arrive at Amsterdam's Schiphol Airport. A few short-haul services fly to Rotterdam, Eindhoven, Maastricht, Groningen, and Enschede.

Car ferries sail from Britain to the Dutch ports of IJmuiden, Rotterdam Europoort, and Hoek van Holland (Hook of Holland). High-speed trains zip in from Paris, Brussels, Cologne, and Düsseldorf to Amsterdam, Rotterdam, and The Hague, and "ordinary" international trains arrive from around Europe. Eurolines operates bus service from many European cities, and there are multiple expressways/motorways from Belgium and Germany.

For more details, see "Getting There & Around," in chapter 3.

Getting Around

Holland is a great place for sightseeing because it's so compact. Whether you choose to drive or use the excellent Dutch public transportation, getting around is relatively easy. Roads and expressways are excellent, and the rail network is one of Europe's finest.

Schedule and fare information about travel by train and other public transportation (*openbaar vervoer*) in the Netherlands is available by calling ✆ **0900/9292,** or visiting **www.9292ov.nl**. For international trains, call ✆ **0900/9296.**

CARDS & FARES

From 2011, or thereabouts, all public transportation in the Netherlands should be using an electronic stored-value card called the **OV-chipkaart.** This card replaces the old system of tickets, "strip cards," and fare zones. "OV" are the initials for *openbaar vervoer,* which is Dutch for public transportation. Three main types of OV-chipkaart are available: reloadable "personal" cards that can be used only by their pictured owner; reloadable "anonymous" cards that can be used by anyone; and non-reloadable "throwaway" cards.

The personal and anonymous cards, both valid for 5 years, cost 7.50€ and can be loaded and reloaded with up to 30€. Throwaway cards, which are likely to be the card of choice for short-term visitors, cost 2.50€ for one ride and 4.80€ for two rides. Electronic readers on Metro and train station platforms, and onboard trams and buses, deduct the correct fare; just hold your card up against the reader at both the start and the end of the ride. Reduced-rate cards are available for seniors and children 4 to 11; children 3 and under ride free.

Purchase cards from the local transit company's offices and ticket booths in the big cities, from Netherlands Railways booths in train stations, from automats at Metro and train stations, and from automats onboard some trams. Not every kind of card is available from each of these sources. Note that the cards are valid throughout the Netherlands, no matter where you purchase them.

BY TRAIN

All major tourist destinations in Holland are within 2½ hours of Amsterdam via **Nederlandse Spoorwegen/NS** (✆ **0900/9292;** www.ns.nl), Holland's national rail system. Generally clean and on time, Netherlands Railways trains are a good way to travel with the Dutch, who use them even for short journeys to the next town up the line. In addition to Amsterdam, other destinations easily reached by train for anyone arriving at Amsterdam's Schiphol Airport include The Hague (35 min.), Rotterdam (27 min. by high-speed Fyra train, and 45 min. by ordinary InterCity train), and Utrecht (33 min.).

An improved **Thalys** and a new **Fyra** high-speed train service, operating on a high-speed rail line that entered service in 2009, has significantly reduced the travel time

One Day at a Time

A better bet than the OV-chipkaart for short-term visitors who plan to use public transportation a lot may be the 1-day or multi-day cards issued by many local public transportation authorities, including those in Amsterdam, Rotterdam, and The Hague. With these cards, you pay only once and you can hog trams, buses, and Metro trains all day long if you want to.

between Paris, Brussels, Rotterdam, The Hague, and Amsterdam. Fast InterCity trains and the slow *stoptrein* (stop train) handle the rail network's bread-and-butter services.

Dutch trains run so often that you can just go to the station and wait for the next one—your wait will be short. At even the smallest stations, there is half-hour service in both directions, and major destination points have between four and eight trains an hour in both directions. Service begins as early as 5am (slightly later on Sun and holidays) and runs until around 1am. A special night-train service operates between Utrecht and Rotterdam, via Amsterdam, Schiphol, Leiden, and The Hague.

If all or most of your travel will be by rail, consider purchasing a discounted ***weekendretour*** (weekend round-trip) ticket, or a ***dagkaart*** (day card) or ***5-dagkaart*** (5-day card). The two card options have **"OV"** variants that permit the use of other public transportation modes, such as the tram, bus, and Metro, for an additional charge. A 1-day ***Railrunner*** unlimited travel pass can be purchased for children 4 to 11 (up to a maximum three children per adult 20 and older) for 2.50€ per child (children 3 and under ride free).

These various tickets and cards can be purchased only from train stations in Holland. You can get most tickets from in-station automats (ticket machines); tickets purchased from the station ticket counters cost 0.50€ per ticket over the automat price.

Note: Tickets cannot be purchased onboard Dutch trains. The fine for riding a train without a valid ticket is 35€, plus the fare.

BY BUS

Most regional service is slow because buses stop at so many places en route, and you may have to change at an intermediate town or city on the way. Traveling by train is faster, but it is possible to travel long distances using the bus, and most regional bus companies have express lines between important destinations. Regional and intercity bus service is operated by **Connexxion** (✆ **0900/266-6399;** www.connexxion.nl); **Arriva** (✆ **0900/202-2022;** www.arriva.nl); **Veolia** (✆ **088/076-1000;** www.veolia-transport.nl); and **Qbuzz** (✆ **0900/728-9965;** www.qbuzz.nl).

BY CAR

Driving in Holland is easy—except in the cities and towns where traffic congestion can be ulcer-inducing. Outside of these, *snelwegen* (expressways/motorways) and local roads are excellent; they're well planned (as you'd expect from the efficient Dutch), well maintained, and well signposted. However, they are often jam-packed with traffic, particularly during the twice-daily rush hours, so avoid these times if possible.

Surprisingly enough, the biggest problem on the roads is other drivers: Many Dutch cast off their usual social skills and conscience when they get behind the wheel of a vehicle and become as bad tempered, erratic, and downright dangerous as, well, as the Belgians, whose roadway recklessness is infamous.

In all the big cities—not just Amsterdam, The Hague, and Rotterdam—tight restrictions on parking and vigorous enforcement of the rules make using public transportation a better option than going by car.

RENTALS Rental cars are available from **Avis** (✆ **800/331-2112** in the U.S., or ✆ 0900/235-2847 in Holland; www.avis.nl); **Budget** (✆ **0900/1576;** www.budget.nl); **Europcar** (✆ **0900/0540;** www.europcar.nl); and **Hertz** (✆ **800/654-3001**

in the U.S., or © 020/201-3512 in Holland; www.hertz.nl). All four companies have desks at Amsterdam's Schiphol Airport, and rental offices (or agencies) in Rotterdam, The Hague, Utrecht, Maastricht, and other towns and cities. Rates begin at around 50€ a day for a no-frills, subcompact auto with a stick shift and unlimited mileage. You pay as much as 200€ a day for a fully equipped luxury car like a BMW.

DRIVING RULES To drive in the Netherlands, you need only a valid passport, a driver's license, and registration for the car you drive. The minimum age for drivers is 18. The speed limit is 120kmph (75 mph) on expressways, 100kmph (62 mph) on some marked stretches of expressway near cities, 50kmph (31 mph) in cities and urban areas, and 80kmph (50 mph) in the outskirts of towns and cities. Lower limits might be posted. Traffic approaching from the right has the right of way, unless the road you are on has signposts with an orange diamond. Pedestrians on the crosswalks always have the right of way. Watch out for bicycle riders, who are vulnerable road users but don't always act like it.

ROAD MAPS Adequate road maps for Holland and street maps for major cities are available from local VVV tourist information offices. Road maps are published by the **ANWB** and **KNAC** motoring organizations, and by various private concerns—among them the excellent Michelin map nos. 210 and 211, which cover the country and are available from bookstores and some news vendors.

BREAKDOWNS/ASSISTANCE If you're a member of a national automobile club, like the American Automobile Association, you're automatically entitled to the services of **ANWB.** This organization sponsors a fleet of yellow Wegenwacht vans (© **088/269-2888;** www.anwb.nl), a sort of repair shop on wheels that you see patrolling the highways. There are special yellow call boxes on all major roads to bring them to your assistance. Emergency call boxes marked POLITIE will bring the police.

BY PLANE

Holland is too small to permit financially viable scheduled air service between the airports of Amsterdam Schiphol, Rotterdam The Hague, Eindhoven, Maastricht Aachen, Groningen, and Enschede, and there is no such service. In any case, you get around quicker by train or car.

BY BICYCLE

Holland has 16 million people and 11 million bicycles. To fully engage in the Dutch experience, you must climb aboard a pedal-bike and head out into the wide green yonder. Local tourist offices have marked out many biking tour routes and publish descriptive booklets and maps.

Biking in Holland is safe, easy, and pleasant. Almost all roads have designated bike paths, often separated from the road by a screen of trees or bushes, and there are separate traffic lights and signs for bikes. (Mopeds, called *brommers* in Holland, and motor scooters also use the bicycle paths.) An unpleasant surprise for those who think an absence of hills makes for easy riding is that in a totally flat landscape, nothing blocks the wind—which is great when the wind is behind you, but not so great when it's blowing in your face. Netherlands Railways (© **0900/9292;** www.ns.nl) has some handy arrangements for bicycles. You can rent bikes from many train stations around the country and drop them off at another station.

BY BOAT

With all the water in its seas, lakes, rivers, and canals, it's no surprise that Holland has plenty of waterborne transportation. The most visible indicators of this are the many boat tour options available in and from cities like Amsterdam, Rotterdam, Arnhem, and Maastricht—to name just a few. To these you can add slow harbor ferries and fast jetfoil and jet-catamaran services in and around Amsterdam and Rotterdam.

In addition, there are car-ferry or passengers-only ferry services to the Wadden Sea islands of Texel, Vlieland, Terschelling, Ameland, and Schiermonnikoog; across the Westerschelde between Vlissingen and Breskens; and on the big lake near Amsterdam known as the IJsselmeer. Multiple tiny ferries—many of them little more than pontoons—shuttle back and forth at points where there is no bridge along rivers like the Maas, Waal, Neder Rijn, IJssel, and Amstel.

Many of these options are detailed in the destination chapters.

AMSTERDAM

13

Easygoing and prosperous, the Dutch capital is the natural focus of a visit to the Netherlands. The historic center—a graceful cityscape of waterways, bridges, and venerable town houses—recalls Amsterdam's 17th-century Golden Age as the command post of a vast trading network and colonial empire, when wealthy merchants constructed gabled residences along neatly laid-out canals.

A delicious irony is that some of the placid old structures now host brothels, smoke shops, and extravagant nightlife. The city's inhabitants, heirs to a live-and-let-live attitude, which is based on pragmatism as much as a long history of tolerance, aim to control what they cannot effectively outlaw. They permit licensed prostitution in the Rosse Buurt (Red Light District) and the sale of hashish and marijuana in designated "coffeeshops."

Tolerance may have been a long-term tradition, but recent years have seen growing tensions between some Dutch and some members of ethnic minorities in Amsterdam, where migrants and their descendants and foreign residents now outnumber native locals. And both the coffeeshops and the red-light haunts have been under pressure as the city works to improve its quality of life and reduce the negative values in its portfolio; see p. 21 in chapter 2 for more details.

In any case, don't think Amsterdammers drift around town in a drug-induced haze. They are too busy zipping around on bikes, in-line skating through Vondelpark, eating ethnic dishes, or simply watching the parade of street life from a sidewalk cafe. Small entrepreneurs have revitalized old neighborhoods like the Jordaan, turning distinctive houses into offbeat stores and bustling cafes, hotels, and restaurants. Meantime, the city government and big entrepreneurs have been redeveloping the old harbor waterfront along the IJ waterway in a shiny, modern style that's a long way from the spirit of Old Amsterdam.

Between dips into Amsterdam's artistic and historical treasures, be sure to take time to absorb the freewheeling spirit of Europe's most vibrant city.

ORIENTATION

Arriving

BY PLANE

For details on air travel to Amsterdam, see chapters 3 and 12. The country's main international airport is **Amsterdam Airport Schiphol**

(✆ **0900/0141** from inside Holland, or 31-20/794-0800 from outside, for both general and flight information; www.schiphol.nl), 13km (8 miles) southwest of the center city. After you deplane, moving sidewalks will take you to the main terminal building, where you pass through Passport Control, Baggage Reclaim, and Customs, into Schiphol Plaza. Tourist information is available from the **Holland Tourist Information** desk (daily 7am–10pm) in Schiphol Plaza.

> **Impressions**
>
> ***While Amsterdam may box your Puritan ears, this great, historic city is an experiment in freedom.***
>
> **—ABCNews.com, 2000**

Trains depart from Schiphol station, downstairs from Schiphol Plaza, for Amsterdam's Centraal Station. Departures range from one per hour at night to six per hour at peak times. The one-way fare to Centraal Station is 3.70€ in second class and 6.30€ in first class; the trip takes around 20 minutes.

The **Connexxion Hotel Shuttle** (✆ **038/339-4741;** www.schipholhotelshuttle.nl) runs daily every 10 to 30 minutes from 6am to 9pm, between the airport and about 100 Amsterdam hotels. No reservations are needed, and buses depart from in front of Schiphol Plaza. Buy tickets from the Connexxion desk inside Schiphol Plaza or onboard from the driver. The fare is 15€ one-way and 25€ round-trip; children 4 to 14 pay half the adult fare.

Taxis from the airport are operated by **Schiphol Taxi** (✆ **0900/900-6666;** www.schipholtaxi.nl). They are metered and charge around 40€ to the center of Amsterdam.

BY TRAIN

For details on traveling to Holland by train, see chapters 3 and 12. Trains arrive in Amsterdam at **Centraal Station,** on an artificial island on the IJ waterway. Centraal Station is the point of origin for most city trams (streetcars) and Metro trains, and a departure point for taxis, canalboat tours, passenger ferries, water taxis, the Canal Bus, and the Museum Quarter Line boats. It houses an office of Amsterdam Tourist Information (a second office is outside on Stationsplein) and a GWK Travelex currency-exchange office. Schedule and fare details on rail travel in Holland are available from the information office inside the station; information is also available by dialing ✆ **0900/9292,** or visiting www.9292ov.nl. Call ✆ **0900/9296** for international trains. Each of these phone services costs 0.70€ per minute.

Tram stops are on either side of the main station exit. A **taxi stand** is in front of the station. (For details on transportation within the city, see "Getting Around," below.)

BY BUS

International buses arrive at Amstel bus station, outside Amstel rail station (Metro: Amstel). From here, there are Metro connections to Centraal Station. For the Leidseplein area, take the Metro toward Centraal Station and get out at the Weesperplein station; then go aboveground to take tram no. 7 or 10.

BY CAR

European expressways E19, E35, E231, and E22 reach Amsterdam from Belgium and/or Germany.

Amsterdam by the Numbers

Amsterdam has a population of 750,000. The Old City, inside the arc of the Singelgracht canal, covers an area of 8 sq. km (3 sq. miles), containing 44,000 dwellings that house 80,000 people. The residents share this central space with 8,000 historical monuments, 2,000 stores, 1,500 cafes and restaurants, and 200 hotels. Every working day, more than two-thirds of a million people pour into the center city by public transportation, bicycle, and car.

Visitor Information

Amsterdam's tourist information organization is the **Amsterdam Tourism & Convention Board,** P.O. Box 3901, 1001 AS Amsterdam (Mon–Fri 9am–5pm; © **0900/400-4040,** or 31-20/551-2525 from outside the Netherlands; fax 020/201-8850; www.iamsterdam.nl). This organization operates two **Amsterdam Tourist Information** offices: one on platform 2B inside Centraal Station, open Monday to Wednesday from 9am to 8pm, Thursday to Saturday from 8am to 8pm, and Sunday and holidays from 9am to 6pm; and one in front of the station, at Stationsplein 10, open daily 8am to 9pm (tram for both: 1, 2, 4, 5, 9, 13, 16, 17, 24, 25, or 26). The 0900 phone number costs 0.40€ a minute. Calls made from outside the Netherlands are at the usual international rate.

Amsterdam Tourist Information can help you with almost any question about the city. It also provides brochures, maps, and the like, and reserves hotel rooms. Pick up a copy of ***Time Out Amsterdam Day*** for 2.95€. This monthly magazine is full of details about the month's art exhibits, concerts, and theater performances, and lists restaurants, bars, dance clubs, and more.

City Layout

Amsterdam's center is small enough that its residents think of it as a village. Finding your way around can be confusing, however, until you get the hang of it. The concentric rings of major canals are the center city's defining characteristic, along with several important squares that act as focal points. The city has 160 canals—more than Venice—with a combined length of 76km (47 miles), spanned by 1,281 bridges. The best-known canals are those of the 17th-century *Grachtengordel* (Canal Belt, or Canal Ring): Herengracht, Prinsengracht, and Keizersgracht. To these three, UNESCO in 2010 added the 15th-century Singel when it inscribed the *Grachtengordel* on the list of World Heritage Sites.

A map is essential. You need to know that in Dutch *-straat* means "street," *-gracht* means "canal," *-plein* means "square," *-markt* means market or market square, *-dijk* means dike, and *-laan* means "boulevard." All of these are used as suffixes attached directly to the name of the thoroughfare (for example, Princes' Canal becomes *Prinsengracht*).

STREET MAPS The most cost-effective map is Amsterdam Tourism & Congress Bureau's **Amsterdam City Map,** available from VVV Amsterdam offices for 2€. It shows every street and canal, tram routes and stops, museums and churches, and more. It goes about as far out as the ring road. For even more detailed coverage of the entire city and suburbs, buy the **Falk Amsterdam City Map** for 9.95€.

Neighborhoods in Brief

The city of Amsterdam can be divided into six major neighborhoods and five lesser outlying districts.

Centrum (Old Center) The oldest part of the city, around the Dam and Centraal Station, includes the major downtown shopping areas and such attractions as the Royal Palace, the Amsterdam Historical Museum, and the canalboat piers.

Het IJ (the Waterfront) Centered on Centraal Station and stretching east and west along both banks of the IJ channel, this fast-redeveloping area covers the artificial islands, warehouses, and installations of Amsterdam's old harbor (the new harbor lies west of the city).

Grachtengordel (Canal Belt) The semicircular, multistrand necklace of waterways constructed during the 17th century includes elegant gabled houses, many restaurants, antiques stores, and small hotels, plus such sightseeing attractions as the Anne Frankhuis and the canal-house museums.

Leidseplein The city's most happening nightlife square and its surroundings are a trove of performance venues, movie theaters, restaurants, bars, cafes, and hotels.

Rembrandtplein Like Leidseplein, but on a reduced scale, this lively square is home to hotels, restaurants, cafes, and nightlife venues.

Jordaan This nest of small streets and canals is west of the center city, outside the major canals. Once a working-class neighborhood, it has become a fashionable residential area with a slew of upscale boutiques and restaurants. Its indigenous inhabitants are alive and well, and show no sign of succumbing to the gentrification going on around them.

Museum District & Vondelpark A gracious residential area surrounds three major museums: the Rijksmuseum, the Van Gogh Museum, and the modern-art Stedelijk Museum. The area includes Vondelpark, the Concertgebouw concert hall, many restaurants and small hotels, and Amsterdam's most elegant shopping streets, Pieter Cornelisz Hooftstraat and Van Baerlestraat.

Amsterdam-Zuid (South) This very prestigious 20th-century residential area is the site of a number of hotels, particularly along Apollolaan, a boulevard the locals have dubbed the "Gold Coast" for its wealthy inhabitants and stately mansions.

Amsterdam-Oost (East) In this residential area on the far bank of the Amstel River, you'll find the maritime and tropical museums, and Artis, the local zoo.

Amsterdam-West The district west of the Singelgracht covers a lot of ground but doesn't have much to recommend in the way of sights.

Amsterdam-Noord (North) Across the IJ channel from Centraal Station, *Noord* has up until now been a largely uninteresting "dormitory" district. That's beginning to change, but for now most of the interesting developments in this area are along what used to be the old harbor, and these are featured under the "Waterfront" heading.

GETTING AROUND

When you look at a map of Amsterdam, you may think the city is too large to explore on foot. This isn't true: It's possible to see almost every important sight on a 4-hour walk, and most people should be able to cover the center city on foot, though not all at once. Be sure to wear comfortable walking shoes, since those charming cobbles can get under your soles and on your nerves. When crossing the street, watch out for trams and bicycles; be particularly careful when crossing bike lanes.

By Public Transportation

From 2011, or thereabouts, all public transportation in the Netherlands should be using an electronic stored-value card called the **OV-chipkaart,** which replaces the old system of tickets, "strip cards," and fare zones. For details about how this card works, see "Getting There & Getting Around," in chapter 12.

In addition, Amsterdam has some details specific to the city. The central information and ticket sales point for GVB Amsterdam, the city's public transportation company, is **GVB Tickets & Info,** Stationsplein (✆ **0900/9292;** www.gvb.nl), in front of Centraal Station.

FARE INFORMATION Purchase cards from the GVB Tickets & Info office, GVB and Netherlands Railways ticket booths in Metro and train stations, automats at Metro and train stations, and automats onboard some trams. Not every kind of card is available from each of these sources. Note that the cards are valid throughout the Netherlands, no matter where you purchase them.

A better bet than a standard OV-chipkaart for short-term visitors who plan to use public transportation a lot is a 1-day or a multi-day card issued by the GVB: 24 hours (7.50€), 48 hours (11.50€), 72 hours (15€), 96 hours (18€), 120 hours (23€), 144 hours (26€), and 168 hours (29€).

Reduced-rate cards are available for seniors and children 4 to 11; children 3 and under ride free.

Should you plan to splash out on a 1-, 2-, or 3-day **I amsterdam Card** (see "Your Passport to Amsterdam," later in this chapter), remember that this affords "free" use of public transportation, so don't purchase additional cards. The same applies if you purchase the **All Amsterdam Transport Pass** associated with travel on the Canal Bus (see "On the Water," below).

Teams of roving inspectors do their best to keep everyone honest. The fine for riding without a valid card is 38€, plus the fare for the ride, payable on the spot.

BY TRAM Half the fun of Amsterdam is walking along the canals. The other half is riding the smooth blue-and-gray trams that roll through most major streets. There are 16 tram routes in the city. Ten of these (lines 1, 2, 4, 5, 9, 13, 16, 17, 24, and 26) begin and end at Centraal Station, and one (line 25) passes through, so you know you can always get back to that central point if you get lost and have to start over. The other tram routes are 3, 7, 10, 12, and 14.

Most trams have an access door that opens automatically. Board toward the rear, following arrowed indicators outside the tram that point the way to the door. To board a tram that has no such arrowed indicators, push the button on the outside of the car beside any door. Getting off, you may need to push a button with an open-door graphic or the words DEUR OPEN. Tram doors close automatically and they do it quite quickly, so don't dawdle.

BY BUS An extensive bus network operated by GVB (see above) complements the trams. Many bus routes begin and end at Centraal Station. It's generally faster to go by tram, but some points in the city are served only by bus. Regional and intercity bus service from Amsterdam is operated by **Connexxion** (✆ **0900/266-6399;** www.connexxion.nl) and **Arriva** (✆ **0900/202-2022;** www.arriva.nl).

BY METRO Four lines—50, 51, 53, and 54—run partly overground and bring people in from the suburbs, but from Centraal Station you can use Metro trains to reach both Nieuwmarkt and Waterlooplein in the central zone. You may want to take them simply as a sightseeing excursion, though few of the sights on the lines are worth going out of your way for.

BY TRAIN The rail network is not as useful within Amsterdam as are the tram, bus, and Metro—but sensitive souls might like that they can ride in a first-class car or compartment. In addition to the Centraal Station hub, there are seven train stations in the city: Zuid, RAI (the city's main convention center), and Amstel in the south; Muiderpoort in the east; and Lelylaan, De Vlugtlaan, and Sloterdijk in the west. Because the transportation network is tightly integrated, all train stations are served by two or more modes of public transportation.

By Taxi

Officially, you can't hail a cab from the street, but often taxis will stop if you do. If you're having trouble, find one of the strategically placed taxi stands sprinkled around the city, or call **Taxi Centrale Amsterdam** (✆ **020/777-7777;** www.tca-amsterdam.nl). Taxis are metered. TCA's base fare begins at 7.50€ when the meter starts and, after 2km (1¼ miles), runs up at 2.20€ a kilometer, or 3.55€ a mile; after 25km at 1.75€ a kilometer, or 2.80€ a mile; and after 50km at 1.45€ a kilometer, or 2.35€ a mile. This includes service; round it up if you like, or tip for good service, like help with your luggage, or for a helpful discourse.

On the Water

With all the water in Amsterdam, it makes sense to use it for transportation. As a side benefit, this affords the unique view of the city from the water.

BY WATER BUS Two separate services bring you to many of the city's top museums and other attractions. **Canal Bus** (✆ **0900/333-4442;** www.canal.nl) operates four routes—Green, Red, Blue, and Orange. Passes for adults cost 22€ for 24 hours, 33€ for 48 hours, and 44€ for 72 hours; children 4 to 12 travel for half the adult price, and children 3 and under are free. An **All Amsterdam Transport Pass,** valid on the Canal Bus, trams, buses, and the Metro, costs 28€ a day and is available from GVB Tickets & Info, VVV tourist information offices, and the Canal Bus company. It's a good value only if you make extensive use of the Canal Bus and GVB public transportation.

The **Hop On Hop Off Museum Line** (✆ **020/530-1090;** www.lovers.nl) operates a scheduled service every 30 to 45 minutes from Centraal Station to Prinsengracht, Leidseplein, Museumplein, Herengracht, the Muziektheater, and the Eastern Dock. A day ticket is 20€ for adults, 10€ for children 4 to 12, and free for children 3 and under. Tickets afford reduced admission to some museums and attractions.

BY WATER TAXI Water taxis do more or less the same thing as landlubber taxis, except they do it on the water. To order one, call **VIP Watertaxi Amsterdam** (✆ **020/535-6363;** www.water-taxi.nl), or pick one up from the dock outside Centraal Station (near the VVV office). To and from points in the city center, a water taxi for between one and eight passengers costs 20€ per half-hour; to and from points outside the city center, the rate is 50€ per half-hour.

BY FERRY Free **ferries** for passengers and two-wheel transportation connect the center with Amsterdam-Noord (North), across the IJ channel. These short crossings are ideal microcruises for the cash-strapped; they afford fine views of the harbor. Ferries depart from the Waterplein-West dock on De Ruijterkade, behind Centraal

bicycling IN AMSTERDAM

It takes a while to get used to moving smoothly and safely through the whirl of trams, cars, buses, trucks, fellow bikers, and pedestrians, particularly if you're on a typically ancient and much-battered *stadfiets* (city bike), also known as an *omafiets* (grandmother bike)—the only kind that makes economic sense here, since anything fancier will attract a crowd of people wanting to steal it. It's better to develop your street smarts slowly.

The first rule: Don't argue with trams—they bite back, hard. The second rule: Cross tram tracks perpendicularly so your wheels don't get caught in the grooves, which could pitch you out of the saddle. And the third rule: Don't crash into civilians (pedestrians). That's about it. Like everyone else, you'll likely end up making up the rest of the rules as you go along.

Station. Another ferry goes west to NDSM Island, a 20-minute trip that doesn't pass any points of particular interest but still affords a decent view of the harbor.

By Bicycle

Follow the Dutch example and rent a bicycle—there are more than 550,000 on the streets of Amsterdam to keep you company. Bike-rental rates are around 12€ per day or 50€ per week; a deposit of around 50€ or a credit card authorization is required. **MacBike** (**© 020/620-0985;** www.macbike.nl) rents a range of bikes, including tandems and six-speeds. The company has rental outlets at: Stationsplein 5 (tram: 1, 2, 4, 5, 9, 13, 16, 17, 24, 25, or 26), Centraal Station; Waterlooplein 199 (tram: 9 or 14); and Weteringschans 2 (tram: 1, 2, 5, 7, or 10), at Leidseplein. **Bike City,** Bloemgracht 68–70 (**© 020/626-3721;** www.bikecity.nl; tram: 13, 14, or 17), near the Anne Frankhuis, is another good choice. **Damstraat Rent-a-Bike,** Damstraat 20–22 (**© 020/625-5029;** www.bikes.nl; tram: 4, 9, 14, 16, 24, or 25), is centrally located near the Dam. Feminists both male and female might want to give their business to **Zijwind Fietsen,** a women's cooperative, at Scheldestraat 168 (**© 020/673-7026;** www.zijwind.com; tram: 25), though it's a bit out from the Center.

Warning: Bicycle theft is common. Always lock both your bike frame and one of the wheels to something solid and fixed.

By Car

Don't rent a car to get around Amsterdam. You'll regret both the expense and the hassle. The city is a jumble of one-way streets, narrow bridges, and no-parking zones, and street parking is hard to come by. Parking fees are expensive. Street parking in the city center costs 3€ to 5€ an hour, depending on time and location, payable at nearby automats; if you're staying longer than 6 hours, it's more economical to buy a day ticket (also available from automats). Reduced-rate permits are available from many hotels.

The cost of transgression is high: 51€ plus an hour's parking charge, payable within 48 hours. If the parking operatives think your car constitutes enough of an obstacle, they tow your car to the **Cition** car-pound at Daniël Goedkoopstraat 7–9 (**© 14-020** for information, or 020/251-3737 for reception; www.cition.nl; Metro: Spaklerweg), open 24 hours a day, way out in the boonies of the southeastern Over-Amstel district, and they charge you 58€ for every 24-hour period (or portion thereof) that it's out there, plus the towing charge. You pay parking fines at the car-pound office, or at a second office, De Clercqstraat 42–44 (tram: 3, 13, or 14).

Outside the city, driving is a different story, and you may want to rent a car to tour the nearby countryside.

RENTALS See "Getting There & Getting Around," in chapter 12, for details.

[FastFACTS] AMSTERDAM

Airport See "Orientation," earlier in this chapter.

Area Code Amsterdam's area code is **020;** use this when calling from within the Netherlands but not in Amsterdam. When making local calls in Amsterdam, simply leave off the area code and dial only the phone number. When calling from outside the Netherlands, the area code for Amsterdam is **20.**

Business Hours See "Fast Facts: Holland," in chapter 21. Thursday is *koopavond* (late shopping evening) in Amsterdam, when many stores stay open to 9pm.

Doctors & Dentists For urgent but nonemergency medical care, and for urgent dental care, call the **Central Doctors Service** (✆ **020/592-3434**).

Embassies & Consulates For embassies of English-speaking countries in The Hague, see "Fast Facts: Holland," in chapter 21. In Amsterdam, the consulate of the **United States** is at Museumplein 19 (✆ **020/575-5309;** http://amsterdam.usconsulate.gov; tram: 3, 5, 12, or 16); the consulate of the **United Kingdom** is at Koningslaan 44 (✆ **020/676-4343;** www.britain.nl; tram: 2).

Emergencies For police assistance, an ambulance, or the fire department, call ✆ **112.** For routine police matters, visit a district police office—a centrally located one is at Lijnbaansgracht 219 (✆ **0900/8844;** tram: 1, 2, 5, 7, or 10), off Leidseplein.

Hospitals Two hospitals with emergency service are the **Onze-Lieve-Vrouwe Gasthuis,** Oosterpark 9 (✆ **020/599-9111;** www.olvg.nl; tram: 3, 7, or 10), in Amsterdam Oost (East); and the **Academisch Medisch Centrum (AMC),** Meibergdreef 9 (✆ **020/566-9111;** www.amc.uva.nl; Metro: Holendrecht), in Amsterdam-Zuidoost (Southeast).

Internet Access Many hotels, coffeehouses (note that this generally doesn't mean pot-selling "coffeeshops"), and other businesses offer Internet access. Dedicated cybercafes have virtually disappeared from the Amsterdam scene.

Mail Most offices of **TNT Post** (✆ **076/527-2727;** www.tntpost.nl) are open Monday to Friday from 9am to 5pm. The office at Singel 250, at the corner of Raadhuisstraat (tram: 13, 14, or 17), is open Monday to Friday from 7:30am to 6pm, and Saturday from 7:30 to 9:30am. See "Fast Facts: Holland," in chapter 21, for more info.

Newspapers & Magazines English-language newspapers and magazines are available from the **American Book Center,** Spui 12 (✆ **020/625-5537;** www.abc.nl; tram: 1, 2, or 5), and **Waterstone's,** Kalverstraat 152 (✆ **020/638-3821;** tram: 4, 9, 14, 16, 24, or 25). Newsstands at Schiphol Airport and Centraal Station stock many international publications.

Toilets See "Fast Facts: Holland," in chapter 21. Should you have a toilet emergency in Amsterdam, a comfortable place to find relief is the NH Grand Hotel Krasnapolsky, across the square from the Royal Palace on the Dam. Just breeze in as if you own the "Kras," swing left past the front desk and along the corridor, pass the Winter Garden restaurant, and then go up a short stairway.

Safety In Amsterdam, if it isn't bolted to the floor, somebody will try to steal it—and even if it is bolted to the floor, somebody will try to steal it. Watch out for pickpockets on trams, buses, and the Metro, and in train and Metro stations. Constant public announcements at Centraal Station and Schiphol Airport warn about pickpockets, and signs on the trams say in a multitude of languages ATTENTION: PICKPOCKETS. Consider wearing a money belt. Women should wear their purses crossed over their shoulders so they hang in front, with the clasps or zippers facing in.

Violence does happen in Amsterdam, but it's not a violent city. Drug-related crime is prevalent. Most crime, like pickpocketing, is nonviolent, relatively minor, and opportunistic. Stolen bicycles are a big problem here! Mugging and armed robbery do happen, though incidents are not common.

There are some risky areas, especially in and around the Red Light District. Be leery of walking alone after dark through narrow alleyways and along empty stretches of canal. Don't use ATMs at night in quiet areas. It's wise to stay out of Vondelpark at night, but there are cafes on the edge of the park that are busy until closing time.

The rules about not walking alone in poorly lit and unpeopled areas at night apply here, especially to women. Although Amsterdam is generally safe, incidents of harassment do occur, and rape isn't unheard of. Public transportation is usually busy even late at night, so you generally won't have to worry about being alone in a tram or Metro train. But if you feel nervous, sit close to the driver when possible. Many local women go around by bicycle at night.

Note: Listing some of the possible dangers together like this can give a misleading impression of the threat from crime in Amsterdam. There is no need to be afraid to do the things you want to do. Amsterdammers aren't afraid. Just remember to exercise the usual rules of caution and observation that apply in any big city. Report any crime committed against you to the police, most of whom speak English.

Also see "Crime & Safety," in chapter 3.

WHERE TO STAY

Is your preference old-world charm combined with luxurious quarters? Glitzy modernity with every conceivable amenity? Small family-run hotels? A bare-bones room that frees up scarce cash for other purposes? Amsterdam has all of these, and more. Many hotels offer significant rate reductions between November 1 and March 31, with the exception of the Christmas and New Year periods. The city has many charms in the off season, when the calendar is full of cultural events. Traditional Dutch dishes are offered that aren't available in warm weather; the streets, cafes, restaurants, and museums are filled more with locals than with visitors.

RESERVATIONS Should you arrive without a reservation, VVV Amsterdam tourist offices will help you for 4€, plus a refundable room deposit. They can find you something, even at the busiest periods, but it may not be exactly what, or where, you want. You can reserve ahead of time with the **Amsterdam Tourism & Convention Board,** P.O. Box 3901, 1001 AS Amsterdam (✆ **020/201-8880;** fax 020/201-8850; reservations@atcb.nl; www.iamsterdam.com). Online reservations are free; those made by phone, fax, or e-mail cost 14€, with an additional 14€ to change a reservation.

The Old Center

VERY EXPENSIVE

Sofitel Amsterdam the Grand ★★ In a fully modernized courtly building that since the 15th-century has been a convent, a royal guesthouse, headquarters of the

A Down-to-Earth Warning

Elevators are hard to shoehorn into the cramped confines of a 17th-century canal house and cost more than some moderately priced and budget hotels can afford. Many simply don't have them. If lugging your old wooden sea chest up six flights of steep, narrow stairs is liable to void your life insurance, you better make sure an elevator is in place and working. Should there be no elevator and you have trouble climbing stairs, ask for a room on a low floor. Or think positively and regard the stairs as your workout for the day.

Amsterdam Admiralty, and the city's Town Hall, the Grand is grand indeed. To reach the lobby, walk through a courtyard with a fountain, then pass through a brass-and-wood revolving door. Sip afternoon tea in the lounge amid Art Deco and stained-glass windows; Oriental rugs grace black-and-white marble floors. Such elegance, and only a few blocks south of the Red Light District. Individually styled and furnished rooms reflect the different phases of the building's past and are the last word in plush. Views are of 17th-century canals, the garden, or the courtyard. The contemporary French restaurant **Bridges** sports an abstract expressionist mural, *Inquisitive Children* (1949), by Cobra-movement artist Karel Appel. This hotel has been awarded a Green Key certificate for environmental awareness and sustainable practices.

Oudezijds Voorburgwal 197 (off Damstraat), 1012 EX Amsterdam. ✆ **800/515-5679** in the U.S. and Canada, or 020/555-3111. Fax 020/555-3222. www.thegrand.nl. 177 units. 550€–650€ double; from 800€ suite. AE, DC, MC, V. Valet parking 50€. Tram: 4, 9, 14, 16, 24, or 25 to Spui. **Amenities:** Restaurant; snack bar; lounge; bar; airport transfer; babysitting; concierge; health club & spa; heated indoor pool; room service. *In room:* A/C, TV, hair dryer, minibar, Wi-Fi (free).

EXPENSIVE

Die Port van Cleve ★ One of the city's oldest hotels—it actually started life in 1864 as the first Heineken brewery—stands right across the street from the Royal Palace on the Dam. The ornamental facade, with its turrets and alcoves, is original and has been fully restored. Likewise, the interior was completely renovated a few years back. The guest rooms are relatively small, and in general are furnished in a plain way that doesn't quite complement the building's handsome looks. Watch out for noise from the busy (or bustling, if you prefer) street, in rooms at the front—especially in summer, when you may want the windows open due to the absence of air-conditioning. You won't eat much more traditionally Dutch than in the **Brasserie de Poort,** and you can drink in the **Bodega de Blauwe Parade** watched over by a feast of Delft blue tiles.

Nieuwezijds Voorburgwal 176–180 (behind the Royal Palace), 1012 SJ Amsterdam. ✆ **020/714-2000.** Fax 020/714-2001. www.dieportvancleve.com. 121 units. 175€–350€ double; from 425€ suite. AE, DC, MC, V. No parking. Tram: 1, 2, 5, 13, or 17 to the Dam. **Amenities:** Restaurant; bars; babysitting; concierge; executive rooms; room service. *In room:* TV, hair dryer, Wi-Fi (free).

Hotel Amsterdam-De Roode Leeuw Close to the Dam, this hotel, founded in 1911, has an 18th-century facade. Its guest rooms are super-modern and have thick carpets and ample wardrobe space. Those at the front tend to get more light but are subjected to more street noise; some have balconies. The award-winning in-house **De Roode Leeuw** restaurant (daily 11am–11:30pm) serves traditional Dutch cuisine, and a glassed-in heated terrace overlooking the Dam is a pleasant and relaxing spot

Where to Stay in Amsterdam

Acacia **20**
Agora **13**
Amsterdam Wiechmann **14**
Amstel Botel **21**
Apollofirst Hampshire Classic **2**
Arena **31**
Bicycle Hotel Amsterdam **3**
Bilderberg Garden Hotel **2**
Bilderberg Hotel Jan Luyken **6**
Bridge Hotel **30**
citizen M Amsterdam City **1**
De Filosoof **9**
Die Port van Cleve **17**
The Dylan Amsterdam **15**
Eden Amsterdam American **10**
Estheréa **16**
Fusion Suites **8**
Hotel Amsterdam-De Roode Leeuw **23**
Keizershof **12**
King's Villa Hotel **4**
Lloyd Hotel **25**
Museumzicht **7**
NH Schiller **27**
Orfeo **11**
Piet Hein **5**
Prinsenhof **29**
Seven Bridges **28**
Sint Nicolaas **22**
Sofitel Amsterdam The Grand **26**
The Toren **18**
Van Onna **19**
Winston **24**

Information
Post office
Railway
Metro Station

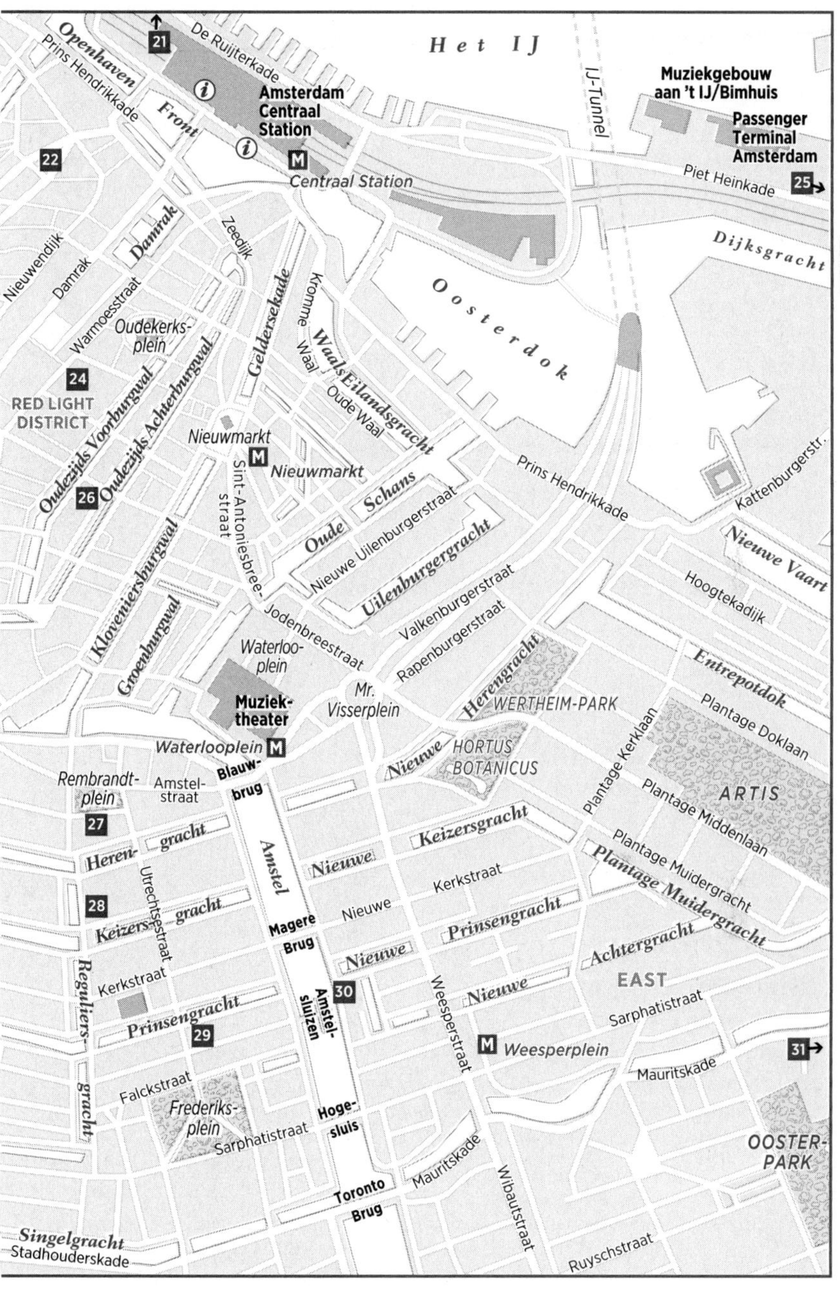

Het IJ
Openhaven
Prins Hendrikkade
De Ruijterkade
Amsterdam Centraal Station
Front
Centraal Station
IJ-Tunnel
Muziekgebouw aan 't IJ/Bimhuis
Passenger Terminal Amsterdam
Piet Heinkade
Dijksgracht
Oosterdok
Damrak
Nieuwendijk
Zeedijk
Geldersekade
Kromme Waal
Waalseilandsgracht
Oude Waal
Warmoesstraat
Oudekerks-plein
RED LIGHT DISTRICT
Oudezijds Voorburgwal
Oudezijds Achterburgwal
Nieuwmarkt
Sint-Antoniesbree-straat
Oude Schans
Nieuwe Uilenburgerstraat
Uilenburgergracht
Prins Hendrikkade
Kattenburgerstr.
Nieuwe Vaart
Hoogtekadijk
Kloveniersburgwal
Groenburgwal
Jodenbreestraat
Valkenburgerstraat
Rapenburgerstraat
Waterloo-plein
Muziek-theater
Mr. Visserplein
Herengracht
WERTHEIM-PARK
Entrepotdok
Plantage Doklaan
Plantage Kerklaan
HORTUS BOTANICUS
Nieuwe
Waterlooplein
Blauw-brug
Rembrandt-plein
Amstel-straat
ARTIS
Plantage Middenlaan
Plantage Muidergracht
Heren-gracht
Amstel
Keizersgracht
Nieuwe
Kerkstraat
Utrechtsestraat
Keizers-gracht
Magere Brug
Nieuwe
Prinsengracht
Nieuwe
Achtergracht
EAST
Reguliers-gracht
Kerkstraat
Prinsengracht
Amstel-sluizen
Weesperstraat
Nieuwe
Sarphatistraat
Weesperplein
Mauritskade
Falckstraat
Frederiks-plein
Sarphatistraat
Hoge-sluis
Mauritskade
OOSTER-PARK
Toronto Brug
Wibautstraat
Singelgracht
Stadhouderskade
Ruyschstraat
21
22
24
25
26
27
28
29
30
31

for a beer. This hotel has been awarded a Green Key certificate for its environmental awareness and sustainable practices.

Damrak 93–94 (beside the Dam), 1012 LP Amsterdam. ✆ **020/555-0666.** Fax 020/620-4716. www.hotelamsterdam.nl. 79 units. 110€–325€ double. AE, DC, MC, V. No parking. Tram: 4, 9, 14, 16, 24, or 25 to the Dam. **Amenities:** Restaurant; cafe; room service. *In room:* A/C, TV, hair dryer, Internet (7.50€/hr., 15€/day), minibar.

MODERATE

Sint Nicolaas ★★ Named after Amsterdam's patron saint, this hotel is close to Centraal Station. Heavy tram, bus, and car traffic passing by outside is the downside to an otherwise convenient location. Originally, the building was a factory that manufactured ropes and carpets; it later housed harbor offices. New owners have upgraded the interior to near-boutique status, affording a level of comfort that's rarely achieved by Amsterdam hotels in this price range. This applies especially if you score a rate at the lower end of a scale that's skewed upward by the "deluxe doubles"—and, bear in mind, a thin amenities roster. Each room has a different character, with the regular ones emphasizing classic comforts, warm colors, prints, and exposed wood beams; and the deluxe doubles sporting cool blacks, grays, and whites.

Spuistraat 1A (at Nieuwendijk), 1012 SP Amsterdam. ✆ **020/626-1384.** Fax 020/623-0979. www.centrehotels.nl. 27 units. 95€–250€ double. Rates include continental breakfast. AE, DC, MC, V. Limited street parking. Tram: 1, 2, 5, 13, or 17 to Martelaarsgracht. **Amenities:** Lounge; bar. *In room:* TV, hair dryer, Wi-Fi (free).

INEXPENSIVE

Winston Maybe too close to the Red Light District for some people's taste, and on a slightly seedy street, this is a step up from grunge class, with a hang-loose, alternative rep. You might even hear some (pretty fanciful) comparisons with New York's Chelsea. Local artists have created paintings, photographs, and other works of what you might call art for the hallways and guest rooms. Sparely furnished, the rooms vary in size, holding from two to six beds, and are tolerably clean and well maintained. None have a view worth looking out the window for. Bathrooms are small but have most of the necessary bits and pieces in them, and those rooms that don't have a bathtub do have a shower. The **Belushi's** bar is a fun meeting place, and the next-door **Winston Kingdom** club has daily live music or DJs.

Warmoesstraat 129 (off Damrak), 1012 JA Amsterdam. ✆ **020/623-1380.** Fax 020/639-2308. www.winston.nl. 69 units. 69€–136€ double. Rates include buffet breakfast. AE, DC, MC, V. No parking. Tram: 4, 9, 14, 16, 24, or 25 to the Dam. **Amenities:** Restaurant; bar; bikes; Wi-Fi (free). *In room:* TV (some rooms), no phone.

The Waterfront

EXPENSIVE

Lloyd Hotel ★ Located in the redevelopment zone of the old harbor east of Centraal Station, the Lloyd was an emigrants' hotel from 1921 to 1935. Each of its rooms has a different shape, style, and modern decor, and with rooms of various classes, the hotel straddles all categories except "Very Expensive." Its most expensive rooms, which are the largest, have a view of the water or a specially designed interior (or both). The mattresses are firm, but only a few rooms have king-size doubles—one does, however, have a bed that "sleeps" eight. The hotel's **Culturele Ambassade** houses art exhibits; modern artworks are scattered around the property; and there's an attic library. Two restaurants aim to make it cool to dine in a hotel: **Snel,** fast and affordable, is open 24/7; **Sloom** is leisurely and expensive—order whatever you heart desires, and the kitchen will aim to cook it.

Oostelijke Handelskade 34, 1019 BN Amsterdam (at IJhaven). ✆ **020/561-3636.** Fax 020/561-3600. www.lloydhotel.com. 117 units, 106 with bathroom. 95€ double without bathroom; 140€–450€ double with bathroom. AE, DC, MC, V. Parking 25€. Tram: 10 or 26 to Rietlandpark. **Amenities:** 2 restaurants; bar; babysitting; bikes; room service. *In room:* TV, Wi-Fi (free).

INEXPENSIVE

Amstel Botel ☺ Where better to experience a city on the water than on a boat-hotel moored permanently to a dock on the IJ waterway northwest of Centraal Station? The Botel is popular largely because of that extra thrill added by sleeping on the water—and modest rates (for Amsterdam) don't hurt. This retired inland-waterway cruise boat has cabins on four decks connected by an elevator. The bright, modern rooms are no-nonsense but comfortable, and the showers are small. Be sure to ask for a room with a view on the water, to avoid the uninspiring quay. To get here, take the NDSM Ferry for foot passengers and two-wheel transportation from behind Centraal Station to the NDSM dock, and you'll see it floating in front of you. A free shuttle bus goes between the Botel and the station when the ferry's not running.

NDSM-Pier 3, 1033 RG Amsterdam. ✆ **020/626-4247.** Fax 020/639-1952. www.amstelbotel.com. 175 units. 69€–94€ double. AE, DC, MC, V. Limited free parking on quay. Boat: NDSM Ferry from Centraal Station. **Amenities:** Bar; bikes; Internet (in bar, .20€/min.). *In room:* TV.

The Canal Belt

VERY EXPENSIVE

The Dylan Amsterdam ★★★ The Asian-influenced decor at this prestigious canal-side boutique hotel is arguably the most stylish in town. Its setting started out as a 17th-century theater (Vivaldi once conducted here, and the serene **Dylan Lounge** still sports the theater's original brick floor). All the guest rooms and suites have the usual array of luxury amenities and are individually decorated with different colors and themes. No. 5 is a blue Japanese-style room with a deep soaking tub and traditional sliding screens. Only three rooms have a canal view, so if this is important to you, specify it—and be ready to pay handsomely for the privilege. Style here occasionally trumps substance: the water fountain–style sinks in a few of the rooms look grand, but their design makes them somewhat hard to use. The superlative French restaurant **Vinkeles** (p. 293) draws admirers on its own account.

Keizersgracht 384 (at Runstraat). 1016 GB Amsterdam. ✆ **020/530-2010.** Fax 020/530-2030. www.dylanamsterdam.com. 41 units. 395€–695€ double; from 900€ suite. AE, DC, MC, V. Limited street parking. Tram: 1, 2, or 5 to Spui. **Amenities:** Restaurant; lounge; bar; bikes; boat rental; concierge; exercise room; room service. *In room:* A/C, TV, hair dryer, minibar, Wi-Fi (free).

EXPENSIVE

Estheréa ★★ ☺ If you like to stay at elegant, not-too-big hotels, you're sure to be pleased by the Estheréa. It's been owned by the same family since its beginnings and, like many Amsterdam hotels, was built within a group of neighboring 17th-century canal houses. The familial touch shows in attention to detail and a breezy yet professional approach. It has an elevator, a rarity in these old Amsterdam homes. In the 1940s, the proprietors spent a lot of money on wood paneling, crystal chandeliers, and other structural additions; younger family members who took over the management have had the good sense to leave it all in place. Wood bedsteads and dresser-desks lend warmth to the regularly renovated and upgraded guest rooms, which vary considerably in size; a few are quite small. Most rooms accommodate two guests, but some rooms have more beds, which makes them ideal for families.

Singel 303–309 (near Spui), 1012 WJ Amsterdam. ✆ **020/624-5146.** Fax 020/623-9001. www.estherea.nl. 92 units. 191€–314€ double. AE, DC, MC, V. Parking 55€. Tram: 1, 2, or 5 to Spui. **Amenities:** Lounge; bar; babysitting; concierge; room service. *In room:* TV, hair dryer, minibar, Wi-Fi (10€/24 hr.).

The Toren ★★ With its antique elegance in two side-by-side buildings dating from 1617 on a posh stretch of canal, this relatively small family-run boutique hotel, completely restyled in 2008 by local interior design guru Wim van de Oudeweetering, is justifiably considered one of Amsterdam's "hidden treasures." If you're a devotee of less-is-more design, though, you might feel that it's more than a tad overdone. The style varies hugely from room to room (which makes a visit before signing up a useful exercise)—a medley of red, gold, and black, from plush Italianate to something that comes perilously close to resembling a classy 19th-century bordello, but with a whirlpool bathtub. There's no restaurant, but if you have the means to lodge here, you should have no problems picking up the tab for room service from elegant French partner restaurant **Christophe** (p. 292), just around the corner on Leliegracht.

Keizersgracht 164 (near Leliegracht), 1015 CZ Amsterdam. ✆ **020/622-6033.** Fax 020/626-9705. www.thetoren.nl. 38 units. 180€–275€ double; 350€–400€ suite. AE, DC, MC, V. Limited street parking. Tram: 13, 14, or 17 to Westermarkt. **Amenities:** Bar; babysitting; room service. *In room:* A/C, TV, hair dryer, high-speed Internet, minibar, Wi-Fi (16€/day).

MODERATE

Agora ★ Old-fashioned friendliness is the keynote at this efficiently run and well-maintained lodging, a block from the Flower Market. The hotel occupies a canal house built in 1735 that has been fully restored. Furniture from the 1930s and 1940s mixes with fine mahogany antiques. Bouquets greet you as you enter, and a distinctive color scheme creates an effect of peacefulness and drama at the same time. There's an abundance of overstuffed furniture, and nearly every guest room has a puffy armchair you can sink into after a day of sightseeing. Those with canal views cost the most, but the extra euros are worth it, though the hustle and bustle out on the street can make them somewhat noisy by day. The large family room has three windows overlooking the Singel. Those rooms that don't have a canal view look out on a pretty garden. There's no elevator.

Singel 462 (at Koningsplein), 1017 AW Amsterdam. ✆ **020/627-2200.** Fax 020/627-2202. www.hotelagora.nl. 16 units. 75€–159€ double. Add 5% city tax. Rates include buffet breakfast. AE, DC, MC, V. Limited street parking. Tram: 1, 2, or 5 to Koningsplein. *In room:* TV, hair dryer, Wi-Fi (free).

Amsterdam Wiechmann It takes only a moment to feel at home in the antique-adorned Wiechmann, a classic, comfortable, casual sort of place. Besides, the location is one of the best you'll find in this or any price range: 5 minutes in one direction is the Kalverstraat shopping street; 5 minutes in the other, Leidseplein. Most of the guest rooms—all of them nonsmoking—are standard, with good-size twin beds or double beds, and some have big bay windows. Room furnishings are modern. The higher-priced doubles have a view of the Prinsengracht. The breakfast room has hardwood floors, lots of greenery, and white linen cloths on the tables. There's no elevator.

Prinsengracht 328–332 (at Looiersgracht), 1016 HX Amsterdam. ✆ **020/626-3321.** Fax 020/626-8962. www.hotelwiechmann.nl. 37 units. 90€–165€ double. Rates include continental breakfast. MC, V. Limited street parking. Tram: 1, 2, or 5 to Prinsengracht. **Amenities:** Lounge; bikes. *In room:* TV, Wi-Fi (free).

Seven Bridges ★★ Proprietors Pierre Keulers and Günter Glaner have made the Seven Bridges, named for its view of seven arched bridges, one of Amsterdam's canal-house gems. Each room is furnished with antiques from the 17th to the 20th centuries, plush carpets, handmade Italian drapes, hand-painted tiles, wood-tiled floors, and Impressionist art reproductions. The biggest room, a quad on the first landing, has high ceilings, a big mirror over the fireplace, an Empire onyx table, antique leather armchairs, an array of potted plants, and a huge marble-floored bathroom. Attic rooms have sloped ceilings and exposed wood beams, and basement rooms are big and bright. Rooms at the front overlook a canal, and those at the rear overlook a garden. There's no elevator, and no breakfast room; breakfast is served in room in only 8 of the 11 rooms.

Reguliersgracht 31 (at Keizersgracht), 1017 LK Amsterdam. ✆ **020/623-1329.** Fax 020/624-7652. www.sevenbridgeshotel.nl. 11 units. 90€–250€ double. Rates include full breakfast served in room (in 8 rooms only). AE, MC, V. Limited street parking. Tram: 4 to Keizersgracht. *In room:* TV, hair dryer, Wi-Fi (free).

INEXPENSIVE

Keizershof ★ Owned by the genial de Vries family, this hotel in a four-story canal house from 1672 has just four beamed rooms, named after old Hollywood stars—though a greater claim to fame is that members of the Dutch royal family were regular visitors in its prehotel days. Several other touches make a stay at this nonsmoking hotel memorable: From the street-level entrance, a steep wooden spiral staircase built from a ship's mast leads to guest rooms—there's no elevator. There are, however, a television and a grand piano in the cozy lounge. In good weather, take breakfast, which includes excellent omelets and pancakes, in the flower-bedecked courtyard. Because the hotel has so few rooms, you need to book well ahead.

Keizersgracht 618 (at Nieuwe Spiegelstraat), 1017 ER Amsterdam. ✆ **020/622-2855.** Fax 020/624-8412. www.hotelkeizershof.nl. 4 units. 90€–105€ double with bathroom; 65€ double without bathroom. Rates include Dutch breakfast. MC, V. Limited street parking. Tram: 16, 24, or 25 to Keizersgracht. *In room:* Hair dryer, no phone.

Prinsenhof ★ This modernized canal house near the Amstel River offers rooms with beamed ceilings and basic—yet tolerably comfortable—beds. Front rooms look out onto Prinsengracht, where colorful houseboats are moored. Breakfast takes place in an attractive blue-and-white dining room. The proprietors, Rik and André van Houten, take pride in their hotel and will make you feel welcome. There's no elevator, but a pulley hauls your luggage up and down the stairs.

Prinsengracht 810 (at Utrechtsestraat), 1017 JL Amsterdam. ✆ **020/623-1772.** Fax 020/638-3368. www.hotelprinsenhof.com. 11 units, 6 with bathroom. 95€ double with bathroom; 65€ double without bathroom. Rates include buffet breakfast. AE, MC, V. Limited street parking. Tram: 4 to Prinsengracht. *In room:* No phone.

Leidseplein

EXPENSIVE

Eden Amsterdam American ★★ One of the most fanciful buildings on Amsterdam's long list of monuments, this castlelike mix of Venetian Gothic and Art Nouveau has been a prominent landmark and a popular meeting place for Amsterdammers since 1900. While the exterior must always remain an architectural treasure curiosity of turrets, arches, and balconies, the interior (except that of the cafe, which is also protected) is modern and chic. Rooms are subdued and refined, superbly furnished, and gifted with great vistas: Some have a view of the Singelgracht, while others overlook kaleidoscopic Leidseplein. The location, in the thick of the action and near many major attractions, is one of the best in town. Famous **Café Americain** is one of Europe's most elegant eateries (p. 295). There is also the **Bar Americain,** which has a closed-in terrace looking out on Leidseplein.

Leidsekade 97 (at Leidseplein), 1017 PN Amsterdam. ✆ **020/556-3000.** Fax 020/556-3001. www.edenamsterdamamericanhotel.com. 175 units. 130€–290€ double; from 415€ suite. AE, DC, MC, V. No parking. Tram: 1, 2, 5, 7, or 10 to Leidseplein. **Amenities:** Restaurant; bar; concierge; electric scooters; exercise room; room service; sauna. *In room:* A/C, TV, hair dryer, Internet (1€/hr.), minibar.

MODERATE

Orfeo One of the city's longest-standing gay lodgings has, for more than 30 years, been providing basic, practical facilities and friendly, helpful service. The front desk is in a cozy and sociable lounge, and there is a marble-floored breakfast room. Only three guest rooms have a full bathroom, some with beamed ceilings; others share a shower and/or toilet. One of the perks is a small in-house Finnish sauna. The largest concentration of center-city restaurants is right at the doorstep.

Leidsekruisstraat 12–14 (off Leidseplein), 1017 RH Amsterdam. ✆ **020/623-1347.** Fax 020/620-2348. www.amsterdamorfeohostel.com. 19 units, 3 with bathroom. 120€–150€ double with bathroom; 55€–95€ double without bathroom. Rates include continental breakfast. AE, MC, V. Limited street parking. Tram: 1, 2, or 5 to Prinsengracht. **Amenities:** Restaurant; bar; Wi-Fi (free). *In room:* TV, minibar.

Rembrandtplein

EXPENSIVE

NH Schiller ★ An Amsterdam gem from 1912, this fully restored hotel boasts a blend of Art Nouveau and Art Deco in its public spaces that is reflected in tasteful decor and furnishings in the guest rooms. Its sculpted facade, wrought-iron balconies, and stained-glass windows stand out on the often brash Rembrandtplein. The hotel takes its name from the painter Frits Schiller, who built it in 1912, and whose outpourings of artistic expression, in the form of 600 portraits, landscapes, and still lifes, are displayed in the halls, rooms, stairwells, and public areas. Brasserie Schiller is a gracious oak-paneled dining room, and Café Schiller (see "Trendy Cafes," later in this chapter) is one of Amsterdam's few permanent sidewalk cafes. This hotel has been awarded a Green Key certificate for its environmental awareness and sustainable practices.

Rembrandtplein 26, 1017 CV Amsterdam. ✆ **020/554-0700.** Fax 020/624-0098. www.nh-hotels.com. 92 units. 95€–203€ double; from 161€ suite. AE, DC, MC, V. Limited street parking. Tram: 4, 9, or 14 to Rembrandtplein. **Amenities:** Restaurant; lounge; 2 bars; babysitting; executive rooms; room service. *In room:* TV, hair dryer, minibar, Wi-Fi (11€/24 hr.).

The Jordaan

INEXPENSIVE

Acacia ★ This hotel faces an unfashionable canal just a block from Prinsengracht, but the friendly couple who run the fully nonsmoking Acacia have worked hard to make it welcoming and clean, and they're justifiably proud of the result. The simple, well-kept, and comfortable rooms, all of which have canal views, have been equipped with new beds, writing tables, and chairs. The large front-corner rooms, shaped like pie slices, sleep as many as five and have windows on three sides. A couple of studios have tiny kitchenettes. Breakfast is served in a cozy Old Dutch room with windows on two sides. There's no elevator.

Lindengracht 251 (at Lijnbaansgracht), 1015 KH Amsterdam. ✆ **020/622-1460.** Fax 020/638-0748. www.hotelacacia.nl. 14 units. 80€–90€ double. Rates include continental breakfast. MC, V (5% charge). Limited street parking. Tram: 3 or 10 to Marnixplein. *In room:* TV, Wi-Fi (free).

Van Onna Consisting of three canal houses, the center one dating from 1644, this hotel has grown over the years, but genial owner Loek van Onna continues to keep prices reasonable. Mr. van Onna has lived here since he was a boy and will gladly regale you with tales about the building's history. Accommodations vary considerably, with the best rooms in the newest building. However, even the oldest, plainest rooms have character, and all are both neatly furnished and clean. Whichever building you wind up in, request a front room overlooking the canal. The hotel is nonsmoking. There's no elevator.

Bloemgracht 102–104 and 108 (off Prinsengracht), 1015 TN Amsterdam. ✆ **020/626-5801.** www.hotelvanonna.com. 41 units. 90€ double. Rates include continental breakfast. No credit cards. Limited street parking. Tram: 13, 14, or 17 to Westermarkt. *In room:* No phone.

Museum District & Vondelpark

EXPENSIVE

Bilderberg Hotel Jan Luyken ★ One block from the Van Gogh Museum and from the elegant Pieter Cornelisz Hooftstraat shopping street, this is best described as a small boutique hotel with many of the amenities and facilities of a large one—though without the large guest rooms. Everything is done with perfect attention to detail. The Jan Luyken maintains a balance between its sophisticated lineup of facilities (double sinks and bidets, elevator, lobby bar with fireplace, and meeting rooms for business) and an intimate and personalized approach that's appropriate to a 19th-century neighborhood. That residential feel extends to the rooms, which look much more like those in a well-designed home than in a standard hotel.

Jan Luijkenstraat 58 (near the Rijksmuseum), 1071 CS Amsterdam. ✆ **020/573-0730.** Fax 020/676-3841. www.janluyken.nl. 62 units. 99€–159€ double; from 500€ suite. Add 5% city tax. AE, DC, MC, V. Limited street parking. Tram: 2 or 5 to Hobbemastraat. **Amenities:** Wine bar; lounge; babysitting; bikes; concierge; room service; spa (small). *In room:* A/C, TV, hair dryer, minibar, Wi-Fi (17€/24 hr.).

Fusion Suites ★★★ It seems almost a crime of *lèse majesté* to describe this superb luxury guesthouse-residence, hosted by a devoted couple, as a B&B, though technically that's what it is. On two floors of an 1893 mansion, a block from the northern edge of Vondelpark's panhandle, the four spacious suites have chic designer furniture mixed with antiques, and views that look out on similar 19th-century mansions at the front or lush gardens at the rear. Each suite is individually styled, using natural materials as much as possible, a characteristic emphasized by the use of Coco-Mat beds.

Roemer Visscherstraat 40 (at Eerste Constantijn Huygensstraat), 1054 EZ Amsterdam. ✆/fax **020/618-4642.** www.fusionsuites.com. 4 units. 245€–275€ suite. Rates include full breakfast. AE, DC, MC, V. Tram: 1 to Eerste Constantijn Huygensstraat, or 3 or 12 to Overtoom. *In room:* Minibar, Wi-Fi (free).

MODERATE

De Filosoof ★★ On a quiet street facing Vondelpark, this hotel might be the very place if you fancy yourself something of a philosopher. One of the proprietors, a philosophy professor, has chosen and displayed posters, painted ceilings, framed quotes, and unusual objects to represent philosophical and cultural themes, and the garden is a kind of grove of academe. Each guest room is dedicated to a mental maestro—Aristotle, Plato, Goethe, Wittgenstein, Nietzsche, Marx, and Einstein are among those who get a look in—or are based on motifs like Eros, the Renaissance, astrology, and women. You can even consult your private bookshelf of philosophical works, or join in a weekly philosophy debate. Rooms in an annex across the street are larger; some open onto a private terrace.

Anna van den Vondelstraat 6 (off Overtoom, at Vondelpark), 1054 GZ Amsterdam. ✆ **020/683-3013.** Fax 020/685-3750. www.sandton.eu. 38 units. 105€–180€ double. Rates include buffet breakfast. AE, MC, V. Limited street parking. Tram: 1 to Jan Pieter Heijestraat. **Amenities:** Lounge. *In room:* TV, Wi-Fi (free).

King's Villa Hotel ★ On Vondelpark's edge in a quiet residential district, this hotel in a renovated circa-1900 Art Nouveau mansion is a good choice. Both inside and out, it's as near as you can get in Amsterdam to staying in a country villa. Furnishings and decor are tasteful, and combine Louis XIV and Liberty styles while featuring stained-glass windows and Murano chandeliers. The house also has a private garden and terrace. It's about a 10-minute walk through Vondelpark to Leidseplein.

Koningslaan 64 (off Oranje Nassaulaan), 1075 AG Amsterdam. ✆ **020/673-7223.** Fax 020/675-0031. www.kingsvillahotel.nl. 22 units. 130€–240€ double. AE, MC, V. Limited street parking. Tram: 2 to Valeriusplein. **Amenities:** Lounge; bikes; Wi-Fi (free). *In room:* A/C, TV/DVD, hair dryer, minibar.

Piet Hein Facing Vondelpark, and close to Amsterdam's important museums, this appealing, well-kept Art Nouveau villa hotel is named after a 17th-century Dutch admiral who captured a Spanish silver shipment. Its spacious rooms have all been modernized recently and are furnished with a subtle nautical theme. Half the rooms overlook the park; two second-floor double rooms have semicircular balconies. Lower-priced rooms are in an annex behind the main hotel. In summer the bar sets tables and chairs out on the garden terrace.

Vossiusstraat 52–53 (off van Baerlestraat), 1071 AK Amsterdam. ✆ **020/662-7205.** Fax 020/662-1526. www.hotelpiethein.nl. 65 units. 135€–250€ double. Rates include continental breakfast. AE, DC, MC, V. Limited street parking. Tram: 3, 5, or 12 to Van Baerlestraat. **Amenities:** Bar; room service. *In room:* TV, hair dryer, Wi-Fi (free).

INEXPENSIVE

Museumzicht This hotel in a Victorian house across from the back of the Rijksmuseum is ideal for museumgoers on a budget. The breakfast room commands an excellent view of the museum with its numerous stained-glass windows. Robin de Jong, the proprietor, has filled the guest rooms with an eclectic furniture collection, from 1930s English wicker to the present day. There's no elevator, and the staircase up to reception is pretty steep.

Jan Luijkenstraat 22 (facing the Rijksmuseum), 1071 CN Amsterdam. ✆ **020/671-2954.** Fax 020/671-3597. www.hotelmuseumzicht.nl. 14 units, 3 with bathroom. 115€ double with bathroom; 55€–85€ double without bathroom. Rates include continental breakfast. AE, DC, MC, V. Limited street parking. Tram: 2 or 5 to Hobbemastraat. **Amenities:** Lounge; room service (coffee and tea); Wi-Fi (free). *In room:* No phone.

Amsterdam South

EXPENSIVE

Bilderberg Garden Hotel ★ Amsterdam's most personal five-star hotel is set in a leafy corner along the Amstelkanaal. Because of its excellent restaurant, the Garden considers itself a "culinary hotel," an idea that extends to the rooms, whose color schemes are salad green, salmon pink, cherry red, and grape blue—choose whichever suits you best. The rooms themselves are furnished and equipped according to high standards and with refined taste. Bathrooms are marble, and each executive room has a Jacuzzi tub. The spectacular lobby has a wall-to-wall fireplace with a copper-sheathed chimney. A deserved reputation attaches to the superb French-Mediterranean **Mangerie de Kersentuin (Cherry Orchard)** restaurant; all things considered, its menu is reasonably priced. The **Kersepit (Cherry Pit)** is a cozy bar with an open fireplace and a vast range of Scotch whiskeys.

Dijsselhofplantsoen 7 (at Apollolaan), 1077 BJ Amsterdam. ✆ **020/570-5600.** Fax 020/570-5654. www.gardenhotel.nl. 124 units. 225€–325€ double. AE, DC, MC, V. Limited street parking. Tram: 5 or 24 to Apollolaan. **Amenities:** Restaurant; bar; babysitting; bikes; concierge; room service. *In room:* A/C, TV, hair dryer, minibar, Wi-Fi (10€/hr., 17€/day).

MODERATE

Apollofirst Hampshire Classic The small, elegant Apollofirst, a family-owned hotel set amid the Amsterdam school architecture of Apollolaan, advertises itself as the "best quarters in town in the town's best quarter." Their claim may be debatable, but the Venman family's justifiable pride in their establishment is not. All the accommodations are quiet, spacious, and grandly furnished. Bathrooms are fully tiled. Rooms at the back overlook the well-kept gardens of the hotel and its neighbors, and the summer terrace, where guests can have a snack or a cocktail.

Apollolaan 123–127 (off Minervalaan), 1077 AP Amsterdam. ✆ **020/577-3800.** Fax 020/675-0348. www.hampshire-hotels.com. 40 units. 135€–185€ double; 295€ suite. Rates include continental breakfast. AE, DC, MC, V. Limited street parking. Tram: 5 or 24 to Apollolaan. **Amenities:** Bar; babysitting; room service. *In room:* TV, hair dryer, Wi-Fi (8.50€/day).

citizenM Amsterdam City ★ If you consider yourself a mobile citizen—better make that netizen, since only online reservations are accepted—this hotel could be the perfect Amsterdam node for you. Admittedly, a location in the business-orientated World Trade Center zone in Amsterdam-Zuid (South) means you'll miss out on lodging in the bustling heart of one of the world's most exciting cities. But the hotel's ultra-modern design (which wouldn't look too out of place on Coruscant), touch-control room installations, king-size double beds, and moderate prices, and the area's relative tranquillity, are among a bunch of persuasive plus-points. Besides, there's a fast-tram connection into the center of town.

Prinses Irenestraat 30 (at Beethovenstraat), 1077 WX Amsterdam. ✆ **020/811-7090.** www.citizenmamsterdamcity.com. 215 units. 72€–166€ double. AE, DC, MC, V. Limited street parking. Tram: 5 to Prinses Irenestraat/Beethovenstraat or Station-Zuid. **Amenities:** Restaurant; bar. *In room:* TV, Wi-Fi (free).

INEXPENSIVE

Bicycle Hotel Amsterdam ★★ The young owners of this establishment have found a niche, catering mainly to visitors who wish to explore Amsterdam on bicycles. They help guests plan biking routes through and around the city. You can rent bikes for 7.50€ daily, with no deposit required, and stable your trusty steed indoors. The guest rooms have new carpets and plain but comfortable modern furnishings; some have kitchenettes and small balconies, and there are large rooms for families. The hotel is a few blocks from the popular Albert Cuyp street market, in the hip De Pijp neighborhood. Two old bicycles hang 6m (20 ft.) high on the hotel's facade, and there are always bikes parked in front. There's no elevator.

Van Ostadestraat 123 (off Ferdinand Bolstraat), 1072 SV Amsterdam. ✆ **020/679-3452.** Fax 020/671-5213. www.bicyclehotel.com. 16 units, 8 with bathroom. 60€–120€ double with bathroom; 50€–80€ double without bathroom. Rates include Dutch breakfast. AE, MC, V (4% charge). Parking 25€. Tram: 3, 12, or 25 to Ceintuurbaan/Ferdinand Bolstraat. **Amenities:** Lounge; bikes; Wi-Fi (free). *In room:* TV.

Amsterdam East

MODERATE

Arena ★ A converted Roman Catholic orphanage from 1890 houses a friendly, stylish, youth-oriented hotel. Although the exterior bears a passing resemblance to Dracula's castle, the interior proves they really knew how to do orphanages in those days. Monumental marble staircases, cast-iron banisters, stained-glass windows, marble columns, and original murals have all been faithfully restored. The rambling spaces where the dormitories once were now house stylish doubles and twins. Spare modern rooms, some that are split-level and some that sport timber roof beams and wooden floors, are individually decorated by young up-and-coming Dutch designers. The Continental cafe-restaurant **To Dine** looks a little like an upgraded cafeteria but has a great alfresco terrace in the garden and an attached bar, **To Drink.** Hotel guests get discounted admission to the nightclub **To Night,** which spins music from the 1960s onward in the old orphanage chapel.

's-Gravesandestraat 51 (at Mauritskade), 1092 AA Amsterdam. ✆ **020/850-2410.** Fax 020/850-2415. www.hotelarena.nl. 127 units. 100€–175€ double; 225€–325€ suite. Rates include buffet breakfast. AE, DC, MC, V. Parking 25€. Tram: 7 or 10 to Korte 's-Gravesandestraat. **Amenities:** Restaurant; bar. *In room:* TV, Wi-Fi (3.50€/hr., 10€/day).

Bridge Hotel ★ The bridge in question is the famous **Magere Brug (Skinny Bridge)** over the Amstel River. This small, tastefully decorated hotel likely provides guests with more space per euro than any other hotel in town. Its pine-furnished rooms seem like studio apartments, with couches, coffee tables, and easy chairs arranged in lounge areas in such a way that there's plenty of room left between them and the beds for you to do your morning exercises. There's no elevator.

Amstel 107–111 (near Theater Carré), 1018 EM Amsterdam. ✆ **020/623-7068.** Fax 020/624-1565. www.thebridgehotel.nl. 46 units. 105€–175€ double; 195€–295€ apt. Rates include continental breakfast. AE, DC, MC, V. Limited street parking. Tram: 7 or 10 to Weesperplein. **Amenities:** Lounge. *In room:* TV, Wi-Fi (free).

WHERE TO DINE

If cities get the cuisine they deserve, Amsterdam's ought to be liberal, multiethnic, and adventurous. Guess what? It is. A trading city with a true melting-pot character, Amsterdam has absorbed culinary influences from far and wide, and rustled them all up to its own satisfaction. You'll find just about every international cuisine type on the city's restaurant roster—in Amsterdam, they say, you can eat in any language. Better yet, many of these eateries satisfy the sturdy Dutch insistence on getting maximum value out of every euro. Dutch cooking, of course, is part of all this, naturally, but you won't be stuck with *biefstuk* (beefsteak) and *kip* (chicken) every day, unless you want to be.

The Old Center

VERY EXPENSIVE

Excelsior ★★ CONTINENTAL One of Amsterdam's most eminent restaurants derives its reputation from French master chef Jean-Jacques Menanteau's Michelin-starred and critically acclaimed cuisine, together with superb service. It's more than a little formal. Crystal chandeliers, elaborate moldings, crisp linens, fresh bouquets of flowers, and picture windows with great views of the Amstel River help give this refined place a baronial atmosphere. Respectable attire (jackets for men) is required.

If your budget can't compete with that of the royalty and showbiz stars who dine here, try the three-course *middagmenu* (lunch menu), or the *menu du théâtre* in the evening, which make fine dining more affordable.

Nieuwe Doelenstraat 2–8 (in the Hotel de l'Europe, facing Muntplein). ✆ **020/531-1705.** www.leurope.nl. Reservations recommended on weekends. Main courses 34€–44€; fixed-price menus 55€–95€. AE, DC, MC, V. Mon–Fri 7–11am, 12:30–2:30pm, and 7–10:30pm; Sat–Sun 7–11am and 7–10:30pm. Tram: 4, 9, 14, 16, 24, or 25 to Muntplein.

EXPENSIVE

De Silveren Spiegel MODERN DUTCH/FRENCH The two houses that compose one of the oldest restaurants in Amsterdam were built in 1614 for wealthy soap maker Laurens Jansz Spieghel. It's typical Old Dutch inside, with a bar downstairs and dining rooms where bedrooms used to be, and it emanates a Dutch tidiness that's very welcoming. The menu at "The Silver Mirror" offers updated preparations of traditional seafood and meat dishes, such as baked sole filets with wild spinach, and trilogy of lamb with ratatouille—but just as in the old days, the lamb, from Texel, is still Holland's finest. Be sure to try the Zaanse mustard.

Kattengat 4–6 (off Singel). ✆ **020/624-6589.** www.desilverenspiegel.com. Main courses 27€–29€; fixed-price menus 40€–53€. AE, MC, V. Mon–Sat 5:30–10:30pm. Tram: 1, 2, 5, 13, or 17 to Martelaarsgracht.

D'Vijff Vlieghen ★ MODERN DUTCH The "Five Flies" is a kind of Old Dutch theme park, with nine separate dining rooms in five canal houses decorated with objects from Holland's Golden Age. Each room has a different character. For example, the Rembrandt Room has four original etchings by the artist; the Glass Room has a collection of Golden Age handmade glassware; and the Knight's Room is adorned with 16th-century armor and accoutrements. The chef is out to convey the culinary excellence inherent in many traditional Dutch recipes and products, in an updated, "New Dutch" form, employing organic ingredients when possible.

Spuistraat 294–302 (at Spui; entrance at Vliegendesteeg 1). ✆ **020/530-4060.** www.d-vijffvlieghen.com. Main courses 22€–39€; seasonal menu 26€–53€. AE, DC, MC, V. Daily 5:30pm–midnight. Tram: 1, 2, or 5 to Spui.

MODERATE

Haesje Claes ★ DUTCH If you're yearning for a cozy Old Dutch environment and hearty Dutch food at moderate prices, try this inviting place. Lots of nooks and crannies decorated with wood paneling, Delftware, wooden barrels, brocaded benches, and traditional Dutch hanging lamps with fringed covers give an intimate, comfortable feel to the setting. The menu covers a lot of ground, from canapés to caviar, but you have the most luck with Dutch stalwarts ranging from omelets to tournedos. Try *hutspot* (stew), *stampot* (mashed potatoes and cabbage), and various fish stews, including those with IJsselmeer *paling* (eel).

Spuistraat 273–275 (at Spui). ✆ **020/624-9998.** www.haesjeclaes.nl. Main courses 16€–26€; *Neerlands Dis* (authentic Dutch) menu 28€. AE, DC, MC, V. Daily noon–10pm. Tram: 1, 2, or 5 to Spui.

In de Waag ★ CONTINENTAL Dissections were once carried out on the top floor of De Waag, the public weigh house, which had earlier been the Sint-Antoniespoort Gate in the city walls. Nowadays, dissections are of a culinary nature. This castlelike structure holds one of Amsterdam's most stylish cafe-restaurants, in an area that's becoming hipper by the minute. It's an indelibly romantic place, the long banquet-style tables ablaze with light from hundreds of candles in the evening. You can mix easily with other diners. If you're not hungry, drop by for just a coffee or a drink.

Where to Dine in Amsterdam

Albatros Seafoodhouse & Vis Restaurant **6**
Amsterdam **1**
Bolhoed **7**
Bordewijk **3**
Café Américain **20**
Café Luxembourg **19**
Café-Restaurant De Duvel **24**
Christophe **12**
De Belhamel **5**
De Kas **38**
De Luwte **13**
De Prins **10**
De Silveren Spiegel **32**
D'Vijff Vlieghen **17**
Eetsalon Van Dobben **28**
Excelsior **29**
Fifteen Amsterdam **35**
Gare de l'Est **36**
Golden Temple **25**
Haesje Claes **16**
Hostaria **9**
In de Waag **30**
Kantjil & de Tijger **18**
Kilimanjaro **37**
Lof **4**
Memories of India **27**
Nam Kee **31**
Pancake Bakery **8**
Pier 10 **33**
Sal Meijer **23**
Spanjer & van Twist **11**
't Blaauwhooft **2**
't Stuivertje **14**
Tempo Doeloe **26**
Vertigo **21**
Vinkeles **15**
Wildschut **22**
Wilhelmina-Dok **34**

(i) Information
Post office
Railway
M Metro Station

13 AMSTERDAM | Where to Dine

Nieuwmarkt 4. ✆ **020/422-7772.** www.indewaag.nl. Main courses 17€–25€; fixed-price menu 34€. AE, DC, MC, V. Daily 10am–1am. Metro: Nieuwmarkt.

Kantjil & de Tijger ★ INDONESIAN Unlike the many Indonesian restaurants in Holland that wear their ethnic origins on their sleeves, literally, with waitstaff decked out in traditional costume, the "Antelope and the Tiger" is chic, modern, and cool. Moreover, it attracts customers who like their Indonesian food not only chic, modern, and cool, but good as well. The two bestsellers in this popular place are *nasi goreng Kantjil* (fried rice with pork kabobs, stewed beef, pickled cucumbers, and mixed vegetables) and the 20-item *rijsttafel* for two. Finish off your meal with the multilayered cinnamon cake or (try this at least once) the coffee with ginger liqueur and whipped cream.

Spuistraat 291–293 (beside Spui). ✆ **020/620-0994.** www.kantjil.nl. Reservations recommended on weekends. Main courses 11€–16€; *rijsttafels* (for 2) 40€–50€. AE, DC, MC, V. Mon–Fri 4:30–11pm; Sat–Sun noon–11pm. Tram: 1, 2, or 5 to Spui.

Lof ★★ CONTINENTAL It's hard to pin down this fashionable, vaguely French/Italian eatery. For one thing, there's no menu. Its youthful chefs describe their creations as *cuisine spontane*—they go to the markets, spontaneously pick out whatever's fresh, and impulsively figure out what to do with it back at base. But the name means "praise" in Dutch, and that sounds about right, since the results are invariably admirable. The choice is deliberately limited, not quite take-it-or-leave-it, but not too far away. Choose from two or three starters, then three main courses—meat, fish, and vegetarian—and finish with a *torte*. You dine on one of two levels, at plain tables in a cozy setting with bare brick walls and a view of proceedings in the open kitchen.

SECRETS OF THE rijsttafel

The Indonesian feast **rijsttafel** is Holland's favorite meal, and has been ever since the United East India Company sea captains introduced it to the wealthy burghers of Amsterdam in the 17th century. The rijsttafel (literally "rice table") originated with Dutch plantation overseers in Indonesia, who liked to sample selectively from Indonesian cuisine.

The basic concept of a rijsttafel is to eat a bit of this and a bit of that, blending the flavors and textures. A simple, unadorned bed of rice is the base and the mediator between spicy meats and bland vegetables or fruits, between sweet and sour tastes, soft and crunchy textures. Although a rijsttafel for one is possible, this feast is better shared by two or by a tableful of people. In the case of a solitary diner or a couple, a 17-dish rijsttafel will be enough food; for four or more, order a 24- or 30-dish rijsttafel and you experience the total taste treat.

Among the customary dishes and ingredients of a rijsttafel are *loempia* (classic Chinese-style egg rolls); *satay* or *sateh* (small kabobs of pork, grilled and served with a spicy peanut sauce); *perkedel* (meatballs); *gado-gado* (vegetables in peanut sauce); *daging smoor* (beef in soy sauce); *babi ketjap* (pork in soy sauce); *kroepoek* (crunchy, puffy shrimp toast); *serundeng* (fried coconut); *roedjak manis* (fruit in sweet sauce); and *pisang goreng* (fried banana). Beware of one very appealing dish of sauce with small chunks of what looks to be bright-red onion—that is *sambal badjak,* or simply *sambal,* and it's hotter than hot.

Haarlemmerstraat 62 (west of Centraal Station). ✆ **020/620-2997.** Main courses 23€; fixed-price menu 35€. AE, DC, MC, V. Tues–Sat 7–11pm (or later). Tram: 1, 2, 5, 13, or 17 to Martelaarsgracht.

INEXPENSIVE

Café Luxembourg ★ INTERNATIONAL "One of the world's great cafes," wrote the *New York Times* about this bohemian, see-and-be-seen grand cafe, where the waitstaff wear starched white aprons. Unlike other cafes in Amsterdam, which often draw a distinctive clientele, the Luxembourg attracts all kinds of people because it offers amazingly large portions of food at reasonable prices. Soups, sandwiches, and such dishes as meatloaf are available. Special attractions often include choices like Chinese dim sum and *satay ajam* (Indonesian grilled chicken in a peanut sauce). Sunday in particular, but also on other days, it's a good place to do breakfast over the day's papers and a cup of strong coffee. You're encouraged to linger and relax. In summer, there's sidewalk dining.

Spuistraat 24 (at Spui). ✆ **020/620-6264.** www.cafeluxembourg.nl. Salads and specials 7.50€–13€; lunch 4.90€–9.90€; main courses 9.50€–16€. AE, DC, MC, V. Sun–Thurs 9am–1am; Fri–Sat 9am–2am. Tram: 1, 2, or 5 to Spui.

Nam Kee ★ CHINESE In the heart of Amsterdam's small but growing Chinatown, Nam Kee has a long interior with few obvious graces and little in the way of decor. Don't let the drab, neon-lit dining room dissuade you from trying the very good, fresh food here. People come for authentic, excellent, modestly priced food from a 140-item menu. Those steamed oysters with black bean sauce and the duck with plum sauce are to die for. The Peking duck—always an indicator of quality in a Chinese restaurant—is satisfyingly crisp-skinned. Service is fast, so you won't have long to wait for a table, and they're open late.

Zeedijk 111–113 at Nieuwmarkt. ✆ **020/624-3470.** www.namkee.nl. Main courses 5.75€–16€. AE, DC, MC, V. Daily 11:30am–midnight. Metro: Nieuwmarkt.

The Waterfront

EXPENSIVE

Fifteen Amsterdam ★ FUSION British celeb-chef Jamie Oliver has brought his unique restaurant concept from London to the old Brazilië building in a harbor redevelopment zone east of Centraal Station. His Amsterdam hotspot has drop-dead gorgeous staff, clientele, and food, with dishes like a salad of the day with figs, prosciutto, Gorgonzola, and toasted almonds on field greens; seafood risotto; and pan-fried calves' liver with balsamic figs. Though Jamie doesn't often preside in person, you can try his eclectic-fun cooking concept in the vast dining room. You can also dine outdoors on a waterside terrace.

Pakhuis Amsterdam, Jollemanhof 9 (at Oostelijke Handelskade). ✆ **020/509-5015.** www.fifteen.nl. Main courses 18€–21€. AE, MC, V. Mon–Sat noon to 3pm and 5:30pm–1am. Tram: 25 or 26 to Passenger Terminal Amsterdam.

MODERATE

Gare de l'Est ★★ FRENCH/MEDITERRANEAN Originally a coffeehouse for workers at the docks, this distinctive detached house—with a conservatory extension and a large sidewalk terrace—is reason enough to take a ride to what's now a fashionable part of town. As the restaurant's name indicates, the cuisine is French traditional, though you'll notice Mediterranean touches. Service is both relaxed and knowledgeable, and the fixed-price menu is an excellent value. The strict three-course formula leaves no room for choice—except for the main course—but plenty for market-fresh ingredients and culinary creativity. There's literally no way to know what will be on the daily changing menu.

Cruquiusweg 9 (at the Eastern Harbor). ✆ **020/463-0620.** www.garedelest.nl. Reservations recommended on weekends. Fixed-price menu 32€. AE, DC, MC, V. Daily 6–11pm. Tram: 7 or 10 to Zeeburgerdijk.

Pier 10 ★ FRENCH/INTERNATIONAL Perched on an old pier on Het IJ behind Centraal Station, this restaurant can't help being romantic. It has great views of the IJ waterway from its big outdoor terrace and from the *serre* (glassed-in room) at the end of the pier. The coming and going of harbor ferries, cruise liners, and workaday barges on the ship channel adds a dash of nautical bustle to the scene, making this one of only a few restaurants where you're aware of the sea and port traffic that was once Amsterdam's lifeblood. Candlelight softens the funky diner decor, and the fanciful international-eclectic food—salads of all kinds, new herring, steak, and fish—ebbs and flows like the tides in Het IJ.

De Ruyterkade, Steiger 10 (behind Centraal Station). ✆ **020/427-2310.** Reservations recommended on weekends. Main courses 20€–22€. AE, DC, MC, V. Daily noon–3pm and 6:30pm–1am. Tram: 1, 2, 4, 5, 9, 16, 17, 24, 25, or 26 to Centraal Station.

Wilhelmina-Dok ★★ ☺ MEDITERRANEAN Just across the IJ channel from Centraal Station, this waterside eatery has an old-fashioned maritime look from its plain wood tables, wood floors, and oak cabinets, and large windows serve up views across the boat-speckled waterway. Most tables on the outdoor terrace are sheltered from the wind in a glass-walled enclosure. The thin menu favors plain cooking and organic products and concentrates on a few broadly Italian, French, or Spanish items with an occasional dash of the Maghreb. Or settle back with just a beer and a snack. On Monday evenings in summer, you can take in movies on an outdoor screen.

Noordwal 1 (at IJplein). ✆ **020/632-3701.** www.wilhelmina-dok.nl. Reservations recommended on weekends. Main courses 18€–21€; chef's menu 28€. AE, DC, MC, V. Daily 11am–midnight. Ferry: IJveer from Waterplein-West behind Centraal Station to the dock at IJplein; then go right, along the dike-top path.

INEXPENSIVE

't Blaauwhooft 🎁 DUTCH/CONTINENTAL A plain neighborhood brown cafe in the gentrified Westelijke Eilanden (Western Islands) district has been transformed into a great *eetcafé* (cafe with food) by the simple expedient of adding a kitchen and a menu. It partakes of the village-y setting on these tranquil islands—which feel isolated despite a location just west of Centraal Station—and brings its own cozy atmosphere to the party. There's a nice sidewalk terrace on the square, though with an uninspiring view of trains coming and going into Centraal Station on the adjacent elevated rail line. The kitchen finds its comfort zone in Dutch standbys like Zeeland mussels, but runs to ostrich steak and some adventurous salads.

Hendrik Jonkerplein 1 (Bickerseiland, off Haarlemmerhouttuinen). ✆ **020/623-8721.** www.blaauwhooft.nl. Main courses 9€–18€; *dagschotel* (plate of the day) 12€. No credit cards. Daily 3–10pm. Bus: 18 or 22 to Haarlemmerhouttuinen.

The Canal Belt

EXPENSIVE

Christophe ★★ MODERN FRENCH/MEDITERRANEAN French chef Jean-Joel Bonsens expertly wields tangy Mediterranean flourishes to create an updated version of classic French cuisine. His ultrarefined food, served in a main dining room

An Amsterdam Dinner Cruise

A dinner cruise is a delightful way to combine sightseeing and leisurely dining. During these 2½-hour canal cruises, enjoy a five-course dinner that includes a cocktail, wine with dinner, coffee with bonbons, and a glass of cognac or a liqueur to finish. Reservations are required. The cruises cost around 60€–100€ for adults, and 30€–50€ for children 4–12. See "Organized Tours," later in this chapter, for details on the tour-boat lines.

of modern flair, employs traditional Mediterranean ingredients—figs, truffles, olives, anchovies, peppers, saffron, and more—in exciting new ways. North African *tajine* and Italian *pata negra* ham have a place on the menu, alongside French "staples" like roast Vendée duck. Bonsen rings the changes seasonally, so what you get depends on when you visit. You get a flavor of what's on offer from dishes like the tuna carpaccio with salted lemon, the roasted pheasant in a crust of green peppers and cardamom, and the roasted turbot with turnip.

Leliegracht 46 (between Prinsengracht and Keizersgracht). ✆ **020/625-0807.** www.restaurantchristophe.nl. Main courses 29€–36€; fixed-price menus 36€–66€. AE, DC, MC, V. Tues–Sat 6:30–10:30pm. Tram: 13, 14, or 17 to Westermarkt.

Vinkeles ★ CONTEMPORARY FRENCH If you dress up in black to celebrate (and I don't mean a tux), then head for this ultrahip, Michelin-star restaurant in an unlikely setting: the converted bakery of a 17th-century almshouse. Its restrained tones soften some of the harsher edges of the überchic designer hotel the Dylan (p. 279). The decor includes a bare section of the bakery's brick wall, along with ovens and other fittings, all of which add to the sense of dining in an old Amsterdam canal house. Top chef Dennis Kuipers, who has an instinct for the right taste combinations and the know-how to put them together so they hit the spot, whips up dishes such as roasted Anjou pigeon with five spices and dried apricots. Dining outside in fine weather in the tree-shaded courtyard is an added plus.

Keizersgracht 384 (in the Dylan Amsterdam Hotel, at Runstraat). ✆ **020/530-2010.** www.vinkeles.com. Reservations required. Main courses 29€–44€; fixed-price menu 45€. AE, DC, MC, V. Mon–Fri 7–11am, noon–2pm, and 6:30–11pm; Sat 7–11am and 6:30–11pm. Tram: 13, 14, or 17 to Westermarkt.

MODERATE

Bolhoed ★ VEGETARIAN Forget the corn sheaf–'n'–brown rice image affected by so many vegetarian restaurants. Instead, garnish your healthful habits with tangy flavors and a dash of zest. Latin style, aboriginal art, world music, ethnic exhibits, evening candlelight, and a fine view of the canal from each of the two plant-bedecked rooms in this former hat store—*bolhoed* is Dutch for bowler hat—distinguish a restaurant for which "vegetarian" is a tad too wholesome-sounding. Service is delivered with equal amounts of gusto and attention. If you want to go the whole hog, so to speak, and eat vegan, most of Bolhoed's dishes can be prepared this way, and most are made with organic produce; the wine is organic, too. In fine weather, dine right beside the canal.

Prinsengracht 60–62 (near Noordermarkt). ✆ **020/626-1803.** Main courses 13€–17€; fixed-price menus 13€–19€. No credit cards. Sun–Fri noon–11pm; Sat 11am–11pm. Tram: 13, 14, or 17 to Westermarkt.

De Belhamel ★★ 🎁 CONTINENTAL Classical music complements a graceful Art Nouveau setting at this two-level restaurant overlooking the photogenic junction of the Herengracht and Brouwersgracht canals. The tables fill up quickly most evenings, so make reservations or go early. The menu changes seasonally (game is a big deal here in the fall), but here's a sampling of dishes that recently appeared: puffed pastries layered with salmon, shellfish, crayfish tails, and chervil beurre blanc to start; and beef tenderloin in Madeira sauce with zucchini *rösti* and puffed garlic for a main course. Or order a vegetarian dish. Try for a window table and take in the superb canal views. The waitstaff is occasionally a bit too laid-back, and when it's full, the acoustic peculiarities of the place mean that it can get noisy.

Brouwersgracht 60 (at Herengracht). ✆ **020/622-1095.** www.belhamel.nl. Main courses 11€–27€; fixed-price menus 30€–45€. AE, MC, V. Sun–Thurs 6–10pm; Fri–Sat 6–10:30pm. Tram: 1, 2, 5, 13, or 17 to Martelaarsgracht.

De Luwte ★★ INTERNATIONAL "Graceful" is the word that seems to best sum up this fine restaurant, though that quality never descends into stiffness. Grace exudes from the Florentine wall murals, floor-to-ceiling Art Deco lamps, drapes, hangings, ceiling mirrors painted with flowers and vines, a candle on every table, and, not least of all, from its elegant canal-side location. And De Luwte avoids being starchy because of its characteristically Amsterdam exuberance and buzz. In either of the twin rooms, try for a window table looking out on the handsome little Leliegracht canal. The menu ranges across the globe, from a Dutch and Mediterranean foundation; look to order items such as the vegetarian coconut curry crepes filled with spinach, lentils, and nuts, or stir-fried guinea fowl with nuts and bok choy.

Leliegracht 26–28 (btw. Keizersgracht and Herengracht). ✆ **020/625-8548.** www.restaurantdeluwte.nl. Main courses 16€–20€; fixed-price menu 32€. AE, MC, V. Daily 6–11pm. Tram: 13, 14, or 17 to Westermarkt.

Spanjer & van Twist ★ 🎁 CONTINENTAL This place would almost be worth the visit for its name alone, so it's doubly gratifying that the food is good, too. The interior is typical neighborhood-*eetcafé* style, with the day's specials chalked on a blackboard, a long table with newspapers at the front, and the kitchen visible in back. High standards of cooking put this place above others of its kind. The eclectic menu changes seasonally, but to give you an idea of its range, I've come fork to face here with Thai fish curry and *pandan* rice, *saltimbocca* of trout in white-wine sauce, and artichoke mousseline with tarragon sauce and green asparagus. In fine weather, dine under the trees on an outdoor terrace beside the tranquil Leliegracht canal.

Leliegracht 60 (off Keizersgracht). ✆ **020/639-0109.** www.spanjerenvantwist.nl. Main courses 14€–16€. MC, V. Sun–Thurs 10am–1am; Fri–Sat 10am–2am (only light snacks after 11pm). Tram: 13, 14, or 17 to Westermarkt.

Tempo Doeloe ★★ INDONESIAN For authentic Indonesian cuisine, this place is hard to beat. It's got a *batik* ambience that's restrained Indonesian, and fine china. Try the small meat, fish, and vegetable dishes of three different rijsttafel options, from the 15-plate vegetarian rijsttafel *sayoeran* and the 15-plate rijsttafel *stimoelan,* to the sumptuous 25-plate rijsttafel *istemewa*. You get dishes like *gadon dari sapi* (beef in a mild coconut sauce and fresh coriander), *ajam roedjak* (chicken in a strongly seasoned sauce of chiles and coconut), *sambal goreng oedang* (small shrimps with Indonesian spices), and *atjar* (sweet-and-sour Indonesian salad). For great individual dishes, go for the *nasi koening* or any of the vegetarian options. ***One caution:*** When something on the menu is described as *pedis,* meaning hot, that's *exactly* what it is.

Utrechtsestraat 75 (btw. Prinsengracht and Keizersgracht). ✆ **020/625-6718.** www.tempodoeloe restaurant.nl. Reservations required. Main courses 14€–25€; rijsttafel 28€–36€; fixed-price menu 27€–45€. AE, DC, MC, V. Daily 6–11:30pm. Tram: 4 to Keizersgracht.

INEXPENSIVE

De Prins ★★ DUTCH/FRENCH This cozy *eetcafé*, housed in a 17th-century canal house across the water from the Anne Frankhuis, has a smoke-stained, brown-cafe style, but its food could easily grace a much more expensive restaurant. De Prins offers an unbeatable price-to-quality ratio for typically Dutch/French menu items, and long may it continue to do so. The youthful clientele is loyal and enthusiastic, quickly filling up the relatively few tables. This is a quiet neighborhood place—nothing fancy or trendy, but very appealing in a local way. There's a bar on a slightly lower level than the restaurant. From March to September, De Prins spreads a terrace along the canalside.

Prinsengracht 124 (at Egelantiersgracht). ✆ **020/624-9382.** www.deprins.nl. Main courses 11€–17€; *dagschotel* 12€. AE, DC, MC, V. Daily 10am–1 or 2am (kitchen to 10pm). Tram: 13, 14, or 17 to Westermarkt.

Golden Temple ★ VEGETARIAN In its fourth decade of tickling meat-shunning palates, this temple of organic taste is one of the best vegetarian (and vegan) options in town. If anything, the atmosphere is a tad too hallowed, an effect enhanced by an absence of decorative flourishes that's Zen-like in its purity. The menu livens things up, with its unlikely roster of delicately spiced Indian, Middle Eastern, and Mexican dishes. Multiple-choice platters are a good way to go. For the Indian *thali,* select from choices like *sag paneer* (homemade cheese in a spinach and onion sauce) and *raita* (cucumber and yogurt dip); the Middle Eastern platter has stalwarts like falafel, chickpea-and-vegetable stew, and vegetable *dolmas.* Side dishes are as varied as guacamole, couscous, and *pakora.*

Utrechtsestraat 126 (2 blocks south of Prinsengracht). ✆ **020/626-8560.** www.restaurantgolden temple.com. Main courses 14€–16€; mixed platter 16€. MC, V. Daily 7am–10pm. Tram: 4 to Prinsengracht.

Pancake Bakery ☺ BAKERY In a 17th-century canal warehouse, this two-story restaurant with winding staircases and exposed beams serves some of the most delicious and unusual pancakes you'll ever taste. There are several dozen varieties, and almost all constitute a full meal. The large pancakes come adorned with all sorts of toppings, both sweet and spicy. Choices include salami and cheese, cheese and ginger, curried turkey with pineapple and raisins, honey nuts and whipped cream, and ice cream and *advokaat* (a Dutch eggnoglike cocktail). One of the bestsellers is the "American" pancake: with fried chicken, sweet corn, peppers, carrots, Cajun sauce, and salad. In summer, a few tables are placed in front overlooking the canal, but beware: All the syrup, honey, and sugar being passed around tends to attract bees and hornets.

Prinsengracht 191 (at Prinsenstraat). ✆ **020/625-1333.** www.pancake.nl. Reservations required for large groups. Pancakes 5.95€–14€ (4.95€–6.95€ for kids). AE, MC, V. Daily noon–9:30pm. Tram: 13, 14, or 17 to Westermarkt.

Leidseplein

MODERATE

Café Americain ★ CONTINENTAL The lofty dining room here is a national monument of Art Nouveau and Art Deco. Since its opening in 1900, the place has been a hangout for Dutch and international artists, writers, dancers, and actors. *Tout* Amsterdam once liked to be seen here, but now it's mostly for tourists. Don't let that

Real Cutups

In the 1960s, satirist Gerrit Komrij described the Café Americain's notoriously brusque waiters as "unemployed knife-throwers."

worry you: It's still great. Leaded stained-glass windows, newspaper-littered reading tables, bargello-patterned velvet upholstery, frosted-glass Tiffany chandeliers from the 1920s, and tall carved columns are all part of the dusky sit-and-chat atmosphere. Seafood specialties include monkfish, perch, salmon, and king prawns; meat dishes include rack of Irish lamb and rosé breast of duck with creamed potatoes. Jazz lovers can stock up on good music and food at the Sunday jazz brunch.

Leidsekade 97 (in the Amsterdam American Hotel, at Leidseplein). ✆ **020/556-3000.** www.edenamsterdamamericanhotel.com. Main courses 16€–23€. AE, DC, MC, V. Daily 10:30am–midnight. Tram: 1, 2, 5, 7, or 10 to Leidseplein.

Rembrandtplein

MODERATE

Memories of India INDIAN The Khan family proprietors earned their spurs in the crowded and intensely competitive London market for Indian cuisine, and then brought their award-winning formula to Amsterdam. That formula is simple, really: Serve top-flight Indian food in a setting that gives traditional Indian motifs a modern slant, charge moderate prices, and employ an attentive waitstaff. The menu is pretty straightforward, with the usual tandoori and curry dishes, but it pushes the boat out a bit with some fish items, like the Indian Ocean pomfret in a roasted coriander-seed sauce. Takeout service is available.

Reguliersdwarsstraat 88 (at Vijzelstraat). ✆ **020/623-5710.** www.memoriesofindia.nl. Main courses 12€–22€; fixed-price menus 18€–28€ a head. AE, DC, MC, V. Daily 5–11:30pm. Tram: 4, 9, or 14 to Rembrandtplein.

The Jordaan

EXPENSIVE

Bordewijk ★★ FRENCH This restaurant is justly regarded as one of the best in the city. The decor is tasteful, with green potted plants offsetting the severity of the white walls and metallic black tables. Service is relaxed yet attentive, and on mild summer evenings, you can't beat dining alfresco on the canal-side terrace. But the real treat is the food. An innovative chef accents French standards with Mediterranean and Asian flourishes to create an elegant fusion of flavors. The menu changes often but might include something like these: Bresse pigeon with fresh morel mushrooms and polenta, salted rib roast with bordelaise sauce, serrano ham marinated in wine and vinegar and served with fresh pasta, or even Japanese-style raw fish.

Noordermarkt 7 (at Prinsengracht). ✆ **020/624-3899.** www.bordewijk.nl. Reservations required. Main courses 24€–29€; fixed-price menu 39€–72€. AE, MC, V. Tues–Sun 6:30–10pm. Tram: 1, 2, 5, 13, or 17 to Martelaarsgracht.

MODERATE

Albatros Seafoodhouse & Vis Restaurant ★ SEAFOOD The Atlantic and North Sea fish served here have the great virtue of being grilled, poached, and fried in the simplest manner possible, then served in a relaxed neighborhood atmosphere amid ship-ahoy decor. In summer, you can dine on a narrow sidewalk terrace and watch seagulls and albatrosses flying overhead, while soaking up the atmospheric Jordaan, where there's little traffic and locals chatting on stoops. Try the mixed seafood salad, the raw herring, or the sea bass.

Westerstraat 264 (at Lijnbaansgracht). ✆ **020/627-9932.** www.restaurantalbatros.nl. Reservations recommended on weekends. Main courses 16€–23€ (some prices set daily). AE, DC, MC, V. Thurs–Mon 6–11pm. Tram: 3 or 10 to Marnixplein.

Hostaria ★ ITALIAN Owners Marjolein and Massimo Pasquinoli have transformed this tiny space on a lively Jordaan street into a piece of authentic Italy, and a showcase for the kind of cuisine Italian mothers wish they could equal. When you sit down, Marjolein brings a dish of garlicky tapenade and warm bread. For an appetizer, you might select a balanced fish soup with a slice of salmon, or lightly grilled eggplant slices with fresh herbs. The *zuppa di gamberone con l'acquetta,* a plate of prawns and shellfish from the market, is terrific. Choose from a variety of wonderful homemade pastas—the tagliatelle with arugula and truffles is a particular treat—and of *secondi piatti* such as veal stuffed with Italian sausage or duck cooked Roman style.

Tweede Egelantiersdwarsstraat 9 (off Egelantiersgracht). ✆ **020/626-0028.** Reservations recommended on weekends. Main courses 17€–23€; fixed-price menu 34€. No credit cards. Tues–Sun 6–10pm. Tram: 13, 14, or 17 to Westermarkt.

't Stuivertje MODERN DUTCH Tucked down a narrow Jordaan side street, this small and personable neighborhood eatery is invariably filled with locals. Meals come from an open kitchen in an agreeably plain, intimate room, with wood chairs and tables, and a small bar. Black-and-white photographs of American stars, like Ol' Blue Eyes, hang on the walls with contrasting Old Dutch prints. The limited menu reflects the restaurant's authentic Amsterdam style, featuring classic Dutch dishes with that extra tasty little something, as in the *gegrilde varkensfilet met een cantherellen-roomsaus* (grilled pork filet in a chanterelles-cream sauce). There are vegetarian choices, daily specials, and a seasonal menu.

Hazenstraat 58 (off Lauriergracht). ✆ **020/623-1349.** www.hetstuivertje.nl. Main courses 13€–25€; fixed-price menu 24€. AE, MC, V. Tues–Sun 5:30–11pm. Tram: 7 or 10 to Marnixstraat.

Local Heroes

To eat a genuine Dutch *broodje* (sandwich) in a real *broodjeswinkel* (sandwich shop), go to the ever-crowded Eetsalon Van Dobben, Korte Reguliersdwarsstraat 5–9 (✆ 020/624-4200; www.vandobben.nl; tram: 4, 9, or 14), off Rembrandtplein, where you might try a smoked-eel sandwich. Locals come here for these and herring, liverwurst, croquets, or ox-tongue sandwiches. Simpler roast beef and Gouda sandwiches are also available. Some patrons swear by the platter of giant meatballs. It's open Monday to Saturday from 9:30am to 1am (to 2am Sat), and Sunday from 11:30am to 8pm.

Should Amsterdam's shortage of good pastrami on rye get to you, head out to Amsterdam-Zuid (South), to the great kosher sandwich shop Sal Meijer ★, Scheldestraat 45 (✆ 020/673-1313; www.sal-meijer.com; tram: 12 or 25), off Churchill-laan. The sandwiches start at 2.95€; the plate of the day begins at 15€. Sal's is open Sunday to Thursday from 10am to 7:30pm, and Friday from 10am to 2pm.

Museum District & Vondelpark

MODERATE

Café-Restaurant De Duvel ★ INTERNATIONAL Invariably packed with hip locals, "The Devil" is a friendly neighborhood *eetcafé* (bar with eats) that serves more-than-decent food in a cozy red dining room in the trendy De Pijp district, close to Sarphatipark. Indonesian chicken saté, salad with prawns tempura, and beef filet in a mustard mousseline are some of the typical dishes—a bit wider-ranging than your standard Continental fare, but nothing overly adventurous—on a menu that changes every 3 months yet rarely goes without some kind of pasta, seafood, and chicken offering. The bar side of things is at least as important as the restaurant, and the kitchen closes before midnight.

Eerste van der Helststraat 59–61. ✆ **020/675-7517.** www.deduvel.nl. Main courses 13€–17€. AE, DC, MC, V. Mon 4pm–1am; Tues–Thurs 11am–1am; Fri–Sat 11am–3am; Sun noon–1am. Tram: 3, 12 or 25 to Ceintuurbaan/Ferdinand Bolstraat.

Vertigo ★ MEDITERRANEAN In the vaulted basement of a monumental, late-19th-century villa on Vondelpark's edge, this tree-shaded, animated cafe-restaurant shares premises with the Film Instituut Nederland and its EYE film theater, which is due to move to Amsterdam-Noord (North) at the end of 2011. Hence the portraits of screen legends on the walls and the classic scenes of movie dining on the menu; the name is even a reference to Hitchcock's classic movie. On summer days, the outside terrace on the edge of Vondelpark is a favored time-out spot for in-line skaters and joggers, and you can expect to share your table and make instant acquaintances with just about everyone within earshot. At other times, you can enjoy the southern European–inspired cuisine in an intimate, candlelit setting inside. The menu, which changes often, has fish, meat, and vegetarian options, plus some fresh pastas.

Vondelpark 3 (at Vondelstraat). **020/612-3021.** www.vertigo.nl. Reservations recommended on weekends. Main courses 12€–20€; fixed-price menu 25€. AE, MC, V. Daily 10am–1am. Tram: 1 or 6 to Eerste Constantijn Huygensstraat, or 2, 3, 5, or 12 to Van Baerlestraat.

Wildschut ★ CONTINENTAL One of those places that keeps its chic reputation through thick and thin, this cafe-restaurant occupies a curved dining room at the junction of van Baerlestraat and Roelof Hartstraat, not far from the Concertgebouw. During the summer, Amsterdam's bold and beautiful come to see and be seen on the terrace. It gets crowded here on Friday and Saturday evenings, so be prepared to join the standing throng while waiting for a table. The food is straightforward but good, ranging from BLTs to vegetarian lasagna to American rib-eye with green-pepper sauce.

Roelof Hartplein 1–3 (off van Baerlestraat). ✆ **020/676-8220.** www.goodfoodgroup.nl. Main courses 15€–18€. MC, V. Mon–Thurs 9am–1am; Fri 9am–3am; Sat 10:30am–3am; Sun 9:30am–midnight. Tram: 3, 5, 12, or 24 to Roelof Hartplein.

Amsterdam South

EXPENSIVE

De Kas ★★ CONTINENTAL Despite a precocious, aren't-we-fabulous house style, this eatery merits a traipse out to the edge of town. The converted 1926 greenhouse with a smokestack, on open ground in South Amsterdam, is light, breezy, and spacious. You get just a couple of variations on a three-course, daily changing fixed menu. Organic Mediterranean-style greens and herbs come fresh from an adjacent working hothouse and the restaurant's own farm, and meat is sourced daily from nearby animal-friendly organic producers. Persnickety attention to detail is the norm in the kitchen, and service is attentive enough that the waitstaff seem to be acquainted personally with every item on your plate.

Kamerlingh Onneslaan 3 (close to Amstel station). ✆ **020/462-4562.** www.restaurantdekas.nl. Reservations required. Fixed-price lunch 38€; fixed-price dinner 50€; chef's table 125€. AE, DC, MC, V. Mon-Fri noon-3pm and 6:30-10pm; Sat 6:30-10pm. Tram: 9 to Hogeweg.

Amsterdam East

INEXPENSIVE

Kilimanjaro ★AFRICAN This chic restaurant on the ground floor of a narrow old house not far from the Maritime Museum has few tables, and it serves such authentically good food—a variety of African specialties, such as Senegalese lamb curry, crocodile steak (very snappy), and *doro wat* (spicy Ethiopian chicken sautéed in red-pepper sauce and served with a spinach salad). The simple decor of high ceilings, white walls, and colorful tablecloths smartly manages to avoid the usual colonial jungle-cabana look.

Rapenburgerplein 6 (at Prins Hendrikkade). ✆ **020/622-3485.** Reservations required. Main courses 11€-17€; *dagschotel* 15€. AE, DC, MC, V. Tues-Sun 5-10pm. Bus: 22, 42, or 43 to Kadijksplein.

Amsterdam West

MODERATE

Amsterdam ★  CONTINENTAL Based in a century-old water-pumping station complete with diesel-powered engine, the inventively named Amsterdam has taken a monument of Victorian industrial good taste and transformed it into a model of contemporary good eats. You dine amid a buzz of conviviality in the large, brightly lit former pumping hall, which had been so carefully tended by the water workers that some of its elegant decoration didn't even need repainting. Service is friendly, and the good food is moderately priced. The fried sweetbreads are popular. If you're sharing and feeling flush, spring for a seafood platter of lobster, crab, clams, and more. The Amsterdam is a little bit out from the center of town, but it's easily worth the tram ride.

Watertorenplein 6 (off Haarlemmerweg). ✆ **020/682-2666.** www.cradam.nl. Reservations recommended on weekends. Main courses 12€-18€; seafood platters (for 2) 33€-65€. AE, DC, MC, V. Sun-Thurs 11am-1am; Fri-Sat 11am-2am (meals served to 11:30pm). Tram: 10 to van Hallstraat.

Picnic Picks

You can pick up almost anything you might want for a picnic—from cold cuts to freshly packed sandwiches to a bottle of wine—at the Albert Heijn supermarket, at the corner of Leidsestraat and Koningsplein, near Spui (tram: 1, 2, or 5), open Monday to Friday from 9am to 8pm and Saturday from 9am to 6pm. Then head over to Vondelpark, only a 10-minute walk. In summertime, you might even catch a free concert at the outdoor theater there. At the branch of Albert Heijn on Museumplein, across the street from the Concertgebouw (tram: 3, 5, 12, or 16), haul your brown bag right up onto the sloping, grass-covered roof, which is a prime spot for sunbathing, hanging out, and picnicking, and has a great view of Museumplein.

SEEING THE SIGHTS

For sightseers in Amsterdam, the question is not simply what to see and do, but rather how many of this intriguing city's marvelous sights you can fit into the time you have. There are miles and miles of canals to cruise, hundreds of narrow streets to wander, countless historic buildings to visit, more than 40 museums holding collections of everything from artistic wonders to obscure curiosities, not to mention all the diamond cutters and craftspeople to watch as they practice generations-old skills . . . the list is as long as every tourist's individual interests.

Your very first stop on any sightseeing excursion, of course, should be the tourist office—the staff there has information on anything you might want to know and some things you might not even have known you wanted to know. One absolute must-do in Amsterdam is a **canalboat cruise** (see "Organized Tours," later in this chapter). The view of the elegant canal houses from the water is unforgettable.

The Top Attractions

Anne Frankhuis ★★★ You shouldn't miss seeing and experiencing the Anne Frank House. In this typical Amsterdam canal house, with steep interior stairs, eight people from three separate families lived together in near silence for more than 2 years during World War II. This hiding place that Otto Frank found for his family, the van Pels family, and Fritz Pfeffer kept them safe until it was raided by Nazi forces tragically close to the end of the war, its occupants deported to concentration camps. It was in this house that Anne, whose ambition was to be a writer, kept her famous diary as a way to deal with both the boredom and her youthful array of thoughts, which had as much to do with personal relationships as with the war and the Nazi terror raging outside. Visiting the rooms in which she hid is a moving and eerily real experience.

During the war, the building was an office and warehouse, and its rooms are still as bare as they were when Anne's father returned, the only survivor of the eight *onderduikers* (divers, or hiders). Nothing has been changed, except that protective Plexiglas

YOUR passport TO AMSTERDAM

To get the most out of your trip, consider purchasing the **I amsterdam Card.** The card is valid for 1 day for 38€, 2 days for 48€, and 3 days for 58€. It affords free travel on public transportation; free admission to more than 40 museums and attractions, including the Rijksmuseum or the Van Gogh Museum (not both), and discounted admission to more museums and attractions; a free canalboat cruise; discounted excursions, including reduced rates on the Hop On Hop Off Museum Boat and the Canal Bus; and discounts at some restaurants and stores.

Before purchasing one, think about whether you'll get your money's worth. Remember, this is Holland, where the local fondness for the coin of the realm is proverbial and killer bargains are thin on the ground. You'll have to work yourself pretty hard to come out ahead, jumping on and off trams, buses, and canalboats, and running into and out of museums.

The card is available from Holland Tourist Information at Schiphol Airport and from Amsterdam Tourist Information offices in the city.

panels now protect the wall on which Anne pinned up photos of her favorite actress, Deanna Durbin, and of the little English princesses Elizabeth and Margaret. As you tour the building, it's easy to imagine Anne's experience growing up in this place, awakening as a young woman and writing down her secret thoughts.

To avoid lines, get here early—this advice isn't as useful as it used to be, because everybody is both giving it and heeding it, but it should still save you some waiting time. An even better strategy is to go in the evening on a night when the museum stays open until 9 or 10pm—it's generally quieter and less crowded. Next door at no. 265–267 is a separate wing for temporary exhibits.

Prinsengracht 263 (at Westermarkt). ✆ **020/556-7105.** www.annefrank.org. Admission 8€ adults, 4€ children 10–17, free for children 9 and under. Mid-Mar to June and 1st 2 weeks of Sept Mon–Fri 9am–9pm, Sat 9am–10pm; July–Aug daily 9am–10pm; mid-Sept to mid-Mar daily 9am–7pm (Jan 1 noon–7pm; Dec 25 noon–5pm; Dec 31 9am–5pm). Closed Yom Kippur. Tram: 13, 14, or 17 to Westermarkt.

Rijksmuseum ★★★ The country's premier museum is still working through a decade-long project to refit itself for the 21st century. Until renovations are done (they're expected to be completed in 2013), most of the museum is closed, but key paintings and other works from the 17th-century Dutch Golden Age collection can be viewed in the Philips Wing, under the banner of The Masterpieces. Even in its reduced circumstances, the "State Museum" is one of the leading museums in the land. But remember: Most of the collection, which totals some seven million individual objects (only a small fraction of which would be displayed at any given time), will be "invisible" to visitors for at least another few years.

Architect Petrus Josephus Hubertus Cuypers (1827–1921), the "grandfather of modern Dutch architecture," designed the museum in a monumental, gabled Dutch neo-Renaissance style. Cuypers, a Catholic, slipped in a dab of neo-Gothic, too, causing the country's Protestant King William III to scorn what he called "that cathedral," and the building opened in 1885 to a less-than-enthusiastic public reception.

The Rijksmuseum contains the world's largest collection of paintings by the Dutch Old Masters, including the most illustrious of all, a single work that all but defines Holland's Golden Age. That painting is ***The Militia Company of Captain Frans Banning Cocq and Lieutenant Willem van Ruytenburch*** (1642), better known as ***The Night Watch,*** by Rembrandt. The scene it so dramatically depicts is surely alien to most of the people who flock to see it: gaily uniformed militiamen checking their weapons and accoutrements before moving out on patrol. Artists van Ruisdael, van Heemskerck, Frans Hals, Paulus Potter, Jan Steen, Vermeer, de Hooch, Terborch, Gerard Dou, and many more also are represented in the museum. The range is impressive—individual portraits, guild paintings, landscapes, seascapes, domestic scenes, medieval religious subjects, allegories, and the incredible (and nearly photographic) Dutch still lifes.

The Day Watch?

Rembrandt's *The Night Watch* (1642) actually shows a daytime scene. Centuries of grime dulled its luster until restoration revealed sunlight glinting on the militia company's arms.

Two rare furnished 17th-century dollhouses should be a highlight for children, bringing the Dutch Golden Age to life for them in a way no amount of "real" stuff could. In addition, some of the museum's finest pieces of antique Delftware and silver are exhibited.

What to See & Do in Amsterdam

13

Seeing the Sights

AMSTERDAM

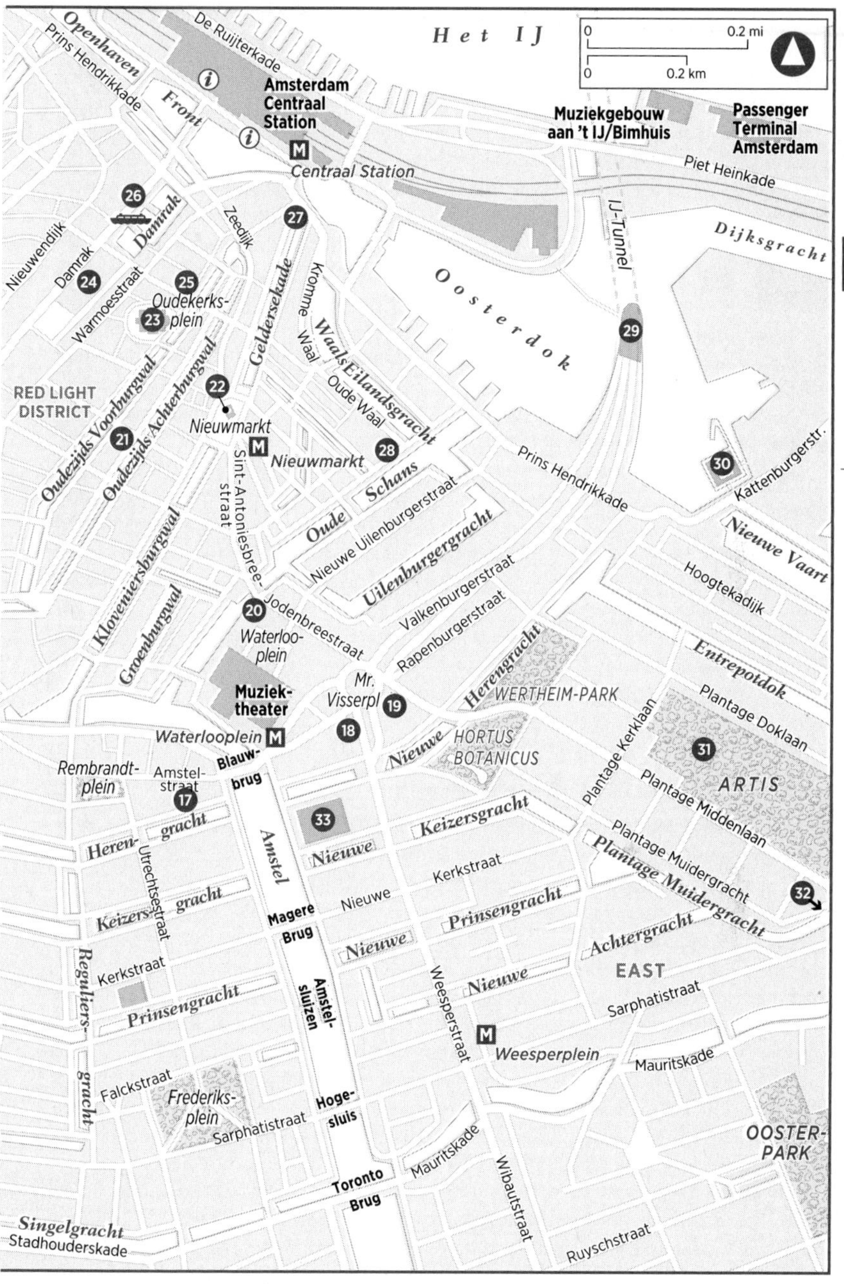
Het IJ
0.2 mi
0.2 km
Amsterdam Centraal Station
Centraal Station
Muziekgebouw aan 't IJ/Bimhuis
Passenger Terminal Amsterdam
Piet Heinkade
Dijksgracht
Oosterdok
IJ-Tunnel
De Ruijterkade
Openhaven
Prins Hendrikkade
Front
Damrak
Nieuwendijk
Zeedijk
Warmoesstraat
Oudekerks-plein
Geldersekade
Kromme Waal
Oude Waal
WaalsEilandsgracht
RED LIGHT DISTRICT
Oudezijds Voorburgwal
Oudezijds Achterburgwal
Nieuwmarkt
Sint-Antoniesbreestraat
Oude Schans
Nieuwe Uilenburgerstraat
Uilenburgergracht
Kattenburgerstr.
Nieuwe Vaart
Hoogtekadijk
Kloveniersburgwal
Groenburgwal
Jodenbreestraat
Valkenburgerstraat
Rapenburgerstraat
Waterloo-plein
Muziek-theater
Mr. Visserpl
Herengracht
WERTHEIM-PARK
Entrepotdok
Plantage Doklaan
Plantage Kerklaan
HORTUS BOTANICUS
Nieuwe
Waterlooplein
Blauwbrug
Rembrandt-plein
Amstel-straat
ARTIS
Plantage Middenlaan
Plantage Muidergracht
Heren-gracht
Utrechtsestraat
Amstel
Keizersgracht
Nieuwe
Kerkstraat
Keizers-gracht
Magere Brug
Prinsengracht
Achtergracht
EAST
Reguliers-gracht
Kerkstraat
Prinsengracht
Amstel-sluizen
Weesperstraat
Sarphatistraat
Weesperplein
Mauritskade
Falckstraat
Frederiks-plein
Sarphatistraat
Hoge-sluis
OOSTER-PARK
Toronto Brug
Mauritskade
Wibautstraat
Singelgracht
Stadhouderskade
Ruyschstraat
13
AMSTERDAM
Seeing the Sights

Philips Wing, Jan Luijkenstraat 1B (at Museumplein). ✆ **020/674-7000.** www.rijksmuseum.nl. Admission 12.50€ adults, free for children 18 and under. Daily 9am–6pm. Closed Jan 1. Tram: 2 or 5 to Hobbemastraat.

Van Gogh Museum ★★★ Walking through the rooms of this contemporary (1973) building is a moving experience. The museum displays, in chronological order, more than 200 van Gogh paintings. As you move through the rooms, the canvases reflect the artist's changing environment and much of his inner life, so that gradually van Gogh becomes almost a tangible presence standing at your elbow. You'll see the early, brooding *The Potato Eaters* and *The Yellow House,* and the painting known around the world simply as *Sunflowers,* though van Gogh actually titled it *Still Life with Fourteen Sunflowers.* By the time you reach the vaguely threatening painting of a flock of black crows rising from a waving cornfield, you can almost feel the artist's mounting inner pain.

Don't "Go"

Gogh is not pronounced *Go,* as Americans incorrectly say it, nor is it *Goff,* as other English speakers would have it, but *Khokh* (the *kh* sounds like the *ch* in the Scottish pronunciation of *loch*—a kind of clearing-your-throat sound).

In addition to the paintings, there are nearly 600 drawings by van Gogh, on permanent display in the museum's new wing. This free-standing, multistory, half-oval structure, designed by the Japanese architect Kisho Kurokawa, is constructed in a bold combination of titanium and gray-brown stone, and is connected to the main building by a subterranean walkway.

Note: Lines at the museum can be long, especially in summer—try going on a weekday morning. Allow 2 to 4 hours to get around once you're inside.

Paulus Potterstraat 7 (at Museumplein). ✆ **020/570-5200.** www.vangoghmuseum.nl. Admission 10€ adults, 2.50€ children 13–17, free for children 12 and under. Sat–Thurs 10am–6pm; Fri 10am–10pm. Closed Jan 1. Tram: 2, 3, 5, or 12 to van Baerlestraat.

More Museums & Galleries

Amsterdams Historisch Museum (Amsterdam Historical Museum) ★★ To better understand what you see as you explore the city, a visit to this brilliantly executed museum is especially worthwhile. Its location, the restored 17th-century former Burger Weeshuis (City Orphanage), is already notable. Gallery by gallery, century by century, you learn how a small fishing village founded around 1200 became a major sea power and trading center. The main focus is on the city's 17th-century Golden Age, when Amsterdam was the wealthiest city in the world, and some of the most interesting exhibits are of the trades that made it rich. You can view famous paintings by the Dutch Old Masters in the context of their time.

There are plenty of hands-on exhibits and some neat video displays. A scale model from around 1677 shows a then-new Stadhuis (Town Hall) on the Dam, now the Royal Palace. Some outer walls and the roof have been removed to allow you a bird's-eye look inside, which makes a later visit to the palace that much more enjoyable.

If you don't feel like visiting the museum but crave some historic art and architecture, stroll through the **Schuttersgalerij (Civic Guards Gallery).** This narrow, sky-lit, two-story passageway linking Kalverstraat to the hidden Begijnhof courtyard (see "Sights of Religious Significance," below) is just outside the museum and is signed at various points around it. Under the walkway's glass roof, you'll see 15 bigger-is-better, 17th-century paintings showing the city's heroic musketeers, the Civic Guards. One of the best is *Captain Joan Huydecoper's Company Celebrating the Peace of Münster* (1648), by Govert Flinck. Admission is free, and hours are the same as for the museum.

Kalverstraat 92, Nieuwezijds Voorburgwal 357, and Sint-Luciënsteeg 27 (next to the Begijnhof). ✆ **020/523-1822.** www.ahm.nl. Admission 10€ adults, 7.50€ seniors, 5€ children 6–18, free for children 5 and under. Mon–Fri 10am–5pm; Sat–Sun and holidays 11am–5pm. Closed Jan 1, Apr 30, and Dec 25. Tram: 1, 2, 4, 5, 9, 14, 16, 24, or 25 to Spui.

Hermitage Amsterdam A visit to Amsterdam can offer you some of the experiences of a trip to St. Petersburg. Opened in 2004 in the neoclassical Amstelhof, the Amsterdam branch of Russia's renowned State Hermitage museum recalls links between the two canal-threaded cities that date back centuries. Surrounding a central courtyard, it's flanked on two sides by canals and on a third by the Amstel River. Holland even gets some of its own cultural patrimony back again here, if only on loan, since the Hermitage has 600 paintings by Dutch and Flemish Old Masters. The Neerlandia Building, which was built next to the Amstelhof in 1888 as a home for indigent married couples, houses a Hermitage for Children exhibit.

Amstel 51 (at the Amstel River). ✆ **0900/4376-48243** or 020/530-7488. www.hermitage.nl. Admission 7.50€ adults, free for children 16 and under. Thurs–Tues 10am–7pm; Wed 10am–8pm. Closed Jan 1 and Dec 25. Tram: 9 or 14 to Waterlooplein.

Joods Historisch Museum (Jewish Historical Museum) ★ In the heart of what was once Amsterdam's thriving Jewish Quarter, this museum is housed in the restored Ashkenazi Synagogue complex—a cluster of four former synagogues. It contains a collection of paintings, decorations, and ceremonial objects that was confiscated during World War II and patiently reestablished in the postwar period. Through its objects, photographs, artworks, and interactive displays, the museum tells three intertwining stories—of Jewish identity, Jewish religion and culture, and Jewish history in the Netherlands. It presents the community in both good times and bad and provides insights into the Jewish way of life over the centuries. Leave time to appreciate the beauty and size of the buildings themselves, which include the oldest public synagogue in Europe. There are frequent temporary exhibits of international interest. The museum cafe is a great place to have a cup of coffee and a pastry, or a light kosher meal.

Nieuwe Amstelstraat 1 (at Waterlooplein). ✆ **020/531-0310.** www.jhm.nl. Admission 9€ adults, 6€ seniors and students, 4.50€ children 13–17, free for children 12 and under; combined admission with the Portuguese Synagogue (p. 310) 12€ adults, 6€ children 13–17, free for children 12 and under. Daily 11am–5pm (Jan 1 noon–5pm). Closed Jewish New Year (2 days) and Yom Kippur. Tram: 9 or 14 to Waterlooplein.

Museum Het Rembrandthuis (Rembrandt House Museum) ★ This isn't the place to see Rembrandt's greatest masterpieces; those are at the Rijksmuseum. But without a doubt, this is the best place to get an intimate sense of the artist himself. Bought by Rembrandt in 1639 when he was Amsterdam's most fashionable portrait painter, the house, which has 10 rooms, is a shrine to one of the most remarkable artists the world has ever known. In this house, Rembrandt's son Titus was born and his wife, Saskia, died. The artist was bankrupt when he left it in 1658. Not until 1906 was the building rescued from a succession of subsequent owners and restored as a museum.

Contemporary restoration has returned the house to the way it looked when Rembrandt lived and worked here. The rooms are furnished with 17th-century objects and furniture that, as far as possible, match the descriptions in Rembrandt's 1656 petition for bankruptcy. His printing press is back in place, and you can view 250 of his etchings and drawings hanging on the walls. Temporary exhibits are mounted in a modern wing next door.

Jodenbreestraat 4 (at Waterlooplein). ✆ **020/520-0400.** www.rembrandthuis.nl. Admission 9€ adults, 6€ students, 2€ children 6–17, free for children 5 and under. Daily 10am–5pm. Closed Jan 1. Metro: Waterlooplein. Tram: 9 or 14 to Waterlooplein.

Museum Van Loon This magnificent patrician house was owned by the van Loon family from 1884 to 1945. On its walls hang more than 80 family portraits, including those of Willem van Loon, one of the founders of the United East India Company; Nicolaas Ruychaver, who liberated Amsterdam from the Spanish in 1578; and another, later, Willem van Loon, who became city mayor in 1686. Among other treasures are a family album in which are tempera portraits of all living van Loons painted at two successive dates (1650 and 1675), and a series of commemorative coins struck to honor seven different golden wedding anniversaries celebrated between 1621 and 1722. The house's restored period rooms are filled with richly decorated paneling, stucco work, mirrors, fireplaces, furnishings, porcelain, medallions, chandeliers, rugs, and more. The garden has carefully tended hedges and a coach house modeled on a Greek temple.

Keizersgracht 672 (near Vijzelstraat). ✆ **020/624-5255.** www.museumvanloon.nl. Admission 7€ adults, 5€ students and children 6–18, free for children 5 and under. Wed–Mon 11am–5pm. Tram: 16, 24, or 25 to Keizersgracht.

Museum Willet-Holthuysen This museum offers another rare opportunity to visit an elegant 17th-century canal house This particular house, built in 1687, was renovated several times before its last inhabitant gave it and its contents to the city in 1889. Among the most interesting rooms are a Victorian-era bedroom on the second floor, a large reception room with tapestry wall panels, and an 18th-century basement kitchen that's still so completely furnished and functional you could swear the cook had merely stepped out to go shopping. In the dining salon, the table under the chandelier is set for a meal being served some 300 years too late.

Herengracht 605 (near the Amstel River). ✆ **020/523-1822.** www.willetholthuysen.nl. Admission 7€ adults, 5.25€ seniors, 3.50€ children 6–18, free for children 5 and under. Mon–Fri 10am–5pm; Sat–Sun and holidays 11am–5pm. Closed Jan 1, Apr 30, and Dec 25. Tram: 4, 9, or 14 to Rembrandtplein.

Ons' Lieve Heer op Solder (Our Lord in the Attic) ★ After Amsterdam's 1578 Protestant *Alteratie* (Changeover), Roman Catholics fell into disfavor. Forced to worship in secret, they devised ingenious ways of gathering for Sunday services. This museum in the middle of the Red Light District incorporates the most amazing and best preserved of these clandestine places of worship. The church is in the attic of one of the oldest canal houses you can visit, which was transformed between 1661 and 1663 by wealthy Catholic merchant Jan Hartman to house a church. Seeing a rambling old canal house furnished much as it would have been in the mid-18th century, with heavy oak furniture, Delft tiles, and period paintings, makes a visit of an hour or two here worthwhile by itself. Worshipers entered by a door on a side street and climbed a narrow flight of stairs to the hidden third-floor church, with its large baroque altar, religious statuary, pews to seat 150, an 18th-century spinet-size pipe organ, and two narrow upper balconies. It's still used for services and concerts.

Other rooms contain a trove of magnificent religious vessels, like 17th-century monstrances in gold and silver.

Oudezijds Voorburgwal 40 (near the Oude Kerk). ✆ **020/624-6604.** www.opsolder.nl. Admission 7€ adults, 5€ students, 1€ children 5–18, free for children 4 and under. Mon–Sat 10am–5pm; Sun and holidays 1–5pm. Closed Jan 1 and Apr 30. Tram: 1, 2, 4, 5, 9, 13, 16, 17, 24, 25, or 26 to Centraal Station.

Scheepvaartmuseum (Maritime Museum) ★★ ☺ ***Note:*** This museum is closed for renovation until the summer of 2011; some of the service information provided below is likely to change when the museum reopens.

A bonanza for anyone who loves ships and the sea, the Scheepvaartmuseum is housed in a former arsenal of the Amsterdam Admiralty dating from 1656 and overlooks the busy Amsterdam harbor. Surrounding the inner courtyard are 25 rooms with ship models, charts, instruments, maps, prints, and paintings—a chronicle of Holland's abiding ties to the sea through commerce, fishing, yachting, navigational development, and war. Brief texts explain each exhibit, and desks with more extensive information are found in every room.

A full-size replica of the *Amsterdam,* a three-masted United East India Company sailing ship which foundered off Hastings in 1749 on her maiden voyage to the fabled Spice Islands (Indonesia), is moored at the museum's wharf. Other ships that can be seen include a steam icebreaker, a motor lifeboat, and a herring lugger. Environmentalists will want to go aboard Greenpeace's retired environmental combatant *Rainbow Warrior.* You reach this museum by taking a 20-minute walk along the historical waterfront, the Nautisch Kwartier (Nautical Quarter).

Kattenburgerstraat 7 (in the Oosterdok). ✆ **020/523-2222.** www.scheepvaartmuseum.nl. Admission 9€ adults, 7€ seniors, 4.50€ children 6–17, free for children 5 and under. Tues–Sat 10am–5pm (also Mon during school vacations); Sun noon–5pm. Closed Jan 1, Apr 30, and Dec 25. Bus: 22, 42, or 43 to Kattenburgerplein.

Stedelijk Museum ★★ ***Note:*** The Stedelijk Museum is closed for renovations and expansion until 2011; some of the service information provided below is likely to change when the museum reopens.

The city's modern-art museum has works by Dutch painters such as Karel Appel, Willem de Kooning, and Piet Mondrian, and by Calder, Oldenburg, Rosenquist, Warhol, and more. It houses the largest collection outside Russia of Kasimir Malevich's abstract paintings, but it centers its exhibits around the De Stijl, Cobra, post-Cobra, nouveau réalisme, Pop Art, color-field painting, zero, minimalist, and conceptual schools. The museum cafe features a giant Appel mural from 1956. Depending on your level of interest in modern art, you could spend from 4 hours to all day here.

The Mondrian paintings displayed here include his *Composition in Red, Black, Blue, Yellow, and Gray* (1920), and, by way of variation, *Composition in Blue, Red, Black, and Yellow* (1922)—the gray's still there, but he chose not to mention it in the title. Van Gogh gets in on the act, too, with his *Montmartre* (1887), *Carnations* (1888), and *The Diggers* (1889). These are alongside a handful of paintings by Chagall, Cézanne, Picasso, Renoir, Monet, and Manet, but the primary focus is on post-1945 art. Not all of the collection is on display all the time, and it's possible that you won't see many—or even any—of these. Despite the names mentioned here, the Stedelijk is not the place to see van Goghs or works by French Impressionists.

Paulus Potterstraat 13 (at Museumplein). ✆ **020/573-2911.** www.stedelijk.nl. Admission 9€ adults; 4.50€ seniors, students, and children 7–16; free for children 6 and under; 23€ family. Daily 10am–6pm. Closed Jan 1. Tram: 2, 3, 5, 12, 16, or 24 to Museumplein.

Tropenmuseum (Tropical Museum) ★★ ☺ One of Amsterdam's more intriguing museums is run by the Royal Tropical Institute, a foundation devoted to the study of the cultures of tropical areas around the world. The building complex alone is worth the trip to Amsterdam East and the Oosterpark (East Park); its heavily ornamented facade is an amalgam of Dutch architectural styles—turrets, stepped gables, arched windows, and delicate spires—and the monumental galleried interior court is one of the most impressive spots in town.

The most interesting exhibits are the walk-through model villages and city-street scenes that capture moments in the daily lives of such places as India and Indonesia; the exhibit on the tools and techniques used to produce batik, the distinctively dyed Indonesian fabrics; and the displays of the tools, instruments, and ornaments that clutter a tropical residence. There's a permanent exhibit on people and the environment in West Asia and North Africa. Part of the premises is given over to the children-only Kindermuseum—the Tropical Museum Junior—with its educational and interactive exhibits.

Linnaeusstraat 2 (at Mauritskade). ✆ **020/568-8200.** www.tropenmuseum.nl. Admission 9€ adults, 7.50€ seniors, 5€ students, 4€ children 6–17, free for children 5 and under, 25€ family. Daily 10am–5pm (to 3pm Dec 5, 24, and 31). Closed Jan 1, Apr 30, May 5, and Dec 25. Tram: 7, 9, 10, or 14 to Mauritskade.

Historical Buildings & Monuments

A massive edifice of colored brick and stone enclosing three arcades roofed in glass and iron, **Beurs van Berlage,** Beursplein 1 (✆ **020/530-4141;** www.beursvanberlage.nl; tram: 4, 9, 14, 16, 24, or 25), at Damrak, was originally the city's Stock Exchange. Completed in 1903, architect Hendrik Petrus Berlage's building was a revolutionary break with 19th-century architecture and is well worth visiting as a prime example of the Amsterdam School, contemporaneous with the work of Frank Lloyd Wright in America. Today, the Beurs is used as a space for concerts, conferences, and exhibits. Admission and open hours vary.

The **Munttoren** (tram: 4, 9, 14, 16, 24, or 25), on Muntplein, sits at a busy traffic intersection on the Rokin and Singel canals. In 1487, the Mint Tower's base was part of the Reguliers Gate in the city wall. In 1620, Hendrick de Keyser topped it with an ornate, lead-covered tower, from which a carillon of Hemony brothers bells sings out gaily every hour and plays a 1-hour concert on Fridays at noon. The tower got its present name in 1672, when it housed the city mint.

Constructed in the 14th century, **De Waag (Weigh House),** in Nieuwmarkt (✆ **020/557-9898;** www.waag.org; Metro: Nieuwmarkt), is the city's only surviving medieval fortified gate. It later became a guild house. Among the guilds lodged here was the Surgeon's Guild, immortalized in Rembrandt's painting *The Anatomy Lesson of Dr. Nicolaes Tulp* (1632), which depicts a dissection being conducted in the upper-floor Theatrum Anatomicum. Most of De Waag now houses a specialized educational and cultural institute and is rarely open; admission (when it's possible at all) is free (except in the case of occasional special exhibits). You can, however, visit the exceptional cafe-restaurant **In de Waag** (p. 287) on the ground floor.

The tilting **Montelbaanstoren** (Metro: Nieuwmarkt), the "leaning tower of Amsterdam," a fortification at the juncture of the Oude Schans and Waalseilandsgracht canals, dates from 1512. It's one of few surviving elements of the city's once-powerful defensive works. In 1606, Hendrick de Keyser added an octagonal tower and spire. The building now houses local Water Authority offices.

Gay Remembrance

The ***Homomonument,*** Westermarkt (tram: 13, 14, or 17), a sculpture group of three pink granite triangles near the Anne Frankhuis, is dedicated to the memory of gays and lesbians killed during World War II or as a result of oppression and persecution because of their sexuality. People visit to remember those who have died of AIDS.

Not far away, at the corner of Geldersekade and Prins Hendrikkade, stands the **Schreierstoren** (Metro: Centraal Station), built in 1480 and once a strong point in the city wall. Its name, which means Tower of Tears, comes from the tears allegedly shed by wives as their men sailed away on voyages from which they might never return. A stone tablet on the wall shows a woman with her hand to her face. Another tablet, placed in 1945, records the 350th anniversary of the *Eerste Schipvaart Naar Oostindië 1595* (First Ocean Voyage to the East Indies 1595). The tower's ground floor now houses a traditional bar, the **V.O.C. Café.**

A Palatial Residence

Koninklijk Paleis (Royal Palace) ★★ Dominating the Dam is the 17th-century, neoclassical facade of the Royal Palace. The building was originally designed by Jacob van Campen as a town hall, but in 1808, when Napoleon Bonaparte's younger brother Louis reigned as king of the Netherlands, it became a palace and was filled with Empire-style furniture. During the summer, you can visit the high-ceilinged Citizens' Hall, the Burgomasters' Chambers, and the Council Room. Since the return to the throne of the Dutch House of Orange, this has been the official palace of the reigning king or queen of the Netherlands. However, it's used only for occasional state receptions or official ceremonies (Queen Beatrix lives at Huis ten Bosch in The Hague).

Dam. ✆ **020/620-4060.** www.paleisamsterdam.nl. Admission 7.50€ adults; 6.50€ seniors, students, and children 5–16; free for children 4 and under. Generally July–Aug Tues–Sun 11am–5pm; Sept–June Tues–Sun noon–5pm (open days and hours vary; check before going). Closed during periods of royal residence and state receptions. Tram: 1, 2, 4, 5, 9, 13, 14, 16, 17, 24, or 25 to the Dam.

Sights of Religious Significance

A cluster of small homes around a garden courtyard, the **Begijnhof ★★**, Spui (✆ **020/625-8853;** www.begijnhofamsterdam.nl; tram: 1, 2, or 5), dates from the 14th century and is one of the best places to appreciate the earliest history of the city, when Amsterdam was a destination for religious pilgrims and an important center of Catholic nunneries. The Begijnhof itself was not a convent, but a home for pious laywomen known as *begijnen* (beguines), involved in religious and charitable work. It remained in operation even after the about-face changeover of the city from Catholicism to Protestantism in the late 16th century. The last *begijn* died in 1971. Opposite the front of the Begijnhof's English Church is a secret Catholic chapel built in 1671 and still in use. In the southwest corner of the cloister, at no. 34, stands **Het Houten Huys,** one of Amsterdam's pair of surviving timber houses, built around 1425. You're welcome to visit the Begijnhof daily 9am to 5pm. Seniors now reside in the 47 old homes, and their privacy and tranquillity must be respected. Access is on Gedempte Begijnensloot, an alleyway off Spui. Admission is free.

Nieuwe Kerk (New Church) This beautiful church was built in the last years of the 14th century. Many of its original priceless treasures were removed or painted over in 1578 when it passed into Protestant hands, but much of the church's original grandeur has since been recaptured. In 1814, the king first took the oath of office and was inaugurated here (Dutch royalty are not crowned). The church has a stately arched nave, an elaborately carved altar, a great pipe organ that dates from 1645, several noteworthy stained-glass windows, and sepulchral monuments for many of Holland's most revered poets and naval heroes.

Dam (next to the Royal Palace). ✆ **020/626-8168.** www.nieuwekerk.nl. Admission varies with different events; free when there's no exhibit. Daily 10am–6pm (to 10pm Thurs during exhibits). Tram: 1, 2, 4, 5, 9, 13, 14, 16, 17, 24, or 25 to the Dam.

Oude Kerk (Old Church) ★★ Construction on this late-Gothic church began in 1250. Rembrandt's wife, Saskia, is buried here. The church contains a magnificent organ from 1724 and is used regularly for organ recitals. Nowadays, the pretty little gabled almshouses around the Oude Kerk feature red-fringed windows through which the scantily dressed ladies of the Red Light District can be seen. Climb the 70m (230-ft.) church tower, which holds a carillon of 17th-century Hemony bells, on an hourly guided tour for great views of Old Amsterdam.

Oudekerksplein 23 (at Oudezijds Voorburgwal). ✆ **020/625-8284** for the church, or 020/689-2565 for the tower. www.oudekerk.nl. Admission: church 7.50€ adults; 5.50€ seniors, students, and children 5–13; free for children 4 and under; tower 6€ (minimum age 12). Church Mon–Sat 11am–5pm; Sun 1–5:30pm. Tower Sat–Sun 1–5pm; tours every 30 min. Metro: Nieuwmarkt.

Portugese Synagoge (Portuguese Synagogue) Sephardic Jews fleeing Spain and Portugal during the 16th and early 17th centuries established a neighborhood east of the center known as the Jewish Quarter. In 1665, they built an elegant Ionic-style synagogue within an existing courtyard facing what is now a busy traffic circle. The building was restored in the 1950s. Today it looks essentially like it did 320 years ago, with its women's gallery supported by 12 stone columns to represent the Twelve Tribes of Israel, and the large, low-hanging brass chandeliers that together hold 1,000 candles, all of which are lighted for the private weekly services.

Mr. Visserplein 3 (at Waterlooplein). ✆ **020/624-5351.** www.esnoga.com. Admission 6.50€ adults, 5€ seniors and students, 4€ children 13–17, free for children 12 and under; combined admission with the Jewish Historical Museum (see earlier in this chapter) 12€ adults, 6€ children 13–17, free for children 12 and under. Apr–Oct Sun–Fri 10am–4pm; Nov–Mar Sun–Thurs 10am–6pm, Fri 10am–2pm. Closed Jewish holidays. Tram: 9 or 14 to Mr. Visserplein.

Westerkerk (West Church) ★ The Dutch Renaissance–style Westerkerk is where Rembrandt was buried, and it holds the remains of his son Titus. This is also where Queen Beatrix said her marriage vows in 1966. Hendrick de Keyser designed the building, and construction began in 1620, but when he died a year later, his son Pieter took over, and the church opened in 1631. Get the best views of Amsterdam by climbing the 186 interior steps or taking the elevator to the top of the Westertoren on a guided tour; the 85m (279-ft.) church tower, dubbed Lange Jan (Long John), is Amsterdam's tallest. On its top is the blue, red, and gold imperial crown of the Holy Roman Empire, a symbol bestowed by the Habsburg emperor Maximilian. The tower's carillon is among the city's most lyrical.

Westermarkt. ✆ **020/624-7766** for the church, 020/689-2565 for the tower. www.westerkerk.nl. Admission: church free; tower 6€. Church Apr–Sept Mon–Sat 11am–3pm. Tower Apr–Oct Mon–Sat 10am–5:30pm; tours every 30 min. Tram: 13, 14, or 17 to Westermarkt.

Other Sites & Attractions

Artis ★★ ☺ For something to do with the kids, Artis is a safe bet. Established in 1838, the oldest zoo in the Netherlands houses more than 6,000 animals—including, of course, the usual tigers, leopards, elephants, camels, and peacocks. But for no extra charge, there's much more here. Visit the excellent Planetarium (closed Mon morning), the Geological and Zoological Museum, an Insectarium, and a Butterfly Garden. The Aquarium is superbly presented, particularly the sections on the Amazon River, coral reefs, and Amsterdam's own canals. Finally, there's a children's farm, where kids help tend to the needs of resident sheep, goats, chickens, and cows. For a snack or lunch, try the Artis Restaurant.

Plantage Kerklaan 38–40 (at Plantage Middenlaan). ✆ **020/523-3400.** www.artis.nl. Admission 19€ adults, 17€ seniors, 15€ children 3–9, free for children 2 and under. Apr–Oct daily 9am–6pm (to sunset Sat June–Aug); Nov–Mar daily 9am–5pm. Tram: 9 or 14 to Plantage Kerklaan.

Heineken Experience The experience unfolds inside the former Heineken brewing facilities, which date from 1867. Before the brewery stopped functioning in 1988, it was producing more than 100 million liters (26 million gal.) of beer annually. The fermentation tanks, each capable of holding a million glassfuls of Heineken, are still there, along with the multistory malt silos and all manner of vintage brewing equipment and implements. You "meet" Dr. Elion, the 19th-century chemist who isolated the renowned Heineken "A" yeast, which gives the beer its taste. In one amusing attraction, you stand on a moving floor, facing a large video screen, and get to see and feel what it's like to be a Heineken beer bottle—one of a half-million every hour—careening on a conveyor belt through a modern Heineken bottling plant. Best of all, in another touchy-feely presentation, you "sit" aboard an old brewery dray-wagon, "pulled" by a pair of big Shire horses on the video screen in front of you, that shakes, rattles, and rolls on a mini tour of Amsterdam.

Stadhouderskade 78 (at Ferdinand Bolstraat). ✆ **020/523-9435.** www.heinekenexperience.com. Admission 15€; children 17 and under admitted only when accompanied by an adult. Daily 11am–7pm (last admission 5:30pm). Closed Jan 1, Apr 30, and Dec 25 and 26. Tram: 16, 24, or 25 to Stadhouderskade.

Madame Tussauds ★ ☺ The Amsterdam version of the famed London attraction has its own cast of Dutch characters (Rembrandt, Queen Beatrix, Mata Hari), among a parade of international names (Kennedy, Churchill, Gandhi, Obama, and many more). Exhibits bring you "face to face" with the powerful and famous and let you step into the times, events, and moments that made them so. In the Grand Hall, styled to look like a reception room in a Dutch manor around 1700, are images of world leaders, royalty, artists, writers, and religious leaders. Those portrayed are brought to life with memorabilia such as paintings, smoking cigarettes, or pictures of the most memorable moments of their lives.

Dam 20. ✆ **020/522-1010.** www.madametussauds.nl. Admission 21€ adults, 16€ children 5–15, free for children 4 and under. Daily generally from 10 or 11am to between 4:30 and 8:30pm, depending on the season and the day. Closed Apr 30. Tram: 4, 9, 14, 16, 24, or 25 to the Dam.

Science Center NEMO ★ ☺ A fount of science and technology, NEMO is in a strikingly modern building in the Eastern Dock, designed by Italian architect Renzo Piano, which seems to reproduce the graceful lines of an ocean-going ship. The center is a hands-on experience as much as a museum, with games, experiments, demonstrations, workshops, and theater and film shows. You learn how to steer a supertanker safely into port, boost your earnings on the floor of the New York Stock

The Narrow View

The **narrowest house** in Amsterdam is at **Singel 7.** It's just 1m (3.3 ft.) wide—barely wider than the front door. However, it's a cheat. Only the front facade is really so narrow; behind this it broadens out to more usual proportions. The *genuine* narrowest house is **Oude Hoogstraat 22,** near Nieuwmarkt. With a typical Amsterdam bell gable, it's 2m (6½ ft.) wide and 6m (20 ft.) deep. A close rival is nearby at **Kloveniersburgwal 26,** the cornice-gabled **Kleine Trippenhuis,** 2.4m (8 ft.) wide.

Exchange, and execute a complicated surgical procedure. One exhibit will even try to make you understand the basis of sexual attraction. Internet-linked computers on every floor help provide insights. In NEMO's digital world, you can play with images, sounds, text websites, and your own imported material.

Oosterdok 2 (off Prins Hendrikkade, over the south entrance to the IJ Tunnel). ✆ **020/531-3233.** www.e-nemo.nl. Admission 12€, free for children 3 and under. July–Aug daily 10am–5pm; Sept–June Tues–Sun 10am–5pm (also Mon during school vacations). Closed Jan 1, Apr 30, and Dec 25. Bus: 22, 42, or 43 to Kadijksplein.

Alternative Museums

Hash Marihuana & Hemp Museum ★ This museum will teach you everything you ever wanted to know, and much you maybe didn't, about hash, marijuana, and related products. One way it does this is by having a cannabis garden on the premises. Plants at various stages of development fill the air with an unmistakable, heady, resinous fragrance. Some exhibits shed light on the medicinal uses of cannabis and on hemp's past and present-day uses as a natural fiber. Among several artworks in the museum's collection is David Teniers the Younger's painting, *Hemp-Smoking Peasants in a Smoke House* (1660).

Oudezijds Achterburgwal 148 (Red Light District). ✆ **020/624-8926.** www.hashmuseum.com. Admission 9€ adults, free for children 12 and under. Daily 10am–11pm. Closed Jan 1, Apr 30, and Dec 25. Tram: 4, 9, 14, 16, 24, or 25 to the Dam.

Sexmuseum Amsterdam Behind its faux-marble facade, this museum isn't as sleazy as you might expect, apart from one room covered with straight-up pornography. Otherwise, presentation tends toward the tongue-in-cheek. Exhibits include erotic prints and drawings, and trinkets like tobacco boxes decorated with naughty pictures. Teenage visitors seem to find the whole place vastly amusing, judging by the giggling fits at the showcases. Spare a thought for the models of early erotic photography—slow film speeds in those days made for uncomfortably long posing times!

Damrak 18 (near Centraal Station). ✆ **020/622-8376.** www.sexmuseumamsterdam.com. Admission 4€ ages 16 and older. Daily 9:30am–11:30pm. Tram: 1, 2, 4, 5, 9, 13, 16, 17, 24, 25, or 26 to Centraal Station.

The Jordaan

Few spectacular sights clutter the beguiling old Jordaan district—just west of the northern reaches of the Canal Belt—though 800 of its buildings are protected monuments. This neighborhood of narrow streets and canals, and tightly packed houses, was built in the 17th century for craftsmen, tradesmen, and artists. Some streets used to be canals, until these were filled in during the 19th century. The charming area provides an authentic taste of Old Amsterdam.

Its modest nature remains even though renewal and gentrification proceed apace, bringing an influx of offbeat boutiques, quirky stores, cutting-edge art galleries, and trendy restaurants. The name Jordaan may have come from the French *jardin* (garden), from Protestant French Huguenot refugees who settled here in the late 17th century. Indeed, many streets and canals are named for flowers, trees, and plants.

The Waterfront ★

Amsterdam's waterfront, a narrow shipping channel called Het IJ, takes its name from a river that used to flow into the Zuiderzee hereabouts until, centuries ago, its course was washed away by an expanding sea. Then, last century, the Zuiderzee transformed into a freshwater lake called the IJsselmeer (after the IJssel River that still flows into it farther east).

Amsterdam's biggest redevelopment project is underway in the IJ's Eastern Harbor, once a major part of Amsterdam Port. City government touts the project as "a new life on the water." Java-Eiland, KNSM-Eiland, and other artificial islands and peninsulas have been cleared of most of their warehouses and other harbor installations. Modern housing and infrastructure take their place. A visit here is a good way to see how Amsterdam sees its future, away from its Golden Age heart.

A fast-tram service (line 26) connects Centraal Station with the old Eastern Harbor's redeveloped districts along Het IJ. Among its stops are ones for the Muziekgebouw aan 't IJ and Bimhuis concert halls, the Passenger Terminal Amsterdam cruise-liner dock, and the Eastern Islands' new residential, shopping, and entertainment zones. The line goes out as far as the new IJburg suburb, on an artificial island in the IJsselmeer's southern reaches.

Some of the redevelopment focus has now switched to the Western Harbor, west of Centraal Station.

The Red Light District

This warren of streets and old canals (known as De Rosse Buurt or De Wallen in Dutch) around Oudezijds Achterburgwal and Oudezijds Voorburgwal by the Oude Kerk, a testament to the city's tolerance and pragmatism, is on most people's sightseeing agenda. However, a visit to this area is not for everyone, and if you're liable to be offended by the sex industry exposed in all its garish colors, don't go. If you do choose to go, exercise some caution because the area is a center of crime, vice, and drugs. As always in Amsterdam, there's no need to exaggerate the risks; in fact, the nightclubs' own security helps keep the brightly lit areas quite safe. Plenty of tourists visit the Red Light District and suffer nothing more serious than a come-on from one of the prostitutes.

In recent years, as part of Project 1012, a program named for the Red Light District's zip or post code that's aimed at cleaning up its "unsavory" side, the city government has forced the closure of 20% of the red-light windows, with a further 20% to go, reducing the number from just over 500 to just under 300. The properties have been bought up and rented out as fashion boutiques and other upscale small businesses. Some of the more raucous sex clubs may also be shuttered. The intention is to concentrate the Red Light District into a smaller geographical area; reduce the role of organized crime in the business, with its attendant features of violent pimps, human-trafficking, and sex slavery; and offer alternatives to make the district more attractive both to Amsterdammers and to visitors who are in town for more than sex tourism. One effect of project 1012 is that the city has booked "tens of millions" of euros in lost revenues from prostitution.

Despite the decreased numbers, it's still extraordinary to view the hookers in leather and lace sitting in their storefronts, listening to their iPods while waiting for customers. The district reflects Dutch pragmatism; if you can't stop the oldest trade in the world, you can at least confine it to a particular area and impose health and other regulations on it. And the fact is that underneath its tacky glitter, the Red Light District contains some of Amsterdam's prettiest canals and loveliest old architecture, plus some excellent bars and restaurants, secondhand bookstores, and other specialty stores (not all of which work the erogenous zones). To get there, take tram no. 4, 9, 14, 16, 24, or 25 to the Dam, and then pass behind the Grand Hotel Krasnapolsky.

Green Amsterdam

Amsterdam is not a notably green city, particularly in the Old Center. Still, the city as a whole has plenty of parks, including the celebrated **Vondelpark ★★**. You'll find Frisbee flipping, in-line skating, pickup soccer and softball, open-air performances, smooching in the undergrowth, and picnics. Best of all, it's free, or as the Dutch say, *gratis*. The Vondelpark lies southwest of Leidseplein, with the main entrance adjacent to the Leidseplein, on Stadhouderskade.

To enjoy scenery and fresh air, head out to the giant **Amsterdamse Bos (Amsterdam Wood) ★**, in the southern suburb of Amstelveen. This is nature on the city's doorstep. The park was laid out during the Depression years as a public works project. The **Bezoekerscentrum** (**Visitor Center; ✆ 020/545-6100;** www.amsterdamsebos.nl), at the main entrance on Amstelveenseweg, traces the park's history and gives information about its wildlife; it's open daily (except Dec 25–26) noon to 5pm, and admission is free. At a large pond called the **Grote Vijver,** you can rent small boats (**✆ 020/644-5119**). The **Openluchttheater (Open-Air Theater)** often has performances on summer evenings. The best way to get to the **Amsterdamse Bos** from the center is to take Connexxion bus no. 170 or 172 from outside Centraal Station.

Organized Tours

BY BOAT **Canalboat cruises ★★** last approximately an hour. Boats depart at regular intervals from *rondvaart* (excursion) piers in key locations around town. The majority of launches are docked along Damrak and Prins Hendrikkade near Centraal Station, on Rokin near Muntplein, and at Leidseplein. Tours leave daily every 15 to 30 minutes during the summer season (9am–9:30pm) and every 45 minutes in winter (10am–4pm). Prices vary from company to company, but a basic 1-hour tour is around 10€ to 13€ for adults, 5€ to 7€ for children 4 to 12, and free for children 3 and under.

The canal tour-boat lines are: **Amsterdam Canal Cruises** (✆ 020/626-5636; www.amsterdamcanalcruises.nl); **Canal Company** (✆ 0900/333-4442; www.canal.nl); **Holland International** (✆ 020/625-3035; www.hir.nl); **Gray Line** (✆ 020/535-3308; www.graylineamsterdam.com); **Rederij Boekel** (✆ 020/612-9905; www.rederijkooij.nl); **Rederij Hof van Holland** (✆ 020/623-7122; www.rederijkooij.nl); **Rederij Lovers** (✆ 020/530-5412; www.lovers.nl); **Reederij P. Kooij** (✆ 020/623-3810; www.rederijkooij.nl); **Rederij Plas** (✆ 020/624-5606; www.rederijplas.nl); and **Blue Boat Company** (✆ 020/679-1370; www.blueboat.nl).

Some lines offer specialized tours and services. These include the **Hop On Hop Off Museum Line** and the **Canal Bus** (see "Getting Around," earlier in this chapter), the **Artis Zoo Express** (which plies a regular furrow between Centraal Station and the Artis Zoo), cruises amid the Eastern Islands' modern architecture, Red Light District cruises, dinner cruises, jazz cruises, candlelight cruises with wine and cheese, night cruises, and more.

BY WATER BIKE If the canalboat cruise whets your appetite to ramble the canals on your own, you can rent sturdy paddleboats, called canal bikes, from (by a strange coincidence) **Canal Bike,** Weteringschans 24 (✆ **0900/333-4442;** www.canal.nl). Canal bikes seat two or four and come with a detailed map, route suggestions, and a bit of information about the places you pedal past. The four Canal Bike moorings are at Leidseplein (tram: 1, 2, 5, 7, or 10); Westerkerk, near the Anne Frankhuis (tram: 13, 14, or 17); Stadhouderskade, beside the Rijksmuseum (tram: 7 or 10); and Toronto Bridge on Keizersgracht, near Leidsestraat (tram: 1, 2, or 5). You can rent a canal bike at one mooring and leave it at another. The canals can be busy with tour boats and other small craft, so go carefully, particularly under bridges. Rental is 8€ per person hourly for one or two people, 7€ per person hourly for three or four people. You need to leave a deposit of 50€.

BY BICYCLE You're going to look conspicuous taking one of the guided tours offered by **Yellow Bike,** Nieuwezijds Kolk 29, off Nieuwezijds Voorburgwal (✆ **020/620-6940;** www.yellowbike.nl). Because you'll be biking on a yellow bicycle along with a dozen other people on yellow bikes. In compensation, you'll have a close encounter with Amsterdam or the nearby countryside. There are multiple tour options, with the shortest (2 hr.) costing 19€.

Mike's Bike Tours, Kerkstraat 134 (✆ **020/622-7970;** www.mikesbiketoursamsterdam.com), offers tours of 2½ to 3 hours around the canals in town and a ride outside the city to see windmills and a cheese farm and clog factory. The cost is 18€ for adults and 16€ for seniors and students; there's a reduction of 5€ if you bring your own bike. March to November, meet daily at 4pm near the reflecting pool behind the Rijksmuseum (tram: 2 or 5); December to February, you need to book in advance (minimum three people).

BY BUS For many travelers, a quick bus tour is the best way to launch a sightseeing program in a strange city, and though Amsterdam offers its unique alternative—a canalboat cruise—you might want to get your bearings on land. Good sightseeing lines are: **Keytours,** Paulus Potterstraat 8 (✆ **020/305-5333;** www.keytours.nl); and **Lindbergh,** Damrak 26 (✆ **020/622-2766;** www.lindbergh.nl). In addition, these lines provide a variety of half- and full-day tours into the surrounding area, particularly between April and October, and there are special excursions at tulip time and at the height of the summer season. Rates vary from company to company and with the particular tour on offer. Typical half-day tours begin around 22€, and full-day tours are 48€; children 4 to 13 are generally charged half fare, and children 3 and under go free.

BY FOOT Though you could see most of Amsterdam's important sights in one long walking tour, it's best to break the city into shorter walks. Luckily, the tourist office has done that for you. For 3€, purchase a brochure outlining one of three walking tours: City Center, Jewish Amsterdam, and the Jordaan; a fourth brochure, which costs 1€, covers the Pijp district.

Many companies offer specialized walking tours. **Let's Go** (www.letsgo-amsterdam.com) offers a range of 90-minute guided walks that cost around 15€ per head.

Skating on the Street

Strap on in-line skates for the regular Friday Night Skate (www.fridaynight skate.com). In summer, this attracts thousands of skaters. It begins at 8pm from the Vondelpark and takes a 15km (9-mile) route through the city.

BY HORSE & CARRIAGE These romantic, kid-friendly vehicles run by **Karos** (✆ **020/691-3478;** www.karos.nl) depart from just outside the Royal Palace on the Dam for traipses through the Old City, along the canals, and into the Jordaan. Tours operate April to October daily 11am to 6pm (to 7pm July–Aug), and on a limited schedule in winter. Rides are 35€ for 20 minutes, 45€ for 30 minutes, and 65€ for 45 minutes.

SPORTS & RECREATION

BASEBALL Honk if you like baseball (the game is called *honkbal* in Holland). The **Amsterdam Pirates** (www.amsterdampirates.nl) aren't the greatest practitioners of the sport, but they have their moments, as you can see at **Sportpark Ookmeer,** Herman Bonpad 5 (✆ **020/616-2151;** bus: 19 or 192).

BASKETBALL **ABC Amsterdam** (www.amsterdambasketball.nl) play their home games at **Sporthallen Zuid,** Burgerweeshuispad 54 (✆ **020/423-1818;** tram: 16 or 24), close to the Olympic Stadium.

BOATING & SAILING Sailboats, kayaks, and canoes can be rented on the Sloterplas Lake from **Watersportcentrum De Duikelaar,** Noordzijde 41 (✆ **020/613-8855;** www.deduikelaar.nl; tram: 7, 13, or 14). From March 15 to October 15, you can go to the Loosdrecht lakes, southeast of Amsterdam, to rent sailing equipment from **Ottenhome,** Zuwe 20, Kortenhoef (✆ **035/582-3331;** www.ottenhome.nl; bus: 106 from Weesp). Canoes can be rented in **Amsterdamse Bos** (see above), south of the city, for use in the park lakes only.

BOWLING Try **Knijn Bowling,** Scheldeplein 3 (✆ **020/664-2211;** www.knijn bowling.nl; tram: 12 or 25).

FITNESS & WELLNESS Head to **Splash** (www.splashhealthclubs.nl), Looiersgracht 26–30 (✆ **020/624-8404;** tram: 7, 10, or 17), and Lijnbaansgracht 241 (✆ **020/422-0280;** tram: 7 or 10). The **Body Tuning Clinic,** Jan Luijkenstraat 40 (✆ **020/662-0909;** www.bodytuningclinic.nl; tram: 2 or 5), will take excellent care of the outer you. At **Sauna Deco,** Herengracht 115 (✆ **020/623-8215;** www.saunadeco.nl; tram: 1, 2, 5, 13, or 17), in Dutch style, you sweat together in mixed facilities. Soothe away a hard day's stress at **Koan Float,** Herengracht 321 (✆ **020/555-0333;** www.koanfloat.nl; tram: 1, 2, or 5), while floating in warm saline water in a soundproof fiberglass capsule with light switches, ambient music, and a two-way intercom.

GOLF Among public courses in or near Amsterdam are: 9-hole **Golfbaan Sloten,** Sloterweg 1045 (✆ **020/614-2402;** www.golfbaansloten.nl; bus: 145); 18-hole **Waterlandse Golf Club,** Buikslotermeerdijk 141 (✆ **020/636-1010;** www.waterlandsegolfclub.nl; bus: 31, 33, or 38); and **Golfbaan Spaarnwoude,** Het Hoge Land 2, Velsen-Zuid (✆ **020/538-5599;** www.golfbaanspaarnwoude.nl; bus: 82).

HORSEBACK RIDING From the comfort of its upper-floor cafe, watch horses being put through their paces in a sawdust-strewn arena at the regal **De Hollandsche Manege,** Vondelstraat 140 (✆ **020/618-0942;** www.dehollandschemanege.nl; tram: 1). Opened in 1882, this fusion of plaster, marble, and gilded mirrors was inspired by Vienna's Spanish Riding School. In addition to being a spectator, you can ride. Trot along to edge-of-town **Hippisch Centrum Sonnenburgh,** Nieuwe Kalfjeslaan 25 (✆ **020/643-1342;** bus: 142, 166, 170, 171, or 172); or to nearby **Manege Nieuw Amstelland,** Jan Tooropplantsoen 17 (✆ **020/643-2468;** www.nieuwamstelland.nl; bus: 142, 166, 170, 171, or 172).

ICE SKATING Skating on Amsterdam's ponds and canals (see "Skating on the Canals," below) won't be easy unless you're willing to shell out for a new pair of skates—there are very few places that rent them. One that does is **Jaap Eden IJsbanen,** Radioweg 64 (✆ **0900/724-2287;** www.jaapeden.nl; tram: 9); you can rent skates here from November to February.

IN-LINE SKATING **De Skate Dokter Amsterdam** has a rent shop for in-line skates in Vondelpark, at the Amstelveenseweg entrance (✆ **06/2157-5885;** www.skatedokter.nl; tram 2).

JOGGING The two main jogging areas are **Vondelpark** in the center city and **Amsterdamse Bos** on the southern edge of the city. You can run along the Amstel River. If you choose to run along the canals, as many do, watch out for uneven cobbles, loose paving stones, and dog poop.

SOCCER Soccer (known as football in Europe, and *voetbal* in Dutch) is absolutely the biggest game in Holland. Ajax Amsterdam is invariably the best team in the land, and often is among the best in Europe. Ajax plays home matches at a fabulous modern stadium with a retractable roof, the **Amsterdam ArenA,** ArenA Blvd. 1, Amsterdam Zuidoost (✆ **020/311-1333;** www.amsterdamarena.nl; Metro: Strandvliet/ArenA). There's an on-site Ajax Museum.

SQUASH Squash courts are at chic **Squash City,** Ketelmakerstraat 6 (✆ **020/626-7883;** www.squashcity.nl; bus: 18, 21, or 22), west of Centraal Station.

SWIMMING Amsterdam's state-of-the-art swimming facility is **Het Marnix,** Marnixplein 1 (✆ **020/524-6000;** www.hetmarnix.nl; tram: 3 or 10), which opened in 2006 and has two heated pools along with a fitness center and spa, and a cafe-restaurant. A handsome, refurbished place from 1911, close to the Rijksmuseum, the **Zuiderbad,** Hobbemastraat 26 (✆ **020/678-1390;** tram: 2 or 5), has times set aside for those who like to swim in their birthday suit. **De Mirandabad,** De Mirandalaan 9 (✆ **020/546-4444;** tram: 25), features an indoor pool with wave machines, slides, and other amusements, and an outdoor pool that's open May to September.

Skating on the Canals

In winter, when the temperature drops low enough for long enough, the canals of Amsterdam become sparkling highways through the city. This doesn't happen very often, but if it does, the Dutch get their skates on. Classical music plays over the ice, and little kiosks are set up to dispense heartwarming liqueurs. Just be cautious when skating under bridges, and in general don't go anywhere the Dutch themselves don't.

TENNIS Find indoor courts at **Frans Otten Stadion,** IJsbaanpad 43 (✆ **020/662-8767;** www.fransottenstadion.nl; tram: 16), close to the Olympic Stadium. For indoor *and* outdoor courts, try **Sportcentrum Amstelpark,** Koenenkade 8, Amsterdamse Bos (✆ **020/301-0700;** www.amstelpark.nl; bus: 166, 170, 171, or 172), which has 36 courts.

SHOPPING

Bargain hunters won't have much luck (except at the flea markets), but shopping in Amsterdam definitely has its rewards. Best buys include diamonds and traditional Dutch products, such as Delftware, pewter, crystal, and old-fashioned clocks. No matter what you're looking for, you're sure to be impressed with the range of possibilities Amsterdam offers. Shopping can easily be integrated into your Amsterdam experience because the center city is small enough that stores and other attractions are often right beside each other.

The Shopping Scene

Major shopping streets in Amsterdam, many of which are closed to traffic, include **Kalverstraat,** from the Dam to Muntplein (inexpensive and moderately priced stores); **Rokin,** parallel to Kalverstraat (quality fashions, art galleries, antiques stores); **Leidsestraat** (upmarket stores for clothing, china, gifts); **Pieter Cornelisz Hooftstraat** and **van Baerlestraat,** near Museumplein (designer fashions, accessories, china, gifts); and **Nieuwe Spiegelstraat,** near the Rijksmuseum (art and antiques).

Malls have sprung up across the city. **Magna Plaza** has filled the former main post office, just behind the Dam, with four floors of exclusive and useful stores. The **Kalvertoren** occupies a prime site at the corner of Kalverstraat, near the Munt; a cafe at the top offers a bird's-eye view of Amsterdam's rooftops.

STORE HOURS Regular hours are Monday from 10 or 11am (some stores don't open at all in the morning) to 6pm; Tuesday, Wednesday, and Friday from 9am to 6pm; Thursday from 9am to 9pm; and Saturday from 9am to 5pm. Many stores stay

NINE GREAT little streets

If your idea of a good shopping day includes browsing through homegrown designer clothes stores, fashion boutiques, and funky specialty stores, garnished with cool little cafes, salons, and galleries, cut a west-to-east path through the northern *Grachtengordel* (Canal Belt). Begin at Westermarkt and crisscross Herengracht, Keizersgracht, and Prinsengracht. By doing so, you'll pass through the *Negen Straatjes* (Nine Streets or, since *straatjes* is the diminutive of *straten,* which means streets, the Nine Little Streets). These 17th-century side streets connect the stately big canals in this part of town.

The streets are grouped in three lines of three, on the canal stretches that lie between Westermarkt and Raadhuisstraat in the north, and Leidsegracht and Beulingstraat in the south. From north to south, they are: Reestraat, Hartenstraat, and Gasthuismolensteeg; Berenstraat, Wolvenstraat, and Oude Spiegelstraat; and Runstraat, Huidenstraat, and Wijde Heisteeg. For more information about the Nine Streets, visit **www.theninestreets.com** and **www.de9straatjes.nl**.

open on Sunday as well, usually from noon to 5pm. Many supermarkets are open daily from 8am to 8pm, or even 10pm.

Shopping A to Z

ANTIQUES

If you're interested in an artistic view of Amsterdam or the Dutch countryside, the fine antiquarian **Mathieu Hart ★★**, Rokin 122 (✆ **020/623-1658;** www.hartantiques.com; tram: 4, 9, 14, 16, 24, or 25), in business since 1878, stocks color etchings of Dutch cities alongside rare old prints, 18th-century Delftware, and grandfather clocks. Inside the brocaded display cases and richly carved cabinets of **Premsela & Hamburger ★**, Rokin 98 (✆ **020/624-9688;** www.premsela.com; tram: 4, 9, 14, 16, 24, or 25), which opened in 1823, is a variety of exquisite silver baubles, ranging from 19th-century English saltcellars to 18th-century tea strainers, and Art Deco silverware. The **Looier Kunst & Antiek,** Elandsgracht 109 (✆ **020/624-9038;** www.looier.nl; tram: 7, 10, or 17), is an indoor antiques market spread through several old warehouses, where hundreds of individual dealers rent small stalls and corners to show their wares.

> **Impressions**
>
> ***I challenge you to find anything open 24 hours a day in this supposedly world-class city. Indeed, most shops close by 6p.m.—precisely when people leaving work might actually want to patronize them.***
>
> **—Russell Shorto, director of Amsterdam's John Adams Institute, *The Times Magazine,* 2009**

ART

Art from around the world (particularly from Africa and Asia) and all kinds of ethnic jewelry are displayed at **Italiaander Galleries,** Prinsengracht 526 (✆ **020/625-0942;** tram: 1, 2, or 5). For ceramics and glassware, **Galerie Carla Koch ★**, Detroit Building (6th Floor), Veemkade 500 (✆ **020/673-7310;** www.carlakoch.nl; tram: 26), employs some of the raciest design talent in Amsterdam.

BOOKS

For English-language publications, there's the **American Book Center ★**, Spui 12 (✆ **020/625-5537;** www.abc.nl; tram: 1, 2, or 5); **Waterstone's,** Kalverstraat 152 (✆ **020/638-3821;** www.waterstones.com; tram: 1, 2, 4, 5, 14, 16, 24, or 25); and **Athenaeum Boekhandel & Nieuwscentrum,** Spui 14–16 (✆ **020/514-1460;** www.athenaeum.nl; tram: 1, 2, or 5), which carries a big selection of books and international magazines and newspapers.

CRAFTS & GIFTS

In the **Blue Gold Fish,** Rozengracht 17 (✆ **020/623-3134;** tram: 13, 14, or 17), there's no real rhyme or reason behind the items for sale. Still, there's unity in its diversity and in the more-or-less fantastic design sensibility that goes into each piece. For more traditional choices, **'t Curiosa Winkeltje,** Prinsengracht 228 (✆ **020/625-1352;** tram: 13, 14, or 17), sells assorted knickknacks such as colored bottles and glasses, modern versions of old tin cars and other children's toys from the 1950s and earlier, big plastic butterflies, lamps shaped like bananas, and many other such useful things. Shop at **Nieuws Innovations,** Prinsengracht 297 (✆ **020/627-9540;** tram: 13, 14, or 17), for all kinds of offbeat souvenirs, such as pens in the shape of fish, washcloths in the form of hand-glove puppets, spherical dice, and many other hard-to-define but colorful little bits and pieces.

The Lowdown on Delftware

Those ubiquitous earthenware items in the familiar blue-and-white "Delft" colors have almost become synonymous with Holland. Souvenir stores, specialty stores, and department stores have Delftware products in the widest variety of forms imaginable. If an object has particular appeal, by all means buy it—but be aware that unless it meets certain specifications, you are not carting home an authentic piece of the hand-painted earthenware pottery that has made the Delft name illustrious.

DELFTWARE

Two upscale stores of **Jorrit Heinen ★★** (www.jorritheinen.com) offer a good selection of quality porcelain from De Koninklijke Porcelyne Fles (Delft), Koninklijke Tichelaars (Makkum), Heinen, and more: Prinsengracht 440 (✆ **020/627-8299;** tram: 1, 2, or 5), and Muntplein 12 (✆ **020/623-2271;** tram: 4, 9, 14, 16, 24, or 25). A wide selection of hand-painted Delftware of every conceivable type can be found at the well-stocked emporium **Galleria d'Arte Rinascimento,** Prinsengracht 170 (✆ **020/622-7509;** www.delft-art-gallery.com; tram: 13, 14, or 17).

DEPARTMENT STORES

De Bijenkorf ★, Dam 1 (✆ **0900/0919;** www.bijenkorf.nl; tram: 4, 9, 14, 16, 24, or 25), Amsterdam's stateliest department store, holds a vast array of goods in all price ranges and some good eateries. Another well-stocked store is **Vroom & Dreesmann (V&D),** Kalverstraat 203 (✆ **0900/235-8363;** www.vd.nl; tram: 4, 9, 14, 16, 24, or 25). The store of choice for Amsterdam's power shoppers, **Metz&Co ★★**, Leidsestraat 34–36 (✆ **020/520-7020;** www.metzandco.com; tram: 1, 2, or 5), sells modern furniture, fabrics, and other such items. The in-store rooftop cafe Metz, designed by De Stijl architect Gerrit Rietveld in 1933, affords fine panoramic views.

DESIGN STORES

Loading up your luggage with the kind of cool chairs, tables, and other furniture from the innovative Dutch designers at **Droog,** Staalstraat 7B (✆ **020/523-5050;** www.droog.com; tram: 4, 9, 14, 16, 24, or 25), likely isn't viable, but you can ship your purchase or settle for accessories that embrace the same design sensibility. Designer furniture and other *objets* by young Dutch fashioners of the irresistible-but-impractical draw aficionados to **Frozen Fountain ★**, Prinsengracht 645 (✆ **020/622-9375;** www.frozenfountain.nl; tram: 1, 2, or 5).

DIAMONDS

Amsterdam diamond cutters have an international reputation for high standards. When you buy from them, you'll be given a certificate listing the weight, color, cut, and identifying marks of the gem you purchase. These stores offer diamond-cutting and polishing tours, and sales of the finished product: **Amsterdam Diamond Center,** Rokin 1–5 (✆ **020/624-5787;** www.amsterdamdiamondcenter.com; tram: 4, 9, 14, 16, 24, or 25); **Coster,** Paulus Potterstraat 2–8 (✆ **020/305-5555;** www.costerdiamonds.com; tram: 2 or 5); and **Gassan,** Nieuwe Uilenburgerstraat 173–175 (✆ **020/622-5333;** www.gassandiamonds.com; Metro: Waterlooplein).

FASHIONS

Large for Amsterdam, Jordaan designer outlet **Megazino,** Rozengracht 207–213 (✆ **020/330-1031;** tram: 13, 14, or 17), sells everything from Armani, Gucci, and Prada to Calvin Klein and Dolce & Gabbana—all at 30% to 50% off the original price. It's a great place to burn some plastic without breaking the bank. The 17th-century Klein Trippenhuis, a protected historical monument, is the counterintuitive setting for **Webers Holland ★**, Kloveniersburgwal 26 (✆ **020/638-1777;** www.webers holland.nl; Metro: Nieuwmarkt), an avant-garde, sexy, humorous, and in-your-face store for women.

You're likely to bump into media stars, gallery owners, and the moneyed creative crowd of both sexes in the small boutique **Van Ravenstein,** Keizersgracht 359 (✆ **020/639-0067**; www.van-ravenstein.nl), buying the latest creations by Dutch and Belgian designers and fashion houses Viktor & Rolf, Maison Martin Margiela, Dirk Bikkembergs, Dries Van Noten, Anne Demeulemeester, and more. **Analik,** Hartenstraat 36 (✆ **020/422-0561;** www.miauw.com; tram: 13, 14, or 17), is owned by one of Amsterdam's renowned designers, Analik. One room is filled with small pieces of clothing for young and skinny women, the other with funky handbags and other accessories designed by local Dutch artists.

FLOWER BULBS

Gardeners will find it well-nigh impossible to leave Amsterdam without at least one purchase from the **Flower Market ★**, on Singel Canal at Muntplein (Tram: 4, 9, 14, 16, 24, or 25), open daily year-round. Just be certain the bulbs you buy carry with them the obligatory phytosanitary certificate clearing them for entry into your home country.

FOOD & DRINK

Jacob Hooy & Co., Kloveniersburgwal 10–12 (✆ **020/624-3041;** www.jacobhooy.nl; Metro: Nieuwmarkt), opened in 1743 and operated for the past 130 years by the same family, is a wonderland of fragrant smells that offers more than 500 different herbs and spices and 30 different teas, sold loose by weight, plus health foods, homeopathic products, and natural cosmetics. In a store from 1839, **Simon Levelt,** Prinsengracht 180 (✆ **020/489-9406;** www.simonlevelt.nl; tram: 13, 14, or 17), specializes in coffee and tea. Devotees of the legal "narcotic" from Columbia and other coffee-producing nations will be tempted by the smell of freshly roasted coffee beans at **Geels & Co. ★**, Warmoesstraat 67 (✆ **020/624-0683;** www.geels.nl; tram: 4, 9, 14, 16, 24, or 25), a coffee-roasting and tea-importing establishment that has been going strong since 1864.

H.P. de Vreng en Zonen, Nieuwendijk 75 (✆ **020/624-4581;** www.oud amsterdam.nl; tram: 1, 2, 5, 13, or 17), has an extensive selection of special Dutch liqueurs and gins. To recover from the aftereffects of these fine distilled spirits, head for **De Waterwinkel,** Roelof Hartstraat 10 (✆ **020/675-5932;** www.dewaterwinkel.nl; tram: 3, 5, 12, or 24), a one-of-a-kind store that stocks a massive range of mineral waters from around the world. Fresh, handmade pralines in a plethora of shapes and styles—pure, milk, and white chocolate—are laid out for perusal at the two branches of **Puccini Bomboni,** Singel 184 (✆ **020/427-8341;** www.puccinibomboni.com; tram: 1, 2, 5, 13, or 17), and Staalstraat 17 (✆ **020/626-5474;** tram: 9 or 14).

JEWELRY

At **Galerie Ra,** Vijzelstraat 80 (✆ **020/626-5100;** www.galerie-ra.nl; tram: 16, 24, or 25). Owner Paul Derrez specializes in stunning modern jewelry in gold and silver, and goes a bit further, turning feathers, rubber, foam, and other materials into pieces he describes as "playful." **BLGK Edelsmeden,** Hartenstraat 28 (✆ **020/624-8154;** www.blgk.nl; tram: 13, 14, or 17), sells affordable designer jewelry. Some of its pieces represent a fresh spin on classic forms; others are more innovative.

MARKETS

Awnings stretch over 15 stalls of brightly colored blossoms, bulbs, and potted plants at the **Bloemenmarkt (Flower Market)** ★, Singel, between Koningsplein and Muntplein. Partly floating on a row of permanently moored barges, this is one of Amsterdam's stellar spots, the most atmospheric place to buy fresh-cut flowers, bright and healthy-looking plants, ready-to-travel packets of tulip bulbs, and all the necessary accessories for home gardening. The market is open daily 8am to 8pm.

At the **Albert Cuypmarkt,** Albert Cuypstraat, you'll find just about anything and everything your imagination can conjure up. It's open Monday to Saturday from 9am to 6pm. Every Friday from 10am to 6pm, there's a **Book Market** on Spui. The **Farmer's Market,** also known as the Bio Market, takes place every Saturday from 9am to 5pm on Noordermarkt and caters to Amsterdam's infatuation with health foods and natural products. Thorbeckeplein hosts a **Sunday Art Market** April to October on Sundays from 11am to 6pm, with local artists showing their wares.

The **Waterlooplein Flea Market** ★ is Amsterdam's classic market, offering everything from cooking pots to mariner's telescopes to decent historical prints of Dutch cities. It's open Monday to Saturday from 10am to 5pm.

SEX

Absolute Danny, Oudezijds Achterburgwal 78 (✆ **020/421-0915;** www.absolute danny.com; Metro: Nieuwmarkt), brings an artistic slant to everything from S&M clothing and accessories in leather and latex to sexy lingerie. All but guaranteeing your apparel of choice, **Condomerie Het Gulden Vlies** ★, Warmoesstraat 141 (✆ **020/627-4174;** www.condomerie.com; tram: 4, 9, 14, 16, 24, or 25), stocks a vast range of condoms, in all shapes, sizes, and flavors, from common brands to flashy designer fittings.

SHOES

When it comes to fanciful footwear, trendies hotfoot to **Antonia by Yvette,** Gasthuismolensteeg 18 (✆ **020/320-9443;** www.antoniabyyvette.nl; tram: 1, 2, 5, 13, 14, or 17), for hip Dutch designer shoes by the likes of Hester Vlamings. There are no classic shoes at **Betsy Palmer** ★, Rokin 9–15 (✆ **020/422-1040;** www.betsy palmer.com; tram: 4, 9, 14, 16, 24, or 25), but there's an incredible collection of trendy women's footwear, with obscure but fun brands.

SMOKING ARTICLES

Run by the same family since 1826, warm, wood-paneled **P.G.C. Hajenius,** Rokin 96 (✆ **020/623-7494;** www.hajenius.com; tram: 4, 14, 16, 24, or 25), is virtually a museum of antique tobacco humidors (not for sale) and has a beautiful selection of distinctively Dutch blends for sale. Pipes of all description are displayed, and fine Sumatra and Havana cigars are kept in a room-size glass humidor.

AMSTERDAM AFTER DARK

Nightlife is centered on the **Leidseplein** and **Rembrandtplein** areas, both of which have a large and varied selection of restaurants, bars, and nightspots. The **Rosse Buurt (Red Light District)** serves up its unique brand of nightlife, and adjoining this is **Nieuwmarkt,** a popular alternative hangout.

If you want to attend any of Amsterdam's theatrical or musical events (including rock concerts), getting tickets should be your first task upon arrival. **Amsterdams Uitburo (AUB) Ticketshop,** Leidseplein 26 (© **0900/0191,** or 020/621-1288 from outside the Netherlands; www.uitburo.nl; tram: 1, 2, 5, 7, or 10), at the corner of Marnixstraat, can reserve tickets for almost every venue in town, for a reservations charge of 2€–4.65€ per ticket at their office, 2.50€ online, and 3€ by phone. The AUB office is open Monday to Wednesday and Saturday from 10am to 6pm, Thursday from 10am to 9pm, and Sunday from noon to 6pm.

> **Impressions**
>
> ***It often seems to me that the night is much more alive and richly colored than the day.***
>
> **—Vincent van Gogh, 1888**

Prices for after-dark entertainment in Amsterdam tend to be modest. Many nightspots only charge for drinks, though others have a nominal cover charge.

The Performing Arts

CLASSICAL MUSIC

Amsterdam's top orchestra—indeed, one of the world's top orchestras—is the famed **Royal Concertgebouw Orchestra** (www.concertgebouworkest.nl), whose home is the **Concertgebouw ★★★**, Concertgebouwplein 2–6 (© **0900/671-8345;** www.concertgebouw.nl; tram: 3, 5, or 12). World-class orchestras and soloists are only too happy to appear at the Grote Zaal (Great Hall) of the Concertgebouw because of its perfect acoustics. No matter where you sit, the listening is impeccable. Chamber and solo recitals are given in the Kleine Zaal (Little Hall). Tickets are from 17€ to 100€. The main concert season is from September to mid-June, but during July and August, there's the Robeco Summer Series, world class but with seats priced from 10€ to 35€.

The city's other symphony orchestra, the **Netherlands Philharmonic Orchestra** (© **020/521-7500;** www.orkest.nl), or the "NedPho," doesn't lag far behind its illustrious cousin. The orchestra's official home is the **Beurs van Berlage,** Damrak 213 (© **020/531-3350;** www.beursvanberlage.nl; tram: 4, 9, 14, 16, 24, or 25), formerly the Amsterdam Stock Exchange. This venue hosts chamber-music concerts and recitals in a large hall that used to be the trading floor. Tickets are 15€ to 75€.

At the other end of the musical spectrum, lovers of avant-garde and experimental music should head to the **Muziekgebouw aan 't IJ,** Piet Heinkade 1 (© **020/788-2000;** www.muziekgebouw.nl; tram: 25 or 26), which opened in 2005 in a spectacular piece of modern architecture on the IJ waterfront, east of Centraal Station. Here you can savor modern and old jazz, electronic, and non-Western music, as well as small-scale musical theater, opera, and dance. The waterside terrace of the cafe-restaurant is one of the most idyllic in town. Tickets are 10€ to 65€. A next-door annex to the Muziekgebouw is the home of the Bimhuis jazz and improv music club (see below).

OPERA & DANCE

Artistic director Pierre Audi has built up the **Netherlands Opera** (www.dno.nl) and its repertoire. The company performs at the superb modern **Muziektheater,** Waterlooplein 22 (✆ **020/625-5455,** or 020/551-8100 for 24-hr. info line; www.hetmuziektheater.nl; tram: 9 or 14). This theater is also used by the **National Ballet** (www.het-nationale-ballet.nl), which performs large-scale classical ballet repertoire and contemporary work, and by the **Netherlands Dance Theater** (www.ndt.nl), which is based in The Hague and is noted for its groundbreaking modern repertoire. Most performances begin at 8:15pm; tickets cost 10€–110€.

After-Dark Attire

If you intend to go to the opera, a classical-music concert, or the theater, don't worry about what to wear. Amsterdam has a very informal dress code. You might want to dress up, and in fact many people do, but it's not likely that you'll be turned away for being "improperly" dressed.

THEATER

Homegrown theater productions are almost always in Dutch, with the main city theater being the **Stadsschouwburg,** Leidseplein 26 (✆ **020/624-2311;** www.stadsschouwburgamsterdam.nl; tram: 1, 2, 5, 7, or 10).

Because English is so widely spoken, Amsterdam is a favorite venue for road shows from the United States and England. Theaters that often host English-language productions include: **Felix Meritis,** Keizersgracht 324 (✆ **020/626-1311;** www.felixmeritis.nl; tram: 1, 2, or 5); **Frascati,** Nes 63 (✆ **020/626-6866;** www.theaterfrascati.nl; tram: 4, 9, 14, 16, 24, or 25), which focuses on modern theater; **Koninklijk Theater Carré,** Amstel 115–125 (✆ **0900/252-5255;** www.theatercarre.nl; tram: 7 or 10); and **DeLaMar,** Marnixstraat 402 (✆ **0900/335-2627;** www.delamar.nl; tram: 1, 2, 5, 7, or 10).

Showtime is usually 8:15pm, and ticket prices vary widely.

Comedy Theater

Boom Chicago ★, Leidsepleintheater, Leidseplein 12 (✆ **020/423-0101;** www.boomchicago.nl; tram: 1, 2, 5, 7, or 10), brings delightful English-language improvisational comedy to Amsterdam. *Time* magazine compared it to Chicago's celebrated Second City comedy troupe. Dutch audiences don't have much problem with the English sketches; they often seem to get the point ahead of the native English-speakers in attendance. Spectators are seated around candlelit tables for eight people, and you can have dinner and a drink while you enjoy the show. Tickets are 15€ to 35€, not including dinner. The restaurant is open at 7pm. The box office is open daily from noon to 8:30pm.

The Club & Music Scene

JAZZ & BLUES

In Amsterdam, jazz and blues groups hold forth in bars, and the joints start jumping at around 11pm. **Bimhuis ★**, Piet Heinkade 3 (✆ **020/788-2188;** www.bimhuis.nl; tram: 25 or 26), at the Muziekgebouw aan 't IJ, on the waterfront, east of Centraal Station, is for the serious contemporary jazz connoisseur. Tickets are 10€ to 30€.

Equally recommended are **Jazz Café Alto,** Korte Leidsedwarsstraat 115, off the Leidseplein (✆ **020/626-3249;** www.jazz-cafe-alto.nl; tram: 1, 2, 5, 7, or 10); Amsterdam's "home of the blues," **Maloe Melo** ★, Lijnbaansgracht 163 (✆ **020/420-4592;** www.maloemelo.nl; tram: 7, 10, or 17), where the music varies from sounds created by capable amateurs to those cooked up by an occasional big name; and **Bourbon Street,** Leidsekruisstraat 6–8 (✆ **020/623-3440;** www.bourbonstreet.nl; tram: 1, 2, 5, 7, or 10), which hosts a mix of local and traveling blues talent.

DANCE CLUBS

Amsterdam's dance scene isn't wildly volatile, but places do come and go. **Akhnaton,** Nieuwezijds Kolk 25 (✆ **020/624-3396;** www.akhnaton.nl; tram: 1, 2, 5, 13, or 17), does African music and salsa. **Paradiso,** Weteringschans 6–8 (✆ **020/626-4521;** www.paradiso.nl; tram: 1, 2, 5, 7, or 10), has live music followed by dance parties. **Escape,** Rembrandtplein 11 (✆ **020/622-1111;** www.escape.nl; tram: 4, 9, or 14), is a large venue with several dance floors.

Guest-list entry only on some nights makes Hong Kong–style club **Jimmy Woo** ★, Korte Leidsedwarsstraat 18 (✆ **020/626-3150;** www.jimmywoo.com; tram: 1, 2, 5, 7, or 10), occasionally hard to get into; it attracts a slow-burning crowd, but both the music and the vibes get hotter the later it gets. A waterfront power station from 1899 houses hip club **Panama** ★★, Oostelijke Handelskade 4 (✆ **020/311-8686;** www.panama.nl; tram: 10 or 26), which hosts big-name DJs and special events for dressed-to-impress 30- to 40-something professionals.

A 17th-century orphanage chapel is the unlikely setting for **Tonight** ★★, 's Gravesandestraat 51 (✆ **020/850-2400;** www.hotelarena.nl; tram: 7 or 10), where DJs rustle up sounds from the '60s to the '90s. Seriously trendy **Home,** Wagenstraat 3–7 (✆ **020/620-1375;** www.clubhome.nl; tram: 4, 9, or 14), is where big names from the Dutch film, theater, and TV scene like to see and be seen.

ROCK & POP

Big stars and large-scale productions are occasionally featured at **Koninklijk Theater Carré** (see "Theater," above). Rock stars strut their stuff at the giant **Amsterdam ArenA,** ArenA Blvd. 1, Amsterdam Zuidoost (✆ **020/311-1313;** www.amsterdamarena.nl; Metro: Bijlmer/ArenA), the Ajax soccer club's stadium in the city's southeastern suburbs, which has a sliding roof to keep out the ubiquitous Dutch rain. Near Amsterdam ArenA, the smaller **Heineken Music Hall** ★, Arena Blvd. 590 (✆ **0900/687-4242;** www.heineken-music-hall.nl; Metro: Bijlmer/ArenA), hosts more intimate concerts. Performers have included Avril Lavigne, Alanis

Vondelpark Open-Air Theater

From June to mid-August, the stage at the Vondelpark Openluchttheater (✆ 020/428-3360; www.openluchttheater.nl) is set for theater, all kinds of music (including concerts by the Royal Concertgebouw Orchestra), dance, operetta, and more. The events are free, but reserving a seat costs 2.50€ per person. Bring a picnic and enjoy an enchanting evening under the stars.

Melkweg: A Multidimensional Venue

A sometime hippie haven in an old dairy factory, Melkweg, Lijnbaansgracht 234A (© 020/531-8181; www.melkweg.nl; tram: 1, 2, 5, 7, or 10), near Leidseplein, houses an art center, dance floor, cinema, theater, concert hall, photo gallery, and exhibit space. The cover charge is 5€ to 10€ plus a 3.50€ monthly club membership. The box office is open Monday to Friday from 1 to 5pm, and Saturday and Sunday from 4 to 6pm.

Morissette, Duran Duran, the Black Eyed Peas, Michael Bolton, Marilyn Manson, and Meat Loaf, among others.

For ticket info, go to **Mojo Concerts** (© **015/212-1980;** www.mojo.nl), and (online only) to **Livenation** (www.livenation.nl).

The Bar & Cafe Scene

BROWN CAFES

You'll see brown cafes *(bruine kroegen)* everywhere: on street corners, at canal intersections, and down narrow little lanes. They look as if they've been there forever. These are the favorite local haunts and are quite likely to become yours as well—they're positively addicting. Brown cafes will typically sport lace half-curtains at the front window and ancient Oriental rugs on tabletops (to sop up any spills from your beer). Wood floors, overhead beams, and plastered walls blend into a murky brown background, darkened by centuries of smoke from Dutch pipes. Frequently there's a wall rack with newspapers and magazines, but they get little attention in the evening, when conversations flow as readily as *pils* (beer). *Jenever,* the potent Dutch gin, is on hand in several different flavors, some served ice cold—but never on the rocks. Excellent Dutch beers, and expensive imported brews, are available as well.

Your hotel neighborhood is sure to have at least one brown cafe close at hand. Far be it for me to set any sort of rigid itinerary for a *kroegentocht* (pub crawl), but you might want to look into the following: **Hoppe,** Spui 18–20 (© **020/420-4420**), a student and journalist hangout since 1670, which still has sawdust on the floor and is always packed; **Kalkhoven,** at Prinsengracht and Westermarkt (© **020/624-8649**), a serious drinker's bar that dates back to 1670; **Cafe 't Smalle,** Egelantiersgracht 12 (© **020/623-9617**), in the Jordaan district on the canalside, a bar in a former distillery and tasting house that dates from 1786; **Café Chris,** Bloemstraat 42 (© **020/624-5942**), a tap house since 1624; **Gollem,** Raamsteeg 4 (© **020/626-6645**), which sells more than 200 different beers; **De Karpershoek,** Martelaarsgracht 2 (© **020/624-7886**), which dates from 1629 and was once a favorite hangout of sailors; and **Papeneiland,** Prinsengracht 2 (© **020/624-1989**), a 300-year-old establishment filled with character and a secret tunnel leading under the Brouwersgracht that was used by 17th-century Catholics.

TASTING HOUSES

The decor will still be basically brown and typically Old Dutch—and the age of the establishment may be even more impressive than that of its beer-swilling brown-cafe neighbors—but in a *proeflokaal* (tasting house), you usually order *jenever* (Dutch gin, taken neat, without ice) or another product of the distillery that owns the place. To drink your choice of spirit, custom and ritual decree that you lean over the bar, with your hands behind your back, to take the first sip from your well-filled *borreltje* (small drinking glass).

Tasting houses to look for include: **De Admiraal,** Herengracht 319 (✆ **020/625-4334**); **De Drie Fleschjes,** Gravenstraat 18 (✆ **020/624-8443**), behind the Nieuwe Kerk; **De Ooievaar,** Sint Olofspoort 1 (✆ **020/420-8004**), on the corner with Zeedijk near Centraal Station; and **Het Proeflokaal,** Pijlsteeg 35 (✆ **020/639-2695**), a wonderful little place that undoubtedly looks much as it did when it opened in 1680.

TRENDY CAFES

Every city has its hip venues, where those out to impress can preen their feathers against a fitting backdrop. Amsterdam is no exception. The places listed below offer contemporary designs and often cocktails instead of beer.

Seymour Likely, Nieuwezijds Voorburgwal 250 (✆ **020/627-1427**), behind the Royal Palace at the Dam, has a constantly changing decor. Subdued lighting, dark wood surfaces, and red tones infuse **bubbles&wines ★**, Nes 37 (✆ **020/422-3318**), a fancy champagne and wine bar a few minutes' walk from the Dam.

Café Schiller ★, Rembrandtplein 36 (✆ **020/624-9864**), has enduringly attracted artistic and literary types to its stunning Art Nouveau setting. Chic **Lux,** Marnixstraat 403 (✆ **020/422-1412**), draws in a healthy dose of locals to the otherwise touristy Leidseplein area; sit on the upper level to enjoy a sweeping view of the place.

Soft chairs, long banquettes, and chandeliers draw a hip, youthful crowd to **Cafe Kale de Derde ★★**, Ferdinand Bolstraat 18–20 (✆ **020/470-0651**), in the Pijp district, to sip mojitos and other cocktails, graze on plates of tempura, and dance to

SMOKING coffeeshops

Tourists often get confused about "smoking" coffeeshops and how they differ from "nonsmoking" ones. Well, to begin with, "smoking" and "nonsmoking" don't refer to cigarettes—they refer to hashish and marijuana. Smoking coffeeshops not only sell cannabis, most commonly in the form of hashish, they provide a place where patrons can sit and smoke it all day long if they so choose. Generally, these smoking coffeeshops are the only places in Amsterdam called "coffeeshops"—regular cafes are called cafes or *eetcafés*.

You're allowed to possess up to 5 grams of hashish or marijuana for personal use, and coffeeshops are forbidden to sell more than this amount to each customer. Each coffeeshop has a menu listing the different varieties of hashish and marijuana it stocks. In addition, there are joints *(stickies)* for sale, rolled with tobacco. Coffeeshops are not allowed to sell alcohol, so they sell coffee, tea, and fruit juices. You're even allowed to bring along and smoke your own stuff, so long as you buy a drink.

In a typically Dutch compromise over the tobacco ban enacted in 2008, patrons of smoking coffeeshops are permitted to puff joints, but not cigarettes, cigars, or pipes. For details on the Dutch government's controversial plans to prevent foreigners from patronizing coffeeshops, turn to "Holland Today," in chapter 2.

DJs on Friday and Saturday nights. A similar spirit infuses nearby **Helden,** Eerste Van der Helststraat 42 (✆ **020/673-3332**), at Quellijnstraat, where a young, well-heeled crowd sinks into the sofas and sips martinis and mojitos over soft music.

The Gay & Lesbian Scene

The gay scene in Amsterdam is strong, and there is no lack of gay bars and nightspots in town; for lesbians, the scene is a little harder to uncover. Amstel and Amstelstraat at Rembrandtplein, the Jordaan, and to a limited extent the edge of the Red Light District are the likeliest zones to check out. Most of the city's gay spots are in well-defined areas. For old-style camp, look along the Amstel near Muntplein and on Halvemaansteeg. Trendier places are along Reguliersdwarsstraat. Casual locals head for Kerkstraat, on both sides of the crossing with Leidsestraat. Heavy-duty types get it on in the Red Light District.

One of the city's oldest gay bars, **Amstel FiftyFour,** Amstel 54 (✆ **020/623-4254**), off Rembrandtplein, though not hip, is engagingly convivial, and regulars occasionally break into song. **Getto,** Warmoesstraat 51 (✆ **020/421-5151**), in the Red Light District, attracts an equal mix of boys and girls with its hip interior and such events as "Club Fu" karaoke (first Mon of every month) and bingo (every Thurs).

At casual **Spijker,** Kerkstraat 4 (✆ **020/620-5919**), the pinball machine and pool table are focal points, and video screens show an amusing juxtaposition of cartoons and erotica. Lively bar staffers keep the atmosphere relaxed with a varied selection of music and stiff drinks, and happy hour draws the crowds in daily from 5 to 7pm. The after-work drinks venue **Web,** Sint-Jacobsstraat 6 (✆ **020/623-6758**), has a raunchy atmosphere and plenty of space to talk. Tuesday is "beer bust" (an intense beer-drinking session), and Wednesday is prize-draw night.

Once a female-only enclave, **Saarein2,** Elandsstraat 119 (✆ **020/623-4901**), in the Jordaan, is now open to both genders. Attractions include pool, darts, pinball, and Continental food. Lesbian bar **Vive-la-Vie,** Amstelstraat 7 (✆ **020/624-0114**), off Rembrandtplein, attracts a young, lively crowd prior to club-hopping time, and lipstick isn't forbidden. The sidewalk terrace offers summertime relaxation. Gay dance venue **Cockring,** Warmoesstraat 96 (✆ **020/623-9604**), in the Red Light District, lays down no-nonsense, hard-core, high-decibel dance and techno music on the dance floor. More relaxed beats in the sociable upstairs bar make for a welcome break.

More Entertainment

In Amsterdam you'll find a dozen or more first-run features, most of them Hollywood's finest, in English with Dutch subtitles. Admission prices are around 9€, depending on the day, the time, and the movie. The **Theater Tuschinski,** Reguliersbreestraat 26–34 (✆ **0900/1458;** tram: 4, 9, or 14), is worth a visit to view its restored Art Deco style from 1921, when it first opened as a variety theater. On the upper balconies, you sit on plush chairs and can sip champagne during the movie.

Visit **Holland Casino Amsterdam,** in the Lido, Max Euweplein 62 (✆ **020/521-1111;** tram: 1, 2, 5, 7, or 10), at Leidseplein, for European gambling, with an emphasis on the quiet games of roulette, baccarat, punto banco, blackjack, and others, though there are abundant one-armed bandits and blackjack, poker, and bingo machines. You need correct attire to get in (jacket and tie or turtleneck for men), and you have to bring your passport to register at the door. The minimum age is 18. The

Closure Blues

The chic end of Amsterdam's gay scene had an attack of the vapors in 2010, when a prominent local business went bust, taking down a bunch of the city's trendiest gay watering holes. Hardest hit was the Reguliersdwarsstraat strip, which overnight went from vital scene to virtual desert. Distraught ex-patrons were left wondering where to go at night. In time, new bars and dance venues will replace those that were lost. To keep up with developments on Reguliersdwarsstraat, turn to **www.reguliers.net**.

casino is open daily (except May 4 and Dec 31) from 12:30pm to 3am. Admission is 5€. Wednesday is "ladies day," and admission is free for all female visitors.

The Red Light District

Prostitution is legal in the Netherlands, and in Amsterdam most of it is concentrated in the Red Light District. Even if you don't want to play, this is a place you may want to see at night, when the red lights reflect from the canals' inky surfaces. Lots of visitors come here out of curiosity or just for fun. There's no problem with wandering around—if you don't mind the weird-looking, sad-sack males hanging around on the bridges—and you don't need to worry much about crime as long as you stick to busier streets and keep an eye out for pickpockets. Visiting women going around in groups of two or more won't be noticed any more than anyone else, but a single female might be subject to misrepresentation.

The Red Light District, known in Dutch as Rosse Buurt, isn't very big. It's centered on the western half of the **Oudezijds Voorburgwal** and **Oudezijds Achterburgwal** canals. Ironically, the **Oude Kerk,** the city's venerable Old Church (p. 310), stands watch over this passable representation of Sodom and Gomorrah.

"Ladies of ill repute" populate the many red-fringed window parlors; they're minimally dressed, and they tap (or pound) on the windows as potential customers go by. Then there are peep-show joints with private cabins, dark and noisy bars, theaters offering a popular form of performance art, bookstores filled with the illustrated works of specialists in a wide range of interpersonal relationships, video libraries, and dedicated apparel and appliance stores. In recent years, as part of a continuing effort to clean up the "unsavory" side of Amsterdam, the city council forced the closure of roughly a third of the red-light windows and bought up properties to be rented as fashion boutiques and other upscale small businesses; for more information, see "The Red Light District" earlier in this chapter.

HAARLEM & NOORD-HOLLAND

14

The landscape around Amsterdam in Noord-Holland (North Holland) province affords a taste of the cultural and natural variety of the Netherlands. There are the dikes that brought this improbable country into being, the polder (the Dutch word for land reclaimed from water) landscape, windmills, wooden shoes, tidy farms, yacht-filled harbors on the IJsselmeer (a large freshwater lake), flower fields reaching to the wide Dutch horizon, and sandy beaches looking out to the North Sea.

In the west is the venerable and graceful city of Haarlem; in the east are remnants of strategic fortifications that protected medieval crossing points. In other places, you can climb tall towers and view museums that recreate the local life of yesteryear, ride a steam train, eat fish by the harbor, and see giant locks and tiny canals.

Everywhere in Noord-Holland is an easy day trip from Amsterdam, but there's so much to see that you need to make several trips to do the region justice. For details of tours from Amsterdam by bus and out-of-town trips by bicycle, see "Organized Tours," in chapter 13.

HAARLEM ★★

18km (11 miles) W of Amsterdam

By being thoroughly provincial, prosperous, and conservative (meaning there's only a tiny red-light district here), Haarlem gets along nicely without the many hassles that go with the nearby capital's famously tolerant and often eccentric lifestyle. The small city (pop. 150,000) has a similar 17th-century ambience, though since it was founded probably in the 10th century, it is older than Amsterdam. You can easily get around this quaint, quiet center of music and art—it's home to one of Holland's premier art museums—on foot. Besides, Haarlem is close to the North Sea beaches and to the bulb fields, at the heart of an area dotted with elegant manor houses and picturesque villages.

Essentials

GETTING THERE **Trains** depart at least every half-hour from Amsterdam Centraal Station for Haarlem; the ride takes 15 minutes. A

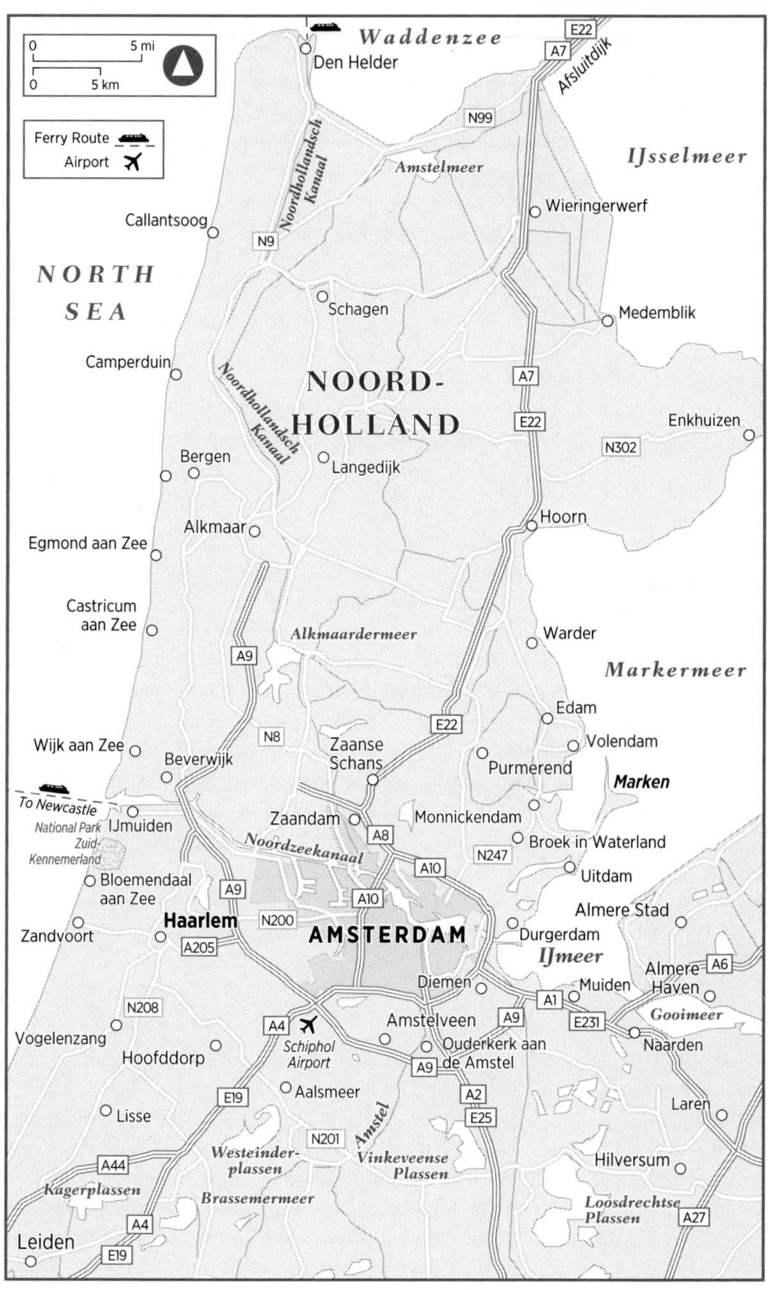

0 5 mi
0 5 km
Ferry Route
Airport
Waddenzee
Den Helder
Afsluitdijk
IJsselmeer
Amstelmeer
Noordhollandsch Kanaal
Wieringerwerf
Callantsoog
NORTH SEA
Schagen
Medemblik
Camperduin
NOORD-HOLLAND
Enkhuizen
Bergen
Langedijk
Alkmaar
Hoorn
Egmond aan Zee
Castricum aan Zee
Alkmaardermeer
Warder
Markermeer
Edam
Volendam
Wijk aan Zee
Beverwijk
Zaanse Schans
Purmerend
Marken
To Newcastle
IJmuiden
National Park Zuid-Kennemerland
Zaandam
Monnickendam
Noordzeekanaal
Broek in Waterland
Uitdam
Bloemendaal aan Zee
Almere Stad
Haarlem
AMSTERDAM
Zandvoort
Durgerdam
IJmeer
Diemen
Muiden
Almere Haven
Gooimeer
Amstelveen
Vogelenzang
Ouderkerk aan de Amstel
Naarden
Hoofddorp
Schiphol Airport
Aalsmeer
Laren
Lisse
Amstel
Westeinder-plassen
Vinkeveense Plassen
Hilversum
Kagerplassen
Brassemermeer
Loosdrechtse Plassen
Leiden

round-trip ticket is 7€ in second class and 12€ in first class. By **car** from Amsterdam, take N200/A200 west.

VISITOR INFORMATION The **City Marketing Haarlem/VVV Informatiecentrum,** Verwulft 11, 2011 GJ Haarlem (✆ **0900/616-1600;** fax 023/534-0537; www.vvvhaarlem.nl), is in the center of town, at the intersection of Grote Houtstraat and Gedempte Oude Gracht. The office is open Monday to Friday from 9:30am to 5:30pm, Saturday from 10am to 5pm, and Sunday from noon to 4pm.

What to See & Do

Haarlem is the little sister city of Amsterdam. Granted municipal status by Count Willem II of Holland in 1245, it was where Frans Hals, Jacob van Ruisdael, and Pieter Saenredam were living and painting their famous portraits, landscapes, and church interiors during the same years that Rembrandt was living and working in Amsterdam.

THE GROTE MARKT & STADHUIS

The old center is a 5- to 10-minute walk from the graceful Art Nouveau rail station from 1908, most of it via pedestrian-only shopping streets. First-time visitors generally head straight for the **Grote Markt ★★★**, the beautiful central market square, adjacent to the **Sint-Bavokerk** (**Church of St. Bavo;** see below). Most points of interest in Haarlem are within easy walking distance of the Grote Markt. The monumental buildings around the tree-lined square, which date from the 15th to the 19th centuries, are a visual minicourse in the development of Dutch architecture. Here stands Haarlem's 14th-century **Stadhuis (Town Hall),** Grote Markt 2 (✆ **023/511-5115**), a former hunting lodge of the counts of Holland rebuilt in the 17th century, and containing a magnificent tapestry of the Crusades, *The Capture of Damietta* (1629) by Josef Thienpont of Oudenaarde—just one of Haarlem's many historical connections with the Belgian region of Flanders.

OTHER TOP SIGHTS

Frans Hals Museum ★★ The finest attraction in Haarlem, this might even be a high point of your trip to Holland. The galleries here are the halls and furnished chambers of the Oudemannenhuis (1608), a home for retired gentlemen designed by Ghent architect Lieven de Key, with a courtyard garden. The famous paintings by Frans Hals (ca. 1580–1666) and other Masters of the Haarlem School hang in settings that look like the 17th-century houses they were intended to adorn. Hals, who died here, is best known for works such as *The Laughing Cavalier* (1624) and *The Gypsy Girl* (1630)—neither of which is in the museum—but he earned his bread and butter by painting portraits of members of the local Schutters (Musketeers) Guild. Typified by his *Officers of the Militia Company of St. George* (ca. 1627), five such works, whose style inspired van Gogh, hang in the museum, along with six more paintings by Hals.

Look out for a peculiar painting, *The Monk and the Beguine* (1591) by Cornelisz van Haarlem: It depicts a monk squeezing a beguine nun's bare breast, and has been interpreted variously as a satire on lecherous behavior in cloisters or as being symbolic of purity and virginity. You'll also see fine collections of antique silver, porcelain, and clocks. Among other pieces is a superb dollhouse from around 1750—though "dollhouse" seems an inadequate description for an exquisitely detailed miniature replica of a merchant's house.

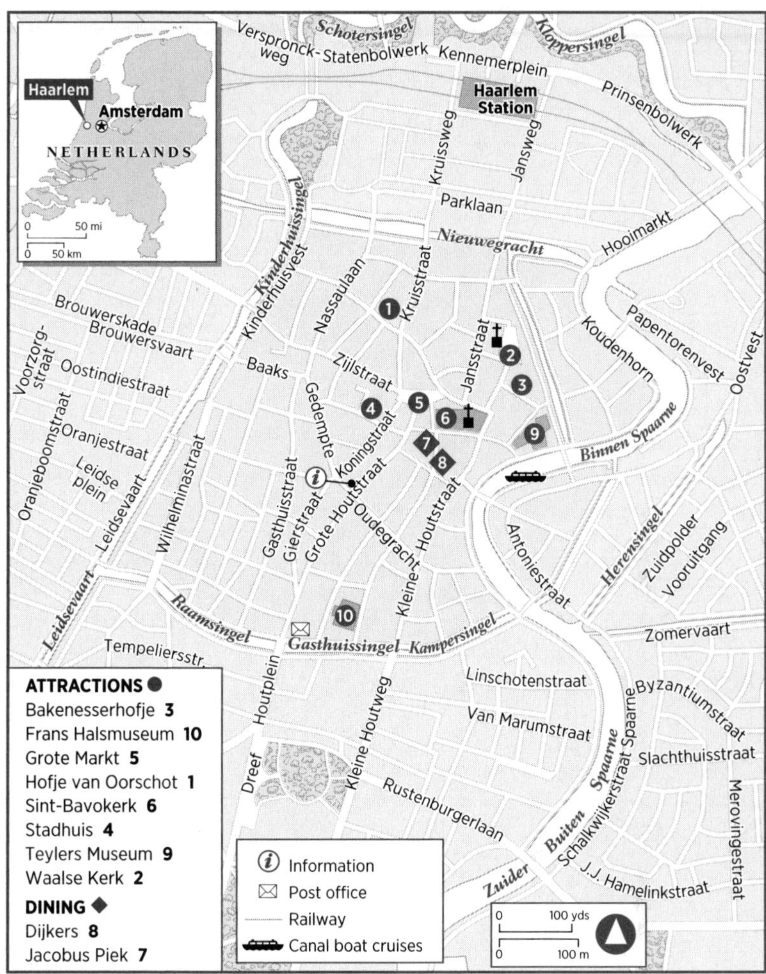

Groot Heiligland 62. ✆ **023/511-5775.** www.franshalsmuseum.nl. Admission 7.50€ adults, 3.75€ ages 19–24, free for children 18 and under. Tues–Sat 11am–5pm; Sun and holidays noon–5pm. Closed Jan 1 and Dec 25.

Sint-Bavokerk (Saint Bavochurch) ★ Walking to the center of town from Haarlem station, you catch only glimpses of the high-towered St. Bavo's Church, also known as the Grote Kerk (Great Church), looming above the narrow streets. But the moment you reach the Grote Markt, it's revealed in all its massive splendor. The colossal late-Gothic church was begun in 1445 under the direction of Antwerp's city architect, Evert Spoorwater. It was basically complete by 1520 and so has a rare unity of structure and proportion. The interior is light and airy, with tall whitewashed walls and sandstone pillars. Its elegant wooden tower is covered with lead sheets and adorned with gilt spheres.

Look for the tombstone of painter Frans Hals, who was probably born in Antwerp around 1580 and who lived and worked for most of his life in Haarlem, where he died in 1666. Search, too, for a cannonball that has been embedded in the wall ever since it came flying through a window during the Spanish siege of Haarlem (1572–73). Don't miss the famous Christian Müller organ, built in 1738. Mozart played this magnificent instrument in 1766 when he was just 10 years old and is said to have shouted for joy—when you see it, you may be struck dumb at the thought of little Wolfie reaching for one of the 68 stops. Handel, Mendelssohn, Schubert, and Liszt also visited Haarlem to play the organ. You can enjoy the organ in a free recital Tuesday at 8:15pm from May to October; in July and August there's an additional free recital on Thursday at 3pm. From May to October, church services using the organ take place Sunday at 10am; from June to October, there's an additional 7pm Vespers and Cantata service.

Oude Groenmarkt 23. ✆ **023/553-2040.** www.bavo.nl. Admission 2€ adults, 1.25€ children 12–16, free for children 11 and under. June–Sept Mon–Sat 10am–4pm, Sun 10am–7pm; Oct–May Mon–Sat 10am–4pm.

Teylers Museum The oldest public museum in the Netherlands was established here in 1784 by a private collector. It contains a curious collection of displays: drawings by Michelangelo, Raphael, and Rembrandt (which are exhibited in rotation); fossils, minerals, and skeletons; and instruments of physics and an odd assortment of inventions, including the largest electrostatic generator in the world (1784).

Spaarne 16. ✆ **023/516-9060.** www.teylersmuseum.eu. Admission 9€ adults, 2€ children 6–17, free for children 5 and under. Tues–Sat 10am–5pm; Sun and holidays noon–5pm. Closed Jan 1 and Dec 25.

MORE PLACES OF INTEREST

Belgium's French-speaking Walloons weren't left out of Haarlem's feast of Flemish history and culture, as may be seen in the 16th-century **Waalse Kerk (Walloon Church),** at the Begijnhof. Built by Walloon and French Protestant refugees so they could practice their religion in peace and in French, the church is surrounded by the Begijnhof, a cluster of little houses that started out as a Catholic foundation for pious laywomen. Its rooms have been put to use by less pious modern laywomen—they host the minimally clad working girls of Haarlem's small *rosse buurt* (red-light district).

Haarlem counts one of the finest tallies of *hofjes* (almshouses) of any Dutch city. These charitable establishments around secluded courtyards were constructed from medieval times onward to house poor and retired persons. There are 20 of them scattered around town. Two worth visiting in the central zone close to the Grote Markt are the **Hofje van Oorschot,** in Kruisstraat; and the **Bakenesserhofje,** founded in 1395, in Wijde Appelaarsteeg.

CANALBOAT TOURS

An ideal way to view Haarlem is by canal tour boat. Tours are operated by **Post Verkade Cruises** (✆ **023/535-7723;** www.postverkadecruises.nl), from the Spaarne River dock next to the Gravenstenenbrug, a handsome lift bridge. From April to October Tuesday to Sunday, boats depart hourly from noon to 4pm on a 45-minute cruise. Tickets are 9.50€ for adults, 4.50€ for children 3 to 12, and free for children

Hot Jets

How about a jetfoil ride to the seacoast? **Fast Flying Ferry (✆ 0900/266-6399;** www.connexxion.nl), runs a scheduled service on the North Sea Canal between Amsterdam and Velsen-Zuid. At the nearby seaport of IJmuiden (connected with the Velsen-Zuid jetfoil dock by frequent bus service), you can view the three great locks of the **Noordzeekanaal,** and visit the **fish auctions** at Halkade 4, Monday to Friday from 7 to 11am. Jetfoils depart from a dock behind Amsterdam Centraal Station, Monday to Friday every half-hour from 7am to 10pm, and Saturday to Sunday from 7am to 6:30pm; the ride takes 30 minutes. Round-trip tickets are 9.40€ at peak times and 8€ at off-peak times for adults, 6.20€ for seniors and children 4 to 11, and free for children 3 and under.

2 and under. In addition, there are longer cruises that go outside of town, candlelight cruises, and more.

Where to Dine

Dijkers INTERNATIONAL Near the start of a short but chic shopping street a block south of the Grote Markt, this tiny restaurant, popular with locals, serves an unlikely mix of Italian and Asian dishes, from Thai green curry to lighter fare such as club and toasted sandwiches—the mozzarella-and-prosciutto club sandwich is an excellent choice for a quick bite at lunch. A bright, orange-toned designer-ish setting with transparent plastic chairs sits nicely with the breezy service. On warm sunny days, a few tables are set out on the sidewalk.

Warmoesstraat 5–7 (off Oude Groenmarkt). ✆ **023/551-1564.** www.restaurantdijkers.nl. Main courses 14€–23€; *dagschotel* (plate of the day) 12€. AE, MC, V. Wed–Mon 10am–10pm.

Jacobus Pieck ★ DUTCH/INTERNATIONAL This popular cafe-restaurant on one of Haarlem's best shopping streets has a lovely shaded terrace in the garden for fine-weather days. Inside it's bustling and stylish. Outside or in, you get excellent food from the open kitchen for reasonable prices, and friendly, mostly efficient service, though at the busiest times it can be slow. At lunchtime, try one of the generous sandwiches, burgers, or particularly good salads; at dinner a daily changing menu typically includes dishes ranging from pastas and Middle Eastern or Asian dishes to wholesome Dutch standards.

Warmoesstraat 18 (off Oude Groenmarkt). ✆ **023/532-6144.** www.jacobuspieck.nl. Main courses 13€–18€; *dagschotel* 12€. AE, MC, V. Mon 11am–4pm; Tues–Sat 11am–4pm and 5:30–10pm.

ZANDVOORT

24km (15 miles) W of Amsterdam; 7km (4½ miles) W of Haarlem

If you feel like drawing a breath of fresh sea air and you don't have much time for it, do what most Amsterdammers do: Head for Zandvoort (*Zand*-fort). On the North Sea coast just west of Haarlem, the resort is brash and brassy in the summer, though it can look forlorn out of season.

Essentials

GETTING THERE **Trains** depart hourly from Amsterdam Centraal Station for Zandvoort (the station's name is Zandvoort aan Zee). You transfer at Haarlem, where the Zandvoort train is usually waiting on the adjacent platform. During summer months, extra trains go direct from Centraal Station. In either case, the ride takes around 30 minutes, and a round-trip ticket is 9.20€ in second class and 16€ in first class. By **car** go via Haarlem, on N200/A200/N200, but be ready for long traffic lines in summer.

VISITOR INFORMATION **VVV Zandvoort,** Bakkerstraat 2B (at Kerkstraat), 2042 HK Zandvoort (✆ **023/571-7947;** fax 023/571-7003; www.vvvzk.nl), is in the center of town. The office is open Monday to Friday from 9am to 5pm, Saturday from 10am to 5pm, and Sunday from 11am to 4pm.

What to See & Do

There's not much more to Zandvoort than its **beach,** but what a beach! In summer, this seemingly endless stretch of smooth sand is lined with dozens of temporary beach cafe-restaurants (*paviljoenen*). Adjoining the mainstream section of the beach is a naturist stretch, where the shocking sight of a clothed individual can generate considerable moral outrage, and a stretch that has been ceded, more or less, to gays.

Windsurfing is pretty good at Zandvoort, which hosts international competitions in this sport and in catamaran sailing. The Dutch Formula One Grand Prix motor race used to be run at **Circuit Park Zandvoort,** Burg van Alphenstraat 108 (✆ **023/574-0740;** www.cpz.nl), in the north of the town. For now the circuit hosts only smaller events. If you come on a summer weekend, you might find a Formula Three training session or a Porsche meeting underway.

Equally racy, though less noisy, is **Holland Casino Zandvoort,** Badhuisplein 7 (✆ **023/574-0574;** www.hollandcasino.com), in the center behind the seafront promenade. There's roulette, blackjack, punto banco, slot machines, and more. The dress code is "correct" (collar and tie for men), and the minimum age is 18. You need your passport to get in. The casino is open daily (except May 4 and Dec 31) from 12:30pm to 3am. Admission is 5€; Wednesday is "ladies day," and admission is free for all female visitors.

Solitude amid surroundings of natural beauty can be found by walking among the 2,500 hectares (6,178 acres) of sand dunes, deciduous and pine forest, grassland, and small lakes in the **Nationaal Park Zuid-Kennemerland** (✆ **023/541-1123;** www.npzk.nl), north of town. Reinforced by native vegetation, the dunes play an important part in the sea defense system and have been designated nature reserves. You can have an active fresh-air experience here, strolling along pathways—once used by fishermen's wives bringing their menfolks' catch from the coast to market—through the woods on the landward side and westward across the dunes toward the sea. A variety of plants, some of them rare, occupies this relatively small area, and you can spot up to 230 species of birds, including rare crossbills and sea eagles. The beach is never far away.

Adjoining the national park is a quiet beach resort called **Bloemendaal aan Zee.** It's only 4km (2½ miles) from Zandvoort, so you can walk there—along the beach or on the diketop promenade. You can also take the bus that departs every half-hour or so from outside Zandvoort rail station. Hotspot **Grand Café-Restaurant Tropen**

BY THE SIDE OF the zuiderzee

Only in Holland could you say, "This used to be a sea." The IJsselmeer actually was once a sea, until the Dutch decided they didn't want it to be one any longer, since it was always threatening to flood Amsterdam and other towns and villages along its low-lying coastline.

For centuries the Dutch have been protecting themselves from encroaching seas and snatching more land to accommodate their expanding population. One of their most formidable challenges was the Zuiderzee (Southern Sea), an incursion of the North Sea that washed over Frisian dunes to flood vast inland areas between A.D. 200 and 300. Over the centuries, the Zuiderzee continued to expand, and in the 1200s a series of storms drove its waters far inland.

As early as the 1600s, there was talk of driving back the sea and reclaiming the land it covered. Parliament got around to authorizing the project in 1918, and in the 1920s, work was begun. In 1932, in an unparalleled feat of engineering, the North Sea was sealed off, from Noord-Holland to Friesland, by the 30km (19-mile) Afsluitdijk (Enclosing Dike), and the saltwater Zuiderzee became, in time, the freshwater IJsselmeer. Since then, a vast area has been pumped dry, converting fishing villages into farming villages and joining islands to the mainland.

aan Zee, Zeeweg 80 (✆ **023/573-1700;** www.tropenaanzee.nl), is the place to people-watch, do lunch, sip a sundowner, and loosen up to DJ beats after dark. You can munch on snacks or dine on full meals.

Even in winter, it's an Amsterdam tradition to take the train to Zandvoort, stroll up and down the shore for an hour or so, then repair to one of the town's cafes, such as **Het Wapen van Zandvoort,** Gasthuisplein 10 (✆ **023/822-3780;** www.wapenvanzandvoort.nl), and the next-door **Café Alex,** Gasthuisplein 9A (✆ **023/571-9205**), a few blocks back from the seafront, in the heart of town.

THE WESTERN IJSSELMEER SHORE ★★

Some of Holland's most emblematic places—Hoorn, Edam, Marken, Urk, Stavoren—lie along the shores of the great lake called the IJsselmeer. Painterly light washes through clouds, and luminous mists seem to merge water and sky. Cyclists test both speed and endurance against its 400km (250-mile) circumference, zipping round in bright Lycra blurs, or plodding along on the dike-top, immersed in wind, rain, or shine. The IJsselmeer (pronounced *Eye*-sel-meer) has a surface area of around 1,200 sq. km (460 sq. miles), and hosts fleets of traditional *boter* and *skûtsje* sailing ships, modern sailboats, powerboats, and canoes. Its waters are an important feeding ground for migrating and resident birds.

This section covers the IJsselmeer's western shore, the part that lies in Noord-Holland province. To complete the "Golden Circle" of the great lake, see "The Eastern IJsselmeer Shore," in chapter 16, and "Lelystad & the Noordoostpolder," in chapter 17.

At Home in Waterland

Midway along the road from Amsterdam to Monnickendam, the village of Broek in Waterland, a protected monument, is worth a stop for its charming green- and gray-painted 17th- and 18th-century timber houses clustered around a church and the little Havenrak lake. In the 18th century, so obsessive were the locals about cleanliness, they were even to be seen scrubbing the trees. Look for the pagoda-style Napoleonhuisje (1656), a lakeside pavilion named for a visit by an admiring Napoleon in 1811.

Volendam, Marken ★ & Monnickendam

Volendam 18km (11 miles), Marken 16km (10 miles), Monnickendam 14km (9 miles) NE of Amsterdam

Volendam and Marken have long been combined on bus-tour itineraries from Amsterdam as a kind of "packaged Holland and costumes to go." Many people would even attach that damning label "tourist trap" to these two lakeside communities. Yes, they're touristy (in particular during summer months), but it's possible to have a delightful day in the bracing air here, where a few residents (fewer all the time) may be seen in traditional dress. Monnickendam is between them.

ESSENTIALS

GETTING THERE **Arriva** buses depart every 15 to 30 minutes from outside Amsterdam Centraal Station. Nos. 110, 112, 116, and 118 go to Volendam; nos. 111 and 115 go to Monnickendam; and no. 111 goes on to Marken. The ride to Volendam takes 35 minutes; to Monnickendam, 30 minutes; and to Marken, 45 minutes. The round-trip fare is 7.50€.

By **car,** go north on N247. When driving to Marken, which was once an island, you cross a 3km (2-mile) causeway from Monnickendam. You leave your car in a parking lot outside the main village before walking through the narrow streets to the harbor. April to October, a passenger-and-bike ferry, the ***Marken Express*** (**© 0299/363-331;** www.markenexpress.nl), sails every hour or so daily 11am to 6pm between Volendam and Marken. The ride takes 30 minutes, and fares are 7.50€ round-trip and 5€ one-way for adults, 4.50€ round-trip and 4€ one-way for children 4 to 11, and free for children 3 and under; bicycles are carried for an additional 1€ one-way.

VISITOR INFORMATION **VVV Volendam,** Zeestraat 37, 1131 ZD Volendam (**© 0299/363-747;** fax 0299/368-484; www.vvv-volendam.nl), is just off Julianaweg in the heart of town. The office is open mid-March to September Monday to Saturday from 10am to 5pm, and Sunday from 11am to 4pm; October Monday to Saturday from 10am to 5pm; and November to mid-March Monday to Saturday from 10am to 3pm.

WHAT TO SEE & DO

A small, Catholic town on the mainland, **Volendam** lost most of its fishing industry to the enclosure of the Zuiderzee. It is geared now for tourism in a big way and has souvenir stores, boutiques, gift stores, cafes, and restaurants. Lots of people come to town to pig out on the town's near-legendary *gerookte paling* (smoked eel) and to visit such attractions as the **fish auction, diamond cutter, clog maker,** and **house** with a room entirely wallpapered in cigar bands. Still, Volendam's boat-filled harbor, tiny streets, and traditional houses have an undeniable charm. If you must have a snapshot of yourself in the traditional Dutch costume—local women wear white caps with wings—this is a good place to do it.

Volendam's rival, **Marken,** is Protestant and was an island until a narrow causeway connected it to the mainland in 1957. It remains insular. Smaller and less rambunctious than Volendam, it is rural, with clusters of farmhouses dotted around the polders. Half of Marken village, Havenbuurt, consists of green-and-white houses on stilts grouped around a tiny harbor. A **clog maker** works in summer in the village car park. Four old smokehouses in the other half of the village, Kerkbuurt, serve as the **Museum Marken,** Kerkbuurt 44–47 (✆ **0299/601-904;** www.markermuseum.nl), which covers traditional furnishings, costumes, and more. The museum is open April to September Monday to Saturday from 10am to 5pm and Sunday from noon to 4pm, and October Monday to Saturday from 11am to 4pm and Sunday from noon to 4pm. Admission is 2.50€ for adults, 1.25€ for children 5 to 12, and free for children 4 and under.

For a pleasant stroll (in fine weather) of an hour or two, take the road that leads past Havenbuurt, through the peaceful heart of the former island, to a white-painted **lighthouse** on the IJsselmeer shore. Then, go left along the dike, all the way back to Havenbuurt—where you arrive conveniently right next to the harborfront cafe-restaurant **De Taanderij** (see below).

Marken does not go gushy for the tourists. It merely feeds and waters them, and allows them to wander its pretty streets gawking at the locals as they go about their daily routines of hanging out laundry, washing windows, and shopping for groceries. Some residents occasionally wear traditional dress—for women, caps with ribbons and black aprons over striped petticoats—but as much to preserve the custom as for the tourists.

In contrast to its two neighbors, **Monnickendam** doesn't pay much attention to tourists at all, but gets on with its own life as a boating center and with what's left of its fishing industry, as you can see in its busy **harbor.** Take a walk through streets lined with gabled houses and make a stop to admire the 15th-century late Gothic **Sint-Nicolaaskerk (St. Nicholas's Church),** at Zarken 2. Be sure to visit the **Stadhuis (Town Hall),** at Noordeinde 5, which began as a private residence in 1746 and has an elaborately decorated ceiling.

Across the street, a 15th-century tower, the **Speeltoren,** Noordeinde 4 (✆ **0299/652-203;** www.despeeltoren.nl), has a carillon that chimes every hour, accompanied by a parade of mechanical knights. Inside used to be the town museum, **Museum de Speeltoren,** Noordeinde 4 (✆ **0299/652-203;** www.despeeltoren.nl). The museum is closed until early 2012 at the earliest (and quite likely until some later date), for reconstruction and reorganization. When it reopens as **Waterlandsmuseum De Speeltoren,** its collection will have expanded beyond Monnickendam to cover the history, art, and crafts of Noord-Holland province's Waterland region, north of Amsterdam. Check the museum's website (alas it's in Dutch only, but the announcement of the reopening might be easy to interpret), or with VVV Volendam (see "Visitor Information," above).

Perchance to Dream

To overnight in style in Volendam and Monnickendam, ask at the VVV offices about sleeping aboard one of the old Dutch wooden IJsselmeer *boters* and *skûtsjes* (sailing ships) in the harbor (this option is not available in Marken). It makes for a romantic, if somewhat cramped, way to spend the night.

WHERE TO STAY

Best Western Hotel Spaander ★ This old-fashioned hotel has real harbor flavor to go with its lakeside setting. The public spaces have an Old Dutch interior look, appropriate to a lodging that started out in 1881, and the entire space is a kind of art gallery, speckled with a thousand 19th-century paintings. Its guest rooms, however, are modern, brightly furnished, comfortable, and attractive. The hotel's two dining rooms, an old-style inn and an elegant sun lounge, serve local IJsselmeer and other Dutch specialties, like smoked eel. The outside terrace cafe is great when the weather is fine.

Haven 15–19 (north end of the harbor), 1131 EP Volendam. ✆ **0299/363-595.** Fax 0299/369-615. www.spaander.com. 79 units. 95€–169€ double; 169€ suite. Rates include continental breakfast. AE, DC, MC, V. Parking 5€. **Amenities:** 2 restaurants; 2 bars; exercise room; small heated indoor pool; sauna; smoke-free rooms. *In room:* TV, hair dryer, Wi-Fi (free).

WHERE TO DINE

De Taanderij ★ DUTCH/FRENCH For lunch, try this little *eethuis* (cafe serving food) at the end of the harbor. Seafood dishes and Dutch meals are served. Especially good for snacks are the traditional Dutch treats—*koffie en appelgebak met slagroom* (coffee with apple pie and cream) and *poffertjes* (small fried pancake "puffs" coated with confectioners' sugar and filled with syrup or liqueur). The inside is an elegant and cozy interpretation of Old Marken style. When the weather is good, a terrace will be spread at the harborside, where you can absorb the sunshine, the tranquil view over the IJsselmeer and, of course, the luscious goodies on the menu.

Havenbuurt 1, Marken. ✆ **0299/602-206.** Main courses 15€–19€; snacks 4€–13€. AE, DC, MC, V. Apr–Sept daily 10am–10pm; Oct–Mar Tues–Sun 11am–7pm.

Edam ★

18km (11 miles) NE of Amsterdam; 2km (1¼ mile) N of Volendam

Just inland from the IJsselmeer, Edam (pronounced *Ay*-dam) has given its name to one of Holland's most famous cheeses. Don't expect to find it in the familiar red skin, however—that's for export. In Holland, the cheese's skin is yellow. This pretty little town (pop. 7,000), a whaling port during Holland's Golden Age in the 17th century, is centered around canals you cross by way of drawbridges, with views on either side of canal houses, gardens, and canal-side teahouses.

ESSENTIALS

GETTING THERE There is frequent bus service by **Arriva.** Bus nos. 110, 112, 113, 116, and 118 depart from outside Amsterdam Centraal Station for the 35-minute ride; the round-trip fare is 7.50€. By **car,** go north on N247, via Monnickendam and Volendam (see above).

VISITOR INFORMATION **VVV Edam** is at the Stadhuis (Town Hall), Damplein 1, 1135 BK Edam (✆ **0299/315-125;** fax 0299/315-127; www.vvv-edam.nl), in the center of town. Should you wish to tour a local Edammer cheese factory, this is where you get the details. The office is open mid-March to June and September to October Monday to Saturday from 10am to 5pm; July to August Monday to Saturday from 10am to 5pm and Sunday from 11am to 3:30pm; and November to mid-March Monday to Saturday from 10am to 3pm.

WHAT TO SEE & DO

If you've arrived here after mingling with the floods of tourists in Volendam, Monnickendam, and Marken, Edam will make a pleasant change of pace. Except during the Wednesday cheese market, it's not a huge draw for tourists. You get to explore a pretty canal-side town with some handsome old buildings without this distraction, and Edam is well worth a few hours of strolling.

This was once a port of some prominence, and a visit to the modest **Edams Museum,** Damplein 8 (✆ **0299/372-644;** www.edamsmuseum.nl), opposite the former Town Hall (and with a section in the Town Hall), gives you a peek not only at its history but also at some of its most illustrious citizens of past centuries. Look for the portrait of Pieter Dirkszoon, a one-time mayor and proud possessor of what is probably the longest beard on record anywhere. An intriguing feature of this merchant's house from around 1530 is the cellar, which is actually a box floating on water, constructed that way so changing water levels wouldn't upset the foundations of the house. The museum is open April to October, Tuesday to Saturday from 10am to 4:30pm, and Sunday from 1 to 4:30pm. Admission is 3€ for adults, 1.50€ for seniors, 1€ for children 13 to 17, and free for children 12 and under.

Take a look at the lovely "wedding room" in the **Stadhuis (Town Hall).** The **Speeltoren (Carillon Tower)** from 1561 tilts a bit and was very nearly lost when the church to which it belonged was destroyed.

The Cheese Market

Edam wouldn't really be Edam without a *kaasmarkt* (cheese market)—and the cheese in question is Edammer, naturally. The market takes place each Wednesday in July and August, from 10:30am to 12:30pm on Kaasmarkt, outside the gaily decorated **Kaaswaag (Cheese Weigh House),** dating from 1592, which features a cheese-making display during these months.

WHERE TO STAY & DINE

Hotel-Restaurant De Fortuna Most of the rooms in this hotel look out on either a quiet garden or the small canal, 't Boerenverdriet, in back. They are country-style cozy, with pine furnishings, beds draped with handmade patchwork quilts, and exposed timber ceiling beams. You eat breakfast in the step-gabled main house, and weather permitting, you can lounge on the tree-fringed canal-side terrace. The on-site restaurant serves specialties of game and fish; its special dinner menu, for which reservations are required, is 35€–45€.

Spuistraat 3, 1135 AV Edam. ✆ **0299/371-671.** Fax 0299/371-469. www.fortuna-edam.nl. 23 units. 98€–140€ double. AE, DC, MC, V. **Amenities:** Restaurant; bar; lounge; bikes. *In room:* TV, hair dryer, minibar.

Hoorn ★★

32km (20 miles) NE of Amsterdam; 17km (11 miles) N of Edam

Hoorn (rhymes with *mourn*) is one of the legendary names in Dutch maritime history. Even now, with the open sea no longer on its doorstep, it remains orientated toward the water and is a busy IJsselmeer sailing center. While touring the graceful streets of the Golden Age town, in particular those around the central square, the Rode Steen, be sure to visit the old harbor, the Binnenhaven. Hoorn (pop. 69,000) is the hometown of Willem Cornelisz Schouten, who in 1616 rounded South America's southernmost tip, which he named Kap Hoorn (Cape Horn) in his hometown's honor.

ESSENTIALS

GETTING THERE **Trains** depart at least every hour from Amsterdam Centraal Station to Hoorn; the ride takes from 33 to 45 minutes, and a round-trip ticket is 14€ in second class and 24€ in first class. **Arriva bus** nos. 114 and 117 depart between two and fours times hourly from outside Amsterdam Centraal Station for the 1-hour ride; the round-trip fare is 11€. By **car** from Amsterdam, take E22/A7 north.

VISITOR INFORMATION **VVV Hoorn** is at Veemarkt 44, 1621 JC Hoorn (✆ **0229/218-343;** fax 0229/215-023; www.vvvhoorn.nl), close to the rail station and the center of town. The office is open May to August Monday from 1 to 6pm, Tuesday to Wednesday and Friday to Saturday from 9:30am to 5:30pm, and Thursday from 9:30am to 9pm. September to April, hours are Monday from 1 to 5pm and Tuesday to Saturday from 10am to 5pm.

WHAT TO SEE & DO

The **Westfries Museum,** Rode Steen 1 (✆ **0229/280-022;** www.westfriesmuseum.nl), housed in a building from 1632, contains a wide-ranging historical collection that includes armor, weapons, paper cuttings, costumes, toys, naive paintings (these embody a style that is deliberately childlike), coins, medals, jewels, civic guards' paintings, and porcelain. A second-floor exhibit details the town's maritime history, with an emphasis on ships and voyages of the United East India Company (V.O.C.). There are fine tapestries and 17th- and 18th-century period rooms. A collection of Bronze Age relics is exhibited in the basement. The museum is open Monday to Friday from 11am to 5pm and Saturday and Sunday from 1 to 5pm; it's closed January 1, April 30, and December 25. Admission is 5€ for adults, 3.50€ for seniors and children 5 to 16, and free for children 4 and under.

During summer months, an antique steam tram, the **Museumstoomtram Hoorn-Medemblik** (✆ **0229/214-862;** www.museumstoomtram.nl) transports visitors through the pretty West Friesland farm country between Hoorn and Medemblik (see below), a 1-hour ride. It departs from a station at van Dedemstraat 8 in Hoorn. Round-trip tickets are 19€ for adults, 14€ for ages 4 to 12, and free for children 3 and under.

WHERE TO DINE

De Hoofdtoren ★ DUTCH Boat lovers will want to sit on the terrace of this cafe-restaurant in an old defense tower, on the edge of Hoorn's busy harbor, surrounded by traditional IJsselmeer sailing ships and by pleasure boats large and small. The tower, which dates from about 1500, protected the harbor entrance, and its interior retains many antique features. Traditional Dutch fare and grilled specialties,

BY bicycle TO HOORN

For a great day trip from Amsterdam, go by bike along the IJsselmeer shore to Hoorn, and return by train with your bike. (Do this on a halfway decent bike, not a decrepit old Amsterdam bike.) Riding along between the polders and the lake is a perfect Dutch experience—but you need to be ready for some vigorous pedaling. You can't get lost if you stay on the road that runs along the IJsselmeer and keep the lake to your immediate right.

Board the IJ ferry at the dock behind Centraal Station and cross to Amsterdam-Noord (North). Take Durgerdammerdijk, a road leading east alongside the IJsselmeer shore to Durgerdam, a lakeside village huddled below water level behind a protective dike, with its roofs sticking up over the top. Ride either next to the houses and the polders or up on the dike-top path, immersed in wind, rain, and shine—and with fine lake views.

Beyond Uitdam, go either left on the lakeside road through Monnickendam to Volendam or right on the causeway to Marken. The first option cuts overall distance because Marken is a dead end and you need to come back across the causeway. But in summer, you can take the *Marken Express* passenger boat (see "Essentials" under "Volendam, Marken & Monnickendam," earlier in this chapter).

Go inland a short way along a canal that runs from the lakeside dike to Edam, famed for its cheese. Cross over the canal on the bridge at Damplein in Edam's center, and go back along the far bank to regain the IJsselmeer shore. Up ahead is a straight run north to Hoorn through the pastoral villages of Warder, Etersheim, Schardam, and Scharwoude.

After exploring Hoorn—or flopping down exhausted in a cafe—follow the green-painted signs pointing the way to the station for the train ride back to Amsterdam.

both meat and fish, are served at dinner. During the day, you can order lunch or snacks.

Hoofd 2. ✆ **0229/215-487.** www.hoofdtoren.nl. Main courses 17€–25€. AE, DC, MC, V. Daily 10am–10pm.

De Waag FRENCH This grand cafe in the monumental Weigh House from 1609 is open for breakfast, lunch, and dinner. It stands on a square that is among the finest in the country, surrounded by 17th-century buildings from the town's heyday. You can still see the antique weighing scales in the wood-beamed interior.

Rode Steen 8. ✆ **0229/215-195.** www.dewaaghoorn.nl. Main courses 13€–24€. AE, DC, MC, V. Mon–Thurs 11am–midnight, Fri–Sun 11am–1am.

Enkhuizen ★

44km (27 miles) NE of Amsterdam; 15km (9 miles) NE of Hoorn

A 400-boat herring fleet once sailed out of Enkhuizen, and so important was this fish to the town's prosperity that images of three herring grace its coat of arms. Then in 1932 came the Enclosing Dike (see below), closing off the North Sea. Enkhuizen's population has declined from 30,000 in its 17th-century heyday to 18,000 today, and the town looks to leisure boating, tourism, and bulb growing for its livelihood. It does pretty well in all three respects, and it boasts one of the country's most fascinating open-air museums, a must-see stop on any itinerary that passes this way.

ESSENTIALS

GETTING THERE **Trains** depart twice hourly from Amsterdam Centraal Station, going via Hoorn. The ride takes just under 1 hour; a round-trip ticket is 19€ in second class and 32€ in first class. By **car** from Amsterdam, drive to Hoorn, and then take N302 or N506 northeast.

VISITOR INFORMATION **VVV Enkhuizen** is at Tussen Twee Havens 1, 1601 EM Enkhuizen (✆ **0228/313-164;** fax 0228/315-531; www.vvvenkhuizen.nl), at the harbor. The office is open mid-April to October daily 9am to 5pm.

WHAT TO SEE & DO

The town is orientated toward its harbors, Oosterhaven, Oudehaven, Buitenhaven, and Spoorhaven, which are protected by the 16th-century **Drommedaris** defense tower, which now houses a restaurant. Behind the waterfront, the handsome old center is worth a leisurely stroll along Westerstraat between the 15th- to 16th-century **Westerkerk,** also known as the **Sint-Gomaruskerk,** and the 17th-century **Stadhuis (Town Hall).** You can do a pleasant walk along the moated 16th- to 17th-century defense walls on the west side of town, along Vest.

Enkhuizen is connected by road across the IJsselmeer, 31km (19 miles) atop the Markerwaarddijk to Lelystad (see "Lelystad & the Noordoostpolder," in chapter 17). This dike originally was built to enclose a vast drainage project, the Markerwaard Polder, in the southwestern reaches of the lake, but the plan was canceled for financial and environmental reasons, and the Markermeer is still open water.

An Outstanding Museum of Tradition

Zuiderzeemuseum ★★★ ☺ Take a step back in time at this remarkable museum, and come face to face with bygone ways of life in the fishing ports around the old Zuiderzee from 1880 until the sea was transformed into the freshwater IJsselmeer in 1932. You'll need to set aside a half-day at least to get the most out of a visit here. Information desks, restrooms, souvenir stores, and restaurants are on-site.

The open-air **Museumpark** ★★★, the best part of the experience, stands on the IJsselmeer shore at the northeast edge of town. It contains more than 130 old buildings—farmhouses, public buildings, stores, a church, and more—furnished in period style, and some sporting tiled interiors. These have been shipped intact from lakeside communities or rebuilt on-site to form a cobblestone-street village. A pair of bottle-shaped limekilns employed seashells as the raw material for making quicklime. To the north, a working windmill twirls its sails atop the dike. Nearby is a functioning smokehouse, where workers preserve herring by smoking them over smoldering wood chips before packing them in barrels. The village church hails from the onetime island of Wieringen, which now lies inland northwest of Enkhuizen. In the sail maker's store, you can watch sails being made that later will grace traditional Zuiderzee *boter* and *skûtsje* sailing ships. In a group of houses from Urk on the IJsselmeer's eastern shore (see "Lelystad & the Noordoostpolder," in chapter 17), daily scenes from around 1905 are reenacted. Don't miss the apothecary and its ornamental "gapers"—painted heads with open mouths—in the window. Among other functioning concerns are a grocery store, a cheese warehouse, a post office, a bakery, a painter's store, and a steam laundry.

Just south of the Museumpark is a recreation of Marken harbor (see above), with smokehouses for preserving herring and eels standing on the dike, and fishing boats

IJsselmeer Ferries

Enkhuizen is the hub for two passenger-and-bike ferries that ply the IJsselmeer during summer months (roughly Apr–Oct). MS *Friesland* (1956), operated by Stoomtram Hoorn-Medemblik (✆ 0229/214-862; www.museumstoomtram.nl), shuttles up and down the coast between Enkhuizen and Medemblik (see below), a 90-minute trip. Fares are 16€ round-trip and 9.30€ one-way for adults, 12€ round-trip and 7€ one-way for children 4 to 12, and free for children 3 and under. Bikes cost 2.60€ both one-way and round-trip.

MS *Bep Glasius* (1966), operated by Rederij V&O (✆ 0228/326-667; www.veerboot.info), sails on the cross-IJsselmeer route between Enkhuizen and Stavoren (see "The Eastern IJsselmeer Shore," in chapter 16), a 90-minute trip. Fares are 13€ round-trip and 9.80€ one-way for adults, 7.60€ round-trip and 6.20€ one-way for children 4 to 11, and free for children 3 and under. Bikes cost 4.90€ one-way and 6.90€ round-trip.

The main ferry dock in Enkhuizen is at Veerhaven, a few steps from the train station and the VVV tourist office. In addition, both ferries call at the Zuiderzeemuseum.

tied up at the dock. From here you can walk a short way to the indoor **Binnenmuseum ★★**, housed in the Peperhuis (Pepper House), a Dutch Renaissance building from 1625 that was used as offices and a warehouse by the Enkhuizen Chamber of the United East India Company (V.O.C.). In a former warehouse, you'll see numerous examples of the old fishing boats that provided the incomes on which Zuiderzee villagers largely depended, and old sailboats (including one that the kids can play on). Other rooms have been fitted out in the varied styles of houses from around the Zuiderzee and other parts of Holland.

Wierdijk 12–22. ✆ **0228/351-111.** www.zuiderzeemuseum.nl. Admission 14€ adults, 14€ seniors, 8.40€ children 4–12, free for children 3 and under, 35€ family. Full museum daily 10am–5pm. Museumpark fully operational Apr–Oct. Closed Jan 1 and Dec 25. Museumpark: Apr–Oct a free ferry boat departs every 15 min. from a dock on Tussen Twee Havens, next to Enkhuizen rail station and the VVV tourist office; and from a dock close to the museum's parking lot on Zijlweg, off the Enkhuizen–Lelystad dike road.

Medemblik

46km (29 miles) NE of Amsterdam; 14km (9 miles) NW of Enkhuizen

A small IJsselmeer town with busy twin harbors that already was a going concern by the year 700, Medemblik later joined the powerful Hanseatic League trading federation.

There are two great ways to get to Medemblik in the summer. One is onboard the 1956 **passenger-and-bike ferry** *Friesland* from Enkhuizen (see above). Tickets are 16€ round-trip and 9.30€ one-way for adults, 12€ round-trip and 7€ one-way for children 4 to 12, and free for children 3 and under. An equally atmospheric way is from Hoorn (see above) by **antique steam tram.** Tickets are 20€ round-trip and 15€ one-way for adults, 11€ round-trip and 8.30€ one-way for children 4 to 12, and free for children 3 and under. Both the boat and the tram are operated by **Stoomtram Hoorn-Medemblik** (✆ **0229/214-862;** www.museumstoomtram.nl).

Tourist information is available from **VVV Medemblik,** Kaasmarkt 1, 1671 BH Medemblik (✆ **0227/542-852;** fax 0227/540-967; www.vvvmedemblik.nl).

Adjacent to Medemblik's Oosterhaven (East Harbor)—twin to the Westerhaven (West Harbor)—is the moated **Kasteel Radboud,** Oudevaartsgat 8 (✆ **0227/541-960;** www.kasteelradboud.nl), originally an 8th-century castle refortified by the count of Holland in 1289 against a possible rebellion by the troublesome Frisians. The remaining section has been restored to its 13th-century state and is well worth a visit. The castle is open May to mid-September Monday to Saturday from 11am to 5pm and Sunday from 2 to 5pm; and mid-September to April Sunday from 2 to 5pm (and during school vacations 11am–5pm). Admission is 5€ for adults, 3€ for seniors and children 5 to 13, and free for children 4 and under.

Afsluitdijk (Enclosing Dike) ★

62km (39 miles) N of Amsterdam; 19km (12 miles) N of Medemblik

It's hard to grasp what a monumental work the great barrier that separates the salty Waddenzee from the freshwater IJsselmeer is until you drive its 30km (19-mile) length. The Afsluitdijk connects the provinces of Noord-Holland and Friesland, and by drastically shortening the coastline, it affords greater protection from the sea for Amsterdam and other low-lying towns around the shore of what was once the dangerous Zuiderzee (Southern Sea). Dr. Cornelis Lely came up with the plans in 1891, but construction was delayed for 25 years while he tried to convince the government to allocate funding.

Massive effort went into building the dike, which is 100m (328 ft.) wide and stands 7m (23 ft.) above mean water level. Many communities around the shores of what used to be the saltwater Zuiderzee lost their livelihood when access to the open sea was shut off. Some of the fishing boats that now sail the IJsselmeer hoist dark-brown sails as a sign of mourning for their lost sea fishing.

Midway along the dike's length, at the point where it was completed in 1932, stands a **monument** to the men who put their backs to the task, and a memorial to Dr. Lely. You can stop for a snack at the cafe in the monument's base and pick up an illustrated booklet that explains the dike's construction. For those crossing over by bicycle or by foot, there's a bike path and a pedestrian path.

ZAANSE SCHANS ★★

16km (10 miles) NW of Amsterdam

On the east bank of the Zaan River, this living-history experience is a replica 17th- to 18th-century village made up of houses, windmills, and workshops that were moved to the site when industrialization leveled their original locations. The aim is to recreate the way of life along the Zaan in the 17th century. Pictures of the windmills and the distinctive green-painted houses grace many a Holland brochure. Most of the buildings on the 8-hectare (20-acre) site are inhabited by people who can afford and appreciate their antique timbers, and who have the patience for the summertime crowds that pour from fleets of tour buses.

The Zaanstreek (Zaan District) has a fascinating history of shipbuilding and other crafts that is told in the architecturally novel **Zaans Museum ★**, Schansend 7 (✆ **075/681-0000;** www.zaansmuseum.nl), at the entrance to the site. Timber was

Get Your Clogs On

Clogs are still a fixture in many farming areas, where they're much more effective against wetness and cold than leather shoes or boots. They are, too, a tourist staple, and if you plan to buy a pair, Zaanse Schans is a good place to do it. Traditionally, those with pointed toes are for women and rounded toes are for men. All must be worn with heavy socks, so when buying, add the width of one finger when measuring for size.

the foundation of wealth along the Zaan in the 16th and 17th centuries. A burgeoning Dutch merchant marine and navy needed the wood, and the invention of a wind-powered sawmill here in 1592 provided the power. The museum is open daily 9am to 5pm (closed Jan 1 and Dec 25). Admission is 7.50€ for adults, 6€ for seniors, 4€ for children 4 to 17, and free for children 3 and under. Pick up a brochure here that features an artist's-impression bird's-eye view of the entire site, with each important location identified. This makes self-guided exploration a snap.

To the pleasure of just walking through Zaanse Schans, add a visit to one or more of the five working **windmills** (out of a total of eight) on the site: a sawmill, and mills specialized in producing paint, vegetable oil (two mills), and the renowned Zaanse mustard (three smaller mills are speckled around). At one time, the Zaanstreek had more than 1,000 windmills. Only 15 have survived, including these eight. A short tour shows you just how these wind machines worked.

Visit, too, **Museumwinkel Albert Heijn,** Kalverringdijk 5, a working reconstruction—with old-style candies and other items for sale—of an Oostzaan store from 1887 that was the beginning of Holland's largest supermarket chain. If you are at all interested in cookies and candy and in old recipes for the same, step inside the **Bakkerijmuseum (Bakery Museum),** Zeilenmakerspad 4, in an old house called De Gecroonde Duykevater. And to get an idea of how a well-heeled Zaan resident lived, visit **Museum Het Noorderhuis,** Kalverringdijk 17, a merchant's house from 1670 containing furnishings, utensils, and costumes that date from a period 2 centuries later.

Even if you are in a hurry, be sure to make time for the **Nederlandse Uurwerk (Dutch Clock) Museum,** Kalverringdijk 3, which displays timepieces from the period 1500 to 1900, and a workshop. Then there's the **Klompenmakerij (Clog Maker's Workshop),** a workshop where wooden *klompen* (clogs) are made and sold; and **De Catherina Hoeve Kaasmakerij,** which does likewise with cheese.

Most of these mini museums and other attractions are open March to October daily 10am to 5 or 6pm, and November to February Saturday and Sunday from around 11am to 4pm. Open hours for other sites are more restricted. Admission (where it's not free) varies from to 1€ to 2.50€ for adults, 0.50€ to 1€ for children 5 to 12, and is free for children 4 and under.

For a view from a different perspective, take a 45-minute **cruise** on the Zaan River aboard **Rederij de Schans** tour boat (**✆ 065/3294-467;** www.rederijdeschans.nl). Boats depart from a dock next to the De Huisman windmill, April to September hourly every day from 10am to 4pm. Cruises are 6€ for adults, 3€ for children 3 to 12, and free for children 2 and under.

windmill WAYS

Picture Holland in your mind. Now try to picture it without windmills. See? It's almost impossible. The Netherlands isn't the only country to harness passing wind in this way, but it seems to have secured exclusive worldwide rights to the image. Tulips, clogs, and cheese all have their places in Dutch mythology, but without windmills, much of this low-lying country would not even exist.

Windmills first appeared in the 13th century, transforming the rotation of their sails into mechanical energy via a system of cogs and gears. They were employed to grind wheat, barley, and oats; crush seeds to create mustard and vegetable oil; hull rice and peppercorns; and power sawmills and other industrial machinery. Most important of all, windmills kept the fertile polder land dry by pumping away surplus water and draining it into the rivers by way of a network of stepped canals.

Of the many thousands that once stood in towns and villages, and in rows on the dikes, fewer than a thousand working examples survive today. The two most famous multiple-windmill scenes in the country are the industrial windmills at Zaanse Schans (see above) and the polder-drainage windmills at Kinderdijk (see "Windmills of Kinderdijk," in chapter 15).

To get you to Zaanse Schans, trains depart every 15 minutes or so from Amsterdam Centraal Station via Zaandam to Koog-Zaandijk station, from where it's a 1km (⅔-mile) walk, across the Zaan River, to Zaanse Schans. The train ride takes 17 minutes, and a round-trip ticket is 5.20€ in second class and 8.80€ in first class. Or take **Connexxion** bus no. 91 from outside Amsterdam Centraal Station for the 40-minute ride direct. By **car** from Amsterdam, take A8 north and then switch to A7/E22 north to exit 2, from where you follow the signs to Zaanse Schans.

WHERE TO DINE

De Hoop Op d'Swarte Walvis ★★ FRENCH/CONTINENTAL A stellar restaurant with a mouthful of a name borrowed from a 19th-century local whaling ship, the "Hope for the Black Whale" occupies a refined brick building that now stands amid Zaanse Schans's green-painted houses, having been originally constructed as an orphanage in nearby Westzaan. Its glass pavilion and memorable outdoor terrace overlook the Zaan River and the waterside villas on the far bank. Gastronomes can expect an unforgettable treat from the hands of master chef Marco Krispijn, with subtle mixtures of superior produce prepared to perfection.

Kalverringdijk 15, Zaanse Schans. ✆ **075/616-5629.** www.dewalvis.nl. Main courses 24€–29€; 4-course *menu du chef* 49€. AE, DC, MC, V. Sun–Fri noon–10pm; Sat 6–10pm.

Nearby Places of Interest

Across the river from Zaanse Schans, in **Zaandijk,** riverside Lagedijk is a well-preserved example of an old-style Zaanstreek street. At its northern end, the **Honig Breethuis,** a merchant's house from 1706 furnished in Old Zaan style, holds the **Zaans Historisch Museum,** Lagedijk 80 (✆ **075/621-7626;** www.honigbreethuis.nl). Paintings, furnishings, religious items, traditional costumes, Chinese porcelain, and more afford an idea about life in the Zaan district around this period. The museum is open April to September Tuesday to Friday and Sunday from 1 to 5pm, and October to March Tuesday to Friday and Sunday from 1:30 to 4pm. Admission is 4€ for adults, 3€ for seniors and children 13 to 17, 2€ for children 4 to 12, and free for children 3 and under.

South of Zaandijk lies Koog aan de Zaan, and adjoining this town to its south is **Zaandam,** the Zaanstreek's main town, an important shipbuilding center in the 17th century. In 1697, Czar Peter the Great of Russia worked incognito for a few days at a Zaandam shipyard as "Peter Mikhailov," studying Dutch shipbuilding methods, which the avid nautical student considered the world's finest. He stayed at the humble timber home of a local blacksmith, Gerrit Kist. In 1895, Czar Nicholas II had it enclosed inside a brick shelter. The **Czaar Peterhuisje,** Krimp 23–24 (**✆ 075/681-0000;** www.zaansmuseum.nl), is the oldest surviving house of the Zaan district. It contains souvenirs of Peter's stay, including an exhibit on his life, the small bed into which the "Czar of All the Russias" squeezed his 2.1m (7-ft.) frame, and displays recounting the history of the district and of shipbuilding on the Zaan. Peter visited Zaandam again in 1698 and twice in 1717, each time paying Kist a visit. The house is open Tuesday to Sunday from 10am to 5pm. Admission is 3€ for adults, 2.50€ for seniors, 2€ for children 4 to 17, and free for children 3 and under. A **statue** of Peter at work on a ship stands on Damplein, the town's main square.

TULIPS & CHEESE

After windmills come tulips and the cheeses of Edam and Gouda as standard-bearers of Dutch national pride. The places to see tulips in their full glory are in the extensive bulb fields of the **Bollenstreek** and at **Keukenhof,** where vast numbers of tulips and other flowers create a dazzling tapestry of color. (Keukenhof is actually just across the province line in neighboring Zuid-Holland.) Edam (see "The Western IJsselmeer Shore," earlier in this chapter) and Gouda (see chapter 15) have more than cheese making to occupy their time, but the town of Alkmaar is a pretty good stand-in, for its weekly cheese market's sheer and unabashed hokum.

Bulb Fields

The heaviest concentration of bulb fields is in the **Bollenstreek (Bulb District) ★**, a strip of land 16km (10 miles) long and 6km (4 miles) wide, between Haarlem and Leiden. In the spring, it's a kind of a Dutch rite of passage to traipse through this colorful district and view the massed, varicolored regiments of tulips on parade. Every year from around the end of January to late May, the fields are covered at various times with tulips, crocuses, daffodils, narcissi, hyacinths, lilies, and more.

Flower Power

During Holland's 17th-century "tulip mania," when trading in bulbs was a lucrative business and prices soared to ridiculous heights, a single tulip bulb could be worth as much as a prestigious Amsterdam canal house, with a garden and coach house thrown in.

Viewing the flowers is easy. Just follow the signposted **Bollenstreek Route** (60km/37 miles) by car or bike. Stalls along the roads sell flower garlands; do as the natives do and buy one for yourself and another for the car. VVV tourist information offices in the area can provide detailed information about the route. To get to the bulb fields from Amsterdam, drive to Haarlem; then south on N206 through De Zilk and Noordwijkerhout, or on N208 through Hillegom, Lisse, and Sassenheim. Alternatively, go south from Amsterdam on A4/E19, past Schiphol Airport, to exit 4 (Nieuw-Vennep), and then northwest on N207 for 8km (5 miles) until you hit N208.

Other bulb-growing centers are scattered around Noord-Holland, with an important concentration in the Hoorn-Medemblik area. If you are interested in the original plants, **Hortus Bulborum,** Zuidkerkenlaan 23A, Limmen (© **0251/231-286;** www.hortus-bulborum.nl), a specialized tulip garden 30km (19 miles) northwest of Amsterdam, has recreated some of the older varieties. Here you can see the flowers that are so prominent in the floral still-lifes painted by 17th-century artists, fancifully shaded in flaming patterns and with names like Semper Augustus and Bruin Anvers. The garden is open April 6 to May 16 Monday to Saturday from 10am to 5pm and Sunday from noon to 5pm. Admission is 3.50€ for adults, 2.50€ for seniors, and free for children 11 and under.

Holland's Grandest Garden

Keukenhof ★★★ Flowers at their peak and these gardens both have short seasons, but if you're here in the spring, you'll never forget a visit to this park. A meandering, 32-hectare (79-acre) wooded green in the heart of the bulb-producing region is planted every fall by the major Dutch growers (each plants his own plot or establishes his own greenhouse display). Then, come spring, the bulbs burst forth and produce not hundreds of flowers, or even thousands, but millions (almost eight million at last count) of tulips and narcissi, daffodils and hyacinths, bluebells, crocuses, lilies, amaryllis, and many others. The blaze of color is everywhere in the park and in the greenhouses, beside the brooks and shady ponds, along the paths and in the neighboring fields, in neat little plots and helter-skelter on the lawns. Keukenhof claims to be the greatest flower show on earth—and it's Holland's annual spring gift to the world. ***Tip:*** There are four cafes on-site where you can grab a quick bite to eat.

Stationsweg 166A, Lisse. © **0252/465-555.** www.keukenhof.nl. Admission 15€ adults, 7€ children 4–11, free for children 3 and under. 3rd week of Mar to 3rd week of May daily 8am–7:30pm. Special train/bus connections via Haarlem and Leiden.

A Gargantuan Flower Auction

Selling flowers and plants nets around 1.5 billion€ a year at the **Bloemenveiling (Flower Auction) ★**, Legmeerdijk 313 (© **0297/393-939;** www.floraholland.com), in the lakeside community of Aalsmeer, 18km (11 miles) southwest of Amsterdam, close to Schiphol Airport. Every day the auction vends some 19 million cut flowers and two million plants, in 12,000 varieties, from 7,000 nurseries, representing 30% of the trade worldwide. So vast is the auction "house" that 120 soccer fields would fit inside.

> **Impressions**
>
> ***Aalsmeer is an auction house in the sense that Shanghai is a city or Everest a mountain.***
>
> ***—National Geographic,* Apr 2001**

Get here early to see the biggest array of flowers in the distribution rooms and to have as much time as possible to watch the computerized auctioning process. The bidding on flowers goes from high to low. Mammoth bidding clocks are numbered from 100 to 1. As many as 1,500 buyers sit in rows in the five auditorium-style auction halls; they have microphones to ask questions and buttons to push to register their bids in the computer. As bunches of tulips, daffodils, or whatever go by on carts, they are auctioned in a matter of seconds. The first bid, which is the first one to stop the clock as it works down from 100 to 1, is the only bid.

The auction is open Monday to Friday from 7 to 11am. Admission is 5€ for adults, 3€ for children 6 to 11, and free for children 5 and under. To get there from Amsterdam, take the train to Schiphol Station, and then **Connexxion** bus no. 198 from outside Schiphol Plaza to the auction entrance; the ride takes an hour. By car, take A4/E19 south to the Hoofddorp junction, and then go southeast on N201.

Alkmaar

30km (19 miles) N of Amsterdam

Every Friday morning during the long Dutch summer season, a steady parade of tourists arrives to visit the famous cheese market in this handsome, canal-lined town (pop. 94,000), founded in the 10th century. It's quite a show they're on their way to see. For other towns with a cheesy disposition, see also the sections on Edam, earlier in this chapter, and on Gouda, in chapter 15.

GETTING THERE **Trains** depart every 15 minutes or so from Amsterdam Centraal Station to Alkmaar; the ride takes around 35 minutes. A round-trip ticket is 13€ in second class and 22€ in first class. By **car** from Amsterdam, take A8, N246, N203, and A9 north.

VISITOR INFORMATION **VVV Alkmaar** is at Waagplein 2, 1811 JP Alkmaar (✆ **072/511-4284;** fax 072/511-7513; www.vvvalkmaar.nl), in the center city. The office is open April to September Monday to Thursday and Saturday from 10am to 5pm, and Friday from 9am to 5pm; and October to March Monday from 1am to 5pm and Tuesday to Saturday from 10am to 5pm.

WHAT TO SEE & DO

At the Friday morning **Kaasmarkt (Cheese Market)** ★ in Waagplein, yellow-skinned Edam, Gouda, and Leidse (Leiden) cheeses are piled high on the cobblestone square. The carillon in the 16th-century **Waaggebouw (Weigh House)** tower showers the streets each hour with tinkling Dutch folk music, accompanying a jousting performance of attached mechanical knights. The square is filled with sightseers, barrel organs, souvenir stalls, and a tangible excitement. White-clad *kaasdragers* (cheese porters) dart around, wearing colored lacquered straw hats in red, blue, yellow, or green as a sign of which of four sections of their more than 400-year-old guild they belong to. Porters, who are not permitted to smoke, drink, or curse while on duty, are so proud of their standards that every week they post on a "shame board" the name of any carrier who has indulged in profanity or has been late arriving at the auction.

The bidding process is carried on in the traditional Dutch manner of hand clapping to bid the price up or down, and a good solid hand clap to seal the deal. Then, once a buyer has accumulated his lot of cheeses, teams of porters move in with their shiny, shallow barrows and, using slings that hang from their shoulders, carry the golden wheels and balls of cheese to the scales in the Weigh House for the final tally of the bill. The market is held from the first Friday of April to the first Friday of September from 10am to 12:30pm; art and craft markets piggyback on the cheese market but run longer.

The history of Dutch cheese and how the various cheeses are produced is the theme of the **Hollands Kaasmuseum,** in the Waaggebouw, Waagplein 2 (✆ **072/55-5516;** www.kaasmuseum.nl). It's open April to October Monday to Saturday from 10am to 4pm (from 9am Fri during the Cheese Market season); Christmas and New Year holidays from 10am to 4pm; and Easter, Pentecost, and Ascension Day holidays from 10:30am to 1:30pm. Admission is 3€ for adults, 1.50€ for children 5 to 12, and free for children 4 and under.

DEN HELDER & TEXEL

The harbor town and navy base of Den Helder, at the tip of Noord-Holland province, is the gateway to the island of Texel.

Den Helder

67km (42 miles) N of Amsterdam; 31km (19 miles) NW of Medemblik

Den Helder holds the country's most important navy base. It still is home to its Royal Naval College (the Dutch Annapolis) and host of the annual Navy Days, the national fleet festival, in July. It's a reasonably endowed resort in its own right, with plenty of adjacent beach space, and takes delivery of more hours of sunshine annually than any other place in the country.

ESSENTIALS

GETTING THERE **Trains** depart every half-hour from Amsterdam Centraal Station for Den Helder; the ride takes around 75 minutes, and a round-trip ticket is 24€ in second class and 41€ in first class. By **car** from Amsterdam, take A8, A9, and N9 north.

VISITOR INFORMATION **VVV Den Helder,** Bernhardplein 14, 1781 HH Den Helder (✆ **0223/625-544;** fax 0223/614-888; www.vvvkopvannoordholland.nl), is next to the rail station. The office is open Monday from 10:30am to 5:30pm, Tuesday to Friday from 9:30am to 6pm, and Saturday from 9:30am to 5pm.

WHAT TO SEE & DO

Marinemuseum (Navy Museum) ★ For an insight into the Royal Netherlands Navy's illustrious past, by way of models, marine paintings, weapons and equipment, and some real live warships, visit this extensive facility just 200m (656 ft.) west of the Texel ferry dock. Among several retired combatants on display is the steam-and-sail ram *De Schorpioen,* built in France for the Dutch navy in 1868. Now tied to a dock, the *Scorpion* was once a vessel with a sting in its bow, where a below-the-water-line ram could deal fatal blows to enemy ships—not that it ever did. The steam engine still works, and you can visit the captain's cabin and crew's quarters. Equally fascinating is the dry-landed coastal attack submarine *Tonijn (Tunny),* which has a torpedo emerging from its front tube and which you can board to experience the claustrophobic quarters of a submariner's world.

Hoofdgracht 3. ✆ **0223/657-534.** www.marinemuseum.nl. Admission 6€ adults, 3€ children 5–15, free for children 4 and under, 15€ family. May–Oct Mon–Fri 10am–5pm, Sat–Sun and holidays noon–5pm; Nov–Apr Tues–Fri 10am–5pm, Sat–Sun and holidays noon–5pm. Closed Jan 1 and Dec 25.

Other Attractions

While you're in navy mode, visit the **Nationaal Reddingmuseum Dorus Rijkers (Dorus Rijkers National Lifeboat Museum),** Oude Rijkswerf, Willemsoord 60G

Ice Hazard

Den Helder has the dubious distinction of being possibly the only port in the world that ever lost a fleet to a company of horsemen. That unique event took place in January 1795, when the Dutch navy found itself stuck fast in the frozen waters of the roads between Den Helder and Texel. French cavalry simply rode out to the ships and captured them.

(✆ **0223/618-320;** www.reddingmuseum.nl), which chronicles the Lifeboat Service's history. The museum is open April to October and Christmas school vacation Monday to Friday from 10am to 5pm and Saturday and Sunday from noon to 5pm; November to mid-December, it's open Sunday from noon to 5pm (closed Jan 1 and Dec 25). Admission is 6€ for adults, 5€ for children 4 to 17, free for children 3 and under, and 18€ for a family.

The Bulb District between Leiden and Haarlem (see above) may be better known, but the largest area of bulb fields in the country is in the hinterland of Den Helder—and the serried ranks of spring tulips look as colorful here as there.

Texel ★

69km (43 miles) N of Amsterdam; 4km (2½ miles) N of Den Helder

A short ferry ride from Den Helder, family-orientated Texel (pronounced *Tess*-uhl) is the largest and most populated of the Wadden Islands archipelago. With just 14,000 permanent inhabitants (outnumbered three to two by sheep that are the source of the prized Texel lamb), that's not saying much. Texel, 24km (15 miles) long and a maximum of 9km (6 miles) wide, has a varied landscape of tidal gullies, sand dunes, and rolling meadows, and its entire North Sea shoreline is one long beach. It has some of the serenity intrinsic to islands, even allowing for the many visitors who pour in during summer months to fill up the island's extensive roster of hotels, vacation homes, apartments, and camping sites.

For the other Wadden Islands—Vlieland, Terschelling, Ameland, and Schiermonnikoog—which lie in Friesland province, see chapter 16.

ESSENTIALS

GETTING THERE The **TESO** line (✆ **0222/369-600;** www.teso.nl) operates car-ferry service from Den Helder across the Marsdiep Strait to 't Horntje on Texel—a 20-minute ride. In Den Helder, **Connexxion** bus no. 33 shuttles between the rail station and the ferry dock (a 10-min. ride). Ferries depart hourly at peak times, and reservations are not accepted. Round-trip fares for cars, including two passengers, are 18€ Friday to Monday, and 12€ Tuesday to Thursday; for passengers alone, round-trip fares are 2.50€, and free for children 3 and under. Bicycles and mopeds cost 2.50€ in addition to the passenger's fare.

May to September, a passengers-only tourist boat operates between De Cocksdorp in the north of Texel and neighboring Vlieland, a 25-minute crossing that opens up the possibility of island hopping through the Wadden chain.

VISITOR INFORMATION **VVV Texel,** Emmalaan 66, 1791 AV Den Burg (✆ **0222/314-741;** fax 0222/310-054; www.texel.net), lies just off the main road from the ferry dock into the island's main town. The office is open Monday to Friday from 9am to 5:30pm, and Saturday from 9am to 5pm.

GETTING AROUND **Cars** are permitted on Texel, and **buses** connect the villages and the main beaches, but there's no doubt that the best way to get around and to respect the island's environment is to go by **bicycle.** These can be brought over free on the ferry, or rented from dozens of outlets around the island.

WHAT TO SEE & DO

Beaches, sailing, biking, hiking, and bird-watching are the big attractions on Texel, yet eating, drinking, and partying have a place, too. To gain an insight into Texel's centuries-long relationship with the sea, head to nearby Oudeschild on the island's east coast, to visit the **Maritiem & Jutters Museum,** Barentszstraat 21 (© **0222/314-956;** www.texelsmaritiem.nl), at the small town's harbor. The museum is open July to August Tuesday to Saturday from 10am to 5pm and Sunday from noon to 5pm, and September to June Monday to Saturday from 10am to 5pm and Sunday from noon to 5pm. Admission is 6.25€ for adults, 4.75€ for children 5 to 14, and free for children 4 and under.

You're allowed to freely visit the large area of dunes and forest on the island's west coast comprising the **Nationaal Park Duinen van Texel ★**, so long as you stick to the marked trails. Guided tours in the national park are conducted by wildlife biologists from **EcoMare,** Ruijslaan 92 (© **0222/317-741;** www.ecomare.nl), a Wadden Islands research center located amid the sand dunes just south of the main coastal village, De Koog. EcoMare's visitor center houses a small natural history museum that features the geology and plants of Texel, and its wildlife of land, sea, and air. The Wadden Sea is rich in seals, and EcoMare has a seal rehabilitation facility that cares for weak and injured animals until they are strong enough to be returned to the sea. An additional rehabilitation project cares for birds affected by pollution and other hazards. The center is open daily 9am to 5pm. Admission is 9€ for adults, 6.25€ for children 4 to 13, and free for children 3 and under.

Some 300 bird species have been observed on Texel, of which around 100 breed on the island. Among the avian stars are oyster catchers, Bewicks swans, spoonbills, eider ducks, Brent geese, avocets, marsh harriers, snow buntings, ringed plovers, kestrels, short-eared owls, and bar-tailed godwits. You can observe these and more in **De Schorren, De Bol,** and **Dijkmanshuizen,** three protected nature reserves that may be entered only on tours conducted by guides from EcoMare.

WHERE TO DINE

Het Vierspan DUTCH/FRENCH The warm welcome here, on a pretty corner occupied by the island's top restaurants, is complemented by a homely interior and well-prepared dishes based on local ingredients. Don't miss out on the local Texel lamb, succulent and salty from grazing the sea-sprayed grass. Other specialties here include game and mushrooms.

Gravenstraat 3, Den Burg. © **0222/313-176.** Main courses 13€–18€. MC, V. Wed–Mon 6–11pm.

CASTLE COUNTRY

In earlier times, the territory southeast of Amsterdam was a place of strategic importance, as evidenced by the grand military constructions still standing today, such as the 13th-century Muiderslot moated castle in Muiden—itself a handsome village of

AN american LIFE

American artist William Henry Singer (1868–1943) chose to live and paint in the clear light of Holland rather than follow his family's traditional path to fame and fortune via the steel mills of Pittsburgh. He settled in suburban Laren, a haven for artists of the Laren, Hague, and Amsterdam schools, 26km (16 miles) southeast of Amsterdam. Among the town's star residents was Dutch Impressionist Anton Mauve (1838–88), an uncle of Vincent van Gogh.

Singer's home, a 1911 villa he called the Wild Swans, is now the **Singer Museum,** Oude Drift 1 (✆ **035/539-3939;** www.singerlaren.nl). It houses Impressionist-influenced paintings by Singer and his collection of works by American, Dutch, French, and Norwegian artists. The museum is open Tuesday to Sunday from 11am to 5pm (closed Jan 1 and Dec 25). Admission is 10€ for adults, 7€ for children 13 to 17, and free for children 12 and under. To get here from Hilversum and Naarden, take bus no. 109, which stops at the museum.

gabled houses along the waterfront at the mouth of the Vecht River—and the star-shaped fortifications of Naarden.

Muiderslot ★ A 14th-century fairy-tale castle with a moat, turrets, and stout walls with crenellations, Muiderslot perches on the bank of the Vecht River, just outside the small IJsselmeer harbor town of Muiden, 13km (8 miles) southeast of Amsterdam. Count Floris V of Holland, who in 1275 granted toll privileges to the vibrant new settlement of Aemstelledamme (Amsterdam), built the castle around 1280, and he was murdered here by rival nobles in 1296. Muiderslot is where poet Pieter Cornelisz Hooft found both a home and employment—and inspiration for romantic and lofty phraseology—when he served here as castle steward and local bailiff for 40 years in the early 17th century. The castle is furnished essentially as Hooft and his artistic friends, known in Dutch literary history as the Muiderkring (Muiden Circle), knew it. You'll find distinctly Dutch carved cupboard beds, heavy chests, fireside benches, and mantelpieces.

Herengracht 1, Muiden. ✆ **0294/256-262.** www.muiderslot.nl. Admission 11€ adults, 6.25€ children 4–12, free for children 3 and under. Apr–Oct Mon–Fri 10am–5pm, Sat–Sun and holidays noon–6pm; Nov–Mar Sat–Sun noon–6pm (last tour 5pm at all times). Bus: Connexxion bus no. 157 departs every 15 min. or so from outside Amsterdam Amstel station for the 20-min. ride to Muiden; from there, walk 1km (½ mile) north through Muiden to the castle. By car from Amsterdam, take A1/E231 east.

Naarden

19km (12 miles) E of Amsterdam

The highlight of this small town is that it has one of Holland's best-preserved rings of old military fortifications.

ESSENTIALS

GETTING THERE **Trains** depart every 15 minutes or so from Amsterdam Centraal Station to Naarden-Bussum station; the ride takes around 25 minutes, and a round-trip ticket is 8.10€ in second class and 14€ in first class. By **car** from Amsterdam, take E231/A1 east.

VISITOR INFORMATION **VVV Naarden,** Adriaan Dortsmanplein 1B, 1411 RC Naarden (✆ **035/694-2836;** fax 035/694-3424; www.vvvhollandsmidden.nl), is located inside the walls of the old town. The office is open May to October Monday to Saturday from 10am to 5pm, Saturday from 10am to 3pm, and Sunday from noon to 3pm; November to April, it's open Monday to Saturday from 10am to 2pm.

WHAT TO SEE & DO

Much in the spirit of locking the barn door after the horse had bolted, the surviving inhabitants of Naarden erected their double fortifications, in the shape of a beautiful 12-pointed-star, after the town was brutally sacked and its populace put to the sword by Don Fadrique Álvarez de Toledo and his Spanish troops in 1572. The inhabitants might have spared themselves the trouble, since the French were able to storm the works in 1673.

Beneath the Turfpoort, one of six bastions, you can visit the casemates (artillery vaults) that house the **Nederlands Vestingmuseum (Dutch Fortification Museum),** Westwalstraat 6 (✆ **035/694-5459;** www.vestingmuseum.nl), filled with cannon, muskets, accoutrements, and documentation. The museum is open mid-March to October Tuesday to Friday from 10:30am to 5pm and Saturday, Sunday, and holidays from noon to 5pm; November to mid-March Sunday from noon to 5pm; the Saturday before Christmas to the Sunday after New Year Tuesday to Friday from 10:30am to 5pm, and Saturday and Sunday from noon to 5pm. It's closed January 1, December 25 and 31. Admission is 5.50€ for adults, 4.50€ for seniors, 3€ for children 5 to 12, and free for children 4 and under.

Take in the town's 15th-century late-Gothic **Grote Kerk (Great Church),** Marktstraat (✆ **035/694-9873**), noted for its 45m-high (148-ft.) tower, fine acoustics, and annual pre-Easter performances of Bach's *St. Matthew Passion.* The church is open June to September daily 1 to 4pm. Admission is free.

THE HAGUE, ROTTERDAM & ZUID-HOLLAND

Zuid-Holland (South Holland) province takes in a cluster of important cities and towns, all within about an hour's drive or train ride from Amsterdam. Roads pass through a landscape straight out of a painting by one of the Dutch Masters. You'll see flat green fields ribboned with canals and distant church spires piercing a wide sky.

15

Amsterdam might be the national capital, but **The Hague** has always been the seat of national government and the official residence of the Dutch monarchs. The city's seacoast resort, **Scheveningen,** makes something of a stab at being Holland's Deauville or Biarritz.

Brash **Rotterdam** has been commercial to the core from the beginning. Most of its historically significant buildings, along with most of the city, were destroyed in World War II Nazi bombings. Rebuilding was a remarkable feat of modern urban planning. High-rise towers, with straight lines and right angles, mold an oddly attractive open cityscape. Rotterdam has one of the world's busiest ports on its doorstep.

The Hague and Rotterdam, for all their geographical proximity, are about as different as two cities easily can be. Zuid-Holland's trio of venerable art towns have more in common. The triangle formed by **Delft, Gouda,** and **Leiden** makes for leisurely sightseeing, with distances short enough to allow you to visit all three from a base in Amsterdam, The Hague, or Rotterdam. Better yet, stay overnight in any one of the three.

THE HAGUE ★★★

50km (31 miles) SW of Amsterdam; 22km (14 miles) NW of Rotterdam; 54km (34 miles) W of Utrecht

Stately and dignified, The Hague (pop. 480,000) is an easy day trip from Amsterdam, but some travelers prefer it as a more relaxed sightseeing base. 's-Gravenhage, to give the city its full name, or more commonly Den Haag, is a cosmopolitan town bursting with style and culture, full of parks and elegant homes. Its 18th-century French look suits its role as a diplomatic center and the site of the International Court of Justice, housed in the famous Peace Palace.

Three royal palaces grace the city. In the beginning, the counts of Holland chose a small village named Haag (from the Dutch for "hedge") as the setting for their hunting lodge, which was why the town was later called 's-Gravenhage (the Count's Hedge). Lush greenery from the original hunting grounds remains in the city's parks, gardens, and forests.

Essentials

GETTING THERE

BY PLANE Amsterdam's **Schiphol Airport,** 40km (25 miles) away, also serves The Hague (see "Getting There & Around," in chapter 3, and "Orientation," in chapter 13). Train service frequently runs from the airport to The Hague, with up to six trains an hour during the day and one an hour at night; the ride takes around 35 minutes, and a one-way ticket costs 7.40€ in second class and 13€ in first class. A taxi from Schiphol to The Hague city center takes 30 minutes in light traffic and costs around 80€.

BY TRAIN The Hague has excellent rail connections from around the Netherlands, with up to six trains arriving hourly from Amsterdam, Rotterdam, and Utrecht. The fastest InterCity trains take around 50 minutes from Amsterdam, 40 minutes from Utrecht, and 20 minutes from Rotterdam. The city has two main stations, **Den Haag Centraal Station** and **Den Haag HS;** most city sights are closer to Centraal Station, but some trains stop only at HS. The one-way fare from Amsterdam is 10€ in second class and 17€ in first class. In 2010 a complete refurbishment of the old station building at Den Haag HS began; it's due to be completed during the course of 2011.

BY CAR From Amsterdam and the north, take A4/E19; from Rotterdam and the south, take A13/E19; and from Utrecht and the east, take A12/E30. You'll want to avoid all three *snelwegen* (expressways) during the morning and evening peak hours, when the designation can seem like a bad joke. At other times, you should be able to go from both Amsterdam and Utrecht in under an hour and from Rotterdam in around 20 minutes.

VISITOR INFORMATION

VVV Den Haag, Hofweg 1 (mailing address: Postbus 85456, 2508 CD Den Haag; ✆ **070/361-8860;** fax 070/361-7915; www.denhaag.nl; tram: 1 or 16), faces the Binnenhof (Parliament) in the center of town. The office is open Monday to Friday from 9:30am to 6pm, Saturday from 9:30am to 5pm, and Sunday from 11am to 6pm.

GETTING AROUND

Public transportation in the city is operated by **HTM** (✆ **0900/9292;** www.htm.net). Centraal Station (tram: 2, 3, 4, 6, 8, 9, 10, 15, 16, or 17) is the primary interchange point for bus and tram routes, and HS station (tram: 1, 8, 9, 10, 11, 12, 15, 16, or 17) the secondary node. Going by tram is the quickest way to get around town, but some points are served only by bus. Note that tram line 1 goes from the North Sea coast at Scheveningen, through The Hague, and all the way to Delft. Regional bus service is handled by **Connexxion** (✆ **0900/266-6399;** www.connexxion.nl). For details on using the **OV-chipkaart** stored-value card for getting around by public transportation in Holland, see "Getting There & Around," in chapter 12.

Taxis operated by **HTMC** (✆ **070/390-7722;** www.htmc.nl) wait at stands outside both main rail stations and at other strategic points around town.

Zuid-Holland

SPECIAL EVENTS

The **State Opening of Parliament,** during which the queen delivers a speech from the throne in the Hall of the Knights (see below), is worth being in town for. On Prinsjesdag (Day of the Princes), the third Tuesday in September, she departs from Noordeinde Palace in a golden coach—like Cinderella—drawn by eight high-stepping royal horses, escorted by military corps, bands, local authorities, and a blaze of street pageantry, to proceed to the Binnenhof, where she officially opens Parliament with an address to both houses of the States General in the Hall of the Knights.

What to See & Do

One of the pleasures of spending a day or more in The Hague is walking through its pleasant streets, matching your pace to the unhurried leisure that pervades the city. Stroll past the mansions that line Lange Voorhout, overlooking a broad avenue of poplar and elm trees, and notice how these spacious, restrained structures differ from Amsterdam's gabled, ornamented canal houses. Window-shop or get down to serious buying in the covered shopping arcades and store-lined pedestrians-only streets. Take time to loiter in the more than 30 sq. km (12 sq. miles) of parks, gardens, and other green spaces within the city limits. To go farther, hop on a tram for the short ride out to The Hague's seacoast resort, Scheveningen.

THE TOP ATTRACTIONS

Binnenhof & Ridderzaal (Inner Court & Hall of the Knights) ★★ The magnificent Binnenhof, the 13th-century hunting lodge of the counts of Holland, is the center of Holland's political life. It now houses the First and Second Chamber of the Staaten-Generaal (States General), the two houses of the Dutch Parliament. At the cobblestoned courtyard's heart is the beautiful, twin-towered Hall of the Knights, measuring 38×18m (125×59 ft.) and soaring 26m (85 ft.) to its oak roof. Since 1904 its immense interior, adorned with provincial flags and leaded-glass windows depicting the coats of arms of Dutch cities, has hosted the queen's annual address to Parliament (third Tues in Sept) and official receptions. Adjacent to the Ridderzaal are the former quarters of the Stadhouder (Head of State).

When Count of Holland Willem II was crowned king of the Romans and emperor-elect of the Holy Roman Empire in 1248, he appointed the Binnenhof, his late father's palace, the official royal residence, thereby providing the city with what is considered its foundation year. Willem's son, Floris V, added the massive Ridderzaal in 1280.

Visit the Parliament exhibit in the reception room of the Hall of Knights, and join a guided tour to visit the hall and, government business permitting, one of the chambers of Parliament. It's worthwhile to visit the courtyard and the Hall of the Knights, which you can do easily in an hour; the tour of Parliament isn't all that exciting, so don't fret if you miss it. Be sure to check out the view from the outside of the Binnenhof, across the rectangular **Hofvijver (Court Lake),** which has a fountain and a tiny island.

Binnenhof 8A. ✆ **070/364-6144.** www.binnenhofbezoek.nl. Admission: courtyard and Ridderzaal reception hall free; guided tours 4€ or 6€ adults, depending on the tour (book in advance by phone, and call ahead to be sure tours are going the day you intend to visit). Mon–Sat 10am–4pm. Closed holidays and special events. Tram: 1, 10, 16, or 17 to Buitenhof.

Gemeentemuseum Den Haag (The Hague Municipal Museum) ★ Housed in a honey-toned brick building (1935) by architect Hendrik Petrus Berlage, this fine museum has plenty to see. Top billing goes to the world's most comprehensive collection—more than 50 works—by De Stijl artist Piet Mondrian, among them his last painting, the unfinished *Victory Boogie Woogie* (1944), an abstract representation of New York. Other rooms cover 19th-century Dutch Romantic art, the Impressionist Hague School, and 20th-century art, and there are a few works by van Gogh, Monet, and Picasso, and prints and drawings by Karel Appel and Toulouse-Lautrec. For decorative arts, there's ceramics from Delft, China, and the Middle East; Dutch and Venetian glass; silver; period furniture; and an intricate 1743 dollhouse. The music department has antique instruments from Europe—harpsichords, pianos, and more—and from around the world, and an impressive library of scores, books, and prints. New underground rooms are used for temporary fashion exhibits. Plan to spend a couple hours here.

Stadhouderslaan 41 (close to the Nederlands Congres Centrum, north of the center). ✆ **070/338-1111.** www.gemeentemuseum.nl. Admission 10€ adults, 6.50€ students, free for children 18 and under. Tues-Sun 11am–5pm. Closed Jan 1 and Dec 25. Tram: 17 to Gemeentemuseum.

Mauritshuis ★★ Once the residence of Count Johan Maurits van Nassau-Siegen, court dandy, cousin of the ruling Oranje-Nassaus, and governor-general of Dutch

The Hague & Scheveningen

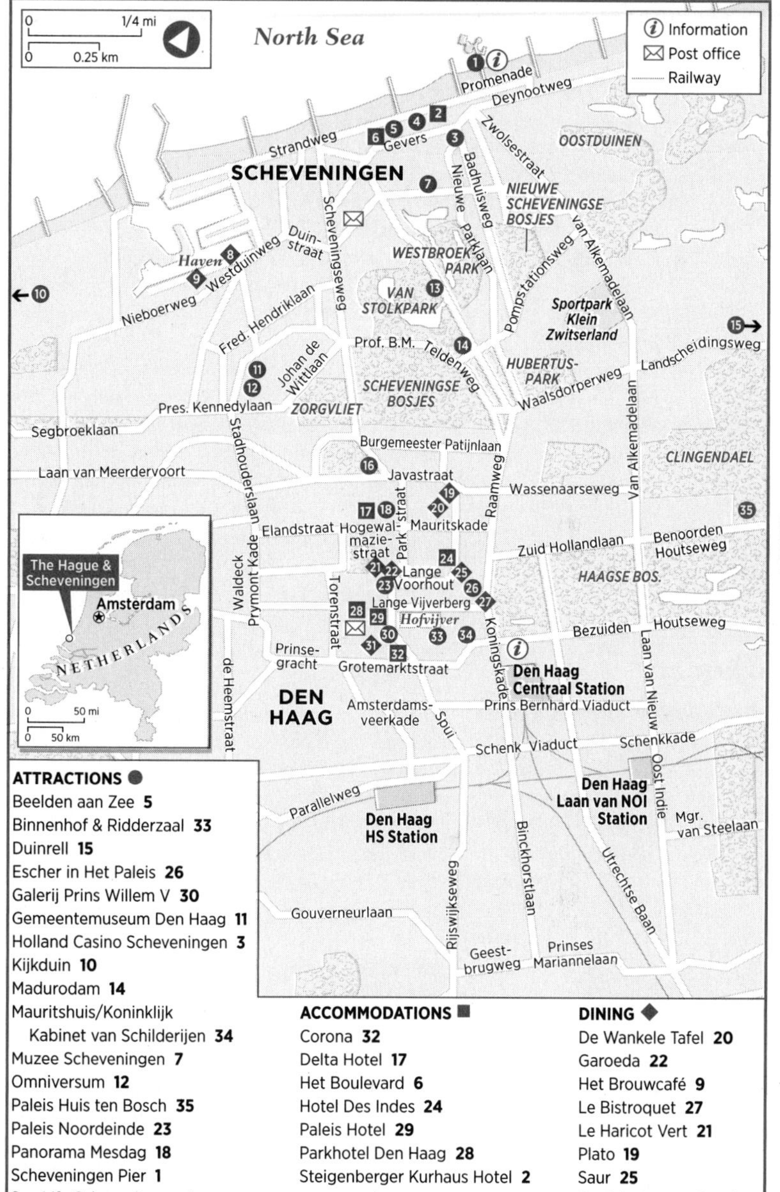

ATTRACTIONS ●
Beelden aan Zee **5**
Binnenhof & Ridderzaal **33**
Duinrell **15**
Escher in Het Paleis **26**
Galerij Prins Willem V **30**
Gemeentemuseum Den Haag **11**
Holland Casino Scheveningen **3**
Kijkduin **10**
Madurodam **14**
Mauritshuis/Koninklijk Kabinet van Schilderijen **34**
Muzee Scheveningen **7**
Omniversum **12**
Paleis Huis ten Bosch **35**
Paleis Noordeinde **23**
Panorama Mesdag **18**
Scheveningen Pier **1**
Sea Life Scheveningen **4**
Vredespaleis (Peace Palace) **16**
Westbroekpark **13**

ACCOMMODATIONS ■
Corona **32**
Delta Hotel **17**
Het Boulevard **6**
Hotel Des Indes **24**
Paleis Hotel **29**
Parkhotel Den Haag **28**
Steigenberger Kurhaus Hotel **2**

DINING ◆
De Wankele Tafel **20**
Garoeda **22**
Het Brouwcafé **9**
Le Bistroquet **27**
Le Haricot Vert **21**
Plato **19**
Saur **25**
Stadsherberg 't Goude Hooft **31**
The Harbour Club **8**

Brazil, this small but delightful neoclassical mansion from 1637 rises out of the Hofvijver pond. It houses the **Koninklijk Kabinet van Schilderijen (Royal Cabinet of Paintings),** a stunning collection of 15th- to 18th-century Low Countries art, given to the nation by King Willem I in 1816. The intimate rooms are set on two floors, and some have illuminated ceilings. It almost feels like you're viewing a private collection. ***Note:*** The Mauritshuis is due to close in mid-2012 for two years of reconstruction and refurbishment, during which it will be connected by way of an underground corridor to a new annex in part of the Art Deco building across Korte Vijverberg, at Plein 26. During the period of closure, important works from the collection will be displayed at other venues around The Hague.

Famous works include paintings by Rembrandt, Frans Hals, Johannes Vermeer, Jan Steen, Peter Paul Rubens, and Hans Holbein the Younger. Highlights are Rembrandt's *The Anatomy Lesson of Dr. Nicolaes Tulp* (1632), and Vermeer's meticulous *View of Delft* (ca. 1660), in which cumulous clouds roil the skies above the neat little town, and *Girl with a Pearl Earring* (ca. 1660).

The first floor is mainly given over to Dutch and Flemish religious paintings, and portraits by Holbein and Rubens. Look out in particular for Rogier van der Weyden's disturbingly realistic *The Lamentation* (ca. 1450), depicting Christ being taken down from the cross. As the first of the "Flemish Primitives," van der Weyden did more than his share of setting off the whole Low Countries art boom. Works by Rembrandt, Vermeer, and a riotous Steen are upstairs. You could easily spend a day here, but a morning or afternoon provides a powerful impression of the wealth and breadth of a great art tradition.

Korte Vijverberg 8 (next to the Binnenhof). ✆ **070/302-3456.** www.mauritshuis.nl. Admission 12€ adults, free for children 18 and under. Apr–Sept Mon–Sat 10am–5pm, Sun and holidays 11am–5pm; Oct–Mar Tues–Sat 10am–5pm, Sun and holidays 11am–5pm. Closed Jan 1 and Dec 25. Tram: 1, 10, 16, or 17 to Buitenhof.

Vredespaleis (Peace Palace) This imposing building (1913), largely paid for by Andrew Carnegie, houses the International Court of Justice, the Permanent Court of Arbitration, and the International Law Academy. Its furnishings were donated by countries around the world. The palace is open for guided tours only. Reserve a tour at least a day or two ahead of time (✆ **070/302-4137;** fax 070/302-4234; guided tours@carnegie-stichting.nl). If you can do it a week ahead, you'll have a better chance of getting a place. English is sure to be spoken by the guide, but it can't hurt to confirm this for your chosen time, and note that the Peace Palace's museum is only visited on the 11am and 3pm tours.

Carnegieplein 2 (at Scheveningseweg). ✆ **070/302-4242.** www.vredespaleis.nl. Admission 5€ adults, 3€ children 5–13, free for children 4 and under; add 3€ per person for the museum visit. Guided tours Mon–Fri 10am, 11am, 2pm, 3pm, and 4pm (there isn't always a 4pm tour). Tours last 50 min. without the museum visit and 1½ hr. with. Tram: 1 or 10 to Vredespaleis.

THE ROYAL PALACES

The working palace for Queen Beatrix and her staff, the splendid neoclassical **Paleis Noordeinde** (www.koninklijkhuis.nl; tram: 1 or 10), on Noordeinde, just west of Lange Voorhout, dates from 1553. It was elegantly furnished when William of Orange's widow was in residence, but it became almost derelict by the beginning of the 19th century. In 1815 restoration brought it back to a state suitable for the residence of King Willem I. The palace isn't open to visitors, but you can view it from the street.

Queen Beatrix's official royal residence is **Paleis Huis ten Bosch (House in the Woods Palace),** in the Haagse Bos, or Hague Woods (www.koninklijkhuis.nl; bus no. 24). For many years, it had been the royal family's summer residence, and originally a small, rather plain structure consisting of several rooms opening from a domed central hall. Prince Willem IV added the two large side wings in the 1700s. The palace isn't open to visitors, but you can view it from the park.

MORE MUSEUMS & GALLERIES

Escher in Het Paleis (Escher at the Palace) Paleis Lange Voorhout (1764), formerly a royal winter palace, now houses a museum honoring the Dutch graphic artist M.C. (Maurits Cornelis) Escher (1898–1972). Escher produced hundreds of lithographs, woodcuts, and engravings, and more than 2,000 drawings and sketches. The museum in the heart of town doesn't have them all, but it has a fair sampling, and a computer-animation section on the top floor. Plus, you get to see inside one of The Hague's palaces (see "The Royal Palaces," above), and even if it's a small, second-tier one, a visit is still worthwhile.

Lange Voorhout 74 (off Korte Voorhout). ✆ **070/427-7730.** www.escherinhetpaleis.nl. Admission 7.50€ adults, 5€ children 7–15, free for children 6 and under, 20€ family. Tues–Sun 11am–5pm. Closed Jan 1, Prinsjesdag (3rd Sat in Sept), and Dec 25. Tram: 10, 16, or 17 to Korte Voorhout.

Galerij Prins Willem V ★ This elegant little gallery, which reopened in 2010 after a long period of refurbishment, is a separate annex of the Mauritshuis (see above), and if you have a ticket to that museum, you'll get in here free. The country's first purpose-built art gallery opened in 1774 to display the private collection of Prince of Orange Willem V. Most of the 150 paintings by Dutch Old Masters from the period dubbed the "Golden Age" are the gallery's original occupants, arranged in the cluttered style of the time. There are few internationally known works, but all the paintings are interesting and have a cumulative impact. Look out for Jan Steen's shiver-inducing *The Toothpuller* (1651), and give thanks for modern dentistry. An hour here should do it.

Buitenhof 33 (across from the Binnenhof). ✆ **070/302-3435.** www.mauritshuis.nl. Admission 5€ adults, free for visitors 12 and under, free for visitors with a Mauritshuis ticket. Tues–Sun noon–5pm. Closed Jan 1 and Dec 25. Tram: 10, 16, or 17 to Buitenhof.

Panorama Mesdag ★ ☺ If you don't have time to visit Scheveningen, you can still hit the beach here, in a way. The panoramic painting, with a circumference of 119m (390 ft.), may take your breath away; in any case, it feels like a breath of fresh sea air. You walk through a dark passageway, up a stairway, and out onto a circular platform—and suddenly, you're in the fishing village of Scheveningen, in 1880. Its dunes, beach, fishing boats, and everything else in the village are three-dimensional, an illusion enhanced by the artificial dunes that separate you from the painting. The panorama was the work of The Hague school artist Hendrik Willem Mesdag, with the assistance of his wife and two other artists.

Zeestraat 65 (at Sophialaan). ✆ **070/364-4544.** www.panorama-mesdag.com. Admission 6.50€ adults, 5.50€ seniors and students, 3€ children 3–12, free for children 2 and under. Mon–Sat 10am–5pm; Sun and holidays noon–5pm. Closed Jan 1 and Dec 25. Tram: 1 or 10 to Mauritskade.

ESPECIALLY FOR KIDS

Madurodam ★ ☺ To see "Holland in a Nutshell," head to the wooded dunes linking The Hague and the coastal resort of Scheveningen. This enchanting display of a miniature, fictitious city sprawls over 170 hectares (420 acres) in the Scheveningse Bosjes (Scheveningen Woods). Typical Dutch townscapes and famous landmarks are replicated on a scale of 1:25. You'll see little versions of famous Dutch places, such as the Anne Frankhuis and Rijksmuseum in Amsterdam; The Hague's own Binnenhof and Mauritshuis; Rotterdam's Euromast; the Stadhuis (Town Hall) in Gouda; the Valkhof in Nijmegen; and much, much more. The wonder of it all is that this is a working miniature world: Trains run, ships move, planes taxi down runways, bells ring, the barrel organ plays, there's a town fair in progress, and 50,000 tiny lamps light up when darkness falls.

George Maduroplein 1 (at Koninginnegracht). ✆ **070/416-2400.** www.madurodam.nl. Admission 15€ adults, 14€ seniors, 11€ children 3–11, free for children 2 and under. Apr–June daily 9am–8pm; July–Aug daily 9am–11pm; Sept–Mar daily 9am–6pm. Tram: 9 to Madurodam.

Omniversum ☺ In Holland's only IMAX theater, ultra-large-format documentary films are projected onto a screen on the inside of a giant dome, for an audience who settle back in 300 comfortable chairs to watch the show, immersed in dramatic digital images and waves of surround-sound audio effects. A new film is screened every hour from a roster of six or seven titles covering subjects as diverse as geographical treasures such as the Alps and the Grand Canyon, animals, underwater exploration, and flight and space travel. The films themselves are in Dutch, but an English translation is available via headphones.

President Kennedylaan 5 (at Stadhouderslaan). ✆ **0900/666-4837.** www.omniversum.nl. Admission 9.75€ adults, 7.50€ children 4–11, free for children 3 and under, 30€ family; additional 4.75€ to view a second film on the same day. Mon 11am–3pm; Tues–Wed 11am–5pm; Thurs and Sun 11am–9pm; Fri–Sat 11am–10pm; holidays and school vacations 10am–10pm (the times are from first to last screening; the box office opens an hour before the first screening). Tram: 17 to Gemeentemuseum.

Where to Stay

VERY EXPENSIVE

Hotel Des Indes ★★ Highly recommended for its elegant accommodations and a location in the center of the oldest part of the city, this palatial old-world hotel has been brought right up to date. It started out as the residence of a certain Baron Willem Joseph van Brienen van de Groote Lindt (1760–1839) and became a hotel in 1881. Since then it has welcomed royalty, diplomats, and celebrities, and has held a consistently prominent place in The Hague's upper-crust social life. Its classically decorated guest rooms are the ultimate in comfort. Public rooms are lavishly fitted with marble, polished wood, chandeliers, and velvet upholstery. The gracious lobby lounge is a favorite place for genteel residents of The Hague to meet up. Continental **Restaurant DesInDes** is as valued by locals as by visitors and guests.

Lange Voorhout 54–56 (close to the Escher Museum), 2514 EG Den Haag. ✆ **070/361-2345.** Fax 070/361-2350. www.hoteldesindesthehague.com. 92 units. 225€–475€ double; from 595€ suite. AE, DC, MC, V. Parking 35€. Tram: 1 or 10 to Kneuterdijk. **Amenities:** Restaurant; bar; lounge; babysitting; concierge; health club; indoor pool; room service. *In room:* A/C, TV, hair dryer, Internet (19€/day), minibar.

EXPENSIVE

Parkhotel Den Haag ★★ This Art Deco–style, centrally located hotel is on a quiet street, with doors opening from the spacious entrance lobby to a walled-in street-side terrace in fine weather. The grandiose breakfast room overlooks the gardens of the Noordeinde royal palace, and the hotel has its own gardens, which together should make for some restful moments. The early-20th-century monument has original yellow brick and tile features on the staircases that demand a constant process of preservation. Its attractive guest rooms have full marble bathrooms. Some double rooms are small, so if space is important to you, check out the room first.

Molenstraat 53 (at the Paleistuin), 2513 BJ Den Haag. ✆ **070/362-4371.** Fax 070/361-4525. www.parkhoteldenhaag.nl. 123 units. 175€–325€ double; from 475€ suite. Rates include buffet breakfast. AE, DC, MC, V. Parking 23€. Tram: 17 to Noordwal. **Amenities:** Restaurant; bar; lounge; bikes; room service. *In room:* TV, hair dryer, minibar, Wi-Fi (free).

MODERATE

Corona ★ Once in part a lively coffeehouse, Koffyhuys van Dalen, this charming hotel set in three 17th-century buildings is across the street from the Binnenhof and the Hofvijver pond outside the Parliament. Public rooms feature contemporary decor, with touches of handsome marble and mahogany in the lobby. The guest rooms, which come in different plush variations, such as traditional English style and East Indies colonial style, are done in soft pastel colors with graceful window drapes. Today politicians, antiques dealers, and gourmets congregate here, as they have done for more than a century. The elegant **Brasserie-Restaurant Corona** is a favorite retreat for the good and the great in government circles. In balmy weather, part of the restaurant becomes a sidewalk terrace.

Buitenhof 39–42 (off Hofweg), 2513 AH Den Haag. ✆ **070/363-7930.** Fax 070/361-5785. www.corona.nl. 36 units. 110€–175€ double. Some rates include buffet breakfast. AE, DC, MC, V. Parking 20€. Tram: 1, 10, 16, or 17 to Buitenhof. **Amenities:** Restaurants; bar; room service. *In room:* TV, hair dryer, minibar, Wi-Fi (20€/day).

Paleis Hotel ★ In a quiet setting behind the royal family's Noordeinde Palace, this intimate boutique hotel takes the "palace" part of its moniker seriously, with a look that's classical yet not stuffy. It has spacious and elegant guest rooms furnished with soft chairs and settees, tasteful drapes and fabrics, subdued lighting, art works, a proportion of genuine antique furniture among the reproductions, and other signs of attention to detail. Bathrooms are on the small side but fitted out beautifully. The central location is good both for shopping (the pedestrian shopping promenade is nearby) and for sightseeing.

Molenstraat 26 (behind Paleis Noordeinde), 2513 BL Den Haag. ✆ **070/362-4621.** Fax 070/361-4533. www.paleishotel.nl. 20 units. 185€–295€ double. AE, DC, MC, V. Limited street parking. Tram: 17 to Gravenstraat. **Amenities:** Bar; sauna. *In room:* A/C (some), TV, hair dryer, minibar, Wi-Fi (15€/day).

INEXPENSIVE

Delta Hotel Here you'll find a smart designer feel without the stiff price tag; the walls often host exhibitions by local artists. The rooms and their attached bathrooms are small and furnished with a Zen-like simplicity that's at least a step up from hostel-style plain. It's in one of The Hague's nicest neighborhoods, so there's a good selection of local bars and restaurants, but the hotel's own street, despite being central, is quite quiet. There's no elevator.

Anna Paulownastraat 8 (off Kortenaerkade), 2518 BE Den Haag. ✆ **070/362-4999.** Fax 070/345-4440. www.deltahotel.info. 11 units. 85€–125€ double. Rates include buffet breakfast. AE, DC, MC, V. Limited street parking. Tram: 1 or 10 to Mauritskade. *In room:* TV, hair dryer.

Where to Dine

EXPENSIVE

Saur ★ FRENCH/SEAFOOD A relaunch at the end of 2008 gave this intimate restaurant in the heart of the city a more contemporary style, thereby helping Saur to maintain the high regard in which it has been held since it first opened in 1928. Meat eaters won't feel entirely left out amid the delectable array of fish, shellfish, and crustacean delicacies on the menu—an excellent rack of lamb is among the dishes aimed at them. In summer there's sidewalk dining on a corner of the tree-shaded square out front.

Lange Voorhout 51 (at Tournooiveld). ✆ **070/361-7070.** www.saur.nl. Main courses 16€–44€; fixed-price menus 35€–69€. AE, DC, MC, V. Mon–Fri noon–11pm; Sat 6pm–midnight. Tram: 10, 16, or 17 to Korte Voorhout.

MODERATE

Garoeda ★ INDONESIAN If it's *rijsttafel* you're hankering for, you couldn't find better than what's served at this multi-level Indonesian restaurant in an Art Nouveau building in the center of town. It's been in business since 1949. There's a cafe section on the ground floor, and the main restaurant occupies the next two floors. The waitstaff are dressed smartly in traditional Javanese silks, adding a classy touch to the authentic cooking and the setting of Balinese carved wood and Oriental art. Lunch gets especially crowded, so make a reservation or come early or late.

Kneuterdijk 18A. ✆ **070/346-5319.** www.garoeda.nl. Reservations recommended for lunch. Main course items 6.25€–13€; rijsttafel 21€–35€. AE, DC, MC, V. Mon–Sat 11am–11pm; Sun 4–11pm. Tram: 1 or 10 to Kneuterdijk.

Le Bistroquet ★★ FRENCH/INTERNATIONAL This small restaurant in the center of town is one of The Hague's best, with lovely table settings in a quietly elegant setting. In summer, you can dine on a terrace shaded by linden trees. The menu is mostly French. Lamb, fish, and fresh vegetables are featured. Good choices include Irish salmon with lobster ravioli in a Thai curry sauce, and lamb filet with cashews, French beans, and a marjoram sauce.

Lange Voorhout 98 (next door to the U.S. embassy). ✆ **070/360-1170.** www.bistroquet.nl. Reservations recommended on weekends. Main courses 25€–38€; fixed-price dinner menus 39€–49€. AE, DC, MC, V. Mon–Fri noon–2pm and 6–10pm; Sat 6–10pm. Tram: 10, 16, or 17 to Kneuterdijk.

Le Haricot Vert ★ BELGIAN/FRENCH A warm bistro ambience awaits visitors to this quality restaurant, a long-standing city favorite. In the summertime, tables are set outside on the sidewalk of the narrow pedestrians-only street. Indulge in the three-course menu and you'll be spoiled with enormous plates holding tasty selections of the best seasonal meat, fish, or vegetable dishes. A strong lineup of French wines is at the sommelier's fingertips.

Molenstraat 9A–11 (behind Paleis Noordeinde). ✆ **070/365-2278.** www.haricotvert.nl. Main courses 17€–27€; fixed-price menus 27€–35€. AE, DC, MC, V. Mon–Sat 6–11pm. Tram: 1 or 10 to Kneuterdijk.

Plato INTERNATIONAL A restaurant that has perfected its formula and hums every night with keen return visitors, Plato is just north of the city center. The many mirrors make the place seem larger than it really is and reflect a decor that's a mix of wood-floor bistro-chic and breezy rattan. Most dishes on the menu can be ordered in small or large portions, according to your capacity or appetite, and you can choose the most appropriate from a list of five combo possibilities. The main-course menu is limited to those five, however—a pair each of meat and fish dishes, and something Continental, like pasta, that might double as a vegetarian option.

Frederikstraat 32 (at Mauritskade). ✆ **070/363-6744.** www.restaurant-plato.nl. Main courses 15€–25€; fixed-price menus 20€–33€. AE, MC, V. Mon–Fri 5–11pm; Sat–Sun 3–11pm. Tram: 8 or 9 to Dr. Kuyperstraat.

Stadsherberg 't Goude Hooft ★★ DUTCH/CONTINENTAL There's a definite Old Dutch flavor to this wonderful, large, happy cafe-restaurant overlooking the city's old market square. Originally, back in 1423, it was a tavern. In 1660, it was transformed into a coffeehouse, and then in 1939 a cafe-restaurant. The wooden beams, brass chandeliers, and rustic chairs and tables blend harmoniously with the stained-glass windows, medieval banners, and wall murals. There's a large, pleasant sidewalk cafe on the Green Market square. An extensive menu ranges from snacks to light lunches to full dinners. Look out for fine menu dishes like the guinea fowl with thyme sauce and the red perch with saffron sauce. This is a good place to drop by for a cocktail and snack, a beer, or a coffee.

Dagelijkse Groenmarkt 13 (at the Grote Kerk). ✆ **070/346-9713.** www.tgoudehooft.nl. Main courses 21€–30€. AE, DC, MC, V. Mon–Sat 8am–1am; Sun 10am–midnight. Tram: 17 to Gravenstraat.

INEXPENSIVE

De Wankele Tafel VEGETARIAN Organic-food fanatics and vegetarians will love chowing down at the casual "Wobbly Table." It's run by a dedicated crew that takes their veggie lifestyle seriously enough to do it right, but not so seriously that it can't be fun. Meals served in the small, minimalist dining room have a world-cuisine flavor, and though there aren't many options, they're sure to have something Asian with rice, and Latin American with beans.

Mauritskade 79 (off Frederikstraat). ✆ **070/364-3267.** www.wankeletafel.nl.nu. Main courses 9€–13€; menu of the week 15€. No credit cards. Tues–Sat 4:30–9:30pm. Tram: 8 or 9 to Dr. Kuyperstraat.

Shopping

Interesting shopping areas include Oude Molstraat and Denneweg in the center city, where there's a concentration of authentic Dutch stores. Connected to Centraal station, the modern Babylon shopping mall has two floors with more than 60 stores, restaurants, and a luxury hotel.

A network of pedestrian streets offers a big selection of stores on Spuistraat, Vlamingstraat, Venestraat, and Hoogstraat. The covered **Passage** (www.depassage.nl; tram: 17), Holland's oldest "mall," is an elegant 19th-century arcade running from Spuistraat to Gravenstraat, a block from the Binnenhof. Two upmarket department stores nearby are worth checking out: **De Bijenkorf,** Wagenstraat 32 (✆ **0900/0919;** www.bijenkorf.nl; tram: 2, 3, 4, or 6), an example of functional early-20th-century architecture; and the stiffly chic **Maison de Bonneterie,** Gravenstraat 2 (✆ **070/330-5300;** www.debonneterie.nl; tram: 17).

Noordeinde and Oude Molenstraat are home to fashion boutiques, antiquarian booksellers, and expensive delicatessens. Leading off from Lange Voorhout, Denneweg and Frederikstraat are lined with high-priced antiques, interior-design stores, and specialist boutiques. One of the largest interior-design stores is **Loft Interiors,** Denneweg 56 (✆ **070/346-4842;** www.loft.nl; tram: 1 or 10), part of which is in a stunning 1899 iron-and-glass showroom.

Among the top shopping attractions are a number of fine antiques stores and a weekly **antiques and book market** (tram: 1 or 10) that runs mid-May to September on Thursday from 10am to 6pm and Sunday from 10am to 5pm under the canopy of trees on Lange Voorhout, north of the Binnenhof; October to mid-May, the market pulls up stakes and moves to the south side of the Binnenhof, on Plein (tram: 1, 8, or 9), for the same days and times. Year-round on Wednesday, there's an **organic farm market** (tram: 1 or 16) on Hofplaats from 11am to 6pm.

The Hague After Dark

Spuiplein, several blocks west of Centraal Station, is the city's modern cultural square. Here you'll find the **Dr. Anton Philipszaal** and the attached **Lucent**

Danstheater, Spuiplein 150 (✆ **070/880-0333;** www.philipszaal.nl; www.ldt.nl; tram: 5, 9, or 15), where The Hague's Residentie Orchestra and the renowned Netherlands Dance Theater perform. If you're more into jazz, modern, and experimental music, check out **Paard van Troje,** Prinsegracht 12 (✆ **070/360-1838;** www.paard.nl; tram: 2, 3, 4, or 6).

The Hague's natural formality somewhat subdues its nightlife, but there is a thriving bar and cafe culture. Plein, a large square in front of the Tweede Kamer (lower house of Parliament), is a favorite for recess with politicians and civil servants. If you want to combine eating and drinking, and hide in a quiet walled garden, head for close-by **Schlemmer,** Lange Houtstraat 17 (✆ **070/360-9000;** www.ropeni.nl; tram: 10, 16, or 17). The Grote Markt square is lined with busy bars and restaurants, ranging from traditional brown cafes to trendy designer spots. **De Zwarte Ruiter,** Grote Markt 27 (✆ **070/364-9549;** www.zwarteruiter.nl; tram: 2, 3, 4, or 6), is a popular drinking and eating place that makes a good starting point, especially since there's often live contemporary rock music on offer. One of The Hague's oldest lesbian and gay bars is **Cafe De Landman,** Denneweg 48 (✆ **070/346-7727;** www.cafedelandman.nl; tram: 8 or 9).

SCHEVENINGEN ★

5km (3 miles) NW of The Hague center

A chic beach resort with a notoriously hard-to-pronounce name, Scheveningen sports a cast of upscale restaurants, accommodations in all price ranges, designer boutiques, and abundant nighttime entertainment. Visitors often stay at Scheveningen and make the 10-minute drive or tram ride into The Hague. Until early in the 19th century, this was a sleepy fishing village set amid the dunes on the North Sea coast. But as its beaches began to attract vacation crowds, Scheveningen evolved into an internationally known watering hole, and it's now a part of The Hague. The magnificent and beautifully restored 19th-century waterfront Kurhaus Hotel still draws celebrities from around the globe. Gamblers flock to the resort's casino, where tuxedoed croupiers ply their craft.

Essentials

GETTING THERE There is frequent **tram** service from The Hague by lines 1 or 9 to the seafront at Gevers Deynootplein in front of the Kurhaus Hotel; line 11 to the beach between the Kurhaus and the fishing harbor; and lines 10 or 17 to the harbor area. Although there's no real reason to choose the **bus** over the tram, bus line 22 goes to the resort from outside Den Haag Centraal Station.

By **car** from The Hague, you can take numerous alternative routes to the resort; the most direct is on Scheveningseweg from the Peace Palace, through the Scheveningse

Code Name: Scheveningen

Just try to pronounce Scheveningen (*Skhay*-ven-ing-uhn) correctly! The name is so difficult to say that during World War II the Dutch underground used it as a code name for identification—the Germans just couldn't get it right.

Rising Roses

In the Rosarium in Westbroekpark (tram: 9), more than 20,000 roses from 300 different varieties bloom each year between July and September. It's open daily from 9am to 1 hour before sunset, and admission is free.

Bosjes (Scheveningen Woods). Going by **bicycle** is even better, and there are several special signposted bicycling routes.

VISITOR INFORMATION Tourist information is available from VVV Den Haag's **Informatiepunt Scheveningen** on the Pier (tram: 1 or 9), open mid-May to August daily from 11am to 5pm. For mail, phone, fax and website details, see "Visitor Information" for The Hague, earlier.

SPECIAL EVENTS The harbor, lined with restaurants that serve up just-caught seafood, is where the Dutch herring season is launched with a colorful Vlaggetjesdag (Flag Day) celebration each year on the first or second Saturday in June. Some fishermen and their wives dress up in traditional costume. The herring boats return with the first of the new season's catch, amid much fanfare.

What to See & Do

Stroll on dunes, splash in the waves, go deep-sea fishing in the North Sea, and more. The beach zone is called Scheveningen Bad—but it looks pretty good. A 3km (2-mile) promenade borders the wide, sandy beach and has as its highlight the **Scheveningen Pier ★** (✆ **070/306-5500;** www.pier.nl; tram: 1 or 9), jutting out onto the North Sea. It first opened in 1901 and was rebuilt in 1961 after being destroyed in World War II. There's plenty to do here, from a casino, cafe-restaurant, and 60m-high (197-ft.) observation tower, to a "play island" for kids, and a bungee-jump that drops you toward the water from a crane atop the observation tower (see "Sea Sports & Recreation," below).

In the **Muzee Scheveningen,** Neptunusstraat 90–92 (✆ **070/350-0830;** www.museumscheveningen.nl; tram: 1 or 9), you learn about the history of the old fishing village. The museum is open Tuesday to Saturday (also Mon July to mid-Aug) from 10am to 5pm and Sunday from noon to 5pm. Admission is 6€ for adults, 5€ for seniors, 3€ for children 4 to 12, and free for children 3 and under.

At **Sea Life Scheveningen,** Strandweg (aka the Boulevard) 13 (✆ **070/354-2100;** www.sealife.nl; tram: 1), an aquarium just west of the Kurhaus Hotel, you'll observe denizens of the deep, including sharks, swimming above your head in a walk-through underwater tunnel. The aquarium is open daily July to August from 10am to 8pm, February to June and September to November from 10am to 7pm, and December to January from 10am to 6pm; it's closed December 25. Admission is 15€ for adults, 13€ for seniors and visitors with disabilities, 9€ for children 3 to 11, and free for children 2 and under.

A few blocks from the Kurhaus, a museum inside the dunes, almost hidden by giant masks looking out to sea, offers a peaceful oasis amid the seaside entertainment. This museum, **Beelden aan Zee (Sculptures on the Seafront),** Harteveltstraat 1 (✆ **070/358-5857;** www.beeldenaanzee.nl; tram: 1), just off the seafront Boulevard, is dedicated to sculptures of the human body. There are changing exhibitions by modern sculptors from around the world and an impressive permanent collection.

A Great Theme Park

For a theme park with rides galore—roller coasters, carousels, treetop cable cars, and a tropical water paradise—head for **Duinrell ★**, Duinrell 1 (✆ **070/515-5255**; www.duinrell.com), at Wassenaar, 5km (3 miles) north of The Hague. Water activities include luge runs, the centrifugal Waterspin, and floating plastic frogs. In addition to the amusement park, covered tropical swimming pools are ideal for wet-weather days with kids. The park is open April to October daily from 10am to 5pm; the pool is open throughout the year. September to March, you can ski on an outdoor artificial ski slope. Admission is 19€ for adults, 15€ for seniors, and free for children 3 and under. In summer, bus no. 491 goes to the park from The Hague Centraal Station and other points in the city center.

The halls are different shapes, and some exhibits are outside on the patios. Wherever you are in the museum, you'll be aware of the surrounding dunes and the wind playing in the grass. From the highest terrace, you can even glimpse the sea. The museum is open Tuesday to Sunday from 11am to 5pm. Admission is 9.50€ for adults, 4.75€ for children 13 to 18, and free for children 12 and under.

Scheveningen's southern neighboring beach resort, **Kijkduin,** is quieter and more family-oriented. Its main attractions are the sea and dunes.

Sea Sports & Recreation

The North Sea's fair-to-middling waves make surfing fun for both the initiated and the uninitiated, who might prefer boogie boards. A wet suit is not an option but a necessity, unless you want to experience hypothermia. Rent surfboards and wet suits from **Hart Surfshop,** Vissershavenweg 55B (✆ **070/354-5583;** www.hartbeach.nl; tram: 11), which runs a beach hut and surf school during the summer season. The oddly named **Go Klap,** Dr. Lelykade 44 (✆ **070/354-8679;** www.goklap.nl; tram: 11), rents surfboards, other windsurfing gear, and sea kayaks. For windsurfing and kite-surfing lessons, in and out of season, contact **Kitesurfschool Harry Vogelezang,** Vissershavenweg 62 (✆ **070/358-4800;** www.kitesurfschool.nl; tram: 11), just east of the harbor.

Head out from the harbor for a deep-sea fishing day trip aboard a converted trawler, operated by **Rederij Groen,** Dr. Lelykade 1D (✆ **070/355-3588;** www.rederijgroen.nl; tram: 11).

Are you up for a plunge toward the cold gray waters of the North Sea? **Bungy Jump Holland** (✆ **070/350-6863;** www.bungy.nl) can accommodate you, with a 60m (197-ft.) freefall from their jump point on Scheveningen Pier. Jump times (weather permitting) are April to June and September to October Saturday and Sunday from noon to 8pm, and July and August Wednesday to Sunday from noon to 11pm.

Where to Stay

Het Boulevard ★ Perched atop the sea dunes at Scheveningen, within walking distance of the Palace Promenade, this hotel has a commanding sea view from its sun lounge/restaurant and some of the guest rooms, which all are plainly furnished in a clean-cut, modern style. The hotel has special family rooms for those with young children.

Herring Days

Scheveningen may be the place most obsessed with herring in this herring-obsessed land. On the first Saturday in June, fishing boats compete to land the season's first *nieuwe haring* (new herring) during the annual, colorful Vlaggetjesdag (Flag Day) event. The fresh-caught fish is considered a delicacy; it's eaten whole (minus the head and the tail!), or chopped with minced onion if you're squeamish. Year-round the fish are pickled as *maatjes.* Buy herring from sidewalk vendors, beachfront fish stands, and trailers towed onto the beach. See "Eating & Drinking in Holland," in chapter 2.

Seinpostduin 1, 2586 EA Scheveningen. ✆ **070/354-0067.** Fax 070/355-2574. www.boulevard-hotel.nl. 30 units. 85€–150€ double. Rates include buffet breakfast. AE, DC, MC, V. Limited free parking. Tram: 1 to Badhuiskade. **Amenities:** Restaurant; bar. *In room:* TV, Wi-Fi (free).

Steigenberger Kurhaus Hotel ★★★ The five-star Kurhaus is the undisputed grande dame of the North Sea coast. Its leather-bound guest register, which opens with the signature of the 13-year-old Queen Wilhelmina, is filled with the names of the world's greats and illustrated by leading artists who embellished their signatures with original drawings. The Kurhaus's Kurzaal concert hall has seen performances by leading musical artists as disparate as violinist Yehudi Menuhin and the Rolling Stones. The guest rooms, many with balconies facing the sea, are spacious and have elegant decor and furnishings, including trouser presses. The splendid **Kandinsky** restaurant, where the dining room walls are "decorated" with signed lithographs by abstract artist Wasily Kandinsky (1866–1944), has earned an international reputation. The **Kurzaal** has lavish lunch and dinner buffets. The Kurzaal Café is for drinks and light meals.

Gevers Deynootplein 30, 2586 CK Scheveningen. ✆ **070/416-2636.** Fax 070/416-2646. www.kurhaus.nl. 253 units. 295€–345€ double; 330€–475€ executive double; from 700€ suite. Rates include full breakfast. AE, DC, MC, V. Valet parking 35€. Tram: 1 or 9 to Kurhaus. **Amenities:** 2 restaurants; bar; lounge; babysitting; concierge; access to nearby health club & spa; room service. *In room:* TV, hair dryer, minibar, Wi-Fi (free).

Where to Dine

Het Brouwcafé DUTCH/SEAFOOD This microbrewery puts up three or four of its house-brand beers, depending on the season, and an impressive selection of domestic and foreign beers. The atmosphere is lively thanks to all this free-flowing beer, and the food is scrumptious and filling, too. The fixed-price three-course menu changes weekly and might include mouthwatering lasagna with tuna and lemon sole as a main course. Many dishes can be ordered as a starter or a main course, and alongside fish dishes, there are meat and vegetarian choices.

Dr. Lelykade 28. ✆ **070/354-0970.** www.hetbrouwcafe.nl. Main courses 13€–19€. AE, DC, MC, V. Daily 11am–11pm. Tram: 11 to Statenlaan.

The Harbour Club ★ SEAFOOD While some seafoodies mourned the passing of the traditional old restaurant Ducdalf from this spot on Scheveningen's yacht harbor, others like the cut of its successor's jib. You dine amid a thoroughly modern *joie de vivre* in a trendily rambling interior of bare brick walls, or outside by the water's edge. The kitchen can handle everything from sushi through *nouvelle*-style grilled North Sea fish—and oyster or mixed-shellfish platters—to surf-and-organic turf.

Dr. Lelykade 5-13. ✆ **070/891-3224.** www.theharbourclub.nl. Main courses 20€-45€; fixed-price menus 25€-45€. AE, DC, MC, V. Daily 11am–1am. Tram: 11 to Statenlaan.

Scheveningen After Dark

Tuxedoed croupiers provide blackjack and roulette at **Holland Casino Scheveningen,** Kurhausweg 1 (✆ **070/306-7777;** www.hollandcasino.com; tram: 1 or 9), across from the restored 19th-century Kurhaus Hotel. There's also punto banco, slot machines, and more. The dress code here is "correct" (collar and tie for men), and the minimum age is 18. You need your passport to get in. The casino is open daily (except May 4 and Dec 31) from 12:30pm to 3am. Admission is 5€; Wednesday is "ladies day," and admission is free for all female visitors.

Look for nightclubs at Gevers Deynootplein in front of the Kurhaus, and for theater productions at the **Circustheater,** which may include opera, ballet, and musical theater.

If it can be played on a piano, you might hear it at **Crazy Pianos,** Strandweg 21–29 (✆ **070/322-7525;** www.crazypianos.com; tram: 1 or 9), with its gaudy neon signs that attract revelers along the waterfront. The formula, which includes eating, drinking, and dancing, appeals to patrons of all ages.

ROTTERDAM ★★

58km (36 miles) SW of Amsterdam; 23km (14 miles) SE of The Hague

Although just an hour from Amsterdam by train, Rotterdam is Holland's most futuristic city, centuries away from the capital in both appearance and personality. Here, instead of the usual Dutch web of little streets, alleyways, and winding canals, there's an abundance of fascinating modern architecture, spacious and elegant malls, and one of the world's busiest ocean harbors. This bustling metropolis (pop. 590,000) is fascinating to see, particularly when you consider the city was a living monument to Holland's Golden Age until it was bombed to rubble during World War II. Traces of Old Rotterdam survive most vividly in only two areas—Delfshaven (Delft Harbor) and Oude Haven (Old Harbor).

At the war's end, rather than try to recreate the old, Rotterdammers looked on their misfortune as an opportunity and approached their city as a clean slate. They relished the chance to create an efficient, workable modern city. The results, though not always elegant, are a testimony to their ability to find impressive solutions.

Essentials

GETTING THERE **Rotterdam The Hague Airport** (✆ **010/446-3444;** www.rotterdam-airport.nl), at Zestienhoven, 4km (2½ miles) north of Rotterdam, has scheduled flights from a few places in Europe. In the unlikely event you fly into here, bus no. 33 goes from the airport to the center of town in 20 minutes for 1.40€; a taxi to downtown is around 20€. If, as is far more likely, you fly into Amsterdam's **Schiphol Airport** (see "Getting There & Around," in chapter 12), Netherlands Railways has fast train service (50 min.) from Schiphol to Rotterdam, for a fare of 13€ one-way in second class and 23€ in first class.

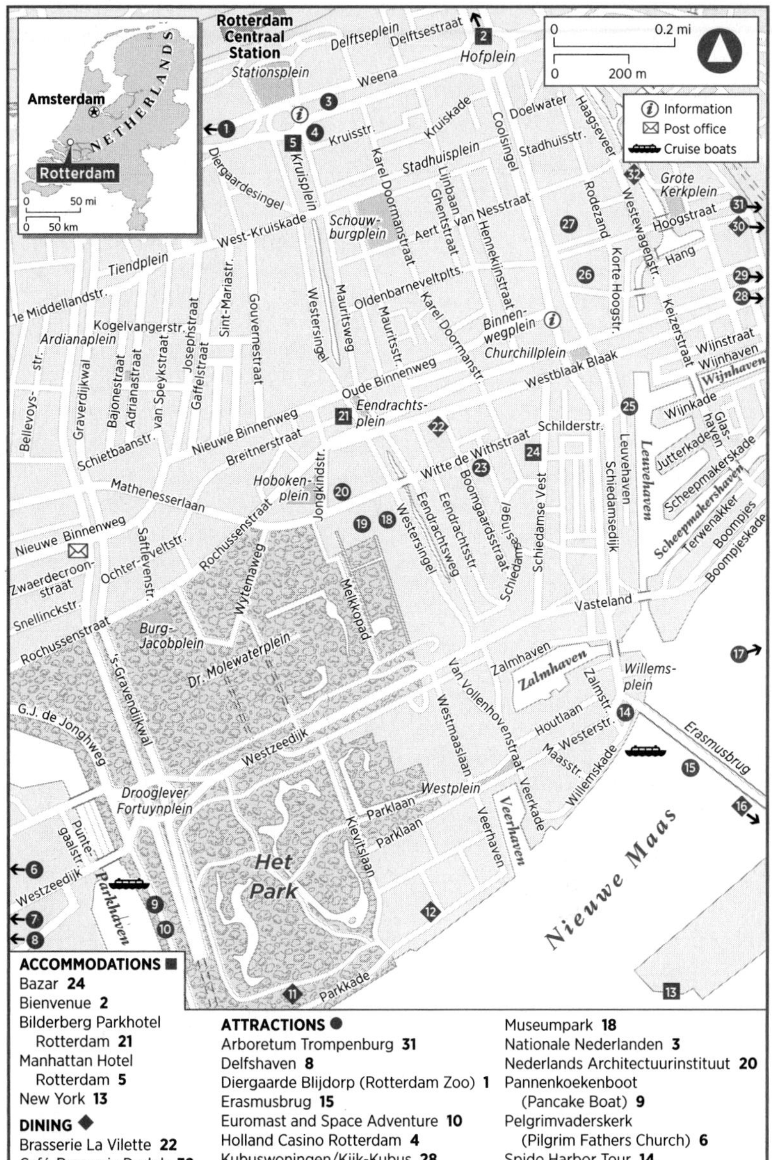

ACCOMMODATIONS ■

Bazar **24**
Bienvenue **2**
Bilderberg Parkhotel Rotterdam **21**
Manhattan Hotel Rotterdam **5**
New York **13**

DINING ◆

Brasserie La Vilette **22**
Café-Brasserie Dudok **32**
Café-Restaurant Rotterdam **16**
Dewi Sri **12**
In den Rustwat **30**
Parkheuvel **11**

ATTRACTIONS ●

Arboretum Trompenburg **31**
Delfshaven **8**
Diergaarde Blijdorp (Rotterdam Zoo) **1**
Erasmusbrug **15**
Euromast and Space Adventure **10**
Holland Casino Rotterdam **4**
Kubuswoningen/Kijk-Kubus **28**
Maritiem Museum Rotterdam **25**
Museum Boijmans Van Beuningen **19**
Museum De Dubbelde Palmboom/ Zakkendragershuisje **7**
Museum Het Schielandshuis **26**
Museumpark **18**
Nationale Nederlanden **3**
Nederlands Architectuurinstituut **20**
Pannenkoekenboot (Pancake Boat) **9**
Pelgrimvaderskerk (Pilgrim Fathers Church) **6**
Spido Harbor Tour **14**
Tropicana **29**
Willemsbrug **17**
Witte de With Center for Contemporary Art **23**
World Trade Center **27**

There's frequent **train** service to Rotterdam Centraal Station from around the Netherlands, and from Paris and Brussels. Construction is currently underway on a new station building that's due to be completed in 2012. From Amsterdam, two to six trains depart each hour round the clock. On **NS Hispeed *Fyra*** trains, the ride takes 40 minutes; on ordinary InterCity trains, around 70 minutes. The one-way fare from Amsterdam is 13€ in second class and 23€ in first class.

Working People

So hardworking are Rotterdammers, they're said to be "born with their sleeves already rolled up."

By **car** from Amsterdam, take A4/E19, and then A13/E19.

VISITOR INFORMATION **ROTTERDAM.INFO,** Coolsingel 195–197, 3012 AG Rotterdam (© **0900/403-4065;** fax 010/271-0128; www.vvvrotterdam.nl), close to the junction with Westblaak, is open Monday to Thursday and Saturday from 9:30am to 6pm, Friday from 9:30am to 9pm, and Sunday from 10am to 5pm. The **VVV Rotterdam Info Cafe** in the Grand Café-Restaurant Engels, Stationsplein 45 (Weena entrance), is open Monday to Saturday from 9am to 5:30pm and Sunday from 10am to 5pm.

GETTING AROUND Rotterdam's sprawling size and large gaps between genuine points of interest makes it a city to be explored on foot one area at a time, using the extensive **RET** (© **0800/6061;** www.ret.nl) public transportation network of bus, tram, and Metro (which runs on north-south and east-west axes) to move from one area to another. The VVV tourist office can furnish a map of public transportation routes.

You can get around the city's extensive waterfront using waterbuses operated by **RET Fast Ferry** (see above for RET contact information) and **Watertaxi Rotterdam** (© **010/403-0303;** www.watertaxirotterdam.nl).

Taxi stands are sprinkled throughout the city. For a pick-up, call **Rotterdamse Taxi Centrale** (© **010/462-6060;** www.rtcnv.nl) or **Taxi Rotterdam** (© **065/133-5755;** www.taxirotterdam.com).

SPECIAL EVENTS The festival year kicks off with the **Rotterdam International Film Festival** (© **010/890-9090;** www.filmfestivalrotterdam.com), which has established a reputation over 3 decades for presenting quality independent films. During 10 days in late January or early February, huge numbers of film buffs find their way to cinemas around the center city to watch one or more of about 300 films shown on 15 screens.

Every year for 3 days in July, jazz greats from around the world gather in Rotterdam for the **North Sea Jazz Festival** (© **0900/1010-2020,** or 31-20/511-0070 from outside Holland; www.northseajazz.com). This nonstop extravaganza features star performances by internationally acclaimed musicians, in some 200 concerts of jazz, free jazz, blues, bebop, and world music, at the giant Ahoy venue.

Another annual festival worth looking out for is the multicultural **Summer Carnival** (© **010/404-9630;** www.zomercarnaval.nl) and its colorful street parade, on the last weekend of July.

What to See & Do

Rotterdam's modern urban planning has resulted in an unusually effective use of city-center space. Particularly attractive are the shingle paths and lazy lawns in the landscaped **Museumpark,** which serves as a central focus for two of the museums mentioned below. Between visits, stretch your legs or sit down and have a picnic.

THE TOP ATTRACTIONS

Euromast and Space Adventure ★★ ☺ This slender tower, 188m (617 ft.) tall, is indisputably the best vantage point for spectacular views of the city and the harbor. A superfast elevator brings you up to the viewing platform. On a clear day, you can see for 30km (19 miles) from the Euroscoop platform. More than that, though, the tower contains interesting exhibits, a restaurant 100m (328 ft.) above the harbor park, and an exciting Space Cabin ride that emulates a rocket takeoff.

Parkhaven 20 (at Het Park). ✆ **010/436-4811.** www.euromast.nl. Admission 8.90€ adults, 5.70€ children 4–11, free for children 3 and under. Apr–Sept daily 9:30am–11pm; Oct–Mar daily 10am–11pm. Tram: 8 to Euromast/Erasmus MC.

Maritiem Museum Rotterdam ★ ☺ Dedicated entirely to the history of Rotterdam Harbor, this marvelous museum consists of two sections: the main building, and *De Buffel,* a beautifully restored warship from 1868. Constantly changing exhibits give you new insight into the close relationship between the Dutch and the sea. In the museum harbor basin, some 20 vessels—dating from 1850 to 1950—are moored. There's a bookstore and a coffeeshop.

Leuvehaven 1 (at the harbor). ✆ **010/413-2680.** www.maritiemmuseum.nl. Admission 7.50€ adults, 4€ children 4–16, free for children 3 and under. Tues–Sat 10am–5pm (also Mon July–Aug and school vacations); Sun and holidays 11am–5pm. Closed Jan 1, Apr 30, and Dec 25. Metro: Beurs or Churchillplein.

Museum Boijmans van Beuningen ★★★ Art lovers will enjoy this collection of works by 16th- and 17th-century Dutch and Flemish artists, such as Rubens, Hals, Rembrandt, and Steen. They share wall space with an international contingent that includes Salvador Dalí and Man Ray, Titian and Tintoretto, Degas and Daumier. Other galleries hold international modern art, sculpture, porcelain, silver, glass, and Delftware, and regular exhibits of prints and drawings. After viewing the collections, you can stroll through the tree-shaded sculpture garden and adjacent Museumpark.

Museumpark 18–20 (at Westersingel). ✆ **010/441-9400.** www.boijmans.rotterdam.nl. Admission 10€ adults, 5€ students, free for children 18 and under, free for all Wed. Tues–Sat 10am–5pm; Sun and holidays 11am–5pm. Closed Jan 1, Apr 30, and Dec 25. Metro: Eendrachtsplein.

Museum Het Schielandshuis Almost lost between towering office blocks is the Schielandshuis, a rare central-zone survivor from the 17th century. The building has been gloriously restored and now shows off Rotterdam's cultural heritage. Period rooms are filled with furnishings rescued from mansions destroyed during World War II. The Atlas Van Stolk, a vast collection of prints and drawings relating to Dutch history, occupies an entire floor. An interesting minor exhibit is Holland's second-oldest clog shoe (the oldest was found in Amsterdam), dating from the second half of the 13th century and made from alder wood.

Korte Hoogstraat 31 (off Coolsingel). ✆ **010/217-6767.** www.hmr.rotterdam.nl. Admission 5€ adults, free for children 17 and under. Tues–Sun 11am–5pm. Closed Jan 1, Apr 30, and Dec 25. Metro: Beurs.

OTHER MUSEUMS & ATTRACTIONS

Arboretum Trompenburg 🎁 This gorgeous garden has evolved from a family-owned 19th-century estate into a peaceful oasis east of the center city that is kept in good order by an army of gardeners. Originally landscaped as an English country garden, the arboretum today has more than 4,000 trees, bushes, and perennials. Oak, pine, cedar, hostas, and rhododendron are particularly well represented, and there are a rose garden, goldfish pond, aviary, and glasshouse full of cacti and succulents. With a variety of bridges and benches, the garden is a perfect antidote to exhaustion-inducing sightseeing.

Honingerdijk 86 (off Maasboulevard). ✆ **010/233-0166.** www.trompenburg.nl. Admission 5.50€ adults, free for children 12 and under (up to 4 kids, who must be accompanied by an adult). Apr–Oct Mon–Fri 9am–5pm, Sat–Sun 10am–4pm; Nov–Mar Mon–Fri 9am–5pm, Sat 10am–4pm, Sun noon–4pm. Closed Dec 23–Jan 7 (the closed dates might vary by a few days). Tram: 21 to Woudestein.

Museum De Dubbelde Palmboom On Voorhaven, in the old port district, is this historical museum, which consists of twin converted warehouses and displays objects unearthed during the excavations of Rotterdam. Craftspeople work in the old **Zakkendragershuisje (Grain Sack Carriers Guild House)** next door, using copies of 17th- and 18th-century molds to cast beautiful plates, bowls, tea urns, and other utensils. Their products make great gifts.

Voorhaven 12 (at the harbor). ✆ **010/476-1533.** www.hmr.rotterdam.nl. Admission 5€ adults, free for children 17 and under. Tues–Fri 10am–5pm; Sat–Sun and holidays 11am–5pm. Closed Jan 1, Apr 30, and Dec 25. Metro: Delfshaven.

Witte de With Center for Contemporary Art ★ Despite being located in a somewhat staid-looking building in the center of town, the city's museum of modern art keeps its changing exhibits program at the cutting edge of modern trends in art and photography, both Dutch and international.

Witte de Withstraat 50 (at Boomgaardsstraat). ✆ **010/411-0144.** www.wdw.nl. Admission 5€ adults; 2.50€ seniors, students, and children 12–18; free for children 11 and under. Tues–Sun 11am–6pm. Metro: Eendrachtsplein.

MODERN ARCHITECTURE

Rotterdam has some spectacular modern architecture. Just outside Centraal Station you encounter the office of the **Nationale Nederlanden** insurance corporation, the city's highest skyscraper at 152m (499 ft.). Down Coolsingel is the bottle-green **World Trade Center.** A city landmark near the Old Harbor is a geometric chaos of quirky, cube-shaped apartments balancing atop tall concrete stalks; the elevated, tree house–like yellow **Kubuswoningen (Cube Houses)** were designed by Dutch architect Piet Blom in the early 1970s. One of these quirky, lopsided little abodes, the **Kijk-Kubus (Look-Cube),** Overblaak 70 (✆ **010/414-2285;** www.kubuswoning.nl; Metro: Blaak), is open for visits daily from 11am to 5pm. Admission is 2.50€ for adults, 2€ for seniors and students, 1.50€ for children 4 to 12, and free for children 3 and under.

Two prominent bridges span the Nieuwe Maas River: the dark-red **Willemsbrug,** and a single-span suspension bridge called the **Erasmusbrug** and nicknamed "the Swan" (or, if you're not quite as charmed by its looks, "the Dishwashing Brush").

Housed in a striking building dating from 1993 at the edge of Museumpark, the **Nederlands Architectuurinstituut (Netherlands Architecture Institute),** Museumpark 25 (✆ **010/440-1358;** www.nai.nl; Metro: Eendrachtsplein), explores all aspects of modern architecture. It houses a large archive of architectural drawings, sketches, models, photographs, books, and journals. The institute is open Tuesday to Saturday from 10am to 5pm and Sunday and holidays from 11am to 5pm (closed Jan 1, Apr 30, and Dec 25). Admission is 8€ for adults, 5€ for seniors, and free for children 18 and under.

DELFSHAVEN

Not all of Rotterdam is spanking new. Take the Metro to the tiny harbor area known as **Delfshaven (Delft Harbor),** a neighborhood the German bombers missed, and from where the Puritans known as Pilgrims embarked on the first leg of their trip to Massachusetts. This is a pleasant place to spend an afternoon. Wander into the 15th-century **Pelgrimvaderskerk (Pilgrim Fathers Church),** Aelbrechtskolk 20 (✆ **010/477-4156;** www.pilgrimfatherschurch.nl), in which the Pilgrims prayed before departure, and where they are remembered in special services every Thanksgiving Day. The church is open irregularly; admission is free. Then peek into antiques stores and galleries, and check on the progress of this historic area's housing renovations.

ESPECIALLY FOR KIDS

Diergaarde Blijdorp ★★ ☺ Rotterdam Zoo inhabits a large enclosed plaza in the city's northern Blijdorp district, containing elephants, crocodiles, reptiles, amphibians, and tropical plants and birds. An Asian section houses Javanese monkeys, a bat cave, and exotic birds. The Oceanium section presents a submarine world inhabited by sharks, jellyfish, and other creatures of the deep brought here from around the world.

Blijdorplaan 8 (at Abraham van Stolkweg). ✆ **010/443-1495.** www.rotterdamzoo.nl. Admission 19€ adults, 16€ children 3–9, free for children 2 and under. Apr–Sept daily 9am–6pm; Oct–Mar Mon–Sat 9am–5pm, Sun and school vacations 9am–6pm. Bus: 32 to Abraham van Stolkweg.

Tropicana ☺ East of the Willems Bridge on the north bank of the Maas, this water-based amusement park simulates a luxuriant tropical setting. It has recreational facilities such as a swimming pool, a wave pool, a sauna, water slides, hot whirlpools, a wild-water strip, and a swimmers' bar.

Maasboulevard 100 (at Oosterkade). ✆ **010/402-0700.** www.tropicana.nl. 15€ adults, 12€ children 4–12, free for children 3 and under. Mon–Fri 10am–10pm; Sat–Sun and holidays 10am–8pm. Closed Jan 1, Apr 30, and Dec 25. Metro: 1 to Oostplein.

Organized Tours

An essential part of the Rotterdam experience is taking a **Spido Harbor Tour ★★** (✆ **010/275-9988;** www.spido.nl; Metro: Leuvehaven). You board a boat that seems large in comparison to the canal launches of Amsterdam—two tiers of indoor seating and open decks—and then feel dwarfed by the hulking oil tankers and container ships that glide into their berths along the miles of docks. The vast **Europoort** (pronounced the same as "port" in English) was created when its several harbors were opened directly to the sea, 32km (20 miles) away, by the dredging of a deepwater channel that accommodates even the largest oil tankers. April to September, departures from a dock below the Erasmus Bridge are every 30 to 45 minutes from 9:30am to 5pm; October to March, departures are limited to two to four times a day. The basic tour, offered year-round, is a 75-minute sail along the city's waterfront; between April and September, it's possible to take an extended (2¼-hr.) trip daily at 10am and 12:30pm. On a limited schedule in July and August, you can make all-day excursions along Europoort's full length and to the Delta Works sluices. Tours start at 9.50€ for adults, 5.80€ for children 4 to 11, and free for children 3 and under.

Combine harbor sightseeing with a taste of a Dutch treat—pancakes—aboard the **Pannenkoekenboot (Pancake Boat) ★**, Parkhaven (✆ **010/436-7295;** www.pannenkoekenboot.nl; tram: 8), moored at the foot of the Euromast. It's a way to combine a romantic evening view of Rotterdam from the water with a plain but

GRAND harbor

The Port of Rotterdam handles more ships and more cargo every year than any other port in Europe—40,000 ships and 420 million metric tons of cargo. A dredged channel, the Nieuwe Waterweg (New Waterway) connects Rotterdam with the North Sea and forms a 32km-long (20-mile) deepwater harbor known as Europoort. Holland owes a fair piece of its prosperity to the port, which employs directly 86,000 people. But the port has a dark side, too: Rotterdam is a center for big-time international drug-dealers and gunrunners.

You may think visiting a harbor is boring business on a vacation, but Rotterdam is one of the most memorable sights in Holland. Container ships, bulk carriers, tankers, sleek greyhounds of the sea, and careworn tramps are waited on by a vast retinue of machines and people. Trucks, trains, and barges, each carrying a little piece of the action, hurry into and out of the hub.

satisfying Dutch meal. As soon as the boat weighs anchor, there's a free-for-all at the pancake buffet, with as many plain, bacon, or apple pancakes as you can eat. Departures are Saturday at 8pm. The 3-hour cruise is 24€ for adults, 19€ for children 3 to 12, and free for children 2 and under.

Where to Stay

Bazar ★★ On a busy street near the main museums, the main floor of this place oozes with the atmosphere of *1,001 Nights*—golden pillars, frilly textiles, open-worked shutters, Persian rugs, stained-glass lamps, and brass fittings. By way of thematic variation, there's an African floor and a South American floor. The rooms follow these cues in both design and spirit, making for a distinctive experience, so long as you feel comfortable in whichever ambience you're given. If not, ask to change. Higher-priced rooms have balconies. The ground-floor international cafe-restaurant Bazar doubles as hotel reception.

Witte de Withstraat 16 (at William Boothlaan), 3012 BP Rotterdam. ✆ **010/206-5151.** Fax 010/206-5159. www.hotelbazar.nl. 27 units. 80€–125€ double. Rates include Middle Eastern breakfast. AE, DC, MC, V. Limited street parking. Tram: 7 or 20 to Museumpark. **Amenities:** Restaurant; bar. *In room:* TV, hair dryer, minibar, Wi-Fi (8€/day).

Bienvenue This small budget hotel is one of the best in its price range. It's within easy walking range (400m/¼ mile) of the city's main train station. The bright guest rooms are plain but serviceable and clean, and have carpets, comfortable beds, showers (two bathrooms have tubs), and include a few three- and four-person rooms. There's a tree-shaded canal in front of the hotel, and rooms at the back open onto the terrace. Steep stairs and lack of an elevator might be a problem for some people.

Spoorsingel 24 (2 blocks north of Centraal Station), 3033 GL Rotterdam. ✆ **010/466-9394.** Fax 010/467-7475. www.hotelbienvenue.nl. 10 units, 7 with bathroom. 66€ double without bathroom; 78€ double with bathroom. Rates include buffet breakfast. AE, DC, MC, V. Limited street parking. Metro: Centraal Station. *In room:* TV, Wi-Fi (free).

Bilderberg Parkhotel Rotterdam ★ For city-center convenience, you can't do better than this high-rise, which offsets its none-too-interesting modern lines by being set in a private garden in a moderately leafy part of town. The spacious guest rooms (some of which are air-conditioned) are luxurious, furnished with soft couches, comfortable beds, and elegant bathrooms. With their spruce greens and browns, they afford an echo of the trees and grass beyond the window. The hotel's **Restaurant 70** has won deserved praise in the city for the flair of its contemporary French/Mediterranean cuisine, and for its restful garden terrace.

Westersingel 70 (at Eendrachtsplein), 3015 LB Rotterdam. ✆ **010/436-3611.** Fax 010/436-4212. www.parkhotelrotterdam.nl. 189 units. 175€–320€ double; from 795€ suite. AE, DC, MC, V. Parking 18€. Metro: Eendrachtsplein. **Amenities:** Restaurant; bar; babysitting; exercise room; room service; sauna. *In room:* TV, hair dryer, minibar, Wi-Fi (17€/day).

Manhattan Hotel Rotterdam ★★ Welcome to a lodging where the "heavenly bed" was specially designed, the minibar is called an "electronic refreshment center," and laptop safes are provided. Shiny, modern, and somewhat impersonal, the hotel, which takes up the first 14 floors of the 32-story Millennium Tower, is the latest in five-star accommodations. It stands at the heart of a district of theaters, restaurants, stores, and a casino. The rooms are hushed oases of relative luxury. Rooms are big—in some of the upper-floor rooms, you might need a bullhorn to cast your voice into the remotest nooks and crannies.

Weena 686 (opposite Centraal Station), 3012 CN Rotterdam. ✆ **010/430-2000.** Fax 010/430-2001. www.manhattanhotelrotterdam.com. 230 units. 315€–350€ double; from 525€ suite. AE, DC, MC, V. Valet parking 18€. Metro: Centraal Station. **Amenities:** Restaurant; bar; concierge; executive rooms; exercise room; room service. *In room:* TV, hair dryer, minibar, Wi-Fi (22€/day).

New York ★★ This building, one of Europe's first skyscrapers, was constructed at the beginning of the 20th century to house the headquarters of the Holland-America shipping line, which sailed to New York. Many of the city's emigrants passed through these portals with their trunks. The reception rooms retain some of their original features. In the bright guest rooms, which encompass a surprising range of styles, furnishings combine the old and the new; some rooms have stunning balcony views. The downstairs cafe-restaurant has a great view over the river and docklands. Open all day, it serves both teatime treats and dinner.

Koninginnenhoofd 1 (at Cruise Terminal Rotterdam), 3072 AD Rotterdam. ✆ **010/439-0500.** Fax 010/484-2701. www.hotelnewyork.nl. 72 units. 99€–260€ double. AE, DC, MC, V. Limited street parking. Metro: Wilhelminaplein. **Amenities:** Cafe-restaurant; room service. *In room:* TV, minibar, Wi-Fi (17€/day).

Where to Dine

Eating out in Rotterdam affords visitors a chance to try Michelin-star dining, traditional Dutch food, and a range of world and fusion cuisines that complement the city's status as a great international port. The waterfront along the Nieuwe Maas River boasts a variety of chic dining possibilities.

VERY EXPENSIVE

Parkheuvel ★★ FRENCH/INTERNATIONAL Scenically located at the border between the park in which Rotterdam symbol Euromast stands and the Nieuwe Maas waterway, Parkheuvel occupies a modern semicircular building with tables that afford a scenic view of passing ships. Patron and chef Erik van Loo has earned a pair of Michelin stars for inventive, French-based cuisine with an added European dimension. The seafood dishes are particularly astounding: Try the starter of *carpaccio* of sea bass, or a lobster salad with sun-dried tomatoes and arugula. Main courses range from *turbot gratinée* to poached filet of beef with truffles.

Heuvellaan 21 (in Het Park). ✆ **010/436-0766.** www.parkheuvel.nl. Reservations recommended on weekends. Main courses 30€–55€; fixed-price menus 50€–125€. AE, DC, MC, V. Mon–Fri noon–2:30pm and 6:30–10pm; Sat 6:30–10pm. Tram: 8 to Euromast/Erasmus MC.

EXPENSIVE

In den Rustwat ★★★ FRENCH You'd swear you're in the country at the "Rest Some," but then, back in the 16th century, this thatched farmhouse-style restaurant used to be an inn. Patron/cuisinier Marcel van Zomeren has turned it into one of the city's top establishments. Using only the freshest organic ingredients, he keeps himself and his staff inspired by constantly adapting the menu to seasonal produce. A salad of Bresse pigeon breast with poached quail's eggs and a ravioli of pigeon and gooseliver is an example of a starter, which might be followed by crisp sautéed sea bass filet on a bed of warm tomatoes and young vegetables. Van Zomeren has no specialties—everything he prepares is special.

Honingerdijk 96 (next to Arboretum Trompenburg). ✆ **010/413-4110.** www.idrw.nl. Reservations recommended on weekends. Main courses 25€–28€; lunch menu 33€; evening menus 43€–58€. AE, DC, MC, V. Tues–Fri noon–3pm and 6–10pm; Sat 6–10pm. Tram: 21 to Woudestein.

MODERATE

Brasserie La Vilette ★ CLASSIC FRENCH Elegant and filled with potted plants and flowers, this center-city oasis has soft rose-colored walls and starched white table linen. Service is both polished and friendly. For starters, try the filet of beef *carpaccio*. The grilled sea bass with lobster sauce makes a fine main course, and the crème brûlée with ice cream flavored with sweet Pedro Ximenez sherry is a tempting dessert.

Westblaak 160 (at Boomgaardsstraat). ✆ **010/414-8692.** www.lavilette.nl. Main courses 22€–25€; fixed-price menus 40€–48€. AE, DC, MC, V. Mon–Fri noon–2pm and 6–10pm; Sat 6–10pm. Metro: Eendrachtsplein.

Café-Brasserie Dudok ★ DUTCH/CONTINENTAL Named after the Dutch modernist architect Willem Marinus Dudok, who designed the building, this stylish modern cafe in the heart of town is flooded with light through large windows. Snacks and Continental meals are served at tables on two levels. It's a popular meeting place for breakfast, lunch, and afternoon coffee, and renowned for its apple pie.

Meent 88 (off Coolsingel). ✆ **010/433-3102.** www.dudok.nl. Main courses 15€–21€. AE, DC, MC, V. Mon–Thurs 8am–midnight; Fri 8am–10pm; Sat 9am–9:30pm; Sun 10am–9:30pm. Metro: Stadhuis.

Café-Restaurant Rotterdam ★★ DUTCH As I savored the delicious flavors of skin-fried cod with truffle purée and spinach, a dramatic sunset lit up the low-lying barges gliding down the Nieuwe Maas outside. You might not be so lucky, but this cafe-restaurant—a jewel in Rotterdam's crown where royalty, dockworkers, and visitors can feel equally at home—is a good choice at any time. The architecture of the light-flooded old cruise-ship terminal on Kop van Zuid peninsula and the potted olive trees give its four floors a special atmosphere. The menu covers a lot of European ground, from pasta to shellfish, and mixes influences from around the world.

Wilhelminakade 699. ✆ **010/290-8440.** www.caferotterdam.nl. Main courses 23€–24€; fixed-price menus 28€–32€. AE, DC, MC, V. Mon–Thurs 11am–midnight; Fri–Sat 11am–1am; Sun 10am–midnight. Metro: Wilhelminaplein.

INEXPENSIVE

Dewi Sri ★ INDONESIAN Soberly decorated Dewi Sri has been making culinary magic since 1977, in a merchant's house dating from 1880 along the Nieuwe Maas. There are plenty of individual choices for those who know their way around an Indonesian menu, while for newcomers the 14-dish Sumatra rijsttafel affords a wide-ranging insight into traditional Indonesian cuisine.

Westerkade 20 (at Het Park). ✆ **010/436-0263.** www.dewisri.nl. Main courses 8€–12€; rijsttafel 25€. AE, DC, MC, V. Mon–Fri noon–2:30pm and 5:30–10:30pm; Sat–Sun 5–10:30pm. Tram: 7 to Westplein.

Shopping

Shop till you drop in Rotterdam. Cutting-edge fashion is the thing in boutiques on and around cool Witte de Withstraat. On the Lijnbaan car-free shopping promenade, you'll find dozens of small fashion boutiques. The historic **Delfshaven** area is a storehouse for antiques.

For sexy designer lingerie, head to **Marlies Dekkers,** Witte de Withstraat 2 (✆ **010/280-9184;** www.marliesdekkers.nl; Metro: Eendrachtsplein), which stands out on cool Witte de Withstraat not so much for its location in a tastefully converted former bank building as for the hot lingerie and beachwear from the Dutch designer's Undressed collection in the window. Chic fashion boutique **Prague,** Van Oldenbarneveltstraat 138 (✆ **010/213-5269;** www.prague-by-louis-dijksman.nl; Metro: Eendrachtsplein), trades intimacy for the space to showcase the creations, for men and women, of a multitude of intriguing fashion designers—the list is headed by Ann Demeulemeester, Dries van Noten, and Haider Ackerman, and extends to little-known Japanese designers.

Department stores are located on Coolsingel and Hoogstraat. The classy **De Bijenkorf** department store, Coolsingel 105 (✆ **0900/0919;** www.bijenkorf.nl; Metro: Beurs), has five floors selling women's and men's fashions and accessories, cosmetics, household items, books, toys, CDs, DVDs, and more. Its bright Continental restaurant, La Ruche, is worth visiting. On one side, it opens onto the new Beurstraverse mall, which runs below street level and has a mix of chain stores and small stores.

With more than 12,000 different products on its shelves, the large supermarket **Gimsel,** Mariniersweg 9–33 (✆ **010/404-7342;** www.degroenepassage.nl; Metro: Blaak or Oostplein), takes shopping for "bio" food and drink far beyond its cottage-industry roots. This is just one of the organic or alternative stores in the Groene Passage green shopping center. Close to Rotterdam's curious Cube Houses (see "Modern Architecture," earlier in this chapter), **De Man van Drank,** Hoogstraat 54A (✆ **010/411-2879;** www.bierenco.nl; Metro: Blaak or Oostplein), stocks a vast selection of beers of distinction, including all the main Dutch beers and those from microbreweries, along with Belgian, German, English, American, and more, plus seasonal, rare, and real ales.

On the trendy south bank of the Nieuwe Maas, the **Entrepot,** a 19th-century bonded warehouse, enjoys a new lease on life. In this place that defines the idea of fun shopping, you find distinct colonial overtones at **Jumbo,** Vijf Werelddelen 33 (✆ **010/485-0111;** www.jumbosupermarkten.nl), the city's largest supermarket. A colonnade of diverse restaurants overlooks a small marina and faces a row of interior design stores.

Back in the center city, a huge **general market** brings alive the Binnenrotte area on Tuesday from 8am to 5:30pm, Friday from noon to 6pm, Saturday from 8am to 5pm, and a scaled-down version on Sunday (mid-Apr to Dec) from noon to 5pm. Lovers of antiques, bric-a-brac, and old books should make their way to the **Sunday market** (Metro: Leuvehaven) amid the mini-Manhattan architecture on Schiedamsedijk, along Leuvehaven harbor in the center of town; the market is open mid-May to mid-September Sunday from 11am to 5pm.

Rotterdam After Dark

Rotterdam has all kinds of nightlife, but the dance-club scene leads the way—pack your clubbing duds to wear among Holland's hottest dance venues.

THE PERFORMING ARTS

The world-class **Rotterdam Philharmonic Orchestra** plays at the concert hall (and convention center) **De Doelen,** at Kruisstraat 2 (✆ **010/217-1717;** www.dedoelen.nl; Metro: Centraal Station), which opened in 1966 and in addition hosts jazz, world music, and other concerts.

THE CLUB & MUSIC SCENE

From converted center-city cinemas to converted harbor warehouses, Rotterdam has the space for techno, trance, and other fancy moves. Most clubs don't get going until midnight, when bars are getting ready to close, and keep going until about 5am.

The **Baja Beach Club,** Karel Doormanstraat 10–12 (✆ **010/289-9800;** www.baja.nl; Metro: Centraal Station), guarantees a sunny ambience, even when it rains, and the bar staff of tanned, muscular males and tanned shapely females in beachwear effortlessly slip into the role of entertainers, while dancers groove to laid-back rhythms from live music or DJs. Techno, electro sounds, party nights, and events like fashion shows are on the agenda at centrally located **Off_Corso,** Kruiskade 22 (✆ **010/411-3897;** www.off-corso.nl; Metro: Stadhuis), a converted cinema southwest of Hofplein, with bars and seating on several levels. Visuals are projected onto a screen on the main dance floor.

With multiple dance floors, secluded lounges, reserved VIP areas, and music from live bands and DJs, nearby **Thalia Lounge,** Kruiskade 31 (✆ **010/214-2547;** www.thaliarotterdam.nl; Metro: Stadhuis), is aimed at sophisticated over-25s. It's willing to experiment, for example with "sushi-samba," a mix of Asian and Latin. **Maastheater,** Boompjes 751 (✆ **010/413-4091**), a waterside disco where DJs dictate the music styles, is popular with students.

A place where the Rotterdam gay scene parties the nights away is the **Gay Palace ★★**, Schiedamsesingel 139 (✆ **010/414-1486;** www.gay-palace.nl; Metro: Leuvehaven). Jazz cats should make their way to **Dizzy's ★**, Gravendijkwal 127 (✆ **010/477-3014;** www.dizzy.nl), an informal, long-established cafe where live music is the name of the game. If you want to see a global pop star, take a ride to **Ahoy,** Ahoyweg 10 (✆ **0900/235-2469;** www.ahoy.nl; Metro: Zuidplein). Megastars perform here to capacity audiences of 10,000.

BARS & CAFES

Bars range from the city's most traditional watering holes at old-world Delfshaven to shiny modern places along the river.

Dating from a respectably venerable 1912, **Café de Oude Sluis,** Havenstraat 7 (✆ **010/477-3068;** www.trilobiet.nl/sluis; Metro: Delfshaven), is a slice of Delfshaven's old harbor scene, with its brown wall carvings and bric-a-brac; at the first hint of sunshine, tables and chairs appear along the harbor wall. A few doors along, **Proeflokaal de Ooievaar,** Havenstraat 11 (✆ **010/476-9190;** Metro: Delfshaven), is Rotterdam's only *jenever* "sampling room," stocking dozens of Dutch and Belgian gin varieties. Its intimate surroundings merit the prized Dutch description *gezellig,* meaning warm and cozy, and it occasionally hosts small-scale live-music concerts.

WINDMILLS OF KINDERDIJK ★

The sight of windmill sails spinning in the breeze stirs the soul of a true Hollander. Kinderdijk (www.kinderdijk.nl), a tiny community between Rotterdam and Dordrecht, on the south bank of the Lek River, has 19 water-pumping windmills; that means 76 mill sails, each with a 14-yard span, all revolving on a summer day. It's a spectacular sight, and one important enough for Kinderdijk to have been placed on UNESCO's World Heritage list.

By regulating the level of water, Kinderdijk's windmills guarded the fertile polders (reclaimed land) of the Alblasserwaard, which were constantly at risk of returning to the water. The Windmill Exposition Center at Kinderdijk treats its subjects as more than just pretty faces and gives a detailed explanation of windmills' technical characteristics and the part they played in the intricate system of water control. It also looks at the people and the culture that developed on the polders.

The mills operate on Saturday afternoons in July and August from 2:30 to 5:30pm; the visitors' mill is open April to October Monday to Saturday from 9:30am to 5:30pm. To get to Kinderdijk from Rotterdam, take **Arriva** bus no. 90 from Keizerswaard in the south-Rotterdam IJsselmonde district (tram: 2 or 23). Or board a fast jet-catamaran operated by **Waterbus** (✆ **0900/899-8998;** www.fastferry.nl), from a dock at the city's Erasmusbrug to the De Schans dock at Ridderkerk, for the local ferry across to Kinderdijk. If you're driving, take N210 east to Krimpen aan de Lek, from where a small car ferry crosses over the Lek River to Kinderdijk.

In the city's hip Meent district, **Level,** Pannekoekstraat 76A (✆ **010/280-0788;** www.levelrotterdam.nl; Metro: Blaak), is a state-of-the-art cocktail bar, decked out in a warm shade of Holland's trademark orange national color. Its staff can shake up more than 60 cocktails, many of them exotic examples. Under the low bar lights at ultracool **Toko94,** Witte de Withstraat 94B (✆ **010/240-0479;** www.toko94.com; Metro: Eendrachtsplein), cocktail "mixologists" shake up a tidal wave of tropical drinks to accompany Caribbean and Asian food, alongside jazz and other laid-back music.

OTHER VENUES

Try your luck at **Holland Casino Rotterdam,** Plaza Complex, Weena 624 (✆ **010/206-8206;** www.hollandcasino.nl; Metro: Centraal Station). There's roulette, blackjack, punto banco, slot machines, and more. The dress code here is "correct" (collar and tie for men), and the minimum age is 18. You need your passport to get in. The casino is open daily (except May 4 and Dec 31) 12:30pm to 3am. Admission is 5€; Wednesday is "ladies day," and admission is free for all female visitors.

DELFT ★★

10km (6 miles) SE of The Hague; 14km (9 miles) NW of Rotterdam; 35km (22 miles) W of Gouda; 30km (19 miles) SW of Leiden; 55km (34 miles) SW of Amsterdam

Delft (pop, 96,000) is perhaps the prettiest town in all of Holland. The facades of the Renaissance and Gothic houses here reflect age-old beauty, a sense of tranquillity

THOSE DELFT pottery BLUES

Porcelain from the factories at Delft can be wonderful, even if it's not cheap. With a lowercase *d*, "delftware" is an umbrella name for all Dutch hand-painted earthenware pottery resembling ancient Chinese porcelain, whether it is blue and white, red and white, or polychrome, and regardless of the Dutch city in which it was produced. Delftware, or Delft Blue (with a capital *D*), refers to the predominantly, but not exclusively, blue-and-white products of three Delft-based firms: **De Koninklijke Porceleyne Fles** (see below); **De Delftse Pauw,** Delftweg 133, Rijswijk (✆ **015/212-4920;** www.delftpottery.com; tram: 1); and **De Candelaer,** Kerkstraat 13 (✆ **015/213-1848;** www.candelaer.nl; bus: 80 or 82).

Genuine Delftware is for sale in specialized stores (De Delftse Pauw sells its pottery only from its workshop and by mail order), but it is far more interesting to go to the workshops and see how they are made. Little has changed over the centuries, and all the decorating is still done by hand. This makes it quite pricey, but each piece is a unique product, made by craftsmen. Some of the numerous copies of De Porceleyne Fles and De Delftse Pauw products are nearly equal in quality, while others miss by miles the delicacy of the brush stroke, the richness of color, or the sheen of the secret glazes that make the items produced by these firms so highly prized.

To be sure that you're looking at a *real* Delft vase from De Koninklijke Porceleyne Fles, look on the bottom for the distinctive three-part hallmark: an outline of a small pot, above an initial *J* crossed with a short stroke, above the scripted word *Delft.* For De Delftse Pauw, look for three blue stars separated by a drafting compass, above the scripted text *D.P Delft.* And for De Candelaer, there will be the company's candle-and-candlestick symbol, the scripted text *D.C. Delft,* and the initials of the artist.

pervades the air, and linden trees bend over its gracious canals. Indeed, it's easy to understand why Old Master Jan Vermeer chose to spend most of his life surrounded by Delft's gentle beauty.

A good part of Holland's history is preserved in memorials in Delft. William the Silent, who led the Dutch insurrection against Spanish rule, was assassinated in the Prinsenhof and now rests in a magnificent tomb in the Nieuwe Kerk; every member of the House of Oranje-Nassau since King Willem I has been brought here for burial. Two of Holland's greatest naval figures, admirals Maarten Tromp and Piet Hein, are entombed in the Oude Kerk.

Of course, to many visitors, Delft means just one thing—the distinctive blue-and-white earthenware still produced by the meticulous methods of old. Every piece of true Delftware is hand-painted by skilled craftspeople. A different Delft exists on the modern campus of the town's Technical University, noted for the excellence of its scientist and engineer graduates, among the latter being many of the world-class Dutch hydraulic engineers.

Essentials

GETTING THERE There's frequent **train** service from around Holland to Delft, with up to six trains an hour from Amsterdam (one is direct and the others require a

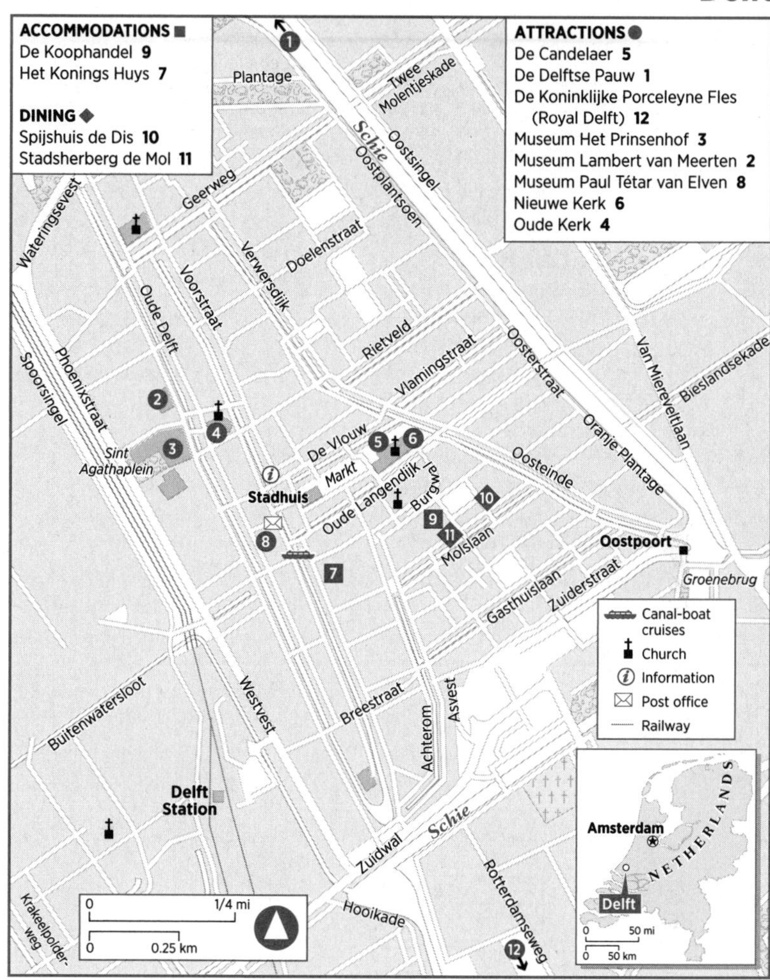

transfer in Rotterdam) and eight an hour from Rotterdam. The ride from Amsterdam takes around 1 hour; a one-way ticket is 11€ in second class and 19€ in first class. From Rotterdam, it's 15 minutes, and 3€ and 5.10€, respectively. From The Hague you can go by tram; it's a 15-minute ride that costs 1.50€ one-way. By **car,** the town is just off A13/E19, the expressway from The Hague to Rotterdam.

VISITOR INFORMATION Delft's **Touristen Informatie Punt (TIP),** Hippolytusbuurt 4, 2611 HN Delft (✆ **0900/515-1555** from inside Holland, 31-15/215-4051 from abroad; fax 015/215-4055; www.delft.nl), is in the center of town. The office is open April to September Sunday and Monday from 10am to 4pm, Tuesday to Friday from 9am to 6pm, and Saturday from 10am to 5pm; October to

March, hours are Sunday from 10am to 3pm, Monday from 11am to 4pm, and Tuesday to Saturday from 10am to 4pm.

What to See & Do

The best way to absorb Delft's special ambience is by strolling its streets. Around every corner and down every street, you step into a scene that might have been composed for the canvas of a great artist. Supplement your walks with a leisurely tour of the canals via the numerous water taxis that operate during the summer. The town's large main square, the Markt, is a zoo on market day (Thurs), but on quieter days, you get space to see how picturesque it is.

THE TOP ATTRACTIONS

De Koninklijke Porceleyne Fles (Royal Delft) ★ The Delft Blue porcelain embossed with the DE PORCELYNE FLES stamp you likely came to town to check out is made here by a traditional and painstaking method. Watch the hand painting of each item, and see an audiovisual show that explains the entire process. Delft potters have been at it since the 1640s, when they met the competition of Chinese porcelain imported by the East India Company. And if you thought the trademark blue-and-white colors were the only Delft, here is where you see exquisite multicolored patterns. Your purchases can be packed carefully and shipped home directly from this workshop.

Rotterdamseweg 196 (at Jaffalaan). ✆ **015/251-2030.** www.royaldelft.com. Admission 8€ adults, free for children 12 and under. Apr–Oct daily 9am–5pm; Nov–Mar Mon–Sat 9am–5pm. Closed Jan 1 and Dec 25 and 26. Bus: 40, 63, 121, or 129 to Jaffalaan.

Museum Het Prinsenhof ★ The Prinsenhof (Prince's Court), on the banks of Delft's oldest canal, Oude Delft, dates from the late 1400s and was originally a convent. This is where William I of Orange (William the Silent) lived from 1572 and had his headquarters in the years when he helped found the Dutch Republic, and where an assassin's bullets ended his life in 1584 (you can see a pair of bullet holes from the fusillade that felled him in the stairwell). The interior William would have known has been recreated, and a museum preserves the record of Dutch struggles to throw off the yoke of Spanish occupation between 1568 and 1648. There are impressive tapestries, silverware, pottery, and paintings—among the latter are five other versions of the *View of Delft,* painted by contemporaries of Vermeer.

Sint-Agathaplein 1 (north of Markt, near Oude Kerk). ✆ **015/260-2358.** www.prinsenhof-delft.nl. Admission 7.50€ adults, 4€ students and children 12–16, free for children 11 and under. Tues–Sat 11am–5pm. Closed Jan 1, Easter Mon., Apr 30, and Dec 25. Tram: 1 or 19 to Prinsenhof.

Museum Lambert van Meerten You'll find in this canal-side Dutch neo-Renaissance mansion (1893) a fascinating collection of Delft earthenware, including 7,000 old Delft tiles, along with antique Chinese porcelain, paintings, furniture, and other interior design elements. All are housed in an elegant, wood-paneled, gray sandstone mansion, named for the wealthy gin distiller and art lover who helped to design it, and who assembled its collection of Dutch Golden Age art and antiques during his lifetime (1842–1904).

Oude Delft 199 (north of Markt, near Prinsenhof). ✆ **015/260-2358.** www.lambertvanmeerten-delft.nl. Admission 3.50€ adults, 1.50€ students and children 12–16, free for children 11 and under. Tues–Sun 11am–5pm. Closed Jan 1, Easter Mon., Apr 30, and Dec 25. Tram: 1 or 19 to Prinsenhof.

Museum Paul Tétar van Elven The 19th-century artist van Elven (1823–96) lived and worked here, and the furnishings are just as he left them. The 17th-century-style studio looks like it's ready for the artist to enter and pick up his brushes. Van

Elven was a noted copyist, and a lot of his reproductions hang on the walls. Except for a subpar Vermeer on the second floor, most of them are excellent, especially the Rembrandts and the Paulus Potter on the first floor. The furniture and porcelain collections are interesting, too.

Koornmarkt 67 (just south of the Markt). ✆ **015/212-4206.** www.delftmusea.nl. Admission 3.50€ adults, 2€ children 13–16, free for children 12 and under. Tues–Sun 1–5pm. Bus: 80 or 82 to Markt.

HISTORIC CHURCHES

Two church spires grace the Delft skyline. One belongs to the **Nieuwe Kerk (New Church) ★**, Markt 80 (✆ **015/212-3025;** www.nieuwekerk-delft.nl), which isn't all that new, since it was begun in 1383 and finally completed in 1510. Inside is the magnificent tomb of William the Silent, surrounded by 22 columns and decorated with figures representing Liberty, Justice, Valor, and Religion. The royal dead of the House of Oranje-Nassau lie in a crypt beneath the remains of the founder of their line. There's a marvelous panoramic view of the town from the 109m-high (358-ft.) church tower, the second tallest in the country.

The other, slightly leaning spire is attached to the **Oude Kerk (Old Church),** Heilige Geestkerkhof 25 (✆ **015/212-3015;** www.oudekerk-delft.nl), founded around 1200 and dating mostly from the 13th and 14th centuries. The tower is embellished with four corner turrets and is noted for its 27 stained-glass windows by Joep Nicolas. Inside are the tombs of the artist Jan Vermeer and his family, and his friend Antoni van Leeuwenhoek, the inventor of the microscope (and perhaps, on occasion, Vermeer's model).

Both churches are open April to October Monday to Saturday from 9am to 6pm, November to January Monday to Friday from 11am to 4pm and Saturday from 11am to 5pm, and February to March Monday to Saturday from 10am to 5pm. Combined admission is 3.50€ for adults, 3€ for seniors, 1.50€ for children 6 to 12, and free for children 5 and under. Admission to the Nieuwe Kerk tower is 3€ for adults, 2.50€ for seniors, 1.50€ for children 6 to 12, and free for children 5 and under.

Where to Stay

De Koophandel Centrally located in a 16th-century building, this hotel boasts a connection to Delft's most famous son: Reynier Jansz Vos, the father of artist Jan Vermeer, was born here in 1591. The guest rooms are small and furnished in contemporary style but have been designed so that this comes across as intimate rather than as cramped. Some of them have views through leaded windows on the bustling, tree-shaded square—which on long summer nights can throw up a noise problem from the sidewalk terraces of the square's plentiful restaurants and cafes. There's no elevator, so you'll need to climb a steep staircase to your room.

Beestenmarkt 30 (at Molslaan), 2611 GC Delft. ✆ **015/214-2302.** Fax 015/214-0674. www.hoteldekoophandel.nl. 25 units. 109€–114€ double. Rates include buffet breakfast. AE, DC, MC, V. Limited street parking. Bus: 80 or 82 to Markt. *In room:* TV, hair dryer, Wi-Fi (free).

Het Konings Huys Plain but functional rooms mark this family-owned budget hotel that boasts both a good location and a friendly approach as its prime assets. For a lively accommodation, ask for a room with a view on the square; for peace and quiet, head instead to the rear of the building. The in-house cafe and restaurant has a decent selection of Dutch and Belgian beers, a good if not particularly imaginative Dutch and Continental menu, and a heated sidewalk terrace on the Markt.

Markt 38–42 (near the Stadhuis/Town Hall), 2611 GV Delft. ✆ **015/212-5115.** Fax 015/213-6069. www.hetkoningshuys.eu. 16 units (10 with bathroom). 59€ without bathroom; 81€ double with bathroom. AE, DC, MC, V. Limited street parking. Bus: 80 or 82 to Markt. **Amenities:** Restaurant; bar. *In room:* TV, Wi-Fi (free).

Where to Dine

Spijshuis de Dis ★ DUTCH Some great Dutch cooking is dished up at this atmospheric restaurant east of the market. Look for traditional plates presented in modern variations. These include Bakke Pot—a stew made from three kinds of meat (beef, chicken, and rabbit) in beer sauce, served in the pan; V.O.C. Mussels (named after the Dutch initials for the East India Company), prepared with garlic and spices such as ginger and curry; and asparagus in season (May–June).

Beestenmarkt 36 (2 blocks from the Markt). ✆ **015/213-1782.** www.spijshuisdedis.com. Main courses 18€–23€; fixed-price menu 30€. AE, DC, MC, V. Thurs–Tues 5–9:30pm. Bus: 80 or 82 to Markt.

Stadsherberg de Mol TRADITIONAL DUTCH Food is served here, in a building that dates from 1563, in the medieval manner: in wooden bowls from which you eat with your hands. Prices are moderate and quantities copious. Live music and dancing add to the fun.

Molslaan 104 (off Beestenmarkt). ✆ **015/212-1343.** www.stadsherbergdemol.nl. Main courses 12€–18€. MC, V. Tues–Sun 6–11pm. Bus: 80 or 82 to Markt.

GOUDA ★

40km (25 miles) S of Amsterdam; 25km (16 miles) NE of Rotterdam

In addition to its famous cheese, Gouda (pronounced *Khow*-dah) is noted for its candles: Every year, in the middle of December, the market and the Town Hall are ravishingly candlelit (see "When to Go," in chapter 12). Gouda (pop. 72,000) has a handsome Old Town.

Essentials

GETTING THERE There's frequent **train** service from around Holland to Gouda, with up to four trains an hour from Amsterdam (one is direct and the others require a transfer in Rotterdam) and eight an hour from Rotterdam. The ride from Amsterdam takes 55 minutes; a one-way ticket is 10€ in second class and 17€ in first class. From Rotterdam it's around 20 minutes, and 4.50€ and 7.70€, respectively. By **car,** the town is just off A13/E19, the expressway from The Hague to Rotterdam.

VISITOR INFORMATION **VVV Gouda,** Lange Tiendeweg 29–31, 2801 KE Gouda (✆ **0900/468-3288;** fax 0182/550-308; www.vvvgouda.nl), is open Monday from 1 to 5:30pm, Tuesday to Friday from 9:30am to 5:30pm, Saturday from 10am to 4pm, and Sunday (July–Aug) noon to 4pm.

What to See & Do

Try to come here on a Thursday morning between 10am and 12:30pm from about the third week in June to the first week in September, when the lively **Goudse Kaasmarkt (Gouda Cheese Market)** ★ brings farmers driving farm wagons painted with bright designs and piled high with round cheeses in orange skins. Walk to the back of the **Stadhuis (Town Hall)** to sample the Gouda cheese. This gray stone building, with stepped gables and red shutters, is reputed to be Holland's oldest Town

Gouda

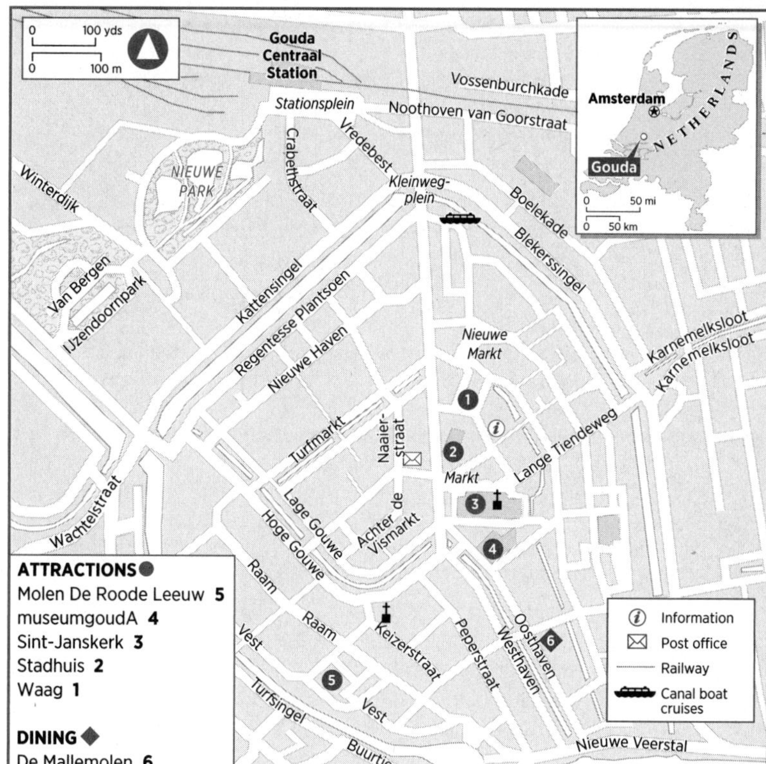

Hall, and parts of its Gothic facade date from 1449. Gouda is noted for its candles, and every year from the middle of December, the Markt and the Town Hall are festively lit by candles.

West of the Markt is an impressive and indelibly Dutch sight. The **Molen De Roode Leeuw (Red Lion Windmill)** ★, Vest 67 (✆ **0182/522-041;** www.flourpower.nl), a grain mill from 1727, has been completely renovated and is now grinding away again. Go out on the platform to watch the vanes swish past, while inside, the huge wooden cogwheels and beams work the millstones. There's a store inside (open Thurs–Sat 9am–4pm) where you can buy all kinds of ground flour.

THE TOP SIGHTS

museumgoudA ★ The jewel of the collections at this museum in the Catharina Gasthuis (1665), a former hospital near Sint-Janskerk, is a gold chalice Countess Jacqueline of Bavaria presented to the town's Society of Archers in 1465. Its whereabouts were unknown for more than a century before it was recovered in the Town Hall's attic and brought here. There are colorful guild relics, antique furniture, antique pipes, and *plateel,* a colorful pottery that is Gouda's answer to Delftware, as well as a terra-cotta plaque whose Latin inscription proclaims that the humanist

Smoke It & See

Gouda has been the center of a thriving clay-pipe industry since the 17th century. One local style of pipe has a pattern on the bowl that's invisible when the pipe is new and only appears as the pipe is smoked and darkens. It's called a "mystery pipe," because the designs vary and buyers never quite know what they're getting.

Erasmus may have been born in Rotterdam but was conceived in Gouda. There's limited wheelchair access.

Achter de Kerk 14 (at Oosthaven). ✆ **0182/331-000.** www.museumgouda.nl. Admission 5€ adults, free for children 18 and under. Wed–Fri 10am–5pm; Sat–Sun noon–5pm. Closed Jan 1, Apr 30, and Dec 25.

Sint-Janskerk (Church of St. John) ★ Holland's longest church, this majestic 15th-century building holds some of Europe's most beautiful stained-glass windows—64 in all, with a total of 2,412 panels. Some date back as far as the mid-1500s. To see the contrast between that stained-glass art of long ago and the work being carried out today, take a look at the most recent window, no. 28A, commemorating the World War II years in Holland.

Achter de Kerk 16 (south of Markt). ✆ **0182/512-684.** www.sintjan.com. Admission 3.50€ adults, 2.50€ seniors, 2.25€ students, 2€ children 5–12, free for children 4 and under. Mar–Oct Mon–Sat 9am–5pm; Nov–Feb Mon–Sat 10am–4pm.

Waag (Weighing House) ★ ☺ This monumental Weighing House, dating from 1669, is the pride of the town. An exhibit inside tells the story of cheese using interactive audiovisual media. You'll get to know all about the manufacturing process, from grass through cow through milk to cheese, and have a chance to taste the finished product. The museum explains the importance of Gouda as a center of Dutch dairy production.

Markt 35–36. ✆ **0182/529-996.** www.goudakaas.nl. Admission 3.50€ adults, 3€ children 5–12, free for children 4 and under, 10€ family. Apr–Oct Tues–Wed and Fri–Sun 1–5pm; Thurs 10am–5pm.

Where to Dine

De Mallemolen ★ CLASSIC FRENCH This excellent traditional restaurant is on what's known as "Rembrandt's corner." There's an antique windmill on the same street. The restaurant has an Old Dutch look, though the cuisine is chiefly French. Dishes include tournedos with gooseliver in a red-wine sauce.

Oosthaven 72. ✆ **0182/515-430.** www.mallemolen.com. Reservations recommended on weekends. Main courses 20€–25€; fixed-price menus 19€–52€. AE, DC, MC, V. Wed–Sun 5–11pm.

LEIDEN ★

36km (22 miles) SW of Amsterdam; 20km (12 miles) NE of The Hague

Stately yet bustling, the old heart of Leiden is classic Dutch, filled with handsome, gabled brick houses along canals spanned by graceful bridges. The Pilgrims lived here for 11 years before sailing to North America. Leiden's proudest homegrown moment came in 1574, when it became the only Dutch town to withstand a Spanish siege. This is also the birthplace of the Dutch tulip trade and of Rembrandt. The oldest

Leiden

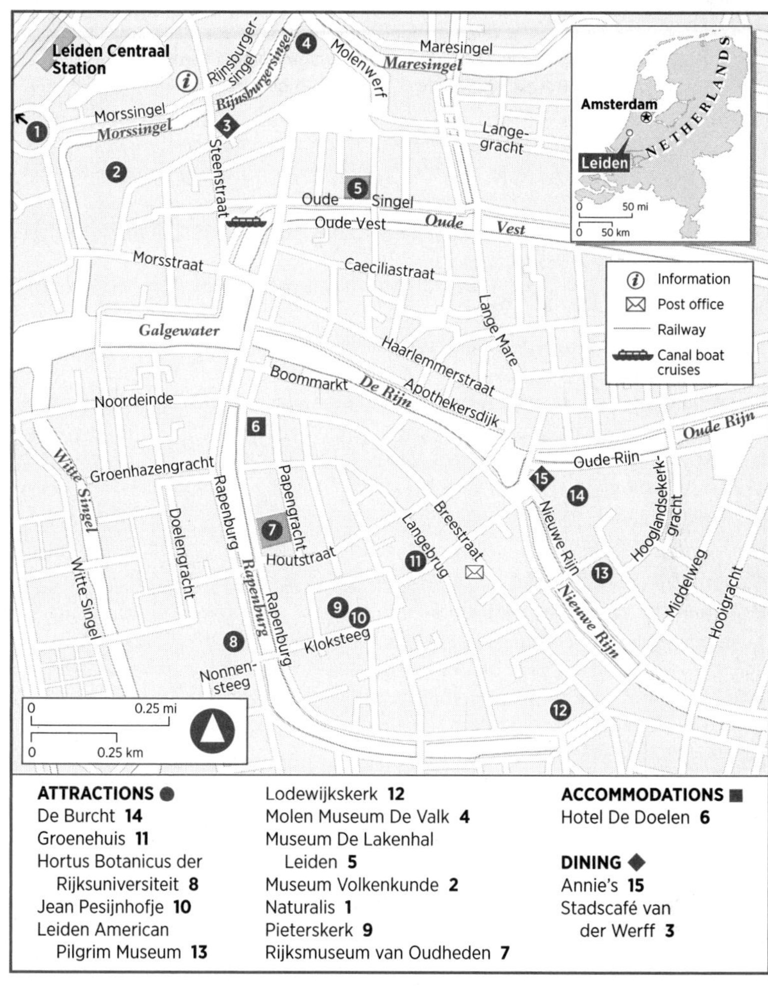

university in the Netherlands is here, too, founded in 1575. With 14 academic-leaning museums, covering subjects ranging from antiquities, natural history, and anatomy to clay pipes and coins, Leiden seems perfectly justified in calling itself Holland's *Museumstad* (Museum City).

Essentials

GETTING THERE Up to eight **trains** per hour run from Amsterdam Centraal Station to Leiden Centraal Station. The ride takes around 35 minutes, and the round-trip fare is 15€ in second class and 26€ in first class. The center of Leiden is a walk of around 1.5km (1 mile) south from the station. By **car,** take A4/E19.

Intelligence Test

As a reward for their heroic resistance during the 1574 Spanish siege, Prince William of Orange offered the people of Leiden a choice—a tax break or a university. They chose the university.

VISITOR INFORMATION **VVV Leiden,** Stationsweg 41, 2312 AV Leiden (✆ **071/516-6000;** fax 071/516-6009; www.vvvleiden.nl), is just outside the train station. The office is open Monday to Friday from 8am to 6pm, Saturday from 10am to 4pm, and Sunday from 11am to 3pm.

What to See & Do

In 1606, the great artist Rembrandt van Rijn was born in Leiden. He later moved to Amsterdam, where he won fame and fortune—and later suffered bankruptcy and obscurity. In his hometown, a **Rembrandt Walk** takes in the site of the house (since demolished) where he was born, the Latin School he attended as a boy, and the first studio where he worked. A descriptive booklet is available from VVV Leiden for 4€.

A 13th-century citadel, **De Burcht,** still stands on a mound of land in the town center between two branches of the Rhine, Oude and Nieuwe, providing a great view of the rooftops around.

THE TOP MUSEUMS

Museum De Lakenhal Leiden ★ This fine 17th-century guildhall is home to Leiden's municipal museum. Its collection of paintings by Dutch artists of the 16th and 17th centuries includes works by Lucas van Leyden, Rembrandt, Steen, and Dou. Temporary modern art exhibitions are organized regularly. The cloth merchants' guild (the original occupants of the building) is represented in historical exhibits; the guild's splendid meeting hall is on the first floor.

Oude Singel 28–32 (at Lange Scheistraat). ✆ **071/516-5360.** www.lakenhal.nl. Admission 7.50€ adults, 4.50€ seniors, free for children 17 and under. Tues–Fri 10am–5pm; Sat–Sun and holidays noon–5pm (Oct 3 only 10am–noon). Closed Jan 1, and Dec 25.

Museum Volkenkunde (National Ethnography Museum) ★ Between 1823 and 1830, German-born Philipp Franz von Siebold collected 5,000 varied objects from a Japan that was still closed to the outside world except for the Dutch trading post on Deshima island in Nagasaki Bay, where he was post physician. From this basis, the collection has grown to take in much of the world outside of Europe. Von Siebold differed from other collectors because he had a passion for understanding and identifying with the Japanese way of life, which extended to other lands and cultures.

Steenstraat 1 (at Sint-Aagtenstraat). ✆ **071/516-8800.** www.rmv.nl. Admission 8.50€ adults, 6€ seniors and children 13–18, free for children 12 and under, free for all on Wed. Tues–Sun (also Mon on national holidays and at some other times) 10am–5pm. Closed Jan 1, Apr 30, Oct 3 and 4, and Dec 25.

Naturalis (National Museum of Natural History) Displays here trace and explain the development of the natural world, from its mineral treasures to ecosystems to modern energy generation. Pickled specimens sit alongside stuffed and painted ones in the overview of plant and animal life. Kids love the simpler displays that let them look at topsoil through a periscope, and there's plenty of computer-based interactivity, too.

walking IN FATHERS' FOOTSTEPS

To touch base with the Pilgrims, who lived in Leiden between 1609 and 1620, pick up the VVV brochure ***A Pilgrimage Through Leiden: A Walk in the Footsteps of the Pilgrim Fathers.*** The walk starts at the **Lodewijkskerk (Louis Church),** which was used as a meeting place by the cloth guild. William Bradford, who became the governor of New Plymouth, was a member of this guild.

The walk takes you past the site of the **Groenehuis (Green House)** on William Brewstersteeg, where, in an attached printing shop, William Brewster's and Thomas Brewer's Pilgrim Press published the religious views that so angered King James and the Church of England. Plaques at the Late Gothic, **Pieterskerk (Peter's Church),** in a square off Kloksteeg, memorialize the Pilgrims, who worshiped here and who lived in its shadow. Special Thanksgiving Day services are held each year in honor of the little band of refugees.

Across the street from the church, at Kloksteeg 21, the **Jean Pesijnshofje,** an almshouse constructed in 1683, occupies the ground where earlier stood the Groene Poort (Green Close), a cluster of small houses in which Rev. John Robinson and 21 Pilgrim families lived. Robinson was forced to stay behind because of illness and is buried in the Pieterskerk. The almshouse is named for Jean Pesijn, a Belgian Protestant who joined the Leiden community along with his wife, Marie de la Noye, and whose son Philip would sail for North America in 1621, where his surname would in time contract to Delano.

On July 21, 1620, the first group of 66 Pilgrims who were leaving boarded barges at Rapenburg Quay for the trip by canal from Leiden to the harbor of Delft, now Delfshaven in Rotterdam. From there they sailed on the *Speedwell* for England, where the *Mayflower* awaited them.

At the **Leiden American Pilgrim Museum,** Beschuitsteeg 9 (✆ **071/512-2413;** www.pilgrimhall.org), in a 16th-century house where one of the Pilgrim families may have lodged, you'll hear a recorded commentary about the Pilgrims and see photocopies of documents relating to their 11-year residence in Leiden. The museum is open Wednesday to Saturday from 1 to 5pm. Admission is 3€, and free for children 5 and under.

Adults should enjoy anthropological displays comparing cultural views of nature: ancient Egypt, the post-Renaissance Western world, China, and Islam. Equally intriguing is the Treasure Room on the fifth floor, for its cases of precious stones and examples of extinct animals and birds that fell into taxidermists' hands.

Darwinweg 2 (close to the train station). ✆ **071/568-7600.** www.naturalis.nl. Admission 11€ adults, 10€ seniors, 9€ children 13–17, 7€ children 4–12, free for children 3 and under. Daily 10am–5pm. Closed Jan 1, Apr 30, Oct 4, and Dec 25.

Rijksmuseum van Oudheden (National Museum of Antiquities) ★★ No visit to Leiden is complete without seeing this museum, the most comprehensive of its kind in the Netherlands. It opened in 1818, and over the years, it has acquired an impressive collection of Egyptian, Near East, Greek, and Roman artifacts. It's still a center for archaeological research. The first exhibit to catch your eye will be the magnificent "Egyptian Temple of Taffeh" from the 1st century A.D.—the museum's gem. Greek and Roman sculpture are well represented, and there are some beautiful examples of Greek decorated ceramics. The top floor provides an overview of the

Roots of a Love Affair

In the spring of 1594, a highly respected yet perennially disgruntled botanist, Carolus Clusius, strode purposefully into the Hortus Botanicus, his research garden at the University of Leiden. He stopped beside a flower bed where an experiment begun the year before was coming to fruition, and cast a critical eye over splashes of color nodding their heads in the spring breeze. Clusius was no great admirer of humanity, but flowers were something else, so we may suppose that his dyspeptic disposition softened for a moment as he paused to admire the first tulips ever grown in Holland. A nation's love affair with a flower had begun.

archaeological finds in the Netherlands from prehistoric times to the early Middle Ages.

Rapenburg 28 (at Houtstraat). ✆ **071/516-3163.** www.rmo.nl. Admission 9€ adults, 7.50€ seniors, 5.50€ children 13–17, free for children 12 and under, 25€ family. Tues–Sun (also Mon on national holidays and during school vacations) 10am–5pm. Closed Jan 1, Apr 30, and Dec 25.

OTHER ATTRACTIONS

Hortus Botanicus der Rijksuniversiteit (University Botanical Garden) ★ The first tulip bulbs were brought to Holland in 1593 by the botanist Carolus Clusius, who planted them at the Hortus Botanicus in Leiden. Tulips soon became highly popular, especially among the aristocracy. The Hortus is near the Weddesteeg, the small street where Rembrandt was born. This garden was established by students and professors of the University of Leiden in 1590. Researchers grew tropical trees and plants such as banana plants, ferns, and flesh-eating plants in greenhouses. Many of the old specimens are still thriving today. The original garden has been reconstructed in the Clusius Garden. There's a minimalist Japanese garden.

Rapenburg 73 (at Nonnensteeg). ✆ **071/527-7249.** www.hortus.leidenuniv.nl. Admission 6€ adults, 3€ children 4–12, free for children 3 and under. Apr–Oct daily 10am–6pm; Nov–Mar Tues–Sun 10am–4pm. Closed Jan 1, Oct 3, and last week of Dec.

Molen Museum (Windmill Museum) de Valk This small museum, in a monumental windmill nicknamed "the Falcon," which sticks up like a sore thumb on Molenwerf in the middle of town, contains exhibits dedicated to various types of windmills. The focus is on the history of grinding grain and on the construction and workings of a corn mill.

Tweede Binnenvestgracht 1 (at Lammermarkt). ✆ **071/516-5353.** http://molendevalk.leiden.nl. Admission 3€ adults, 1.70€ seniors and children 6–15, free for children 5 and under. Tues–Sat 10am–5pm; Sun and holidays 1–5pm.

Where to Stay

Hotel de Doelen This hotel is situated on one of the most beautiful and stately canals in Old Leiden. Part of the building was formerly a patrician's house, dating from 1638. The higher-priced rooms have open hearths; with their high ceilings, they're grand and comfortable. A wonderful painted ceiling fresco is in the breakfast room.

Rapenburg 2 (at Breestraat), 2311 EV Leiden. ✆ **071/512-0527.** Fax 071/512-8453. www.dedoelen.com. 16 units. 105€ double. AE, DC, MC, V. Limited street parking. *In room:* TV, minibar, Wi-Fi (16€/day).

LIVING history

For a fun and educational excursion for the whole family, visit the fascinating historical theme park **Archeon ★**, Archeonlaan 1 (✆ **0172/447-703;** www.archeon.nl), 12km (7½ miles) east of Leiden, on the southern edge of Alphen aan den Rijn. You follow the trail of human development and join people in their everyday activities through the ages. You visit a Stone Age settlement populated by hunter-gatherers, and walk through a Roman village on your way to the amphitheater to watch a contest between gladiators. The last stop is a medieval town, where you watch artisans at work and are taken to the marketplace by a group of beggars and musicians to watch a farce unfold.

The park is open April to October Tuesday to Sunday (and some Mon) from 10am to 5pm. Admission is 17€ for adults, 16€ for seniors, 15€ for children 4 to 10, and free for children 3 and under; it's 1.75€ per person extra weekends in July and August. Take the train to Alphen aan den Rijn; you then need either to take a **Connexxion** taxi from outside the station (✆ **0900/200-0150**), or walk for 2.4km (1½ miles). By car, take N11 from Leiden to Alphen aan den Rijn.

Where to Dine

Annie's DUTCH/CONTINENTAL This lively restaurant at water level has vaulted cellars that are a favorite eating spot for both students and locals, who spill out onto the canal-side terrace in fine weather. When the canals are frozen, the view is enchanting, as skaters practice their turns. The dinner menu is simple but wholesome. During the day, enjoy sandwiches or tapas.

Hoogstraat 1A (at Oude Rijn). ✆ **071/512-5737.** www.annies.nu. Main courses 13€–28€. MC, V. Sun-Mon noon–1am; Tues and Thurs–Fri 11am–1am; Wed and Sat 10am–1am.

Stadscafé van der Werff ★ CONTINENTAL A relaxed cafe-restaurant in a grand 1930s villa on the edge of the old town, this place is popular with the town's students and ordinary citizens alike. Even if you're not enjoying dinners like Indonesian satay or surf-and-turf *kalfsbiefstukje met gebakken gambas en een kreeftensaus* (beefsteak with fried prawns in a lobster sauce), while away your evening just having a drink and reading a paper.

Steenstraat 2 (off Beestenmarkt). ✆ **071/513-0335.** www.stadscafevanderwerff.nl. Main courses 14€–20€. AE, DC, MC, V. Daily 9am–1am.

16 FRIESLAND, GRONINGEN & DRENTHE

Holland's three northern provinces were home to the earliest settlers of what is now the Netherlands. Almost another world, **Friesland** (*Freess*-luhnd) has customs and a language all its own. Which is not to say the people are not Dutch; they are, but *first* they are Frisian. In the windmill-speckled north of the province are ancient earth dwelling mounds, or *terpen,* constructed on land that was subject to frequent floods many centuries ago, before dike building began. In the southwest is a cluster of lakes, and in the southeast are woodlands and moorlands covered in heather. Four of Holland's five Wadden Islands belong to Friesland.

Although not as varied, **Groningen** has its share of historical sites, among them its own mound villages. The provincial capital, the city of Groningen, has the vibrant atmosphere of a university town, with architectural touches from a history that stretches back beyond the 12th century. The past is most eloquent at places like the 15th-century Menkemaborg manor house in Uithuizen, the fortress town of Bourtange, a 15th-century monastery, and any number of picturesque old villages.

Sparsely populated **Drenthe** is a green, tranquil, rural haven. The Dutch have dubbed this land of deep forests, broad moors, small lakes, and villages *Mooi Drenthe* (Beautiful Drenthe). It hosts prehistoric *hunebedden* (giants' beds), huge megalith constructions that served early inhabitants as burial sites. Farming provides a satisfactory living in Drenthe, to judge from the size of farmhouses and barns. Church spires, which elsewhere stick up through the haze on the horizon, are mostly hidden behind the trees of a province that hosts three national parks: Drentsche Aa, Drents-Friese Wold, and Dwingelderveld.

LEEUWARDEN (LJOUWERT)

111km (69 miles) NE of Amsterdam

Be sure to take time to look around Friesland's pleasant, unassuming capital. But don't make a visit to Leeuwarden a substitute for getting out into the province's wide-open spaces. It may be the provincial center, but the town's burghers themselves affirm wryly that visitors wash up on their

doorstep only when it rains. An important trading town as far back as the 11th century, on a gulf of the Wadden Sea that has since been drained, Leeuwarden (pop. 92,000) is a university town and has a large student community.

Essentials

GETTING THERE Leeuwarden is the hub of Friesland's thin rail network and has good connections from around the country. Two **trains** arrive hourly from Amsterdam; the ride takes around 2 hours and 20 minutes (transfer in Amersfoort), and a one-way ticket is 24€ in second class and 41€ in first class. The train and bus stations are both on Stationsplein, south of the city center.

By **car** from Amsterdam, the shortest way—a distance by road of 137km (85 miles)—is on A7/E22 north across the Afsluitdijk, and then north and east on N31 and A31.

VISITOR INFORMATION **VVV Leeuwarden,** Sophialaan 4, 8911 AE Leeuwarden (✆ **0900/202-4060;** www.vvvleeuwarden.nl), is 2 blocks north of the rail station. The office is open Monday from noon to 5:30pm, Tuesday to Friday from 9:30am to 5:30pm, and Saturday from 10am to 4pm.

Independent Spirits

Frisian (Frysk) is spoken by two-thirds of the 600,000 inhabitants of Friesland, which is known to the natives as Fryslân. Road signs are in both Dutch and Frisian (I've put the Frisian name for localities in this chapter in parentheses after the Dutch). These highly independent folk have their own flag, their own national anthem, and their own sense of belonging to a nation that long predated the Netherlands. They even have their own *nasjonale slokje* (national drink): potent, heart-warming Beerenburger herbal bitter.

What to See & Do

Fries Museum ★ Friesland's "national" museum started in 1881 in the Eysinga House, the 18th-century home of a local nobleman, which has since been extended several times. The ground-floor rooms have been restored to their appearance when Mr. Eysinga lived here with his family. On the second floor is a series of stylized 19th-century period rooms and folk costumes. The third floor holds a collection of colorfully painted traditional Hindeloopen furniture. A gallery of paintings includes Rembrandt's portrait of his wife, Saskia, the mayor's daughter—they were married in 1634 in the nearby village of Sint-Anna Parochie (St. Anne). Finally, don't miss the exhibit on the World War I spy Mata Hari (see "Mata Hari," below), the highlight of which is a period recreation of a Parisian salon.

A subterranean tunnel leads to a museum annex in the Renaissance **Kanselarij (Chancellery)** from 1571, the seat of the Frisian High Court of Justice during the reign of King Philip II of Spain (1555–81). Here you can trace the history of the Frisians by way of prehistoric objects dating back to the Ice Age and medieval and Renaissance treasures, and peruse a collection of modern Frisian art. A statue of Emperor Charles V adorns the roof. In the Kanselarij attic is the moving **Verzetsmuseum Friesland/Frisian Resistance Museum** (✆ **058/212-0111;** www.verzetsmuseum.nl; same admission and hours). A collection of photos, personal mementos, and other items documents the bravery of the Frisian Resistance in World War II and the daily rigors of life under Nazi occupation.

Turfmarkt 11 (east of the Stadhuis, across the canal). ✆ **058/255-5500.** www.friesmuseum.nl. Admission 6€ adults, 3€ children 13–17, free for children 12 and under, free to all Wed. Tues–Sun 11am–5pm. Closed Jan 1 and Dec 25. Bus: 31 to Wortelhaven.

Keramiekmuseum Princessehof (Ceramics Museum) In the 18th century, this elegant neoclassical building in the center of town was the home of Princess Maria Louiza van Hessen-Kassel (1688–1765), the mother of Stadhouder of the Netherlands William IV and widow of Prince of Orange Jan Willem Friso. One of the rooms, the Nassau-Kamer, is preserved just as it was in her time. The museum holds what's said to be the world's largest collection of tiles, among them Dutch, Spanish, Portuguese, and Persian work, and a marvelous collection of Chinese porcelain and ceramics.

Grote Kerkstraat 11 (3 blocks northwest of the Stadhuis). ✆ **058/294-8958.** www.princessehof.nl. Admission 8€ adults, 6€ children 13–18, free for children 12 and under. Tues–Sun 11am–5pm. Closed Jan 1, Apr 30, and Dec 25. Bus: 12 or 36 to Boterhoek.

Mata Hari

The most famous figure in Leeuwarden's history was born here in 1876 as Margaretha Geertruida Zelle, but gained notoriety as Mata Hari. Margaretha grew up in a wealthy family and at the age of 19 married an army officer and left for the Dutch East Indies. She returned to Holland in 1902.

With her marriage falling apart, Margaretha left for Paris, where she performed as an Asian dancer. There she adopted the name "Mata Hari"—meaning "eye of the day" or "sun" in Malaysian. Her nude dancing became a sensation. During World War I, she had affairs with high-ranking Allied officers and allegedly passed pillow-talk military secrets to the Germans. In any case, her naiveté and yarn spinning led to her downfall. She was executed by the French in 1917.

MORE PLACES OF INTEREST

A bronze plaque placed by the DeWitt Historical Society of Ithaca, New York State, adorns Friesland's **Provinciehuis (Provincial House)** at Tweebaksmarkt 52. The house, a few blocks south of the Fries Museum, dates from 1570 and has a 1784 facade. The plaque was presented in 1909 to the people of Leeuwarden in gratitude for their having been the first to vote for recognition of the fledgling United States in 1782. (Holland was the first country to extend recognition to the U.S.) A letter written by John Adams in 1783 expresses his personal thanks. Another document of interest relates to Petrus Stuiffsandt, the same Peter Stuyvesant who had such an important role in America's beginnings, and who was born in Friesland. The Provinciehuis is open at variable times; inquire at the VVV office. Admission is free.

Just west, beside the canal at Korfmakerspijp, is a statue of **Mata Hari.**

A NEARBY NATIONAL PARK

Head out of town south and southeast on N31 to the marshes, lakes, and water channels in the **Nationaal Park De Alde Feanen (The Old Fens) ★**. If pottering around in peat bogs is your thing, you'll love this place. In typical Dutch style, the park is small—it covers just 25 sq. km. (9½ sq. miles)—though it won't seem so on the ground, or on the water. Yet it covers an important wetlands resource and is filled with rare plants, waterbirds, and aquatic life. You can get around by boat, hiking, or bicycling. The park's **Bezoekerscentrum (Visitor Center)** is at Koaidyk 8A, Earnewoude (Earnewâld; ✆ **0511/539-618;** www.dealdefeanen.nl), on the park's eastern edge.

Boat tours are operated from Eernewoude by **Rondvaardij Princenhof** (✆ **0511/539-334;** www.rondvaardij-princenhof.nl). The line's menu of cruise options begins with a basic 2-hour tour in the national park that's 9.50€ for adults, 5.50€ for children 5 to 12, and free for children 4 and under.

Where to Stay

Eden Oranje Hotel ★ You'd never suspect that the Oranje, which looks ultracontemporary on both the outside and the inside, has been standing in this great location across the street from the train station since 1879, within an easy walk of nearly everything you'll want to see in Leeuwarden. It now belongs to the Eden chain, and all of the guest rooms have been updated. Even the largest are not overly spacious,

Tale from the Crypt

The crypt of the village church in Wieuwerd (Wiuwert), 12km (7½ miles) southwest of Leeuwarden, evidently has the power to prevent corpses from decomposing. Four from an original 11 naturally mummified bodies dating from the early 17th century can be seen—nobody seems to know what happened to the other seven! The church is open April to October Monday to Saturday from 10 to 11:30am and 1 to 4:30pm; admission to the crypt is 1.50€, and free for children 5 and under.

but neither are they cramped. Lots of locals come to dine at the sophisticated French/Dutch restaurant, **Van Buren.**

Stationsweg 4 (facing the rail station), 8911 AG Leeuwarden. ✆ **058/212-6241.** Fax 058/212-1441. www.edenhotelgroup.com. 78 units. 75€–155€ double. AE, DC, MC, V. Parking 10€. Bus: All buses to Leeuwarden Station. **Amenities:** Restaurant; bar; room service. *In room:* A/C, TV, minibar, Wi-Fi (10€/day).

Where to Dine

Coffee Club De Waag ★ LIGHT FARE In the atmospheric 16th-century Weigh House, on a canalside packed with inexpensive eateries, this friendly little coffeehouse is worth visiting for the location alone. During the summer, you can drink your coffee and eat a snack on a terrace overlooking the canal that runs along the town's main shopping street.

Nieuwestad 148 (at Waagplein). ✆ **058/215-9352.** Snacks 4€–10€. MC, V. Mon–Sat 10am–6pm. Bus: 31 to De Waag.

A LUXURY CHÂTEAU-HOTEL NEARBY

Bilderberg Landgoed Lauswolt ★★ On the edge of the village of Beetsterzwaag (Beetstersweach) is this gracious three-story château dating from 1868. Green lawns and huge shady trees surround the lovely place, and an 18-hole golf course is just across the way. The grounds contain beautiful forest walks, and the decor—in both public rooms and guest rooms—is elegant. A high level of service, a pool, and the La Prairie wellness center just add to the attractions here. The restaurant, **De Heeren van Harinxma,** where you dine by candlelight in a paneled dining room overlooking a garden, enjoys a top reputation throughout this part of Holland and is a member of the prestigious Alliance Gastronomique Néerlandaise.

Van Harinxmaweg 10, 9244 CJ Beetsterzwaag (45km/28 miles southeast of Leeuwarden). ✆ **0512/381-245.** Fax 0512/381-496. www.bilderberg.nl. 65 units. 175€–275€ double; from 350€ suite. AE, DC, MC, V. Free parking. Take N31 from Leeuwarden to Drachten, then join Expwy. A7, heading toward Heerenveen, and take the Beetsterzwaag exit (no. 28). Pass through the center of Beetsterzwaag, and look for the hotel on its outskirts, on the right. **Amenities:** Restaurant; bar; nearby golf course; health club; heated indoor pool; room service; sauna; tennis courts. *In room:* TV, minibar, Wi-Fi (13€/day).

Franeker (Frjentsjer)

17km (11 miles) W of Leeuwarden

Once an important Frisian cultural and trading center, Franeker is today an enchanting small town. A young Peter Stuyvesant, who would later govern the Dutch Nieuw Nederland (New York State) colony from 1646 to 1664, studied at the now-closed university here. In the center of town, stop to admire the **Stadhuis (Town Hall),** from 1591, a fine example of Northern Dutch Renaissance architecture.

Of Blades & Ice

Ice skating stirs the blood of any true Frisian, and no event stirs it more than the Elfstedentocht (Eleven Cities Tour), a tough ice-skating hypermarathon that follows the canals on a loop of just under 200km (124 miles) through 11 medieval Frisian towns, beginning in Bolsward (Boalsert). The first race was run in 1909, and it has been run only 14 times since, when the canals freeze solidly enough. When it was last run, in 1997, it drew 16,000 skaters and a half-million onlookers. In 1985, skater Evert van Benthem clocked a record time for the tour, getting around in 6 hours and 47 minutes; but Henk Angenet's time of 6 hours and 49 minutes in 1997 yielded a faster average speed on that year's slightly longer course.

Koninklijk Eise Eisinga Planetarium ★ Franeker's highlight is this simple, restored period house of wool comber Eise Eisinga. Over a period of 7 years between 1774 and 1781, Eisinga spent his leisure hours building a scale representation of the solar system on his ceiling. An amateur astronomer, he wanted to prove to fearful neighbors that the planetary conjunction of May 8, 1774, didn't mean the end of the world was nigh. Guides are on hand to explain the "Royal Planetarium's" mechanism, which still functions and was accurate for the knowledge of that time, before the discovery of Uranus, Neptune, and Pluto.

Eise Eisingastraat 3 (at Groenmarkt). ✆ **0517/393-070.** www.planetarium-friesland.nl. Admission 4.50€ adults, 4€ seniors, 3.75€ children 5–14, free for children 4 and under. Apr–Oct Sun–Mon 1–5pm, Tues–Sat 10am–5pm; Nov–Mar Tues–Sat 10am–5pm, Sun 1–5pm. Closed Jan 1 and Dec 25.

THE EASTERN IJSSELMEER SHORE ★★

From the long barrier of the Afsluitdijk, the east shore of Holland's great lake curves south through a string of historic towns that shelter behind the coastal dike. To complete the "Golden Circle" of the IJsselmeer, see "The Western IJsselmeer Shore," in chapter 14, and "Lelystad & the Noordoostpolder," in chapter 17.

Makkum

30km (19 miles) W of Leeuwarden; 17km (11 miles) SW of Franeker

A small harbor town 8km (5 miles) south of the Afsluitdijk, Makkum has been home to tile makers and ceramics craftspeople since the 1500s. Getting there by bus from Leeuwarden takes around an hour. Take Connexxion Qliner bus no. 350 from Leeuwarden bus station; transfer at the Afsluitdijk to Connexxion bus no. 96 for Makkum. It's a lot easier to get around by car in these parts.

WHAT TO SEE & DO

Connoisseur, polychrome Makkumware ceramics—fully the equal of Delftware—are produced at the workshop of **Koninklijke Tichelaar Makkum ★**, Turfmarkt 65 (✆ **0515/231-341;** www.tichelaar.nl), a pottery maker founded in 1572 (if not earlier), and owned by the Tichelaar family since 1689. Guides take you through the entire production process, in which craftspeople employ the same procedures as in

A Frisian Heritage Trail

The engaging Aldfaers Erf (Forefathers' Heritage) Route passes through a trail of restored antique buildings—a grocery, schoolhouse, bakery (which serves Frisian pastries), church, bird museum, farm, and more—in the villages of Exmorra, Allingawier, Ferwoude, and Piaam, which lie in the triangle formed by Makkum, Workum, and Bolsward. The route of around 20km (12 miles) is clearly signposted on minor roads and through villages, and the buildings are open May to September daily 10am to 5pm. A map and a ticket for all sights cost 7.95€ for adults, 4.50€ for children 5 to 16, free for children 4 and under, and 23€ for a family. Purchase the map and ticket from any of the sights from Stichting Aldfaers Erf, Meerweg 4, Allingawier (✆ 0515/231-631; www.aldfaerserf.nl), open April to October Tuesday to Sunday from 10am to 5pm.

the 17th century. Watch the exquisite designs being painted by hand. Tichelaars is sold in specialized stores all over the country. At the salesroom, you can buy anything from a simple tile to a larger piece with an elaborate design. To distinguish genuine Royal Tichelaar Makkumware from generic Makkumware knock-offs, look for the company's hallmark of two scripted *T*s overlapped like crossed swords. The workshop is open Monday from 1 to 5:30pm, and Tuesday to Saturday from 10am to 5pm. Admission is free.

Makkum's **Waag (Weigh House),** a square, towerlike structure in the heart of town dating from 1698, constructed of brick and topped with an elegant steeple, was used for weighing cheese and butter. Its ground floor has quaint, oval windows; the upper floors have shuttered windows.

Heading south from Makkum to **Workum (Warkum),** take in the intriguing modern art of beloved local artist Jopie Huisman (1922–2000). The **Jopie Huisman Museum,** Noard 6 (**✆ 0515/543-131;** www.jopiehuismanmuseum.nl), is open April to October Monday to Saturday from 10am to 5pm and Sunday and holidays from 1 to 5pm; November to December and February to March, it's open daily from 1 to 5pm. Admission is 6€ for adults, 2€ for children 6 to 12, and free for children 5 and under.

Hindeloopen (Hylpen) ★★

39km (24 miles) SW of Leeuwarden; 20km (12 miles) S of Makkum

Like something out of a Dutch fairy tale, this tiny 13th-century Hanseatic League trading port on the IJsselmeer is filled with charming houses and crisscrossed by small canals with wooden bridges. Talented craftspeople from the village have for centuries adorned their homes, furniture, cupboard beds, and even wooden coat hangers with vivid colors and intricately entwined vines and flowers. It's thought the designs were originally brought from Scandinavia by Hindeloopen sailors who sailed the North Sea in the days when the IJsselmeer was the Zuiderzee.

ESSENTIALS

GETTING THERE Hourly **trains** go from both Leeuwarden and Stavoren (see below) to Hindeloopen station, just outside the village; the ride takes 40 minutes from Leeuwarden and 9 minutes from Stavoren. From the station, it's a walk of just under 2km (1¼ miles) into Hindeloopen; or take Connexxion bus no. 102. **Cars** are not allowed in many of the village's narrow streets.

VISITOR INFORMATION **VVV Hindeloopen,** Nieuwstad 26, 8713 JL Hindeloopen (✆ **0514/851-223;** www.vvvhindeloopen.nl), is on the village's eastern edge. The office is open Monday to Friday from 10am to 5pm and Sunday from 11am to 4pm.

Clogged Up

Friesland is a great country for clogs. Farmers, country folk, and even some townspeople wear the genuine—as distinct from the tourist—version of these traditional shoes, made from poplar wood and leather. They do so not as an affectation but as plain, functional footgear.

WHAT TO SEE & DO

A good place to view Hindeloopen's decorative designs is the **Museum Hindeloopen,** Dijkweg 1 (✆ **0514/521-420;** www.museumhindeloopen.nl), across from the village's 17th-century **Grote Kerk (Great Church),** on the northwest edge of town. Each room presents a varied collection of period furniture and local costumes. There's a splendid selection of Dutch tiles, and every wooden surface seems covered in bright designs. The museum is open April to October Monday to Friday from 11am to 5pm and Saturday, Sunday, and holidays from 1:30 to 5pm. Admission is 3€ for adults, 2.25€ for seniors, 1.80€ for children 6 to 16, free for children 5 and under, and 7.50€ for families.

Alternatively, you could visit one of the village workshops and see for yourself how the furniture is decorated. **Het Roosje,** Nieuwstad 44 (✆ **0514/521-251;** www.roosjehindeloopen.com), is a workshop established in 1894 that specializes in woodcarving.

WHERE TO DINE

't Kalkoentje ★ TRADITIONAL DUTCH The magical "Little Turkey" makes for a more interesting choice than the more touristy (but still good) eateries that shelter behind Hindeloopen's lakeshore dike. Here the views are of the town's quaint streets and 17th-century Great Church, and the nearest water is a narrow canal of the kind the Dutch call a *sloot,* above which the restaurant's balcony terrace perches. Inside is a convivial Old Dutch scene of brick pillars, stone walls, ship models, and an open-hearth fire in the middle. The menu is replete with hearty fish and meat dishes—the turkey filet would seem an appropriate choice.

Buren 1 (across from the Grote Kerk). ✆ **0514/521-257.** www.kalkoentje.com. Main courses 17€–23€. MC, V. Mar Tues–Thurs and Sat–Sun noon–10pm; Apr–June Tues–Fri 10am–10pm, Sat–Sun noon–10pm; July–Aug Mon–Sat 10am–10pm, Sun noon–10pm; Sept–Oct Tues–Thurs 10am–10pm, Sat–Sun noon–10pm. Closed Nov–Feb (except for pre-booked groups).

Stavoren (Starum) ★

46km (29 miles) SW of Leeuwarden; 7km (4½ miles) SW of Hindeloopen

Founded in 500 B.C. and once a capital of the ancient Frisian kings, then a medieval mercantile center and member of the powerful Hanseatic League, Stavoren has shriveled considerably from those heady days. Yet it remains a handsome small harbor town, for fishing boats and pleasure craft. Small boats and antique Frisian *skûtsje* sailing vessels shuttle through the town's Johan Friso Canal between the IJsselmeer and the Frisian lakes.

An hourly **train** from Leeuwarden stops in end-of-the-line Stavoren. In summer months, the MS *Bep Glasius* (1966), a passenger-and-bike ferry operated by **Rederij V&O** (✆ **0228/326-667;** www.veerboot.info), crosses over to and from Enkhuizen on the IJsselmeer's western shore, a 90-minute trip, from where there are train connections with Amsterdam (see "The Western IJsselmeer Shore," in chapter 14). Fares are 13€ round-trip and 9.80€ one-way for adults, 7.60€ round-trip and 6.20€ one-way for children 4 to 11, and free for children 3 and under. Bikes cost 4.90€ one-way and 6.90€ round-trip.

Visitor information is available from **VVV Stavoren,** Stationsweg 7, 8715 ES Stavoren (✆ **0514/682-424;** www.stavoren.nl). The office is open mid-April to October Monday to Saturday 9:15am to noon and 1:30 to 6pm, and Sunday 9:15 to 10:30am, 1:30 to 2:30pm, and 5:30 to 6pm.

SNEEK (SNITS) ★

20km (12 miles) SW of Leeuwarden; 26km (16 miles) NE of Stavoren

The placid inland waterways—lakes, canals, and rivers—around Sneek (pronounced *Snayk,* like "snake") have made this Friesland's most important sailing center, with a marina and sailing schools in the bustling town (pop. 33,000).

Essentials

GETTING THERE **Trains** go from Leeuwarden to Sneek, a 20-minute ride, every half-hour. By **car** from Leeuwarden, take A32 south to junction 15, and then go west on N354.

VISITOR INFORMATION **VVV Sneek,** Marktstraat 18, 8601 CV Sneek (✆ **0515/414-096;** fax 0514/423-703; www.vvvsneek.nl), is in the center of town. The office is open Monday to Friday from 9:30am to 6pm (to 9pm Thurs Apr–Sept), and Saturday from 9:30am to 5pm.

What to See & Do

In the old, canal-ringed center of town, note the rococo facade on the 16th-century **Stadhuis (Town Hall)** on Marktstraat, which is close to the landmark **Martinikerk (St Martin's Church),** from the same century.

Interested in ships and the sea? Spare some time for the **Fries Scheepvaartmuseum (Frisian Maritime Museum),** Kleinzand 14 (✆ **0515/414-057;** www.friesscheepvaartmuseum.nl), in a canal-side house from 1844 east of Markstraat. The first part focuses on Friesland's maritime traditions on the sea, lakes, and inland waterways. Models of old sailing ships, marine paintings, reconstructed boat interiors, and more allow you to just about smell the salt tang of the sea. Antique local silver, paintings, and recreated house interiors are in the second part. The museum is open Monday to Saturday from 10am to 5pm and Sunday from noon to 5pm (closed Jan 1, Easter Sunday, Pentecost Sunday, Ascension Thursday, and Dec 25). Admission is 3€ for adults, 2.50€ for seniors, 1€ for children 6 to 12, and free for children 5 and under.

Astride the entrance to the port in the south of the old town rise the twin octagonal turrets of the brick Renaissance **Waterpoort,** a gate from 1613 and the only remains of the town's defense walls, which were razed in the 18th century.

Sailing Days

During 2 weeks in July and August, Friesland falls under the spell of the Skûtsjesilen (Skûtsje Sailing) races between traditional flat-bottomed sailing barges. These boats, 20m (66 ft.) long, once used for transporting goods on the Zuiderzee, race on the lakes around Sneek and on the IJsselmeer from Stavoren. More than a dozen boats compete, dating from 1910 to 1930. They don't look too maneuverable, but the crews have an arsenal of tricks designed to outwit their rivals. **VVV Sneek** (see above) can provide information on dates and places, or visit the race organizers at **www.skutsjesilen.nl.**

THE FRIESE MEREN (FRISIAN LAKES) ★

The constellation of lakes south of Sneek—Pikmeer, Snekermeer, Heegermeer, Slotermeer, and Tjeukemeer—is the main tourism region in Friesland. In the summer, you can rent powerboats, sailboats, rowboats, and canoes. The lakes are connected by rivers and canals so you can easily move between them.

Among the most attractive places around is **Sloten (Sleat),** beautifully sited on a tree-fringed canal south of the Slotermeer. The village's narrow streets lined by 17th-century houses make for a pleasant stroll. Just west of here is the forested **Gaasterland** district, which contains a hamlet called Nieuw Amerika and is good for hiking.

Southeast of the lakes, at **Wolvega (Wolvegea),** snap a picture of the statue of Peter Stuyvesant, the governor of Nieuw Nederland (New York State), who was born in 1592 at the hamlet of Scherpenzeel (Skerpenseel), 10km (6 miles) west.

THE WADDENZEE COAST

Traveling north through Friesland along the Waddenzee (Wadden Sea) coast, you won't actually see much of the sea unless you walk up onto the sea dike from time to time for a better view. The Wadden Sea is an important European staging area on bird migration routes, a stopover zone where waterfowl as well as shore and wading birds rest and feed. In 2009 the sea was declared a UNESCO World Natural Heritage site.

Harlingen (Harns)

24km (15 miles) W of Leeuwarden

This bustling seaport and former whaling town (pop. 16,000), founded in the 9th century, hunkers down behind a dike on the Wadden Sea. Fishing boats, cargo ships, and ferries to the offshore Wadden Islands shuttle in and out of the busy harbor, and canalboats and recreational craft ply the van Harinxma Canal that leads east to Leeuwarden.

ESSENTIALS

GETTING THERE **Trains** depart every half-hour from Leeuwarden to Harlingen; the ride takes 23 minutes. By **car** from Leeuwarden, take N383 and A31 west.

VISITOR INFORMATION **TIP Info Harlingen,** Grote Bredeplaats 17B, 8861 BA Harlingen (✆ **0517/430-207;** fax 0517/434-592; www.harlingen-friesland.nl), is off Zuiderhaven, close to the harbor. The office is open Monday from 1 to 5pm, Tuesday to Friday from 10am to 5pm, and Saturday from 10am to 4pm.

WHAT TO SEE & DO

Harlingen is a maze of canals filled with fishing boats and recreational craft, and lined with gabled 16th- to 18th-century houses and warehouses in its carefully preserved old center. Close to the ferry dock is one of several statues around Holland that represent the legend of the boy who saved the community from a calamity by sticking his finger in a leaking dike.

Moderately interesting seafaring and whaling exhibits, ship models, seascape paintings, antiques, porcelain, and silver are all to be seen in the **Hannemahuis,** Voorstraat 56 (✆ **0517/413-658;** www.hannemahuis.nl), in the 18th-century Hannemahuis. The municipal museum is open Tuesday to Friday from 11am to 5pm and Saturday, Sunday, and holidays from 1:30 to 5pm (closed Jan 1, Easter Sun, Apr 30, Pentecost Sun, and Dec 25 and 31). Admission is 3.50€ for adults, 1.50€ for children 6 to 16, and free for children 5 and under.

Since 1973, craftspeople have produced and painted by hand traditional-style Frisian pottery and tiles at the **Harlinger Aardewerk- en Tegelfabriek,** Voorstraat 84 (✆ **0517/415-362;** www.harlinger.nl), in the heart of the Old Town. The workshop is open Monday to Friday from 8am to 6pm and Saturday from 9am to 5pm; admission is free. Should you need to choose between a visit to this workshop or to Tichelaar in Makkum (see earlier in this chapter), Tichelaar produces the more prestigious wares, but Harlinger's are perhaps more individual.

WHERE TO STAY & DINE

Hotel-Restaurant Anna Casparii This charming canal-house hotel on the north bank of the yacht harbor has comfortable and attractive guest rooms. Ask for one with a view of the boat dock. The moderately priced restaurant specializes in seafood fresh off the boats that sail into the town's harbor. Bikes are available to rent for 10€ a day.
Noorderhaven 69 (4 blocks east of the island ferry terminal), 8861 AL Harlingen. ✆ **0517/412-065.** Fax 0517/414-540. www.annacasparii.nl. 14 units. 93€–120€ double. Rates include Dutch breakfast. AE, DC, MC, V. Limited street parking. **Amenities:** Restaurant; lounge; bikes. *In room:* TV, minibar.

Dokkum

19km (12 miles) NE of Leeuwarden; 42km (26 miles) NE of Harlingen

The northernmost terminus of the Eleven Cities Tours (see "Of Blades & Ice," earlier in this chapter), Dokkum is a pleasant small town, constructed on two *terpen* (earthen mounds). You can reach Dokkum on Connexxion bus no. 50 from Leeuwarden, a half-hour ride.

Remnants of the town's 16th-century walls and moat date from a period when the town was a seaport. St. Boniface, the English monk Wynfryth, was martyred here in 754 while on a mission to convert the pagan Frisians. That's about it history-wise until 1618, when Dokkum was made headquarters of the Friesland Admiralty.

Water Beds

Harlingen has three highly unusual lodging options that fit right in with its seaport heritage: the Vuurtoren van Harlingen, a retired lighthouse; the Reddingsboot in Harlingen, a retired lifeboat; and the Havenkraan van Harlingen, in the cabin of a retired harbor crane. For more information, contact Dromen aan Zee (✆ 0517/414-410; www.vuurtoren-harlingen.nl).

Frisian High

Climb Friesland's highest elevation, in the Fochteloërveen (Fochtelerfean) fenlands, near Appelscha (Appelskea), in the province's southeast. This original natural landscape, covering 26sq. km (10 sq. miles), has been awarded European Natura 2000 protected status. Unless you have a bad case of vertigo, you won't get dizzy up there—it's just 26m (85 ft.) above sea level.

In the restored former Admiralty building, from 1618, on the waterfront in the heart of town, the **Museum Het Admiraliteitshuis,** Diepswal 27 (✆ **0519/293-134;** www.museumdokkum.nl), exhibits a mixed bag of antiquities, antiques, and Frisian folk art and traditional costumes. The museum is open Tuesday to Saturday from 1 to 5pm. Admission is 4€ for adults, 2€ for children 6 to 16, and free for children 5 and under.

AROUND DOKKUM

The scenic north Friesland country around Dokkum is speckled with windmills, and with villages and farmhouses constructed atop *terpen.* Friesland makes a big deal of its hundreds of *terpen,* but you'd have to be a genuine enthusiast for these small man-made hillocks to want to go out of your way to visit more than a few. Most of them are between 2 and 6m (6½–20 ft.) high. **Hoogebeintum (Hegebeintum),** 10km (6 miles) west of Dokkum, boasts the highest *terp,* 9m (30 ft.) above sea level, and a beautiful 17th-century church.

Southeast of Dokkum is the neat little village of **Veenklooster,** with thatched cottages around a *brink* (green), and a nearby abbey, the **Fogelsanghstate,** from 1725, which houses a branch of Leeuwarden's Fries Museum. **Bergumermeer** and Klein Zwitserland (Little Switzerland) are to the south.

Going northeast from Dokkum brings you to the **Lauwersmeer,** a man-made freshwater lake that was an inlet of the Waddenzee until it was cut off in 1969 by a barrier dam. Its sheltered waters provide a haven for birds, and for sailing and other watersports. Cross the dam-top road to Lauwersoog in Groningen province, from where ferries sail to Schiermonnikoog (see below).

WADDENEILANDEN (FRYSKE EILANNEN) ★★

The five beautiful and highly individual Wadden Islands—low-lying, dune-laden, windswept barrier islands—are connected by ferry across the Waddenzee (Wadden Sea) from adjacent mainland harbors. This shallow sea's depth ranges from about 1 to 3m (3–10 ft.), and at low tide it virtually disappears. The Dutch treasure these small islands as romantic getaways. On a line curving north and east, they are: Texel, Vlieland, Terschelling, Ameland, and Schiermonnikoog. Texel belongs to Noord-Holland and is covered separately (see "Den Helder & Texel," in chapter 14). The remaining four islands belong to Friesland.

These havens of wild natural beauty encompass miles of white sand on wide beaches along the North Sea coasts, marshes, and wetlands that are sanctuaries for thousands of migratory seabirds, seals sunning on sandbanks, rare plants, old villages, and museums connected with the sea and seafarers. Most vacationers visit between the spring and fall; only a hardy few brave the winter gales.

The best way to get around is by bicycle. You can rent bikes on the islands, though they get scarce during the busiest periods. The island VVV offices have information on bungalows, campsites, bed-and-breakfasts, and hotels.

Vlieland (Flylân)

A thin strip of beach and dunes, 19km (12 miles) long and a maximum of 3km (2 miles) wide, Vlieland (pop. 1,200) is an ideal hide-out. Carefree and almost car-free, Vlieland is virtually deserted, except in summer. The only disturbance here is the plangent cry of seabirds—and an occasional howling flyover by Royal Netherlands Air Force F-16 Fighting Falcon jets on training sorties.

ESSENTIALS

GETTING THERE **Rederij Doeksen** (✆ **0900/363-5736;** www.rederij-doeksen.nl) operates ferry and jet-catamaran service from Harlingen (see above). A Connexxion **bus** shuttles between Harlingen train station and the harbor, connecting with the ferries to Vlieland and Terschelling (see below). The ferry ride to Vlieland takes 1½ hours one-way. A round-trip ticket is 23€ for adults, 20€ for seniors, 11€ for children 4 to 11, and free for children 3 and under. Private cars are not transported on the Vlieland ferry (except those belonging to permanent residents). The jetcat crosses over in 45 minutes, for an additional 6€ one-way for passengers of all ages. In addition, there is jet-cat service from Terschelling (30 min.) and a passenger boat from Texel (25 min.) and Terschelling (25 min.).

VISITOR INFORMATION **VVV Vlieland,** Havenweg 10, 8899 BB Vlieland (✆ **0562/451-111;** fax 0562/451-361; www.vlieland.net), is next to the ferry dock. The office is open Monday to Friday from 9am to 12:30pm and 1:30 to 5pm, and Saturday from 9:30 to 11:45am; in addition, Saturday afternoon, Sunday, and evenings after 5pm when the ferries arrive and depart.

WHAT TO SEE & DO

There's not a lot to see and do; that's the main attraction here. Sunbathing—the island has what's said to be Europe's longest naturist beach—bird-watching (at least they're *supposed* to be watching birds through those binoculars), biking, and hiking among the dunes and forests are the key activities. An important bird sanctuary is the **Natuurgebied De Kroon's Polders;** look out for **De Posthuys,** a cafe from 1837, on the edge of the reserve.

In the old-time whaling port of **Oost-Vlieland (East-Flylân),** the island's only village (its one-time sister village West-Vlieland vanished beneath the waves in 1736), the 16th-century **Trompshuys,** Dorpstraat 99 (✆ **0562/451-600;** www.trompshuys.nl), named for the 17th-century admiral Cornelis Tromp (though the house never belonged to him), hosts a local history museum, with a collection of antique clocks and other items. The museum is open May to September Tuesday to Friday from 11am to 5pm and Saturday from 2 to 5pm; October to April Tuesday to

> **For Whom the Bell Tolls**
>
> **Lloyds of London's Lutine Bell, rung when a vessel insured by the company was reported missing, came from the British bullion ship *HMS Lutine,* which shipwrecked on sandbanks between Vlieland and Terschelling in 1799.**

Saturday from 2 to 5pm. Admission is 2.75€ for adults, 2.50€ for seniors, 2€ for children 6 to 16, and free for children 5 and under.

The **Informatiecentrum De Noordwester,** Dorpstraat 150 (✆ **0562/451-700;** www.denoordwester.nl), has displays on the island's flora and fauna, and can give advice on the best places for observing the hundred or so species of birds that show up here. The information center is open on a complex monthly schedule that ranges from 10am to 5pm in high summer to 2 to 5pm in winter; it's closed from early January to mid-February. Admission is 4.50€ for adults, 3€ for children 4 to 12, and free for children 3 and under.

The VVV office organizes guided tours on an observation vehicle, the **Vliehorsexpres.**

Terschelling (Skylge) ★★

The most accessible of Friesland's four Wadden Islands, Terschelling (pop. 5,000) is a strip of beach, dunes, nature reserves, and pine forest. It's 29km (18 miles) long and a maximum of 4km (2½ miles) wide. Large and popular enough to have some things for visitors to do besides soak up the sun and admire the natural beauty, the island can be quite busy, though not crowded, in summer.

ESSENTIALS

GETTING THERE **Rederij Doeksen** (✆ **0900/363-5736;** www.rederij-doeksen.nl) operates car-ferry and jet-catamaran service from Harlingen (see above). A Connexxion **bus** shuttles between Harlingen rail station and the harbor, connecting with the ferries to Terschelling and Vlieland (see above). The ferry trip to Terschelling takes 2 hours one-way. A round-trip ticket is 23€ for adults, 20€ for seniors, 11€ for children 4 to 11, and free for children 3 and under. Taking a car is possible but not encouraged—the fare for an ordinary car alone begins at 81€ round-trip and goes up in stages to 299€ for a large auto and trailer, plus charges for above-average height and width; reservations are essential. The jetcat crosses over in 45 minutes, for an additional 6€ one-way for passengers of all ages. In addition, there is jet-cat service from Vlieland (30 min.) and a passenger boat from Ameland (3 hr.).

VISITOR INFORMATION **VVV Terschelling,** Willem Barentszkade 19A, 8881 BC West-Terschelling (✆ **0562/443-000;** fax 0562/442-875; www.vvvterschelling.nl), overlooks the harbor. The office is open May to October Monday to Saturday from 9:30am to 5:30pm, and November to April Monday to Friday from 9:30am to 5pm and Saturday from 10am to 3pm.

WHAT TO SEE & DO

West-Terschelling (West-Skylge), the island's main village, a former whaling center set in a sheltered bay on the coast facing the mainland, is dominated by the square, yellowish-colored **Brandaris Lighthouse,** 54m (177 ft.) high and constructed in 1594. A look into the lives of the islanders of yesteryear is available at **'t Behouden Huys Museum,** Commandeurstraat 30–32 (✆ **0562/442-389;** www.behouden-huys.nl), in the gabled houses constructed in 1668 for two sea captains. You'll find period rooms and displays about whaling and other local traditions. The museum is open April to mid-June and October Monday to Friday from 10am to 5pm and Saturday from 1 to 5pm (and Sun mid-June to Sept). Admission is 3€ for adults, 2€ for seniors and children 5 to 13, and free for children 4 and under.

To learn more about local geography, wildlife, and plants, visit the **Centrum voor Natuur en Landschap,** Burgemeester Reedekkerstraat 11 (✆ **0562/442-390;** www.natuurmuseumterschelling.nl). A small aquarium recreates North Sea and Wadden

A Gift from America

Cranberry pie and cranberry wine are Terschelling specialties. These are produced from berries originally brought from America, allegedly by way of a barrel washed up after a North Sea storm and tossed away in disgust by its finder, who had hoped for something stronger.

Sea environments. The center is open April to October Monday to Friday from 9am to 5pm and Saturday and Sunday from 2 to 5pm, and November to March Tuesday, Saturday, Sunday, and school vacations from 2 to 5pm. Admission is 5.50€ for adults, 3.50€ for seniors and children 4 to 12, and free for children 3 and under. An important nature reserve and bird sanctuary, **De Boschplaat ★**, occupies the eastern half of the island (access is restricted during the breeding season, mid-Mar to mid-Aug).

More thrilling is sand-sailing on the North Sea beaches, aboard a wheeled sand-yacht that can sail along at an impressive clip when the wind is strong, as it often is. Rent one on the beach from **Blokarten** (✆ **06/2533-2885;** www.sporteventsterschelling.nl).

Ameland (It Amelân)

Ameland (pop. 3,500), 24km (15 miles) long and a maximum of 4km (3 miles) wide, can be thought of as the "median" Wadden Island—not as busy nor as varied as Texel and Terschelling, not as quiet and remote as Vlieland and Schiermonnikoog, but every bit as scenic as the other four. For many visitors, it's the ideal compromise.

ESSENTIALS

GETTING THERE **Wagenborg Passagiersdiensten** (✆ **0900/455-4455** for information, or 0519/546-111 for reservations; www.wpd.nl) operates car-ferry service from a dock 4km (2½ miles) north of Holwerd (Holwert), which is itself 22km (14 miles) north of Leeuwarden. The ferry trip takes 45 minutes one-way. April to September, the round-trip fare is 13€ for adults, 12€ for seniors, 6.90€ for children 4 to 11, and free for children 3 and under; fares from October to March are around 10% cheaper. Taking a car is possible but not encouraged; the summer fare for an ordinary car begins at 84€; reservations are required. In addition, passenger boats sail from both Terschelling and Schiermonnikoog (3 hr. in both cases).

Connexxion buses connect both Groningen and Leeuwarden rail stations with the ferry dock. Going by **car** from Leeuwarden, take N357 north.

VISITOR INFORMATION **Ameland,** Bureweg 2, 9163 KE Nes (✆ **0519/546-546;** fax 0519/546-547; www.vvvameland.nl), is close to the ferry terminal. The office is open April to October Monday to Friday from 9am to 5pm and Saturday from 10am to 3pm.

WHAT TO SEE & DO

The main village and ferry port, **Nes,** in the middle of the south coast, has 17th- to 18th-century sea captains' houses. In Nes the **Natuurcentrum ★**, Strandweg 38 (✆ **0519/542-737;** www.amelandermusea.nl), takes you close to the island's natural history. It has a weather station and an aquarium containing denizens of the North Sea and Wadden Sea. The center is open April to October and during Christmas/New Year school vacation Monday to Friday from 10am to 5pm, and Saturday and

Sunday from 1 to 5pm; and November to December (outside of Christmas/New Year school vacation) Wednesday to Saturday from 1 to 5pm. Admission is 5.75€ for adults, 4€ for children 5 to 12, and free for children 4 and under.

In **Hollum,** on the west coast, the **Cultuur-Historisch Museum Sorgdrager,** Herenweg 1 (✆ **0519/554-477;** www.amelandermusea.nl) is in a sea captains' house from 1751. It employs cultural history as a cover for what's essentially a museum of whaling, an industry that once was the island's bread and butter. The museum is open mid-February to October Monday to Friday from 10am to noon and 1 to 5pm and Saturday and Sunday from 1:30 to 5pm (closed weekends Jul–Aug), and November to mid-February Wednesday to Saturday from 1:30 to 5pm. Admission is 3€ for adults, 2.50€ for children 5 to 12, and free for children 4 and under. Check out the cemetery of the village's old church for gravestones decorated with images of whaling ships.

Nearby, the **Reddingsmuseum Abraham Fock,** Oranjeweg 18 (✆ **0519/542-737;** www.amelandermusea.nl), takes as its theme the sometimes grim, sometimes buoyant, but always uplifting history of the local lifeboats and the crews who risked—and often enough, lost—their lives. The museum is open mid-February to October Monday to Friday from 10am to noon and 1 to 5pm, and Saturday and Sunday from 1:30 to 5pm (closed weekends Jul–Aug); and November to mid-February Wednesday to Saturday from 1:30 to 5pm. Admission is 4€ for adults, 3€ for children 5 to 12, and free for children 4 and under.

Birds do their avian thing in the **Oerduinen** and **Het Hon** nature reserves on the east coast. Get your own bird's-eye view aboard a light aircraft from **Ameland Rondvluchten** (✆ **0519/554-644;** www.ameland-rondvluchten.nl), just north of **Ballum,** a village between Nes and Hollum. The cost of a flight for up to three adults, or two adults and two children, runs from 98€ for 15 minutes to 270€ for 60 minutes.

Schiermonnikoog (Skiermûntseach) ★

Wild, scenic, remote, and invariably all but deserted, the easternmost and smallest of the Wadden Islands, Schiermonnikoog (pop. 1,000), 17km (11 miles) long and a maximum of 6km (4 miles) wide, was declared a national park in 1988.

ESSENTIALS

GETTING THERE **Wagenborg Passagiersdiensten** (✆ **0900/455-4455** for information, or 0519/546-111 reservations; www.wpd.nl) operates ferry service from **Lauwersoog,** 36km (22 miles) northeast of Leeuwarden. Buses connect both Leeuwarden and Groningen rail stations with Lauwersoog. The ferry trip takes 45 minutes one-way. April to September, the round-trip fare is 13€ for adults, 12€ for seniors, 7.25€ for children 4 to 11, and free for children 3 and under; fares from October to March are around 10% cheaper. A bus meets the ferry and takes passengers to the island's only village, also called Schiermonnikoog. If you're **driving,** you'll have to leave your car at Lauwersoog (only residents are permitted to ship their cars across). In addition, a passenger boat sails from Ameland (3 hr.).

VISITOR INFORMATION **VVV Schiermonnikoog,** Reeweg 5, 9166 PW Schiermonikoog (✆ **0519/531-233;** fax 0529/531-325; www.vvvschiermonnikoog.nl), is on the village's main street. The office is open May to September Monday to Friday from 9am to 1pm and 2 to 6pm, and Saturday from 10am to 1pm and 2 to 4pm; and October to April Monday to Friday from 9am to 1pm and 2 to 5:30pm, and Saturday from 10am to 1pm and 2 to 4pm.

walking ON WATER

At low tide, the Wadden Sea virtually disappears, the seabed becomes visible, and seabirds feast on mollusks in the sand. Then the Wadden Islands seem even closer to the mainland, and if you feel like walking the mud flats, from May to October join a Wadlopen (Wadden Walking) trip and plow across to one of the islands. ***Warning:*** **Don't try this without an official guide—there is a real danger of being caught by a fast-incoming tide.** With a guide, it is generally safe, but every once in a while a group needs to be picked up by lifeboat.

Weather permitting, you start walking at ebb tide. Soon the mainland looks far away, and you feel lost in the middle of a salty mire trying to suck your feet in deeper with every step. But your attention will be drawn to the unusual landscape as you realize you're actually walking on the bottom of a sea, and in a few hours all this will disappear under water again. If you're lucky, you'll see seals disporting in pools or soaking up rays on a sandbar. When you reach the island, you need to wait for high tide to be able to go back by boat.

Tours cost 8€ to 33€ a head and range from an easy round-trip of a few hours on the flats to difficult hikes to the islands lasting around 8 hours (including the wait for the boat). Wear shorts and close-fitting, ankle-high shoes or boots. The trips are popular; groups may be as large as 75 to 100 people, so you need to book ahead. Contact **Wadloopcentrum Fryslân** (✆ **0518/451-491;** www.wadlopen.net), in Holwerd, or **Stichting Wadloopcentrum Pieterburen** (✆ **0595/528-300;** www.wadlopen.com), in Pieterburen.

WHAT TO SEE & DO

On the sheltered Wadden Sea coast, **Schiermonnikoog** village dates from the early 18th century, and life here doesn't seem to have sped up much since then. A statue known as the *Schiere Monnik (Gray Monk)* recalls the island's early history as a refuge of Cistercian monks, and two nearby complete whale jawbones, its 18th-century heyday as a whaling center.

The **Nationaal Park Schiermonnikoog ★★** covers most of the island and is a treasure for its isolation, wild scenery, and migratory birds, and because of its flora—half of all native Dutch plant species can be found here. Housed in an old lighthouse, a short walk or bike ride from the village, the national park's **Bezoekerscentrum (Visitor Center),** Torenstreek 20 (✆ **0519/531-641;** www.nationaalpark.nl/schiermonnikoog), can provide information about wildlife on the island and offer guided tours. The center is open April to October Monday to Saturday from 10am to noon and 1:30 to 5:30pm; November to March, hours are reduced to Saturday from 1:30 to 5:30pm. Admission is 1€ for adults and free for children 11 and under.

A great way to get around the island's dunes, beaches, woodlands, and polders is aboard the **Balgexpress,** a tractor-drawn observation trailer, which departs from the Visitor Center.

WHERE TO STAY & DINE

Graaf Bernstorff This hotel and apartment complex has luxuriously appointed rooms and apartments. The on-site restaurant has a more Continental feel than the traditionally Dutch Van der Werff (see below). Main courses start at 16€. During the day, you can get snacks on the terrace or at the bar.

Reeweg 1, 9166 PW Schiermonnikoog. ✆ **0519/532-000.** Fax 0519/532-050. www.bernstorff.nl. 69 units. 110€–210€ double. Rates include Dutch breakfast. AE, DC, MC, V. **Amenities:** Restaurant; bar. *In room:* TV, minibar.

Hotel-Pension Van der Werff ★ There's a sort of stuffiness here, which somehow lends to this rambling superhotel's charm. Games and sagging leather armchairs are in the lounge. Guest rooms are up-to-date, with some elegant features. The restaurant, with its wood-paneled walls and rich decor, is like a colonial officers' dining room. Guests can take the free hotel shuttle—sometimes an old charabanc is pressed into service—to and from the ferry dock.

Reeweg 2, 9166 PX Schiermonnikoog. ✆ **0519/531-203.** Fax 0519/531-748. www.hotelvanderwerff.nl. 55 units. 105€–115€ double. Rates include buffet breakfast. DC, MC, V. **Amenities:** Restaurant; lounge. *In room:* TV.

GRONINGEN ★

144km (90 miles) NE of Amsterdam; 51km (32 miles) E of Leeuwarden

The capital city of Groningen province, Groningen (pop. 185,000) is commercially and industrially important, and sits atop one of the world's largest natural gas fields. Cars are banned from the Old Town, which is enclosed by a moat. Part of this zone was destroyed during World War II, but much of its medieval and 16th- and 17th-century heritage survived. The University of Groningen was founded in 1614, and a student population of 45,000 gives the town a lively character.

Essentials

GETTING THERE There are **trains** every half-hour to Groningen from Amsterdam Centraal Station (transfer at Amersfoort); the ride takes around 2 hours and 20 minutes. One-way fares are 25€ in second class and 42€ in first class. From Leeuwarden, there are three direct trains an hour, a fast train (35 min.) and two slow trains (49 min); one-way fares are 8.80€ in second class and 15€ in first class. The train and bus stations in Groningen adjoin each other 1km (½ mile) south of the center of town. By **car** from Amsterdam, take A1/E231 southeast to the Muiderberg intersection, switch to A6 north to its intersection with A7/E22, and then take this expressway northeast to Groningen. An alternative route is A7/E22 north from Amsterdam, across the IJsselmeer on the Afsluitdijk, north and east on N31 and A31 to Leeuwarden, and then east on N355.

VISITOR INFORMATION **VVV Groningen,** Grote Markt 25, 9712 HS Groningen (✆ **0900/202-3050;** fax 050/311-3855; www.vvvgroningen.nl), is on the main square in the center of town. The office is open Monday to Friday from 9am to 6pm and Saturday from 10am to 5pm; July and August, hours are extended to Sunday from 11am to 3pm.

What to See & Do

Among Groningen's highlights is its handsome central square, the **Grote Markt,** graced by the 1810 neoclassical **Stadhuis (Town Hall).** Adjacent to this, at Waagplein 1, is the sparkling 1635 Renaissance **Goudkantoor (Gold Office),** which first housed a tax office, then a hallmarking bureau for precious metals, and now hosts a restaurant (see below). Should your Latin be rusty, the inscription on the building, DATE CAESARI QUARE SUNT CAESARIS, was spoken by Jesus and translates as: "Give unto Caesar that which is Caesar's."

THE TOP ATTRACTIONS

Groninger Museum ★★ Emerging like some exotic alien plant out of the gray waters of the Verbindingskanaal, the museum (1994) adds a surprising touch to this sober northern city. Italian architect Alessandro Mendini dreamed up a structure as quirky and varied as the contents. Playful, garish, disjointed, all jutting beams and cantilevered panels, each of the four pavilions has a different style, thanks to designers as varied as Philippe Starck, Michele de Lucchi, and Vienna bureau Coop Himmelbau. One appears to be the victim of an exploded paint box, and another, as the locals say, of a plane crash. These surround a golden tower in which a spiral staircase leads upward, its walls and balustrade a mosaic of small, varicolored tiles. After all this, you might find it hard to focus your attention on the collection. Each pavilion pursues a different theme: local archaeological finds and the history of the city and province; Eastern ceramics; decorative arts; and paintings—including works from the Expressionists of the Groningen school and a watercolor by Vincent van Gogh, *Drawbridge in Nieuw-Amsterdam* (1883)—prints, and sculpture from the 16th century to the present. A visit here should last 2 hours and 5 minutes: 2 hours for looking around, and 5 minutes for gazing slack-jawed in front of the building before you enter.

Museumeiland 1 (opposite the rail station). ✆ **050/366-6555.** www.groningermuseum.nl. Admission 8€ adults, 7€ seniors and students, 3€ children 5–15, free for children 4 and under. Tues–Sun 10am–5pm (to 10pm Fri). Closed Jan 1 and Dec 25. Bus: All buses to Groningen train station.

Martinitoren ★ The 15th-century **Martinikerk (St. Martin's Church),** across from the Grote Markt, is not easily missed, thanks to its lofty tower. Begun in 1469, completed in 1482, and reworked in 1627, the church is 97m (318 ft.) high from its base to the tip of a weather vane in the shape of St. Martin's horse, and that makes it the fourth tallest in Holland. Climb D'Olle Grieze (the Old Gray Man), as the tower is known locally, for fine panoramic views over the city and the low-lying country roundabout. A 17th-century Hemony carillon frequently rings out. Inside the church are 16th-century frescoes depicting the Christmas and Easter stories, and an impressive organ from 1480.

Martinikerkhof 3 (at Grote Markt). ✆ **050/311-1277.** www.martinikerk.nl. Admission: church free; tower 3€ adults, 2€ children 4–11, free for children 3 and under. Church open irregularly. Tower Apr–Oct Mon–Sat 11am–5pm (Sun 11am–5pm July–Aug); Nov–Mar daily noon–4pm. Bus: All buses to Grote Markt.

Noordelijk Scheepvaartmuseum (Northern Maritime Museum) ★ Housed in two medieval buildings, this museum traces the rich history of northern Holland's shipping industry, through models, instruments, charts, paintings, and more. There's a fine section on Groningen's medieval Hanseatic trading period.

Brugstraat 24 (at Hoge der A). ✆ **050/312-2202.** www.noordelijkscheepvaartmuseum.nl. Admission 4€ adults, 2.50€ seniors and children 7–15, free for children 6 and under. Tues–Sat 10am–5pm; Sun and holidays 1–5pm. Closed Jan 1, Apr 30, Aug 28, and Dec 25. Bus: 3, 8, 15, 33, 35, 39, 88, 619, or 637 to A Kerk.

Comfort Station

If you find yourself caught short in Groningen, relax, and take some time to appreciate a modern-design masterpiece. The *Urinoir* (1996), by Rem Koolhaas, in Kleine der A-straat, may not attract the same crowds as a van Gogh, but those who pass this way might well derive a certain satisfaction from the experience.

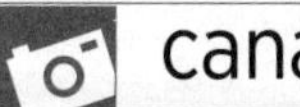

canal TOURS

April to October, the tour boats of **Rondvaartbedrijf Kool** (✆ **050/312-8379;** www.rondvaartbedrijfkool.nl) operate 1-hour cruises through Groningen's canals. These depart from a dock at Stationsweg 1012, outside Groningen train station, right next to the Groninger Museum (p. 414). A basic tour is 9€ for adults, 6€ for children 4 to 11, and free for children 3 and under.

Or, during the same months, propel yourself around on a canoe or a water bike from **'t Peddeltje** (✆ **050/313-0661;** www.tpeddeltje.nl), from a dock under the Herebrug bridge, just east of the Groninger Museum. The price per boat for two ranges from 8€ to 20€.

ALMSHOUSES

With more than 30 *hofjes* (almshouses) within the city limits, Groningen shares with Amsterdam and Leiden the distinction of hosting the greatest number of these charitable medieval institutions in the country. Constructed around courtyards, these clusters of small cottages still provide homes for the poor and the aged. The **Heilige Geestgasthuis (Holy Ghost Guesthouse),** Pelsterstraat 43, dating from 1267, is the oldest in town. Founded in 1405, the **Sint-Geertruidsgasthuis (St. Gertrude's Guesthouse),** Peperstraat 22, started out as a lodging for pilgrims who came to Groningen to pay homage to a relic—a supposed arm of John the Baptist in the Martinikerk—and later became homes for seniors. There's a handsome courtyard garden behind the gate. Until midway through the 17th century, the **Sint-Anthonygasthuis (St. Anthony's Guesthouse),** Rademarkt 29/1–30, functioned in part as an asylum for the mentally ill. Its redbrick-and-sandstone gate dates from 1644.

PARKS & GARDENS

The beautiful Renaissance **Prinsentuin** garden was established in 1625 behind the Prinsenhof building at Martinikerkhof 23, which was a monastery before becoming the seat of the bishop of Groningen in 1568. Later taken over for a royal residence, then used as a television and radio studio, the venerable building will house a four-star hotel from 2012. The hedges surrounding the herb beds, the rose garden, and a sundial are the result of more than 250 years of topiary. The garden is open April to mid-October daily 10am to sundown; admission is free.

When the city fortifications were demolished in the 19th century, part of the terrain in the north of the Old Town was given over to a pretty park, the **Noorderplantsoen,** laid out in the English landscape style.

TWO SCENIC LAKES NEARBY

The **Paterswoldsemeer,** a lake on Groningen's southern edge, is a sailing and watersports center with a vacation village on its shores. Just 8km (5 miles) southeast of here, the **Zuidlaardermeer** attracts watersports enthusiasts. In October the nearby village of **Zuidlaren** is the setting for one of Holland's largest horse fairs.

Where to Stay

De Doelen ★ Standing on bustling Grote Markt, this hotel is about as centrally located as you can get. The attractive guest rooms are done in muted colors and feature soft carpets and a mixture of period and modern furniture. The VIP rooms are outfitted with a private sauna and Jacuzzi, and are air-conditioned; the other rooms have to do without.

Grote Markt 36, 9711 LV Groningen. ✆ **050/312-7041.** Fax 050/314-6112. www.hotel-dedoelen.nl. 59 units. 85€–180€ double. Breakfast included only in VIP rooms. AE, DC, MC, V. Limited street parking. Bus: All buses to Grote Markt. **Amenities:** Restaurant; lounge. *In room:* A/C (some rooms), TV, minibar.

Familiehotel Paterswolde ★★ Set in a wooded 12 hectares (30 acres) on the western shore of the Paterswoldsemeer lake, just outside Groningen, this fine hotel provides a restful respite from the city. For all its country-villa exterior, it sports an up-to-date interior and offers spacious and bright guest rooms that have a soothing yet contemporary style. There's a cozy bar, and the fine **Fleurie** restaurant serves Continental cuisine.

Groningerweg 19 (a 10-min. drive south of Groningen), 9765 TA Paterswolde. ✆ **0347/750-451.** Fax 050/309-1157. www.familiehotelpaterswolde.nl. 65 units. 100€–200€ double. AE, DC, MC, V. Free parking. Bus: 52 from Groningen rail station stops outside the hotel. By car, take A28 toward Assen; at the Haren intersection, follow the signs for Paterswolde. **Amenities:** Restaurant/brasserie; bar; babysitting; bikes; health club; heated indoor pool; room service; sauna. *In room:* A/C, TV, minibar, Wi-Fi (16€/day).

NH Hotel de Ville ★ Three old houses have been converted into this modest though up-to-date hotel that fits nicely into the bustling ambiance of the town's central university district. Many rooms overlook the quiet gardens at the rear of the block. You'll probably want to check out a few rooms, since the smallest ones are a tight squeeze indeed, and even some of the larger ones don't have much in the way of furnishings or style. On site is a relaxed French brasserie-style restaurant, **Bistro 't Gerecht,** that's more than a cut above your standard hotel eatery, and is well worth going out of your way for, and a breakfast room/bar set in a glass conservatory. Breakfast is served in the garden on fine summer days.

Oude Boteringestraat 43–45 (at Groningen University), 9712 GD Groningen. ✆ **050/318-1222.** Fax 050/318-1777. www.nh-hotels.com. 43 units. 122€–135€ double; 212€–282€ suite. Rates include buffet breakfast. AE, DC, MC, V. Parking 18€. Bus: 1, 3, 5, 8, 11, 22, 40, or 42 to Grote Markt/Waagstraat. **Amenities:** Restaurant; bar; lounge; bikes; room service. *In room:* TV, hair dryer, minibar, Wi-Fi (11€/day).

Schimmelpenninck Huys ★★ This grand mansion, with origins that date back to around 1100, was transformed from a derelict pile into an elegant hotel in the late 1980s, but it still retains many historical features and has been extended into neighboring buildings. The light, spacious rooms have modern furniture that blends with the classical atmosphere, and the most expensive ones come equipped with a Jacuzzi. The Mediterranean-French restaurant **La Classique** in the Empire Room, which dates from 1723, has a French-style garden terrace in the summer and is well worth visiting even if you are not a guest here. Much the same can be said of the Greek restaurant La Femme Grecque in the 14th-century wine cellar. In addition, there is an Art Nouveau lounge.

Oosterstraat 53 (several blocks south of Grote Markt), 9711 NR Groningen. ✆ **050/318-9502.** Fax 050/318-3164. www.schimmelpenninckhuys.nl. 26 units. 108€–145€ double; 155€–215€ suite. AE, DC, MC, V. Free parking. Bus: 1, 3, 5, 6, 8, 11, 22, 40, 42, 52, 61, or 65 to Oosterstraat. **Amenities:** 3 restaurants; lounge. *In room:* TV, minibar, Wi-Fi.

Where to Dine

Muller ★★ FRENCH For an exquisite experience amid classic French surroundings, close to the university, come to Muller, arguably Groningen's finest restaurant.

Chef Jean-Michel Hengge is the proud possessor of a Michelin star. He uses local produce as often as seems reasonable for a restaurant that is, after all, French, and this includes game in season. The five-course chef's menu makes good use of the day's best market finds. Menu items include roasted Bresse pigeon and monkfish filet.

Grote Kromme Elleboog 13 (off Turftorenstraat). ✆ **050/318-3208.** www.restaurantmuller.nl. Main courses 28€–34€; fixed-price menus 60€–85€. AE, DC, MC, V. Tues–Sat 6–10pm. Bus: 23 to Oude Kijk in 't Jatstraat.

EXPLORING AROUND GRONINGEN

The towns and places below can easily be visited on day trips from Groningen by car or bus, some by train, and others by bike or canoe if you have the time and energy for it.

Warffum

20km (12 miles) N of Groningen

Warffum is typical of the "mound villages" constructed above flood level in past centuries. Before local people became expert at building dikes to hold back the water, they constructed mounds to provide places of safety for their families and livestock. Such a man-made mound, known as a *terp* (pl. *terpen*) in Friesland, and as a *wierde* (pl. *wierden*) or *warft* (pl. *warften*) in Groningen, often holds one of the oldest settlements in the area and looks like an island rising a little way above the surrounding polderland.

There are local trains and buses from Groningen to Warffum; by car, go north on N361 to Winsum, and then north and east on N363.

Just outside the village, **Openluchtmuseum Het Hoogeland,** Schoolstraat 4 (✆ **0595/422-233;** www.hethoogeland.com), is an open-air museum that holds fascinating relics from the mound settlements, medieval costumes, and other objects. It's open April to October Tuesday to Saturday from 10am to 5pm and Sunday from 1 to 5pm. Admission is 6€ for adults, 2€ for children 6 to 11, and free for children 5 and under.

Uithuizen

23km (14 miles) N of Groningen; 8km (5 miles) E of Warffum

A mound village with a 13th-century church that contains a beautiful organ from 1700, Uithuizen is worth a quick look just for itself. But the main reason for coming here is to visit the nearby Menkemaborg manor house. There are frequent trains and buses from Groningen; by car, take N46 north and then N999.

Deathly Silence

In the countryside just south of Uithuizen is a tiny hamlet with a name that says it all. It's called Doodstil (Dead Quiet).

Menkemaborg ★★ A double-moated fortified manor house that dates back to the 14th century, this is the finest surviving example of such a *borg,* as the country seats of the local lords of Groningen were called. It was

Pedaling Pleasure

Groningen province's tranquil Waddenzee coastline—from Lauwersoog to Eemshaven, it's a distance of around 50km (31 miles)—makes a fine setting for a bicycling tour. From the dike, you get views offshore to Schiermonnikoog and the low-lying, uninhabited islets of Rottumerplaat and Rottumeroog.

extensively reconstructed in the early 18th century and its interior has changed little since then, though the elegant furnishings, paintings, and fittings are a combination of Menkemaborg's own from this period and notable antiques drawn from other manors. Five rooms in which the upper crust could live in style are open to view, as is the kitchen where the lower orders labored with a mass of cooking utensils to keep things that way. The **1939–1945 Museum** on the grounds evokes the World War II period through a collection of armaments and military vehicles. The estate's formal gardens, which include a rose garden and a labyrinth, are a compelling attraction. A pancake restaurant occupies the old carriage house.

Menkemaweg 2 (1km/½ mile east of Uithuizen). ✆ **0595/431-970.** www.menkemaborg.nl. Admission: mansion and gardens 6€ adults, 2€ children 6–12, free for children 5 and under; gardens only 4€ adults, 1.50€ children 6–12, free for children 5 and under. Mar–June and Sept Tues–Sun 10am–5pm; July–Aug daily 10am–5pm; Oct–Dec Tues–Sun 10am–4pm.

Delfzijl

26km (16 miles) NE of Groningen; 19km (12 miles) SE of Uithuizen

The port town of Delfzijl (pop. 28,000) has a busy, colorful harbor and looks out across the Eems estuary toward Germany. From here, seagoing vessels sail up the Eems Canal to Groningen.

There are frequent trains and buses from Groningen; by car, go northeast on N360. Tourist information is available from **VVV Delfzijl,** J. van den Kornputplein 1, Delfzil (✆ **0596/618-104**).

In the town is the **Muzeeaquarium,** Zeebadweg 7A (✆ **0596/632-277;** www.muzeeaquarium.nl). Here you find North Sea aquatic life, corals, shells, and a geological museum with fossils, minerals, and archaeological and maritime exhibits. The aquarium is open daily 10am to 4:30pm (closed Jan 1, Apr 30, and Dec 25 and 26). Admission is 4.50€ for adults, 4€ for seniors, 2.75€ for children 4 to 12, and free for children 3 and under.

East of Delfzijl, the shore of the **Dollard,** a wide bay rimmed by mud flats, is a great place to observe wading birds.

WHERE TO STAY & DINE

Boven Groningen Rooms at this unpretentious, family-run hotel in the center of town, between the train station and the shops, are small but clean and bright, with whitewashed walls and up-to-date furnishings. A walk of just a few minutes brings you to the harbor and to Delfzijl's little (indeed, very nearly nonexistent) beach. On the premises is a good, brasserie-style in-house cafe-restaurant that serves traditional Dutch dishes, as well as a three-course *dagmenu* (day menu) for 23€.

Waterstraat 78 (1 block south of the train station), 9934 AX Delfzijl. ✆ **0596/618-771.** Fax 0596/617-147. www.bovengroningen.com. 60 units. 88€ double. Rates include continental breakfast. AE, DC, MC, V. Free parking. **Amenities:** Restaurant; bar. *In room:* TV, Wi-Fi (11€/day).

Slochteren

16km (10 miles) E of Groningen

This village is at the center of Groningen's natural gas field. Its star attraction is the lovely Fraeylemaborg estate. To get here by car from Groningen, take N360 toward Delfzijl, turn right onto N986 just outside the city, and then take N387. **Qbuzz** bus no. 78 goes from Groningen bus station, a 45-minute ride.

Fraeylemaborg ★ Comparable with Menkemaborg (see above), this 16th-century moated manor house, surrounded by attractive woods and gardens in the 19th-century English landscape style, is a fine surviving example of a Groningen *borg*. The interior has a wealth of richly decorated period rooms from the 18th and 19th centuries. You'll find collections of Asian porcelain and an exhibit about the Dutch royal house of Oranje-Nassau.

Hoofdweg 30 (on the eastern edge of Slochteren). ✆ **0598/421-568.** www.fraeylemaborg.nl. Admission 5€ adults, 2.50€ children 6–12, free for children 5 and under. Tues–Fri 10am–5pm; Sat–Sun and holidays 1–5pm. Closed Jan 1.

Heiligerlee

30km (19 miles) E of Groningen

The village of Heiligerlee is known to every Dutch schoolchild because one of the most famous battles in the country's history was fought here. On May 23, 1568, Count Louis (Lodewijk) of Nassau defeated a Spanish army in a battle that sparked the Eighty Years' War, which in turn led to the formation of the free Republic of the Netherlands.

To get here from Groningen by car, take A7/E22 east to exit 46. Local trains and buses go from Groningen via nearby Scheemda.

A multimedia exhibit at the **Museum Slag bij Heiligerlee (Battle of Heiligerlee Museum),** Provincialeweg 55 (✆ **0597/418-199;** www.slagbijheiligerlee.nl), takes you back to the famous battle of 1568 and the war that ensued. The museum is open April Tuesday to Sunday from 1 to 5pm, May to mid-September Tuesday to Saturday from 10am to 5pm and Sunday from 1 to 5pm, and mid-September to October Tuesday to Friday and Sunday from 1 to 5pm. Admission is 3.50€ for adults, 1.50€ for children 6 to 17, and free for children 5 and under.

Just across the street, in the former Van Bergen Bell Foundry, from 1795, which cast more than 10,000 bells, ranging from the smallest of dinner bells to massive church and carillon bells, is the **Klokkengieterijmuseum,** Provincialeweg 46 (✆ **0597/418-199;** www.klokkengieterijmuseum.nl). Exhibits explain the history of bell casting, and there are demonstrations (by appointment only) and carillon concerts. The museum is open April Tuesday to Sunday from 1 to 5pm, May to September Tuesday to Saturday from 10am to 5pm and Sunday from 1 to 5pm, and October

Illustrious Son

The greatest Dutch navigator, Abel Tasman (1603–59), was born in the village of Lutjegast, 20km (12 miles) west of Groningen. In 1642, he discovered Tasmania and New Zealand, and the following year he reached Tonga and Fiji.

Tuesday to Friday and Sunday from 1 to 5pm. Admission is 3.50€ for adults, 1.50€ for children 6 to 17, and free for children 5 and under.

Combined admission to both museums is 5€ for adults, 2.50€ for children 6 to 17, and free for children 5 and under.

Leek

14km (9 miles) SW of Groningen

Just northeast of this small town (pronounced *Lake*)—reached in 24 minutes by **Qbuzz** bus no. 85 from Groningen—stands the wooded estate of **Landgoed Nienoord** (✆ **0594/512-604;** www.landgoednienoord.nl). It's on the border of the Leekstermeer, a lake that offers swimming and sailing. At the heart of the estate, **Kasteel Nienoord,** a handsome manor house that was reconstructed in 1887 after fire and general deterioration had all but ruined the 1525 original, houses the **Nationaal Rijtuigmuseum (National Carriage Museum),** Nienord 1 (✆ **0594/512-260;** www.rijtuigmuseum.nl). This holds a wonderful collection of antique horse-drawn carriages, stagecoaches, and sleighs; the uniforms and accessories of their drivers; and related paintings and prints. The museum is open April to October Tuesday to Friday from 10am to 5pm and Saturday and Sunday from 1 to 5pm. Admission is 5€ for adults and free for children 17 and under.

Around the estate, you'll find several other attractions. **Familiepark Nienoord,** Nienoord 10 (✆ **0594/512-230;** www.landgoednienoord.nl), is a park with rides and other activities for children. Swim both indoors and outdoors in a "subtropical pool" at **Nienoord Zwemkasteel,** Nienoord 12 (✆ **0594/517-500;** www.landgoednienoord.nl). The park is open April to October daily 10am to 6pm (or later). Admission is 6€, and free for children 2 and under.

Haren

6km (4 miles) S of Groningen

The premier attraction in Haren is its botanical garden. **Qbuzz** bus no. 50 goes from Groningen to Haren in 12 minutes.

Hortus Haren ★ Exotic flowers and plants of all climates, from alpine to tropical, are collected at the botanical garden of the University of Groningen, which has been here since the middle of the 17th century. Visit a greenhouse where plants from the tropical rainforests are kept, and its section devoted to tropical insects. Among different European gardens is a recreation of a Celtic garden. The Hidden Kingdom of Ming is a replica of a Ming dynasty (1368–1644) Chinese imperial garden. You can sip Chinese tea in the teahouse.

Kerklaan 34. ✆ **050/537-0053.** www.hortusharen.nl. Admission 4.50€ adults, 2€ children 4–12, free for children 3 and under. Daily 9:30am–5pm. Closed Jan 1 and Dec 25.

ASSEN

24km (15 miles) S of Groningen

With all due respect to the capital of Drenthe province, Assen (pop. 64,000) is a pleasant enough town but contains little of historical importance or unmissable visitor interest. It is, though, a good base from which to make forays into Drenthe's rural tranquillity—an ancient landscape in which life flourished long before the land on which most Dutch now live was reclaimed from the sea.

A MOVING side trip FROM ASSEN ★

After the German army occupied the Netherlands in World War II, **Kamp Westerbork,** a refugee camp for German Jews south of Assen, became a transit center for Jews, Gypsies, Resistance fighters, and other victims on their way to Nazi death camps. In memory of the 102,000 people transported from here, an equal number of stones have been laid out on the camp's parade ground. At the **Memorial Center** (✆ **0593/592-600;** www.kampwesterbork.nl), exhibits and film footage afford some idea of their fate. Among those who "transited" through Westerbork were Anne Frank and the members of the group who had shared her secret hiding place in Amsterdam (p. 300). Anne and her sister Margot were sent first to Auschwitz and finally to Bergen-Belsen.

The camp terrain is open permanently; the museum is open Monday to Friday from 10am to 5pm and Saturday, Sunday, and holidays from 1 to 5pm (from 11 am Apr–Aug); it's closed January 1 and December 25 and 31. Admission to the camp is free; to the museum it is 5€ for adults, 2.50€ for children 8 to 18, and free for children 7 and under. To drive there from Assen, take the minor road parallel to A28/E232 south to Hooghalen, and then turn east for 4km (2½ miles). Or go by train to Beilen, and then take bus no. 22 from outside the station to the center of Hooghalen, from where the camp is a signposted, 15-minute walk.

The nearby **Westerbork Synthesis Radio Telescope,** an array of 14 connected radio telescopes, is a fantastic and—after the sad experience of visiting the camp—uplifting sight.

Essentials

GETTING THERE Up to three **trains** an hour run from Groningen to Assen station, a little way east of the center of town. The ride takes 18 minutes, and one-way fares are 5.10€ in second class and 8.70€ in first class. By **car,** take A28/E232 south or the parallel and more scenic N372.

VISITOR INFORMATION **VVV Assen,** Marktstraat 8–10, 9401 JH Assen (✆ **0592/243-788;** fax 0592/241-852; www.ditisassen.nl), is in the center of town. The office is open Monday from 1 to 6pm, Tuesday to Thursday from 9am to 6pm, Friday from 9am to 9pm, and Saturday from 9am to 5pm.

What to See & Do

Drents Museum ★ ***Note:*** The museum is closed for renovation until late 2011; the practical information provided here was the latest available and is subject to change. The provincial museum is spread out over five neighboring historic buildings on the town's main square, including the church of the Cistercian Convent of Maria-in-Campis from 1260, and the former provincial Gouvernementsgebouw (Government Building) from 1885. Among many archaeological finds on display are Stone Age objects from Drenthe's *hunebedden* (megaliths), weapons, pottery, Roman sarcophagi, and Celtic and Merovingian jewelry. Among the well-preserved items recovered from Drenthe's peat bogs is the mummified corpse of Het Meisje van Yde (the Yde Girl). The highlight of the art collection is Vincent van Gogh's oil painting *Peat Boat with Two Figures* (1883).

Biking the Wide Green Yonder

The bicycle might have been invented with Drenthe in mind. A myriad of bike paths, signed routes, and remote byways lead deep into the heart of farming country, heathland, and forest. Local tourist offices have details of suggested bicycling routes. Other routes touch the main towns, Assen and Emmen, and yet others weave in and out of *hunebed* territory.

Brink 1 (at Jacob Cramerplein). ✆ **0592/377-773.** www.drentsmuseum.nl. Admission 6€ adults, 4€ seniors and students, 3€ children 5–15, free for children 4 and under. Tues–Sun and Mon national holidays 11am–5pm. Closed Jan 1 and Dec 25. Bus: 7 or 8 to Kloosterhof.

MORE PLACES OF INTEREST

Just south of the center, the large **Asserbos** public park contains the remnants of an ancient oak forest, though only around one-tenth of the park's area is covered by original forest, the remainder having been planted in 1760. On the grounds is a children's farm.

Farther south, just outside of town, is Holland's national **TT (Tourist Trophy) Circuit** (www.tt-assen.com), where the annual Dutch Grand Prix motorcycle race takes place on the last Saturday in June. On preceding days, Assen's peaceable streets fill up with leather-clad bikers and fab-looking bikes from around Europe.

EMMEN

32km (20 miles) SE of Assen

Drenthe's largest town (pop. 109,000) is a delightful mix of old buildings left over from its village origins and new ones reflecting its prosperity. It has dubbed itself "Vlinderstad" (Butterfly Town), by way of drawing attention to some of the most notable denizens of its large zoo (see below).

Essentials

GETTING THERE Going by **train** from Assen is not a good way to get to Emmen, because the roundabout ride via Zwolle can take as long as 2 hours. **Qbuzz** bus no. 25 departs every half-hour or so from Assen, and the ride take just 1 hour. By **car,** take N376 east from Assen to Rolde, and then go southeast to its intersection with N381; then go east on this highway and its continuation, N364, into Emmen.

VISITOR INFORMATION **Tourist Info Emmen,** Hoofdstraat 22, 7811 EP Emmen (✆ **0591/649-712;** www.touristemmen.nl), is in the center of town. The office is open Monday from 1 to 5pm and Tuesday to Saturday from 10am to 5pm.

A Great Zoo

Noorder Dierenpark (Northern Zoo) ★ ☺ Animals from around the world roam freely at this large zoo, in habitats that have been made as natural as can be for a park in the middle of Drenthe. For instance, cliffs, pebble beaches, and realistic underwater scenery are the setting in which Humboldt penguins disport. Among the nearly 500 different species here, you'll see elephants, tigers, white rhinoceroses, giraffes, hippopotamuses, impalas, apes, baboons, kangaroos, and snakes. On the children's farm, there are a bunch of cute domesticated animals. Emmen takes its

STONE AGE giants

Drenthe can count more than 50 Stone Age chambered tombs or temples called *hunebedden* on its territory. These fascinating monuments consist of large, freestanding stones, or megaliths, often capped by lateral stones. They are scattered along a stretch of scenic, relatively high ground known as the Hondsrug (Dog's Back). The terminal moraine of a long-vanished Ice Age glacier, the Hondsrug's rugged spine angles northwest from Emmen to the southeastern edge of Groningen. Discoveries of pottery, tools, jewelry, and other items have enabled archaeologists to date the tombs to around 3400 B.C. and attribute their construction to the farming communities of the Funnel-Beaker Culture, so-called after the characteristic style of pottery they created.

The most interesting hunebedden are along N34, the Emmen-Groningen highway; in the northern reaches of Emmen itself; and around the pretty Hondsrug villages of Odoorn, Borger, Rolde, Eext, Annen, and Anloo. The tourist offices in Emmen and Assen have details on where they are and how to get to them. Equally worth a visit is the **Hunebedcentrum,** Bronnegerstraat 12 (✆ **0599/236-374;** www.hunebedcentrum.nl), in Borger. Close by is the largest hunebed, #D27, which has nine capstones still in place. The center is open Monday to Friday from 10am to 5pm and Saturday and Sunday from 11am to 5pm (closed Jan 1 and Dec 25 and 31). Admission is 6.75€ for adults, 3€ for children 4 to 11, and free for children 3 and under.

moniker of "Butterfly Town" from the magnificent tropical *vlindertuin* (butterfly garden).

Hoofdstraat 18. ✆ **0591/850-855.** www.noorderdierenpark.nl. Admission 19€ adults, 17€ seniors, free for children 3 and under. Mar–May and Oct daily 10am–5pm (to 6pm Sun Apr–May); June–Aug daily 10am–6pm; Sept daily 10am–5:30pm; Nov–Feb daily 10am–4:30pm.

Side Trips from Emmen

BOURTANGE ★

31km (19 miles) NE of Emmen; 17km (11 miles) NE of Ter Apel

This unique fortress village has been restored to its former glory. Constructed from 1580 onward, it withstood many battles over the centuries, only to fall into disrepair as methods of warfare changed. Two wooden drawbridges span a star-shaped moat and lead to traffic-free streets within the ramparts, where you can visit barracks, gunpowder storage rooms, a synagogue, and officers' quarters. Various relics of military life are displayed. The fortress is permanently open, and admission is free. Its museums are open mid-March to mid-November daily 10am to 5pm, and mid-November to mid-March Saturday and Sunday from noon to 5pm. Admission to the museums is 5.50€ for adults, 3.50€ for children 7 to 12, and free for children 6 and under. Bourtange's **Visitor Center** is at Willem Lodewijkstraat 33 (✆ **0599/354-600;** www.bourtange.nl), on the west side of the village. In July and August, military living-history events take place. The highlight is a uniformed reenactment of the 1640 Battle of Bourtange during the Eighty Years' War of liberation from Spain. To get there, take Qbuzz bus no. 73 from Emmen to Ter Appel, where you transfer to bus no. 70; the ride takes 1¼ hours.

VINCENT'S VISION OF drenthe

It would take a van Gogh to capture Drenthe's many moods of landscape and light, especially when the summer fields are heavy with ripening crops. The traditional lives of this area's peasant farmers and peat cutters actually drew Vincent to the province for a 3-month sojourn in 1883, early in his career as a painter. "I am in a wonderful country," he wrote to his brother, Theo.

Vincent lodged for 2 months at a ferry-house-cafe in the village of Nieuw-Amsterdam, 8km (5 miles) south of Emmen. He had to leave because he couldn't afford the rent. Then owned by Hendrik Scholte, the **Van Gogh House,** Van Goghstraat 1 (✆ **0591/555-600;** www.vangogh-drenthe.nl), has been restored to its 1883 condition and contains archival material on the artist. It's open for guided tours Tuesday to Sunday from 1 to 5pm (to 4pm in winter); the last tour is 45 minutes before close. Admission is 4.50€ for adults, 3.50€ for children 5 to 13, and free for children 4 and under.

Among the works van Gogh created during his stay in Drenthe in 1883 is an oil painting, *Peat Boat with Two Figures,* which you can view at the Drents Museum in Assen; and a watercolor, *Drawbridge in Nieuw-Amsterdam,* on display at the Groninger Museum in Groningen.

BARGER-COMPASCUUM

10km (6 miles) E of Emmen

Set outside this village, on 1.6 sq. km (⅔ sq. mile) of the peat moors along the German border, is the **Open-Air Museum Veenpark (Peat Park)** ★, Berkenrode 4 (✆ **0591/324-444;** www.veenpark.nl). At a reconstructed peat cutters' village, 't Aole Compas, watch demonstrations of peat cutting, butter churning, weaving, and clog making, as they were done at the end of the 19th century. There are nostalgic stores and an antique barbershop, and you can take a short canal trip onboard a turf boat. The park is open April to October daily from 10am to 5pm (to 6pm July–Aug). Admission is 13€ for adults, 11€ for seniors, and free for children 4 and under. To get there, take Qbuzz bus no. 26 from Emmen, a 16-minute ride.

SCHOONOORD

12km (7 miles) NW of Emmen

Named after Ellert and Brammert, two giants who once upon a time robbed travelers in these parts, the **Openluchtmuseum Ellert en Brammert,** Tramstraat 73 (✆ **0591/382-421;** www.ellertenbrammert.nl), is a trip down Drenthe's memory lane. Sculptures of Ellert and Brammert stand guard at the gates, behind which are sod huts, a Saxon farmhouse, a tollhouse, an old school, a prison, a smithy, a sawmill, an apiary (bee farm), geological exhibits, and a children's farm. Watch living crafts, like pottery making, and the recreated farming methods of yesteryear, and then enjoy a snack and a drink at an old country inn. Children can relive the legend of the two bandits in their cave hideaway. You'll need at least a couple of hours to make a visit here worthwhile. The museum is open April to October daily 9am to 6pm. Admission is 5€ for adults, 4€ for seniors and children 4 to 11, and free for children 3 and under. To get there, take Qbuzz bus no. 21 from Emmen, a half-hour ride.

ORVELTE

18km (11 miles) NW of Emmen; 6km (4 miles) W of Schoonoord

In a beautiful, forested landscape, **Museumdorp Orvelte ★** is a genuine old village, but one that has been preserved as a living-history monument that gives a fine insight into the way things once were in Drenthe. Rustic, thatched-roof buildings are grouped around the village square, the Brink. Real people live here and go about their daily lives, and though you can visit some houses and buildings that have been opened for display by masters of traditional crafts and trades, like the clog maker, the blacksmith, and the carpenter, others are private and can't be visited. There's an old-fashioned country cafe and a restaurant. For more information, check out the **Visitor Center,** Dorpsstraat 1A (✆ **0593/322-335;** www.orvelte.net).

You can reach Orvelte by signposted country roads off N364 (leave your car at one of the car parks just outside the village), and by bus from Emmen, Assen, and the rail station in nearby Beilen.

17 UTRECHT, GELDERLAND, OVERIJSSEL & FLEVOLAND

These four central provinces form a tapestry of history and scenic beauty. In Utrecht, the smallest of the nation's 12 provinces, châteaux speckle the landscape. The provincial capital, the 2,000-year-old city of Utrecht, is a center of learning and religion, while Amersfoort and Oudewater evoke medieval times.

To the east is the country's largest province, **Gelderland.** The banks of the Rhine, Maas, and Waal rivers, along with national parks, nature reserves, and recreation centers, are vacation venues here. Gelderland beckons with attractions like the Het Loo royal palace and the Netherlands Open-Air Folklore Museum. Noteworthy, too, is Arnhem, where the World War II battle for the Rhine crossing—the famed "bridge too far"—was fought.

A parklike landscape of forests, meadows, and lakes distinguishes rural **Overijssel.** These are punctuated by châteaux, steep-roofed and half-timbered farmhouses, tranquil villages, and picturesque medieval and Hanseatic towns.

Holland's newest province, **Flevoland,** was created on land reclaimed in recent decades from the IJsselmeer and was inaugurated in 1986. The new polders cover 1,800 sq. km (695 sq. miles), sprinkled with old villages that were once islands by themselves, and shiny modern towns like Lelystad. Straight roads run through flat fields traversed by equally straight canals.

UTRECHT ★★

42km (26 miles) SE of Amsterdam

A good starting point for exploring this province is the capital city, with its thriving cultural life. Utrecht's modern face hits you the moment you arrive by train at Utrecht Centraal Station, in the multitiered Hoog Catherijne mall that spreads over a 6-block area to the edge of the Old Town.

Utrecht, Gelderland, Overijssel & Flevoland

But don't let that dampen your interest in visiting this well-preserved city, Holland's fourth largest (pop. 296,000). Utrecht started out in A.D. 47 as the Roman Trajectum at a ford on the Rhine.

The Dutch Republic was established here in 1579. Utrecht had already been a powerful political player from the earliest days of Christianity in the Low Countries, since the English missionary St. Willibrord founded a bishopric here in 695. As a result, this is a city of churches, with many restored medieval religious structures in the old heart of town.

Essentials

GETTING THERE Utrecht is the Dutch rail net's hub; **trains** arrive at Utrecht Centraal Station every 15 minutes or so from Amsterdam, and about as frequently from many other places around the country. The ride from Amsterdam takes 27 minutes; one-way fares are 6.70€ in second class and 11€ in first class. By **car,** take A2/E35 southeast from Amsterdam.

VISITOR INFORMATION **VVV Utrecht** is at Domplein 9, 3512 JC Utrecht (✆ **0900/128-8732;** fax 030/236-0037; www.utrechtyourway.nl), in the center of town. The office is open Monday to Friday from 10am to 6pm, Saturday from 10am to 5pm, and Sunday from noon to 5pm.

SPECIAL EVENTS Every year at the end of August and the start of September, concert halls, churches, and other Utrecht venues are filled with the sounds of Renaissance and baroque music during the **Holland Festival of Early Music Utrecht** (✆ **030/232-9000;** www.oudemuziek.nl), an international event that attracts the world's top performers.

What to See & Do

Unique to Utrecht is its tree-shaded wharf, 5m (16 ft.) below street level, along **Oudegracht,** a canal that winds through the Old Town. Restaurants, stores, and sidewalk cafes have replaced the hustle and bustle of the commercial activity of former times, when Utrecht was a major port along an arm of the Rhine and these quays were used for offloading into the vaulted storage cellars. The adjacent sunken **Nieuwegracht** canal follows a former course of the river. Much of the Old Town has been transformed into a pedestrians-only zone and contains many secondhand bookstores, antiques dealers, cafes, and restaurants.

Centraal Museum ★ The emphasis at this convent-turned-museum is on an impressive collection of Dutch modern art and Dutch 20th-century applied art from the De Stijl group, displayed in the former stables on the grounds. Elsewhere are historical displays about Utrecht, including a preserved Viking longboat found in the city that dates from around 1100 and an exquisite dollhouse from 1680. There are paintings by artists of the 16th-century Utrecht school, in particular those of Jan van Scorel (1495–1562), whose group portraits planted the seeds of a genre that would flower in Holland in the next century. A 2-hour visit should suffice.

Nicolaaskerkhof 10 (at Agnietenstraat). ✆ **030/236-2362.** www.centraalmuseum.nl. Admission 9€ adults, 7.50€ seniors, 4€ children 13–17, free for children 12 and under. Tues–Sun 11am–5pm. Closed Jan 1, Apr 30, and Dec 25. Bus: 2 to Centraal Museum.

Domkerk (Cathedral) ★★ This magnificent cathedral took almost 3 centuries to build, from 1254 to 1517. The nave collapsed during a violent storm in 1674 and was never reconstructed; the choir and transepts survived and remain disconnected from the tower (see below). On the inside, the cathedral bears traces of the fierce wave of iconoclasm that spread over Holland in the second half of the 16th century. There's a battered altarpiece in one of the side chapels. A sandstone Holy Sepulcher, dated 1501, shows a defaced Christ in a tomb under a badly damaged Gothic arch.

Other sights around the Dom are **Bisschopes Hof,** or Bishop's Garden (daily 11am–5pm); and **Dom Kloostergang,** a cloister arcade constructed in the 15th century with magnificent stained-glass windows depicting scenes from the legend of St. Martin. The cathedral cloisters are connected to the former **Chapter House,** where the signing of the 1579 Union of Utrecht (which united the seven Protestant Dutch provinces in their rebellion against Catholic Spanish rule) took place.

Achter de Dom 1. ✆ **030/231-0403.** www.domkerk.nl. Free admission. May–Sept Mon–Fri 10am–5pm, Sat 10am–3:30pm, Sun 2–4pm; Oct–Apr Mon–Fri 11am–4pm, Sat 11am–3:30pm, Sun 2–4pm. Bus: 2 to Domplein.

Domtoren ★ The cathedral's 110m (361-ft.) tower, constructed between 1321 and 1383, dominates Utrecht's skyline and is the tallest in the Netherlands. It stands on the site of St. Willibrord's original 8th-century church and across a square from its mother building, since the nave collapsed during the great storm of 1674, leaving the

Utrecht

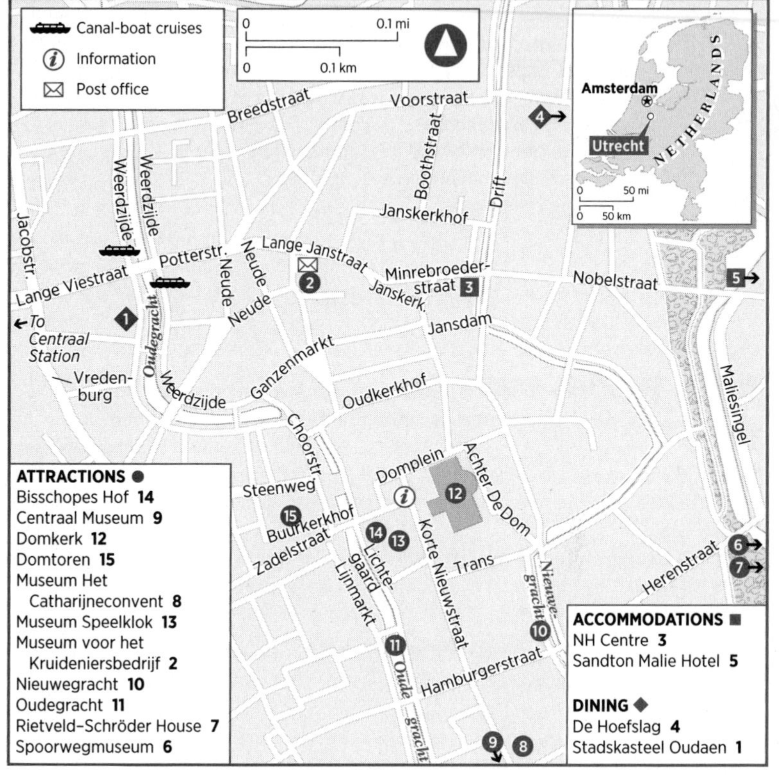

tower unharmed. One of the best views of Utrecht is from the top of the tower, a climb of 465 steps if you have the stamina and the inclination (about halfway up is the 14th-c. St. Michael's Chapel, where you can stop and ease the panting!). The climb goes past the church's 50 massive bells—Europe's largest carillon—which you'll hear all through your stay in Utrecht. Its *bourdon* (largest bell) weighs 10,000 kilograms (11 tons) and has a diameter of 2.7m (9 ft.).

Domplein 9–10. ✆ **030/236-0010.** www.domtoren.nl. Admission 8€ adults, 6.50€ students, 4.50€ children 4–12, free for children 3 and under. Sun–Mon noon–5pm; Fri–Sat 10am–5pm. Bus: 2 to Domplein.

Museum Het Catharijneconvent Housed in the old **St. Catherine's Convent,** in the Old Town's southern reaches, this exceptional collection of medieval religious art—paintings, relics, carvings, and church robes—helps illustrate the development of Christianity in Holland from the 8th century onward. The courtyard of the convent where the museum is housed has a cafe terrace where you can take a meditative pause.

Sweet Satisfaction

Tucked away in a courtyard, the Museum voor het Kruideniersbedrijf, Hoogt 6 (✆ 030/231-6628), at Telingstraat, a grocers' museum upstairs in a tiny grocery store, is the place to satisfy your sweet tooth. The interior and equipment are original; an aroma of cinnamon, ginger, and other spices pervades the air; and the ladies behind the counter serve with old-fashioned friendliness. It's difficult not to buy an ounce or two of each kind of candy or cookie. The museum is open Tuesday to Saturday from 12:30 to 4:30pm. Admission is free.

Lange Nieuwstraat 38 (at Zuilenstraat). ✆ **030/231-3835.** www.catharijneconvent.nl. Admission 12€ adults, 11€ seniors, 7.25€ children 6–17, free for children 5 and under, family 32€. Tues–Fri 10am–5pm; Sat–Sun and holidays 11am–5pm. Closed Jan 1 and Apr 30. Bus: 2 to Catharijneconvent.

Museum Speelklok (Chimes Museum) ☺ Six hundred mechanical music machines from the 17th century to the present—including fairground organs and those barrel organs you see on Dutch streets—are housed in this 13th-century former church. A player piano is controlled by punched rolls. The most overwhelming exhibits are the music-hall organs of yesteryear, to which you can sing and dance at the end of your tour.

Steenweg 6 (at Choorstraat). ✆ **030/231-2789.** www.museumspeelklok.nl. Admission 9€ adults, 8€ seniors, 5€ children 4–12, free for children 3 and under. Tues–Sun, holidays, and Mon during school vacations 10am–5pm. Closed Jan 1, Apr 30, and Dec 25. Bus: 2 to Domplein.

Spoorwegmuseum (Railway Museum) ★ ☺ You don't have to be a train buff to be fascinated by this former rail station and its marvelous collection of more than 60 steam engines, carriages, and wagons. There are moving models, paintings, and films relating to train travel. The multimedia section should have you and the kids stuck to your seats with presentations on the latest high-speed trains, such as the Thalys and the TGV.

Maliebaanstation (at Maliesingel). ✆ **030/230-6206.** www.spoorwegmuseum.nl. Admission 15€ adults, 13€ seniors, 12€ children 3–12, free for children 2 and under. Tues–Sun and Mon during school vacations 10am–5pm. Closed Jan 1 and Apr 30. Bus: 3 to Maliebaan.

Rietveld-Schröder House Constructed in 1924, this family home was something of a shocker at the time and represents a high point of the De Stijl movement that so influenced contemporary art. It was designed by Utrecht architects and designers Gerrit Rietveld and Truus Schröder, and is now a UNESCO World Heritage Site, owned by the Centraal Museum. The plaster exterior bears De Stijl's signature red, yellow, blue, and gray tones, and the innovative interior is a model of space-saving and efficiency. The tour takes in the Rietveld Model Home, across the street at Erasmuslaan 9.

Prins Hendriklaan 50 (at Waterlinieweg). ✆ **030/236-2310.** www.rietveldschroderhuis.nl. Admission (includes same-day admission to Centraal Museum; see above): guided tour 16€ adults, 15€ seniors, 11€ children 13–17, 7€ children 5–12, free for children 4 and under; audiotour 9€ adults, 7.50€ seniors, 4€ children 13–17, free for children 12 and under. Guided tours (hourly) Thurs–Sun 11am–2pm; audiotours (hourly) Wed 11am–4pm, Thurs–Sun 3–4pm. Reservations recommended for both tours. Bus: 4 to Prins Hendriklaan.

BOAT TOURS

One-hour **cruises** on Utrecht's canals are available year-round from **Rederij Schuttevaer** (✆ **030/272-0111;** www.schuttevaer.com), with boats departing from Oudegracht at the corner of Lange Viestraat. Tours are daily every hour on the hour from 11am to 5pm, and are 8.40€ for adults, 6.30€ for children 4 to 12, and free for children 3 and under. From mid-May to September, there are cruises on the Vecht River to the pretty village of Loenen aan de Vecht, with a stop to visit the Terra Nova estate. Another cruise goes along the Kromme Rijn to the Rhijnauwen estate.

Where to Stay

NH Centre ★ This excellent hotel is literally in the shadow of the cathedral and within a 2-minute walk of the canal, with its bi-level wharf, restaurants, and stores. The not overly large guest rooms aim for an intimate feel and have contemporary furniture, soft drapes, and large beds that take up most of the space. Some windows still retain the original early-20th-century stained glass. The bar and lounge have a sidewalk terrace in summer.

Janskerkhof 10 (at Drift), 3512 BL Utrecht. ✆ **030/231-3169.** Fax 030/231-0148. www.nh-hotels.com. 47 units. 100€–200€ double. Rates include buffet breakfast. AE, DC, MC, V. Parking 19€. Bus: 2, 3, 4, 8, or 11 to Janskerkhof. **Amenities:** Restaurant; bar; lounge; bikes. *In room:* A/C, TV, hair dryer, minibar, Wi-Fi (11€/day).

Sandton Malie Hotel ★ Two 19th-century mansions in a quiet residential neighborhood near the university Uithof complex, on the leafy eastern edge of the city, are the setting for this lovely small hotel. The generally small guest rooms have color-coordinated drapes, carpets, and bedspreads, and large windows that let in plenty of light during the day. Some rooms have a balcony. Both the breakfast room and the bar overlook the peaceful garden at the back.

Maliestraat 2 (at Maliebaan), 3581 SL Utrecht. ✆ **030/231-6424.** Fax 030/234-0661. www.sandton.eu. 45 units. 115€–175€ double. Rates include buffet breakfast. AE, DC, MC, V. Limited street parking. Bus: 4, 10, or 11 to Oorsprongpark. **Amenities:** Bar; bikes. *In room:* A/C, TV, hair dryer, minibar, Wi-Fi (free).

Where to Dine

De Hoefslag ★★ INTERNATIONAL/FRENCH This beautiful dining spot, on wooded grounds northeast of Utrecht, is considered by many to be Utrecht's top restaurant. There's a Victorian-garden feel to the lounge, while the dining room is reminiscent of an upscale hunting lodge, with lots of dark wood, an open hearth, and ceiling-to-floor doors opening to the terrace. The De Hoefslag changes its menu daily, deciding on specials after the chef has returned from the market. The seafood is superb, as are the pork, lamb, and game dishes.

Vossenlaan 28, Bosch en Duin. ✆ **030/225-1051.** www.hoefslag.nl. Main courses 35€–50€; fixed-price menus 45€–90€. AE, DC, MC, V. Mon–Sat noon–2:30pm and 5:30–9:30pm. Bus: 59 to Vossenlaan.

Stadskasteel Oudaen CONTINENTAL A medieval fortified town house dating from 1320 has been transformed into this culinary palace. Downstairs, in what was the main hall, you can sit in the cafe and savor beer brewed on the premises according to medieval recipes. Upstairs is the restaurant **Tussen hemel en aarde** ("Between heaven and earth"), with its original fireplace still intact and a rustic tile floor. The menu changes weekly, according to what is freshest and in season.

Oudegracht 99 (at Zakkendragerssteeg). ✆ **030/231-1864.** www.oudaen.nl. Main courses 19€–22€; fixed-price menus 40€–45€. AE, DC, MC, V. Cafe daily 10am–2am. Restaurant Mon–Sat 5:30–10pm.

Side Trips from Utrecht

At the **Loosdrechtse Plassen (Loosdrecht Lakes) ★**, 8km (5 miles) north of Utrecht, old peat diggings brim with water, and the land has been reduced to straggly ribbons between a checkerboard of lakes. These are popular for recreational sailing and watersports, out of the busy harbor at Oud-Loosdrecht. A handsome old village off the western end of the lakes is **Loenen aan de Vecht,** on the bank of the Vecht River.

THREE NEARBY CASTLES

In and around the area between Utrecht and the Loosdrecht lakes are three of the finest castles and stately châteaux in the Netherlands.

Kasteel De Haar ★★ If you have time for only one castle jaunt, make it to richly furnished De Haar. Like most castles, it has had its ups and downs—fires and ransackings and the like—over the centuries, but thanks to an infusion of Rothschild money in the early 1900s, it now sits in all its 15th-century moated splendor in the middle of a gracious Versailles-like formal garden. Craftsmen worked with medieval techniques to an extraordinary degree of detail. Its walls hold many fine paintings and precious Gobelin tapestries of the 14th and 15th centuries; the floors are softened with Persian rugs; and its chambers are furnished in the styles of Louis XIV, XV, and XVI of France.

Kasteellaan 1, Haarzuilens. ✆ **030/677-8515.** www.kasteeldehaar.nl. Admission 8€ adults, 5€ children 5-12, free for children 4 and under. Guided tours hourly July-Aug daily noon-4pm; Sept to late Nov Mon-Fri noon-3pm, Sat-Sun noon-4pm; 1st 2 weeks of Dec Sat-Sun noon-4pm; 2nd 2 weeks of Dec daily noon-4pm; see website for additional tours and children's tours. Bus: GVU bus no. 28, then 127 from Utrecht to Haarzuilens. By car from Utrecht, take the local road west through Vleuten (16km/10 miles).

Kasteel-Museum Sypesteyn A castle turned art gallery and museum, Sypesteyn was reconstructed in the early 1900s on the foundations of a late-medieval manor house destroyed about 1580. Today it holds some 80 paintings dating from the 16th, 17th, and 18th centuries, representing the work of artists such as Paulus Moreelse, Nicolaes Maes, and Michiel van Mierevelt. There are collections of old weapons, glassware, silverware, pottery, porcelain, and furnishings dating from the 16th to the 18th centuries. The parklike grounds are laid out in 17th-century landscape style and include a colorful rose garden.

Nieuw-Loosdrechtsedijk 150, Nieuw Loosdrecht. ✆ **035/582-3208.** www.sypesteyn.nl. Admission 7.50€ adults, 4€ children 8-15, free for children 7 and under. Guided tours hourly Apr-Oct Tues-Fri noon-5pm; Nov-Mar Sat-Sun noon-5pm. Bus: GVU bus no. 122 from Utrecht to Loosdrecht. By car from Utrecht, take N417 north and then the local road northwest to Loosdrecht (17km/11 miles).

The Breukelen Bridge

New Yawkers might want to take in Breukelen, a tiny village on the Vecht River northwest of Utrecht. Treat yourself to crossing the *original* Brooklyn Bridge—all of 6m (20 ft.) long, one car wide, and definitely not for sale!

Slot Zuylen ★ One of Holland's best examples of a medieval castle was constructed in the late 13th century and inhabited until the early 1900s. Since 1952 it has been a museum. Period rooms are furnished in 17th- to 19th-century styles, along with family portraits. A special feature in the landscaped gardens is a so-called "snake

A Painterly Place

Visit the scene of a rich historical canvas, at Wijk bij Duurstede, on the bank of the Neder Rijn, 20km (12 miles) southeast of Utrecht. A windmill at the village was the star of Jacob van Ruysdael's painting *The Mill at Wijk bij Duurstede* (1670), now in Amsterdam's Rijksmuseum. An old windmill standing on the town's riverside ramparts might be the very one he painted.

wall" that creates a sun trap, protecting southern fruit trees from the harsher northern European climate.

Tournooiveld 1, Oud-Zuilen (near Maarssen, 5km/3 miles north of Utrecht). ✆ **030/244-0255.** www.slotzuylen.com. Admission 7€ adults, 6€ students, 4€ children 4–16, free for children 3 and under. Guided tours hourly Mar 15–May 15 and Sept 15–Nov 15 Sat 2–4pm, Sun 1–4pm; guided tours hourly mid-May to mid-Sept Tues–Thurs 11am–4pm; Sat 2–4pm; Sun 1–4pm. Bus: Connexxion bus no. 120 from Utrecht to Oud-Zuilen. By car from Utrecht, take N230 west to Oud-Zuilen (10km/6 miles).

OUDEWATER

18km (11 miles) SW of Utrecht

Back in the 1500s, this charming little village was the scene of some of Europe's most bizarre witch trials. Accused women were weighed on scales in the **Heksenwaag (Witches' Weigh House) ★**, Leeuweringerstraat 2 (✆ **0348/563-400;** www.heksenwaag.nl), to determine whether or not they were witches who, it was believed, lacked souls and so weighed little enough to fly through the air supported on a broomstick. So many women were weighed and convicted of witchcraft that the town's reputation for having accurate scales was in jeopardy. To remedy this, the town fathers devised a system of judging accused witches by having them stand on scales clad only in a paper costume and carrying a paper broom. Present were the mayor, the alderman, the weighmaster, and the local midwife. The weighmaster could then proclaim with confidence that the accused could not possibly be a witch, and a certificate was issued to that effect. Europe's accused witches flocked here in droves. Nowadays, you can step on the Heksenwaag scales (kids love to do this) and walk away with your very own certificate. The Weigh House is open April to October Tuesday to Sunday and holidays from 11am to 5pm. Admission is 4.25€ for adults, 2€ for children 4 to 11, and free for children 3 and under.

As you walk through the quaint village streets, take a look at the storks' nests on the **Stadhuis (Town Hall)** roof. The birds, traditionally associated with the arrival of a new child, have been nesting here for more than 3 centuries.

ZEIST

9km (6 miles) E of Utrecht

Set in a green landscape of parks and forests, this village gem was once a fashionable country retreat for Utrecht's wealthy nobility. Take **Connexxion** bus no. 50 from Utrecht, a 25-minute ride. By **car,** take N237 east, then go south on Utrechtseweg. The tourist information office, **VVV Zeist,** Slotlaan 24, 3701 GL Zeist (✆ **030/697-4007;** www.vvvheuvelrug.nl), is open Tuesday to Saturday from 10am to 5:30pm.

Slot Zeist ★ This castle was constructed between 1677 and 1687 for Prince Willem Adriaan van Nassau. Its plain brick facade conceals a lavish interior designed by

French architect Daniël Marot, who was responsible for decorating Het Loo palace (p. 435). Many of his baroque murals and ceiling paintings have survived, as well as the interior's ornate gilded wood paneling and stucco. The grand drive is lined by elegant houses belonging to the Hernhutters, a Protestant religious order that had its origins in Bohemia and Moravia (today's Czech Republic) in the first half of the 18th century. The large formal gardens were relandscaped in the 19th century to create a pleasant park.

Zinzendorflaan 1. ✆ **030/692-7528.** www.slotzeist.nl. Admission 5€ adults, 4€ seniors and children 5 to 18, free for children 4 and under. Guided tours Sat–Sun 1:30 and 2:45pm. Bus: 50, 58, 71, or 74 to Het Rond/Lageweg.

Where to Stay & Dine in Zeist

Hotel Theater Figi ★ Should you fall for the charms of Zeist, this modern, top-notch hotel ensures a pleasant stay. The guest rooms, quite large, are decorated in a modern, Mediterranean style, and some have balconies. Four cinemas and the cozy brown Theatercafé are part of the hotel complex, accessible via the hotel and through their own street entrances.

Het Rond 2, 3701 HS Zeist. ✆ **030/692-7400.** Fax 030/692-7468. www.figi.nl. 97 units. 185€–225€ double; 285€–335€ suite. AE, DC, MC, V. Free parking. Bus: 50, 58, 71, or 74 to Het Rond/Lageweg. **Amenities:** 2 restaurants; bar; lounge. *In room:* TV, hair dryer, minibar, Wi-Fi (10€/day).

AMERSFOORT ★

42km (26 miles) SE of Amsterdam; 20km (12 miles) NE of Utrecht

Industrial development in the outer districts aside, this medieval town (pop. 140,000) on the Eem River has held onto its ancient character. Indeed, its medieval heart is guarded by a double ring of canals—the only city in Europe to have this feature. The artist Piet Mondrian was born here in 1872.

Essentials

GETTING THERE Up to four **trains** arrive every hour from Amsterdam Centraal Station, and as many as six an hour from Utrecht. By **car,** take A1/E231 southeast from Amsterdam, or A28/E34 northeast from Utrecht.

VISITOR INFORMATION **VVV Amersfoort** is at Stationsplein 9–11, 3818 LE Amersfoort (✆ **0900/112-2364;** fax 033/465-0188; www.vvvamersfoort.nl). The office is open May to September Monday to Friday from 9am to 5:30pm and Saturday from 10am to 4pm, and October to April Monday to Friday from 9am to 5:30pm and Saturday from 10am to 2pm.

What to See & Do

Entering the town, you pass the oldest standing gateway, the **Kamperbinnenpoort,** constructed on the inner canal around 1260. The two other surviving gates are the **Koppelpoort,** a land-and-water gate from around 1400; and the **Monnikendam,** a water gate from 1430, both on the outer canal. Look for examples of 15th-century *muurhuizen* (wall houses) constructed into the ramparts and fortifications. If you visit Amersfoort on a summer Saturday, you may be lucky enough to encounter the colorful trumpeters who show up from time to time.

An impressive landmark is the tall, 15th-century **Onze-Lieve-Vrouwetoren (Our Lady's Tower),** in the west of the old town, which stands 100m (328 ft.) high and is the third-tallest tower in the land; if you're here on a Friday, listen for its carillon concert between 10 and 11am. Other ancient religious buildings include the **Sint-Joriskerk,** started in 1243 and completed around 1534, and the beautifully restored 16th-century **Mariënhof Monastery.**

For an illuminating look at Amersfoort's history, make a brief sojourn among the large collection of objects, models, and displays at the **Museum Flehite,** Westsingel 50 (✆ **033/247-1100;** www.museumflehite.nl). The museum is open Tuesday to Friday from 11am to 5pm and Saturday, Sunday, and holidays from noon to 5pm (closed Jan 1, Easter Sun, Apr 30, Pentecost Mon, and Dec 25). Admission is 7€ for adults, 3.50€ for students, and free for children 17 and under.

A Nearby Attraction for Families

Dolfinarium Harderwijk ★ ☺ Harderwijk, a lakeside town on the Veluwemeer, 26km (16 miles) northeast of Amersfoort, boasts one of Europe's largest sea wildlife centers. There's a dolphin research and rehabilitation station, as well as entertaining performances by the resident dolphins, sea lions, walruses, and seals. Additional highlights include a series of open-air pools, underwater viewing galleries, and a touch tank filled with fish. A visit here is a thrilling day out, especially for families.

Strandboulevard Oost 1, Harderwijk. ✆ **0341/467-467.** www.dolfinarium.nl. Admission 25€ adults, 23€ seniors and children 3–11, free for children 2 and under. Mid-Feb to June and Sept–Oct daily (except Mar Mon–Tues) 10am–5pm; July–Aug daily 10am–6pm. From Amersfoort, two trains every hour go to Harderwijk. By car, take A28/E232; the Dolfinarium is next to the Veluwestrand leisure center and beach, and is clearly signposted all around town.

APELDOORN

76km (47 miles) E of Amsterdam; 40km (25 miles) E of Amersfoort; 26km (16 miles) N of Arnhem

"Royal Apeldoorn" is a title often bestowed on a city (pop. 136,000) that has hosted the likes of Willem III in 1685, Louis Napoleon in 1809, Queen Wilhelmina from 1948 until her death in 1962, and Princess Margriet from 1962 to 1975. It's a city of many parks and gardens, and a good place in which to base yourself for a visit to Hoge Veluwe National Park (see below).

Essentials

GETTING THERE There are two **trains** every hour from Amsterdam Centraal Station and four from Amersfoort; the ride takes 1 hour and 5 minutes and 25 minutes, respectively. By **car,** take A1/E30 east from Amersfoort.

VISITOR INFORMATION **VVV Apeldoorn** is at Deventerstraat 18, 7311 LS Apeldoorn (✆ **055/526-0200;** fax 055/526-0209; www.vvvapeldoorn.nl), a block north of Marktplein in the heart of town. The office is open Monday to Friday from 9am to 5:30pm, and Saturday from 9am to 5pm.

A Royal Retreat

Rijksmuseum Paleis Het Loo ★★ The 1685 Het Loo palace and estate, outside Apeldoorn, has sheltered generations of Dutch royalty, being the favorite summer residence and hunting lodge of Stadhouders (Heads of State) and the royal house of Oranje-Nassau until 1975. Since 1984 it has served as a museum that celebrates the history of the House of Orange. This splendid palace, with its original paneling and colorful damasks, is now an ideal setting for paintings, furniture, silver, glassware, and ceramics, and memorabilia of the royal family. Highlights include the lavish silk-and-damask-embellished private study (1690) and bedroom (1713) of Stadhouder William III, and the dining room (1686), decorated with tapestries illustrating themes of Ovid.

The fascinating vintage car and carriage collection in the stable block includes smooth models like a royal 1925 Bentley. But the jewel in the crown is the formal gardens, a harmonious mélange of plants, flowers, trees, pathways, statues, fountains, and pools. These were restored using the original 17th-century plans and recreating a small-scale Dutch Versailles. They are in four sections: the King's Garden, Queen's Garden, Upper Garden, and Lower Garden.

Koninklijk Park 1, Oude Loo (on the northwest edge of Apeldoorn). ✆ **055/577-2400.** www.paleishetloo.nl. Admission 10€ adults, 3€ children 6–17, free for children 5 and under. Tues–Sun and Mon holidays 10am–5pm. Closed Jan 1. Bus: 10 from outside Apeldoorn train station.

Where to Stay

Bilderberghotel De Keizerskroon ★ This attractive hotel on the edge of town is adjacent to the Het Loo palace. Each of the spacious guest rooms is furnished with a sense of flair, in which the effect of stylish red-and-black furnishings and bedspreads is softened by floral drapes and, in some rooms, sofas. Some rooms have balconies overlooking the landscaped grounds. The fine international restaurant takes some of its design cues and sensibility from the royal palace across the way.

Koningstraat 7, 7315 HR Apeldoorn. ✆ **055/521-7744.** Fax 055/521-4737. www.keizerskroon.nl. 94 units. 125€–225€ double; 270€–350€ suite. AE, DC, MC, V. Free parking. Bus: 10 from outside Apeldoorn train station. **Amenities:** Restaurant; bar; exercise room; health club; heated indoor pool; sauna. *In room:* TV, minibar, Wi-Fi (13€–17€/day).

Hotel Berg & Bos In a quiet, peaceful setting near the Berg en Bos park and Het Loo palace, you'll find comfortable, bright, airy rooms here. While it's not luxury, it's a tolerable approach to it, in a family-owned establishment where things are done just so. Some rooms overlook the garden.

Aquamarijnstraat 58, 7314 HZ Apeldoorn. ✆ **055/355-2352.** Fax 055/355-4782. www.hotelbergenbos.nl. 16 units. 66€–99€ double. Rates include continental breakfast. AE, DC, MC, V. Limited street parking. Bus: 5 from outside Apeldoorn train station. **Amenities:** Restaurant; bar; lounge. *In room:* TV, Wi-Fi (free).

Where to Dine

De Echoput ★★ DUTCH/CONTINENTAL This widely acclaimed restaurant is named after the old well at which travelers once watered their horses (the "echoing well"). It's on the edge of the Royal Wood, about 10km (6 miles) west of Apeldoorn. From the outside, it has the look of a hunting lodge, but inside it's surprisingly modern and sophisticated. The lounge and dining room are decorated in shades of chocolate and pewter. Windows look out on pools and fountains, and forest greenery. The specialty here is seasonal game (fall and winter), and summer specialties include lamb, beef, and poultry.

Amersfoortseweg 86, Hoog Soeren/Apeldoorn (just off the N344 Apeldoorn-Amersfoort Rd.). ✆ **055/519-1248.** www.echoput.nl. Fixed-price menus: lunch 33€; dinner 65€–85€. AE, DC, MC, V. Tues–Fri noon–2pm and 6–9:30pm; Sat 6–9:30pm; Sun 1–9:30pm.

Holland's Largest National Park

A beautiful nature reserve between Apeldoorn and Arnhem, **Nationaal Park De Hoge Veluwe ★★** (✆ **0900/464-3835;** www.hogeveluwe.nl) covers some 55 sq.

km (21 sq. miles) of gently rolling heath, pine and birch woodland, fens, and sand dunes, populated by red and roe deer, wild boar, pine martens, badgers, polecats, and other wildlife, including non-native species like the mouflon Mediterranean wild mountain sheep, along with around 150 different bird species. You can observe the wildlife from hides and observation posts.

In the Saddle

The average Hollander rides about 1,000km (620 miles) annually by bicycle.

The national park has solved its transportation issues in a way that's both user-friendly and nature-friendly. Cars aren't permitted in the reserve, and a fleet of free white bicycles, which you can pick up from one of several convenient spots next to the perimeter car parks, makes getting around both easy and pleasant—though some visitors have an unfortunate tendency to "borrow" other people's bikes as soon as the original rider's back is turned. These bikes are the perfect way to explore the park, and you'll get to see far more than if you go on foot.

A leisurely ride takes you to the splendid **Jachtslot Sint-Hubertus,** an extravagant hunting lodge on the park's northern edge, with a tower that soars high above it. The Art Deco lodge was designed in 1920 by architect Hendrik Petrus Berlage. Inside, stained-glass windows tell the story of St. Hubert, the patron saint of hunters, and the house is full of symbolic references to his life. Stroll through the rose garden or sit on the banks of the swan-shaped lake.

Entrances to the Hoge Veluwe National Park are at Otterloo, Rijzenburg, and Hoenderloo. The park is open daily from 8 or 9am to between 6 and 10pm, depending on the time of year. The St. Hubert Hunting Lodge is open for guided tours April to October daily every half-hour from 11am to 4:30pm (except 1pm), and November to December and February to March Monday to Friday at 2 and 3pm. Admission to the park alone is 7.50€ for adults, 3.75€ for children 6 to 12, free for children 5 and under, and 3€ for a car. Free white bicycles are available at the park entrances. Veolia bus no. 106 departs for the Hoge Veluwe every hour or so from outside both Apeldoorn and Arnhem rail stations.

The reserve has a camping ground, bungalows, other vacation accommodations, and picnic facilities.

Kröller-Müller Museum ★★★ An unexpected treasure is embedded like a flower in the middle of Hoge Veluwe National Park. Perhaps a sunflower or iris would be the appropriate bloom, because the museum is home to 278 works by Vincent van Gogh. This museum is where you find most of the van Gogh paintings that aren't in Amsterdam's Van Gogh Museum (p. 304). Named after the art collector Helene Kröller-Müller, who gathered up some 120 works by van Gogh around the turn of the 20th century, the museum is a friendly rival to the Amsterdam museum. However, the Kröller-Müller's pastoral setting and the light, airy structure of glass-walled pavilions add another dimension to a museum visit. It seems somehow surprising to find paintings like the *Café Terrace in Arles* (1881) hanging on the wall of this isolated place. The collection includes paintings by Mondrian, Picasso, Braques, and Seurat, and Chinese porcelain and Delftware. An adjacent **sculpture garden** hosts pieces by artists such as Rodin, Moore, Dubuffet, and Lipchitz.

Houtkampweg 6, Otterloo. ✆ **0318/591-241.** www.kmm.nl. Admission (includes National Park) 15€ adults, 7.50€ children 6–12, free for children 5 and under. Tues–Sun 10am–5pm. Closed Jan 1.

ARNHEM ★

82km (51 miles) SE of Amsterdam; 55km (34 miles) E of Utrecht; 26km (16 miles) S of Apeldoorn

Gelderland province's capital (pop. 144,000), founded in the 13th century and later a prosperous member of the Hanseatic League trading alliance, Arnhem became a household name when its strategic road bridge over the Neder Rijn (Lower Rhine) became the target of a massive Allied airborne assault during World War II (see the box "A Bridge Too Far," below). The city was destroyed during the fighting and reconstructed after the war.

Essentials

GETTING THERE Up to four **trains** to Arnhem depart every hour from Amsterdam Centraal Station; on some trains, you transfer in Utrecht. The ride takes just over an hour. In addition, there are frequent trains from Apeldoorn and Nijmegen. By **car** from Amsterdam, take A2/E35 southeast to Utrecht and A12/E35 east to Arnhem; from Apeldoorn, go south on A50.

VISITOR INFORMATION **VVV Arnhem** is at Stationsplein 13, 6811 KG Arnhem (✆ **0900/112-2344;** www.vvvarnhemnijmegen.nl), outside the city's rail station. The office is open Monday to Friday from 9:30am to 5:30pm and Saturday from 9:30am to 5pm.

What to See & Do

The road bridge over the Rhine in the center of town is a replica of the bridge destroyed during World War II and is known as the **John Frost Bridge,** in honor of the commander and troops of the British 2nd Parachute Battalion. In September 1944, Lieutenant-Colonel Frost's 600 valiant "Red Devils" took and for 4 days held the north end of the bridge against overwhelming German numbers and firepower.

Contemporary and classic artworks, with an emphasis on modern Dutch painting and sculpture, can be found in the **Museum voor Moderne Kunst (Museum of Modern Art)** ★, Utrechtseweg 87 (✆ **026/377-5300;** www.mmkarnhem.nl; trolley bus: 1). This is housed in a handsome 19th-century villa on the road to Oosterbeek (see below) and has a sculpture garden, a coffee room, and an open-air cafe overlooking the Neder Rijn. The museum is open Tuesday to Friday from 10am to 5pm and Saturday, Sunday, and holidays from 11am to 5pm (closed Jan 1, Apr 30, and Dec 25). Admission is 7€ for adults, 5€ for seniors and students, and free for children 18 and under.

Housed in a graceful 18th-century mansion just south of Gele Rijders Plein, the **Historisch Museum (Historical Museum),** Bovenbeekstraat 21 (✆ **026/377-5300;** www.hmarnhem.nl; trolley bus: 1, 3, 5, or 7), contains artworks, porcelain, and other objects associated with the city's history. The museum is open Tuesday to Friday from 10am to 5pm and Saturday, Sunday, and holidays from 11am to 5pm (closed Jan 1, Apr 30, and Dec 25). Admission is 4.50€ for adults, 3€ for seniors and students, and free for children 18 and under.

ORGANIZED TOURS

Boat trips from Arnhem by **Rederij Eureka** (✆ **0570/615-914;** www.rederij-eureka.nl) depart from a quay below the John Frost Bridge and include daylong excursions on the Rhine and IJssel rivers. Some cruises cross the border into Germany;

Smooth Movers

Arnhem is almost the only place in the Benelux lands where you get to ride trolley buses (Ghent, Belgium, has a single line). The blue, electrically powered trolley buses glide silently through the streets, justifying Arnhem's moniker of *trolleybusstad* (trolley-bus town). There are five lines: 1, 2, 3, 5, and 7; a sixth line, no. 10, is being ramped up. A ride on line 1 from Arnhem to Oosterbeek (see below) combines that environmentally friendly trolley-bus feeling with good views of Arnhem and an interesting destination.

another visits the Dutch Hanseatic towns of Deventer, Doesburg, Zutphen, Zwolle, and Kampen (see "The Hanseatic Towns," below). A day-long cruise that includes coffee and a lunch buffet is 32€ for adults, 23€ for children 4 to 11, and free for children 3 and under.

Places of Interest Outside Arnhem

Northeast of town is **Nationaal Park Veluwezoom ★**, 46 sq. km (18 sq. miles) of pine and silver birch forest and heathland crisscrossed by riding, walking, and biking trails. The national park is an extension of the larger Hoge Veluwe National Park to the west (see "Apeldoorn," above), the two being separated by about 5km (3 miles) and the A50 expressway. The **Visitor Center,** Heuvenseweg 5A, Rheden (✆ **026/497-9100;** www.veluwezoom.nl), is open Tuesday to Sunday (also Mon during school vacations) from 10am to 5pm. Admission is free.

TWO GREAT ESCAPES FOR KIDS

Burgers' Zoo ★ ☺ As you go through the grounds of this safari park covering 40 hectares (99 acres) in the northwestern edge of Arnhem, you'll watch more than 300 animals roam freely behind protective fencing. Its chimpanzee and gorilla enclosures are internationally acclaimed. Tropical rainforest and subtropical desert habitats have been recreated in two enormous greenhouses, together with some of the fauna indigenous to these regions.

Antoon van Hooffplein 1 (near the Nederlands Openluchtmuseum). ✆ **026/442-4534.** www.burgerszoo.eu. Admission 19€ adults, 18€ seniors, 19€ children 4–9, free for children 3 and under. Apr–Oct daily 9am–7pm; Nov–Mar daily 9am–5pm. Trolley bus: 3.

Nederlands Openluchtmuseum ★★ ☺ Don't miss this delightful open-air museum (the European Museum of the Year in 2005), which brings to life Dutch history, customs, dress, and architecture from about 1800 to 1950. On its 44 hectares (109 acres), step-gabled town houses, farmhouses, windmills, antique means of transport, and colorful costumes of the past from around the country have been gathered together. It's a living museum, with frequent demonstrations of old arts and handicrafts.

Schelmseweg 89 (at Hoeferlaan). ✆ **026/357-6111.** www.openluchtmuseum.nl. Admission 14€ adults, 10€ children 4–12, free for children 3 and under. Apr–Oct daily 10am–5pm. By car, take A12/E35 and follow the signs to Arnhem-Noord/Openluchtmuseum. Trolley bus: 3.

OOSTERBEEK

Adjoining Arnhem on the west, Oosterbeek (pronounced *Ohst*-uhr-bayk) in the 19th century was beloved by artists, who built handsome villas here. The village was badly

A bridge TOO FAR

On September 17, 1944, the Allies launched the greatest airborne assault in history: Operation Market Garden. In all, 35,000 paratroops and glider infantry were deployed. The U.S. 101st Airborne Division landed near Eindhoven, and the 82nd Airborne Division parachuted onto the Nijmegen area. After hard and bloody fighting, the Americans captured both cities along with bridges over the Maas and Waal rivers. Meanwhile, the British 1st Airborne Division and the Polish 1st Parachute Brigade landed near Arnhem to capture the key bridge over the Rhine there.

The plan called for a ground force to break through the German front line along the Dutch-Belgian border; roll 100km (62 miles) north along a single road through Eindhoven, Nijmegen, and Arnhem; cross the bridges captured by the airborne; and get across Hitler's last big defensive barrier, the Rhine, before the Germans could react.

As one Allied commander feared, it turned out to be "a bridge too far." The British airborne troops landed close to the tanks and artillery of the German 2nd SS Panzer Corps and were plunged into a fight for survival. Bad weather prevented reinforcements and supplies being flown in on schedule. A single battalion of paratroops made it to the Rhine bridge and held it in 4 days of bitter fighting, but they were finally overwhelmed. The division's tenuous bridgehead across the Rhine at nearby Oosterbeek was lost when the relief column was held up along what was dubbed "Hell's Highway."

The British survivors withdrew across the Rhine on September 27, having suffered 13,000 casualties. American losses were around 3,500.

damaged during heavy fighting that accompanied the September 1944 Allied airborne offensive to capture the Rhine bridge at Arnhem, and was rebuilt after the war. In Oosterbeek is the Airborne Cemetery, where 1,748 of the Allied fallen rest. Local schoolchildren lay flowers on the graves for the annual day of remembrance, in a moving echo of the support Dutch civilians gave their liberators during the battle.

Airborne Museum Hartenstein ★ The former Hotel Hartenstein housed the headquarters of the British 1st Airborne Division during the Battle of Arnhem. Most of that proud command was killed, wounded, or captured while trying to break through to the Rhine bridge at Arnhem and, after the failure of that assault, in a vain effort to maintain a bridgehead on the river's north bank at Oosterbeek. The museum details the week of fierce combat, during which the hotel's environs were under constant attack. Walk the paratroop survivors' withdrawal route south through a park and suburban streets, to the Neder Rijn at Westerbouwing. A passenger-and-bicycle ferry shuttles back and forth across this scenic stretch of the river, to dock near Driel on the south bank. In this village is a monument to Polish paratroops who landed here in the face of heavy German fire.

Utrechtseweg 232 (on the western edge of Oosterbeek). ✆ **026/333-7710.** www.airbornemuseum.com. Admission 8€ adults; 4€ veterans, seniors, and students; 3.50€ children 13–18; 2.50€ children 6–12; free for children 5 and under. Apr–Oct Mon–Sat 10am–5pm, Sun and holidays noon–5pm; Nov–Mar Mon–Sat 11am–5pm, Sun and holidays noon–5pm. Closed Jan 1 and Dec 25. Trolley bus: 1.

NIJMEGEN

58km (36 miles) SE of Utrecht; 15km (9 miles) S of Arnhem

Nijmegen (pop. 160,000) has a long recorded history and boasts dibs on being the oldest city in the Netherlands. In A.D. 104, the Roman Emperor Trajan granted city rights to the trading town of Ulpia Noviomagus Batavorum, which had grown up around a legionary fortress on the empire's Rhine frontier. The city lies in the orchard country of Gelderland's Betuwe (Fertile Wetlands) district, a peninsula between the Neder Rijn and Waal rivers, which in ancient times had been the heartland of the Batavian tribe.

Essentials

GETTING THERE Up to six **trains** depart every hour from Amsterdam Centraal Station to Nijmegen (only one or two of these is a direct train), and a similar number for the short hop south from Arnhem. By **car,** take A52 south from Arnhem.

VISITOR INFORMATION **VVV Nijmegen** is at Keizer Karelplein 32H, 6511 NC Nijmegen (✆ **0900/112-2344;** www.vvvarnhemnijmegen.nl), at the city's Schouwburg (theater). The office is open Monday to Friday from 9:30am to 5:30pm and Saturday from 10am to 5pm.

What to See & Do

Nijmegen's road bridge over the Waal was a key objective of Operation Market Garden during World War II. A combination of the destruction wrought by that battle, and an earlier raid by U.S. bombers that mistakenly struck the city instead of their intended target in Germany, devastated the old heart of town. Postwar reconstruction was mostly along modern lines. Around the handsome **Grote Markt,** look for the 1612 **Waag (Weigh House)** and the **Kerkboog** vaulted passageway from 1545 with a gable from 1605.

The city's strategic position is clearly visible from the **Valkhof (Falcon Court),** a park affording magnificent views. It's high on the south bank of the Waal—this is actually the main continuation of the Rhine, which splits in two after entering Holland—on the site of a 9th-century Frankish castle. Here, too, are the ruins of the 12th-century **Sint-Maartenskapel (St. Martin's Chapel),** and the octagonal **Sint-Niklaaskapel (St. Nicholas's Chapel)** from 1030, dubbed the Carolingian Chapel because of the erroneous belief that Charlemagne ordered its construction. Equally good views are available from the nearby 15th-century **Belvedere,** a watchtower that now houses a restaurant.

Museum Het Valkhof The daring glass structure (1999), worth viewing in its own right, accommodates Nijmegen's historical and art museum, and integrates two older, smaller museums. Nijmegen's Roman period is given major emphasis. The later Frankish era, when Nijmegen was a favorite residence of Charlemagne, is covered, too. In addition, there's an interesting array of fine-art objects and sculptures, and modern art.

Kelfkensbos 59 (at Hunnerpark). ✆ **024/360-8805.** www.museumhetvalkhof.nl. Admission 7€ adults, 5€ seniors, 3.50€ students and children 4–16, free for children 3 and under. Tues–Fri 10am–5pm; Sat–Sun and holidays 11am–5pm. Closed Jan 1 and Dec 25. Bus: 2, 3, 57, 58, 80, or 82.

THE GROESBEEK HEIGHTS

The loftiest peak in this range of hills just off Nijmegen's southeastern flank, along the German border, soars to all of 99m (325 ft.). For the Netherlands, that's more than respectable. In any case, the wooded hills and open country make good strolling and cycling terrain, and host a cluster of surprising attractions.

Museumpark Orientalis ★★ Step back in time, into the world of the New Testament. Life-size period replicas of homes and street scenes from the biblical lands inhabit the 49-hectare (121-acre) museum. The commitment to historical verisimilitude in the dioramas—Jewish, Roman, Greek, and Egyptian homes; a synagogue; a Sea of Galilee fishing village; a stretch of Roman road—is impressive. During the Christmas period, there's a crib exhibit. In the visitor center are archaeological finds and exhibits on Christian, Jewish, and Islamic scriptures. Due to the size of the place, you'll need a few hours to get much out of your visit, and a full morning or afternoon to do it justice. ***Note:*** The park is closed for renovation until early in 2012; the practical information below was in effect at the time of its closure.

Profetenlaan 2 (southeast of town on the Groesbeek road). ✆ **024/382-3110.** www.museumparkorientalis.nl. Admission 10€ adults, 9€ seniors, 6€ children 5–13, free for children 4 and under. Tues–Sun 10am–5pm (Jan 1 noon–5pm; Dec 26–28 10am–8pm). Bus: 5 or 25 from Nijmegen.

Nationaal Bevrijdingsmuseum (National Liberation Museum) 1944–1945 The U.S. 82nd Airborne Division parachuted onto drop zones around Groesbeek to capture the bridges over the Maas River at Grave and the Waal at Nijmegen and open the way for British armor to roll north toward Arnhem. A diorama in the parachute-shaped museum depicts the scene when paratroops crossed the Waal in flimsy assault boats through a hail of fire to take the Nijmegen road bridge. Photographs, films, a slide show, and a model of the area evoke Holland's period of occupation during World War II, leading up to the story that began on September 17, when the skies above Groesbeek suddenly blossomed with thousands of parachutes. Guided tours of the battle zone are available.

Close to the museum, on Zevenheuvelenweg, is the **Groesbeek Canadian War Cemetery,** containing the graves of more than 2,300 soldiers who fell during the final offensive into Nazi Germany in 1945. Between the two, on Wylerbaan, lies the **Canada-Netherlands Memorial Park,** a grove of Canadian maple trees.

Wylerbaan 4, Groesbeek (9.5km/6 miles from Nijmegen). ✆ **024/397-4404.** www.bevrijdingsmuseum.nl. Admission 9.50€ adults, 8€ seniors, 4.50€ children 7–17, free for children 6 and under. Mon–Sat 10am–5pm; Sun and holidays noon–5pm. Closed Jan 1 and Dec 25. Bus: 5 or 25 from Nijmegen.

THE HANSEATIC TOWNS ★

The Hanze Route (Hanseatic Route) runs along the IJssel River, which was the quick way from the Rhine to the Zuiderzee long before the sea was dammed in and became the freshwater IJsselmeer. Seven towns—Doesburg, Zutphen, Deventer, Hattem, Zwolle, Hasselt, and Kampen—along the 125km (78-mile) route through Gelderland and Overijssel played important roles in the international trade of yesteryear and profited handsomely from their membership in the medieval Hanseatic League, a Baltic-based association of more than 150 trading towns and cities in north and northwest Europe. You can tell this today by viewing the many old churches, public buildings, merchants' houses, and gateways that are still standing.

Zutphen

26km (16 miles) NE of Arnhem; 18km (11 miles) SE of Apeldoorn

A handsome walled medieval town, Zutphen (pop. 47,000) stands on the east bank of the IJssel River. From Arnhem, up to four **trains** arrive every hour and **buses** every half-hour or so; by **car,** take N48. For tourist information, visit **VVV Zutphen,** Stationsplein 39, 7201 MH Zutphen (✆ **0575/519-355;** www.vvvzutphen.nl). The office is open Monday from 11am to 5:30pm, Tuesday to Friday from 9am to 5:30pm, and Saturday from 9am to 4pm.

Zutphen's magnificent Gothic **Sint-Walburgiskerk (St. Walburga's Church),** 's-Gravenhof (✆ **0575/514-178**), in the center of town, houses important works of art and the **Librije (Library),** from 1564. The medieval books and manuscripts here are still in use, chained to reading desks.

Zutphen is a gateway into Gelderland's **Achterhoek (Back Corner)** district, which stretches east from the IJssel to the German border. Make a rewarding foray by bicycle or car into this tranquil landscape of farms, forests, and châteaux.

Deventer

14km (9 miles) N of Zutphen; 14km (9 miles) E of Apeldoorn

Just across the province line in Overijssel, Deventer (pop. 98,000) began in the 11th century and later became a fountain of religious and intellectual scholarship, with Thomas à Kempis, Erasmus, and Descartes among those who passed through its monastery school of the Brothers of the Common Life. You still see fine medieval and Renaissance buildings along its streets.

ESSENTIALS

GETTING THERE Up to four **trains** depart every hour from Arnhem via Zutphen. **Buses** leave every half-hour from Zutphen. By **car,** take N348 north from Zutphen.

VISITOR INFORMATION **VVV Deventer** is housed in the **Waag (Weigh House)** at Brink 56, 7411 BV Deventer (✆ **0900/353-5355;** fax 0570/671-544; www.vvvdeventer.nl), in the center of town. The office is open Tuesday to Saturday from 10am to 5pm and Sunday and Monday from 1 to 5pm.

WHAT TO SEE & DO

The old center and the IJssel waterfront are dominated by the magnificent Gothic **Sint-Lebuïnuskerk (St. Lebuin's Church)** ★, Grote Poot (✆ **0570/612-548**), named after an 8th-century Saxon missionary. Its 17th-century Hemony carillon is among the finest in Holland. The church is open Monday to Saturday from 11am to 5pm; admission is free. In the neighboring 17th-century **Stadhuis (Town Hall),** Grote Kerkhof 4 (✆ **0570/649-959**), is a large library of medieval books and manuscripts. It's open Monday to Friday from 10am to 4pm; admission is free.

Objects relating to the area and a marvelous collection of local costumes are exhibited in the **Historisch Museum Deventer,** Brink 58 (✆ **0570/693-783;** www.deventermusea.nl), in the extravagant 1528 **Waag (Weigh House)** on Deventer's main square. The museum is open Tuesday to Saturday from 10am to 5pm and Sunday and holidays from 2 to 5pm (closed Jan 1, Easter weekend, Pentecost, and Dec 25). Admission is 4€ for adults, 1€ for children 2 to 17, and free for children 1 and under.

Ferry Tales

Following the course of the IJssel River, you can cross back and forth from one bank to the other. A good place to do this is the scenic stretch of around 20km (12 miles) between Deventer and Zwolle, and a nice way to do it is by ferry for cars, bicycles, motorcycles, and foot passengers at the villages of Olst and Wijhe, on a crossing that takes just a few minutes.

The **Olst Ferry** (**✆ 0570/561-563;** www.olsterveer.nl) operates Monday to Friday from 7am to 10pm, Saturday from 8am to 10pm, and Sunday and holidays from 9am to 10pm. Farther north, the **Wijhe Ferry** (**✆ 0578/631-169;** www.wijheseveer.nl) operates Monday to Saturday from 6:30am to 9:30pm and Sunday and holidays from 8am to 9:30pm during the summer season (9am–9:30pm during the winter season). By both services, it costs 1.70€ for a car and driver, and 0.30€ for passengers, and there are rates for two-wheelers, cars with trailers, and more.

Organized Tours

Rederij Eureka (**✆ 0570/615-914;** www.rederij-eureka.nl) operates boat trips on the IJssel from Deventer, going north to Kampen and south to Arnhem.

Nearby Places of Interest

Just north of the pretty little village of **Holten,** 19km (12 miles) east of Deventer, are the ancient heathland and forests of the **Sallandse Heuvelrug (Salland Hills) ★**. These rear up all of 76m (249 ft.) at the Holterberg and mark the spot where the northern glaciers ground to a halt during the last ice age. Part of the area is a protected nature reserve, but you can hike and bike in the rest of it.

Zwolle ★

28km (17 miles) N of Deventer; 34km (21 miles) N of Apeldoorn

The capital of Overijssel, Zwolle (pop. 117,000) was founded in the 9th century and flourished during the 14th and 15th. In that boom time, churches and civic buildings were enlarged or embellished, and Zwolle became an important religious and cultural center, and a hub of trade. Thomas à Kempis (1379–1471), who wrote the influential *Imitation of Christ,* was a monk at the Agnietenberg Augustinian monastery north of Zwolle and is buried in the town's Sint-Michaelskerk. The fortified bastions and the distinctive star-shaped moat that makes an island of the Old Town date from the 17th century.

ESSENTIALS

GETTING THERE There are two **trains** every hour from Deventer and from Apeldoorn. **Buses** depart about every 30 minutes from Deventer and every hour from Apeldoorn. By **car,** take N337 north from Deventer, or A50 north from Apeldoorn.

VISITOR INFORMATION **VVV Zwolle,** Grote Markt 20, 8011 LW Zwolle (**✆ 038/421-6198;** www.vvvzwolle.nl), is in the center of town. The office is open Monday from 1 to 5pm, Tuesday to Friday from 10am to 5pm, and Saturday from 10am to 4pm.

WHAT TO SEE & DO

Sint-Michaelskerk (St. Michael's Church) Not to be confused with the small St. Michael's Church just outside the center of town, where Thomas à Kempis is buried, this church dates from 1446. Its dedication to the Archangel Michael, the winged guardian of Israel, is signified by a sculpture portraying him slaying the dragon, as told in the Bible in Revelation, and by a relief on a Romanesque tympanum from around 1200 of Abraham with Michael and two other archangels. The interior is interesting for its octagonal vestry and the massive 4,000-pipe Arp Schnitger organ (1722), which is often used for concerts and recordings.

Grote Kerkplein. ✆ **038/422-2299.** www.grotekerkzwolle.nl. Free admission. May–Oct Tues–Fri 11am–4:30pm, Sat 1:30–4:30pm.

More Places of Interest

Most of the original city wall has been demolished. But you can follow the walkways along what's left and discover Zwolle's hidden charms. Particularly impressive is the redbrick **Sassenpoort (Saxon Gate),** Sassenstraat 53 (✆ **038/421-6626**), a fortified gateway from 1406 adorned with four octagonal towers. It holds an exhibit on the town's history. It's open Friday from 2 to 5pm and weekends and holidays from noon to 5pm; admission is 2€ for adults, 1€ for children 5 to 12, and free for children 4 and under.

Affectionately dubbed the Peperbustoren (Pepperpot Tower), the restored tower (1487) of the massive **Onze-Lieve-Vrouwbasiliek (Basilica of Our Lady),** Ossenmarkt (✆ **038/421-4894;** www.olvbasiliek-zwolle.org), west of the Grote Markt, is Zwolle's primary landmark. Climb it to treat yourself to wide views over the town and the IJssel valley. Inside the 15th-century church are medieval relics and statues. The church is open May to October Monday from 1:30 to 4:30pm and Tuesday to Saturday from 11:30am to 4:30pm, and November to April Monday to Saturday from 1:30 to 3:30pm. Admission is 2€ for adults, 1€ for children 5 to 12, and free for children 4 and under.

Especially for Kids

Ecodrome Zwolle ★ ☺ The different displays at this educational theme park allow you to get close to the earth's nature and environment. You start out in the Geology Pavilion, where you learn about the earth's past, and then head into the Biology Pavilion, to see how plant and animal life started, and how humans began to interact and exercise influence over nature. Along the way, you pass through the Piranha Tunnel for a fish's-eye view of these needle-toothed little monsters, and visit the Rio Negro tropical rainforest and river. You come face to face with dinosaurs in the Dinorama, and you can even dig up fossilized bones.

Willemsvaart 19 (10 min. on foot from Zwolle rail station). ✆ **038/423-7030.** www.ecodrome.nl. Admission 14€ adults, 13€ seniors and children 3–11, free for children 2 and under. Apr–Oct daily 10am–5pm; Nov–Mar Wed, Sat–Sun, and school vacations 10am–5pm. Closed Jan 1 and Dec 25 and 31. Bus: 100S from Zwolle bus station. By car, from A21 take the Zwolle-Zuid junction.

Kampen ★★

13km (8 miles) NW of Zwolle

With its handsome, bustling IJssel River waterfront and more than 500 historical monuments, including medieval merchants' houses, towers, and town gates, Kampen (pop. 50,000) still displays the signature of its boom period from 1330 to 1450, when it was an important member of the Hanseatic League. Golden Age artist Hendrik

Avercamp (1585–1663) lived, worked, and died in the town. Kampen is a good base from which to make bicycle and walking tours of the scenic riverside landscapes and nature reserves around the nearby mouth of the IJssel.

ESSENTIALS

GETTING THERE From Zwolle, two **trains** depart every hour, and **buses** about every half-hour, to Kampen. By **car,** take N50 northwest.

VISITOR INFORMATION **VVV Kampen,** Oudestraat 151, 8261 CL Kampen (✆ **038/331-3500;** www.vvvijsseldelta.nl), is in the center of town. The office is open January to mid-April and October to December Monday and Wednesday to Friday from 10am to 5pm, and Saturday from 10am to 4pm; and mid-April to September Monday to Friday from 9:30am to 5:30pm and Saturday from 10am to 4pm.

WHAT TO SEE & DO

The **Oude Raadhuis (Old Town Hall),** Oudestraat 133 (✆ **038/339-2999**), was reconstructed in 1543 after a fire that grievously damaged the original, built from 1345 to 1350. Pass by for a look at the onion-shaped tower and the oak-paneled 14th-century **Schepenzaal (Aldermen's Chamber),** with its carved-stone chimneypiece from 1545 and bust of Habsburg Emperor Charles V at its center. The Town Hall is open Monday to Friday from 10am to 4pm.

Across the way, the imposing Gothic **Sint-Nicolaaskerk (Church of St. Nicholas),** also known as the **Bovenkerk,** Koornmarkt 28 (✆ **038/331-6453**), achieved its final form around 1500. It has a massive organ with 3,200 pipes, and a tower that's 70m (230 ft.) high.

To get an idea of Kampen's illustrious history, visit the **Stedelijk (Municipal) Museum,** Oudestraat 133 (✆ **038/331-7361;** www.stedelijkemuseakampen.nl). The museum is open Tuesday to Saturday from 10am to 5pm and Sunday from 1 to 5pm. Admission is 5€ for adults; 3€ for seniors, students, and children 12 to 17; and free for children 12 and under.

A few doors along, the **Nieuwe Toren (New Tower),** Oudestraat 146, dating from 1664 and designed by Amsterdam architect Philips Vingboons, has a 47-bell Hemony carillon in its octagonal belfry. For a fine view over the town, climb the 152 interior steps. The tower is open May to August Wednesday and Saturday from 2 to 5pm. Admission is 1€ for adults and free for children 13 and under.

There's no better way to get close to the spirit of those Hanseatic League traders of yore than by stepping aboard the ***Kamper Kogge*** ★, Havenweg 7 (✆ **038/331-0515;** www.kamper-kogge.nl), on the IJssel waterfront. Constructed of oak using original methods, this is a replica of the broad-beamed, deep-draft, single-masted merchant vessels, called cogs, that in the 13th and 14th centuries plied the Hanseatic League's Baltic and North Sea trade routes, connecting Lübeck, Bergen, London, Bruges, and other ports. Each could carry up to 200 tons of bulk cargo—salt, furs, wax, dried and salted fish, grain, cod-liver oil, beer, textiles, and more. The *Kamper Kogge* is open to visitors Monday to Friday from 10am to 5pm, unless it's being used for a special event. To go onboard costs 3€ for adults and 2€ for school-age kids.

Out of the seven original fortified gates in the demolished town walls, three survive. The riverside **Koornmarktspoort,** IJsselkade 1, from the first half of the 14th century, is the oldest gate and for a long time was used as a prison and garrison quarters. West of the center of town, the **Broederpoort,** Tweede Ebbingestraat 50, dates from 1465 and was partly reconstructed between 1615 and 1617 in Renaissance style

Boat People

The Royal Huisman Shipyard at Vollenhove, 14km (9 miles) north of Kampen, builds luxury sailboats for the world's wealthy and world-class racing yachts that have won an occasional Admiral's Cup trophy and Round-the-World Race. Silicon Graphics founder Jim Clark is something of a regular customer. Huisman constructed his 89m (292-ft.) three-masted schooner *Athena,* and the earlier 52m (171-ft.) sloop *Hyperion* (that has since been sold).

after losing its military role when the town defenses were pushed farther out. Like this gate, its near neighbor **Cellebroederpoort,** Tweede Ebbingestraat 1, with twin towers, was constructed in the second half of the 14th century and, between 1615 and 1617, was partly reconstructed for the same reasons. On its town side are two sculptured lions bearing shields.

Giethoorn ★

26km (16 miles) N of Zwolle

This picture-postcard village has no streets, only canals (and walking and bicycling paths). You get here by hourly **bus** from Zwolle. By **car,** take N331 north along the Zwarte Water river to Zwartsluis, and N334 northeast across the beautiful Overijssel lakes. Then leave your car at a car park on the edge of Giethoorn and follow a signposted path to the main canal. Visitor information is available from **VVV Giethoorn,** Eendrachtsplein 1, 8355 DL Giethoorn (✆ **0900/567-4637;** www.ervaarhetwaterreijk.nl). The office is open Monday from 1 to 5pm, Tuesday to Friday from 10am to 5pm, and Saturday from 10am to 4pm.

A rented punt is a romantic way to glide under the village's humpback bridges, past farms, meadows, and enchanting old canal-side cottages with reed-thatched roofs and carefully tended gardens. Should punting seem too much like work, rent a launch with an electric motor and still enjoy the experience in tranquillity.

For an insight into the rural area's way of life, visit the **Museumboerderij (Farmhouse Museum) 't Olde Maat Uus,** Binnenpad 52 (✆ **0521/362-244;** www.oldemaatuus.nl), in an 1826 house decked out with local craft and farming displays. The museum is open Easter to fall school vacations Monday to Saturday from 11am to 5pm and Sunday from noon to 5pm, and during school vacations from the rest of the year from noon to 5pm. Admission is 4€ for adults and 1€ for children.

Just 8km (5 miles) to the west, the now inland village of **Blokzijl,** which lost its port to the IJsselmeer project, is a fair monument to past trading, fishing, and whaling wealth, from its days as a member of the Hanseatic League to the 17th and 18th centuries, when ships of the United East India Company sheltered in its harbor while storms raged on the Zuiderzee. A maritime museum, **In Den Coop'ren Duikhelm (In the Copper Diving Helmet),** Binnenpad 62 (✆ **0521/362-211**), takes as its theme the changing seascape of the Zuiderzee/IJsselmeer and, as its name suggests, has a section on diving. The museum is open March to October daily 10am to 6pm and November to February daily 11am to 5pm. Admission is free.

Northwest of Giethoorn stretches **Nationaal Park De Weerribben,** a protected landscape of reed marshes and moorland crisscrossed by narrow water channels.

Step Back into Staphorst

Staphorst, 16km (10 miles) north of Zwolle on the Meppel road, has colorfully dressed residents living as their ancestors did. This is no tourist act. You seldom get an enthusiastic welcome from these devout and strict Calvinists, especially on Sunday, when the entire population observes a tradition that dates back centuries: With downcast eyes, separate lines of men and women form a silent procession to the churches. No automobiles are allowed into the village on the Sabbath—even bicycle riding is forbidden. Cameras are always frowned upon. Whenever you come to Staphorst—on Sunday or a weekday—be sure to respect the townspeople's conservative ways.

WHERE TO STAY

Kaatjes Résidence ★ Weary travelers on the polders can settle in at this charming 17th-century mansion hotel in the heart of picturesque Blokzijl. You'll see passing boats and bicycles when you look out of one of the big picture windows of the tastefully furnished, comfortable rooms. The finest views are from room nos. 12 and 14. Breakfast is served in a bright winter garden, and on a water-side terrace in the summer. Across the canal, the restaurant (see below) deserves its fine reputation.

Zuiderstraat 1, 8356 DZ Blokzijl. ✆ **0527/208-580.** Fax 0527/208-590. www.kaatjesresidence.nl. 8 units. 129€–225€ double. Rates include buffet breakfast. AE, DC, MC, V. Free parking. **Amenities:** Lounge. *In room:* A/C, TV, minibar, Wi-Fi.

WHERE TO DINE

Kaatje bij de Sluis ★★ CONTINENTAL The name means "Kate's by the Sluice," which is appropriate enough, since it's located right beside a canal sluice and drawbridge in Blokzijl. Across the canal from Kaatjes Résidence, the restaurant deserves its fine reputation. The menu is not extensive and changes seasonally according to what's special and available. You can expect a couple of fish dishes and three or four meat dishes, two of which are likely to be duck and beef tournedos.

Brouwerstraat 20, Blokzijl. ✆ **0527/291-833.** www.kaatje.nl. AE, DC, MC, V. Main courses 42€; fixed-price menus 63€–99€. Tues–Sat 6–10pm.

LELYSTAD & THE NOORDOOSTPOLDER

41km (26 miles) NE of Amsterdam; 30km (19 miles) W of Kampen

This ultramodern town (pop. 74,000) and capital of Holland's newest province, Flevoland, has little—nothing, really—in the way of traditional Dutch character to offer. Yet a number of standout attractions here justify an expedition across the flat, bare polders; indeed, a drive across those polders, wrested from the IJsselmeer during recent decades, has its own peculiar fascination. On Saturdays, vendors on Gordiaandreef in the heart of town hawk everything from smoked eels to crafts to cheese, in a street market that's been voted one of Holland's finest.

To complete the IJsselmeer's "Golden Circle," see "The Western IJsselmeer Shore," in chapter 14, and "The Eastern IJsselmeer Shore," in chapter 16.

Essentials

GETTING THERE Two **trains** arrive at Lelystad Centrum Station every hour from Amsterdam Centraal Station. By **car** from Amsterdam, take A6 northeast; from Kampen, take N307 and N309 west.

VISITOR INFORMATION **Tourist Info Lelystad,** De Meent 14, 8224 BR Lelystad (✆ **0320/278-222;** www.touristinfo.lelystad.nl), is in the center of town. The office is open Monday to Wednesday and Friday from 8:30am to 5pm, Thursday from 8:30am to 5pm and 6 to 8pm, and Saturday from 9am to 4pm.

What to See & Do

Bataviawerf (Batavia Wharf) ★★ ☺ Step aboard the moored, faithful reconstruction of the *Batavia,* a three-masted sailing ship of the Vereenigde Oostindische Compagnie (United East India Company), and imagine yourself en route to the fabled Spice Islands. Launched in 1628 at the V.O.C.'s Amsterdam yard, the original *Batavia* sailed in 1629 on her maiden voyage to the East Indies but struck a reef off Australia and broke up. The survivors' subsequent experience of mutiny, murder, rescue, and retribution electrified Dutch society. This replica, 50m (164 ft.) long, cluttered with spars, sails, and rigging, was constructed here between 1985 and 1995 mostly by unemployed teens using 16th- and 17th-century tools and construction techniques. Tour the ship, and visit the onshore workshops where the ship pieces were assembled.

Currently taking shape at the wharf, amid a clattering of hammers on wood, is a full-size replica of the 80-gun ship-of-the-line *Zeven Provinciën (Seven Provinces),* launched in Rotterdam in 1665 and later the flagship of Adm. Michiel de Ruyter. During a 30-year career, the original ship saw action in many a sea battle in the wars against England and France. Construction of the replica began in 1995.

The Batavia Wharf museum exhibits ships and relics from ships that went to a watery grave in the Zuiderzee as far back as Roman times. Their remains were revealed as water was pumped out to make way for polderland. The process of reconstructing old, sunken ships, after finding and recovering them, is made both visible and accessible to visitors.

Oostvaardersdijk 1–9 (just off the Markerwaard dike rd.). ✆ **0320/261-409.** www.bataviawerf.nl. Admission 11€ adults, 9€ seniors, 5.50€ children 6–12, free for children 5 and under. Daily 10am–5pm. Closed Jan 1 and Dec 25. Bus: D from Lelystad Centrum station.

Nieuwland Poldermuseum ☺ The Dutch themselves have created a fair part of the solid ground their country stands on by taking new land from the sea and draining it to create polders. This fascinating museum affords an understanding of how they did it, in particular around the old Zuiderzee. You learn about the construction of dikes, the pumping process, the final drying-up operation, and making the newly won land habitable. The museum is housed in a building that represents a cross section of a polder dike. Children can get down and dirty with the "Play with Water" interactive exhibit, where they get to construct their own dikes.

Oostvaardersdijk 1–13 (next to the Bataviawerf). ✆ **0320/225-900.** www.nieuwlanderfgoed.nl. Admission 7.50€ adults, 6€ seniors, 3.50€ children 6–17, free for children 5 and under, 16€ family. Tues–Fri and Mon during local school vacations 10am–5pm; Sat–Sun and holidays 11:30am–5pm. Closed Jan 1 and Dec 25. Bus: D from Lelystad Centrum station.

Art of Earth & Sun

In 1977, American sculptor Robert Morris created a kind of modern Stonehenge, with his *Observatorium Robert Morris,* a little way northeast of Lelystad on N307. From inside twin concentric rings of embanked earth, 3m (10 ft.) high, you look through openings that spot the sunrise on the first day of summer, the first day of winter, the vernal equinox (Mar 21), and the autumnal equinox (Sept 23).

NEARBY ATTRACTIONS

All kind of thrills and enjoyment for the whole family are on offer at **Walibi World,** Spijkweg 30 (✆ **0321/329-999;** www.walibiworld.nl), near Biddinghuizen, 22km (14 miles) east of Lelystad. Top billing goes to the Goliath, the highest, longest, fastest, and steepest roller coaster in the Benelux lands. There's plenty of other rides, a minitrain for young children, theme areas like Bugs Bunny World and Sherwood Forest, a Wild West show, and restaurants and snack bars. The park is open April to October daily 10am to 6pm (to 5pm weekdays Apr–May and Sept–Oct). Admission is 29€ for adults; 27€ for seniors, visitors with disabilities, and children 4 to 11; and free for children 3 and under. To get here by bus from Lelystad, take Connexxion bus no. 249 from Lelystad Centrum train station; by car, take N309 and N306.

Just outside Lelystad is Holland's largest wetlands nature reserve, the **Oostvaardersplassen,** covering 60 sq. km (23 sq. miles). While this might not be wildly exciting to everybody, it should be for birders, since every year this area is visited by 100,000 nesting and migrating birds. In recent years, a small number of sea eagles and ospreys have been nesting in the reserve. The marshes lie west of town, on either side of the A6 Amsterdam expressway. There's a visitor center at Knardijk with information and observation hides.

Urk ★

19km (12 miles) N of Lelystad

This quaint fishing village was a Zuiderzee island for more than 700 years, its isolation undisturbed until the IJsselmeer reclamation project joined it to the mainland in 1942. Urk now lies on the west coast of the Noordoostpolder (Northeast Polder), a flat, reclaimed farm-landscape in the north of Flevoland province covering 480 sq. km (185 sq. miles).

ESSENTIALS

GETTING THERE **Buses** leave every hour on average from the bus station outside Lelystad Centrum train station. By **car,** take A6 north from Lelystad, and then go west on N352. While you will certainly encounter cars on the narrow brick-paved streets, it's a good idea to park outside the village and take to your feet.

VISITOR INFORMATION **Tourist Info Urk** is at Wijk 2/2, 8321 EP Urk (✆ **0527/684-040;** http://new.touristinfourk.nl). The office is open April to October Monday to Friday from 10am to 5pm and Saturday from 10am to 4pm, and November to March Monday to Saturday from 10am to 4pm.

WHAT TO SEE & DO

As you walk past picturesque brick homes lining tiny streets, notice the decorated wooden doors and elaborate wrought ironwork. At the long piers in the busy harbor are moored sturdy fishing boats that sail in search of eels. Smoked eel is sold everywhere in Urk, and there's a busy fish market.

Eel Selection

When buying smoked eels, demonstrate your expertise by selecting only the skinny ones (the fat ones aren't as tasty).

The small **Museum Het Oude Raadhuis,** Wijk 2/2 (✆ **0527/683-262;** www.museum.opurk.nl), in the old Town Hall, has exhibits about Urk's ancient and recent history, fishing traditions, and displays of local costumes and architecture. It's open April to October Monday to Friday from 10am to 5pm and Saturday from 10am to 4pm. Admission is 4€ for adults, 3.50€ for seniors, 2€ for children 6 to 12, free for children 5 and under, and 10€ for a family.

Schokland ★

12km (8 miles) E of Urk

Like Urk, this used to be an island, but it was uninhabited by the time the polders were created. Because of the threat of inundation, the island community was evacuated in 1859. Nowadays Schokland seems like a phantom island, outlined by trees emerging from the flat polder, with a lonely church, a cannon that was fired to warn of rising waters, and a few old anchors as witnesses to its past. It's special enough, though, to have been declared a UNESCO World Heritage Site.

Visit the **Museum Schokland,** Middlebuurt 3 (✆ **0527/251-396;** www.schokland.nl), in a church (1834) that stands on slightly raised ground. It holds Bronze Age tools, mammoth bones, and other prehistoric relics, as well as stone coffins from the 1100s and pottery dating as far back as 900. All were discovered on the sea bottom when the polder was drained. The museum is open April to October Tuesday to Sunday (also Mon July–Aug) from 11am to 5pm and November to March Friday to Sunday from 11am to 5pm (closed Jan 1 and Dec 25). Admission is 3.80€ for adults, 3€ for seniors and children 6 to 12, and free for children 5 and under.

ZEELAND, NOORD-BRABANT & LIMBURG

18

History, recreation, and attractive scenery are abundant in the southern Netherlands. The locals share a relaxed view of the world and place emphasis on life's pleasures. They lump Amsterdammers together with the other "cold-blooded" northerners as people too straitlaced to know how to have a good time.

Zeeland's three-part harmony of sea, land, and sky is so smooth it's sometimes hard to say where one begins and another ends. The province's islands have been stitched together by a succession of great dams and barriers that bring a measure of security to the inhabitants of this low-lying delta, where the Rhine, Waal, Maas, and Scheldt rivers drain into the North Sea. Elegant harbor towns like Zierikzee and Veere retain the character of past centuries, when Zeeland's seafarers plied the world's oceans.

Scenic **Noord-Brabant (North Brabant)** has waterways and polders in the north and west; sand drifts, moors, and fir and deciduous forests in the south and east; and tranquil villages and ancient towns.

Limburg is shaped like a leg stepping into the space between Germany and Belgium. Coming into the province from the north, you notice a gradual transformation taking place in the landscape. Gone are the flat Dutch fields interlaced with canals. Contours appear. The change becomes more pronounced the farther south you go and culminates in steep hills. Truth be told, the hills aren't that high, yet in a country where you get a view just by standing on a match, Limburg has hidden depths.

ZIERIKZEE ★

48km (30 miles) SW of Rotterdam

This harbor town on the Oosterschelde (Eastern Scheldt) shore of the one-time islands of Schouwen and Duiveland, now joined together, is among the best-preserved towns in the Netherlands. Just big enough (pop. 11,000) to escape the "sleepy" category, Zierikzee is still guarded by

Zeeland, Noord-Brabant & Limburg

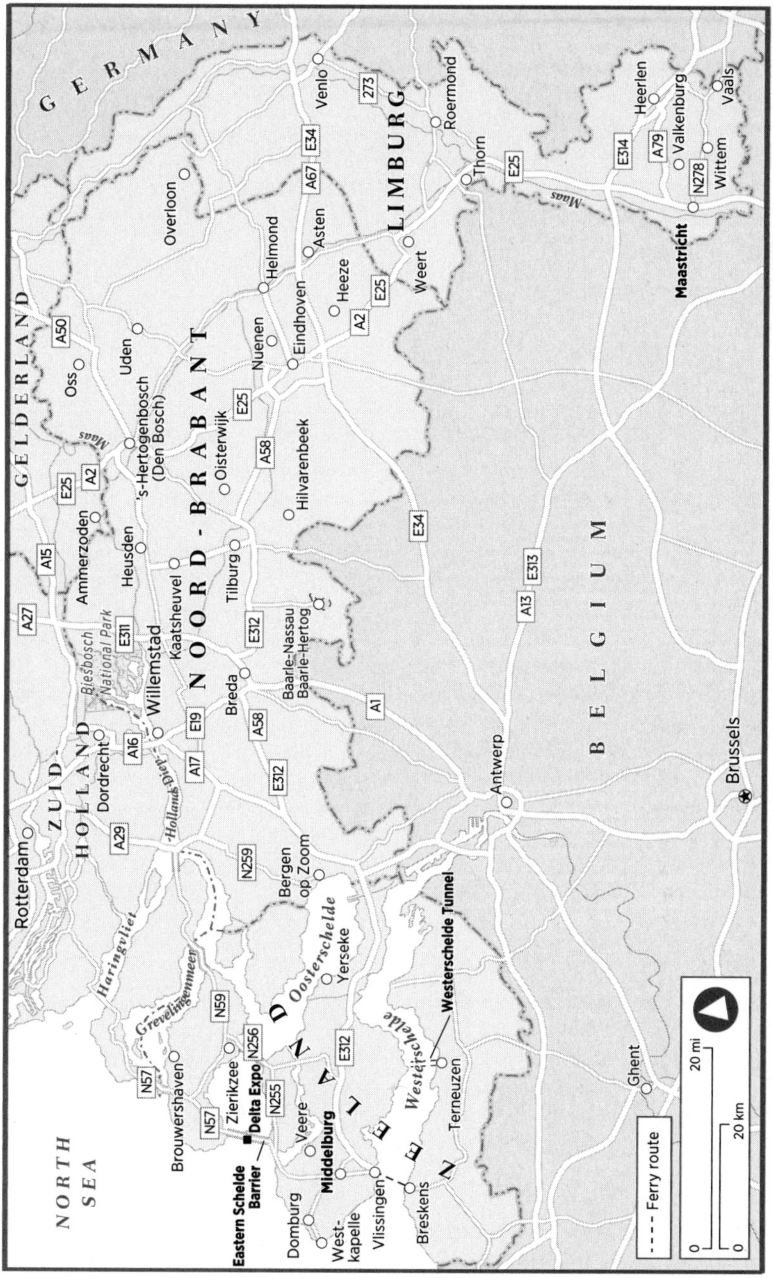

a wall constructed during the Middle Ages and has elegant whitewashed 16th- to 18th-century houses.

Essentials

GETTING THERE **Buses** depart every hour to Zierikzee from outside the train station in nearby Goes. By **car** from Rotterdam, take A29 and N59 south and west. An alternative route, skirting the coast, is N57 south to the junction with N59, and then east on this road into town.

VISITOR INFORMATION **VVV Zierikzee,** Nieuwe Haven 7, 4301 DG Zierikzee (✆ **0900/202-0233;** fax 0111/450-525; www.vvvzeeland.nl), is at the harbor. The office is open Monday to Saturday from 10am to 4pm.

What to See & Do

Strolling Zierikzee's narrow, cobblestone streets, you'll likely find it easy to imagine the everyday life of its citizens in earlier times, especially if you're here for a colorful Thursday market day (8:30am–4pm). The entrance to the old harbor is guarded by two impressive fortified gates, **Zuidhavenpoort** (14th–15th c.) on the south side of the waterway, and **Noordhavenpoort** (15th–16th c.) on the north side.

In the center of the Old Town, the **Stadhuis (Town Hall),** Meelstraat 6 (✆ **0111/454-454**) began around 1550 as a covered market. Its carillon tinkles merrily at frequent intervals. On the corner of Poststraat, across from the Town Hall, is the oldest house in town, the 14th-century **Huis De Haene** (or Templiershuis). Look for the **Sint-Lievensmonstertoren** (**Great Tower;** 1454) on the cathedral, west of the Town Hall. For all its 60m (197 ft.) of height, the tower is actually incomplete, since townspeople lacked the funds to take it up to an intended 204m (670 ft.).

Zierikzee's rich history as a maritime trading town, stretching back to 976, is presented by way of antique model ships and other exhibits at the **Maritiem Museum,** Mol 25 (✆ **0111/454-464;** www.museaschouwenduiveland.nl), across from the Town Hall in the 16th-century 's-Gravensteen building. This was originally the town prison, and its upstairs cells still bear the marks of prisoners who carved their names and other graffiti on the oak walls. The museum is open April to October Monday to Saturday from 10am to 5pm and Sunday from noon to 5pm; November to March, it's open during school vacations only from 10am to 5pm (closed Jan 1 and Dec 25). Admission is 2€ for adults, 1€ for seniors and children 6 to 12, and free for children 5 and under.

Where to Stay

Hostellerie Schuddebeurs ★ Amid an area of villas in the wooded countryside on the edge of the nearby village of Schuddebeurs, you'll find this bungalow-style, 3-centuries-old restored farmhouse. The guest rooms are fitted out in fancy country style, with exposed beams and old-fashioned original or replica furniture. The new wings have some rooms on the ground floor with their own garden terraces. A top-notch French/Dutch restaurant, the centerpiece of various gastronomic arrangements, locally sources many of its products—mussels and oysters from the Oosterschelde, and highly fancied Schouwen lamb, for instance—and in summer you can dine on the garden terraces. Golf is on the menu, too, at a nearby course.

Donkereweg 35, 4317 NL Schuddebeurs (3km/2 miles north of Zierikzee). ✆ **0111/415-651.** Fax 0111/413-103. www.schuddebeurs.nl. 24 units. 130€–169€ double; 214€ suite. AE, DC, MC, V. Free parking. **Amenities:** Restaurant; bar; lounge; nearby golf course. *In room:* TV, minibar, Wi-Fi (free).

Where to Dine

Brasserie Maritime ★ SEAFOOD Overlooking the harbor and Zierikzee's fishing fleet, this informal bar-cafe-restaurant in the town center is a pleasant stop for a meal or for drinks and snacks. The atmosphere inside is an updated brasserie style, with a relatively plain decor of wood tables and long banquettes, placing the emphasis on conviviality and what's served on the plate. Try the sea bass in a pastry crust with dill sauce, or the lamb cutlets with thyme and honey (there are always a few menu dishes for meat eaters). Oysters and lobsters are kept fresh in a special aquarium. Outdoor seating is available in the summer.

Nieuwe Haven 21. ✆ **0111/412-156.** www.brasseriemaritime.nl. Main courses 25€–29€; *fruits de mer* plates 29€–58€. AE, MC, V. May–Aug daily noon–11pm; Sept–Apr Tues–Sun noon–11pm.

Around Schouwen-Duiveland

On a wide Zeeland horizon from which an occasional church steeple rises amid a hazy cluster of red-roofed houses, the former islands of Schouwen and Duiveland are great places to explore by bicycle or car. The handsome little village of **Dreischor,** 7km (4 miles) north of Zierikzee, is a good target for an excursion. It's ringed by a canal and has a 14th- to 15th-century church with a leaning tower at its heart.

Approximately 17km (11 miles) west of Zierikzee is a great North Sea **beach** backed by sea dunes, centered on the resort of Nieuw-Haamstede. It curves around from Westenschouwen in the south to Renesse in the north. Many summer visitors' activities in Zeeland stretch no farther than a stint on this beach. At Westenschouwen is the northern access to the monumental Eastern Scheldt Barrier (see below).

The Oosterschelde estuary is an important feeding ground and stopover point for migrating birds, and bird-watchers flock to these parts to admire them.

The Delta Works ★

For as long as people have lived in Zeeland and in neighboring parts of the delta of the rivers Rhine, Maas, Waal, and Scheldt, their tenancy depended on nature's consent. But on a cold, dark morning—February 1, 1953—that consent was withdrawn. A fierce hurricane sent the North Sea surging through the sea dikes and across the land to a record depth of 4.6m (15 ft.), drowning more than 1,800 people. Following the disaster, construction began on a massive system of sea defenses, known collectively as the **Deltawerken (Delta Works).** This colossal feat of engineering aimed to prevent a repeat performance. It took 3 decades of dredging, dumping, towing, and building to create the network's component parts. Dams on the seaward side close off the former Haringvliet and Grevelingenmeer inlets, now lakes, and more dams and raised dikes protect the mainland coast.

The most impressive among the engineering marvels is the **Eastern Scheldt Barrier—Oosterscheldekering** in Dutch. This string of 65 gigantic sluice-gates, stretching 9km (5½ miles) across the tidal inlet between Schouwen-Duiveland and Noord-Beveland, can be opened and closed during storms. The barrier's towers support a four-lane highway.

Deltapark Neeltje Jans ★★ ☺ Even if you don't think you have any interest in dams, engine rooms, and the like, a visit to the intriguing Delta Expo—on a man-made island called Neeltje Jans in the middle of the Oosterschelde—is well worthwhile. To give visitors an overall view of the massive Delta Works undertaking, a huge scale-model of the complex is accompanied by an easily understood explanation of

> **Impressions**
>
> ***He who cannot master the sea is not worthy of the land.***
>
> **—Dutch saying**

how it all works. You are treated to a film history and map demonstration, after which you descend into the innards of one of the Eastern Scheldt Barrier's 36 sluice-gate engine rooms. In addition, there's a seal basin, a 3-D film, and Holland's largest exhibit on whales. Allow yourself no less than 2 hours, and additional time for a boat tour that takes you around the barrier during the summer months.

Faelweg 5, Neeltje Jans island (15km/9 miles west of Zierikzee, off N57). ✆ **0111/655-660.** www.neeltjejans.nl. Admission 19€ adults, 16€ seniors, free for children 3 and under. Apr-Oct daily 10am-5:30pm; Nov-Mar Wed-Sun 10am-5pm. Bus: 133 from Zierikzee (ride takes 20 min.).

MIDDELBURG ★

74km (46 miles) SW of Rotterdam; 27km (17 miles) SW of Zierikzee

At the center of Zeeland is Walcheren (often still called Walcheren Island even though it has long been connected to the mainland), which holds the bustling provincial capital, Middelburg (pop. 40,000). A medieval town that has restored its 1,000 historical landmarks so successfully you'd think they've stood undisturbed through the centuries, it began as a 9th-century fortress, erected as a defense against Viking raiders. The fortifications expanded into a settlement around 1150, when an abbey was established.

On Thursday, Middelburg's colorful **market day,** mingle in the Markt square with locals, some of whom wear traditional dress.

Essentials

GETTING THERE Two **trains** to Middelburg depart every hour from Amsterdam, Rotterdam, The Hague, and other points. By **car,** take A29 and N259 south from Rotterdam to Bergen op Zoom, and then go west on A58/E312.

VISITOR INFORMATION **Tourist Shop Middelburg** is at Markt 51, 4331 LK Middelburg (✆ **0118/674-300;** fax 0118/674-333; www.touristshop.nl), across from the Town Hall. The office is open Monday from 11am to 6pm, Tuesday to Friday from 9am to 6pm (to 9pm Thurs), Saturday from 9am to 5pm, and the first Sunday of the month from 1 to 5pm.

What to See & Do

Middelburg sights you shouldn't miss include the **picturesque streets** of Spanjaardstraat—crowned by the monumental **Oostkerk (East Church)**—Kuiperspoort, and Bellinkstraat; the 1559 **Vismarkt (Fish Market),** with its Doric columns and little auctioneers' houses, where Thursdays in summer are **arts and crafts market** days; the **Blauwpoort (Blue Gate);** and the **Koepoort (Cow Gate).**

The side of the elaborate **Stadhuis (Town Hall),** Markt (✆ **0118/675-450**), facing the market square is Gothic and dates from the 15th century; the Noordstraat side, from the 17th and 18th centuries, is classic in style. Inside are Belgian tapestries from the 1600s, 17th-century Makkum tiles, and the Middelburg coat of arms. To the left of the main entrance is the vaulted Vleeshal (Meat Hall), which hosts contemporary art exhibits. The Town Hall is open for guided tours April to October Saturday to

Middelburg

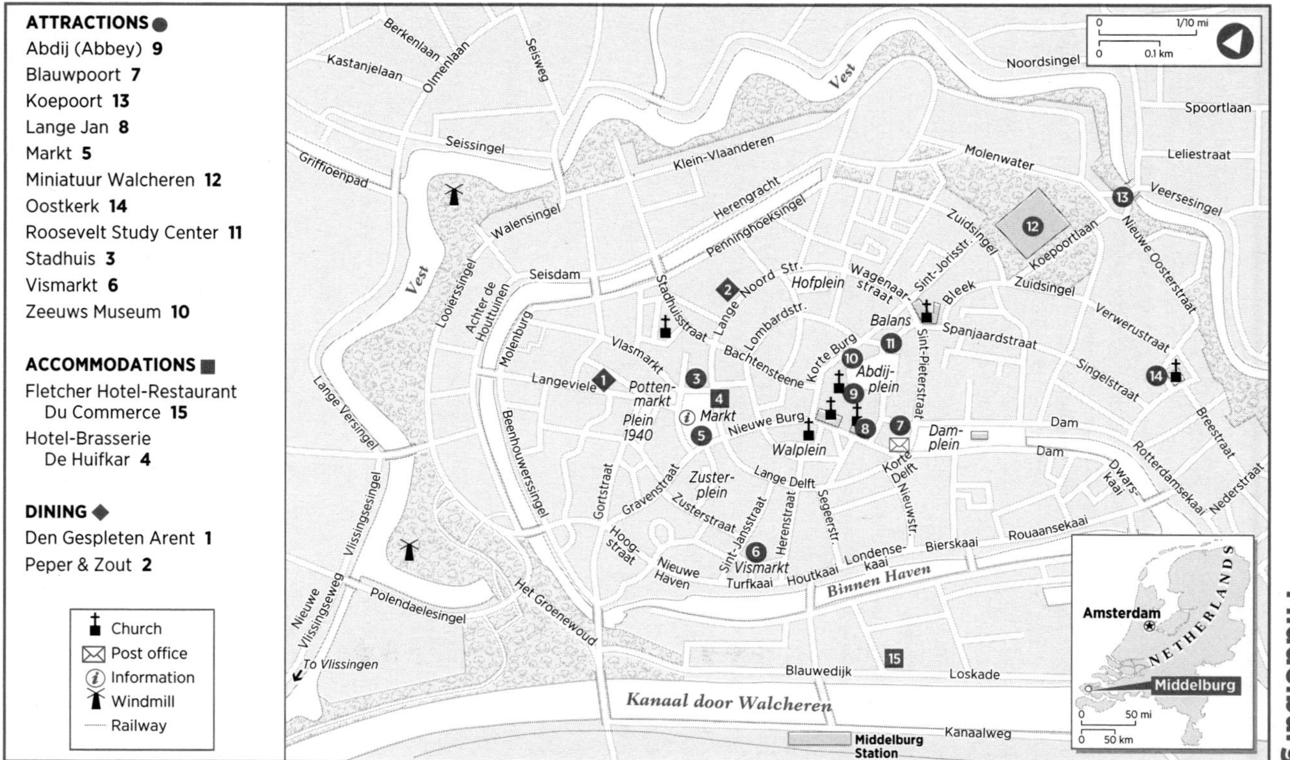
ATTRACTIONS ●
Abdij (Abbey) 9
Blauwpoort 7
Koepoort 13
Lange Jan 8
Markt 5
Miniatuur Walcheren 12
Oostkerk 14
Roosevelt Study Center 11
Stadhuis 3
Vismarkt 6
Zeeuws Museum 10
ACCOMMODATIONS ■
Fletcher Hotel-Restaurant Du Commerce 15
Hotel-Brasserie De Huifkar 4
DINING ◆
Den Gespleten Arent 1
Peper & Zout 2
Church
Post office
Information
Windmill
Railway
0 1/10 mi
0 0.1 km
NETHERLANDS
Amsterdam
Middelburg
0 50 mi
0 50 km
Berkenlaan
Kastanjelaan
Olmenlaan
Seisweg
Noordsingel
Spoortlaan
Leliestraat
Veersesingel
Vest
Seissingel
Griffioenpad
Klein-Vlaanderen
Molenwater
Herengracht
Penninghoeksingel
Walensingel
Zuidsingel
Koepoortlaan
Nieuwe Oosterstraat
Seisdam
Looierssingel
Achter de Houttuinen
Molenburg
Stadhuisstraat
Lange Noord Str.
Hofplein
Wagenaar-straat
Sint-Jorisstr.
Bleek
Verwerustraat
Lombardstr.
Balans
Sint-Pieterstraat
Spanjaardstraat
Singelstraat
Vlasmarkt
Bachtensteene
Korte Burg
Abdij-plein
Langeviele
Potten-markt
Markt
Plein 1940
Nieuwe Burg
Dam-plein
Dam
Breestraat
Walplein
Rotterdamsekaai
Nederstraat
Dwars-kaai
Lange Versingel
Beenhouwerssingel
Gortstraat
Gravenstraat
Zuster-plein
Zusterstraat
Lange Delft
Korte Delft
Nieuwstr.
Segeerstr.
Herenstraat
Sint-Jansstraat
Hoog-straat
Nieuwe Haven
Vismarkt
Turfkaai
Houtkaai
Londense-kaai
Bierskaai
Rouaansekaai
Binnen Haven
Vlissingsesingel
Nieuwe Vlissingseweg
Polendaelesingel
Het Groenewoud
To Vlissingen
Blauwedijk
Loskade
Kanaal door Walcheren
Kanaalweg
Middelburg Station

Living Traditions

The local costume—for women, a long, simple black dress with a blue pinafore—is still worn on occasion in Walcheren and Zuid-Beveland. (In the latter, the women wearing bonnets shaped like conch shells are Protestant, while those wearing trapezoidal bonnets with a light-blue underbonnet are Catholic.) On some holidays, you might happen on the traditional game of *ringsteken,* in which contestants ride on bare horseback and try, as they gallop past, to thrust a pointed stick through a ring dangling from a line strung high between two poles.

Thursday at 11:30am and 3:15pm. Admission is 4.25€ for adults; 3.75€ for seniors, visitors with disabilities, and children 6 to 12; and free for children 5 and under.

Abdij (Abbey) ★ Middelburg's sprawling 13th-century abbey in the center of town had a career of traumatic ups and downs over the centuries, as it went from Catholic to Protestant to secular usages, all the while suffering from fires and careless alterations at the hands of whoever happened to be in charge. What you see today is a replica of the original, reconstructed following World War II bombings. Soaring 87m (285 ft.) into the sky, the 14th-century **Lange Jan (Long John) Tower** can be seen from any point on the island and has magnificent panoramic views from its summit.

Part of the abbey complex is occupied by the **Zeeuws Museum (Zeeland Museum)** ★, which houses a collection of antiquities. Highlights include a Roman altar to pagan sea-goddess Nehallenia recovered from the beach after a storm, a medieval stone coffin that was used for watering cattle, and 16th-century tapestries depicting the victory of Zeeland over the Spanish.

The **Roosevelt Study Center** was established in honor of Theodore, Franklin Delano, and Eleanor Roosevelt, whose ancestors—the Belgian Protestant de la Noyes—emigrated to the New World in the 1640s from the Zeeland town of Tholen. The library here holds extensive research material, including audiovisual and slide presentations. The annual Four Freedoms Medals (based on FDR's famous 1941 "Four Freedoms" speech) are awarded in Middelburg in even-numbered years, and in New York in odd-numbered years.

Abdijplein (at Onder de Toren). Lange Jan: ✆ **0118/615-525.** www.langejanmiddelburg.nl. Admission 4€ adults, free for children 5 and under. Apr–June and Sept–Oct Mon 1–4pm, Tues–Sun 10am–4pm; July–Aug daily 10am–5pm. Zeeuws Museum: ✆ **0118/653-000.** www.zeeuwsmuseum.nl. Admission 8€ adults, free for children 18 and under. Tues–Sun 11am–5pm. Closed Jan 1 and Dec 25. Roosevelt Study Center: ✆ **0118/631-590.** www.roosevelt.nl. Free admission. Mon–Fri 9:30am–12:30pm and 1:30–4:30pm; by appointment only.

Mini Mundi ★ ☺ Play giant at this miniature version of Walcheren Island, where model villages and farms give a different perspective on the area. This marvelous 1:20 scale model is a faithful replication of more than 200 buildings, moving trains and ships, and windmills. A delight for both young and old, it's a good place to visit before exploring Walcheren, where you see the real structures on which these models are based.

Podium 35. ✆ **0118/415-400.** www.minimundi.nl. Admission mid-March to mid-Dec 13€, free for children 2 and under; mid-Dec to mid-March 9.95€, free for children 2 and under. Mid-Apr to June daily 10am–7pm; July–Aug daily 10am–8pm; Sept to mid-Apr some weeks daily 10am–7pm, some weeks Wed and Fri noon–7pm, and Sat–Sun 10am–7pm; school vacations and national holidays daily 10am–7pm; check website to confirm the open hours for the day of your visit. The park is 5km (3 miles) SE of Middelburg, off N57.

Where to Stay

Fletcher Hotel-Restaurant du Commerce Across the Kanaal door Walcheren from the train station and an easy walk from the center of town, this canal-side hotel is in one of the town's most convenient locations. The guest rooms in the century-old building, a cut above merely plain, are bright, clean, and homey. Many of them have a sun-shaded balcony, which adds to the effect of the hotel's minor-resort style. Families might want to reserve the family room, which sleeps four or more. In the mornings, treat yourself to a varied breakfast buffet. For other meals, there's a good restaurant serving Continental food at moderate prices, and a sidewalk terrace to enjoy when the weather is nice.

Loskade 1 (at the Kanaal door Walcheren), 4331 HV Middelburg. ✆ **0347/750-405.** Fax 0118/626-400. www.hotelducommerce.nl. 45 units. 105€–125€ double. Rates include continental breakfast. AE, MC, V. Limited street parking. **Amenities:** Restaurant; bar; bikes; laundry room. *In room:* TV, Wi-Fi (6€/hr.).

Hotel-Brasserie De Huifkar This neat little hotel overlooks the bustling Markt square, right in the heart of town. While not luxurious, the guest rooms are well cared for and are furnished in a bright contemporary style. Downstairs is a decent Dutch brasserie with moderate prices, serving local Zeeland specialties and its own tourist menu. In the summer, you can dine on the lively sidewalk terrace on the Markt.

Markt 19, 4331 LJ Middelburg. ✆ **0118/612-998.** Fax 0118/612-386. www.hoteldehuifkar.nl. 5 units. 80€–90€ double. Rates include Dutch breakfast. AE, DC, MC, V. Limited street parking. **Amenities:** Restaurant; cafe; bar; Wi-Fi (6€/50 min.; unused minutes can be saved). *In room:* TV.

Where to Dine

De Gespleten Arent ★★ FRENCH/CONTINENTAL Meals here, though slightly more expensive than at most local restaurants, are exceptional. The friendly owner has created a warm and intimate atmosphere in this patrician-house setting. Food is prepared with an imaginative use of ingredients from a limited list of main-course options—generally, a pair each of meat and fish dishes.

Vlasmarkt 25–27 (near the Town Hall). ✆ **0118/636-122.** www.degespletenarent.nl. Main courses 28€–29€; fixed-price menus 48€–63€. MC, V. Tues–Sat 6–9pm.

Peper & Zout ★ CONTINENTAL You'll find cozy "Pepper & Salt" on a street next to the Gothic Town Hall. The place is full of small tables decked in yellow and brown. Besides serving almost any variety of fried and grilled fish, the restaurant's specialties include a succulent mussels au gratin Ste. Marie topped by a cream sauce. Meat choices are not neglected, and a tasty local dish is *tournedos* (steak) served with Zeeland mustard.

Lange Noordstraat 8 (close to the Stadhuis/Town Hall). ✆ **0118/627-058.** www.peperenzout.com. Main courses 18€–25€; fixed-price menus 34€–48€. AE, DC, MC, V. Mon and Thurs–Fri noon–2pm and 5:30–9:30pm; Sat–Sun 5:30–9:30pm.

Around Walcheren & Zuid-Beveland

VEERE ★

6km (4 miles) N of Middelburg

On the one-time island of Noord-Beveland, by the shore of a former sea inlet that is now a lake called the Veerse Meer, stands this charming village that was an important port for Scottish wool from the 14th to the 18th century. Those bygone trading links earned Scottish mariners the right to free hospitality—a right they surely took full advantage of. Veere's streets are lined with houses and buildings straight out of the past, and its original fortifications are still intact, the ancient harbor tower now housing an excellent hotel/restaurant (see below).

Buses go every hour from Middelburg. For visitor information, go to **VVV Veere,** Oudestraat 28, 4351 AV Veere (✆ **0118/581-342;** fax 084/215-0844; www.vvvzeeland.nl), in the center of the village. The office is open daily 10am to 4:30pm.

What to See & Do

The Gothic **Stadhuis (Town Hall),** Markt 5, dates in part from 1474—look outside for the *kaak,* an iron brace that locked around a wrongdoer's neck to hold him or her in place as townspeople threw refuse and insults. Over the *kaak* hang the "stones of the law," which an offender was forced to drag through the town in penance. Although today it's stripped to the bare bricks, the **Grote Kerk (Great Church),** Oudestraat 26, constructed between 1405 and 1560, is awe-inspiring for its sheer size.

After a stroll through streets filled with venerable buildings, head for the handsome waterfront and the old harbor, which is now a haunt of leisure-time mariners busy with the comings and goings of sailboats. You'll pass the 16th- to 17th-century **Schotse Huizen (Scottish Houses)** at Kade 25–27, waterfront mansions that belonged to Scottish wool merchants, and arrive finally at the cannon-studded **Campveerse Toren (Campveer Tower),** dating from around 1500, which was the key to the harbor defenses.

A small passenger-and-bicycle ferry operated by **Rederij Dijkhuizen** (✆ **0118/419-367;** www.rederij-dijkhuizen.nl) shuttles back and forth across the Veerse Meer lake between Veere harbor and Kamperland island; the ride takes just 15 minutes. The ferry sails four times a day (10:15am, noon, 3pm, and 5pm) in May to June and September on Tuesday, Thursday, Saturday, and Sunday; and in July and August daily. A one-way ticket costs 3.50€, and is free for children 3 and under.

Where to Stay & Dine

Romantik Hotel-Auberge de Campveerse Toren ★★ You couldn't ask for a more romantic location than the 16th-century waterfront fortress of which this delightful hotel, one of the oldest in the country, is a part. It offers simple but comfortable rooms with good light, wood floors, and antique furniture. The waters of the Veerse Meer are right below the windows. Some rooms are in nearby waterfront annexes, which have their own charm but lack the "wow" factor shared by the four rooms in the main building. In the expensive adjoining French restaurant, perched in a 16th-century tower room overlooking the lake, various gastronomic arrangements are available. The breakfast and dining room have been furnished in a 17th-century

The Zeeland Riviera

The western shore of Walcheren is a string of delightful small seacoast resorts, often called the Zeeland Riviera ★ because of its long stretches of wide, white-sand beaches. A few miles northwest of Vlissingen are Koudekerke, Westkapelle, and Domburg—all family-oriented resorts. Beaches are safe for swimming, and there are activities aplenty, including boating, golf, tennis, fishing, and walks in wooded areas near the beaches. This prime vacation country abounds with accommodations, including upscale hotels, bungalows, rustic cabins, and camping sites.

style, with wooden floors, wainscoted walls, and a huge stone fireplace, creating an intimate atmosphere.

Kaai 2, 4351 AA Veere. ✆ **0118/501-291.** Fax 0118/200-022. www.campveersetoren.nl. 16 units. 128€–175€ double. AE, DC, MC, V. Limited street parking. **Amenities:** Restaurant; bar. *In room:* TV, hair dryer.

VLISSINGEN

6km (4 miles) S of Middelburg

The port town of Vlissingen (in English, the name translates to Flushing) is a popular resort and hosts the Royal Netherlands Navy's southernmost base. Standing on the town beach or atop the waterfront dike, you get a front-row view of the 50,000 seagoing vessels that sail up and down the Scheldt annually—most of these are sailing to or from the ports of Antwerp, Ghent, and Terneuzen, but some head into and out of Vlissingen (pop. 45,000).

Essentials

GETTING THERE There are two **trains** hourly from Rotterdam and Amsterdam to Vlissingen, via Middelburg, and frequent **buses** from Middelburg. By car from Middelburg, drive south on N57.

A pair of **fast ferries,** the *Prinses Máxima* and the *Prins Willem-Alexander,* cross the Westerschelde (Western Scheldt) between Breskens on the coast of Zeeuws-Vlaanderen (Zeeland Flanders) and Vlissingen, opening up easy travel options from the neighboring Belgian seacoast resorts, and from Bruges and Ghent (but when going by car from Zeeuws-Vlaanderen, you need to take the tunnel under the Westerschelde from Ternuizen). The ferries are operated by **Veolia Fast Ferries** (✆ **0900/9292;** www.veolia-transport.nl). A day round-trip ticket is 4.55€ for adults; 2.70€ for seniors and children 4 to 11; 1.60€ for bicycles, scooters, and mopeds; and free for children 3 and under. The ferry ride takes 20 minutes, and there are two departures hourly in both directions.

VISITOR INFORMATION **VVV Vlissingen,** Spuistraat 30, 4381 HS Vlissingen (✆ **0118/715-320;** www.vlissingen.nl), is in the center of town. The office is open Monday from 1 to 5:30pm, Tuesday to Friday from 9:30am to 5:30pm, and Saturday from 9:30am to 5pm.

What to See & Do

In the Old Town, the **Oude Markt** and the neighboring 14th-century **Sint-Jacobskerk (St. James's Church)** are well worth visiting. Also, don't miss a stroll down the **seafront promenade** that's named variously De Ruyter, Bankert, and Evertsen, in honor of those Dutch naval heroes of yore.

The **Reptilienzoo Iguana,** Bellamypark 31–35 (✆ **0118/417-219;** www.iguana.nl), south of Oude Markt, is filled with animals that childhood nightmares are made of but that kids seem to love just the same. It's a fascinating introduction to the lives of reptiles, amphibians, and insects. There are more than 500 specimens from around the world on display, from tiny, creepy scorpions to endless tiger pythons, but they're not all scary—there are also frogs, turtles, and salamanders. In the baby room, eggs hatch and young animals crawl out of their shells. The zoo is open June to September Sunday and Monday from 2 to 5:30pm and Tuesday to Saturday from 10am to 5:30pm, and October to May daily from 1 to 5:30pm (closed Jan 1 and Dec 25). Admission is 8.50€ for adults, 7€ for seniors and children 4 to 11, and free for children 3 and under.

mussel-BOUND

The Oosterschelde's waters are ideal for building mussels. Whiplike branches sticking out of shallow water off Yerseke mark the location of "parcels"—stretches of water where mussels lie on the sandy bottom. In April and May, mussel cutters are busy "planting" mussel-seed: young mussels that will form the next year's crop. By the time they've grown to 4 centimeters (1½ in.), they've joined together in dense mats for mutual support against tidal pull. These are scooped up and moved for 2 weeks to other parcels, dubbed "wet warehouses," which have less sand, for the final growth to maturity. Once they reach 6 centimeters (2½ in.) or larger, they are ready for harvesting, destined for Belgium, Holland, and France. But as any mussel-cutter skipper will tell you: "The biggest ones are for me."

From the start of mussel season in July until it ends the following April, the cutters ply back and forth between port and parcels. On a good outing, a skipper can return to Yerseke with a thousand mussel-tonnes glistening in his hold—a mussel-tonne is 100 kilograms (220 lb.).

muZEEum ★ ☺ The collection of the Zeeland Maritime Museum includes ship models, finds from sunken ships, portraits of Dutch naval heroes, paintings of seascapes and harbor scenes, and more. The stars of the show are a thousand objects recovered by divers from the Dutch East Indiaman *'t Vliegent Hart*, which went down off Vlissingen in 1735.

Nieuwendijk 11 (at the harbor). ✆ **0118/412-498.** www.muzeeum.nl. Admission 8€ adults, 7€ seniors, 5€ children 4-12, free for children 3 and under. Mon-Fri 10am-5pm; Sat-Sun and holidays 1-5pm. Closed Jan 1.

YERSEKE

30km (19 miles) E of Middelburg

This busy little fishing port on the Oosterschelde is noted for its extensive offshore mussel beds (see "Mussel-Bound," below) and oyster farms, and for seafood restaurants that serve up these and other marine delights. Buses go to Yerseke every hour from the train station at Goes.

Where to Dine

Nolet-Het Reymerswale ★★ SEAFOOD Fish can't get much fresher than at this special waterfront restaurant. A member of Holland's prestigious Alliance Gastronomique Néerlandaise association of top restaurants, it sports a Michelin star. Most of what lands on your plate from master chef Danny Nolet's kitchen comes right off the local fishing boats in the harbor below. Het Reymerswale is named after a coastal Zeeland village that vanished beneath the waves around 1500, and the interior is "decorated" with excavated items from the village. Try the decadent oysters and champagne, or a more restrained dish like grilled turbot with a béarnaise sauce.

Burgemeester Sinkelaan 6 (at the Yerseke yacht harbor). ✆ **0113/572-101.** www.nolethetreymerswale.nl. Main courses 33€-65€; fixed-price menus 43€-68€. AE, MC, V. Thurs-Mon noon-2:30pm and 6-9pm.

BERGEN OP ZOOM

47km (29 miles) E of Middelburg

The center of this small town (Zoom rhymes with "home"), close to Zeeland and the Belgian border, is alive with many cafes and restaurants.

Essentials

GETTING THERE The town lies on the Amsterdam-Rotterdam-Vlissingen rail line, with **trains** every half-hour in both directions. By **car,** take A58/E312 east from Middelburg and west from Breda.

VISITOR INFORMATION Contact **VVV Brabantse Wal,** Korte Meestraat 19, 4600 AA Bergen op Zoom (✆ **0164/277-482;** fax 0164/240-176; www.vvvbrabantsewal.nl). The office is open Monday from 1 to 5pm, Tuesday to Saturday from 10am to 5pm, and Sunday (May–Oct) noon to 4pm.

What to See & Do

Part of the monumental **Stadhuis (Town Hall),** on the Grote Markt, is a beautiful 14th-century castlelike structure (reconstructed after being destroyed by a fire). Three more buildings were attached to the complex in subsequent centuries.

Het Markiezenhof (The Marquis's Court) ☺ Remnants of Bergen op Zoom's past as a small but powerful city-state can be found all over the center of town, and this unique palace is perhaps the most impressive example. It was constructed between 1485 and 1525, and was once home to the Marquis of Bergen op Zoom. Behind the striped facade of redbrick and yellow sandstone, you'll find the town's history museum and a kids-oriented fairground museum.

Steenbergsestraat 8 (at Moeregrebstraat). ✆ **0164/277-077.** www.markiezenhof.nl. Admission 7.50€ adults, 6€ seniors, 4€ children 6–12, free for children 5 and under. Tues–Sun 11am–5pm. Closed Jan 1 and Dec 25.

Where to Stay & Dine

Hotel de Draak & Résidence Dagmara ★ Modern comfort awaits you in Holland's oldest hotel, founded in 1397, which now occupies three adjacent buildings—which themselves date from the beginning of the 17th century—overlooking the lively market square in the heart of town. The guest rooms are decorated with antiques and flowery chintzes. Period furniture and a grand old fireplace lend the convivial lounge and bar a medieval character. The on-site French restaurant, **Hemingway Eten & Drinken,** is furnished in a 17th-century style, and you can dine outdoors on a large sidewalk terrace when the weather's good.

A Frontier Fort

If the powerful, star-shaped fortifications surrounding Willemstad, 24km (15 miles) north of Bergen op Zoom, are anything to go by, this handsome small town on the Hollandse Diep waterway once had a strategic importance far beyond its size. Today it is just one of many fortified riverside towns that tell of harsher times, when northern Brabant lay on the front line between the Spanish occupiers of the Lowlands and the free Dutch territories to the north.

Grote Markt 30 and 36–38, 4611 NT Bergen op Zoom. ✆ **0164/252-050.** Fax 0164/257-001. www.hoteldedraak.com. 51 units. 135€–195€ double; 275€ suite. AE, DC, MC, V. Limited street parking. **Amenities:** Restaurant; lounge/bar. *In room:* TV, minibar, Wi-Fi (17€/day).

BREDA

36km (22 miles) NE of Bergen op Zoom; 38km (24 miles) SW of Den Bosch

Breda was granted its town charter in 1252. In 1625 it withstood a 9-month siege before surrendering to Spanish forces. In 1667 the Treaty of Breda (between England, France, the Dutch United Provinces, and Denmark) awarded the New World colonies of Nieuw Amsterdam (New York) and New Jersey to the English. Today life in Breda centers around the bustling Grote Markt.

Essentials

GETTING THERE One direct **train** arrives every hour from Amsterdam, going via Rotterdam and The Hague; there's up to another six per hour involving either one or two transfers. By **car,** Breda lies just off the junction of A16/E19 from Rotterdam and Antwerp (in Belgium this expressway is designated A1/E19), and A27/E311 from Utrecht.

VISITOR INFORMATION **VVV Breda's** main office is at Willemstraat 17–19, 4811 AJ Breda (✆ **0900/522-2444;** fax 076/521-8530; www.vvvbreda.nl), across the street from the train station; it's open Monday from 1 to 5:30pm, Tuesday to Friday from 9:30am to 5:30pm, and Saturday from 10am to 4pm. A second office is on the main square in the center of town, at Grote Markt 38, open Tuesday (July–Aug only) and Wednesday to Friday from 10:30am to 5:30pm, and Saturday from 10:30am to 5pm.

What to See & Do

In the old center, **Kasteel Breda (Breda Castle),** dating from 1536, is now a military academy. On the Grote Markt, the town's main square, the **Grote Kerk (Great Church),** also known as the **Onze-Lieve-Vrouwekerk (Church of Our Lady),** contains the striking sculptured tombs of the lords of Breda Count Engelbrecht I of Nassau-Dillenburg (1380–1442) and his grandson Count Engelbrecht II (1451–1504).

The **Breda's Museum,** Chasséepark Breda, Parade 12–14 (✆ **076/529-9300;** www.breda-museum.org), has an extensive collection focusing on the town's history and on products manufactured in the region. It has a collection of religious objects belonging to the bishop of Tilburg. The museum is open Tuesday to Sunday and

Nobody's Town

Baarle-Nassau/Baarle-Hertog, an oddity of a town 20km (12 miles) southeast of Breda, can't make up its mind whether to be in Belgium or in Holland—so it exists in both. Houses use colored number plates to identify their citizenship. If the figures are blue, the occupants are Dutch; if they're black on a white background with a black, yellow, and red vertical stripe, the occupants are Belgian. Must get confusing!

THE biesbosch NATIONAL PARK ★★

The Nationaal Park de Biesbosch (Forest of Reeds), south of Rotterdam, shared between the provinces of Noord-Brabant and Zuid-Holland, bears the imprint of constant flooding by tidal surges and overflow from the rivers Maas and Waal. Once dry land, this area of marshland, meadows, and willow woods was formed during the great St. Elisabeth flood of 1421, when 16 villages were submerged and what had been polders became an inland sea. It has since been shaped by the interplay between the rivers and the tides. A unique culture developed on these isolated and partly drowned islands, where islanders harvested reeds that grew on the marshy land.

Since 1970, when the Haringvliet Dam, part of the Delta Works (see "The Delta Works," earlier in this chapter), was constructed at the seacoast, the Biesbosch has been a freshwater delta of creeks and inlets on and around the two rivers. An ecologically rich wetland, the Biesbosch is slowly being dried out by the flood-control measures that bring security to the coastal cities.

Its 90 sq. km. (35 sq. miles) of marshes and islands are a habitat that supports a large and varied bird population. A boat trip into the Biesbosch is a journey into a different world from the nearby polders. Kingfishers dart along reed-clogged channels, while a discord of bleeps, twitters, and honks—music to any bird-watcher's ears—escapes from ponds and marshes where heron, storks, geese, spoonbills, ducks, and cormorants make their homes. Beavers, last seen in the wild here in 1826, have been successfully reintroduced. Leisure activities in the Biesbosch include rowing and canoeing along its labyrinth of creeks and hiking.

In Zuid-Holland, the visitor center, **Biesboschcentrum Dordrecht,** Baanhoekweg 53, Dordrecht (✆ **078/630-5353;** www.biesbosch.org), is open May to September daily from 9am to 5pm, and October to April Tuesday to Sunday from 10am to 5pm (closed Jan 1–2 and Dec 25); admission is free. To get there from Rotterdam, on A15/E31 take junction 23, pass through Papendrecht, and then follow the signs. From Breda, take A16 to Dordrecht and N3 toward Papendrecht; then follow the signs east across the Merwede River.

On the Noord-Brabant side, the visitor center, the **Biesbosch Bezoekerscentrum Staatsbosbeheer,** Biesboschweg 4, Drimmelen (✆ **0162/682-233;** www.biesbosch.org), 17km (11 miles) north of Breda, is open Tuesday to Sunday (daily July–Aug) from 10am to 5pm (closed Jan 1 and Dec 25, 26, and 31); admission is free.

holidays from 10am to 5pm (closed Jan 1, Apr 30, and Dec 25). Admission is 5€ for adults, 3.50€ for seniors and children 4 to 13, and free for children 3 and under.

Van Gogh's Birthplace

Art lovers will surely want to stop by the village of **Zundert,** 15km (9 miles) southwest of Breda, on N263. This is the birthplace of Vincent van Gogh (1853–90). There's a touching statue (1963) here of the painter and his devoted brother, Theo, commissioned by the townspeople and sculpted by Ossip Zadkine. The spot where the van Gogh family home stood until it was demolished in 1903 is now occupied by the **Vincent van GoghHuis ★**, Markt 27 (✆ **076/597-8590;** www.vangoghhuis.com), a museum of remembrance of van Gogh and a gallery that has temporary exhibits—but generally not of original van Gogh paintings. It's open Wednesday to

Friday from 10am to 5pm and Saturday and Sunday from noon to 5pm (closed Jan 1, Easter Sun, Apr 30, Corso/Parade Sun, and Dec 25). Admission is 5€ for adults, 3.50€ for seniors, 2€ for students and children 13 to 18, and free for children 12 and under.

DEN BOSCH ('S-HERTOGENBOSCH)

74km (46 miles) SE of Amsterdam; 64km (40 miles) SE of Rotterdam

The full name of the Noord-Brabant provincial capital is 's-Hertogenbosch, meaning the Duke's Wood, but the place is generally referred to simply as Den Bosch—maybe the locals, too, have given up on trying to pronounce the longer version! This cathedral town (pop. 100,000) was given its town charter in 1184. Parts of the center city have retained their medieval atmosphere, in particular around the crooked alleys leading up to the odd triangular market "square," the Markt.

Essentials

GETTING THERE Up to four **trains** arrive in Den Bosch every hour from Amsterdam via Utrecht, and more from Rotterdam, The Hague, and Maastricht. By **car,** take A2/E35 and E25 southeast from Amsterdam.

VISITOR INFORMATION **VVV Meierei & Noordoost-Brabant** is at Markt 77, 5211 JX 's-Hertogenbosch (✆ **0900/112-2334;** fax 073/612-8930; www.vvvdenbosch.nl). The office is open Monday from 1 to 6pm, Tuesday to Friday from 9:30am to 6pm, and Saturday from 9am to 5pm.

What to See & Do

Het Zwanenbroedershuis The Brotherhood of Our Illustrious Lady, a charitable body founded in the 14th century that grew into an organization of considerable influence, is housed in this neo-Gothic building (1847). Membership became a matter of prestige, attracting rich citizens and nobility, including Queen Beatrix and Crown Prince Willem-Alexander. Illuminated books of music especially commissioned for its choir are on display, along with gifts from its members and other memorabilia documenting the Brotherhood's history.

Hinthamerstraat 94 (at Louwschepoort). ✆ **073/613-7383.** www.zwanenbroedershuis.nl. Admission 5€. Guided tours Tues, Thurs, and Sun 1:30 and 3pm.

Sint-Janskathedraal (St. John's Cathedral) ★ Parts of this magnificent cathedral date back to the 1200s, though most of the present Gothic structure was finished in 1529. The cathedral suffered considerable damage during a fire in 1584, when the cupola and its tower collapsed. Some of the original 15th-century frescoes were revealed during restoration, among them those in the ambulatory depicting the Joshua Tree and St. James. Have a look at the 15th-century brass chandelier in the Chapel of the Holy Sacrament on the north side of the choir. The chapel (1497) is lavishly decorated and imbued with a soft light. Notice also the little stone figures on the flying buttresses and up the copings. The 50-bell carillon in the rump of the 13th-century, late-Romanesque tower is played every Wednesday from 11:30am to 12:30pm.

Choorstraat 1 (at Parade). ✆ **073/613-0314.** www.sint-jan.nl. Free admission. Daily 8am–5pm.

NEARBY ATTRACTIONS

De Efteling ★★ ☺ Most remarkable, in this 284-hectare (702-acre) recreational park, is the miniature city with towers, castles, and characters based on just about every fairy tale that ever stirred a child's imagination. Slightly weird and wacky figures, dreamed up by the park's creative team, exist here, too. Many of the characters are animated or played by an actor in costume. Other attractions are exciting water rides and a boating lake, and there are cafeteria-type restaurants. Organization is good, so queuing is kept to a minimum even in busy school-vacation periods.

Europalaan 1, Kaatsheuvel (24km/15 miles west of Den Bosch). ✆ **0900/0161.** www.efteling.nl. Admission 29€ adults, 27€ seniors and visitors with disabilities, free for children 3 and under. Apr–Oct daily 10am–6pm (to 6 or 9pm or midnight July–Aug); Nov–Mar daily 10am to 6 or 8pm. From Den Bosch, take A59 westbound to junction 37, then go south on N261.

Kasteel Ammersoyen ★ One of the best-preserved medieval castles in Holland, this place has had a colorful array of inhabitants over the centuries. It served as a nunnery and later as a depot for a manufacturer of washing machines. The foundation that now owns the castle has restored it and on the inside recreated the plain, austere atmosphere it would have had in the 14th century. Outside, a moat and four sturdy towers are connected to make a square, virtually impregnable building. You enter the castle through the cellar and go up staircases constructed inside the thick walls. Upstairs are a magnificent hall and some smaller tower rooms.

Kasteellaan 1, Ammerzoden (11km/7 miles northwest of Den Bosch). ✆ **073/599-5506.** www.kasteel-ammersoyen.nl. Admission 5€ adults, 3€ children 5–12, free for children 4 and under. Hourly guided tours Apr–Oct Tues–Fri 11am–5pm; Sat–Sun 1–5pm. From Den Bosch, take A2/E25 northbound to junction 19, then N831 westbound.

Safaripark Beekse Bergen ☺ Either stay in your own car or take a guided bus tour through this extensive open-air safari park. Some 125 different species live together here in a natural environment (even though it's not exactly native to many of the species that reside here). Let's see, we're talking about lions, zebras, cheetahs, giraffes, rhinoceroses, wildebeest, jackals, reindeer, and lots more. Since some animals can come right up to your car, you need to be a little bit careful with children here, and keep the windows shut.

Beekse Bergen 1, Hilvarenbeek. ✆ **0900/233-5732.** www.safaripark.nl. Admission Apr–Oct 20€ adults, 13€ seniors and children 3–11, free for children 2 and under; Nov–Mar 14€ adults, 13€ seniors and children 3–11, free for children 2 and under. Dec–Jan daily 10am–4pm; Feb and Nov daily 10am–4:30pm; Mar–June and Sept–Oct daily 10am–5pm; July–Aug daily 10am–6pm (to 9pm some Sat). From Tilburg, go south on N269.

Where to Stay

Eurohotel Den Bosch ★ The family owners of this small central hotel, 2 blocks east of the Markt, have made it a very convivial lodging. Reached by cream-colored marble stairs from the reception, the guest rooms are attractive and intimate, decorated in pastels and print fabrics, and furnished with stylish chairs and comfortable beds. The breakfast room overlooks a bustling pedestrian shopping street.

Kerkstraat 56 (at Torenstraat), 5211 KH 's-Hertogenbosch. ✆ **073/613-7777.** Fax 073/612-8795. www.eurohotel-denbosch.com. 42 units. 119€–159€ double. Rates include buffet breakfast. AE, DC, MC, V. Parking 9€. **Amenities:** Bar. *In room:* TV, Wi-Fi (6€/5 hr.).

Golden Tulip Hotel Central You couldn't ask for a more romantic location than this, just off the city's medieval market square. The family-owned hotel, in business

Star-Shaped Gem

The village of Heusden, 15km (9 miles) northwest of Den Bosch on the Maas River, illustrates North Brabant's penchant for hiding tiny glittering gems in places where you almost have to stumble upon them. Heusden could be a blueprint for the ideal Dutch town. Its windmills, canals, bridges, 16th-century houses, star-shaped defenses, and air of tranquil well-being recall an open-air museum. But Heusden seems unsurprised by its miniature perfection and makes no great fuss about it.

since 1905, is large and modern, but somehow manages to be cozy. The guest rooms are nicely appointed. The Dutch restaurant **De Hoofdwacht** occupies a 14th-century cellar.

Burgemeester Loeffplein 98, 5211 RX 's-Hertogenbosch. ✆ **073/692-6926.** Fax 073/614-5699. www.hotel-central.nl. 132 units. 165€–185€ double; 240€–340€ suite. AE, DC, MC, V. Limited street parking. **Amenities:** 2 restaurants; 2 bars; exercise room; room service. *In room:* A/C, TV, hair dryer, minibar, Wi-Fi (10€/12 hr.).

Where to Dine

De Raadskelder ★ REGIONAL DUTCH For an excellent meal at a moderate price, visit this huge, vaulted cellar restaurant under the Gothic Town Hall. The interior is medieval in theme: Lighting is provided by brass chandeliers and lanterns, and there are massive pillars and a grand stone fireplace. The imaginative menu includes fried pike perch with salsify, black olives, and beurre blanc, and veal stewed in a sauce of kriek lambic (Belgian cherry beer) and celeriac root.

Markt 1A. ✆ **073/613-6919.** www.raadskelder.info. Main courses 20€–35€; fixed-price menus 33€–44€. AE, MC, V. Tues–Sat 10:30am–5pm and 5:30–10:30pm.

Pilkington's BRITISH/CONTINENTAL As you enter this cafe-restaurant in a former convent that has the atmosphere of an English country home, you see a display of luscious cakes, sandwiches, quiches, and homemade pâtés. People sit at small tables along the wall on wicker chairs. At the back, overlooking a lovely garden with clipped hedgerows and rosebushes, is a roofed terrace where you can dine romantically in summer. Seasonal specialties include wild boar, venison, and hare, all with delectable sauces. Try the tasty *speculaas* pudding—made with traditional Dutch spicy biscuits—for dessert.

Torenstraat 5 (across from Sint-Janskathedraal). ✆ **073/612-2923.** www.pilkingtons.nl. Main courses 12€–16€; fixed-price menu 22€. AE, DC, MC, V. Mon 11:30am–5pm; Tues–Sat 10am–10pm; Sun 10am–7pm.

EINDHOVEN

32km (20 miles) SE of Den Bosch; 120km (75 miles) SE of Amsterdam

Its town charter dates from 1232, but Eindhoven limped along for centuries as not much more than a village. Today, it is tomorrow's city, a laboratory for the latest ideas in urban design, and ranks as Holland's fifth-largest city (pop. 200,000)—thanks almost entirely to the giant Philips electronics corporation, which has been headquartered here since 1891. Despite its size, Eindhoven has only a few points of genuine interest for visitors.

Essentials

GETTING THERE **Trains** go to Eindhoven every 30 minutes or so from Amsterdam, Rotterdam, and The Hague, and every hour from Maastricht. By **car,** Eindhoven lies on the main north-south A2/E35-E25 Amsterdam-Maastricht expressway.

VISITOR INFORMATION **VVV Eindhoven** is at Stationsplein 17, 5611 AC Eindhoven (✆ **0900/112-2363;** fax 040/243-3135; www.vvveindhoven.nl). The office is open Monday from 10am to 5:30pm, Tuesday to Friday from 9am to 5:30pm, and Saturday from 10am to 5pm.

What to See & Do

Museum Kempenland Eindhoven Exhibits depicting the history of this city and region are housed here in an Italianate basilica that was constructed between 1917 and 1919. Note the stained-glass windows. There's a collection of 19th- and 20th-century art and sculpture by Dutch and Belgian artists.

Sint-Antoniusstraat 7 (at Gagelstraat). ✆ **040/252-9093.** www.museumkempenland.nl. Admission 4€ adults, 2€ seniors and children 6–18, free for children 5 and under. Tues–Sun 11am–5pm. Bus: 16 to Gagelstraat.

Van Abbemuseum ★ Established in 1936 and since extended with a new wing, this was one of the first museums in Holland to devote itself entirely to contemporary art. It got its start due to local cigar manufacturer Henri van Abbe, who donated his collection of paintings to the city. Look for works by Pablo Picasso, Piet Mondriaan (Mondrian), Marc Chagall, Theo van Doesburg, and other big names in modern art. The work of acquisition continues, and the museum has frequent temporary exhibits of leading-edge art.

Bilderdijklaan 10 (just south of the Dommel River). ✆ **040/238-1000.** www.vanabbemuseum.nl. Admission 9€ adults, 6.50€ seniors, 4€ students and children 13–18, free for children 12 and under. Tues–Sun and Mon holidays11am–5pm (to 9pm Thurs). Closed Jan 1, Apr 30, and Dec 25. Bus: 10, 20, or 24 to Bilderdijklaan.

Where to Dine

De Karpendonkse Hoeve ★★ INTERNATIONAL This first-class restaurant specializes in game in season and always uses the best of local products. It's on the outskirts of town, in an 18th-century farmhouse surrounded by trees and overlooking a small lake. Tables are decked stylishly in green and pink. The menu offers delicacies like a "triple quail fantasy": mousse, sautéed breast and aspic of quail, or brill filet topped with steamed carrot and cucumber with a Noilly Prat sauce. In the summer, you can dine on a terrace overlooking the lake.

Sumatralaan 3 (at Karpendonksche Plas). ✆ **040/281-3663.** www.karpendonksehoeve.nl. Main courses 20€–35€; fixed-price lunch 35€, dinner 77€. AE, MC, V. Mon–Fri noon–2:30pm and 6–9:30pm; Sat 6–9:30pm.

Where to Stay & Dine Nearby

Hostellerie Vangaelen ★ In the village of Heeze, a 20-minute drive from Eindhoven, this 18th-century coaching inn is directly across from a 17th-century château. The place has been redone with a curious Mediterranean touch that disavows its rustic heritage, and the guest rooms, which are all individually styled, have opulent furnishings and tasteful decor. The restaurant serves food with a Mediterranean accent. Weather permitting, you can dine outdoors.

Kapelstraat 48, 5591 HE Heeze (8km/5 miles SE of Eindhoven). ✆ **040/226-3515.** Fax 040/226-3876. www.hostellerie.nl. 14 units. 138€–202€ double. Rates include buffet breakfast. AE, DC, MC, V. From Eindhoven, take A67 east, then exit 34 south to Heeze. **Amenities:** Restaurant. *In room:* A/C, TV, Wi-Fi (free).

Nuenen

Driving N265 east from Eindhoven brings you to the village of Nuenen, 8km (5 miles) from the city; you also can get here on bus no. 121 from outside Eindhoven rail station. Vincent van Gogh lived in Nuenen rectory for 2 years (1883–85), where he fretted about the human condition, created early masterpieces like *The Potato Eaters* (1885), and painted and sketched scenes in and around the village. Visit Nuenen's **Vincentre,** Berg 29 (✆ **040/283-9615;** www.vangoghvillagenuenen.nl). The documentation center is open Tuesday to Sunday from 10am to 5pm (closed Jan 1, 3 days of Carnival, Easter Sun, and Dec 25). Admission is 6€ for adults, 3.50€ for children 6 to 17, and free for children 5 and under.

A Nearby Bell Museum

The small town of Asten, 19km (12 miles) east of Eindhoven, is home to Royal Eijsbouts, the world's leading producer of large-scale carillon and swinging bells. Its bells grace church towers, town halls, university campuses, and memorials in Holland, Belgium, elsewhere in Europe, the United States, and beyond.

Nationaal Beiaard- en Natuurmuseum Asten (Asten National Carillon and Nature Museum) ★ The Eijsbouts bell-foundry's location in the town explains the existence of one half of this fascinating museum, which embraces the centuries-old love in the Low Countries for bells clustered together as musical instruments. Here are displayed the oldest surviving swinging bells in the Netherlands, from the 11th century, and carillon bells cast by the brothers François and Pieter Hemony in the 17th century. The bells are joined by the local nature museum's exhibits.

Ostaderstraat 23, Asten. ✆ **0493/691-865.** www.museumasten.nl. Admission 6€ adults, 5€ seniors, 3€ children 4–15, free for children 3 and under. Tues–Fri 9:30am–5pm; Sat–Mon and holidays 1–5pm. Closed Jan 1, Dec 25, and during Carnival.

MAASTRICHT ★★★

186km (116 miles) SE of Amsterdam; 70km (44 miles) SE of Eindhoven

An exuberant center of history, culture, and hospitality, Maastricht (pop. 118,000) is a city of cafes and churches, and it's hard to tell which of these has the upper hand. Maastricht is generally reckoned to be Holland's most user-friendly city, blessed with a quality of life the northerners can't match. In between eating, drinking, church going, stepping out for Carnival, and hanging onto their rich heritage, the citizens of Maastricht have created a modern, prosperous, and vibrant city. Discovering how they do it all can be quite an education.

The capital of Limburg province—its name is Mestreech in the local Limburgs (Limburgish) language—owes its name and existence to the Maas River and repays the debt with a handsome riverfront. Maastricht traces its roots back to the Roman settlement of Mosae Trajectam, founded in 50 B.C. at a strategic bridge across the Maas at the foot of Sint-Pietersberg (Mt. St. Peter).

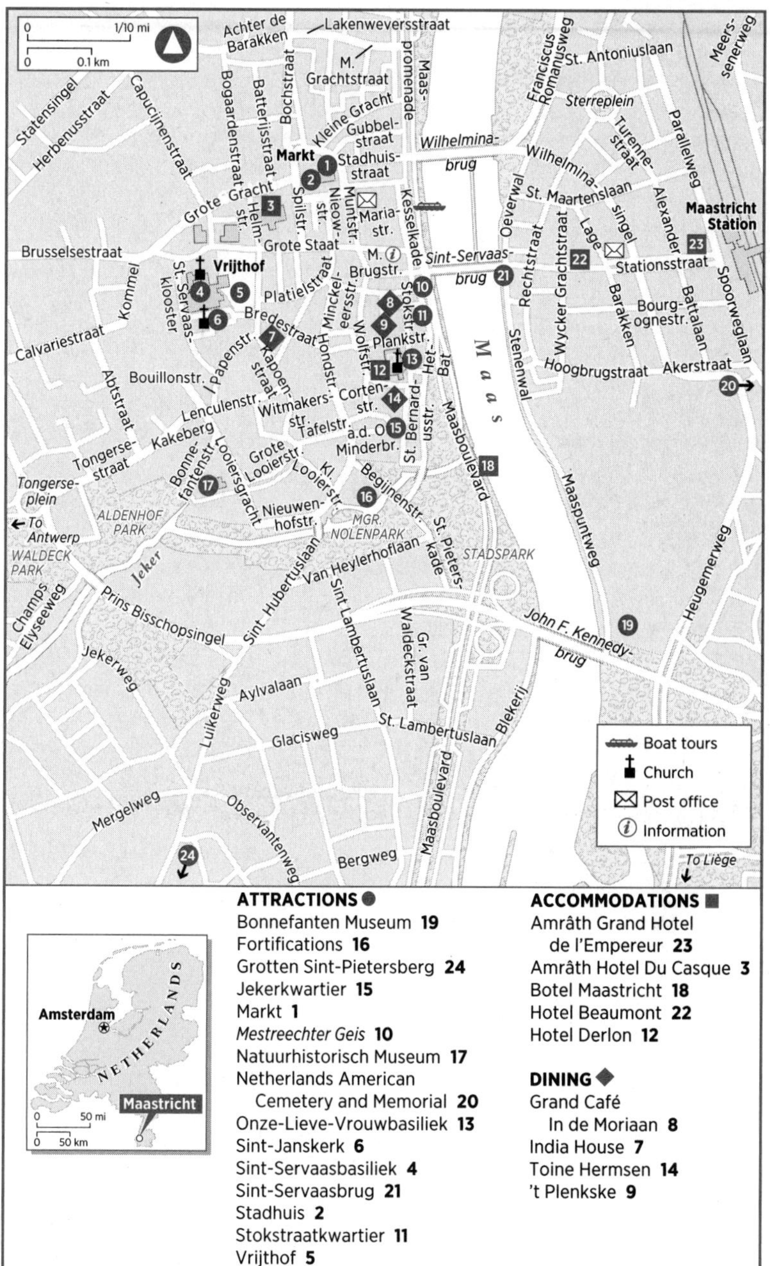

0 1/10 mi
0 0.1 km
Achter de Barakken
Lakenweversstraat
M. Grachtstraat
Maas-promenade
Franciscus Romanusweg
St. Antoniuslaan
Meers-senerweg
Statensingel
Herbenusstraat
Capucijnenstraat
Bogaardenstraat
Batterijsstraat
Bochstraat
Kleine Gracht
Gubbel-straat
Stadhuis-straat
Markt
Wilhelmina-brug
Sterreplein
Turenne-straat
Parallelweg
Wilhelmina-singel
St. Maartenslaan
Grote Gracht
Helm-str.
Spilstr.
str.
Nieuw-str.
Muntstr.
Maria-str.
Kesselkade
Oeverwal
Wyck
Lage
Alexander
Maastricht Station
Brusselsestraat
Grote Staat
M.
Sint-Servaas-brug
Rechtstraat
Grachtstraat
Stationsstraat
Vrijthof
St. Servaas-klooster
Kommel
Platielstr.
Brugstr.
Stokstr.
Bourg-ognestr.
Barakken
Battalaan
Spoorweglaan
Calvariestraat
Bredestraat
Minckel-eersstr.
Plankstr.
Wolfstr.
Het-usstr.
Bat
Maas
Stenenwal
Wycker
Hoogbrugstraat
Akerstraat
Abtstraat
Bouillonstr.
Papenstr.
Kapoen-straat
Hondstr.
Witmakers-str.
Corten-str.
Lenculenstr.
Tafelstr.
a.d. O
Minderbr.
St. Bernard-
Maasboulevard
Maaspuntweg
Tongerse-straat
Kakeberg
Bonne-fantenstr.
Grote Looierstr.
Kl. Looierstr.
Looiersgracht
Begijnenstr.
Tongerse-plein
To Antwerp
ALDENHOF PARK
Nieuwen-hofstr.
MGR. NOLENPARK
St. Pieters-kade
STADSPARK
Heugemerweg
WALDECK PARK
Jeker
Van Heylerhoflaan
Sint Hubertuslaan
Sint Lambertuslaan
Champs Elyseeweg
Prins Bisschopsingel
John F. Kennedy-brug
Gr. van Waldeckstraat
Jekerweg
Aylvalaan
Luikerweg
Glacisweg
St. Lambertuslaan
Blekerij
Mergelweg
Observantenweg
Bergweg
Maasboulevard
To Liège
Boat tours
Church
Post office
Information
ATTRACTIONS
Bonnefanten Museum 19
Fortifications 16
Grotten Sint-Pietersberg 24
Jekerkwartier 15
Markt 1
Mestreechter Geis 10
Natuurhistorisch Museum 17
Netherlands American Cemetery and Memorial 20
Onze-Lieve-Vrouwbasiliek 13
Sint-Janskerk 6
Sint-Servaasbasiliek 4
Sint-Servaasbrug 21
Stadhuis 2
Stokstraatkwartier 11
Vrijthof 5
ACCOMMODATIONS
Amrâth Grand Hotel de l'Empereur 23
Amrâth Hotel Du Casque 3
Botel Maastricht 18
Hotel Beaumont 22
Hotel Derlon 12
DINING
Grand Café In de Moriaan 8
India House 7
Toine Hermsen 14
't Plenkske 9
Amsterdam
NETHERLANDS
Maastricht
0 50 mi
0 50 km

The Lost Musketeer

Maastricht was where d'Artagnan, the hero of Alexandre Dumas's *The Three Musketeers,* lost his life during King Louis XIV's siege of the city in 1673. Dumas's musketeers are fictitious, but the siege actually happened, and d'Artagnan was based on captain of musketeers Comte d'Artagnan Charles de Batz-Castelmore, who was indeed killed at Maastricht.

Essentials

GETTING THERE **Trains** depart twice every hour from Amsterdam, Rotterdam, and The Hague for the approximately 2½-hour journey to Maastricht (trains from Amsterdam are direct; those from Rotterdam and The Hague require a transfer in Eindhoven). By **car,** take A2/E25 southward through Limburg.

VISITOR INFORMATION **VVV Maastricht,** Kleine Staat 1, 6211 ED Maastricht (✆ **043/325-2121;** www.vvvmaastricht.eu), in Het Dinghuis (1470), formerly the local law courts, is both helpful and friendly. The office is open May to October Monday to Saturday from 9am to 6pm and Sunday from 11am to 3pm; November to April, hours are Monday to Friday from 9am to 6pm and Saturday from 9am to 5pm.

GETTING AROUND Outside Maastricht station are stops for city and regional bus service, operated by **Veolia** (✆ **0900/9292;** www.veolia-transport.nl), and a taxi stand. The station is a 15- to 20-minute walk from the Vrijthof square in the center of town, on the far bank of the Maas River.

SPECIAL EVENTS One of the world's premier art and antique shows, the annual **European Fine Art Fair,** is held in March at the Maastricht Exhibition and Congress Center (MECC). Jewelry, silver, carpets, Egyptian and classical antiquities, and 20th-century art are among the items on view. See "Holland Calendar of Events," in chapter 12.

What to See & Do

Going from the rail station to the center city, you cross the Maas River on the pedestrians-only **Sint-Servaasbrug (St. Servatius Bridge),** which dates from 1289 and is one of the oldest bridges in the Netherlands (albeit rebuilt after its destruction in World War II).

The **Vrijthof,** the city's most glorious square, is a vast open space bordered on three sides by restaurants and cafes with sidewalk terraces, and on the fourth by the Romanesque Sint-Servaas Church and the Gothic Sint-Jan's with its soaring red belfry. This square is Maastricht's forum, especially in good weather, when the sidewalk terraces are filled with people soaking up the atmosphere and watching the world go by.

On the market square, the **Markt,** vendors from Holland, Belgium, and Germany gather on Wednesday and Friday mornings to open colorful stalls, watched over by the cheerful little ***'t Mooswief (Vegetable Woman)*** statue. The sober-looking 17th-century **Stadhuis (Town Hall),** in dignified gray stone, is surmounted by a tower containing a 43-bell carillon that breaks into song at every conceivable opportunity and in a special concert on Saturday from 3:30 to 4:15pm.

Maastricht packs 1,590 protected historical monuments inside The **Stokstraatkwartier,** which is also known as the Roman district because the ancient city was in this quarter. It experienced a decades-long restoration that made of its 17th- and 18th-century buildings a baroque shopping and restaurant area. Between here and the medieval wall along the Jeker River lies the **Jekerkwartier,** a haunt of the city's sizeable student population and location of offbeat bars and boutiques. These narrow cobbled alleyways, where the past intersects the present, are an essential element of Maastricht's charm.

Keep your eye out for the little square called **Op de Thermen,** off Stokstraat, a couple of blocks inland from the Maas, where the outline of a Roman thermal bath can be seen on the cobblestones; and for the small, impish ***Mestreechter Geis*** statue in a tiny square at nearby Kleine Stokstraat; he embodies the *joie de vivre* of Maastrichters, and his name in Limburgish means "Spirit of Maastricht."

Walking along the remaining stretches of **fortifications,** in particular the triple line of bastions in the western suburbs and the south wall along the Jeker, it's easy to be impressed by their strength. The besieged could probably afford to poke fun at the besiegers, discounting the improbable chance of them getting inside.

MUSEUMS & OTHER ATTRACTIONS

Bonnefantenmuseum ★ Designed by Italian architect Aldo Rossi, this riverside museum (1995) is instantly recognizable, even amid the relentlessly modern architecture of the Céramique district, for its striking, bullet-shaped dome. Works of art from the Maasland School include sculpture, silverwork, and woodcarvings from the Maas Valley in Limburg and Belgium (where the river is called the Meuse). This art dates as far back as the 13th century and had its apogee during the 15th and 16th centuries. Works by Dutch and Flemish Old Masters include Pieter Brueghel the Younger's *Census at Bethlehem* (1610) and David Teniers the Younger's *Temptation of St. Anthony* (ca. 1640). Archaeological finds dating from 250,000 years ago to the Middle Ages are displayed, with an emphasis on the Roman period. In the Wiebengahal next to the museum are changing exhibits by contemporary artists.

Av. Céramique 250 (next to the John F. Kennedy Bridge). ✆ **043/329-0190.** www.bonnefanten.nl. Admission 8€ adults, 4€ children 13–18, free for children 12 and under. Tues–Sun 11am–5pm. Closed Jan 1, Dec 25, and during Carnival. Bus: 1, 3, 50, or 57 to Bonnefantenmuseum.

Grotten Sint-Pietersberg ★★ Don't miss these mysterious caverns that tunnel into the heart of high cliffs. The Romans and all who came after them took from Mount St. Peter great chunks of marlstone, a type of limestone that's as soft to carve as soap and hardens when exposed to air. Many Maastricht buildings are constructed of marlstone. As more and more marlstone was extracted over the centuries, the Sint-Pietersberg interior became honeycombed with 20,000 passages. From Roman times, to medieval sieges, to the 4 years of Nazi occupation during World War II, these chambers have served as a place of refuge. Many drawings and signatures have been left on the marlstone walls. During World War II, the caves sheltered from the Nazis Dutch masterpieces such as Rembrandt's *The Night Watch* and other treasures. You follow your guide's lantern through a labyrinth of 6- to 12m-high (20- to 39-ft.) tunnels. Stay close to that lantern—tales are told of those who entered the 200km (124 miles) of tunnels and were never seen again (ask about the four monks). The temperature underground is about 50°F (10°C), and it's damp, so bring a cardigan or a coat.

Grotten Zonnenberg: Slavante 1; Grotten Noord: Luikerweg 71. ✆ **043/325-2121.** www.pietersberg.nl. Guided tours 4.95€ adults, 3.95€ children 13–18, free for children 12 and under. Tours in English July–Sept daily 2:45pm. Bus: 4 to Sint-Pietersberg.

Natuurhistorisch Museum (Natural History Museum) Fossils from the marlstone walls of the Sint-Pietersberg Caves (see above) are displayed here. These include skeletons of Mosasaurier dinosaurs and giant turtles. In addition, there are rocks and minerals, and both rough and cut gemstones. The courtyard contains a botanical garden, with beautiful examples of the local flora.

De Bosquetplein 6-7 (near the Music Conservatory). ✆ **043/350-5490.** www.nhmmaastricht.nl. Admission 4.50€ adults, 3€ seniors and children 4–11, free for children 3 and under. Mon–Fri 10am–5pm; Sat–Sun 2–5pm. Closed holidays. Bus: 3, 4, 9, or 34 to Papenstraat.

SIGHTS OF RELIGIOUS SIGNIFICANCE

Onze-Lieve-Vrouwbasiliek (Basilica of Our Lady) ★ The west wing and crypts of this medieval Romanesque cruciform structure date from the 11th century. But the focus for most visitors is the side chapel containing the statue of Our Lady Star of the Sea. The richly robed statue, fronted by a blaze of candles, is credited with many miracles. In the early 1600s, as many as 20,000 pilgrims came to worship at the shrine every Easter Monday. When the Calvinists took power in 1632, the statue went into hiding. Legend has it that in 1699, Our Lady herself established Maastricht's "prayer route" by stepping down from her pedestal and leading a devout parishioner through the muddy streets, and that the morning after the miraculous walk there was indeed mud on the hem of her robe! The church treasury contains a rich collection of tapestries, reliquaries, church silver, and other religious objects.

Onze-Lieve-Vrouweplein. ✆ **043/325-3135.** www.sterre-der-zee.nl. Admission: basilica free; treasury 3€ adults, 2€ seniors and children 6–12, free for children 5 and under. Basilica daily 11am–5pm, except during services. Treasury Easter to mid-Oct Mon–Sat 11am–5pm; Sun 1–5pm. Bus: 3, 4, 9, or 34 to Papenstraat.

Sint-Janskerk (St. John's Church) The sober, whitewashed interior of the city's main Dutch Reformed (Protestant) church, dating from the 14th century and given to the Protestants in 1633, makes a study in contrast with the lavish Catholic decoration at St. Servatius's next door. But there are murals, sculpted corbels of the Twelve Apostles, and grave monuments of local dignitaries and wealthy individuals. Most people come here, though, to climb the 218 narrow, winding steps to the 70m (230-ft.) belfry's windy viewing platform, 43m (141 ft.) above the streets, and for the fine views of the city it affords.

Henric van Veldekeplein (next to the Vrijthof). ✆ **043/325-2121.** Admission: church free; tower 1.50€ adults, 0.50€ children 5–13, free for children 4 and under. Easter to mid-Oct Mon–Sat 11am–4pm. Bus: 3, 4, 9, or 34 to Vrijthof.

Sint-Servaasbasiliek (Basilica of St. Servatius) ★ The oldest parts of this majestic medieval cruciform church, with a rich, glittering interior, date from the year 1000. St. Servatius, Maastricht's first bishop, appointed around 380, is buried in the crypt. Over the centuries, worshipers have honored the saint with gifts, so the Treasury has a collection of incredible richness and beauty, including two superb 12th-century reliquaries fashioned by Maastricht goldsmiths. The basilica's interior is largely Romanesque, and restorations have given it a cool, restrained atmosphere, emphasizing the simple arches and vaults. A statue of Emperor Charlemagne stands in the church. The basilica was enlarged in the 14th and 15th centuries, when the south portal and the entrance to the cloister at Keizer Karelplein were added. These are adorned with statues and intricate stone carvings. The southern tower of the west wall holds Grameer (Grandmother), the largest bell in Holland and a beloved symbol

MAASTRICHT carnival CAPERS

The city seems to have gone mad. A tumult of garishly clad people with painted faces dance and sing through the elegant Vrijthof. Crowds flow and sway through the maze of narrow cobblestone alleyways beyond. Music from a hundred bands merges into a discordant medley of tunes and tempos, and blares out into the chill February air. The city's 500 bars and cafes, popular enough in ordinary times, burst their seams and spill revelers onto the streets, in a display of fervid celebration that contradicts the sober-sided character generally attributed to the Dutch.

Welcome to Maastricht Carnival, an event that dates back to the 15th century. On the Saturday before Ash Wednesday, the mayor of Maastricht hands over the keys of the city to Prince Carnival, who will reign over it and turn it completely upside-down over the next few days. The populace dress up and bring out colorful floats for the parades that take place each day. When the sun goes down, everyone disappears into the cafes and restaurants, continuing the party with wining and dining.

of the city. In the summer, a daily concert is performed on the tower carillon from 8:30 to 9:30pm.

Keizer Karelplein 3 (next to Vrijthof). ✆ **043/321-2082.** www.sintservaas.nl. Admission 3.80€ adults, 2.30€ seniors and students, free for children 17 and under. Treasury and basilica Sept–June Mon–Sat 10am–5pm, Sun 1–5pm; July–Aug Mon–Sat 10am–6pm, Sun 1–5pm. Bus: 3, 4, 9, or 34 to Vrijthof.

A NEARBY U.S. MILITARY CEMETERY

The **Netherlands American Military Cemetery** (✆ **043/458-1208;** www.abmc.gov), at Margraten, 5km (3 miles) east of Maastricht on N278, is the final resting place for 8,301 American service members who lost their lives in Holland in World War II. The Dutch often leave wreaths and flowers behind as symbols of gratitude for the sacrifices that liberated them from Nazi oppressors. The cemetery is open daily 9am to 5pm (closed Jan 1 and Dec 25). Admission is free. Veolia bus no. 50 departs every 15 minutes from outside Maastricht train station for the 20-minute ride to the Militair Kerkhof stop at Margraten.

ORGANIZED TOURS

One of the most pleasant ways to view Maastricht and the riverbanks upstream and down is to take a cruise provided by **Rederij Stiphout,** Maaspromenade 58 (✆ **043/351-5300;** www.stiphout.nl). April to October, generally daily from noon to 4pm on the hour (some days start and/or finish later), and in November and December on Saturday and Sunday at 2 and 4pm, a riverboat leaves the landing stage on Maasboulevard at the Sint-Servaas bridge for a 50-minute cruise past Sint-Pietersberg (you can leave the boat, tour the caves, and catch the next boat to continue the cruise) and on to the sluices at the Belgian border. The fare without the caves tour is 7.20€ for adults, 4.30€ for children 4 to 12, and free for children 3 and under. In addition, there are brunch trips, day trips to Liège, and a romantic "Candlelight Cruise" that includes dancing and dinner; call for schedules and fares. ***Note:*** Reservations are required for all except the basic cruise.

Rederij Stiphout also organizes landlubber tours by **double-decker bus,** departing from the Vrijthof July to September on Tuesday, Wednesday, Friday, and Saturday.

At the VVV tourist office, pick up the **City Walk** and **Fortifications Walk** self-guided tour brochures. From March to November, the VVV conducts **guided walking tours** that depart from the VVV office and cost 5€ for adults and 4€ for children 12 and under. These include walks through the old city and among the fortifications.

Where to Stay

EXPENSIVE

Hotel Derlon ★ This jewel of a four-star hotel sits on one of the loveliest of the city's squares. In the summer, a sidewalk cafe opens under the trees. The hotel is constructed over the city's ancient Roman forum, and there are excavated foundations and objects in its cellar museum. The guest rooms are bright and airy, and nicely blend classic and modern decor. There's a brasserie on the premises.

Onze-Lieve-Vrouweplein 6, 6211 HD Maastricht. ✆ **043/321-6770.** Fax 043/325-1933. www.derlon.nl. 42 units. 195€–270€ double; from 370€ suite. AE, DC, MC, V. Valet parking 30€. Bus: 3, 4, 9, or 34 to Papenstraat. **Amenities:** Restaurant; champagne bar; babysitting; room service. *In room:* A/C, TV, hair dryer, minibar, Wi-Fi (free).

MODERATE

Amrâth Grand Hotel de l'Empereur ★ This lovely old turreted hotel exudes Art Nouveau style and has comfortable, attractive guest rooms, and apartments that can sleep up to four people. Some rooms have trouser presses. A cozy lounge bar draws a local clientele, and there's a fine brasserie. It's handy for the train station, but not so good if you want easy access by foot to the center of town around the Vrijthof, which is 1.5km (1 mile) distant—on the other hand, it's a pleasant walk to and over the Maas, and you can always go by bus from outside the station.

Stationsstraat 2 (across from the train station), 6221 BP Maastricht. ✆ **043/321-3838.** Fax 043/321-6819. www.amrathhotels.nl. 80 units. 159€–195€ double; 285€ suite. AE, DC, MC, V. Parking 18€. All buses to Maastricht train station. **Amenities:** Restaurant; bar; Jacuzzi; heated indoor pool; sauna. *In room:* A/C, TV, hair dryer, minibar, Wi-Fi (16€/day).

Amrâth Hotel DuCasque ★★ There's been an inn at this location since the 15th century. The present family-run hotel carries on the proud tradition, with modern facilities, comfortable rooms, and good old-fashioned friendliness. It faces the lively Vrijthof square; those rooms overlooking the Vrijthof have the finest view in town. The hotel doesn't have its own restaurant, but considering how thickly spread restaurants are around the Vrijthof, that's no great loss.

Helmstraat 14 (at Vrijthof), 6211 TA Maastricht. ✆ **043/321-4343.** Fax 043/325-5155. www.amrathhotels.nl. 41 units. 120€–190€ double. Rates include buffet breakfast. AE, DC, MC, V. Limited street parking. Bus: 3, 4, 9, or 34 to Vrijthof. *In room:* TV, hair dryer, Wi-Fi.

Hotel Beaumont ★ Halfway between the rail station and the river, this well-established hotel, a short walk from the center city, is in its third generation of family ownership. The decor is warmly classical, and the guest rooms are comfortable and attractive. An annex has 40 rooms and a fitness room. The rooms vary considerably in size, decor, and how each one is outfitted. A four-person family room has two bathrooms. The stylish in-house restaurant serves moderately priced meals with Limburg specialties and wines.

Wycker Brugstraat 2 (between the rail station and St. Servaas Bridge), 6221 EC Maastricht. ✆ **043/325-4433.** Fax 043/325-3655. www.beaumont.nl. 121 units. 145€–225€ double. AE, DC, MC, V. Parking 22€. Bus: 1, 2, 3, 4, 5, or 6 to Wilhelminasingel. **Amenities:** Restaurant. *In room:* TV, minibar, Wi-Fi (free).

Eating the Proof

Pampering its collective stomach is a way of life in Maastricht. A culinary fair, the Preuvenemint (www.preuvenemint.nl) showcases this love affair with food annually during the last weekend of August (Fri–Mon). The Vrijthof is filled with stalls set up by top city restaurants, and around 100,000 visitors pile in every year. It's accompanied by a live-music program.

INEXPENSIVE

Botel Maastricht Leggy guests aboard this converted river cruiser likely will appreciate Abraham Lincoln's rueful remark, after spending a night in a cramped U.S. Navy ship's bunk, that "you can't put a long blade into a short scabbard." The Botel's sparely furnished cabins have a compact form factor, but so do its rates, and the shipboard ambience and a nautically themed bar prove attractive to youthful travelers. Try for a cabin on the river side, and then make due allowance for the fact that the Maas isn't the Seine—though, since we're reminiscing about U.S. presidents, the boat does have a view of the John F. Kennedy Bridge.

Maasboulevard 95 (on the Maas, at Stadspark), 6211 JW Maastricht. ✆ **043/321-9023.** Fax 043/325-7998. www.botelmaastricht.nl. 28 units, 20 with bathroom. 44€ double without bathroom; 48€ double with bathroom. No credit cards. Limited street parking. Bus: 4 to Sint-Pieterskade. **Amenities:** Bar. *In room:* No phone.

Where to Dine

Maastricht is filled with good places to eat. Menus tend to be broadminded, drawing as they do on the culinary traditions of at least three nations—and that's just those that serve "local" cuisine. The VVV office provides the *Maastricht Culinair* brochure, for a taste of the best in town.

EXPENSIVE

Toine Hermsen ★ REGIONAL/FRENCH One of the city's top restaurants is the proud possessor of a Michelin star. Expect good portions of impeccable food and superb but relaxed service. The chef cooks up classics of French cuisine and exploits regional seasonal ingredients such as Limburg's famous asparagus and chicory.

Sint-Bernardusstraat 2-4 (corner of Onze-Lieve-Vrouweplein). ✆ **043/325-8400.** www.toinehermsen.com. Reservations required. Main courses 25€–54€; fixed-price menus 25€–65€. AE, DC, MC, V. Mon 6:30–9pm; Tues–Fri noon–2pm and 6:30–9pm; Sat 6:30–9pm. Bus: 3, 4, 9, or 34 to Papenstraat.

MODERATE

India House INDIAN For a change of pace from the city's general focus on regional and French cuisine, try this excellent Indian offering. It easily lives up to the local standard of elegance, in a tastefully reworked town house just off the main square. The line of *balti* menu dishes is superb, and these are backed up by *tandoori* and curry items. Fish and prawn dishes are at the high end of the price range, but opting for vegetarian takes you into "inexpensive" territory.

Bredestraat 45 (off Vrijthof). ✆ **043/325-8186.** www.theindiahouse.info. Main courses 13€–25€; fixed-price menus 25€–29€. AE, DC, MC, V. Wed–Mon 5–11pm. Bus: 3, 4, 9, or 34 to Vrijthof.

't Plenkske ★ REGIONAL DUTCH/FRENCH This fine restaurant, with its light, airy decor—which contrasts neatly with a solid-looking town-house setting—and

Southern Taste

Look out for locally produced asparagus, dubbed the "white gold of Limburg," and for *vlaai,* a handcrafted pie into which goes a lip-smacking quantity of fruit. The province's seven breweries—Bavaria, Brand, Gulpen, Ridder, Leeuw, Alfa, and Lindeboom—make beers that are popular around the country. Last, but by no means least, is white wine, produced in modest quantities by the Apostelhoeve and Slavante vineyards near Maastricht, in the southernmost sliver of the Netherlands, close by the Belgian border.

outdoor patio overlooking the Thermen (site of the city's ancient Roman baths), is a great local favorite. Regional specialties from both Maastricht and Liège are prominent on the menu, with a number of French classics thrown in for good measure. Menu dishes include duck breast with lime sauce, and Limburg lamb with thyme and honey, garnished with garlic marmalade.

Plankstraat 6 (in the Stokstraatkwartier). ✆ **043/321-8456.** www.hetplenkske.nl. Main courses 20€–26€; fixed-price menu 30€. AE, DC, MC, V. Mon–Sat noon–2:30pm and 6–10pm. Bus: 4 to Hondstraat.

INEXPENSIVE

Grand Café In de Moriaan LIGHT FARE The Netherlands's smallest cafe (or so it claims), in a building dating from 1540, was the country's Wine Café of the Year in 1997 and hasn't deteriorated one whit since that *annus mirabilis.* Settle down in the cozy nook inside or, in fine weather, on an outside terrace on Op de Thermen, delineated by hedges and shaded by umbrellas. The menu is on the minimalist side, but the few items that go beyond simple snacks—such as mussels gratin and salade nicoise (for two)—are excellent, and the servings big.

Stokstraat 12 (in the Stokstraatkwartier). ✆ **043/321-1177.** www.indemoriaan.nl. Main courses 5.50€–13€. No credit cards. Mon–Wed 2pm–midnight; Thurs–Sun noon–2am. Bus: 4 to Hondstraat.

Where to Stay & Dine Nearby

Château Neercanne ★ FRENCH Constructed in 1698, this gracious château (restaurant only) stands on a hill above the Jeker River. Its wide stone terrace, where you can dine or have drinks in fine weather, affords views of the scenic Jeker Valley. Inside, tasteful renovations have created a classic, romantic ambience, with baroque wallpaper, shades of beige and burgundy, and Venetian glass chandeliers. Marlstone caves in the hillside serve as wine cellars. Fresh herbs and vegetables from the château's own gardens and the best of local ingredients assure top quality.

Cannerweg 800 (5km/3 miles southwest of Maastricht). ✆ **043/325-1359.** www.chateauhotels.nl. Main courses 25€–35€; fixed-price lunch menus 53€–72€; fixed-price dinner menus 77€–89€. AE, DC, MC, V. Tues–Fri and Sun noon–2:30pm and 6:30–9:30pm; Sat 6:30–9:30pm. Bus: 34 to Cannerweg/Neercanne. From Maastricht, go southwest on N278, turn left on Bieslanderweg.

Kasteel Wittem ★★ For a taste of southern charm at its most alluring, stop by this romantic 15th-century castle, where stately swans adorn the moat. If you're lucky, you'll draw one of the two tower suites (one has panoramic windows in the bathroom). Castle guests over the centuries have included the knights of Julemont, the duke of Burgundy, Prince of Orange William the Silent, Emperor Charles V, any number of other noblemen, and even humble folk like traveling monks. The guest rooms have a cozy charm, with country-style decor and furnishings, and the hotel offers a variety of gastronomic arrangements. The expensive French restaurant (reservations required), paneled in French oak, has a warm, clubby atmosphere.

Wittemer Allee 3, 6286 AA Wittem (16km/10 miles east of Maastricht). ✆ **043/450-1208.** Fax 043/450-1260. www.kasteelwittem.nl. 12 units. 175€ double; 225€ suite. AE, DC, MC, V. Free parking. Bus: 50 to Gulpen, then 21 to Wittem (total 35 min.). From Maastricht, take N278 east through Gulpen; then exit left to Wittem. **Amenities:** 2 restaurants; bar; lounge; Wi-Fi (free). *In room:* TV, hair dryer.

Shopping

One of the specialties of **Olivier Bonbons,** Kesselskade 55 (✆ **043/321-5526;** www.olivierbonbons.nl), is a porcelain reproduction of the city's much-loved Grameer bell filled with luscious chocolates. **Maison Florop,** Heugemerweg 6C (✆ **043/321-2155;** www.florop.com), is an excellent wine shop and delicatessen. A general **street market** takes place on Wednesday and Friday from 8am to 1pm at the Markt; a **food market** is held on Thursday from 2 to 8pm on Stationsstraat, and a **flea market** on Saturday from 10am to 4pm.

Maastricht After Dark

During winter months, the city hosts performances of opera, classical music, dance, and theater (mostly in Dutch). Check with the VVV, and pick up a copy of *Uit in Maastricht* for current happenings.

The city's main venue is the **Theater aan het Vrijthof,** Vrijthof 47 (✆ **043/350-5555;** www.theateraanhetvrijthof.nl); the box office is open Monday to Saturday from noon to 6pm (or until the evening performance begins), and Sunday for 1 hour before the evening performance begins. Among frequent performers here is the highly rated **Limburgs Symfonie Orkest** (**Limburg Symphony Orchestra;** ✆ **043/350-7000;** www.lso.nl). The **Conservatoire,** Bonnefantenstraat 15 (✆ **043/346-6680;** www.hszuyd.nl), hosts regular musical performances by students from the Maastricht Conservatorium.

Maastricht is no place for a teetotaler. Much of the after-dark action takes place in the more than 500 bars and cafes around town. One of the best of these is **In den Ouden Vogelstruys** ★, Vrijthof 15 (✆ **043/321-4888**). The traditional bar's rustic interior and faithful local clientele make it a great place to stop for a drink inside or, in fine weather, on a sidewalk terrace. A light-snacks menu is written in the local dialect, so look out for items like *Mestreechter pâté* and *Ardenner sjink* (ham). Ask about the cannonball that lodged in a wall here in 1653.

North Along the Maas

The Maas slides into the North Sea at Rotterdam, but above all it's the river of Limburg—a silver thread that runs the length of the province. The river has its share of day-trippers on tour boats departing from Maastricht. There are marinas filled to the gunwales with leisure boats, stretches for water-skiers and jet-skiers, and fishermen casting such quantities of hooks it seems miraculous if any fish can run the gauntlet. Hop back and forth cheaply on an armada of little car ferries that link the opposite banks along most of the river's length. North of Maastricht, the stream has been diverted into worked-out gravel quarries, creating the Maasplassen miniature lakes.

Northern Limburg shelters vacation parks and villages in a landscape of wooded hills and broad heaths. At its hourglass waist, it almost feels like you should breathe in to squeeze through the gap between Belgium and Germany.

THORN ★

48km (30 miles) N of Maastricht; 42km (26 miles) SE of Eindhoven

Early-morning mist from the Maas sifting through cobblestone streets adds a ghostly air to the village's whitewashed buildings, which seem to float free from their foundations. Thorn (pronounced *Torn*), dubbed the "White Village," looks almost too good to be true, as if it has been specially treated to preserve the graces of a bygone age. For centuries the village was ruled by women, abbesses of a cloister founded in 992. The nobility of the Holy Roman Empire sent their daughters here to be educated in the ways of a Christian life.

Whether they succeeded or not is uncertain—there were back doors to each of the cottages where the girls lived—but Thorn itself has brought its own uplifting presence safely down the centuries. The old center of the village seems like a page torn straight out of a history book, with its white walls, cobblestone courtyards, and wall-mounted lamps. It's reason enough to be diverted off the highway before the day gets fairly started and stroll through the streets, sniffing the wood-smoke-scented air, freshly baked bread, and a timeless atmosphere that will struggle later to cope with tour-bus crowds.

The nearest rail station to Thorn is Weert (on the Amsterdam-Maastricht line), from where buses connect to Thorn. By car, leave A2/E25 southeast of Weert, and drive southwest.

WHERE TO STAY & DINE

Hotel-Restaurant La Ville Blanche In the placid village center (at any rate, it's placid once the tour groups have left), this small hotel offers nicely done-up guest rooms. From the looks of the neat little building, which somehow looks most suitable for hobbits, you might think they would be all rustic, exposed beams and wood panels. Instead, there's a contemporary but tasteful style, with pastel-toned furnishings and fittings chosen to go well together. Fine Continental food is served in the restaurant, and drinks in the bar in an atmospheric brick cellar.

Hoogstraat 2, 6017 AR Thorn. ✆ **0347/750-423.** Fax 0475/562-828. www.villeblanche.nl. 23 units. 89€–135€ double. Rates include continental breakfast. AE, DC, MC, V. Free parking. **Amenities:** Restaurant; lounge; bar; bikes. *In room:* TV, minibar, Wi-Fi (6€/50 min.).

VALKENBURG ★

13km (8 miles) E of Maastricht

Southern Limburg occupies the highest ground in the Netherlands. Nestled among gently sloping hills where lush forests alternate with pastures unfolding toward the Geul River, Valkenburg is best known for its spa, casino, and a ruined fortress up a steep hill that still seems to guard this bustling small town. Surrounded by parks and farms constructed in Limburg's characteristic half-timbered style, this is where the action is in summertime. Folks generally come to Limburg to unwind, but the pace is faster in Valkenburg. Even the Geul races through town, as though it's just gotten away with the casino takings. Out of season, Valkenburg is more like a ghost town of last summer's dreams.

GETTING THERE From Maastricht, there are up to four **trains** every hour, and two **buses** an hour, from outside Maastricht train station. By **car,** take A79 northeast.

VISITOR INFORMATION **VVV Valkenburg** is at Theodoor Dorrenplein 5, 6301 DV Valkenburg (✆ **0900/555-9798;** fax 043/601-6640; www.vvvzuidlimburg.nl). The office is open Monday to Friday from 9am to 5:30pm, Saturday from 9am to 5pm, and Sunday (July–Sept) from 10am to 4pm.

What to See & Do

Some of Valkenburg's most intriguing sights are hidden. The rocks beneath Valkenburg are like Swiss cheese—for centuries (beginning with the Romans), people have excavated the soft marlstone for use as building material. Nowadays six caves are open to the public.

Gemeentegrot (Cauberg Cavern) Visit this cave either on foot or aboard a little train. The interesting formations within include a subterranean lake that has formed over the centuries. A million years from now, you might see some stalactites and stalagmites.

Cauberg 4 (at Grendeplein). ✆ **043/601-2271.** www.gemeentegrot.nl. Admission 5€ adults, 3.50€ children 4–11, free for children 3 and under. Guided tours Jan to mid-Apr Mon–Fri 11am, 12:30pm, and 2pm, Sat–Sun and holidays every half hour or hour 11am–4pm; mid-Apr to end June and Sept–Oct Mon–Fri every half hour or hour 11am–4pm, Sat–Sun and holidays every half hour 10:30am–4:30pm (and at 4:45pm); July–Aug every 15–30 minutes 10:15am–5pm; 1st 2 weeks Nov Mon–Fri 11am, 12:30pm, and 2pm, Sat–Sun and holidays every half hour or hour 11am–4pm; mid-Nov to Dec 24 (closed Dec 25) daily 1, 2, 3, and 4pm; Dec 26–31 11am and 4pm; check this complex and variable schedule on the website to confirm the open hours for the day of your visit.

Sprookjesbos (Fairy Tale Forest) ★ ☺ Aimed at younger kids, around 2 to 8, this sweet little theme park features children's fairy-tale favorites like Snow White and the Seven Dwarfs, Cinderella, Little Red Riding Hood, and Hansel and Gretel. Most of the "action" takes place in tiny houses and miniature castles dotted at intervals along a winding pathway through a "magical forest"; you stop to look in the doors and windows, behind which mechanical puppets act out scenes from fairy tales. There are a few low-intensity rides, including an artificial river with falls, and a puppet Western show. Older kids will find the park's excitements limited. You need at least 2 hours to get around, longer if you plan on having a picnic or snack.

Sibbergrubbe 2A (off Gulpen Rd.). ✆ **043/601-2985.** www.sprookjesbos.nl. Admission 7.95€ adults, 6.95€ children 2–12, free for children 1 and under. Mid-Apr to 1st week of Sept Mon–Sat 10am–5pm, Sun and holidays 10am–6pm; weekends in Sept after 1st week 10am–5pm. From Valkenburg center, take Gulpen Rd. to southern suburbs, where park is signposted to the right. Parking lot is on Gulpen Rd., about 180m (591 ft.) from park entrance.

Thermae 2000 The waters that simmer below Valkenburg's hills are the source of this futuristic health spa, where you relax completely in the soothing thermal baths, have a session in the sauna, and work out in the fitness center. Extra pampering possibilities include a massage and floating in a warm bath in an herbal bodywrap. There's an excellent hotel here (see below).

Kuurpark Cauberg 25–27. ✆ **043/609-2000.** www.thermae2000.nl. Admission 30€ (Mon–Fri) or 32€ (Sat–Sun) adults, 20€ seniors and students (admission includes all services except massages, floats, and beautician and therapeutic treatments). Daily 9am–11pm.

Where to Stay & Dine

Thermaetel ★ This is the place to overnight in Valkenburg. After checking in, put on your bathrobe and walk to the pool. The price of a room includes admission to the health spa for the length of your stay, including the day you arrive and the day you leave. The water in your hotel room comes from the spa's spring. Every room has a hillside garden terrace. The restaurant offers a tasty array of health-oriented dishes.

Kuurpark Cauberg 25-27, 6301 BT Valkenburg. ✆ **043/609-2001.** Fax 043/609-2011. www.thermae2000.nl. 60 units. 195€-305€ double. Rates include buffet breakfast. AE, DC, MC, V. Parking 8.50€. **Amenities:** Restaurant; bar; lounge; babysitting; health club & spa; heated indoor pool; Wi-Fi (free). *In room:* TV, minibar.

Valkenburg After Dark

Holland Casino Valkenburg, Kuurpark Cauberg 28 (✆ **043/609-9600;** www.hollandcasino.com), on a hilltop across from Thermae 2000, has French and American roulette, blackjack, and mini–punto banco. A separate area has slot machines of all shapes and sizes, plus two restaurants, two bars, and reception rooms. For an entire evening's entertainment, sit down to a dinner show. Note that a dress code is observed (jacket and tie, or turtleneck, for men; dress or dressy pantsuit for the ladies), and you need your passport to show you're over 18 years of age. The casino is open daily (except May 4 and Dec 31) from 12:30pm to 3am. Admission is 5€. Wednesday is "ladies day," and admission is free for all female visitors.

Nearby Places of Interest

You can get legally high in Limburg. At the **Drielandenpunt (Three-Country Point),** near Vaals, in the province's southeast corner, the Netherlands, Belgium, and Germany share a common backyard in the "Land Without Frontiers." The elevation is the highest in Holland, a full 322m (1,056 ft.) above sea level—a veritable mountain!—and affords an excellent opportunity to look across miles of countryside in three different countries. From the timber King Baudouin Tower, surrounded by extensive forest, the German city of Aachen merges with the haze in one direction. In another, the green waves of Belgium's Ardennes Hills wash over the horizon. The "Dutch Alps" are behind you. Vaals is 30km (19 miles) east of Maastricht on N278; the Drielandenpunt is a farther .5km (⅓ mile) south.

Thermenmuseum (Roman Bath Museum) ★ ☺ Sixteen centuries have passed since anyone had a bath in Heerlen—at the city's Roman bath, that is. Ancient Coriovallum's 2nd-century-A.D. *thermae* are among Holland's most important classical sites. Heerlen, which back then was a major point on Roman roads, has preserved the remains of the *sudatorium* (sauna), *natatio* (swimming pool), and gymnasium. Aided by a sound-and-light show depicting "Lucius the Potter" on his first visit to the bath, you can recreate the intricate ritual of a Roman bath, which was such an important part of life in the Empire.

Coriovallumstraat 9, Heerlen (24km/16 miles northeast of Maastricht). ✆ **045/560-5100.** www.thermenmuseum.nl. Admission 6.50€ adults, 6€ seniors, 5.50€ children 4–12, free for children 3 and under. Tues–Fri 10am–5pm; Sat–Sun and holidays noon–5pm. Closed Jan 1, Carnival, and Dec 24–25 and 31. You get to Heerlen by train from Maastricht (4 per hr./22–28 min.); by car on A79.

PLANNING YOUR TRIP TO LUXEMBOURG

This chapter provides some of the nuts-and-bolts information you'll need for getting the most out of a visit to the Grand Duchy of Luxembourg. For information that covers planning information and tips for the Benelux countries in general, see chapter 3.

19

THE REGIONS IN BRIEF

It might seem like stretching a point to speak of regions in a land as small as Luxembourg. Rest assured, the Luxembourgers don't agree! Indeed, they recognize no fewer than five distinctive regions: the central **Bon Pays (Good Country),** comprising Luxembourg City and its environs; the **Luxembourg Ardennes;** the **Mullerthal** (also known as "Little Switzerland"); the valley of the **Moselle River;** and the **Terres Rouges (Red Earth)** country. Once you get to know the place, you'd have to agree they're right. Though elements of all five regions are covered in this book, the emphasis is on Luxembourg City, the Ardennes, and the Moselle Valley—the three areas where most visitors spend their time.

WHEN TO GO

"In season" in Luxembourg, as in the rest of the Benelux countries, means from about mid-April to mid-October. The peak of the tourist season is in July and August, when the weather is at its finest. The weather is never really extreme at any time of year, and if you favor shoulder- or off-season travel, you'll find the Grand Duchy every bit as attractive during those months. Not only are hotels and restaurants cheaper, less crowded, and more relaxed during this time, but some very appealing events are

Visitor Information

For contact details of the Luxembourg tourist offices in the United States and Britain, see "Fast Facts: Luxembourg," in chapter 21.

The Euro

Luxembourg's currency is the euro (see "Money & Costs," in chapter 3).

going on. For instance, theater is most active during winter months in Luxembourg City.

Climate

Luxembourg has a moderate climate, with less annual rainfall than either Belgium or the Netherlands, since North Sea winds have usually wept their tears before they get this far inland. The vineyard-rich Moselle Valley in the southeast has the lowest rainfall, with between 30 and 41 centimeters (12–16 in.), and the western districts have the highest, with around 100 centimeters (39 in.). Late summer temperatures in Luxembourg City average 63°F (17°C). Winter temperatures average 34°F (1°C). Snowfalls, which open up the cross-country and downhill skiing pistes in the Ardennes, are common but not guaranteed.

Luxembourg City's Average Monthly Temperature & Days of Rain

	JAN	FEB	MAR	APR	MAY	JUNE	JULY	AUG	SEPT	OCT	NOV	DEC
TEMP. (°F)	33	34	41	45	54	59	63	63	57	49	39	35
TEMP. (°C)	1	1	5	7	12	15	17	17	14	9	4	2
DAYS OF RAIN (OR SNOW)	20	16	14	13	15	14	14	15	16	15	19	20

Holidays

National holidays in Luxembourg are New Year's Day (Jan 1), Shrove Monday/Carnival (2 days before Ash Wednesday), Easter Monday, May Day (May 1), Ascension (40 days after Easter), Pentecost Monday (1 day after the 7th Sun after Easter), National Day/grand duke's official birthday (June 23), Assumption (Aug 15), All Saints' Day (Nov 1), and Christmas (Dec 25 and 26).

Luxembourg Calendar of Events

For an exhaustive list of events beyond those listed here, check http://events.frommers.com, where you'll find a searchable, up-to-the-minute roster of what's happening in cities all over the world.

MARCH

Carnival, Pétange. Mid-Lent carnival and costume parade. Contact **Administration Communale de Pétange** (✆ **50-12-51-1;** www.petange.lu). Refreshment, or Laetere, Sunday (4th Sun of Lent; 3 weeks before Easter). Generally takes place in March or April: April 3, 2011; March 18, 2012.

Printemps Musical (Musical Spring), Luxembourg City. Festival of music, including classical, jazz, and folk, at venues around the city. Contact **Luxembourg City Tourist Office** (✆ **22-28-09;** www.lcto.lu), or go to www.printempsmusical.lu. March to June.

APRIL

L'Eimaischen, Luxembourg City and Nospelt. Market stalls sell pottery and other items; colorful pottery whistles for children are especially popular. Contact **Luxembourg City Tourist Office** (✆ **22-28-09;** www.lcto.lu). Easter Monday: April 25, 2011; April 9, 2012.

Grevenmacher Liesse Wine Festival, Grevenmacher. Contact **Caves Coopératives des Vignerons de Grevenmacher** (✆ **75-01-75**). Saturday after Easter: April 30, 2011; April 14, 2012.

MAY

Festival International Echternach (classical music). National and visiting orchestras play in Echternach's Basilica and the Church of Saints Peter and Paul. Contact **Festival International Echternach** (✆ **72-83-47;** www.echternachfestival.lu). May to June and September.

Luxembourg

To Amsterdam, Maastricht & Liège
0
5 mi
0
5 km
BELGIUM
GERMANY
FRANCE
N7
Troisvierges
Lieler
Asselborn
Woltz
E421
N18
Clervaux
Our
Clerf
To Brussels
Wiltz
E421
Parc Naturel de la Haute-Sûre
Vianden
N7
Sûre
Esch-sur-Sûre
LUXEMBOURG ARDENNES
Lac de la Haute-Sûre
N5
N19
Diekirch
Sûre
N10
Bigonville
Ettelbruck
Grosbous
Echternach
Holtz
Redange
Mersch
Alzette
To Frankfurt
E29
N8
N7
Wasserbillig
VALLEY OF THE SEVEN CASTLES
N11
Hollenfels
Septfontaines
Ansembourg
Grevenmacher
Eisch
E421
E44
Machtum
Koerich
A1
Steinfort
MOSELLE WINE COUNTRY
Capellen
N10
Moselle
Dommeldange
Wormeldange
A6
E25
Luxembourg
Luxembourg (Findel) Airport
Ehnen
E44
E44
A1
N2
E29
N5
Pétange
Remich
Rodange
A4
N3
Differdange
Wellenstein
Bettembourg
To Paris
Mondorf-les-Bains
Esch-sur-Alzette
Alzette
E25
Dudelange
A3
Rumelange

Octave de Notre-Dame de Luxembourg, Luxembourg City. Two-week pilgrimage from towns and villages around the Grand Duchy to Luxembourg Cathedral, in honor of Our Lady of Consolation. It ends with the Octave Procession. Contact **Luxembourg City Tourist Office** (✆ **22-28-09;** www.lcto.lu). Octave Procession on the fifth Sunday after Easter: May 29, 2011; May 13, 2012.

Fête du Genêt/Geenzefest (Broom Festival), Wiltz. The flower parade and festival includes a street market. Contact **Wiltz Tourist Office** (✆ **95-74-44;** www.touristinfowiltz.lu), or go to www.geenzefest.lu. Monday after Pentecost. Generally takes place in May: June 13, 2011; May 28, 2012.

Procession Dansante (Dancing Procession) ★, Echternach. Internationally renowned centuries-old folk-dancing procession in honor of the Irish monk and missionary St. Willibrord (658–739), the patron saint of Luxembourg. Contact **Echternach Tourist Office** (✆ **72-02-30;** www.echternach-tourist.lu). Tuesday after Pentecost, beginning at 9am. Generally takes place in May: June 14, 2011; May 29, 2012.

Danz Festival Lëtzebuerg ★, Luxembourg City. A weeklong festival of modern dance performed by both local and foreign troupes. Contact **Centre de Création Chorégraphique Luxembourgeois** (✆ **40-45-69;** www.dans.lu). Last week in May.

JUNE

Fête de la Musique ★, multiple locations around the Grand Duchy. Culminating on the summer solstice, June 21, the longest day of the year, Luxembourg City and around 20 other towns and villages in the Grand Duchy put on music performances from all kinds of musical genres. Contact **Fête de la Musique** (✆ **621-39-81-37;** www.fetedelamusique.lu). June 18–21.

Summer in the City ★★, Luxembourg City. A wide-ranging program of open-air events: Music, theater, dance, folklore, markets, and more, with a highlight being the Fête de la Musique evening concerts on place d'Armes. Contact **Luxembourg City Tourist Office** (✆ **22-28-09;** www.lcto.lu). From June 21 until mid-September.

National Day ★★, Luxembourg City. Gala celebration featuring festival activities, the Grand Duke reviewing his guards with all the pomp and ritual of centuries past, and fireworks. Contact **Luxembourg City Tourist Office** (✆ **22-28-09;** www.lcto.lu). June 23.

Riesling Open Wine Festival, Remich. Open-air celebrations and wine tasting. Contact **Remich Tourist Office** (✆ **23-69-84-88;** www.moselle-tourist.lu). End of June to August.

JULY

Festival de Wiltz, Wiltz. International open-air theater performances every Friday, Saturday, and Sunday. Incorporates a music program at the Château de Wiltz. Contact **Festival de Wiltz** (✆ **95-74-41;** www.festivalwiltz.lu). Throughout July.

Remembrance Day, Ettelbruck. Celebration in honor of U.S. Gen. George S. Patton and his Third Army troops, who liberated Luxembourg in World War II. Contact **Musée Général Patton** (✆ **81-03-22;** www.patton.lu). July 6.

Al Dikkrich (Old Diekirch) Festival, Diekirch. Folklore events, music, and street market. Contact **Diekirch Tourist Office** (✆ **80-30-23;** www.diekirch.lu). Second week in July.

AUGUST

Procession of the Holy Virgin, Girsterklaus. Pilgrimage dating back to 1328. Contact **Echternach Tourist Office** (✆ **72-02-30;** www.echternach-tourist.lu). Sunday after August 15.

Fête des Récoltes/Léiffrawëschdag (Grape Harvest Festival), Greiveldange. A folkloric procession, wine tastings, and election of the "Wine Queen" greet the new Moselle grape harvest. Contact **Caves Coopératives des Vignerons de Greiveldange** (✆ **23-69-66-1**). Middle weekend in August.

Schueberfouer, Luxembourg City. A big amusement fair and street market. Contact **Luxembourg City Tourist Office** (✆ **22-28-09;** www.lcto.lu). Three weeks, beginning last week in August.

SEPTEMBER

Fête du Raisin et du Vin (Wine and Grape Festival), Grevenmacher. A splendid folklore procession celebrates the local grape harvest and the new Moselle wine season. Contact **Comité des Fêtes Grevenmacher** (✆ **621-37-26-28;** www.grevenmacher.org). Second weekend in September.

OCTOBER

Luxembourg Festival ★★, Luxembourg City. An extensive program of opera, ballet, classical music, jazz, and more is a highlight of the cultural season. Contact **Luxembourg City Tourist Office** (✆ **22-28-09;** www.lcto.lu), or go to www.luxembourgfestival.lu. Through October to the third week in November.

DECEMBER

Marché de Noël/Krëschtmaart ★, Luxembourg City. Stalls selling all kinds of seasonal crafts, food, and drink—be sure to try the *glühwein* (mulled wine)—are set up on place d'Armes for the annual Christmas Market. There's a parallel **Winterlights** program of concerts and events. Contact **Office des Fêtes, Foires et Marchés** (✆ **47-96-42-94;** www.kreschtmaart.lu). Late November to January 3.

GETTING THERE & GETTING AROUND

Getting There

While getting to Luxembourg is not exactly hard (see "Getting There & Around," in chapter 3), it's not as much of a snap as getting to most other parts of the Benelux lands. Luxembourg City is such a tiny capital it doesn't justify much in the way of intercontinental air service, yet as an important financial hub and seat of some European Union institutions, it does have decent service from many European capitals.

Luxembourg City is served by only one high-speed rail line, the TGV from Paris, but the distances involved are short enough that even the slower trains from neighboring Belgium and Germany don't take very long to arrive.

Getting Around

Good news: Traveling around Luxembourg is easy. Going by car affords maximum flexibility, of course, but the efficient public transportation is an excellent option in such a small country.

BY TRAIN & BUS

The **Chemins de Fer Luxembourgeois** (✆ **24-89-24-89;** www.cfl.lu), or Luxembourg Railways, operates frequent trains throughout the Grand Duchy, with connecting bus service to those points the rails don't reach. Going by train is a great way to get around. Luxembourg's local trains are not luxurious, nor are they exactly speedy, but riding the rails gives you the chance to sit back and let the sights and the scenery unfold around you.

Bus service is efficient and comfortable, and between the main towns, at least, is reasonably frequent. In Luxembourg City, a combination of walking and using the excellent city bus network is the best way to get around.

Information on the best public transportation routes and connections in Luxembourg is available from **Mobilitéits Zentral** (✆ **24-65-24-65;** www.mobiliteit.lu).

A **1-day *billet longue durée* (day ticket),** good for unlimited travel by train and bus, costs 4€. A *carnet* (book) of five 1-day tickets costs 16€. When going by train, these prices are for second-class travel; riding in a first-class compartment costs an additional 2€ per day. On Saturday and Sunday, a ***billet Weekend*** is an even better value, at 6€ for unlimited travel in the Grand Duchy (except when traveling to or from a frontier point). Travelers 61 and over are eligible for a 50% reduction, as are children 6 to 12 (who may be eligible to ride free when accompanied by parents or grandparents); children 5 and under ride free.

BY CAR

Roads in the Grand Duchy are kept in good repair and are well signposted. But beware that some roadways are narrow, and with many curves, especially in the Ardennes.

To park in the "blue zones" of Luxembourg City and some other towns, you may need a **parking disc.** These are cardboard or plastic discs with a revolving hour scale. When you park, you set your arrival time by turning the disc to the appropriate hour, displayed in a slot in the card, so that the parking inspectors know when you have overstayed your welcome. The discs are available from stores and banks, often at no charge. In many other places, there are parking-ticket dispensers.

RENTALS If you plan to rent a car in the Grand Duchy, you need a driver's license valid in your own country. Car rental rates begin at around 60€ a day and 75€ for a weekend. Leading car rental firms in Luxembourg (with rental desks at Luxembourg Airport) are **Avis** (✆ **800/331-2112** in the U.S., or ✆ 43-51-71; www.avis.lu); **Budget** (✆ **43-75-75-1;** www.budget.lu); **Europcar** (✆ **43-45-88;** www.europcar.lu); and **Hertz** (✆ **800/654-3001** in the U.S., or ✆ 43-46-45; www.hertz.be).

GASOLINE Fill up on gas *(benzine)* in Luxembourg. A low rate of tax on gas and diesel means you can save around 25% on gas prices in Luxembourg, compared to the prices in neighboring Germany, Belgium, and France—enough of a difference that drivers from those countries go out of their way to fill up in Luxembourg. The Grand Duchy's main border towns sport long, ugly lines of gas stations along the main roads.

DRIVING RULES Speed limits are 50kmph (31 mph) in towns and villages; 70kmph (44 mph), 90kmph (56 mph), or 110kmph (68 mph) on open country roads (national roads); and 130kmph (81 mph), or 110kmph (68 mph) in rain, on the *autoroute* (expressway/motorway). In all cases, lower limits may be posted. The use of seat belts is compulsory, and tooting the horn is permitted only in case of imminent danger.

ROAD MAPS An excellent road map of the Grand Duchy—which shows camping grounds, swimming pools, and tourist attractions in addition to main roads—is available at no cost from the Luxembourg National Tourist Office in Luxembourg City. Other good road maps include the Ordnance Survey maps (two sheets) and Michelin map no. 214, available from local bookstores and newsstands.

BREAKDOWNS/ASSISTANCE A 24-hour emergency road service is offered by the **Automobile Club du Grand-Duché Luxembourg** (✆ **26-00-0;** www.acl.lu).

BY BICYCLE

The Luxembourg countryside lends itself to biking. You're free to ramble down any road that strikes your fancy, and there are biking trails leading through the most scenic areas. Local tourist offices can provide suggestions for tours on these trails and on less traveled roadways. In addition, tourist offices in Luxembourg City, Diekirch, Echternach, Vianden, and other towns can arrange **bicycle rentals.** Bikes can be transported by train for a small fee, regardless of distance traveled, subject to space availability (which is usually not a problem).

BY FOOT

Walking is a great way to travel through this beautiful land. You can do this on 21 separate signposted walking trails around the Grand Duchy. Known as Sentiers Nationaux (National Trails), these range in length from 13km (8 miles) to 84km (52 miles). Plus, there's the Eifel-Ardennes Trail that crosses the border into Germany. Bookstores carry maps of these and other walking routes, and local tourist offices have brochures of walking tours in their area.

The free Luxembourg Railways' *Rail et Randonnée (Train and Tour)* brochure, available from stations, outlines 40 walking routes connecting stations; you can take the train to one station, follow the walking route to another, and return or go on by train from there. The **Luxembourg Youth Hostels Association,** rue du Fort Olisy 2, 2261 Luxembourg-Ville (✆ **26-27-66-40;** www.youthhostels.lu), issues detailed maps with walking paths marked in red. All youth hostels are on walking paths designated by white triangular signs.

In total, these different kinds of trails and footpaths add up to some 5,000km (3,100 miles) of walks and hikes.

LUXEMBOURG

Once dubbed the "Gibraltar of the North," Luxembourg City stands on a natural fortress. Immensely powerful fortifications constructed around it by a parade of rulers made it for centuries a tough proposition for enemies to assault. These defenses were dismantled in 1867. Today, parks cover ground once occupied by forts, and the city is an attractive mixture of historical interest and contemporary charm. The capital is embedded in the rich farmlands of the Bon Pays (Good Country), a rolling plateau traversed by narrow valleys.

The forested **Luxembourg Ardennes,** in the north of the Grand Duchy, is part of a range of hills that sprawls across international frontiers into Belgium, France, and Germany, gouged by narrow rivers like the Our and the Sûre. South of the Ardennes is Luxembourg's stretch of the **Moselle River,** with its celebrated riverside vineyards and wineries. Both regions are liberally sprinkled with pretty villages, castles, and vacation retreats.

LUXEMBOURG CITY ★★

315km (196 miles) SE of Amsterdam; 189km (117 miles) SE of Brussels; 122km (76 miles) SE of Liège

Luxembourg-Ville (Lëtzebuerg Stad), the Grand Duchy's diminutive capital (pop. 89,000), is a marvelously contrasting mix of the old and the new. The old part of town runs along a deep valley beneath brooding casemates that have lent themselves readily to defense in times of war, while the more modern part of town crowns steep cliffs overlooking the old. The city is the headquarters of the European Court of Justice and the European Investment Bank, and it's one of the three seats of the European Parliament (along with Brussels and Strasbourg).

Despite the many banks and the Euro-office towers, Luxembourg City has retained plenty of small-scale, provincial ambience. Still, 60% of the inhabitants are foreigners, so it has an international feel (at least during the day)—a lot of people commute from neighboring countries because it's expensive to live here.

Essentials

GETTING THERE

For details on travel to Luxembourg City, see "Getting There & Around," in chapter 3.

BY PLANE **Lux Airport** (✆ **24-64-0;** www.lux-airport.lu) is at Findel, 6km (4 miles) northeast of Luxembourg City. Regular flights arrive

What's In a Name?

In this chapter, more for interest than necessity, I have provided the names of towns and places in the Grand Duchy of Luxembourg in both French and in Luxembourg's own language, Lëtzebuergesch. You'll often see Lëtzebuergesch place names in the Grand-Duché du Luxembourg (Grouss-herzogtum Lëtzebuerg), but you'll easily get by with just French.

from all major European capitals and other important cities. City bus line 16 (Eurobus) departs from in front of the terminal building to the city's train station, Gare de Luxembourg, a 25-minute ride. The fare is 1.50€, and one to four buses depart every hour. A taxi (✆ **43-43-43**) to the city center costs around 25€; add 10% from 10pm to 6am, and 25% to 35% (depending on the time) on Sunday and holidays.

BY TRAIN Luxembourg City has rail connections from Belgium, France (including a TGV high-speed train from Paris), and Germany. The main station, **Gare de Luxembourg,** in the southern part of town, has an office of the Luxembourg National Tourist Office (see below), a currency-exchange office, a luggage-storage facility, and stops for city bus lines just outside. For train information (and bus service outside Luxembourg City), contact **Chemins de Fer Luxembourgeois** (✆ **24-89-24-89;** www.cfl.lu).

BY BUS **Eurolines** buses arrive in Luxembourg City from London, Brussels, Paris, and other European cities. The main bus station is in front of the train station (see above).

BY CAR Expressways A1/E44, A4/E25, and A31/E25, and highways N4 and N6, converge on Luxembourg City from Germany, France, and Belgium.

VISITOR INFORMATION The **Luxembourg City Tourist Office,** place Guillaume II 30, 1648 Luxembourg-Ville (✆ **22-28-09;** fax 46-70-70; www.lcto.lu), is in the center of town. The office is open April to September Monday to Saturday from 9am to 7pm and Sunday and holidays from 10am to 6pm; October to March, hours are Monday to Saturday from 9am to 6pm and Sunday and holidays from 10am to 6pm. It provides a free, detailed city map that lists the main attractions.

The Luxembourg National Tourist Office operates a **Bureau d'Acceuil (Welcome Desk)** at Gare de Luxembourg (✆ **42-82-82-20;** fax 42-82-82-38; www.visitluxembourg.lu), open June to September Monday to Saturday from 9am to 7pm and Sunday from 9am to 12:30pm and 1:45 to 6pm; October to May, it's open daily from 9:15am to 12:30pm and 1:45 to 6pm.

Both the English-language weekly magazine 352 *Luxembourg News* and its website, **http://hello.news352.lu**, have sections on local news. For information on cultural and tourist events and exhibits around the Grand Duchy, visit **www.agendalux.lu**.

CITY LAYOUT

The heart of Luxembourg City revolves around two main squares in the Old Town. The small **place d'Armes** was once a parade ground, and this is where you find sidewalk cafes and band concerts during summer months. The larger **place Guillaume II**—dubbed the **Knuedler (Knot)** in Lëtzebuergesch, after the knot in the belt worn by Franciscan monks—is the setting for the Hôtel de Ville (Town Hall), the city tourist office, and for statues of William II and Luxembourg poet Michel

Luxembourg City

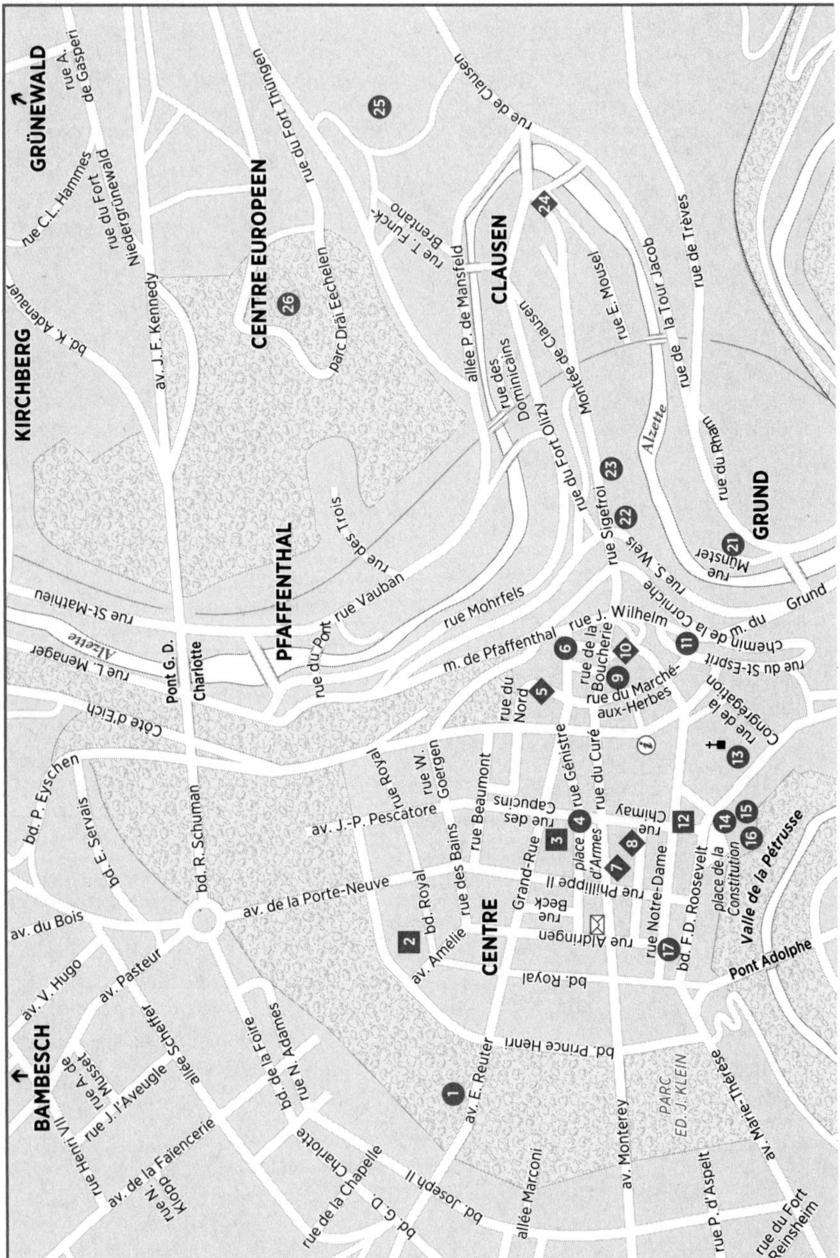

GRÜNEWALD
KIRCHBERG
CENTRE EUROPEEN
PFAFFENTHAL
CLAUSEN
GRUND
CENTRE
BAMBESCH
rue A. de Gasperi
rue C.L. Hammes
rue du Fort Niedergrünewald
bd. K. Adenauer
av. J.F. Kennedy
rue du Fort Thüngen
rue de Clausen
rue T. Funck-Brentano
parc Dräi Eechelen
allée P. de Mansfeld
rue des Dominicains
Montée de Clausen
rue du Fort Olizy
rue E. Mousel
rue de la Tour Jacob
rue de Trèves
rue du Rham
Alzette
rue Sigefroi
rue S. Weis
rue Münster
rue des Trois
rue Vauban
rue du Pont
rue Mohrfels
rue St-Mathieu
rue L. Menager
Pont G. D. Charlotte
Côte d'Eich
m. de Pfaffenthal
rue J. Wilhelm
rue de la Boucherie
rue du Marché-aux-Herbes
rue de la Corniche
chemin de la Congrégation
m. du Grund
rue du St-Esprit
rue de la Congrégation
rue du Nord
rue Génistre
rue du Curé
rue Royal
rue W. Goergen
rue Beaumont
av. J.-P. Pescatore
rue des Capucins
place d'Armes
rue Chimay
bd. P. Eyschen
bd. E. Servais
bd. R. Schuman
av. de la Porte-Neuve
rue des Bains
Grand-Rue
rue Philippe II
rue Notre-Dame
bd. F.D. Roosevelt
place de la Constitution
Valle de la Pétrusse
av. du Bois
bd. Royal
av. Amélie
rue Beck
rue Aldringen
Pont Adolphe
av. V. Hugo
av. Pasteur
allée Scheffer
rue A. de Musset
rue J. l'Aveugle
bd. de la Foire
rue N. Adames
bd. Prince Henri
av. E. Reuter
PARC ED. J. KLEIN
av. Marie-Thérèse
rue Henri VII
av. de la Faïencerie
rue N. Kiopp
rue Charlotte
rue de la Chapelle
bd. G. D. Charlotte
bd. Joseph II
allée Marconi
av. Monterey
rue P. d'Aspelt
rue du Fort Reinsheim

1 2 3 4 5 6 7 8 9 10 11 12 13 14 15 16 17 21 22 23 24 25 26

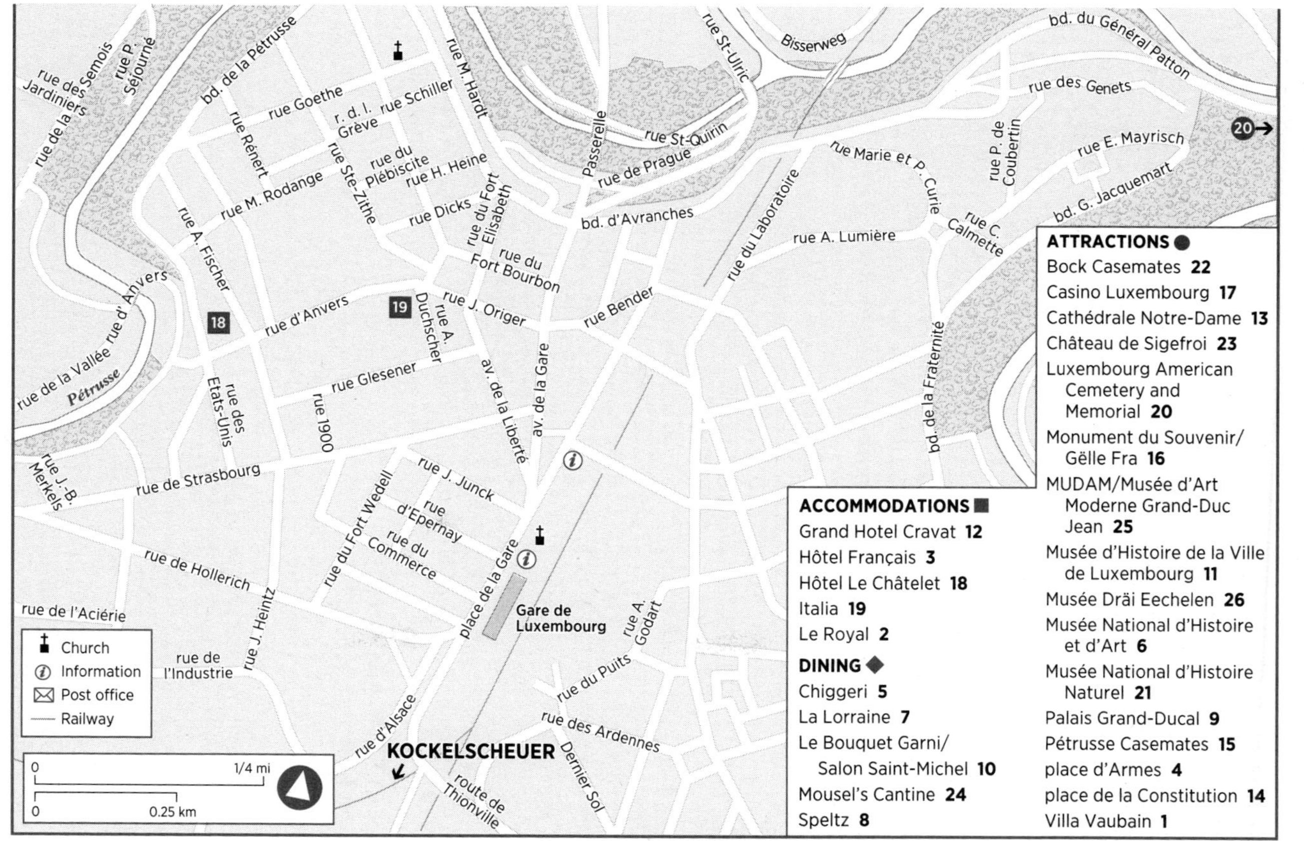
ATTRACTIONS ●
Bock Casemates 22
Casino Luxembourg 17
Cathédrale Notre-Dame 13
Château de Sigefroi 23
Luxembourg American Cemetery and Memorial 20
Monument du Souvenir/ Gëlle Fra 16
MUDAM/Musée d'Art Moderne Grand-Duc Jean 25
Musée d'Histoire de la Ville de Luxembourg 11
Musée Dräi Eechelen 26
Musée National d'Histoire et d'Art 6
Musée National d'Histoire Naturel 21
Palais Grand-Ducal 9
Pétrusse Casemates 15
place d'Armes 4
place de la Constitution 14
Villa Vaubain 1
ACCOMMODATIONS ■
Grand Hotel Cravat 12
Hôtel Français 3
Hôtel Le Châtelet 18
Italia 19
Le Royal 2
DINING ◆
Chiggeri 5
La Lorraine 7
Le Bouquet Garni/ Salon Saint-Michel 10
Mousel's Cantine 24
Speltz 8
Church
Information
Post office
Railway
0
1/4 mi
0
0.25 km
KOCKELSCHEUER
Gare de Luxembourg
20
18
19
Pétrusse
bd. du Général Patton
rue des Genets
rue P. de Coubertin
rue E. Mayrisch
bd. G. Jacquemart
rue C. Calmette
rue Marie et P. Curie
rue A. Lumière
bd. de la Fraternité
rue du Laboratoire
Bisserweg
rue St-Ulric
rue St-Quirin
Passerelle
rue de Prague
bd. d'Avranches
rue Bender
rue J. Origer
rue du Fort Bourbon
av. de la Gare
av. de la Liberté
rue du Fort Elisabeth
rue M. Hardt
rue Dicks
rue H. Heine
rue du Plébiscite
rue Ste-Zithe
r. d. l. Grève
rue Schiller
rue Goethe
rue Rénert
rue M. Rodange
bd. de la Pétrusse
rue P. Séjourné
rue des Jardiniers
rue de Semois
rue de la
rue A. Fischer
rue d'Anvers
rue A. Duchscher
rue Glesener
rue 1900
rue des Etats-Unis
rue de la Vallée
rue J.-B. Merkels
rue de Strasbourg
rue J. Junck
rue d'Epernay
rue du Commerce
rue du Fort Wedell
place de la Gare
rue de Hollerich
rue J. Heintz
rue de l'Aciérie
rue de l'Industrie
rue d'Alsace
route de Thionville
Dernier Sol
rue des Ardennes
rue du Puits
rue A. Godart

Passport to Luxembourg

If you plan to do a lot of sightseeing and traveling on public transportation, both in Luxembourg City and around the Grand Duchy, a sound investment is the LuxembourgCard, available from tourist offices. It comes with a 32-page booklet listing more than 50 attractions offering cardholders free admission, and others offering discounted admission. In addition, the card lets you ride free on buses and trains. Valid for 1, 2, or 3 days, for one person it costs 10€, 17€, and 24€, respectively; a family card for two to five people costs 20€, 34€, and 48€.

Rodange (1827–76); it hosts morning markets on Wednesday and Saturday during the summer. The principal shopping street is **Grand-Rue.**

Main arteries bordering the Old Town are **boulevard Grande-Duchesse Charlotte** to the north and **boulevard Franklin D. Roosevelt** to the south. A pleasant walkway, the **promenade de la Corniche,** connects the Bock Casemates to the Citadelle du St-Esprit fortifications. There are steps, in addition to an elevator, from **place St-Esprit** down to the **Grund (Gronn)** neighborhood in the valley below. Take a stroll alongside the Alzette River, and look up at the fortifications on the hills.

Grund and the neighboring districts of **Clausen** and **Pfaffenthal (Paffendal),** south of the Pétrusse Valley, are among Luxembourg City's oldest, most picturesque sections, and each merits a visit; though be warned—you'll probably want to loiter at least half a day. There is a popular nightlife scene here, and cafes and restaurants, often with open-air terraces in good weather. The ultramodern Euro-zone on the **Kirchberg (Kierchbierg)** plateau, off avenue John F. Kennedy in the northeast of the city, is home to the European Court of Justice, the European Investment Bank, and the Secretariat of the European Parliament.

Belts of dense greenery ring the city, giving visitors an easy, close-at-hand escape from city sightseeing. Take your pick: **Bambesch (Bambësch),** to the northwest, contains play areas for children, tennis courts, and footpaths through the **Grünewald (Gréngewald)** forest; **Kockelscheuer (Kockelscheier),** a village outside the city limits to the south, holds a campsite, ice rink, tennis courts, and a pond for fishing.

GETTING AROUND

BY BUS Because of the city's small size, you may have little need to use the bus network. Service is extensive and efficient but infrequent on some lines. The fare (valid for 1 hr.) is 1.50€; a 10-ticket pack costs 12€. A money-saving **day ticket** for 4€, and a 5-day pack for 16€, available from train stations and the airport, can be used on buses and trains throughout the Grand Duchy. Luxembourg City bus information is available from **AVL** (© **47-96-29-75;** www.autobus.lu).

BY TAXI Taxis charge 2€ per kilometer (3.20€ per mile), with a 10% surcharge from 10pm to 6am, and 25% on Sunday and holidays. Taxi service is available from **Benelux Taxis** (© **800/2-51-51,** or 40-38-40; www.beneluxtaxi.lu).

BY CAR Driving in Luxembourg City isn't difficult, but most in-town attractions are within easy walking distance. My advice? Park your car and save it for day trips outside the city. For information on car rental and driving rules, see "Getting There & Around," in chapter 19. Street parking can present a problem, but there are many parking garages. The city map supplied by the tourist office (see above) has parking areas clearly marked. The three most centrally located underground parking garages are off boulevard Royal near the post office, off rue Notre-Dame, and at place du Théâtre.

ON FOOT Luxembourg City is made for walking—that's really the only way to do it justice. Most major attractions are within .5km (⅓ mile) of the center of town. Beyond that, though, the hilly nature of the city and the distance to other points of interest may start to take a toll. The many green spaces and parks invite either a soul-refreshing sit-down or a leisurely stroll to slow your sightseeing pace.

SPECIAL EVENTS

The **Fête de la Musique** (✆ **621-39-81-37;** www.fetedelamusique.lu) comes to town from June 18 to 21, bringing with it performances of all kinds of musical genres. **Summer in the City** (✆ **22-28-09;** www.summerinthecity.lu) picks up where the Fête leaves off, from June 21 to the middle of September, with free open-air music, theater, cinema, and other events. During the June 23 **National Day** celebration (which kicks off on the previous evening), the grand duke reviews his troops, and city streets ring with merrymaking until well after dark, when the festivities conclude with spectacular fireworks over the Pétrusse Valley.

[FastFACTS] LUXEMBOURG CITY

Airport See "Essentials," above.

Area Code The Grand Duchy of Luxembourg has no area codes.

Currency Exchange Currency-exchange offices are open daily at the airport and at the Gare the Luxembourg. See "Money & Costs," in chapter 3.

Doctors & Dentists Call ✆ **112** for referrals to English-speaking doctors and dentists.

Embassies See "Fast Facts: Luxembourg," in chapter 21.

Emergencies For police assistance, call ✆ **113.** For an ambulance or the fire department, call ✆ **112.**

Hospitals The most important city hospital is the modern **Centre Hospitalier de Luxembourg,** rue Nicolas-Ernest Barblé 4 (✆ **44-11-11;** www.chl.lu; bus no. 22), off route d'Arlon in the northwest of the city.

Mail The main post office, rue Aldringen 25 (✆ **47-65-44-51;** www.pt.lu), is open Monday to Friday from 7am to 7pm and Saturday from 7am to 5pm.

Police In an emergency, call ✆ **113.** For routine matters, go to central police headquarters, rue Glesener 60 (✆ **49-97-45-00;** www.police.public.lu).

Safety Luxembourg City is a safe, low-crime city. There are no dangerous or unsafe areas. That's not to say being a victim of crime is impossible, just that it's extremely unlikely.

What to See & Do

Luxembourg City is a delight for the sightseer. Most attractions are in a compact area, and inexpensive bus tours can take you to places of interest farther afield. One of your greatest pleasures in Luxembourg may come on a balmy summer evening at a sidewalk cafe on tree-shaded **place d'Armes,** as a band plays on the square in front of you.

THE FORTIFICATIONS ★★

Luxembourg City grew up around **Count Sigefroi's 10th-century château** at Montée de Clausen on the Bock promontory. The count's choice of location was astute—the 48m (157-ft.) cliffs overlooking the Alzette and Pétrusse river valleys were persuasive obstacles to invading forces. In time, there came to be three rings of battlements around the city, including the cliff bastions, 15 forts surrounding the bastions, and an exterior wall interspersed with nine more forts, three of them cut right into the rock.

Even more impressive than these aboveground fortifications were the 25km (16 miles) of underground tunnels that sheltered troops by the thousands, and their equipment, horses, workshops, artillery, arms, kitchens, bakeries, and slaughterhouses. Legend says that within these tremendous rocky walls of the fortress sits a beautiful maiden named Mélusine, whose knitting needles control the fate of Luxembourg.

Over the centuries, Burgundian, French, Spanish, Austrian, and German forces took control of these strategic fortifications, each in turn adding to the already formidable defenses. Europe's fears of the city's strength stood in the way of Luxembourg's very freedom and independence. Finally, in 1867, the Treaty of London ordered the dismantling of all these battlements, and what you see today represents only about 10% of the original works.

Visit the impressive **casemates** (✆ **22-28-09**), a UNESCO World Heritage site, by entering from two points: The entrance on Montée de Clausen leads to the **Bock Casemates,** and the entrance on place de la Constitution leads to the **Pétrusse Casemates.** In the Bock Casemates, the **Crypte Archéologique (Archaeological Crypt)** features an audiovisual presentation that runs through the highlights of the Luxembourg fortress's history. The Bock Casemates are open March to October daily from 10am to 5pm; the Pétrusse Casemates are open during school vacations daily from 11am to 4pm. Separate admission for each is 3€ for adults, 2.50€ for children 6 to 18, and free for children 5 and under.

OTHER TOP SIGHTS

Cathédrale Notre-Dame (Cathedral of Our Lady) ★★ This magnificent Gothic structure was constructed between 1613 and 1621. It holds the royal family vault and the huge sarcophagus of Count of Luxembourg John I of Bohemia ("John the Blind"; 1296–1346), in addition to a remarkable treasury (which can only be viewed on request, so ask the sacristan, whose office is on the right as you enter). The cathedral is the scene of the **Octave of Our Lady of Luxembourg,** an annual ceremony on the fifth Sunday following Easter, when thousands of pilgrims arrive to pray for protection to the miraculous statue of the Holy Virgin. They then form a procession to carry the statue from the cathedral through the streets to an altar covered with flowers on avenue de la Porte Neuve, north of place d'Armes.

Bd. Franklin D. Roosevelt (entrance on rue Notre-Dame). Free admission. Daily 10am–noon and 2–5:30pm. Closed to nonworshipers during services.

Musée National d'Histoire et d'Art (National Museum of History and Art) ★ In the 120-plus rooms of a strikingly modern building of white stone and glass, this museum in the oldest part of town holds archaeological, geological, and historical exhibits, and decorative and popular art. Highlights of the collections are the exhibit on the Fortress of Luxembourg, two watercolors by J.M.W. Turner depicting the Old Town in the 19th century, and works of art by later artists including Cézanne, Picasso, Magritte, and Luxembourg's own Joseph Kutter.

A Big Smile for Museums

Some imaginative spirit noticed that if you plotted seven cultural institutions in Luxembourg City, they formed the outline of a smile, and most of them were within a mile (or at any rate, easy walking distance) of each other. This gave rise to the birth of a notion: the **Museumsmile** (www.statermuseeen.lu).

Of the seven, the **Musée National d'Histoire et d'Art,** the **Musée d'Histoire de la Ville de Luxembourg,** the **Musée National d'Histoire Naturelle,** and the **MUDAM/Musée d'Art Moderne Grand-Duc Jean,** are covered in this chapter.

The remaining three are the art galleries **Villa Vaubain,** av. Emile Reuter 18 (**✆ 47-96-45-52;** www.villavauban.lu), and **Casino Luxembourg,** rue Notre-Dame 41 (**✆ 22-50-45;** www.casino-luxembourg.lu); and the fortress museum **Musée Dräi Eechelen,** parc Dräi Eechelen 3 (**✆ 47-93-30-214;** www.mnha.public.lu).

You can get discounted admission to all seven by purchasing a **Muséeskaart** from participating museums and from tourist offices. The card is 50€ for adults, 35€ for seniors and students, 25€ for ages 12 to 25, free for children 11 and under, 75€ for a couple, and 100€ for a family.

Marché-aux-Poissons. ✆ **47-93-30-1.** www.mnha.lu. Admission 5€ adults, 3€ seniors, free for students and children 17 and under, family 8€. Tues–Sun 10am–6pm (to 8pm Thurs).

Palais Grand-Ducal (Palace of the Grand Dukes) ★ The official residence of Luxembourg's constitutional monarch evokes all the opulence of the Grand Duchy's medieval splendor. Since the Grand Ducal Guard was disbanded in the 1960s, the palace has been "guarded" by a solitary soldier from the tiny national army. The oldest part of this interesting and often renovated building dates back to 1572 (its "new" right wing dates from 1741). Next door is the Chamber of Deputies (Luxembourg's Parliament).

Rue du Marché-aux-Herbes 17. ✆ **47-48-74-1.** www.monarchie.lu. Admission only for guided tours 6€ adults, 3€ children (tickets from Luxembourg City Tourist Office on place Guillaume II). Mid-July to early Sept Mon–Fri 2:30–5pm (in English 4:30pm only); Sat 10–11am (not in English).

THREE MORE FINE MUSEUMS

As its name suggests, the **Musée d'Histoire de la Ville de Luxembourg (Luxembourg City Historical Museum) ★**, rue du St-Esprit 14 (**✆ 47-96-45-00;** www.musee-hist.lu), takes you back along the corridors of the city's eventful history from the 10th century onward, by way of original objects and an interactive multimedia display. It's open Tuesday to Sunday from 10am to 6pm (to 8pm Thurs). Admission is 5€ for adults, 3€ for seniors and students, free for children 17 and under, and free for all visitors 6 to 8pm Thursday.

The **Musée National d'Histoire Naturelle (National Museum of Natural History),** rue Münster 25 (**✆ 46-22-33-1;** www.mnhn.lu), housed in the 14th-century Hospice St.-Jean on the bank of the Alzette River, should be of special interest to children. It is invariably overrun with local school groups, due to its inventive dioramas and other exhibits depicting the changing peoples, cultures, geography, and environment of both Luxembourg and the wider world. The museum is open Tuesday to Sunday from 10am to 6pm. Admission is 4.50€ for adults, 3€ for students and children 6 to 18, free for children 5 and under, and 9€ for a family.

Opened in 2006 in a modernist building in the Quartier Européen (European District) and designed by Chinese-American architect I. M. Pei, the **MUDAM (Musée d'Art Moderne Grand-Duc Jean/Grand-Duke Jean Museum of Modern Art),** parc Dräi Eechelen 3 (✆ **45-37-85-960;** www.mudam.lu), presents both permanent and visiting collections of modern art from around the world. It's open Wednesday to Friday from 11am to 8pm and Saturday to Monday from 11am to 6pm. Admission is 5€ for adults, 3€ for seniors and ages 18 to 26, free for children 17 and under, and free for all visitors 6 to 8pm Wednesday.

MORE PLACES OF INTEREST

Place de la Constitution affords a marvelous view of the Pétrusse Valley and the impressive Pont Adolphe that spans it. In the center of the square, the tall **Monument du Souvenir (Remembrance Monument),** a gold-plated female figure on a tall stone obelisk, is a memorial to those who have perished in Luxembourg's wars. Known affectionately as the **Gëlle Fra (Golden Lady),** the monument was erected in 1923, destroyed by the Nazis in 1940, partly reconstructed in 1958, and finally restored to its original form in 1985.

The serene **Luxembourg American Cemetery and Memorial** at Hamm (✆ **43-13-27;** www.abmc.gov), 5km (3 miles) east of Luxembourg City, is the final resting place of 5,076 of the 10,000 American troops who lost their lives in Luxembourg during World War II, in the course of liberating the Grand Duchy and fighting the Battle of the Bulge (1944–45). The identical graves are arranged without regard to rank, religion, race, or place of origin, the only exception being the grave of Gen. George S. Patton (because of the many visitors to his gravesite). To get to the cemetery by car, take boulevard du Général Patton, which becomes N2 outside of town. The cemetery is open daily 9am to 5pm (closed Jan 1 and Dec 25); admission is free.

ORGANIZED TOURS

WALKING TOURS The Luxembourg City Tourist Office organizes a **City Promenade,** a 2-hour guided walking tour through the heart of town, starting out from the tourist office on place Guillaume II. The tour runs April to October daily at noon (in French and German) and 2pm (in English and German); and November to March Monday, Wednesday, Saturday, and Sunday at 1pm (in English, French, and German). It is 9€ for adults, 7€ for seniors and students, 4.50€ for children ages 6 to 18, and free for children under 6.

TRAIN TOURS One of the city's best tours is on the **Pétrusse Express** ★ (✆ **26-65-11;** www.sales-lentz.lu), a *petit train touristique,* a brightly painted "little tourist train" on rubber wheels that takes the weight off your feet when you tour the city. Don't worry: You don't need to be a "little tourist" to step aboard. The train departs twice an hour from place de la Constitution and travels paved pathways through the Pétrusse and Alzette valleys, and on through some of the oldest sections of town to one of the original city gates. Simply sit back and enjoy the passing scenery, or don earphones and listen to a historical commentary (in English, among other languages). The train runs from mid-March to October daily every 30 minutes from 10am to 6pm. The 50-minute ride is 8.50€ for adults, 5€ for children 4 to 15, free for children 3 and under, and 27€ for families.

BUS TOURS The **Hop On-Hop Off** (✆ **26-65-11;** www.sales-lentz.lu) circular bus tour, onboard open-top double-deck buses, brings you to the cathedral, the grand duke's palace, the remains of the fortress, the European Center, and some of Luxembourg's most important avenues. The buses operate from the last week in March to

Band Concerts

From June to October, place d'Armes hosts open-air concerts, performed by either the Grand Ducal Big Band for Military Music or bands from towns around Luxembourg. The program ranges from classical to light classics to show tunes. The concerts usually are on Sunday at 11am and 8:30pm.

October daily, with departures every 30 minutes between 10am and 5pm from place de la Constitution. The fare is 14€ for adults, 11€ for seniors and students, 7€ for children 4 to 15, free for children 3 and under, and 35€ for families.

Where to Stay

VERY EXPENSIVE

Le Royal ★★ The Royal fully deserves its recognized status as one of the Leading Hotels of the World. There isn't much that this hotel doesn't offer in the way of service. It's on the main financial street in the center city, in a leafy district across from a park, a location that will suit those who like that kind of thing. Most, but not all, of the guest rooms are large and tastefully modern in style and have marble bathrooms; with so many rooms, their size and state varies enough that you might want to check yours out before committing. Some rooms have balconies overlooking the park. There are two top-notch restaurants, the international **La Pomme Canelle,** and the Mediterranean-style **Le Jardin,** with terrace dining in summer. The Piano Bar features live music after 6pm.

Bd. Royal 12 (at av. Amélie), 2449 Luxembourg-Ville. ✆ **24-16-16-1.** Fax 22-59-48. www.hotelroyal.lu. 210 units. 380€–520€ double; from 650€ suite. Rates include breakfast on weekends. AE, DC, MC, V. Parking 18€ (free on weekends). **Amenities:** 2 restaurants; bar; free airport transfers; babysitting; concierge; health club; heated indoor pool; room service; sauna; smoke-free rooms. *In room:* A/C, TV, hair dryer, minibar, Wi-Fi (22€/day).

EXPENSIVE

Grand Hotel Cravat ★ This century-old hotel, on a busy boulevard in the heart of town, has retained much of its old-world charm, high standards, and friendly hospitality. It's a classy old place, but that hasn't stopped it from keeping up-to-date, albeit in a chintzy kind of a way. The guest rooms are cozily furnished. Some have balconies overlooking place de la Constitution and the Gëlle Fra monument, and have grand views down into the Pétrusse Valley. Restaurant **Le Normandy** serves fine French cuisine and seafood. In the gracious Le Trianon Bar, you often see Luxembourg's leading businesspeople gathered at the end of the day. Casual meals are served in the traditional Luxembourg brasserie La Taverne.

Bd. Roosevelt 29 (at the Gëlle Fra monument), 2450 Luxembourg-Ville. ✆ **22-19-75.** Fax 22-67-1. www.hotelcravat.lu. 60 units. 350€–435€ double; 500€ suite. Rates include buffet breakfast. AE, DC, MC, V. Limited street parking. **Amenities:** 2 restaurants; bar; babysitting; concierge; room service; smoke-free rooms. *In room:* TV, hair dryer, minibar, Wi-Fi (30€/day).

MODERATE

Hôtel Français Located on one of central Luxembourg City's most bustling squares, this is one of the nicest moderately priced small hotels in town. The guest rooms are decorated in a bright, modern style; though some are on the small side, they are all well laid out. The hotel is in a pedestrian-only zone, but taxis are allowed to drop off and pick up people and baggage. On the ground floor is the popular French/Italian brasserie **Restaurant Français,** with a terrace on the square in summer. Watch out for noise coming up from the sidewalk tables on the square on warm summer evenings when you might want to keep your room window open, or ask for a quieter room at the back. Four of the units are apartments.

Place d'Armes 14 (in the center city), 1136 Luxembourg-Ville. ✆ **47-45-34.** Fax 46-42-74. www.hotelfrancais.lu. 25 units. 99€–140€ double. Rates include continental breakfast. AE, DC, MC, V. No parking. **Amenities:** Restaurant. *In room:* TV, Wi-Fi (free).

Hôtel Le Châtelet ★ This small hotel near the Pétrusse Valley on the edge of the center city, owned and operated by the friendly and gracious Mr. and Mrs. Ferd Lorang-Rieck, is a longtime favorite of visiting academics and businesspeople. Its rooms are divided between two lovely old Luxembourg homes; all have modern, comfortable, and attractive furnishings. The rustic restaurant, a local favorite, serves traditional Luxembourg specialties and a nice variety of fish and meat dishes at moderate prices.

Bd. de la Pétrusse 2 (at rue d'Anvers), 2320 Luxembourg-Ville. ✆ **40-21-01.** Fax 40-36-66. www.chatelet.lu. 48 units. 105€–175€ double. Rates include buffet breakfast. AE, DC, MC, V. Parking 12€. **Amenities:** Restaurant; exercise room; Jacuzzi; sauna; smoke-free rooms. *In room:* TV, Wi-Fi (free).

INEXPENSIVE

Italia This friendly, small hotel (without an elevator) isn't far from the central rail station and is set in a generally quiet area, though rooms at the front can be affected by traffic noise. The comfortable but rather old-fashioned guest rooms are above a decent restaurant that serves Italian and other Continental dishes. There's a long a la carte menu, with outstanding specialties such as *entrecôte ala peperonata* (steak with pepper sauce).

Rue d'Anvers 15–17 (at av. de la Liberté), 1130 Luxembourg-Ville. ✆ **48-66-26-1.** Fax 48-08-07. italia@euro.lu. 20 units. 80€ double. Rates include continental breakfast. AE, MC, V. Limited street parking. **Amenities:** Restaurant; bar; room service; smoke-free rooms. *In room:* TV.

Where to Dine

EXPENSIVE

La Lorraine ★ SEAFOOD/FRENCH The popular, atmospheric La Lorraine excels in its preparation of seafood specialties. There are two dining sections here: Downstairs is a casual and airy brasserie-style room, with an oyster bar in the corner whose wooden roof models the underside of a fishing boat's hull; upstairs, formal elegance reigns in the Art Deco–style main dining room. Bouillabaisse is a standout, and there's a gigantic selection of Breton oysters, but the menu is not limited to fish. There's a deft French touch to the duck with honey-vinegar sauce and the succulent lamb. *Cuisine de nos grand-mères,* says the menu ("Just like grandma used to make").

Place d'Armes 7. ✆ **47-14-36.** www.lalorraine-restaurant.lu. Main courses 18€–47€; fixed-price menus 36€–50€. AE, DC, MC, V. Daily 11:30am–10:30pm.

Le Bouquet Garni/Salon Saint-Michel ★★ FRENCH Bare stone and wood beams mark this critically acclaimed, cozy place in the Old City, down a narrow side street near the Palace of the Grand Dukes. Flawless service and classic French cuisine from Michelin-star chef Thierry Duhr and his wife, Lysiane, combine to make this family-run restaurant one of Luxembourg's most highly regarded. Seafood is the big deal here, but look, too, for meat dishes such as game poultry with truffles in season. The contents of the dessert trolley will make true believers of even the most waistline conscious.

Rue de l'Eau 32 (at rue du Marché aux Herbes). ✆ **26-20-06-20.** www.lebouquetgarni.lu. Reservations required. Main courses 34€–42€; fixed-price lunch 38€–50€, dinner 90€. AE, DC, MC, V. Mon–Fri noon–2pm and 7–10pm; Sat 7–10pm.

MODERATE

Chiggeri ★★ MEDITERRANEAN The upstairs dining room in this rambling mansion on a quiet side street showcases African decorative motifs, like a ceiling-mounted dugout canoe, and elegant table settings. Its seasonal menu features inventive Mediterranean dishes with Asian influences, and there's always a vegetarian option or two. Reserve the bay-window table, for fine views over the Alzette valley. When the weather's good, you'll likely want to dine on the outdoor terrace. Downstairs, a New Age–look cafe serves 30 different kinds of beer. In addition, a Saharan oasis–style *jardin d'hiver* (winter garden) patio-restaurant provides a light, airy space for raclettes, fondues, and other light meals. Different kinds of music, from rock to world music to classical, set an appropriate tone in each of the rooms.

Rue du Nord 15 (off Grand-Rue). ✆ **22-99-36.** www.chiggeri.lu. Main courses 24€–32€; fixed-price lunch 21€–25€, dinner 50€. MC, V. Sun–Thurs 9am–1pm; Fri–Sat 9am–3am.

Speltz ★ FRENCH Set in a wood-paneled town house with two convivial dining rooms, this brasserie serves a line of savory French fare. The menu comprises, so far as is possible, dishes prepared using organic products and ingredients. You'll find a few seafood items, like the *dorade* (bream) in a tomato-and-basilicum sauce, and earthy meat choices, like the filet mignon of roast pork served with organic fries. In good weather, you can dine outdoors on a tree-shaded terrace. The wines on the menu originate from the associated **Vinothèque Speltz,** just across the way at place Guillaume II 22 (✆ **24-47-83-40;** www.vinothequespeltz.com).

Rue Chimay 8 (corner of rue Louvigny). ✆ **47-49-50.** www.speltzluxembourg.com. Main courses 20€–27€; vegetarian plate 12€; fixed-price menus 24€–35€. AE, MC, V. Tues–Sat 11:45am–2pm and 6:45–10pm.

INEXPENSIVE

Mousel's Cantine LUXEMBOURGEOIS Located in a bustling zone of bars and other nightlife, this is an excellent place to sample regional treats. Although much renovated, it still sports a rustic decor, with plain wood tables and oil paintings in the back room. The front room overlooks the quaint street outside. A friendly staff serves up large portions of Luxembourg favorites such as sauerkraut with sausage, potatoes, and ham. To wash down this hearty fare, try a stein of the unfiltered Mousel local brew.

Montée de Clausen 46 (next to the Mousel Brewery, beside the Alzette River). ✆ **47-01-98.** www.mouselscantine.lu. Main courses 11€–23€; *menu du jour* 25€. AE, DC, MC, V. Mon–Sat noon–2pm and 6–10pm.

Shopping

In the Old City, upmarket stores are clustered around **Grand-Rue** and adjacent streets and **rue de la Poste.** Many of Europe's leading designers are represented in boutiques in this area, and there are good art galleries as well. In the station area, **avenue de la Gare,** which joins the Passerelle (bridge) to the new city, is lined with stores, most in the moderate price range.

Souvenir stores abound, selling attractive **handcrafted items, clocks, pottery,** and miscellaneous objects. **Paintings** are featured at many fine galleries in the city. **Porcelain plates,** decorated with painted landscapes of the Grand Duchy, and **cast-iron wall plaques** produced by Fonderie de Mersch, depicting castles, coats of arms, and local scenes, are excellent mementos of a Luxembourg visit. The best place to find all these items is the streets leading off place d'Armes.

Two good sources of English-language books are **Chapter 1,** rue Astrid 42 (✆ **44-07-09;** www.chapter1.lu), and **Librairie Ernster,** rue du Fossé 27 (✆ **22-50-77;** www.ernster.com).

Luxembourg's handmade chocolates are not so well known as those of neighboring Belgium, but the locals are no slouches when it comes to rustling up some fine pralines and other such dainty delights. To prove the point, visit one of the city branches of **Namur** (www.namur.lu), purveyors to the grand-ducal court: rue des Capucins 27 (✆ **22-34-08**), and av. de la Liberté 44 (tel] **49-39-64**). Another good choice is **Oberweis** (www.oberweis.lu), which has multiple city branches; try the central one at Grand-Rue 19–21 (✆ **47-07-03**).

Wednesday and Saturday are bustling and colorful **market days,** when place Guillaume II is awash with the color and exuberance of country folk tending stalls filled with brilliant blooms, fresh vegetables, and a vast assortment of other goods. It will have you pitting your bargain-acquisition skills against the moneymaking instincts of wily traders.

Luxembourg City After Dark

Luxembourg City stays up late, and there are numerous nightspots, jazz clubs, theater performances, concerts, and other after-dark activities to choose from. Clubs come and go rather frequently, so it's a good idea to stop by the tourist office on place Guillaume II and pick up a copy of ***La Semaine à Luxembourg (The Week in Luxembourg)*** to see what's happening during your visit. In addition, get the 352 *Luxembourg News,* an English-language newspaper published every Friday that highlights current events. ***City Luxembourg Agenda*** lists leading entertainment venues in addition to restaurants.

THE PERFORMING ARTS

CLASSICAL CONCERTS, MUSIC & DANCE From May to October, the **Grand Théâtre de la Ville de Luxembourg,** rond-point Robert Schuman (✆ **47-96-39-00;** www.theatres.lu), presents major concert artists from around the world, in addition to concerts by the **Grand Orchestre Philharmonique du Luxembourg** (✆ **22-99-01;** www.opl.lu). There are dance (ballet and modern) performances and musical revues by visiting artists year-round. Tickets are 15€ to 75€. Local **dance** and **jazz** school students have periodic performances at Théâtre des Capucins (see below).

THEATER The Round Tower Players present high-caliber productions (in English) at **Théâtre des Capucins,** place du Théâtre 9 (✆ **47-96-40-54;** www.theatres.lu); tickets are 8€–30€. For classic theater in French, there's the **Théâtre National du Luxembourg,** rte. de Longwy 194 (✆ **26-44-12-70;** www.tnl.lu); tickets are 10€–30€.

DANCE CLUBS

Luxembourg's hottest club, and a self-declared venue for "beautiful people," **Bypass ★★**, rue des Bains 19 (✆ **26-18-78-67;** www.bypass.lu), on the city center's northern edge, attracts hip clubbers to its twin dance floors, Le Club and Le VIP. Next door, **White,** rue des Bains 21 (✆ **26-20-11-40;** www.white.lu), fits in plenty of black decor and welcomes visitors of all shades to its multi-faceted party nights. Popular among students, Grund-district club **Melusina** ★, rue de la Tour Jacob 145 (✆ **43-59-22;** www.melusina.lu), alternates between rock and jazz groups; house spins in the separate Ultra Lounge. There's a trendy restaurant here.

LIVE MUSIC

An invariably busy rock club, **Den Atelier** ★, rue de Hollerich 54 (✆ **49-54-85-1;** www.atelier.lu), close to the city's main train station (Gare de Luxembourg), regularly signs up name local and international performers; ticket prices vary with the standing of the act. Music bar **D:Qliq,** rue du St-Esprit 17 (✆ **26-73-62;** www.dqliq.com), in the Grund district south of the city center, puts on an eclectic mix of musical styles.

BARS

Down in the valley, Grund is blessed with several good pubs: **Scott's Pub,** Bisserwee 4 (✆ **22-64-75;** www.scotts.lu), which serves Guinness and English ale to a mostly expatriate crowd; and **Pygmalion,** rue de la Tour Jacob 19 (✆ **42-08-60**), a typical Irish pub.

A Side Trip to Mondorf-les-Bains (Munnneref) ★

16km (10 miles) SE of Luxembourg City

Luxembourg's only casino and a widely recognized health club are in this spa town. Buses depart every hour from Luxembourg City. By car, take N3 south, and turn east at Frisange.

WHAT TO SEE & DO

Casino 2000 This is the place for gambling. Attached to the casino is a four-star hotel and multiple restaurants, ranging from buffet-style to serious French, and there are dinner/entertainment specials. A dress code requires jacket and tie (or turtleneck) for men and suitable dress for women, and you must have your passport to prove you're over 18.

Rue Th. Flammang. ✆ **23-61-12-13.** www.casino2000.lu. Admission 2.50€ per day. Mon–Sat 7pm–3am; Sun 4pm–3am. Closed Dec 24.

Domaine Thermal ★ This health resort is known for its idyllic location, with vineyards and woods to the east and the Lorraine Hills to the west. Its thermal baths, health center, fitness center, and recreation facilities (tennis, golf, squash, fencing, archery, horseback riding, and an outdoor pool) are all excellent. For several months in 1945, the Palace Hotel, which stood on this site until its demolition in 1988, was codenamed "Camp Ashcan" and held leading Nazis awaiting transit to Nuremberg (Nürnberg) to stand trial for war crimes; among them were Hermann Göring, Joachim von Ribbentrop, Julius Streicher, and field marshals Gerd von Rundstedt and Albert Kesselring.

Av. des Bains. ✆ **23-66-68-80.** www.mondorf.lu. Treatments and activities begin at 45€. Mon 1–8pm; Tues–Fri 10am–8pm; Sat 9am–7pm; Sun and holidays 9am–6pm. Closed Jan 1 and Dec 24–26.

WHERE TO STAY & DINE

Hôtel du Grand Chef ★ Set in a private park facing the spa center, within walking distance of the casino, this gracious hotel occupies the 1852 home of a French

VALLEY OF THE SEVEN castles

It's really just the valley of the Eisch River, but that doesn't have the same panache as "Valley of the Seven Castles," which is what the Luxembourg tourist literature calls it. This scenic little area holds one of Europe's finest concentrations of castles.

Steinfort (Stengefort), 16km (10 miles) northwest of Luxembourg City on N4, is the entry point to the valley. Thereafter your route is northeast to **Koerich (Käerch),** and its ruined medieval castle. As you follow the course of the river (which is really no more than a stream), next up is **Septfontaines (Simmer),** a high-sited village dominated by its ruined 13th-century castle. Below the castle are the seven springs *(sept fontaines)* that give the village its name.

From here the valley road turns east to **Ansembourg (Aansebuerg),** which has two castles: a 12th-century one with later modifications high on a hill, and a 17th-century one in the valley. A little way north is **Hollenfels (Huelmes),** with an 18th-century castle constructed around a 13th-century keep dramatically situated on a cliff top (it's now a youth hostel). From there you go northeast on a minor road to the castle at **Schoenfels (Schëndels).**

Go north now, to **Mersch (Miersch),** the geographical center of the Grand Duchy. In addition to the early feudal Pettingen Castle, you find here the remains of a Roman villa that exhibits mosaics, sculpture, and wall paintings.

The crow's-flight distance from Steinfort to Marsch is just 16km (10 miles), but the winding nature of even the most direct roads will about triple that distance on the ground.

nobleman. Although completely modernized, it has not given up the charm and elegance of its beginnings. If it's peace and quiet you're after, take note that this hotel is a member of the Relais du Silence, and it guards its silence even though it's close to what passes for the "Vegas scene" in Luxembourg. Some rooms have heated terraces, and others have balconies.

Av. des Bains 36, 5610 Mondorf-les-Bains. ✆ **23-66-80-12.** Fax 23-66-15-10. www.grandchef.lu. 40 units. 98€–111€ double; 144€–155€ suite. Rates include buffet breakfast. AE, DC, MC, V. Free parking. **Amenities:** Restaurant; bar; lounge. *In room:* TV, hair dryer, minibar, Wi-Fi (free).

THE LUXEMBOURG ARDENNES ★

This northern region, which spills over from the Belgian Ardennes (see chapter 11), is a treat for nature lovers and a gift for those in search of a quiet vacation. Handsome castles are everywhere in the Ardennes (Ardennen), with especially impressive examples at Clervaux and Esch-sur-Sûre. The area has its share of vacation resort towns, perhaps most notably in medieval Vianden, the proud site of a huge restored fortress surrounded by dense forests. At the Buurgplaatz hill, 5km (3 miles) northeast of Troisvierges (Ëlwen), is Luxembourg's supposed highest point, 559m (1,834 ft.) above sea level—there's even a stone tower with a plaque that says so. In fact the highest point is the Kneiff hill, 1km (⅔ mile) to the east, which tops out at 560m (1,837 ft.)

In places like Berdorf, Clervaux, Ettelbruck, and Wiltz, U.S. forces fought German troops in the Battle of the Bulge (1944–45), and the Ardennes bears more visible scars of World War II than any other part of Luxembourg. Memorials abound to the valiant GIs who fell in these fierce encounters.

While easily explored from a base in Luxembourg City, the Ardennes deserves an extended visit. The region has many fine country inns and small hotels in all price ranges. Reserve accommodations as far in advance as possible in summer; this is a popular vacation spot, and hotel rooms can be hard to come by. Restaurants in the hotels listed (indeed, in most hotels in the Ardennes) are excellent.

Ettelbruck (Ettelbreck)

25km (16 miles) N of Luxembourg City

This handsome old town (pop. 6,000), a crossroads of tourist routes, lies in a bowl-shaped depression amid the rolling hills of the southern Luxembourg Ardennes, at the confluence of the Sûre (Sauer) and Alzette (Uelzecht) rivers. It takes its name from "Attila's Bridge," a river crossing supposedly constructed by Attila the Hun when he and his hard-handed army passed this way in A.D. 451.

On the edge of town in Patton Park is **Patton Square,** on which stands a statue, 3m (10 ft.) high, of U.S. General George Patton. Nearby is a Sherman tank similar to the ones that arrived to liberate Ettelbruck in September 1944. Patton's men then had the job to do all over again at Christmas after the German army overran the town during the Battle of the Bulge.

ESSENTIALS

GETTING THERE Up to four **trains** depart every hour or so to Ettelbruck from Luxembourg City; on the fastest (IR) trains, the ride takes 25 minutes. By **car,** take A7/N7 north.

VISITOR INFORMATION The **Syndicat d'Initiative et du Tourisme** is at rue Abbé Muller 5, 9065 Ettelbruck (✆ **81-20-68;** fax 81-98-39; www.ettelbruck-info.lu), in the heart of town. The office is open Monday and Wednesday to Saturday from 10am to noon and 1 to 5pm.

WHAT TO SEE & DO

General Patton Memorial Museum This museum is dedicated to the flamboyant, hard-driving commander of the U.S. Third Army, whose troops liberated Luxembourg and did so much to turn the tide in the Battle of the Bulge in World War II. More than 1,000 photographs and other documents portray the war years in Luxembourg. Displays of military equipment include items excavated from the Ettelbruck battlefield in recent years.

Rue Dr. Klein 5 (at av. John Fitzgerald Kennedy). ✆ **81-03-22.** www.patton.lu. Admission 5€ adults, 3€ children 14–17, free for children 13 and under. June to mid-Sept daily 10am–5pm; mid-Sept to May Sun 2–5pm.

Diekirch (Dikrech)

5km (3 miles) E of Ettelbruck

Standing mostly on the north bank of the Sûre River, Diekirch (pop. 6,000) was a Celtic stronghold in the days before the Roman legions arrived. There are some good, and not difficult, signed hiking trails in the hills around the town.

ESSENTIALS

GETTING THERE One or two **trains** depart every hour or so from Ettelbruck; the ride takes just 5 minutes. By **car,** take E241/N7 east from Ettelbruck.

VISITOR INFORMATION The **Syndicat d'Initiative** is at place de la Libération 3, 9255 Diekirch (✆ **80-30-23;** fax 80-27-86; www.diekirch.lu), in the center of town. It's open July to August Monday to Friday from 9am to 5pm and weekends from 10am to 4pm; and September to June Monday to Friday from 9am to noon and 2 to 5pm, and Saturday from 2 to 4pm.

WHAT TO SEE & DO

Be sure to view the **Vieille Eglise St-Laurent (Old Church of St. Lawrence)** in the oldest part of town. The church dates originally from the 6th and 8th centuries, although it has been much altered since then. It's open daily 10am to noon and 2 to 6pm; admission is free.

The local tourist office can provide details for a signed circular hike of 7km (4½ miles) from the center of Diekirch, across the Sûre, and into the hills to a prehistoric Celtic **dolmen** (stone tomb), dubbed the Deiwelselter (Devil's Altar).

Musée National de l'Histoire Militaire (National Museum of Military History) ★★ The best Battle of the Bulge museum in either Belgium or Luxembourg displays a series of superb life-size dioramas depicting U.S. and German military forces. The finest of these portrays U.S. troops crossing the icy Sûre River near Diekirch in January 1945, a turning point in the battle. The dioramas afford an eerie insight into what it might have been like to be there, struggling and fighting through the snow. This realistic display is augmented by military equipment, uniforms, weapons, maps, and items such as a tank, artillery pieces, and tracked vehicles. In addition, the museum covers Luxembourg's occupation and liberation, and the history of its army.

Bamertal 10 (off rue du Moulin on the northern edge of town). ✆ **80-89-08.** www.mnhm.lu. Admission 5€ adults; 3€ students, children 10–18, and service members in uniform; free for World War II veterans, visitors with disabilities, and children 9 and under. Daily 10am–6pm. Closed Dec 25 and Jan 1.

Wiltz (Wolz)

40km (25 miles) NW of Luxembourg City; 18km (11 miles) NW of Ettelbruck

Wiltz is split right down the middle, with a difference in height of 150m (492 ft.) between **Oberwiltz** ("uptown") and **Niederwiltz** ("downtown"). This popular vacation town (pop. 4,500), which lies in a beautiful and heavily wooded setting and is a great place for hiking and other outdoor activities, witnessed fierce fighting in December 1944 during the Battle of the Bulge.

ESSENTIALS

GETTING THERE One or two **trains** depart every hour or so from Ettelbruck; the ride takes around 40 minutes. By **car,** take N15 west from Ettelbruck.

VISITOR INFORMATION The **Syndicat d'Initiative et de Tourisme** is at Château de Wiltz, 9516 Wiltz (✆ **95-74-44;** fax 95-75-56; www.touristinfowiltz.lu). The office is open July to August daily 10am to 6pm; September to June, hours are Monday to Friday from 10am to noon and 2 to 5pm, and Saturday from 2 to 5pm.

WHAT TO SEE & DO

Just as the town itself is divided geographically, the town's attractions are divided historically between the medieval and the modern. Witness the 1502 **stone cross** outside the Hôtel de Ville (Town Hall) at whose feet the powerful lords of Wiltz once meted out justice, and the **1944 battle tank** that sits at the bend of the approach road. The 12th-century **Château (Castle),** "modernized" in the 1600s, perhaps best

NATURAL avenues

On a bend of the Sûre River, 6km (4 miles) south of Wiltz, Esch-sur-Sûre has a ruined medieval castle. But it is the **Parc Naturel de la Haut-Sûre ★**, on the village's doorstep, that brings visitors here in large numbers. Though its area of 184 sq. km. (71 sq. miles) is tiny by North American standards, the natural park occupies a significant chunk of Luxembourg's real estate, a protected scenic part of the Grand Duchy in the hills and forests around the waters of the Lac de Haut-Sûre. This is the place for fishing, boating, hiking, horseback riding, and other outdoor activities, including cross-country skiing in winter. There's good bird-watching, too.

For the lowdown, stop by the visitor center in the **Maison du Parc Naturel,** rte. de Lultzhausen 15, Esch-sur-Sûre (✆ **89-93-31-1;** www.naturpark-sure.lu). The center is open Monday to Friday from 10am to noon and 2 to 6pm, and weekends and holidays from 2 to 6pm (at 5pm and closed Wed Nov–Mar); admission is free. The national park is open permanently, and admission is free.

There are buses to Esch every hour or so from both Wiltz and Ettelbruck. By car, take N15 south from Wiltz and northwest from Ettelbruck.

represents the town's dual traditions, since its ancient left wing houses a museum commemorating the fighting in 1944 and 1945. A memorial recalls those killed during and after a general strike protesting military conscription during the Nazi occupation.

The **Eglise Niederwiltz,** a Romanesque and Renaissance church, holds richly ornamented tombs of the counts of Wiltz. A 1743 Renaissance altar made by a local artist stands in the **Eglise Oberwiltz.** A good side trip is southeast through the scenic wooded Wiltz Valley for 11km (7 miles) to the handsome village of **Kautenbach.**

Clervaux (Klierf) ★

48km (30 miles) N of Luxembourg City; 13km (8 miles) NE of Wiltz

The handsome old village (pop. 1,800) occupies an incredibly scenic location in a steep valley of the Clerve River. It is the main—though by no means the only—tourist center in Luxembourg's northern reaches.

ESSENTIALS

GETTING THERE One or two **trains** depart every hour or so from Ettelbruck; the ride takes 25 minutes. By **car,** take E421/N7 north from Ettelbruck.

VISITOR INFORMATION The **Syndicat d'Initiative et de Tourisme** is at the Château de Clervaux, 9701 Clervaux (✆ **92-00-72;** fax 92-93-12; www.tourisme-clervaux.lu).

WHAT TO SEE & DO

Dominating this little town is its 12th-century **Château ★** (✆ **92-96-57**), restored after suffering heavy damage during the Battle of the Bulge. Cut-off U.S. troops held out in this Luxembourg "Alamo" until the Germans used a tank as a battering-ram to break through the timber gates. The castle houses scale models of other medieval fortresses, uniforms and arms from World War II, and Edward Steichen's moving

Family of Man photographic essay. It's open March to December Tuesday to Sunday from 10am to 6pm. Admission to all three exhibits is 7€ for adults, 3.50€ for children 10 to 15, and free for children 9 and under; the cost of visiting one or two exhibits is proportionately less.

WHERE TO STAY & DINE

Hôtel International ★★ A not especially distinguished streetfront leads into this hotel's fully renovated interior, with lots of bright, primary colors, modern art, and a relaxed attitude exemplified by the long list of wellness treatments and packages on offer in the hotel spa. The guest rooms have all-new furnishings; big beds by European standards; and armchairs or sofas that you sink so deep into, you may be reluctant to stand up. The French/International restaurant **Les Arcades** is about as health-inducing as the spa, an impression confirmed by delicate dishes on a limited-choice fixed-price menu (that runs to six courses for the top-end option); **Brasserie Rhino,** both simpler and earthier, emphasizes grilled meat (though not grilled rhino!).

Grand-Rue 10 (on Clervaux's main street), 9710 Clervaux. ✆ **92-93-91.** Fax 92-04-92. www.interclervaux.lu. 51 units. 105€–159€ double; 145€–195€ suite. Rates include buffet breakfast. AE, MC, V. Parking 10€. Free transfers to and from Clervaux train station. **Amenities:** 2 restaurants; piano bar; bikes; nearby golf course; health club & spa; heated indoor pool. *In room:* TV, hair dryer, minibar, Wi-Fi (free).

Vianden (Veianen) ★★

34km (21 miles) NE of Luxembourg City; 18km (11 miles) SE of Clervaux

Vianden straddles the Our River and looks across to Germany's forested Eifel region. In 1871, exiled French writer and Vianden resident Victor Hugo described the village (pop. 1,600) as a "jewel set amid splendid scenery, characterized by two both comforting and magnificent elements: the sinister ruins of its fortress and its cheerful breed of men." Well, the splendid scenery and the fortress are still there, and the populace seems cheerful enough.

ESSENTIALS

GETTING THERE From Ettelbruck, **bus no. 570** goes to Vianden in 25 minutes; from Clervaux, **bus no. 663** makes the 45-minute trip during the summer months. Two **trains** leave every hour from Luxembourg City to Diekirch, which connect with buses (line 570) to Vianden; the ride from Diekirch takes 15 minutes. By **car,** take N7 north from Luxembourg City to Ettelbruck, and then go east on N19 and north on N17.

VISITOR INFORMATION The **Syndicat d'Initiative** is at rue du Vieux Marché 1A, 9419 Vianden (✆ **83-42-57-1;** fax 84-90-81; www.vianden-info.lu). The office is open Monday to Friday from 9am to noon and 1 to 5pm, and Saturday and (July–Sept) Sunday from 10am–2pm.

WHAT TO SEE & DO

For the best view of Vianden's narrow winding streets, castle, and the river valley, take the **Télésiège (chairlift)** that operates from rue du Sanatorium 39 (✆ **83-43-23**), April to October daily 10am to 5 or 6pm. The round-trip fare is 4.25€ for adults and 2.25€ for children.

The **Maison Victor Hugo (Victor Hugo House),** rue de la Gare 37 (✆ **26-87-40-88;** www.victor-hugo.lu), is where the great French writer stayed during his sojourn in Vianden. The **Musée Littéraire Victor Hugo** in the house is open Tuesday to Sunday from 11am to 5pm. Admission is 4€ for adults, 3.50€ for ages 13 to 25, 2.50€ for children 6 to 12, and free for children 5 and under.

Château de Vianden ★ A mighty 9th-century fortress-castle perched on a hill above town draws most of Vianden's visitors. It has been restored to its original plans, so you can now see the 11th-, 12th-, and 15th-century additions that are even more impressive than the earlier sections.

Montée de Château. ✆ **84-92-91.** www.castle-vianden.lu. Admission 7€ adults, 6.50€ seniors and students, 2€ children 6–12, free for children 5 and under, 17€ family. Jan–Feb and Nov–Dec daily 10am–4pm; Mar and Oct daily 10am–5pm; Apr–Sept daily 10am–6pm. Closed Jan 1, Nov 2, and Dec 25.

WHERE TO STAY & DINE

Hôtel-Restaurant Heintz ★ Even though the Heintz occupies one of the Grand Duchy's oldest buildings, a former Trinitarian monastery, you needn't worry about bare cells and being woken up for prayers at 3am. This lovely place, scenically sited about midway downhill between the castle and the river, has modernized rooms, which retain some of the quaint old character and ambience that's typical of Vianden. Twelve rooms face south and have large balconies that afford great views. The restaurant serves local specialties, like the *truite de l'Our* (Our River trout).

Grand-Rue 55, 9410 Vianden. ✆ **83-41-55.** Fax 83-45-59. www.hotel-heintz.lu. 30 units. 62€–96€ double. AE, DC, MC, V. Parking 7€. **Amenities:** Restaurant; bar. *In room:* TV.

Echternach (Lechternach) ★

30km (19 miles) NE of Luxembourg City

This enchanting little town (pop. 5,000) is a living open-air museum, from its patrician houses and picturesque market square to its medieval walls and towers.

ESSENTIALS

GETTING THERE **Bus no. 500** departs every hour or so from Ettelbruck; the ride to Echternach takes 45 minutes. By **car** from Ettelbruck, take N7 then N19 east to Wallendorf-Pont, then go south on N10 to Echternach.

VISITOR INFORMATION The **Syndicat d'Intiative et de Tourisme** is at parvis de la Basilique 9–10, 6401 Echternach (✆/fax **72-02-30;** www.echternach-tourist.lu), opposite St. Willibrord Basilica. The office is open Monday to Friday from 10am to 5:30pm, Saturday from 10am to 4pm, and Sunday from 10am to noon.

WHAT TO SEE & DO

Be sure to take in the **Mairie (Town Hall),** which dates from 1444, and the 18th-century **Abbaye (Abbey)** and **Basilique (Basilica).** Echternach has been the repository of the ages since the missionary St. Willibrord arrived from England in 658 and established the abbey that made this one of the area's earliest centers of Christianity. Allow yourself enough time to soak up the medieval atmosphere that permeates the air.

If you arrive on Pentecost Tuesday—the sixth Tuesday after Easter—you'll encounter the spectacular and unique **Dancing Procession.** Pilgrims from all over Europe come to join this parade, during which they march, chant, sing, and dance to an ancient tune performed by bands. This event mixes religious solemnity with a liberal dose of native gaiety. The procession forms at 9am and ends at the basilica.

WHERE TO STAY & DINE

Hôtel Bel Air ★ This luxury hotel is a member of the Relais & Châteaux hotel chain, which is composed exclusively of converted manor houses and châteaux. It lies in its own large (4-hectare/10-acre) park overlooking the Sûre Valley. The hotel

outdoor PURSUITS

The rivers of the Grand Duchy comprise an anglers' paradise, but one that's strictly controlled by the authorities. Complex regulations govern fishing in private waters and rivers. Licenses are issued by the district commissioners in Luxembourg City, Diekirch, and Grevenmacher, and by a few communal administrations, such as those in Ettelbruck, Vianden, and Wiltz. Check with the local tourist office about the local regulations and licensing before going fishing.

There are marked walking paths throughout the Grand Duchy. During the summer, organized walking tours of 10 to 40km (6–25 miles) are conducted from Luxembourg City. Contact the **Fédération Luxembourgeoise de Marche Populaire,** BP 56, 9201 Diekirch (✆ **621-500-677;** www.flmp-ivv.lu), for more information.

Horseback-riding is a favorite sport in Luxembourg. For a list of stables and riding schools, contact the **Fédération Luxembourgeoise des Sports Equestres,** rte. d'Arlon 3, 8009 Strassen (✆ **48-49-99;** www.flse.lu). The organization puts together horseback tours in Luxembourg City and around the Grand Duchy.

features include lovely terraces and serene wooded walking paths just outside the door. The plainest of the four guest-room types don't quite make it to baronial style, but as you go up the price ladder, you get closer to this conservative ideal, with floral-pattern bedspreads and cozy armchairs.

Rte. de Berdorf 1 (.8km/½ mile outside town), 6409 Echternach. ✆ **72-93-83.** Fax 72-86-94. www.belair-hotel.lu. 39 units. 116€–160€ double; 172€–184€ suite. Rates include buffet breakfast. AE, DC, MC, V. Free parking. **Amenities:** 2 restaurants; lounge; spa; tennis courts. *In room:* TV, hair dryer.

THE MOSELLE VALLEY ★

Luxembourg's vineyard and winery region is set in a landscape that's quite different from that of the Ardennes. A tour of the area will take you along the flat banks of the broad Moselle (Musel) River, with a gentle slope of low hills rising on both sides—the east bank is in Germany, where the river is known as the Mosel. For miles these slopes are covered with vineyards. The riverbanks themselves are alive with campers, boaters, and anglers. Several wineries open their doors to visitors: They take you on a guided tour, explain how their still or sparkling wine is made, and top off your visit with a glass of what comes out of their barrels.

To explore the Moselle Valley, begin at Echternach and follow the well-marked *Route du Vin* (Wine Route) south through Wasserbillig, Grevenmacher, Machtum, Wormeldange, Ehnen, Remich, and Wellenstein. You can do this as an easy day trip by car from Luxembourg City. Should you find yourself beguiled by this part of the country, plenty of accommodations and excellent local restaurants are along the route.

Grevenmacher (Greiwemaacher)

12km (8 miles) SE of Echternach

This scenic Moselle town, on the riverside road southeast of Wasserbillig, is noted for both its wine and its waters. There are regular buses from Echternach. The **Syndicat**

d'Initiative et de Tourisme is at rte. du Vin 10, 6701 Grevenmacher (✆ **75-82-75;** fax 75-86-66; www.moselle-tourist.lu).

For tours of their wine cellars, visit the **Caves Coopératives des Vignerons,** rue des Caves 12 (✆ **75-01-75**). They're open May to August Monday to Saturday from 10am to 5pm (by appointment other months). The tour is 2.75€ for adults, 2€ for children 5 to 14, and free for children 4 and under.

Bernard-Massard, rte. du Vin 22 (✆ **75-05-45-1;** www.bernard-massard.lu), has guided wine tours April to October daily 9:30am to 6pm. The tour is from 4€ to 7€ for adults (depending on how much you drink) and 2.50€ for children 13 and under (includes 1 glass of grape juice). The tourist cruise boat ***Princesse Marie-Astrid*** (✆ **75-82-75;** www.moselle-tourist.lu), which has an onboard restaurant, plows a furrow up and down the Moselle from Grevenmacher, from Easter to the end of September. Cruises range from 4.50€ to 23€, without meals; children 6 to 12 pay half fare, and children 5 and under travel free.

A FINE NEARBY RESTAURANT

Chalet de la Moselle ★ CONTINENTAL This charming chalet restaurant on the Wine Route between Grevenmacher and Ahn has an emphasis on fish and other seafood, and backs this up with a range of meat dishes and a strong wine list. Good choices from the fish list are *moules au Riesling* (mussels in a Riesling sauce) and *sandre aux écrevisses* (pike-perch with crayfish); the Angus rumpsteak in mustard sauce should find favor with meat-eaters.

Rte. du Vin 35, Machtum. ✆ **75-91-91.** www.chaletdelamoselle.lu. Main courses 19€–32€; fixed-price menus 23€–68€. AE, DC, MC, V. Fri–Tues noon–2pm and 7–10pm.

Wormeldange (Wuermeldeng) & Ehnen (Einen)

8km (5 miles) SW of Grevenmacher

By bus and car, it's a quick trip on the riverside road from Grevenmacher to **Wormeldange,** where the **Caves des Crémants Poll-Fabaire,** rte. du Vin 115 (✆ **76-82-11**), are open May to October Monday to Friday from 7am to 8pm, Saturday from 10:30am to 8pm, and Sunday from 3 to 8pm (tastings are on a more restricted schedule). The tour is from 4.50€ for adults, 1€ for children 5 to 14, and free for children 4 and under.

Less than 1km (½ mile) away is **Ehnen.** The pretty village's **Musée du Vin (Wine Museum)** ★, rte. du Vin 115 (✆ **76-00-26**), is set in a beautiful old vintner's mansion that's been lovingly restored. It serves as an info center for the region's wineries. A comprehensive exhibit on viniculture processes now occupies what was once the fermenting cellar. The museum is open April to October Tuesday to Sunday from 9:30 to 11:30am and 2 to 5pm. Admission is 3€ for adults (includes glass of wine), 1.50€ for children 5 to 14, and free for children 4 and under.

WHERE TO STAY & DINE

Hôtel-Restaurant Bamberg ★ This small, family-owned hotel occupies a renovated 19th-century town house overlooking the Moselle. Its guest rooms are furnished in a country style, and the public rooms have a homey feel. The restaurant, which draws locals in addition to visitors, and sources some of its fish from the river and accompanying wines from local wineries, has an old-world atmosphere, with a fireplace, dark wainscoting, and exposed rafters. This is a good place to stop for lunch or dinner, even if you're not staying in the hotel.

Rte. du Vin 131, 5416 Ehnen. ✆ **76-00-22.** Fax 76-00-56. 12 units. 90€ double. Rates include continental breakfast. MC, V. Free parking. **Amenities:** Restaurant. *In room:* TV.

Remich (Reimech)

6km (4 miles) S of Ehnen

On the riverside road south from Grevenmacher, Remich (pop. 3,000) is an important wine center. The **Syndicat d'Initiative et de Tourisme,** rue de la Sapinière 3, 5571 Remich (✆ **23-69-84-88;** fax 23-69-72-95; www.moselle-tourist.lu), at the bus station, is open July to August daily 10am to 5pm. The **Caves St-Martin,** rte. de Stadtbredimus 53 (✆ **23-69-97-74;** www.cavesstmartin.lu), offers an informative tour of the winery's cellars. It's open April to October daily 10am to noon and 1:30 to 6pm. The basic tour is 4€ for adults (detailed tours are available for a higher price), 2.50€ for children 5 to 14, and free for children 4 and under.

WHERE TO STAY & DINE

Hôtel Saint-Nicolas ★ Overlooking the Moselle on a broad promenade beside the river—which makes it particularly convenient if you are cruising—with a view across the water to Germany, this large terraced hotel has guest rooms furnished and decorated in a tasteful contemporary style. Half of the rooms have a whirlpool bath, so if that's important to you, be sure to ask if there's one in your room. The French restaurant, **Lohengrin,** is highly regarded along the Moselle.

Esplanade 31, 5533 Remich. ✆ **26-66-3.** Fax 26-66-36-66. www.saint-nicolas.lu. 40 units. 105€–160€ double. Rates include buffet breakfast. AE, DC, MC, V. Parking 10€. **Amenities:** Restaurant; cocktail bar; lounge; health club; 2 pools (heated indoor and outdoor); spa. *In room:* TV, hair dryer, minibar, Wi-Fi (free).

Wellenstein (Wellesteen)

4km (2½ miles) SW of Remich

Wellenstein's **Caves Coopératives des Vignerons,** rue des Caves 13 (✆ **26-66-14-1**), offers guided tours of the wine cellars. It's open May to October daily 11am to 6pm. The tour is 2.75€ for adults, 2€ for children 5 to 14, and free for children 4 and under.

FAST FACTS

FAST FACTS: BELGIUM

Area Codes See "Telephones," p. 55.

Business Hours Banks are usually open Monday to Friday from 9am to 1pm and 2 to 4:30pm, and some branches are open on Saturday morning. Stores generally are open from 10am to 6pm Monday to Saturday, and some are also open on Sunday. Most department stores have late hours on Friday, remaining open until 8 or 9pm.

Cellphones (Mobile Phones) See "Staying Connected," p. 54.

Drinking & Drug Laws Belgium has rigid prohibitions against the possession and use of controlled narcotic drugs, and a strict enforcement policy that virtually guarantees stiff fines and/or jail sentences for offenders. This can be especially important if you are traveling from neighboring Holland, where the rules are more tolerant and enforcement (for soft drugs) is generally lax. The minimum age for drinking beer and wine in bars and for legally purchasing beer and wine is 16; for drinking hard liquor in bars and for purchasing hard liquor, the minimum age is 18.

Driving Rules See "Getting There & Around," p. 38.

Electricity Belgium uses 230 (220–240) volts AC (50 cycles), compared to 110–120 volts AC (60 cycles) in the United States and Canada. Converters that change 110–120 volts to 220–240 volts are difficult to find in Belgium, so bring one with you.

Embassies The following embassies are all located in the Belgian capital, Brussels:

Australia: rue Guimard 6–8, 1040 Bruxelles (✆ **02/286-05-00;** www.belgium.embassy.gov.au; Métro: Arts-Loi).

Canada: av. de Tervueren 2, 1040 Bruxelles (✆ **02/741-06-11;** www.canadainternational.gc.ca; Métro: Merode).

Ireland: chaussée d'Etterbeek 180, 1040 Bruxelles (✆ **02/282-34-00;** www.embassyofireland.be; Métro: Schuman).

New Zealand: av. des Nerviens 9–31, 1040 Bruxelles (✆ **02/512-10-40;** www.nzembassy.com/belgium; Métro: Schuman).

United Kingdom: av. d'Auderghem 10, 1040 Bruxelles (✆ **02/287-62-11;** http://ukinbelgium.fco.gov.uk/en; Métro: Schuman).

United States: bd. du Régent 27, 1000 Bruxelles (✆ **02/811-40-00;** www.usembassy.be; Métro: Arts-Loi).

Emergencies For police assistance, call ✆ **101.** For an ambulance or the fire department, call ✆ **100.**

Gasoline (Petrol) A gas (petrol) station is a *station-service* in French, and a *benzinestation,* a *pompstation,* or a *tankstation* in Dutch. Gasoline in Belgium is lead-free and sold in two varieties: eurosuper 95 or eurosuper 98 (for its octane number). Diesel is sold in all stations; LPG (liquid petroleum gas) is sold in many. The first hydrogen-fuel pump was installed in 2008. Taxes are already included in the printed price. One U.S. gallon equals 3.8 liters, and 1 imperial gallon equals 4.4 liters.

Holidays & Events See "When to Go," p. 73.

Internet Access See "Staying Connected," p. 54.

Language Belgians speak either French or Dutch (you may hear it called Flemish), and a tiny minority in the east speaks German. English is in effect the second language, and it is taught in the schools from the early grades, with the result that many Belgians speak English quite well. You may speak English in Belgian cities almost as freely as you do at home to anyone in the business of providing tourist services, whether hotel receptionist, waitperson, or (though not always) store assistant. Cab drivers, on the other hand, often hail from ethnic minority communities and might not be so handy with English. In other situations, particularly in the country, and more so in Wallonia than in Flanders, you can't be sure of being able to speak English.

Legal Aid If you get into trouble with the law, your first point of contact is likely to be the police. As a generalization (it won't be true in all cases), the police in Brussels and French-speaking Wallonia are less likely to be sympathetic and "foreigner-friendly," and less likely to speak English, than the police in Dutch-speaking Flanders, and in particular those in tourist hotspots like Bruges and Ghent. If the problem is serious and you are arrested, you have rights similar to those in any Western democracy. You are not required to say anything self-incriminatory, and you will be given access to a court-appointed lawyer or permitted to contact your embassy (see "Embassies," above).

Mail Most offices of **bpost** (✆ **022/01-23-45;** www.bpost.be) are open Monday to Friday from 9am to 5pm. Depending on the speed-of-delivery option you select, postage for a postcard or an ordinary letter up to 50 grams (1¾ oz.) to the U.K., Ireland, and other European countries is 1€ or 0.90€; to the U.S., Canada, Australia, New Zealand, and the rest of the world, it's 1.15€ or 1.05€.

Newspapers & Magazines See "Staying Connected," p. 54.

Passports See p. 36.

Police For emergency police (*police/politie/polizei*) assistance, call ✆ **101.**

Smoking Smoking is officially forbidden in enclosed workplaces, restaurants, and bars that sell food, except in a separate room (where in the case of restaurants and bars it is not permitted to serve food). Other bars and snack bars are not due to be covered by anti-smoking laws until 2014. Trams, buses, and Metro trains are smoke-free. ***Note:*** This being Belgium—where thumbing one's nose at the awesome number of government rules and regulations is a national sport—don't be surprised if nobody takes a bit of notice of the smoking ban anyway.

Taxes There's a value-added tax (TVA) in Belgium of 6% on hotel bills, 12% on some other goods and services, and 21% on restaurant bills. The higher rate is charged on purchased goods, too. If you spend over 125€ in some stores and you are not residing in the European Union, you can recover it by having the official receipt stamped by Belgian Customs on departure. Stores that offer tax-free shopping advertise with a TAX-FREE SHOPPING sign in the window and provide the information you need to recover taxes when you leave the European Union.

Telephones See "Staying Connected," p. 54.

Time Belgium is on Central European Time (CET), which is Coordinated Universal Time (UTC), or Greenwich Mean Time (GMT), plus 1 hour. Clocks are moved ahead 1 hour for daylight-saving Central European Summer Time (CEST) between late March and late October or early November. For example, when it's 6pm in Brussels, it's 9am in Los Angeles (PST), 7am in Honolulu (HST), 10am in Denver (MST), 11am in Chicago (CST), noon in New York City (EST), 5pm in London (GMT), and 2am the next day in Sydney.

For the exact local time from a "speaking clock," dial ✆ **1200.**

Tipping The prices on most restaurant menus already include a service charge of 16%, so it's unnecessary to tip. However, if the service is good, it's customary to show appreciation with a tip. It's enough to round up the bill to the nearest convenient amount, if you wish, rather than leave a full-fledged tip. Otherwise, 10% is adequate, and more than most Belgians would leave. Service charge is included in your hotel bill as well. Taxis include the tip in the meter reading. You can round up the fare if you like, but you need not add a tip unless you have received extra service like help with luggage. Give 20% of the bill to hairdressers (leave it with the cashier when you pay up), and 2€ per piece of luggage to porters.

Toilets In primarily French-speaking Brussels and in Wallonia, these likely will display an H or HOMMES for men, and an F or FEMMES for women; in Dutch-speaking Flanders, it'll be an H or HEREN for men, and a D or DAMEN for women (or there'll be a graphic that should leave no doubt either way). Be sure to pay the person who sits at the entrance to a *toilette*. He or she has a saucer where you put your money, usually around 0.50€.

Visas See "Entry Requirements," in chapter 3.

Visitor Information Before leaving for Belgium, obtain information about the country by contacting the **Belgian Tourist Office** (or its equivalent), which maintains offices around the world. Its Internet address is **www.visitbelgium.com**.

In the **U.S.,** the **Belgian Tourist Office** is at 220 E. 42nd St., Ste. 3402, New York, NY 10017 (✆ **212/758-8130;** fax 212/355-7576).

Residents of Canada can call ✆ **514/457-2888.** For information concerning Brussels and French-speaking Wallonia (not Flanders), Francophone Canadians can contact the **Office de Promotion du Tourisme Wallonie-Bruxelles,** rue de Buade 43, Bureau 525, Quebec Ville, Quebec, G1R 4A2 (✆ **418/692-4939;** fax 418/692-4974; www.belgique-tourisme.qc.ca).

For the **U.K.** and **Ireland,** Brussels and French-speaking Wallonia has its own office: **Belgian Tourist Office Brussels & Wallonia,** 217 Marsh Wall, London E14 9FJ (✆ **020/7537-1132,** or ✆ 0800/954-5245 for the brochure line; fax 020/7531-0393; www.belgiumtheplaceto.be). The separate office for Brussels and Dutch-speaking Flanders is: **Tourism Flanders-Brussels,** 1A Cavendish Sq., London W1G 0LD (✆ **020/7307-7738;** www.visitflanders.co.uk).

In Belgium, for Brussels and the French-speaking Wallonia region (and its mainly German-speaking Ostkantone district), contact the **Office de Promotion du Tourisme de Wallonie et Bruxelles,** rue St-Bernard 30, 1060 Bruxelles (✆ **070/22-10-21** for the brochure line, or 02/509-24-00 for the Belgium-only line; fax 02/513-04-75; www.opt.be). This is an administrative office only; it is not open for walk-in visits.

For Brussels and the Dutch-speaking Flanders region, contact **Toerisme Vlaanderen,** rue du Marché aux Herbes/Grasmarkt 61, 1000 Bruxelles (✆ **02/504-03-90;** fax 02/504-04-48; www.visitflanders.com; Métro: Gare Centrale). The office is open for walk-in visits April to June and September Monday to Saturday from 9am to 6pm and Sunday from 10am to 5pm; July to August, hours are daily 9am to 7pm; and October to March, it's open Monday to Saturday from 9am to 5pm and Sunday from 10am to 4pm.

For passengers arriving at Brussels Airport, there is a tourist information desk in the Arrivals hall. Another desk is in the Arrivals hall for Eurostar, Thalys, and TGV high-speed international trains at Bruxelles-Midi station.

Tourist offices in French-speaking areas are generally known as the Office du Tourisme, and in small places the Syndicat d'Initiative. In Dutch-speaking areas, they're Toerisme "Whatever"—for instance, Toerisme Brugge for Bruges—or VVV followed by the place name. In German-speaking areas, the tourist office is known as the Verkehrsamt.

Water The water from the faucet in Belgium is safe to drink. Many people drink bottled mineral water, though—generally, Belgian brands like Spa and Bru.

Wi-Fi See "Staying Connected," p. 54.

FAST FACTS: HOLLAND

Area Codes See "Telephones," p. 55.

Business Hours Banks are open Monday to Friday from 9am to 4pm (some stay open until 5pm). Some banks open on late-hour shopping nights and Saturday. Stores generally are open Monday from 10 or 11am to 6pm, Tuesday to Friday from 8:30 or 9am to 5 or 6pm, and Saturday to 4 or 5pm. Some stores close for lunch, and nearly all have one full closing day or one morning or afternoon when they're closed—signs are prominently posted announcing closing times. Many stores, especially in the larger towns, have late hours on Thursday and/or Friday evening. In the cities, stores along the main streets are open on Sunday.

Cellphones (Mobile Phones) See "Staying Connected," p. 54.

Drinking & Drug Laws There is no minimum legal drinking age in the Netherlands—but other laws may be used against a parent, guardian, or other third party who permits or causes a minor to abuse alcohol. For purchasing drinks that have less than 15% alcohol by volume, the minimum legal age is 16; for drinks with more than 15% alcohol by volume, the minimum legal age is 18. In both cases, ID must be produced.

The use of controlled narcotic drugs is officially illegal in the Netherlands, but Amsterdam and some other local authorities permit the sale in licensed premises of up to 5 grams (⅕ oz.) of hashish or marijuana for personal consumption, and possession of 30 grams (1 oz.) for personal use. On the other hand, peddling drugs *is* a serious offense.

Driving Rules See "Getting There & Around," p. 261.

Electricity Holland uses 230 (220–240) volts AC (50 cycles), compared to 110–120 volts AC (60 cycles) in the United States and Canada. Converters that change 110–120 volts to 220–240 volts are difficult to find in Holland, so bring one with you.

Embassies & Consulates The following embassies are all located in the Dutch seat of government, The Hague:

Australia: Carnegielaan 4, 2517 KH Den Haag (✆ **070/310-8200;** www.australian-embassy.nl; tram: 1 or 10).

Canada: Sophialaan 7, 2514 JP Den Haag (✆ **070/311-1600;** www.canadainternational.gc.ca; tram: 1 or 10).

Ireland: Scheveningseweg 112, 2584 AE Den Haag (✆ **070/363-0993;** www.irishembassy.nl; tram: 1).

New Zealand: Eisenhowerlaan 77N, 2517 KK Den Haag (✆ **070/346-9324;** www.nzembassy.com/netherlands; tram: 10).

United Kingdom: Lange Voorhout 10, 2514 ED Den Haag (✆ **070/427-0427;** www.britain.nl; tram: 1 or 10).

United States: Lange Voorhout 102, 2514 EJ Den Haag (✆ **070/310-2209;** http://thehague.usembassy.gov; tram: 1 or 10).

In addition, both the U.S. and the U.K. have consulates in the Dutch capital, Amsterdam (see "Fast Facts: Amsterdam," in chapter 13).

Emergencies For police assistance, an ambulance, or the fire department, call ✆ **112.**

Gasoline (Petrol) A gas (petrol) station is a *benzinestation,* a *pompstation,* or a *tankstation* in Dutch. Gasoline is lead-free and sold in two varieties: euro 95 or euro 98 (for its octane number). Diesel is sold in all stations; *autogas,* also known as LPG (liquid petroleum gas), is sold in many. Taxes are already included in the printed price. One U.S. gallon equals 3.8 liters, and 1 imperial gallon equals 4.4 liters. The Netherlands has some of the highest gasoline prices in the world.

Holidays & Events See "When to Go," p. 256.

Internet Access See "Staying Connected," p. 54.

Language Dutch people speak Dutch, of course, but English is the second language of the Netherlands and is taught in school from the early grades. The result is that nearly everyone speaks it well—so you may speak English almost as freely as you do at home, particularly to anyone providing tourist services, whether hotel receptionist, waitperson, or store clerk (cab drivers from ethnic minorities might be a different story). Not every Dutch person speaks English, of course, but you'll usually be able to call on someone to help out.

Legal Aid If you get into trouble with the law, your first point of contact is likely to be the police. Many (but by no means all) Dutch police officers are disposed to go easy with foreigners on minor matters, and many of them will speak English. If the problem is serious and you are arrested, you have rights similar to those in any Western democracy. You are not required to say anything self-incriminatory, and you will be given access to a court-appointed lawyer or permitted to contact your embassy or consulate (see "Embassies & Consulates," above).

Mail Most offices of **TNT Post** (✆ **076/527-2727;** www.tntpost.nl) are open Monday to Friday from 9am to 5pm. Postage for a postcard or an ordinary letter up to 20 grams (¾ oz.) to the U.K. Ireland, and other European countries is 0.79€; to the U.S., Canada, Australia, New Zealand, and the rest of the world, it's 0.95€. A letter weighing from 20 to 50 grams (¾–1¾ oz.) to the U.K. Ireland, and other European countries costs 1.58€; to the U.S., Canada, Australia, New Zealand, and the rest of the world, it's 1.90€.

Newspapers & Magazines See "Staying Connected," p. 54.

Passports See p. 36.

Police Holland's emergency phone number for the police (*politie*) is ✆ **112.**

Smoking Smoking is forbidden in restaurants, bars, cafes, hotel public areas, and most hotel rooms. Exceptions are in separate enclosed areas for smokers, in which staff are not allowed to provide drinks, meals, or other services. Smoking tobacco in "coffeshops" is likewise forbidden, but smoking the pot that is their stock in trade is allowed—don't ask me! Trams, buses, Metro trains, and trains are smoke-free.

Taxes There's a value-added tax (BTW) in Holland of 6% on hotel and restaurant bills (19% on beer, wine, and liquor), and 6% or 19% (depending on the product) on purchases. Visitors residing outside the European Union can recover it by having the official receipt stamped by Dutch Customs on departure. Stores that offer tax-free shopping advertise with a TAX-FREE SHOPPING sign in the window and provide the information you need to recover taxes when you leave the European Union. Refunds are available only when you spend more than 50€ in a participating store.

Telephones See "Staying Connected," p. 54.

Time Holland is on Central European Time (CET), which is Coordinated Universal Time (UTC), or Greenwich Mean Time (GMT), plus 1 hour. Clocks are moved ahead 1 hour for daylight-saving Central European Summer Time (CEST) between late March and late October or early November. For example, when it's 6pm in Amsterdam, it's 9am in Los Angeles (PST), 7am in Honolulu (HST), 10am in Denver (MST), 11am in Chicago (CST), noon in New York City (EST), 5pm in London (GMT), and 2am the next day in Sydney.

For the exact local time from a "speaking clock," dial ✆ **0900/8002.**

Tipping The Dutch government requires that all taxes and service charges be included in the published prices of hotels, restaurants, cafes, nightclubs, salons, and sightseeing companies. Even taxi fares include taxes and a standard 15% service charge. To be absolutely sure in a restaurant that tax and service are included, look for the words *inclusief BTW en service* (BTW is the abbreviation for the Dutch words that mean value-added tax), or ask the waiter.

Dutch waiters and hotel staff often "forget" that a service charge and a tip are in effect the same thing. If you query them, they'll likely tell you that the tip isn't included in the bill—slightly true, since it's not called a tip but a service charge. Customers pay a standard 15% whether they liked the service or not. The tourist office's advice is: "Tips for extra service are always appreciated but not necessary."

To tip like the Dutch, in a cafe or snack bar, leave some small change on the counter or table. In a restaurant, leave 1€ to 2€ per person, or to generously reward good service, 5€ per person or 10% of the tab. Since service can tend toward the lackadaisical, you may need to make due allowance for what constitutes "good." If another staffer takes your payment for the bill, give the tip to your waitperson directly.

In a hotel, tip if you wish for a long stay or extra service, but don't worry about not tipping—you're unlikely to be hassled by a bellboy who lights every lamp in your room until he hears the rattle of spare change.

Should you feel an irrational compulsion to tip taxi drivers, round up the fare by a euro or two, or splash out 5% to 10%.

Toilets The most important thing to remember about public toilets in Holland—apart from calling them *toiletten* (twa-*lett*-en) or "the WC" (Vay-*say*) and not restrooms or comfort stations—is not the usual Male/Female *(Heren/Dames)* distinction (important though that is), but to pay the attendant. He or she has a saucer where you put your money. Toilets usually cost only about 0.40€, and the attendant generally ensures that they are clean.

Visas See "Entry Requirements," in chapter 3.

Visitor Information Before leaving for the Netherlands, obtain information about the country by contacting the **Netherlands Board of Tourism & Conventions (NBTC),** which maintains offices around the world. Their Internet address is **www.holland.com**.

For the **U.S. and Canada,** they're at 215 Park Ave. South, Ste. 2005, New York, NY 10003 (✆ **212/370-7360;** fax 212/370-9507). For **Great Britain** and **Ireland** (no walk-in service), the info is P.O. Box 30783, London WC2B 6DH (✆ **020/7539-7959;** fax 020/7539-7953).

Or contact the organization in Holland (no walk-in service): **Netherlands Board of Tourism & Conventions,** Vlietweg 15, 2260 KA Leidschendam (✆ **070/370-5705;** fax 070/370-5368).

For tourist information when you arrive at Amsterdam's Schiphol Airport and to make hotel reservations, go to the **Holland Tourist Information** desk in Schiphol Plaza (✆ **0900/400-4040**), which is open daily 7am to 10pm.

It used to be that all tourist offices in Holland, from big-city and province-wide offices down to the tiniest village booth, were called "VVV" (pronounced *vay-vay-vay*) followed by the destination's name: VVV Amsterdam, for instance. The letters stand for **Vereniging voor Vreemdelingenverkeer (Association for Visitor Travel).** Triangular blue-and-white vvv signs are still a common sight around the country, but a growing number of places—Amsterdam is one—are adopting different names. Whatever they're called, Dutch tourist offices are efficient and have multilingual attendants on duty. They can reserve local accommodations for you, help with travel arrangements, tell you what's on where, and plenty more.

Water The water from the faucet in Holland is safe to drink. Many people drink bottled mineral water, generically called *spa,* even though not all of it is the Belgian Spa brand.

Wi-Fi See "Staying Connected," p. 54.

FAST FACTS: LUXEMBOURG

Area Codes See "Telephones," p. 55.

Business Hours Banks are open Monday to Friday from 8:30am to noon and 1 to 4:30pm. Stores generally are open Monday to Saturday from 10am to 6pm, and many open on Sunday for shorter hours.

Cellphones (Mobile Phones) See "Staying Connected," p. 54.

Drinking & Drug Laws Luxembourg has rigid prohibitions against the possession and use of controlled narcotic drugs, and a strict enforcement policy that virtually guarantees stiff fines and/or jail sentences for offenders. The minimum age for drinking in bars is 16; there is no minimum age for legally purchasing beer, wine, and hard liquor, but stores might be reluctant to sell to children much under 16 years.

Driving Rules See "Getting There & Around," p. 483.

Electricity Luxembourg uses 230 (220–240) volts AC (50 cycles), compared to 110–120 volts AC (60 cycles) in the United States and Canada. Converters that change 110–120 volts to 220–240 volts are difficult to find in Luxembourg, so bring one with you.

Embassies Australia, Canada, and New Zealand do not have embassies in Luxembourg; for these countries, contact the embassy in Brussels (see "Fast Facts: Belgium," earlier in this chapter). The following embassies are all in Luxembourg City:

Ireland: rte. d'Arlon 28, 1140 Luxembourg-Ville (✆ **45-06-10-1;** www.embassyofireland.lu).

United Kingdom: bd. Joseph II 5, 1840 Luxembourg-Ville (✆ **22-98-64;** http://ukinluxembourg.fco.gov.uk/en).

United States: bd. Emmanuel-Servais 22, 2535 Luxembourg-Ville (✆ **46-01-23;** http://luxembourg.usembassy.gov).

Emergencies For police assistance, call ✆ **113.** For an ambulance or the fire department, call ✆ **112.**

Gasoline (Petrol) A gas (petrol) station is a *station-service* in French. Gasoline in Luxembourg is lead-free and sold in two varieties: eurosuper 95 or eurosuper 98 (for its octane number). Diesel is sold in all stations; LPG (liquid petroleum gas) is sold in many. Taxes are already included in the printed price. One U.S. gallon equals 3.8 liters, and 1 imperial gallon equals 4.4 liters. Due to lower taxation, the price of gas in Luxembourg is around 25% cheaper than in neighboring countries.

Holidays & Events See "When to Go," p. 483.

Internet Access See "Staying Connected," p. 54.

Language The national language, Lëtzebuergesch, has a vaguely German base with overtones of French, yet is distinct from both of those languages. For anyone who isn't a native, forget it—it's a tongue twister. Not to worry; while the language is widely used among Luxembourgers, and although French is most often used in official and cultural activities and German is heard frequently, many Luxembourgers speak at least some English. You're not guaranteed to be able to get by in English in all circumstances, particularly in country areas, however.

Legal Aid If you get into trouble with the law, your first point of contact is likely to be the police. Luxembourg is a low-crime country, and that's how the local police aim to keep it. Police officers might go easy with foreigners on minor matters, and some at least will speak English. If the problem is serious and you are arrested, you have rights similar to those in any Western democracy. You are not required to say anything self-incriminatory, and you will be given access to a court-appointed lawyer or permitted to contact your embassy (see "Embassies," above).

Mail Most offices of **P&T Luxembourg** (✆ **80-02-32-10;** www.pt.lu) are open Monday to Friday from 9am to 5pm. Postage for a postcard or an ordinary letter up to 20 grams (¾ oz.) to the U.K., Ireland, and other European countries is 0.85€; to the U.S., Canada, Australia, New Zealand, and the rest of the world, it's 1.10€.

Newspapers & Magazines See "Staying Connected," p. 54.

Passports See p. 36.

Police For emergency police (*police*) assistance, call ✆ **113.**

Smoking Smoking is officially forbidden in most restaurants and bars. Exceptions are small bars and small restaurants serving light meals—but even in these establishments, smoking is not permitted between noon and 2pm and 7 and 9pm (when most people are having lunch or dinner). Buses and trains are smoke-free.

Taxes There's a value-added tax (TVA) in Luxembourg of 6% or 15% on most goods and services (for a few categories the rates are 3% or 12%). If you spend over 74€ in some stores and you are not residing in the European Union, you can recover it by presenting your receipt and a form to the Luxembourg Customs upon departure. Stores that offer tax-free shopping advertise with a TAX-FREE SHOPPING sign in the window, and provide the information you need to recover taxes when you leave the European Union.

Telephones See "Staying Connected," p. 54.

Time Luxembourg is on Central European Time (CET), which is Coordinated Universal Time (UTC), or Greenwich Mean Time (GMT), plus 1 hour. Clocks are moved ahead 1 hour for daylight-saving Central European Summer Time (CEST) between late March and late October or early November. For example, when it's 6pm in Luxembourg City, it's 9am in Los Angeles (PST), 7am in Honolulu (HST), 10am in Denver (MST), 11am in Chicago (CST), noon in New York City (EST), 5pm in London (GMT), and 2am the next day in Sydney.

Tipping Restaurants and hotels will almost always include a 16% service charge on the bill. If you've had exceptional service, you may want to add a little more; it isn't necessary, but it is common to do so.

Toilets Restrooms often display an H or HOMMES for men, and an F or FEMMES for women (or a graphic that should leave no doubt either way). Be sure to pay the person who sits at the entrance to a *toilette.* He or she has a saucer where you put your money, usually 0.50€.

Visas See "Entry Requirements," in chapter 3.

Visitor Information Before leaving for Luxembourg, obtain information about the country by contacting one of a handful of international offices of the **Luxembourg National Tourist Office.** Their Internet address is **www.visitluxembourg.com**.

For the **U.S.** and **Canada,** the office is at 17 Beekman Place, New York, NY 10022 (✆ **212/888-6664;** fax 212/888-6116).

For the **U.K.** and **Ireland,** the office is at Sicilian House, 7 Sicilian Ave., London WC1A 2QR (✆ **020/7434-2800;** fax 020/7430-1773; www.luxembourg.co.uk).

In Luxembourg, for information covering the "entire" country, you can contact the administrative office of the **Office National du Tourisme,** BP 1001, 1010 Luxembourg-Ville (✆ **42-82-82-20;** fax 42-82-82-38; www.visitluxembourg.lu). If you arrive by train at the Gare de Luxembourg, visit the ONT's **Bureau d'Acceuil (Welcome Desk)** at the station. It's open June to September Monday to Saturday from 9am to 7pm and Sunday from 9am to 12:30pm and 1:45 to 6pm; October to May, it's open daily from 9:15am to 12:30pm and 1:45 to 6pm.

Water You need have no concerns about Luxembourg's water—it's clear, pure, and safe.

Wi-Fi See "Staying Connected," p. 54.

AIRLINE WEBSITES

MAJOR U.S. AIRLINES

American Airlines
www.aa.com

Continental Airlines
www.continental.com

Delta Air Lines
www.delta.com

United Airlines
www.united.com

US Airways
www.usairways.com

INTERNATIONAL & BUDGET AIRLINES

Aer Lingus
www.aerlingus.com

Air Canada
www.aircanada.ca

Air New Zealand
www.airnewzealand.com

BMI Baby
www.bmibaby.com

British Airways
www.british-airways.com

Brussels Airlines
www.brusselsairlines.com

easyJet
www.easyjet.com

Luxair
www.luxair.lu

Qantas Airways
www.qantas.com

Ryanair
www.ryanair.com

South African Airways
www.flysaa.com

Index

C

D

N

O

S

T

U

V